Instructor's Manual
and Resource Kit

to accompany

¿Qué tal?

An Introductory Course

Sixth Edition

Instructor's Manual and Resource Kit

to accompany

¿Qué tal?

An Introductory Course

Sixth Edition

DORWICK • PÉREZ-GIRONÉS • KNORRE • GLASS • VILLAREAL

Chapter-By-Chapter Materials By
Ana María Pérez-Gironés, *Wesleyan University*
William R. Glass

Desenlace Activities By
Edda Temoche-Weldele, *Grossmont College*
Micaela Ramos, *Grossmont College*
Dora Schoenbrun-Fernández, *Grossmont College*

Video Activities By
Mark Porter

Games By
Linda H. Colville, *Citrus College*

Boston Burr Ridge, IL Dubuque, IA Madison, WI New York
San Francisco St. Louis Bangkok Bogotá Caracas Kuala Lumpur
Lisbon London Madrid Mexico City Milan Montreal New Delhi
Santiago Seoul Singapore Sydney Taipei Toronto

McGraw-Hill Higher Education

*A Division of The **McGraw-Hill** Companies*

This is an EBI book.

Instructor's Manual and Resource Kit to accompany
¿Qué tal? An Introductory Course

Published by McGraw-Hill, an imprint of The McGraw-Hill Companies, Inc., 1221 Avenue of the Americas, New York, NY 10020.

This book is printed on acid-free paper.

1 2 3 4 5 6 7 8 9 0 BKM BKM 0 9 8 7 6 5 4 3 2

ISBN 0-07-253536-9

Vice president and Editor-in-chief: *Thalia Dorwick*
Publisher: *William R. Glass*
Sponsoring editor: *Christa Harris*
Development editor: *Pennie Nichols-Alem*
Executive marketing manager: *Nick Agnew*
Senior production editor: *David M. Staloch*
Senior supplements producer: *Louis Swaim*
Compositor: *Eisner/Martin Typographics*
Typeface: *10/12 Palatino*
Printer and binder: *Bookmart*

http://www.mhhe.com

Contents

I. Introduction to *¿Qué tal?*

¿Qué tal?: An Introductory Course is a first-year program that emphasizes the four language skills—speaking, listening, reading, and writing—in a communicative approach to language learning. The goal of *¿Qué tal?* is to help students learn to communicate in Spanish—converse with others, express their own ideas in writing, and read and understand what others have written. The authors assume that effective communication depends on practice and have included meaningful, communicative exercises and activities as well as contextualized practice. Learning about Hispanic cultures is assumed to be an integral part of the language learning process.

The textbook's 18 main chapters are preceded by a three-part preliminary chapter, **Primeros pasos,** which introduces students to the Spanish language, the text format, and the program overall. Each of the text's regular chapters is divided into four **pasos,** highlighted with color tabs for easy reference, with a cultural feature in between **Pasos 2** and **3.** Thus, each regular chapter has the following structure:

Paso 1: Vocabulario
Paso 2: Gramática
Enfoque cultural
Paso 3: Gramática
Paso 4: Un paso más (optional section)

The following features of *¿Qué tal?* and its supplements (Listening Comprehension CD, Workbook/Laboratory Manual and Audio Program, Electronic Workbook/Laboratory Manual, Video, Student CD-ROM, Online Learning Center, Instructor's Manual and Resource Kit, Overhead Transparencies, and Electronic Language Tutor) contribute to the development of communication skills. The optional section, **Paso 4: Un paso más,** includes culminating video, reading, and writing exercises. Instructors may use part or all of this section, according to individual needs, interests, and schedules.

Each chapter is organized around a cultural or practical theme, with grammar, vocabulary, and culture working together as an interactive unit.

The opening page of each chapter establishes the chapter theme with a photograph that highlights both the chapter theme and the country of focus. This page also provides an overview of the vocabulary, grammar, and culture presented in the chapter.

Paso 1: Vocabulario focuses on theme-related vocabulary (family, shopping, and so forth). Since most of the chapter vocabulary is introduced in this first major section of the chapter, a focus on vocabulary is achieved that is separate, to a large extent, from the study of grammar. Once students are familiar with theme vocabulary, most of the grammar exercises in **Pasos 2** and **3** are based on situations related to the chapter theme and are therefore conducive to natural and meaningful language practice.

The theme is also reentered in the recombination activities of the **Un poco de todo** section, in the **Notas culturales** and **En los Estados Unidos y el Canadá...** boxes, and in **Paso 4: Un paso más. Videoteca: En contexto** offers a functionally driven vignette that also relates to the chapter theme. Extensive use of photographs and realia provide realistic and informative glimpses of Hispanic cultures.

Cognate vocabulary and real language are used throughout the text.

The extensive use of cognate vocabulary, especially in the early chapters, increases students' ability to communicate in Spanish while making minimum demands for new vocabulary memorization. Use of cognates helps students cope with their linguistic limitations as beginning language learners and encourages them to make linguistic predictions.

In all sections of the text, even in the more mechanical exercises, an attempt has been made to present students with "real-world" language. In exercises and activities, this means that individual items help students form sentences that they might want to say in real-life situations. Usually the exercise directions or set-up will establish this context. In dialogues and readings, unfamiliar vocabulary and structures are glossed or translated at the bottom of the page (in the case of minidialogues) rather than avoided. In realia, language is minimally glossed and has not been altered (although some—but not all—typographical errors have been fixed), and in this Instructor's Manual, instructors will find suggestions for using realia in ways appropriate to students' language levels at different stages of the course. Thus natural language input is provided, but great care has been taken to ensure that students need not *produce* unfamiliar vocabulary or structures.

Receptive skills provide the basis for the development of productive skills.

Throughout *¿Qué tal?*, attention is paid to the development of all four language skills. Most sections of the text offer students opportunities to work with new vocabulary and grammar concepts in a receptive mode (listening and reading) before having to produce them actively (speaking or writing). The *Instructor's Edition* contains abundant suggestions for listening comprehension activities and listening-based follow-ups to text activities.

Communication is an integral part of each grammar section.

The opportunity for student self-expression is integrated into each grammar section. The **Práctica** exercises are more controlled, form-focused exercises. Even here, however, exercises are set into contexts that infuse them with meaning: a general, "umbrella" situation, a logical sequence of actions, a story, and so on. Many **Práctica** exercises permit some student input within controlled situations. Others are accompanied by brief comprehension activities (in the student text or in the *Instructor's Edition*) that focus students' attention on the meaning of the exercise they have just completed.

Práctica exercises are followed by the **Conversación** section, in which activities encourage students to use the newly learned structures to talk about personally meaningful topics. Thus, students do not have to wait until the end of the chapter or the end of the book to begin expressing themselves with new structures. Many of the **Conversación** exercises consist of interviews or partner/pair and small-group work, providing students an opportunity to share ideas and use Spanish in a natural, relaxed conversational setting.

Chapter and text organization provide for built-in review.

In each chapter, the sections called **Paso 1: Vocabulario** and **Pasos 2** and **3: Gramática** provide a carefully controlled introduction and practice of new materials. The material introduced in these three sections is then combined, reentered, and reviewed in the review exercises of the **Un poco de todo** section, and in the readings, writing exercises, and video activities of **Paso 4: Un paso más.** This systematic reentry and review is designed to reinforce new knowledge and strengthen communication skills.

The **Un poco de todo** sections also provide systematic review of major topics such as **ser/estar,** preterite/imperfect, and so on. **¿Recuerda Ud.?** sections review earlier concepts on which new grammar is based.

A variety of material and exercises provides flexibility.

The exercises and activities in *¿Qué tal?* encourage the development of all four language skills: listening, speaking, reading, and writing. Many exercises lend themselves to either oral or written practice; individual course goals and instructors' preferences will determine how they will be used.

Additional exercises provided in many sections of the *Instructor's Edition* and in the Instructor's Manual and Resource Kit provide supplementary or alternative classroom practice, and individual instructors may select those exercises that best meet the needs of their students.

Ancillary materials—Workbook/Laboratory Manual, Electronic Workbook/Laboratory Manual, the Student CD-ROM, the Online Learning Center, and Electronic Language Tutor—provide additional out-of-class practice. Because the answers to many exercises are provided in the student text, Workbook, and Audio Program, students can check their answers at home and in the laboratory, saving class time for conversation practice. Most ancillary materials also offer many exercises and activities (of a more creative or open-ended nature) for which answers are not provided for students. Instructors may wish to collect these exercises to read and/or grade them as a way of monitoring students' progress.

SUGGESTIONS FOR SECOND-YEAR PROGRAMS

The choice of an intermediate text to use in second-year courses, after using *¿Qué tal?* in the first year, should be determined by the goals of your second-year program. If a focus on grammar is desired, you will want to select a text that has a strong grammar emphasis. If your intermediate program is highly communicative in nature, a text that de-emphasizes grammar in some way may meet your needs.

The following intermediate titles published by McGraw-Hill are appropriate for use in the intermediate sequence following *¿Qué tal?* McGraw-Hill also publishes a wide variety of cultural and literary readers for use as supplements to a text-driven course. Please contact your local McGraw-Hill sales representative for more information on these and other McGraw-Hill titles.

Punto y aparte: Spanish in Review: Moving Toward Fluency (Foerster, Lambright, Alfonso-Pinto: 2003). This program is the ideal bridge for students who have completed first-year or beginning Spanish and plan to go on to upper division course work in the language. It focuses on seven major communicative functions: describing, comparing, reacting and recommending, narrating in the past, expressing likes and dislikes, hypothesizing, and talking about the future.

Pasajes: An Intermediate Spanish Program (Bretz, Dvorak, Kirschner: 2002). This popular component program for intermediate Spanish offers instructors great flexibility. Any of the three volumes—*Lengua, Cultura,* and *Literatura*—can be used alone or in conjunction with each other. For each chapter in *Pasajes,* all three volumes share the same theme, grammar focus, and vocabulary. The Workbook/Laboratory Manual is coordinated with *Pasajes: Lengua* and offers additional practice with vocabulary and structures, as well as listening comprehension, pronunciation practice, and additional readings.

Al corriente: Curso intermedio de español (Blake et al.: 2003). This one-volume intermediate grammar review offers vocabulary development, grammar presentations, and many communicative activities. Authentic readings from journals and literature help students build reading skills.

Nuevos Destinos: Spanish in Review (Medina: 2003). The intermediate-level, video-based *Nuevos Destinos* is a core student textbook and two separate workbooks that make the text appropriate for two different courses: 1) an intensive high beginner course (review of first year), and 2) a second-year grammar review course. *Nuevos Destinos* is a collaboration with McGraw-Hill Higher Education, WGBH, and the Annenberg/CPB Project.

¡De viva voz! Intermediate Conversation and Grammar Review (Thomas: 2001). This second-year communicative text concentrates on conversation, and emphasizes the thematic and lexical structures necessary to support oral changes.

¿Qué te parece? (Lee, Young, Wolf, Chandler: 2000). Appropriate for any communicative or proficiency-based intermediate course, *¿Qué te parece?* offers students and instructors a refreshing change from the traditional topics of first- and second-year texts. Highly interesting and thought-provoking topics provide the framework for a complete grammar review with many task-based activities.

II. Using *¿Qué tal?* to Organize Courses for Language Proficiency

A. THE CONCEPT OF PROFICIENCY

Teaching for proficiency has been a goal of United States government and military language schools for over three decades, and many foreign language professionals in academia have also accepted it enthusiastically as a goal for their own classes. The emphasis on proficiency began largely in response to the findings of the 1979 President's Council on Foreign Languages and International Studies and as the result of the "Common Yardstick" project* and the profession's own growing concerns about foreign language instruction. Proficiency-based standards (as opposed to seat-time requirements) for university graduation and teacher certification continue to gain nationwide attention.

The reactions of the profession, both positive and negative, in professional journals and conferences testify to the interest and lively discussion that this concept has created. Although much of the discussion has centered on *oral* proficiency, the idea of proficiency is not, of course, limited to oral production. It also applies to reading, writing, and listening. Teams of professors working under American Council on the Teaching of Foreign Languages (ACTFL) coordination have written generic guidelines for all skills, and language-specific guidelines are available for the most commonly taught languages.†

B. TEACHING FOR PROFICIENCY: CLASSROOM APPLICATIONS OF THE CONCEPT OF PROFICIENCY

There are several ways to make the standard beginning language class more proficiency oriented. The suggestions that follow are based on the ACTFL Intermediate-level descriptors. No claim is made here that they offer a secret key that will magically unlock the doors to language proficiency, but when used with a textbook such as *¿Qué tal?*, which was developed with these concerns in mind, they can produce excellent results, even with the customary limitations imposed by time and the often excessive number of students in beginning language classes.

1. The ACTFL Intermediate Level

Creating with the language is an important criterion for the Intermediate level, so ways must be found to stimulate original language production. Personalization, contextualization, input-based and open-ended activities, small-group and/or pair work, and opportunities for correction-free self-expression are the keys to progress in this area, as is practice with critical language functions.

---

*This was a multinational effort aimed at developing a set of descriptors of language ability that led to the ACTFL/ETS oral proficiency scale in use today.

†ACTFL's website: http://www.actfl.org. ACTFL's Guidelines can also be found on several websites, such as http://www.sil.org/lingualinks/LANGUAGELEARNING/OtherResources/ACTFLProficiencyGuidelines/ACTFLProficiencyGuidelines.htm.

A. PERSONALIZATION

Students will learn Spanish more enthusiastically and produce it more spontaneously if they are encouraged from the beginning to speak and write about themselves, their families, their friends, their classes, and their favorite activities. Questions and topics that appeal to them will encourage more use of Spanish than will those about which they have no interest or knowledge.

¿Qué tal? gives students extensive opportunities to talk about things of greatest interest to them: their families, homes, school and work experiences, favorite sports, activities, and celebrities, plans for the future, and so on. There are many contextualized activities that call on students to answer questions, complete sentences, interview one another, or talk spontaneously about their tastes and preferences.

B. CONTEXTUALIZATION

Exercises consisting of a series of unrelated questions, fill-in-the-blank statements, and the like are much less effective in stimulating language production than are the interesting, contextualized activities of the sort found in *¿Qué tal?*

Even language use of the simplest kind takes on more meaning when placed in a thematic framework suggestive of a real-life situation. *¿Qué tal?* is filled with such activities. Here is an example of part of a contextualized activity based on the daily routine of Diego and Antonio, friends that students get to know throughout the exercises and activities in *¿Qué tal?* The activity is on page 263 and focuses on the use of **se** for unplanned events.

Un día fatal

¡A Diego y a Antonio todo les salió horrible hoy!
A Diego *se le cayó* la taza de café.
También *se le perdió* la cartera.
A Antonio *se le olvidaron* sus libros y su trabajo cuando fue a clase.
También *se le perdieron* las llaves de su apartamento.

C. INPUT-BASED ACTIVITIES

Second-language acquisition research has recently focused considerable attention on the importance of the development of receptive skills in the broader language learning process. This means not only working on listening and reading skill development, as many good instructors have always done, but more importantly, providing opportunities for students to be exposed to new materials via input-based activities.

Paso 1: Vocabulario sections of *¿Qué tal?* have traditionally provided such activities. An important feature of the Sixth Edition is the inclusion of input activities in the grammar sections as well. For example, the first student text activity in the **Práctica** section on **-ar** verbs (p. 43) permits students to "process" a variety of **-ar** present tense forms in a meaningful context.

Paso 1. Read the following statements and tell whether they are true for you and your classmates and for your classroom environment. If any statement is not true for you or your class, make it negative or change it in another way to make it correct.

MODELO: **Toco el piano. → Sí, toco el piano. (No, no toco el piano. Toco la guitarra.)**

1. **Necesito dinero.**
2. **Trabajo en la biblioteca.**

and so on. **Paso 2** of the same activity provides an opportunity for students to work with the new structure in pairs, using the same sentences that they have become familiar with in **Paso 1.**

D. OPEN-ENDED ACTIVITIES

Exercises and activities in any given part of a text should progress from the more controlled, in which students are expected to supply the correct answer to demonstrate understanding of a concept or mastery of vocabulary, to the open-ended, in which they are encouraged to be inventive and communicate their own ideas. *¿Qué tal?* is rich in such open-ended activities, as can be seen in this one from page 158 in the student text.

> **Una encuesta sobre la comida. Hágales** (*Ask*) **preguntas a sus compañeros de clase para saber si toman las comidas or bebidas indicadas y con qué frecuencia. Deben explicar también por qué toman o *no* toman cierta cosa.**
>
> MODELO: **la carne →** E1: **¿Comes carne?**
> E2: **No *la* como casi nunca porque tiene mucho colesterol.**

No judgment of right or wrong should inhibit language use in these activities, for students must feel free to use Spanish as a natural means of communicating personal thoughts and feelings. For the most part, error correction should be done at a later time, as discussed in letter F.

E. SMALL-GROUP AND PAIR WORK

The difficulty of working on such open-ended activities in the large classes normally found in colleges and universities can be dealt with successfully by dividing students into pairs or small groups. These can be for reading, writing, conversational, or cultural-research assignments, or for a combination of skills. It is helpful to match talented students with those of less advanced language ability so that no team is likely to become the class "star." (This also has the effect of allowing slower learners to receive help from more proficient language students in a nonthreatening situation.) Specific tasks should be assigned and time limits established for each activity. The instructor should "float" from one group to another providing assistance or encouragement as needed, ensuring that Spanish is being used, and making mental (or discreetly written) notes of common errors to be worked on later. Each group or pair must know that some, if not all, of them will be required at the end to share with the class what they have been doing during the activity. If all are called on with equal regularity, it will not matter if any given pair or group is not selected to "report" at the end of a specific activity. A friendly, cooperative, noncompetitive environment must be established in the classroom so that students will want to work together toward proficiency.

F. ERROR CORRECTION

Also critical to developing proficiency is judicious error correction. In real-life situations, errors are allowed to pass uncorrected unless they interfere with communication, at which time conversation usually breaks down. In the classroom the same thing must be allowed to happen, difficult though it may be for the instructor to allow. A good technique is for the instructor to take note of frequently made errors as unobtrusively as possible when they occur (in general class discussions or in small-group work) and bring them up after the open-ended activity session is over. Then additional practice can focus on eliminating the more troublesome problems. Only if errors interfere with communication or threaten to be repeated so frequently as to become ingrained should a "free expression" activity be interrupted for correction.

G. LANGUAGE FUNCTIONS

Other functions essential to reaching the Intermediate level of proficiency are the ability *to ask and answer* questions and *to survive predictable situations.* Throughout *¿Qué tal?* students are given the opportunity to interview each other or to ask questions in the context of communicative activities. Many role-play situations are also suggested—some rather structured, others quite open-ended. Again, instructors can be as creative as they like in providing opportunities for students to practice these critical functions.

Instructors with a proficiency orientation will want to note in addition the following functional features of the Sixth Edition of *¿Qué tal?*

- The presentation of some material traditionally presented as grammar in the **Nota comunicativa** boxes. For example, the **acabar** + **de** + infinitive structure is presented in such a box (p. 158), in the context of a discussion of actions associated with food and mealtimes.
- The emphasis on language functions in grammar section headings, so that students focus on the function they will be learning to perform rather than exclusively on structure.
- The **Videoteca** sections include dialogues and activities related to the video segments from the *¿Qué tal?* **En contexto** portion of the Video Program. **Videoteca** offers practical, real-life situations involving the cultural themes (for example, trying to meet an interesting person) of each chapter or related to everyday linguistic negotiations (for example, asking for directions). **En contexto** features **Lluvia de ideas,** several questions linking the content of this video segment to the student's own life; a **Dictado;** and **Un diálogo original,** a segment that allows the student to reenact and process the new information. Instructors can also use the **Minidramas** portion of the Video Program. Suggestions for use can be found in Section X of this Manual.
- The Conversation Cards (in the Instructor's Manual and Resource Kit).

The goal of all such dialogues and activities is to create the illusion of "real-life" human interaction and to allow students to express their own experiences, opinions, and feelings in Spanish. Such exercises and activities provide an ideal opportunity for small-group or pair practice, and they are often identified as such. In addition, the Instructor's Manual suggests further ways to expand and personalize exercises. Instructors are encouraged to allow spontaneous class discussion and conversations in Spanish to develop out of the information revealed by students as they enjoy the activities in the text.

2. Reducing the First-Year Grammar Load

One frequent response to suggestions like those in the preceding section is, "I'd like to be able to take the time for such activities in my class, but if I do, we'll never finish the book." This is certainly a problem in multiple-section courses in which all students must arrive at the same point by the end of each term, and it is a problem that has often been exacerbated by the philosophy of textbook writers and departmental administrators alike. It is usual for foreign language textbooks to pack a standard canon of grammar into a first-year book, and department heads routinely expect instructors to cover every bit of it in a year. The frustrations that result for both instructors and students are obvious.

There are some very solid reasons for *reducing the amount of grammar presented in beginning courses.* First, it is clearly more likely that students will master the fundamentals of Spanish if they are given time to use vocabulary and structures repeatedly in a variety of contexts. Proficiency in Spanish is not attained merely by knowing about Spanish but by using Spanish as much as possible. Concepts and vocabulary must become second nature to the language learner, and this is not achieved by memorization alone. It is far more effective to reduce the quantity of structures studied and fully master those that *are* taught than to pack the course so heavily with grammar that students spend all their time memorizing new rules and have no time to practice using them.

Second, setting the ACTFL Intermediate level as a reasonable goal for first-year students of Spanish suggests that the most important grammar structures for a first-year course are those necessary to achieve proficiency at that level. This means that the structures that enable students to express their own feelings in a personal way, talk about their own lives, survive basic, predictable situations, ask and answer questions, and in general sustain a good conversation are those that should receive the greatest emphasis in a first-year text. This is not to say that structures such as the imperfect subjunctive and the conditional should never be taught in a first-year course; it merely implies that teachers should not set unreasonable goals for their students. Successful mastery of the preterite and imperfect or of the subjunctive on an achievement test does not necessarily translate into proficiency at advanced levels, where those structures are essential.

¿Qué tal? has taken these factors into account. It places greatest emphasis on those structures essential to achieving proficiency at the Intermediate level. Here are some examples. Concepts such as the past perfect indicative are downplayed, introduced lexically (p. 336 of the student text), and practiced only briefly. Passive **se** constructions are presented for recognition only. Material such as the past subjunctive, *if* clauses, and future verb and conditional verb forms are all presented in later chapters (although parts of these paradigms are presented functionally relatively early in the text, for example, **me gustaría** + infinitive).

Consequently, students work with these secondary structures (secondary for the needs of beginning students), but not as much as with other, more fundamental material. Exposure to the structures, however, means that students have an awareness of them, with in-depth study postponed to the second year. In all probability they will master such material more quickly when the appropriate time comes, and the first year can be devoted to practice with and review of more basic material, where proficiency can more realistically be achieved.

3. Authentic Materials

Realia and authentic texts of all kinds enhance students' receptive skills, reinforce vocabulary, contextualize grammar, provide a basis for real-life conversations, and contribute to cultural understanding. Without authentic materials, a language text is sterile. With them, learning a language can be an enjoyable, enriching, practical experience. Thus, authentic materials have always formed an integral part of *¿Qué tal?*

4. Ancillary Materials

The package of materials that accompanies *¿Qué tal?* provides enormous support to both students and instructors interested in proficiency building. The effectiveness of *¿Qué tal?* will be greatly enhanced by adding or working with any of the components of that package. (See the Preface to the student text for a complete list of the materials that are available.)

C. CONCLUSION

¿Qué tal? is up to date in its approach to teaching Spanish and can be used effectively in proficiency oriented classrooms. To derive the maximum benefits from the materials, instructors are urged to do the following:

- Encourage personalized, open-ended conversation with the class as a whole and with students working in pairs or small groups, and spontaneously, as suggested by thematic vocabulary, realia, and readings.
- Capitalize on the thematic vocabulary sections to enhance students' word power in Spanish.
- Take full advantage of integrated realia and authentic texts, so that students can learn to read Spanish meaningfully.
- Regularly use the student ancillaries and the abundant support materials available to the instructor.
- Above all, ensure that grades are calculated in such a way as to reflect the communication skills students are practicing, in equal proportion to the time spent on them in class.

This approach to teaching for proficiency should make learning Spanish both more enjoyable to students and more functionally productive. The ACTFL Intermediate level is a reasonable goal for first-year college students to achieve, and it is not too much to expect that most students in a class will reach that level in most skills. *¿Qué tal?* provides a framework and an extensive series of communicative activities designed to lead to that level of proficiency. When sufficient time, encouragement, and help are provided, students can achieve the highest level of proficiency possible in one year and establish a solid foundation on which further proficiency can be built.

While believing that their text serves well as a vehicle for proficiency-oriented classes, the authors of *¿Qué tal?* feel that no textbook can promise that students will achieve the proficiency goals set by a language department, by ACTFL, or by any other organization. It remains the individual instructor's task to carefully and consistently implement and supplement in the classroom the proficiency-oriented activities found in the text. It is the authors' hope that the text will be used as they intended: to help students develop proficiency in the four language skills essential to truly communicative language learning and to learn about Hispanic culture within the United States, Canada, and abroad.

III. Teaching Techniques

This section provides detailed explanations of the parts of each chapter in *¿Qué tal?*—what is found in each of them and why—as well as general suggestions for using, elaborating upon, and adapting the text materials and *Instructor's Edition* glosses.

A. PRELIMINARY LESSON: *PRIMEROS PASOS*

The preliminary lesson has three purposes: to make students aware of the importance of the Spanish language; to give them a functional introduction to the language and make it possible for them to speak it from the very first days of class, before any grammar has been formally covered; and to set up the organization of the chapters that follow.

Primeros pasos is divided into three parts. **Primera parte** begins with **Saludos y expresiones de cortesía,** a section with three minidialogues, a number of useful expressions, and several exercises for practicing the new material. It contains the first of the text's **Nota comunicativa** sections. It also provides an introduction to the sounds of Spanish via the alphabet, with a focus on sounds that beginning students need to become aware of immediately to develop good listening and speaking habits. The concept of cognates is presented in **Los cognados,** and cognate adjectives are given simple focused practice with the singular forms of **ser,** set in a functional context (**¿Cómo es usted?**). The **Los cognados** section also contains "Spanish in the United States and in the World," a brief history of the development of the Spanish language, as well as an overview of the importance, wide dispersion, and diversity of modern Spanish, including the Spanish spoken in the United States.

Segunda parte begins with more cognate study (**Más cognados**). In this section, the exercise materials introduce students informally to gender distinctions and forms of the indefinite article. Vowel sounds are presented and practiced for the first time in **Pronunciación. Los números 0–30; hay** continues to develop the concept of gender and introduces **hay** for both statements and questions. In **Gustos y preferencias** only the singular **me/te/le gusta** forms are introduced, and exercises with these memorized forms introduce students to the forms of the definite article and to infinitives. **El mundo hispánico (Parte 1)** picks up the theme of Hispanic culture beginning in **Primera parte,** but in Spanish. The major Spanish-speaking areas of the world are introduced, with the names of countries and capital cities and their populations. The reading introduces **está** for location.

Tercera parte begins with telling time (**¿Qué hora es?**). A list of interrogative words presented throughout **Primeros pasos** is given in **Palabras interrogativas. El mundo hispánico (Parte 2)** reenters the concept of cognates, stressing contextual guessing and introducing students to a system (the underlining of guessable cognates in cultural readings) that will help them build cognate recognition skills throughout the text. Active vocabulary that students should learn before beginning **Capítulo 1** is listed in **Vocabulario: Primeros pasos.**

The First Day of Class

The first day of class can be the most important day of the course, since it sets the tone for what will happen during the rest of the term. Many language instructors like to use the first class meeting to introduce students to both the course and the language. The first day of class can include an introduction to the course, getting to know students, and beginning an active practice of the Spanish language.

1. Introduction to the Course

You may want to include the following items as you briefly discuss the organization of the course, although many of the details can be left until later in the term.

- Introduce yourself and announce your office number, office phone number, and the hours when you will be available to students for individual consultations.
- State the course goals. Will there be equal emphasis on all four language skills (listening, speaking, reading, and writing), or will there be special emphasis on one or more of them? To what extent will cultural content be required learning?
- Distribute the syllabus and briefly discuss materials the students will need for the course (basic book, Workbook/Laboratory Manual, and so on).
- Give general information about testing and grading.
- What are your expectations? Is attendance required? Will written exercises be collected and corrected? Will homework exercises be corrected or discussed in class? What do you expect in terms of class participation and lab attendance?
- Discuss the language laboratory and use of the Audio Program, if appropriate in your program.
- Provide hints on how to study a foreign language. Emphasize the fact that learning a language is learning a skill, more like learning how to swim or ride a bike than like learning history, and that it is important to practice using the language daily. Merely memorizing vocabulary and grammar rules is not enough for learning how to read, write, speak, and understand Spanish.

2. Getting to Know Students

Because language learning is essentially communication practice and requires a lot of risk taking on the part of the learner, it is extremely important for students and instructor to get to know each other and feel comfortable together. There are several ways to establish this kind of rapport.

- Ask students to fill out an information sheet or a file card with whatever information you think would be useful or interesting to know about them: name; high school attended; local address and phone number; language studied previously in high school or college, and for how long; class rank and major; whether they have ever traveled, worked, or studied in another country (if so, where, and for how long); and so on.
- Ask students to wear name tags or put one on their desks, to facilitate the learning of names by all members of the class.
- Plan at least one or two first-day activities in which students practice Spanish with each other and begin to get to know each other. Make an effort to learn as many students' names as you can. This will help subsequent classes run more smoothly and will also demonstrate your interest in your students.

B. CHAPTER SEQUENCE AND TYPES OF ACTIVITIES

Each of the eighteen basic chapters of *¿Qué tal?* is organized according to a fixed sequence. This section of the manual follows the chapter sequence.

1. Chapter-Opening Pages

The first two pages of each chapter serve to introduce students to the cultural theme and the grammar points to be studied in the chapter, as well as to outline the technology-based materials available to students to use or practice. The first page includes a four-color photograph followed by a list of the chapter content and related materials. The *Instructor's Edition* annotations also serve as a springboard for asking questions about the photo. These questions often have students relate the content of the photo to their own lives.

2. *Paso 1: Vocabulario*

This section of each *¿Qué tal?* chapter presents important vocabulary related to the chapter theme and provides vocabulary-building activities. (Only thematically related words are introduced and practiced in this section. A complete list of all new words for the chapter is in the **Vocabulario** at the end of each chapter.) It is assumed that the **Paso 1: Vocabulario** will be studied before the other sections of the chapter. This approach establishes the chapter theme and makes it possible to reenter and thus reinforce these important lexical items throughout the chapter. It also minimizes the amount of active vocabulary introduced later in the **Pasos 2** and **3 Gramática** sections, where emphasis is on the presentation of new grammar. Finally, it ensures that students will have the vocabulary necessary to handle the communicative situations posed throughout the chapter.

Instructors can use the drawing and/or vocabulary list that appears at the beginning of each **Paso 1: Vocabulario** section as a vehicle for the introduction of theme vocabulary. Many instructors feel it is useful first to model pronunciation and then to ask for choral repetition. *Modeling pronunciation* means providing an example of the correct pronunciation of the words or phrases that appear in the list. Students listen and imitate your pronunciation. *Choral repetition* means repetition by the whole class, with students speaking in unison. Beginning with choral repetition provides practice for everyone—an especially important factor in large classes—and allows individual students to reach some level of accuracy and confidence before being called on individually. During choral repetition, you can listen attentively for errors in pronunciation and call attention to them. It is best to deal with such errors as a whole-class activity, rather than drawing attention to individual students.

Once theme vocabulary has been presented, you should concentrate on individual words in the **Paso 1: Vocabulario** drawings and lists. The suggestions in this Manual will call your attention to words of particular interest, words that may cause problems for a variety of reasons, or words that need more explanation. For example, in the theme vocabulary list in **Capítulo 3** (p. 81), you should discuss the differences between a **mercado** and a **tienda,** explain the concept behind the verb **regatear,** and so on.

Certain conventions are observed in the listing of vocabulary, and you will want to bring these to students' attention at the beginning of the course. Nouns are always given with their articles in **Paso 1: Vocabulario** and students should be encouraged to learn the article with the noun as a means of learning the gender of nouns. Both masculine and feminine forms are indicated for adjectives—**alto/a, trabajador(a)**—and for nouns referring to persons—**chico/a, profesor(a)**. The use of a slash (**o/a**) indicates that the **-o** ending of the masculine form is replaced by **-a** in the feminine form. The use of parentheses (**a**) indicates that the **-a** is added to the masculine form to form the feminine.

Practice is just as essential in learning vocabulary as it is in learning grammar, and so vocabulary-building activities have been included in the **Paso 1: Vocabulario** section. The most frequently used types of vocabulary activities in *¿Qué tal?* include the following.

A. FILL-IN-THE-BLANK ACTIVITIES

This type of activity requires students to fill in the blank with the word or phrase that most accurately completes the sentence. For example, in **¿Quién es?** (p. 55), students study the chapter vocabulary list, then complete the sentences with the correct names of members of the family:

1. **La madre de mi padre es mi <u>abuela</u>.**
2. **El hijo de mi tío es mi <u>primo</u>.**

There is only one right answer to the items in this exercise.

In **Conversación C,** (p. 82), some of the items have more than one correct answer, but comprehension of the vocabulary items is still tested. Item 4, for example, can be completed in several ways:

4. **Cuando estoy en casa todo el día, llevo <u>*bluejeans*</u> / <u>una camiseta</u>...**

B. QUESTION/ANSWER (PERSONALIZED QUESTIONS)

In this type of activity, students practice new vocabulary by answering questions based on general knowledge or shared reality (the classroom environment, for example), or by answering questions about themselves and sharing their own experiences or opinions. For example, the questions in **Preguntas** (p. 103) illustrate the wide range of question-answer sequences. Item 1 requires general knowledge: **¿Qué día es hoy?,** and so on. Item 2 draws on shared knowledge: **¿Qué días de la semana tenemos clase?,** and so on. And items 3 and 4 are personalized: **¿Estudia Ud. mucho durante el fin de semana?,** and so on.

C. LOGICAL COMPLETION AND PERSONALIZED COMPLETION

In this type of fill-in-the-blank activity, students practice new vocabulary by completing sentences with logical words and phrases, or according to their own opinions, attitudes, or experiences. There is, of course, no single right answer to this type of exercise, but you can gauge students' command of and understanding of vocabulary items by the appropriateness of their responses.

Conversación B (p. 82) shows the whole range of possibilities for this type of exercise. There is only one logical answer to items 1 through 5, based on the vocabulary list on the previous page. In items 6 through 9, the context is quite controlled and students' answers will be predictable but varied.

8. **La ropa de seda/lana es muy elegante.**

Many items are almost completely personalized.

D. ASSOCIATIONS

In this type of activity, students indicate what words or phrases they associate with other words or phrases. Thus, they make associations between vocabulary items and review vocabulary clusters, for example, **Conversación B** (p. 55): **¿Quién es?** Here, students answer the question that serves as the title of the activity by telling the characteristics they associate with a famous personality, such as Bill Gates.

E. DEFINITIONS

In the first chapters of *¿Qué tal?,* definition activities are passive in nature; students are given a definition or paraphrase of a vocabulary item and respond only with the item defined. Sometimes only the definitions are given and students must supply words on their own, for example, **Conversación B** (p. 151):

B. Definiciones. ¿Qué es?

1. **un plato de lechuga y tomate**
2. **una bebida alcohólica blanca o roja**

In the later chapters of *¿Qué tal?,* definition activities become more active, and students are asked to give simple definitions of new vocabulary items. By this point, they will have a large enough vocabulary to create reasonable definitions, as in **Conversación B** (p. 283). In other definition activities a matching format is used (**Conversación B,** p. 327).

F. VISUAL-BASED ACTIVITIES

Students complete sentences, answer questions, or make statements based on line drawings in the text. This type of activity cues vocabulary items without the use of translation, and without the cue's telling the students the word you want them to practice. Sometimes these activities are very structured, allowing for only one correct answer. Generally, however, they are more open, allowing for increased student creativity while providing a structure for it. In such open-ended activities, students should be encouraged to produce as many answers as possible. Often, several students may express the same idea in very different ways, and that type of repetition should be encouraged, since the goal of the activity is vocabulary practice. Examples of this type of activity include **Conversación B** (p. 38): **Semejanzas** (*Similarities*) **y diferencias.** Here students identify and contrast the two drawings by using a simple formula:

En el dibujo A / En el escritorio del dibujo A, hay _______.

Various answers are possible, but the activity itself is quite controlled by the particular items in the drawing and by the formula given.

Or **Conversación B** (p. 175):

En el aeropuerto. ¿Cuántas cosas y acciones puede Ud. identificar o describir en este dibujo?

In this activity, the only limits are the student's creativity and vocabulary. Since no formula is given, any answer is appropriate.

G. *¿CIERTO O FALSO?* (AGREE OR DISAGREE)

In this type of activity, students indicate whether statements are true or false, or whether they agree or disagree with them. In many cases, students know enough vocabulary and grammar to correct false statements or change statements to ones with which they do agree, for example, **Conversación A** (p. 55). In this activity, correcting false statements is quite simple to do, since students need change only the name in question or the word that describes the relationship. A more complex example of this type of activity is **Conversación B** (p. 324):

Problemas del mundo en que vivimos. Comente las siguientes opiniones. Puede usar las siguientes expresiones para aclarar (*clarify*) **su posición. ¡OJO! Todas las expresiones requieren el uso del subjuntivo o del infinitivo.**

Es/Me parece (*It seems to me*) **fundamental/importantísimo/ridículo/¿ ?**

Me opongo a que (*I am against*)**...**

No creo que...

1. **Para conservar energía debemos mantener bajo el termostato en el invierno y elevarlo en el verano.**

Here, students express personal opinions and attitudes about energy conservation by reacting to a series of statements.

H. MATCHING (MULTIPLE CHOICE)

This type of activity focuses on the recognition of new vocabulary. Students are asked to match new words with their definitions or with their opposites, questions with appropriate answers, or statements with appropriate rejoinders. An example of this kind of activity is **Conversación A** (p. 202), in which students match a situation with an appropriate emotion. You may want to extend this kind of activity by having students continue the conversation initiated by the linking of situation with response:

1. **Es Navidad y alguien le hace a Ud. un regalo carísimo. ¿Cómo se siente? ¿Qué le dice?**

I. SITUATIONS/LOGICAL CONCLUSIONS

In this type of activity, the text provides the situation or context within which to use vocabulary. Students respond to the situation by telling what they would do or say, for example, **Conversación B**

(p. 124): **Consejos** (*Advice*) **para Joaquín.** The situations in this activity are structured enough to lead students in the direction of the use of particular vocabulary items (in this case, weather words and phrases), and yet open enough to permit humor and creativity.

J. SURVEY/SELF-TESTS

In the category of the input-based activities described in Section I is a type of activity best described as a Survey/Self-Test. In these activities, which frequently occur in the **Paso 1: Vocabulario** sections as well as in **Pasos 2** and **3: Gramática,** students check off the answers to a series of questions or responses to items. Typical surveys ask for yes/no answers or for students to rate the frequency with which they do a particular activity.

An example of this type of activity is **Conversación C, Cuando Ud. viaja...** (p. 405):

Paso 1. A continuación hay una lista de las acciones típicas de los viajeros. ¿Hace Ud. lo mismo cuando viaja? Indique las acciones que son verdaderas para Ud.

1. ☐ **Hago una reserva en un hotel (motel) o en una pensión con un mes de anticipación.**
2. ☐ **Confirmo la reserva antes de salir de viaje.**

and so on. The activity offers structured input with the new vocabulary of the chapter (**En un viaje al extranjero**) and, at the same time, is highly personalized, since students respond according to their own experiences.

The advantages and benefits of this type of activity are obvious. Although on the surface the activity seems relatively passive, it is quite engaging and will maintain students' interest. Furthermore, the follow-up activity (**Paso 2. Ahora piensa en su último viaje...**) guides students toward productive use of the vocabulary and grammar. With this type of activity, students *can* produce a brief narrative of their last trip because the texts provide a supportive framework for such an activity. Compare what students can do in this type of activity with the results instructors typically achieve when they ask the class questions like **¿Quién quiere hablar de su último viaje?**

K. *ESTUDIO DE PALABRAS* ACTIVITIES

The purpose of this type of activity is to make students become more aware of word families and word morphology—the forms of related nouns and verbs, for example, **Conversación A** (p. 240): **Estudio de palabras.**

Here, students give the nouns or verbs that correspond to the cue words, indicated by italic letters in the student text (here shown with **respiración... → respira**). You may want to use this type of activity far more often than it occurs in the student text, simply by giving students vocabulary items for which they know related words. In particular, it is a good idea to practice word families when you are presenting the theme vocabulary for a chapter. In this way, students relate new words to words they have already learned, and the new material may seem easier to learn.

L. LOGICAL SEQUENCE ACTIVITIES

In this type of activity, students are given—out of sequence—a series of statements about an event. They demonstrate comprehension of the vocabulary items by putting the sentences into logical or sequential order, for example, **Conversación A** (p. 175):

Imagine que Ud. va a hacer un viaje en avión. El vuelo sale a las siete de la mañana. Usando los números del 1 al 9, indique en qué orden van a pasar las siguientes cosas.

M. CLASSROOM-BASED ACTIVITIES

The people and objects in the classroom provide the basis for this type of activity, for example, **Conversación B** (p. 84):

¿De qué color es?

Paso 1. Tell the color of things in your classroom, especially the clothing your classmates are wearing.

> MODELO: **El bolígrafo de Anita es amarillo. Roberto lleva calcetines azules, una camisa de cuadros morados y azules, *bluejeans*...**

Paso 2. Now describe what someone in the class is wearing, without revealing his or her name. Using your clues, can your classmates guess whom you are describing?

Here, colors are practiced in a natural context. The activity is at once controlled (by the model) and open-ended, since on any given day there will be many interesting kinds of clothing to describe.

N. *ENTREVISTAS*

In most interview activities in the **Paso 1: Vocabulario** sections, the structure of the **Entrevista** is provided by the activity items, for example, **Conversación C, Paso 2** (p. 305):

Ahora entreviste a un compañero/una compañera para saber cuáles son sus preferencias con respecto a este tema.

In **Paso 1,** students were requested to give their own preferences.

Often interview activities will end with the suggestion that students share the information they have learned with the class. This need not be done each time an interview activity is done, nor is it necessary to go around the class and have every student report what he/she has learned. However, instructors who frequently use this type of activity find that a brief share-back phase helps to validate the activity in students' eyes and that it often provides the stimulus for lively conversation.

O. ROLE PLAYS/STORY INVENTION

This open-ended activity allows a great deal of freedom on the part of the students, while providing a highly focused context. After students have had a chance to practice in small groups or pairs, they can act out the text with the rest of the class as an audience. The following example (**Conversación B,** p. 362) focuses on careers.

C. ¿Qué preparación se necesita tener para ser... ? Imagine que Ud. es consejero universitario / consejera universitaria. Explíquele a un estudiante qué cursos debe tomar para prepararse en las siguientes carreras. Consulte la lista de cursos académicos del Capítulo 1 y use la siguiente lista. Piense también en el tipo de experiencia que debe obtener.

In this activity, students should be encouraged to move from merely providing a list of courses and to try to imitate the speech and manner of an academic counselor.

In addition to the vocabulary activities in the student text, many more activities are provided in the suggestions in Section X of this Manual. If those suggestions and the listening-passage model of vocabulary presentation are followed, the following sequence will be observed.

1. Students first hear vocabulary in meaningful contexts.
2. Students verify comprehension of vocabulary and use vocabulary in one-word answers during a meaningful interchange with the instructor.

3. Students incorporate vocabulary into prefabricated sentences (that is, sentences given in the student text).
4. Students use vocabulary in original sentences for communication.

It is a good idea to spread the presentation and practice of vocabulary over two class meetings. A typical sequence to follow would be to present vocabulary during the second half of one class (listening passage or modeling with choral repetition, focus on individual words), and then practice the vocabulary (using the *Instructor's Edition* and student text activities) on the following day. This brief preview of material the day before will prepare students to work on the vocabulary activities as a homework assignment. (For ways to fit this sequence into your classes, see "Lesson Planning," Section V, this Manual.)

Finally, the *Instructor's Edition* points out which **Paso 1: Vocabulario** visuals are included in the set of transparencies. (See also "The Master Organizing Document," Section IX, this Manual.) For some chapters, there are additional (optional) drawings that are appropriate for vocabulary presentation, practice, and discussion.

3. *Pasos* 2 and 3: *Gramática*

In *¿Qué tal?*, grammar is presented in three phases—introduction, explanation, and practice. Each phase has a separate function. In the introductory phase, a minidialogue, cartoon, drawing, or some other similar example serves as a point of departure for each grammar explanation. Then, grammar explanations present and define grammatical terms and give English examples before presenting Spanish forms, functions, and rules. The word **¡OJO!** ("Watch out!") calls students' attention to areas where they should be especially careful when speaking and writing Spanish, since these are areas in which beginning students frequently make mistakes or have special difficulties. The practice phase of each section is divided into two parts—**Práctica** (more controlled practice) and **Conversación** (more open-ended practice).

Early chapters contain more grammar points than do later chapters, to provide for more rapid development of linguistic skills at the beginning of the course and to permit increased use of the supplementary skill-based activities in later chapters. The number of grammar points per chapter is as follows:

CHAPTERS	GRAMMAR POINTS
2	4 points
1, 3–9, 12	3 points
10, 11, 13–16	2 points
17, 18	1 point

Individual grammar sections do not actively practice grammar from any other section in that chapter. Therefore, within a chapter, you can present the individual grammar sections in any convenient order. Most instructors will choose to follow the sequence of grammar points as presented in the text. On occasion, however, increased flexibility may be useful—when you have less than the usual amount of time, for example, or when you have ten minutes left and had anticipated thirty, you may want to present and begin practice on one of the shorter grammar points in the chapter, rather than beginning the longer, more complex one you had planned to do. You will also appreciate this flexibility of presentation when your own style or philosophy requires it.

All grammar points, however, are practiced together later in the chapter—in the **Un poco de todo** activity and in the optional **Paso 4: Un paso más** section that follows. Thus, the overall organization of *¿Qué tal?* has a focused, single-emphasis presentation cycle (**Paso 1: Vocabulario, Pasos 2** and **3: Gramática**) and a recombined or synthesis-application cycle (**Un poco de todo, Paso 4: Un paso más**).

A. *MINIDIÁLOGOS* (MINIDIALOGUES)

The **Minidiálogos** in many of the grammar sections have several purposes: (1) to introduce new grammatical structures in a meaningful context; (2) to add a light touch to the classroom interaction; and (3) to provide short dialogues that can serve as models of conversation. Forms that illustrate a new grammar point are italicized in the **Minidiálogos.**

Because the **Minidiálogos** are short and introduce only one new grammar point, they lend themselves to oral practice. Since they relate to either practical or humorous situations, they are easy to introduce in class and are fun to work with.

A sequence of classroom activities to follow when using the **Minidiálogos** is: (1) presentation, (2) practice, (3) comprehension check, and (4) use of the **Minidiálogo** to introduce a new grammar structure.

(1) Presentation You can assign preparation of the dialogues as homework geared to the presentation of a new grammar section during the next class meeting. Since a dialogue contains only one new grammar point, it should be possible for students to understand it on their own. (The English equivalents of the **Minidiálogos,** which appear at the bottom of the page, will be helpful in this regard.) Some of the **Minidiálogos** also appear on the audio program.

The **Minidiálogos** also lend themselves quite well to in-class presentation and practice. You may want to begin the presentation by explaining briefly the communicative focus of the dialogue. For example, the one on page 33 can be introduced by your saying, "This minidialogue expresses some of the stress we all feel about time demands," or words to that effect. Or, instead of focusing on the communicative content of the minidialogue, you can introduce it by previewing its grammar content: "This minidialogue will help you learn about naming things in Spanish."

Another way to develop the minidialogues in class is to model them yourself. First, read the minidialogue through once aloud, pausing for student comprehension. Next, model each dialogue line, breaking longer sentences into shorter phrases.

Students can repeat the shorter phrases after you and imitate your rhythm, pronunciation, and intonation as closely as possible. As with the presentation of new vocabulary or in pronunciation practice, initial student repetitions should usually be choral. Choral repetition may be followed by half-class, partial-class, or single-row repetition of phrases or lines from the dialogue before you move on to repetition by individual students.

(2) Continuing Practice As a prelude to individual repetition of the dialogues, you can divide the class into groups (according to the number of speakers in the minidialogue) and have students practice choral reading, with each group reading the lines of one speaker. Next, assign individuals roles to read aloud, or ask for volunteers; the rest of the class listens, perhaps with books closed, as individuals read. As an alternative, students can be assigned specific roles to rehearse out of class and then present in class as a dramatization.

(3) Comprehension Check Most **Minidiálogos** are followed by a series of comprehension questions that test students' understanding of the minidialogue. Typically, these comprehension questions also guide students toward using the new grammar point being introduced, but without requiring its active manipulation. For example, in the **Minidiálogo** in Grammar Section 3 (p. 40), students gain passive practice with **-ar** verbs via the minidialogues and by answering the questions, but students are not required to transform the wording when responding to questions or to use verb forms they have not yet seen. Note also that the *Instructor's Edition* frequently contains additional comprehension activities and personalized questions based on the topic of the minidialogue.

(4) Introduction of New Grammar Structures Phrases from the **Minidiálogos** can be used to initiate formal grammar presentation in a more focused way than would be achieved by manipulating new grammar in comprehension questions. Draw students' attention to grammatical patterns by asking several questions of the **¿Cómo se dice _______? ** or **¿Qué significa _______?** type.

You may want to use phrases from the **Minidiálogos** to stimulate inferences about grammatical structures. The minidialogue for **-ar** verbs (p. 40) can be used in this way to help students recognize personal endings. (See "Presenting Grammar" that follows for a more thorough discussion of this kind of presentation.)

Note that not all grammar sections in *¿Qué tal?* are introduced with a **Minidiálogo.** Some use a cartoon or a line drawing that illustrates the grammar point, and the techniques outlined above can still be applied. Occasionally a grammar point is introduced by a series of drawings that can be used to lead the student toward an understanding of the grammar point in question. Reflexive verbs and pronouns (Grammar Section 13, p. 114) is introduced in this way. Each numbered drawing illustrates an aspect of Diego's daily routine with a corresponding numbered statement (**1.** ***Me despierto*** **a las siete y media...**). Students are then asked to talk about their own daily routines according to models given. (See "Presenting Grammar" that follows for a more thorough discussion of this kind of presentation.)

Not all the techniques outlined in this section of the Manual will be appropriate to your course goals. For example, few instructors will have enough class time to cover every **Minidiálogo** in the text by following the four-point sequence described here. You may want to cover one minidialogue thoroughly in each chapter and do only brief coverage of the others; in that case, it would be most logical to focus on the minidialogue for the most important grammar point in the chapter. Alternately, you may want to focus on those dialogues that appeal to your students because they touch on common interests or for some other reason go over particularly well.

B. PRESENTING GRAMMAR

Grammar sections in the Sixth Edition of *¿Qué tal?* are designed to clearly mark what students are supposed to learn. The two-column design separates prose grammar explanations (in the left-hand column) from Spanish examples (in the right-hand column). Spanish charts and paradigms are now contained within an easily identifiable shaded box and placed either in the right-hand column or centered across the page, depending on the space available. Students can therefore, on a first reading, work through the explanations on the left plus examples in the shaded boxes and on the right, then simply scan for the examples when reviewing for a test.

The grammar sections all have single emphases; that is, only one grammar point is presented and practiced in a grammar section. Thus, within each chapter, a step-by-step sequence of grammar-practice, grammar-practice, and so forth, is repeated as many times as there are grammar sections. This single-emphasis presentation and sequence breaks chapter grammar down into manageable chunks, allowing students to absorb difficult concepts bit by bit.

Grammar sections of some complexity are further subdivided for ease of mastery by students, and these subdivided grammar explanations are frequently coordinated with the exercise sections. For example, Grammar Section 17, "Expressing *what* or *whom* • Direct Object Pronouns" (p. 155), is divided into a number of parts: the forms of the direct object pronouns and their general placement (A), the attachment of direct object pronouns to infinitives and present participles (B), the use of direct object pronouns rather than reflexive pronouns with some verbs (C), and the meaning of the neuter pronoun **lo** (D). The bracketed indications throughout (in A, **[Práctica A]**, in B, **[Práctica B]**, and so on) tell students that they are now prepared to do the indicated activities in the **Práctica** section. In this way, students are guided through a complex explanation and given practice at several stages along the way. In this example, note that point D has no bracketed section, since there is no explicit practice of this point in the student text.

In the student text, grammar presentations are done in English to ensure maximum student comprehension and to enable students to study material on their own. Because many students are not familiar with or have forgotten grammatical terms and concepts (subject, infinitive, adjective, direct object, and so on), each new concept is introduced and defined, with examples in English as well as in Spanish and with brief exercises for some of the more difficult concepts. Spanish equivalents of all grammatical terminology (parts of speech, names of verb tenses, and so on) are provided, so that these terms can be used in Spanish directions for exercises and as an aid to students whose instructors prefer to make grammar presentations in Spanish.

One of the best ways to organize clear grammar presentations is to follow the example of the grammar presentations in the text. First, read through the entire explanation of a grammar section to get an overview of the material covered and how the presentation is developed. Next, read the *Instructor's Edition* comments to see what supplementary information, suggestions, and exercises are provided. Jot down the entire sequence of presentation if there is a lot of material. For example, part of the grammar presentation for Grammar Section 3, "Present Tense of **-ar** Verbs," (pp. 40–42) can be outlined as follows:

Step 1.	Grammar Explanation: infinitives and personal endings	[student text]
Step 2.	Suggestions: model, conversational exchange; **bailar** and personal endings; translation activity	[*Instructor's Edition:* Supplementary Materials]
Step 3.	Preliminary Exercises: oral rapid response drill, listening activity, pattern practice (explanation of activity type, activity)	*Instructor's Edition*]
Step 4.	**Práctica A, B**	[student text]
Step 5.	Suggestion	[*Instructor's Edition*]

and so on. Some instructors prefer to follow grammar presentations exactly as they are given in the text. Others prefer to vary presentations somewhat, so that their students have two slightly different presentations to help them understand new material.

In addition to brief, straightforward presentations of the material to be covered, most instructors point out areas of English interference with Spanish—that is, areas in which English-language structures are likely to interfere with mastery of a new pattern in Spanish. For example, English puts object pronouns after conjugated verbs, whereas Spanish places them before conjugated verbs. It is also a good idea to point out areas of Spanish interference, such as cases in which previously mastered Spanish grammar concepts can interfere with learning new Spanish concepts. For example, many students confuse the first and third persons singular of the preterite of regular **-ar** verbs, using **habló** for the **yo** form, since they are used to producing a **yo** form that ends in **-o.**

Brief, simple discrimination activities are also often helpful for students learning to distinguish differences that exist in Spanish but not in English; for example, **saber** versus **conocer, ser** versus **estar,** indicative versus subjunctive, and so on. Many such discrimination exercises are provided in the *Instructor's Edition.*

Whenever new grammar structures are based on previously learned material, it is crucially important to review the "old" material before beginning the new. The **¿Recuerda Ud.?** sections of the student text will alert you to these situations in the grammar sequence and provide students with brief, focused activities with which to review. It is a good idea to follow up their review in class with a quick conversational review of the same material. For example, before presenting **-er** and **-ir** verbs in Grammar Section 7, (p. 71) you might review the **-ar** infinitives that students already know with this brief activity:

¿Qué verbo asocia Ud. con... ? ¿una tienda? ¿la biblioteca? ¿el dinero? ¿la ropa? ¿una fiesta? ¿la boca (touch your mouth)**? ¿la casa? ¿la oficina? ¿el laboratorio de lenguas? ¿la clase?**

Emphasizing review and reentry in this way, when appropriate, will help students to see the grammar structures they are learning as part of a coherent system, *not* as discrete items completely separate from each other.

C. A NOTE ABOUT SPIRALING

A careful scan of the contents of *¿Qué tal?* or of its Index will reveal the extent to which major grammar topics are introduced gradually, or spiraled, throughout the text. Topics treated in this way include **ser** and **estar,** the preterite and the imperfect, the subjunctive, and so on. A hallmark of *¿Qué tal?* since the First Edition, this spiraling technique has many benefits for language learners.

- Students—especially true beginners—are not overwhelmed with all of the details of a major grammar point all at once.
- When topics are spread out over the entire book, and thus over the entire course, review and reentry of them is automatically built into the syllabus.
- Furthermore, with major topics of a more difficult nature, like the subjunctive, students have multiple opportunities to "catch" or gain some functional control of the topic. Thus, when the topic is introduced for the second time, students have a base of knowledge on which to build and can be more successful with difficult material the second time around.

D. *PRÁCTICA* AND *CONVERSACIÓN*

¿Qué tal? provides a two-phase sequence of grammar practice—form-focused practice (**Práctica**) and communicative practice (**Conversación**). The **Práctica** exercises come first, providing drills and basic, easy activities with new constructions. These precommunicative drills tend to be more mechanical and less personalized than the activities in the **Conversación** sections, which are intended to be exactly that—stimuli for speaking. The **Conversación** activities, although still carefully structured, are more communicative and open-ended, so that students can express their thoughts and opinions by answering questions, describing pictures and cartoons, completing sentences, and so on. It is never assumed that all material from either **Práctica** or **Conversación** sections will be used. A variety is provided so that instructors can choose activities that best suit the needs and goals of a class, as well as the tastes and preferences of students.

One of the goals of the more open-ended **Conversación** sections is to help students get to know one another as well as practice Spanish. The authors of *¿Qué tal?* hope that these activities, together with the activities in the **Práctica** sections, will ease the process of language acquisition and lead to spontaneous interactions and a relaxed atmosphere in class. *¿Qué tal?* assumes that such communication is both necessary to and the ultimate goal of language learning and that students have not learned Spanish if they do not progress beyond manipulating the mechanical drills in the text.

(1) The *Pasos* Concept The use of **Pasos** (1, 2, 3, and so on) in *¿Qué tal?* organizes the steps or stages of more complex activities. In essence, the **Pasos** break down an activity into its component parts. A **Pasos** sequence might evolve as follows: **Paso 1** = answer these questions about yourself; **Paso 2** = use them to interview a classmate; **Paso 3** = compare your answers with those of your classmate; **Paso 4** = report what you learned to the class. Most activities organized into **Pasos** are not as complex as that, but the advantage of the **Pasos** approach is clearly demonstrated with this four-step activity. Most students (and instructors, for that matter) would be overwhelmed by direction lines that asked for all that activity. However, when broken down into short, doable stages, the activity not only appears more doable, it *is* in fact easier to implement in the classroom. Experienced instructors who have tried activities that did "too much" will welcome the simplicity of the **Pasos** approach, and neophyte instructors will gain confidence in implementing communicative activities by doing them.

The **Pasos** concept is used in **Paso 1: Vocabulario** activities, and it occurs frequently in materials in both the **Práctica** and **Conversación** phases of grammar practice.

(2) Types of Activities in the *Práctica* Sections Although most of these drills and activities require the manipulation of Spanish as opposed to meaningful communication, their role in language learning is fundamental. Once students have completed the required manipulations, many of the drills can be personalized, extended, or transformed in other ways to extend the usefulness of these relatively simple activities. Suggestions of these kinds of variations are found in the student text or in the *Instructor's Edition.* (*Note:* Also found in the **Práctica** sections are many of the activity types already described for the **Paso 1: Vocabulario** sections.)

(a) Substitution (Pattern) Drill (Instructor's Edition). This type of drill requires the substitution of one word or phrase for another, plus the production of other changes made necessary by the substitution. The word that is substituted can be a noun, adjective, verb, or any other part of speech. In *¿Qué tal?,* these drills are always presented within a context: a general situation that serves as the "umbrella" for several patterns or a two-line conversational exchange that shows the pattern in a natural conversational setting. This is done to make the drill more realistic and to encourage students to think about what they are saying as well as about the forms they are producing. Substitution drills are most frequently used in *¿Qué tal?* to practice new verb forms. For example, (p. 72, *Instructor's Edition*):

En la sala de clase

1. **Yo asisto a clase todos los días.** (*tú, nosotros, Ud., todos los estudiantes, Carlos, vosotros*)
2. **Aprendes español en clase, ¿verdad?** (*nosotros, yo, Ud., la estudiante francesa, Uds., vosotros*)

These pattern drills practice the present tense of regular **-ar** verbs in sentences that might naturally be said in Spanish class, the "umbrella" that serves as the context for the drill items. The individual items are the base sentence in which substitutions are to be made: **Ud. estudia mucho.** The cues are given in parentheses:

Cue: ***nosotros***
Response: **Estudiamos mucho.**
Cue: ***yo***
Response: **Estudio mucho.**

(b) Rapid Response Drills (Instructor's Edition). As its name suggests, the primary purpose of this type of drill is to give students practice in responding very quickly to a stimulus. The drill can be very mechanical in nature, or it can stimulate a conversational situation.

As a preliminary exercise prior to pattern practice in a context, the rapid-response drill can help reinforce the verb stem/personal ending, as in the following drill, which precedes the regular **-ar** verb pattern drills:

Page 42: Explain the purpose of a rapid response drill. Have students give corresponding forms.

yo: bailar, estudiar, trabajar, necesitar,...
tú: buscar, hablar, pagar, tomar

and so on. Here, in a very focused drill situation (one person at a time), students give answers as quickly as possible. Speedy response is important, since students need to learn to respond quickly in common conversational situations. This same technique also works in conversation-oriented drills. For example, **Conversación A** (p. 3):

A. How many different ways can you respond to the following greetings and phrases?

1. **Buenas tardes.**
2. **Adiós.**

and so on. Here, the rapid-response technique might best be used the second time you do this drill in class, perhaps as a review on the following day.

(c) Chain Drill. This type of drill provides very focused question-answer practice. It has the additional advantage of increasing student practice and minimizing the amount of speaking the instructor does. To begin, the instructor indicates the question to be asked and asks a student to initiate the drill sequence. This student asks the question of another student, who answers it. That student

then asks the same question of another student, and so on. The chain continues for as long as seems appropriate. The instructor then provides a second question, and the chain continues. Examples of questions that might work well in this framework include: **¿De dónde eres tú?, ¿Cuántos hermanos (tíos, primos, etcétera) tienes?,** and so on.

(d) Transformation Drills. In this type of activity, one type of sentence or structure is changed into another—affirmative sentences into negative sentences, declarations into questions, present tense to past (future, present perfect, and so on). For example, **Práctica A** (p. 160):

A. Manolo está de mal humor (*in a bad mood*)**. Hoy Manolo está de mal humor y tiene una actitud muy negativa. ¿Qué opina Manolo de las afirmaciones de su esposa Lola sobre las clases y la vida universitaria en general?**

MODELO: LOLA: **Tengo algunos estudiantes excelentes este año.**
MANOLO: **Pues, yo no tengo ningún estudiante excelente este año.**

LOLA:

1. **Hay muchas clases interesantes en el departamento.**

As students perform the indicated transformation, **No hay nada interesante...**, their attention is focused mainly on the grammar point at hand—in this case, the formation of the negative. This kind of drill, along with pattern drills, is an excellent type to use in the initial stages of practice with new material.

(e) Input-based Activities. Input-based activities occur with all major vocabulary and grammar topics in the student text (and in the Workbook/Laboratory Manual as well). In these activities, all or part of a grammar topic is embedded in the items of an activity that has a content focus. For example, in **Práctica A** (p. 204), which occurs in the irregular preterites section, students are asked to tell if a series of statements about **la última Noche Vieja** is true for them or not. Here are some sample items.

1. **Fui a una fiesta en casa de un amigo / una amiga.**
2. **Di una fiesta en mi casa.**
3. **No estuve con mis amigos, sino** (*but rather*) **con la familia.**

and so on. The items provide focused input with irregular preterite verbs, yet the activity for all intents and purposes does not have a grammar focus; rather, students are drawn into the items and answer based on their own experiences.

(f) Sentence Builders. In this type of activity, students create original sentences by selecting one word or phrase from each of the columns provided. Since the verb is usually given in the infinitive form, students must produce the required form according to the subject pronoun they select. Semantic (vocabulary) and syntactic (structural) decisions are also needed to produce logical, grammatically sound sentences. For example, see the sentence builder in **Práctica B,** on page 112 of the student text. In this activity, students demonstrate a knowledge of subject-verb correspondence, the meaning of the infinitives (since not all of the verbs can be combined with all of the suggested predicates), and the conjugated verb/infinitive structure.

In some activities of this type, there will be question marks (**¿ ?**) at the bottom of one or more of the columns. This indicates that students should be creative, supplying words and phrases that are not used in the sentence builder in the text. In this way, what is basically a mechanical activity can be personalized, as time and needs permit.

Note that sentence builders are often included in the **Conversación** sections of early chapters, especially **Capítulos 1–3.** In these chapters, where students have so little to rely on in terms of known vocabulary and structures, it is felt that the sentence builder format is in fact "open" enough to warrant placing the activity type in **Conversación.** As students' language skills and knowledge increase, however, the sentence builder is most commonly found in the **Práctica** sections.

(g) Dehydrated Sentences. This type of activity provides the main elements of a sentence and gives them in the proper order, but the verb is given in the infinitive form or omitted, articles and

prepositions are usually omitted, and adjectives are given in their base (masculine singular) form, for example, **Práctica B** (p. 205):

B. Una Nochebuena en la casa de los Ramírez. Describa lo que pasó en casa de los Ramírez, haciendo el papel (*playing the role*) **de uno de los hijos. Haga oraciones en el pretérito según las indicaciones, usando el sujeto pronominal cuando sea necesario.**

1. **todos / estar / en casa / abuelos / antes de / nueve**
2. **(nosotros) poner / mucho / regalos / debajo / árbol**

and so on. To do this type of activity, students must consider the grammatical and semantic relationships among the words given, add any missing words, and make any necessary changes to supply appropriate verb forms and grammatical agreement. In later chapters, other variables are added, such as giving an adverb based on italicized adjectives, the superlative of italicized adjectives, and so on.

(h) Phrase Cues. This type of activity is similar to dehydrated sentences in that only the base for the sentence or question is given, and students must "flesh out" the item. For example, **Práctica A** (p. 163):

A. Profesor(a) por un día. Imagine que Ud. es el profesor / la profesora hoy. ¿Qué mandatos debe dar a la clase?

MODELOS: **hablar español → Hablen Uds. español.**
hablar inglés → No hablen Uds. inglés.

1. **llegar a tiempo**
2. **leer la lección**

Here, students act as the teacher based on the infinitive phrases that are offered as a guide.

(i) Patterned Conversations. In this type of activity, students work in pairs to simulate a typical conversation. A model dialogue is given, and substitutions to be made in it are indicated in the activity items, for example, in **Práctica D** (p. 62), students must make logical matches between the items listed and the persons suggested.

D. ¡Seamos (*Let's be*) **lógicos! ¿De quién son estas cosas? Con un compañero / una compañera, haga y conteste preguntas según el modelo.**

MODELO: **—¿De quién es el perro?**
—Es de...

Personas: las estudiantes, la actriz, el niño, la familia con diez hijos, el estudiante extranjero, los señores Schmidt

¿De quién es / son... ?

1. **la casa en Beverly Hills**
2. **la casa en Viena**

and so on.

(j) Story Sequences. These activities form a logical sequence or tell a story. At times they are quite simple in format, for example, **Práctica C** (p. 70):

D. ¡Dolores es igual! Cambie Diego → Dolores.

Diego es un buen estudiante. Es listo y trabajador y estudia mucho. Es norteamericano de origen mexicano, y por eso habla español...

When students make the indicated transformation from Diego to Dolores, they will practice adjective agreement. The exercise, however, has its own content. Although on a simple level, it tells a story that can be discussed, continued, expanded, and so on. Note the follow-up comprehension activity in the *Instructor's Edition.*

Story sequences are generally more complex in format, for example, **Práctica B** (p. 188):

B. El día de tres compañeras

Paso 1. Teresa, Evangelina y Liliana comparten un apartamento en un viejo edificio... Describa lo que hicieron, según la perspectiva de cada una.

TERESA Y EVANGELINA:

1. **(nosotras) salir / de / apartamento / a / nueve**
2. **llegar / biblioteca / a / diez**

and so on. When students have completed all items they will have completed a brief narration about a typical day in the roommates' lives. The story has enough content to be accompanied by inferential comprehension items (the **¿Quién lo dijo?** follow-up on p. 189) and can also be repeated with a twist: students retell the story from another point of view, as suggested in **Paso 3.**

In addition, a relatively small number of cloze activities are found in the **Práctica** sections of the Sixth Edition. For a discussion of this type of material, see the **Un poco de todo** section, later on in this section of the manual.

(3) **Types of Activities in the *Conversación* Sections** With the more open-ended activities of the **Conversación** sections, as with many vocabulary-building activities, students should be encouraged to stay within the structures and vocabulary they have already studied and mastered. Clearly, however, as students try to become more creative in their responses and seek to express themselves, they are more likely to make mistakes. (*Note:* Also found in the **Conversación** sections are many of the previously discussed activity formats from **Paso 1: Vocabulario.** Activities similar in format to some **Práctica** sections also occur, although with a much more open structure.)

*(a) Questions (**Preguntas**).* Questions in the **Conversación** sections relate to common knowledge (the weather, geography, history, and so on) or to students' personal experiences and opinions. You can use these questions as a guide to asking questions of individual students in the class; you can ask one student to ask a question of another student; or you can have students work in pairs or small groups, asking each other questions. For more ideas along these lines, see "Question/Answer (Personalized Questions)," in the **Paso 1: Vocabulario** section, this section, this Manual.

(b) Games. Guessing games of all kinds work quite well in beginning language classes, as demonstrated by **Conversación A** (p. 184):

A. ¿Conoce bien a sus compañeros de clase? Piense en una persona de la clase de español que Ud. conoce un poco. En su opinión, ¿a esa persona le gustan o no las siguientes cosas?

	SÍ, LE GUSTA(N).	NO, NO LE GUSTA(N).
1. **la música latina**	☐	☐

and so on. The same activity can be repeated throughout the course. If done later in the term, students' questions will be more complex and interesting.

*(c) **Encuesta** (Survey) Activities.* Survey activities are similar to **Entrevistas** in that students work one-on-one with others to obtain information. The survey, however, adds the twist of interviewing a number of students. Survey activities, although conversational in tone, are still relatively structured, and

students can make of them what their language abilities and interest level permit. See, for example, the survey activity **Conversación C** (pp. 158–159):

Una encuesta sobre la comida. Hágales preguntas a sus compañeros de clase para saber si toman las comidas o bebidas indicadas y con qué frecuencia. Deben explicar también por qué toman o *no* toman cierta cosa.

MODELO: **la carne → E1: ¿Comes carne?**
E2: No la como casi nunca porque tiene mucho colesterol.

1. **la carne**
2. **los mariscos**

and so on. Since a good deal of information about the class as a whole is collected in a survey activity, surveys lend themselves to whole-class discussions as a follow-up.

(d) Situation Activities. Many **Conversación** section activities simply set up a situation or situations to be discussed. For example, the activity on page 260:

Posibilidades. ¿Qué puede Ud. hacer o decir —o qué puede pasar— en cada situación?

1. **A Ud. le duele mucho la cabeza.**
2. **Ud. le pega a otra persona sin querer.**

and so on. The activity can be done by asking individuals to supply responses orally or in writing, by students working in pairs or groups to come up with as many responses as possible, and so on.

Frequently occurring **Conversación**-type activities previously discussed in this Manual include the following:

- **Entrevistas,** frequently containing the suggestion that students report to the class what they have learned during the interview
- Visual-based activities, with *Instructor's Edition* suggestions that encourage students to expand the focus of the activity by telling stories based on the drawings, inventing histories for the persons depicted, and so on
- Personalized completions, many of which can serve as the basis for brief class presentations
- **Preguntas** activities, which can serve as the basis for whole-class discussions or partner/pair work

E. *UN POCO DE TODO*

The activities in this section combine and review the grammatical topics of the chapter as well as much of the vocabulary, thus providing a chapter review. This section, then, forms part of the synthesis-application cycle initiated by the **Videoteca** section.

Some of the **Un poco de todo** exercises are best done orally in class; others are more suited to writing practice; and many can be done either way, depending on course goals, time limitations, and so on.

Activity types from the **Paso 1: Vocabulario, Práctica,** and **Conversación** sections occur here as well. Other formats that are used frequently include the following.

(1) ***Dehydrated Sentences*** This type of activity has already been discussed (see "Types of Activities in the **Práctica** Sections"), but it bears mentioning again since it occurs in the **Un poco de todo** sections with a somewhat different format and purpose.

The dehydrated-sentence activities in the recombinative **Un poco de todo** sections are more complex, requiring decision making not only about correct forms but about tenses and moods, for example, exercise **A** (p. 251):

A. Lo mejor de estar enfermo

Paso 1. Form complete sentences using the words in the order given. Conjugate the verbs in the preterite or the imperfect and add or change words as needed. Use subject pronouns only when needed.

Here students must decide what tense to use to tell about a completed action (preterite), and what tense to use to describe background circumstances (imperfect).

(2) ***Cloze Exercises*** Although cloze procedures are more commonly used for testing purposes than for language practice, it is believed that a modified cloze procedure has great utility for exercise formats as well. The technique is used in many of the **Un poco de todo** sections. Rather than deleting every *nth* word as is common cloze procedure, deletions have been made to focus student attention on current chapter and previous chapter grammar points. A choice is generally offered (**el/la, algo/nada,** and so on), or a base word is given, which the student must then supply in the appropriate form to fit the context (an infinitive, an adjective, and so on).

The topic of these cloze exercises is generally cultural, related to the chapter's cultural theme. Thus when completed, the paragraphs demonstrate not only the language proficiency of the student but also form a complete discussion that adds to students' information about the cultural topic.

Conversely, the cultural information in the paragraph provides the context within which students process language. Care has been taken to ensure that no previously unpresented cultural information is needed for students to be able to complete the exercise.

The advantages to the format as a synthetic exercise are as follows:

- Instructors who have used these and similar paragraphs in their classes report that student interest is maintained by the content of the paragraph, thus taking attention away from the grammatical and vocabulary processing that occurs as students complete the items.
- Systematic review/reentry of particularly troublesome grammatical material is made possible, with relatively little class time spent for the benefits involved. Topics systematically reentered in this way in the **Un poco de todo** cloze paragraphs include **ser/estar,** preterite/imperfect/ subjunctive/ indicative, gender and gender agreement, and so on.

Instructors are encouraged to accept as correct any response that is grammatically and contextually accurate.

An example of this type of exercise is found on page 191 of the student text. The two brief paragraphs of **Recomendaciones para las vacaciones** provide contextual practice with the following grammar topics (review-synthesis topics are marked with an *) as they convey information about Machu-Picchu:

direct/indirect object pronoun discrimination*
affirmative/negative words*
gender*
saber/conocer*
ser/estar*
impersonal **se**
comparative forms*
gustar
present indicative*
impersonal expressions with **ser***
adjective agreement*

4. *Enfoque cultural* Sections

All regular chapters of the Sixth Edition of *¿Qué tal?* contain at least one free-floating **Nota cultural,** a brief cultural note about a limited aspect of the chapter's cultural theme and one that is usually stimulated by something specific in the chapters. The **Notas** are offered in Spanish or in English, depending on the complexity of the information they convey. Key words or concepts in Spanish are included in boldface type for pre-reading scanning and to facilitate comprehension. The **Notas culturales,** however, represent only a small part of the cultural content offered in the Sixth Edition of *¿Qué tal?*

A special cultural section focuses on U.S. and Canadian Hispanics and cultural matters important to them. These features, called **En los Estados Unidos y el Canadá...** highlight people, places, and events that showcase the rich Hispanic tradition found in the United States and Canada and its importance in the daily lives of Hispanics and non-Hispanics alike. Some of the personalities mentioned are well-known, and some are not so well-known. Each, however, stands out in his or her own way in a wide variety of fields: education, art, medicine, business, sports, and so on.

The first several **En los Estados Unidos y el Canadá...** sections are written in English for better comprehension. Then, beginning with **Capítulo 6,** these features are written completely in Spanish. As with **Nota cultural** sections, key words or concepts are in boldface type.

The cultural goals of language study generally lie in two areas, knowledge and attitude. It is important for students to gain some knowledge of the everyday customs of Spanish speakers, as well as knowledge about Hispanic geography, history, and contributions to art, literature, film, and so on. In addition, however, most language instructors are concerned with helping their students come to the realization that "different" is not the same as "dumb," and that all cultural phenomena make sense within the context of the cultures where they occur.

The **Enfoque cultural** section appears between **Pasos 2** and **3** in every chapter. Each **Enfoque cultural** section focuses on a Hispanic country (or countries), providing basic atlas-type data (the official name of the country, capital, population, currency, and languages), as well as some interesting historical, social, or geographical information. It can include the profile of a famous person and, in the case of writers, may contain a short example of his/her writing. For instance, **Capítulo 15,** on Chile, has a section entitled **Conozca a... Gabriela Mistral,** which offers a minibiography of the poet and a short poem, "**Riqueza**" (p. 350).

These brief, country-specific profiles are intended to offer students a first glance of the vast expanse and diversity of the Spanish-speaking world. Instructors should use their knowledge of their program's priorities to assign these cultural capsules the proper weight and amount of time in their curriculum. Treatment options include covering all the **Enfoque cultural** materials briefly, selecting those that seem relevant for particular reasons, assigning them in part or in whole as reading outside of the class, and so on. The *¿Qué tal?* Website offers links relevant to the sites about each country and about specific topics covered in the **Enfoque cultural** sections. These can be further explored or can form the basis for student presentations. When teaching **Enfoque cultural** in class, you may wish to accompany your lesson with cultural footage about the focus country from the video to accompany *¿Qué tal?*

5. *Paso 4: Un paso más*

Although there are numerous reading and writing opportunities throughout the entire chapter in the **Notas culturales,** realia, **Minidiálogos,** and so on, the optional **Paso 4: Un paso más** section focuses specifically on the reading and writing skills. The section also serves as a thematic corollary to the chapter. Each **Paso 4: Un paso más** section includes a **Videoteca** subsection followed by a chapter-culminating activity. In odd-numbered chapters (1, 3, 5, and so on), **A leer** and **A escribir** are offered as culminating activities. New to this edition is the chapter-culminating **A conversar** activity in the even-numbered chapters (2, 4, 6, and so on); this group or pair activity allows students to explore the chapter themes and topics in a conversation setting. You will find additional **A leer** and **A escribir** activities for even-numbered chapters and additional **A conversar** activities for odd-numbered chapters in the Instructor Center of the *¿Qué tal?* Online Learning Center Website.

A. *VIDEOTECA*

In the Sixth Edition of *¿Qué tal?*, the **Videoteca** section includes activities for one of the three segments of the video that accompanies the program: **En contexto.** (The other two are **Minidramas** and **Enfoque cultural.** Suggestions for **Minidramas** can be found in Section X of this Manual. The **Enfoque cultural** footage is referenced in the textbook's **Enfoque cultural** section.) The **En contexto** video segments include some of the theme vocabulary and grammar of the chapter to which they correspond. In those instances where unfamiliar structure and vocabulary appear in the dialogue segments of **Videoteca,** glosses are provided. These dialogue segments are not meant to be memorized. Students always have access to all video segments as well as comprehension activities for all segments on the "Video on CD."

EN CONTEXTO

This video segment, new to the Sixth Edition of *¿Qué tal?*, has a very functional focus. This new video, shot on location in Mexico, Peru, and Costa Rica, is supported by a variety of activities in the textbook.

(1) *Lluvia de ideas* This section is designed to encourage students to anticipate the situation that they are going to watch on the video. This is achieved through a series of personalized questions that tap into the video and the chapter's theme. The goal is to prepare students to understand the video by organizing their thinking in advance, and by activating its vocabulary.

(2) *Dictado* The segments of the **En contexto** situations in the **Videoteca** offer a cloze activity, which students must complete with the exact word they hear in the video. It also provides a working text for practicing role-playing later on.

Many alternatives are available to you for modeling and remodeling the **En contexto** dialogues. You should experiment with all of them throughout the year, combining them in different ways. Some work better at the beginning of the course; some work best with shorter dialogues, and so on. Here are some basic possibilities.

- You read each line and students repeat (sometimes all together, sometimes by assigning a different role to different groups of students, sometimes one student at a time).
- You read with students.
- Students read alone, in a group, or one by one.

It is recommended that you use at least some of the preceding techniques before asking students to act out or read a dialogue aloud in front of the class.

En contexto can also serve as the basis for classroom activities that go beyond listening or pronunciation practice. After presenting them in whatever format you find most effective, classroom activities can be developed following these general guidelines.

- Ask the optional comprehension questions given in "Chapter-by-Chapter Supplementary Materials," Section IX, this Manual.
- Ask students to summarize the content of the dialogue. You should not interfere or ask direct questions at this time, unless incorrect information is given or the class gets "stalled" trying to summarize a particular aspect of the dialogue.
- Use the extension of the dialogue situation found in many chapters of the audio program.
- Encourage students to continue the situation by inventing yet another phase of it or by inventing details about the characters. Students can also create summaries of what happened before the dialogue begins. Their ability to handle this final kind of classroom activity will increase throughout the year. You should also consult the supplementary exercises and dialogues in "Chapter-by-Chapter Supplementary Materials," Section IX, this Manual.

The **En contexto** dialogues also lend themselves quite well to supplementary writing assignments. Two types of writing exercises are especially appropriate.

- *Students rewrite and summarize the dialogue in narrative form.* The dialogue provides the structures and vocabulary that students transform into indirect discourse. You should model this type of activity the first few times you assign it.
- Students write a similar but original dialogue following the vocabulary and structures of the text dialogue, but varying some elements. The ending can be changed; the personality of one of the characters can be varied; students can write the dialogue that would have taken place if one of the speakers had been a member of their own family or a friend; and so on.

(3) ***Un diálogo original*** These brief role-playing situations are designed to give students additional practice with the situations demonstrated in **En contexto.**

Paso 1 asks students to reenact the situation in the video, and **Paso 2** asks students to invent a similar situation of their own.

See the *Instructor's Edition* for suggestions on how to work with the **Un diálogo original** sections.

B. *A LEER*

Readings in the **A leer** sections are both author-written and authentic. In this case, "authentic" indicates that a previously published text was intended to be read by native speakers and that prior to this appearance, it had no didactic purposes for language learning. Other examples of authentic materials in *¿Qué tal?* are realia (typically newspaper and magazine ads) and poetry. The authors of *¿Qué tal?* believe that students should be exposed to authentic readings as early as possible. For this reason, **A leer** sections written by the *¿Qué tal?* authors only appear in **Primeros pasos** and in **Capítulo 1,** where they facilitate students' first reading experiences.

- The author-written readings are what their name implies: commentaries written by the authors of the text about various aspects of the chapter cultural themes. This approach produces reading texts written by language teachers for language learners (rather than material written by and for native speakers of Spanish). The author-written readings contain reentry of vocabulary and chapter grammar points. For this reason, they are written approximately at students' reading level at any point in the text and thus should be relatively easy for students to read.

  As always, special attention has been dedicated to improving the overall quality of the content of the **A leer** and other cultural sections, as well as their language in the Sixth Edition. It is hoped that these commentaries present Hispanic peoples and values as nonstereotypically as possible. However, instructors should keep in mind at all times the variety of Hispanic cultures throughout the world. Few generalizations about any culture are valid 100% of the time, and the readings in *¿Qué tal?* will of necessity contain inaccuracies for some Hispanic cultures. At no time is the content invented or capricious. If individual instructors have no personal experience with a phenomenon described in the materials, it is suggested that they present the information they *are* familiar with as an alternative to the point of view taken by the text's authors.
- Authentic readings are further expanded in the Sixth Edition. Initial contact with authentic materials of this kind can be intimidating to students, since vocabulary and grammar are *not* controlled or "at" student level in reading texts written by native speakers for other native speakers. However, it is hoped that the comprehension activities that accompany these readings set appropriate tasks for students that will enable them to confront and enjoy the authentic-reading experience. It is critical that instructors convey to students the fact that they should not expect to understand the readings word for word and that if they can complete the comprehension activities, they have understood enough. Although beginning students cannot understand everything in readings of this kind, they *can* perform skimming (for general meaning) and scanning (for specific information) kinds of activities. They should be made aware of the fact that such activities are a valuable part of the language-learning process.
- New to the Sixth Edition is a poem now included as an **A leer** reading. As authentic materials, poems reflect the time and culture from which they spring, as does Gustavo Pérez Firmat's poem "Cubanita descubanizada," which presents the Cuban expatriate's sense of loss and displacement. The additional **A leer** sections for **Capítulos 16** and **18,** available on the *¿Qué tal?* Website, offer two more poems.

Another aspect of the readings is the inclusion of reading-strategy sections. The goal of the **Estrategia** sections is to make students aware of reading strategies that they already use in their native language and that they should learn to apply to reading in Spanish. (Occasionally an **Estrategia** section will also focus on an aspect of language that is particular to a given reading: how to recognize derivative adjectives [past participles, for example], and so on. Poetry **Estrategias** help students recognize some of the formal elements of the genre.) Thus the readings can become a vehicle for learning how to read, as well as a source of cultural information.

In all cases, the content of the **Estrategia** sections is geared to the specific reading that it precedes. Instructors should also note that the strategy of guessing words through context is encouraged throughout the book by means of words that are underlined in the readings. As explained in the second **Estrategia** section (p. 24), underlined words should be guessed from context, and students should resist the urge to look them up.

Certain **Estrategia** sections review strategies learned in previous **A leer** sections. These **Repaso de estrategias** sections may use one or more previous strategies appropriate to the current reading to help students review what they already know and to use that knowledge to help them become better readers in Spanish.

Following the **Estrategia** is a section entitled **Sobre la lectura.** Here, information is given on the source of the reading passage: whether author-written or authentic. Information on the type of source used also helps students to understand the audience for whom the piece was written (scientific magazine, popular magazine, and so on). The section that corresponds to **Sobre la lectura** in the poetry **A leer** is **Sobre el autor / la autora.** This section presents biographical information.

The **Comprensión** sections ensure that the activities really help beginning students "get the gist" of the readings, especially the more challenging authentic readings. Instructors familiar with previous editions will note the inclusion of more inferential and more chart-completion activities.

C. *A ESCRIBIR*

The **A Escribir** sections are guided writing exercises related to the cultural content of the **A leer** reading. Whereas the exercise in the **A escribir** relates directly to the reading, it will also relate (or a second exercise will relate) to students, their lives, and experiences. For example, in **Paso 4: Un paso más** (p. 49), where the reading describes Hispanic universities, students are asked to compare their own in the first exercise. Then in the second exercise, students are asked to describe their university for a Hispanic student.

Writing sections in *¿Qué tal?* are guided to give students models and examples when necessary, yet provide them with enough open-ended ideas and suggestions that they can truly express themselves in Spanish. The value of such guided writing exercises, as opposed to free composition, is that the questions or paragraph models lead students toward using vocabulary and structures they already know. Provocative questions can also suggest ideas or thoughts about cultural contrasts.

Finally, it is hoped that instructors will not limit their treatment of reading in the classroom to coverage of the author-written **A leer** readings. These readings, while written in language that is as authentic as possible, are still keyed to the grammar sequence and vocabulary development of *¿Qué tal?*, and as such do not constitute truly authentic reading materials. Research in second-language acquisition suggests that reading should be one of the primary ways of providing students with good language input. It is hoped that instructors using *¿Qué tal?* will cover the more "natural" realia-based readings. They should in addition augment the reading materials found in the text with supplementary readers and with other authentic reading materials from Hispanic cultures, in particular newspaper and magazine articles and features.

D. *A CONVERSAR*

The chapter-culminating group or pair **A conversar** activities that appear in the textbook in even-numbered chapters target chapter theme, vocabulary, and grammar as appropriate, and provide an opportunity for students to further develop listening and speaking skills. These activities involve several steps, all clearly explained in the textbook. Some examples of the tasks that students complete in these sections include developing a house schedule to accommodate the needs and habits of three roommates, ordering a meal in a nice restaurant, an exchange between a pharmacist and an ill client, and exchanges between tourists and others in travel situations. If you and your students enjoy doing these activities and would like additional **A conversar** activities for odd-numbered chapters, you can, as pointed out earlier, find them in the Instructor Center of the *¿Qué tal?* Online Learning Center Website.

6. *En resumen*

En resumen is, as the title suggests, a summary of the key vocabulary and grammar presented in the chapter. It appears at the end of each chapter to be used by students as a quick reference to the materials as they work through the chapter or as a review of the chapter.

A. *GRAMÁTICA*

The **Gramática** subsection is a brief synopsis of the grammar points covered in the chapter. The grammar points are named, and followed by a question or statement to remind students about the structure and what they should know about it.

B. *VOCABULARIO*

The **Vocabulario,** the last section in the basic chapter, lists active vocabulary—that is, all new words in the chapter that are to be learned. The **Vocabulario** list includes the theme vocabulary presented and practiced in the **Paso 1: Vocabulario** section, as well as active vocabulary introduced in the **Pasos 2** and **3: Gramática** sections. Thus, it serves as a ready reference for both students and instructors. Words are listed in the categories of **Los verbos** and **Las palabras adicionales** and by semantic group.

In all chapters of *¿Qué tal?* there are some vocabulary items—either cognates or glossed words—that are used to provide humor or establish the context for an exercise. These words are usually not considered to be active vocabulary and are therefore not listed in the chapter **Vocabulario,** since students do not actively manipulate them. However, instructors who carefully follow the introduction of vocabulary will discover that such background vocabulary often becomes active in a later chapter, especially if it has appeared passively in a number of chapters.

You should also note that in most **Paso 1: Vocabulario** sections, a few words are listed that have already been learned as active vocabulary in previous chapters. For example, the verb **comprar** relates to the shopping theme of **Capítulo 3,** but it was learned as active vocabulary in **Capítulo 1;** such vocabulary is listed with no definition, in an appropriate semantic category, under the heading **Repaso:...** This feature makes explicit one of the ways in which vocabulary is consistently reviewed throughout the chapters of *¿Qué tal?*

When the same word is introduced with a new meaning, it is listed, along with the new definition, in the **Vocabulario** lists. Thus, the verb **sacar** is listed in **Capítulo 9** with the meaning *to take out* (and listed as **sacar la basura**) and in **Capítulo 10** with the meaning *to extract; to stick out* (*one's tongue*).

The Spanish-English vocabulary at the back of the text lists all words used in *¿Qué tal?,* including both active and passive vocabulary. To help instructors prepare tests or supplementary exercises, this vocabulary indicates the chapter in which active vocabulary items are first used as active vocabulary; chapter numbers are not given for passive vocabulary.

IV. Planning a Course Syllabus

A. HOW TO USE *¿QUÉ TAL?* ON THE SEMESTER SYSTEM

As a general guideline, it is suggested that colleges and universities on the semester system cover *¿Qué tal?* in the following manner:

First Term: **Primeros pasos, Capítulos 1–9**
Second Term: **Capítulos 10–18**

The following information will be helpful for planning a detailed course syllabus. Calculations are based on a 15-week semester. Extra hours can be used for review and hourly exams. In the second semester, extra time should also be allotted for the review of the first semester's work before beginning **Capítulo 10.** The use of an additional reading text might also be appropriate in the second semester.

1. Classes Meeting 3 Hours per Week

Approximately 45 contact hours are available during the semester. An average of 4 contact hours can be spent on each chapter.

First Semester:

4 contact hours for **Primeros pasos**	4 hours
4 contact hours × 9 chapters	36 hours
Extra hours	5 hours
	45 hours

Second Semester:

4 contact hours × 9 chapters	36 hours
Extra hours (some of which can be used for chapters that may require more time, such as **Capítulos 10** and **12**)	9 hours
	45 hours

2. Classes Meeting 4 Hours per Week

Approximately 60 contact hours are available during the semester. An average of 5 contact hours can be spent on each chapter.

First Semester:

6 contact hours for **Primeros pasos**	6 hours
5 contact hours × 9 chapters	45 hours
Extra hours	9 hours
	60 hours

Second Semester:

6 contact hours × 9 chapters	54 hours
Extra hours	6 hours
	60 hours

3. Classes Meeting 5 Hours per Week

Approximately 75 contact hours are available during the semester. An average of 6 contact hours can be spent on each chapter.

First Semester:

6 contact hours for **Primeros pasos**	6 hours
6–7 contact hours × 9 chapters	54–63 hours
Extra hours	7–13 hours
	67–82 hours

Second Semester:

6–7 contact hours × 9 chapters	54–63 hours
Extra hours	13–19 hours
	67–82 hours

B. HOW TO USE *¿QUÉ TAL?* ON THE QUARTER SYSTEM

As a general guideline, it is suggested that colleges and universities on the quarter system cover *¿Qué tal?* in the following manner (note that separate suggestions are offered for courses meeting 3 days a week and for those meeting 4 or 5 days).

1. Classes Meeting 3 Days a Week

First Term: **Primeros pasos, Capítulos 1–6**
Second Term: **Capítulos 7–12**
Third Term: **Capítulos 13–18**

2. Classes Meeting 4 or 5 Days a Week

First Term: **Primeros pasos, Capítulos 1–6**
Second Term: **Capítulos 7–12**
Third Term: **Capítulos 13–18**

The following information will be helpful for planning a detailed course syllabus. Calculations are based on a 10-week semester. Extra hours can be used for review, hourly exams, and expanded coverage of the **Paso 4: Un paso más** sections. In the second and third quarters, extra time should also be allotted for the review of the first and second quarter's work before beginning new work. The use of an additional reading text might also be appropriate in the third quarter.

3. Classes Meeting 3 Hours per Week

Approximately 30 contact hours are available during the quarter. An average of 4 contact hours can be spent on each chapter.

First Quarter:

4 contact hours for **Primeros pasos**	4 hours
4 contact hours × 6 chapters	24 hours
Extra hours	2 hours
	30 hours

Second Quarter:

4 contact hours × 6 chapters	24 hours
Extra hours	6 hours
	30 hours

Third Quarter:

4 contact hours × 6 chapters	24 hours
Extra hours	6 hours
	30 hours

4. Classes Meeting 4 Hours per Week

Approximately 40 contact hours are available during the quarter. An average of 5 contact hours can be spent on each chapter.

First Quarter:

5 contact hours for **Primeros pasos**	5 hours
5 contact hours × 6 chapters	30 hours
Extra hours	5 hours
	40 hours

Second Quarter:

5 contact hours × 6 chapters	30 hours
Extra hours	10 hours
	40 hours

Third Quarter:

5 contact hours × 6 chapters	30 hours
Extra hours	10 hours
	40 hours

5. Classes Meeting 5 Hours per Week

Approximately 50 contact hours are available during the quarter. An average of 6 contact hours can be spent on each chapter.

First Quarter:

6 contact hours for **Primeros pasos**	6 hours
6 contact hours × 6 chapters	36 hours
Extra hours	8 hours
	50 hours

Second Quarter:

6 contact hours × 6 chapters	36 hours
Extra hours	14 hours
	50 hours

Third Quarter:

6 contact hours × 6 chapters	36 hours
Extra hours	14 hours
	50 hours

C. HOW TO USE *¿QUÉ TAL?* OVER THREE SEMESTERS

As a general guideline, it is suggested that colleges and universities on the semester system that wish to use *¿Qué tal?* over three semesters cover the book in the following manner (note that separate suggestions are offered for courses meeting 3 days a week and for those meeting 4 or 5 days).

1. Classes Meeting 3, 4, or 5 Days a Week

First Semester: **Primeros pasos, Capítulos 1–6**
Second Semester: **Capítulos 7–13**
Third Semester: **Capítulos 14–18**

The following information will be helpful for planning a detailed course syllabus. Calculations are based on a 15-week semester. Extra hours can be used for review, hourly exams, and other types of activities, such as oral presentations. In the second and third semesters, extra time should also be allotted for review of the first and second semester's work before beginning new work. The use of an additional reading text is also suggested for the third semester.

The use of additional video supplements, such as the *Destinos* video series, along with the *Student Viewer's Handbook, Volumes I and II,* might also be appropriate for schools that wish to use *¿Qué tal?* over three semesters.

2. Classes Meeting 3 Hours per Week

Approximately 45 contact hours are available during the semester. An average of 5 contact hours can be spent on each chapter.

First Semester:

5 contact hours for **Primeros pasos**	5 hours
5 contact hours × 6 chapters	30 hours
Extra hours	10 hours
	45 hours

Second Semester:

5 contact hours × 7 chapters	35 hours
Extra hours	10 hours
	45 hours

Third Semester:	
5 contact hours × 5 chapters	25 hours
Extra hours	20 hours
	45 hours

3. Classes Meeting 4 Hours per Week

Approximately 60 contact hours are available during the semester. An average of 6 contact hours can be spent on each chapter.

First Semester:	
6 contact hours for **Primeros pasos**	6 hours
6 contact hours × 6 chapters	36 hours
Extra hours	18 hours
	60 hours

Second Semester:	
6 contact hours × 7 chapters	42 hours
Extra hours	18 hours
	60 hours

Third Semester:	
6 contact hours × 5 chapters	30 hours
Extra hours	30 hours
	60 hours

4. Classes Meeting 5 Hours per Week

Approximately 75 contact hours are available during the semester. An average of 7 contact hours can be spent on each chapter.

First Semester:	
7 contact hours for **Primeros pasos**	6 hours
6 contact hours × 6 chapters	42 hours
Extra hours	27 hours
	75 hours

Second Semester:	
7 contact hours × 7 chapters	49 hours
Extra hours	26 hours
	75 hours

Third Semester:	
7 contact hours × 5 chapters	35 hours
Extra hours	40 hours
	75 hours

V. Lesson Planning

Careful organization of each class meeting helps even experienced language instructors use their time more efficiently, anticipate many questions, and provide clear explanations. Detailed lesson plans minimize the amount of talking done by the instructor and maximize the opportunity for student practice.

A. TEXTBOOK ADAPTATION

Individual instructors always know their own students better than any group of textbook authors can. For this reason, most instructors do not follow the textbook word for word, but instead emphasize the grammar points and language skills that seem most important for their language program. They select some exercises and activities for classroom practice, assign others to be prepared out of class, create their own variations of some materials, and omit others. This type of decision making is at the heart of good language teaching.

At first reading, it may seem contradictory for the authors of a foreign language textbook to recommend the adaptation of—rather than the slavish use of—the text for effective language instruction, yet this is precisely their recommendation. Factors that make textbook adaptation a virtual necessity include the following:

- the reevaluation of course goals in elementary language courses
- curricular changes such as extending the first-year course over three semesters (four quarters)
- multiple sections of first-year courses, with different language goals in different sections
- the desire to incorporate supplementary materials (readers, video materials, and so on)
- available class time that is insufficient for covering all of the material offered in the text

If instructors are in agreement with the underlying pedagogical assumptions of a first-year text (that is, if they believe that the language learning materials that the text contains truly help students learn a foreign language and are compatible with course goals), then almost any textbook can be adapted to meet the needs of a given problem.

With the increased emphasis on proficiency-oriented instruction, instructors will find readily available many fine books and articles on the topic of textbook adaptation. In addition, since the topic of textbook adaptation has become popular in recent years, attendees at local or national foreign language conferences will often find sessions on the program about this topic. In particular, the ACTFL organization has been active in this area.

Perhaps the most common complaint about textbooks is that they cover too much material. Here again, instructors should feel free to adapt materials to fit their instructional needs. "Covers too much" may mean "presents too many grammar topics." If this is the case, instructors should feel free to omit (or present for passive recognition only) grammar points that they feel are too detailed for first-year students. The omission of entire chapters is also another option. This recommendation is especially appropriate for language programs meeting three hours a week. Alternatively, many institutions choose to cover a beginning textbook over three semesters (or four quarters). There is no need to permit the textbook to define curricular goals, yet this is precisely what happens when "covering the text" or "covering 'x' chapters" is used as a synonym for "first-year Spanish."

"Covers too much" can also mean "presents too many practice materials to be used in one's academic program." Again, textbook adaptation is the logical solution. *¿Qué tal?* contains more material than can be used in most language programs. Some materials (the **Un poco de todo** and the **Paso 4: Un paso más** sections) lend themselves quite well to out-of-class assignments. The abundance of materials has been included for a variety of reasons:

- to be of help to novice instructors, who are less able to create supplementary materials needed for a given situation
- to provide instructors with a wide range of materials from which to choose
- to serve as supplementary materials for students who need more practice or who want to do more

It is the authors' firm belief that providing *more* practice with *less* grammar is one of the keys to effective first-year language instruction, especially in four (or five) skills language programs. The text has been structured to serve as the basis for such programs.

B. SYSTEMATIC LESSON PLANNING

Whereas some instructors are capable of teaching an excellent and engaging class off the top of their heads, most instructors—especially "new" teachers—cannot do so without substantial planning ahead of time. The following four-step approach demonstrates the issues that experienced language teachers think about implicitly or explicitly as they plan their classes. New or inexperienced teachers may wish to follow these steps carefully in planning their first classes.

1. Think Through What You Are Going to Teach

a. What you want to accomplish (content)
b. What students already know about the content
c. How you will present new material
d. What exercises and activities you will use and how you will use them
e. How much time you need for each segment of the class

Be aware of how you sequence material. A typical sequence for new material would be: presentation → drill practice → communicative practice.

When you present a new grammar topic, it may make sense to begin with a brief review of similar or related material. For example, review possession with **de** before introducing the unstressed forms of possessive adjectives in **Capítulo 3.** (**¿Recuerda Ud.?** sections and marginal notes in the *Instructor's Edition* will alert you to such situations.) When introducing new material, strive for clear, concise explanations, and give several pertinent examples; it is a good idea to write down a few.

Activities should also follow a sequence. Ideally, you would follow the presentation of new material with a very brief, focused activity that tests students' ability to use the new material. Easier activities should precede more difficult ones, and activities that are very controlled should precede the open-ended kind, in which students must be creative. The activity materials in *¿Qué tal?,* including those in the *Instructor's Edition,* follow the sequence just described.

A typical class should also include a review of the previous day's material, especially when new material was presented, and a quick preview of new material for the following day. Review can be systematic, featuring grammar activities, but it can also be a simple warm-up activity at the beginning of the class, consisting of a few personalized questions that practice the vocabulary or grammar point emphasized in the previous day's lesson. Even though a preview of new material can be as simple as the modeling and choral repetition of new vocabulary items, this kind of brief introduction will give students a head start.

A general sequence to follow in planning each class would be: review → new material (main emphasis) → preview of new material. The sample lesson plans in this section of the manual and the charts in the next section follow this sequence.

2. Write Down Your Plan

Check your plan to see that you have a variety of classroom activities, as well as a balance of the language skills and cultural material appropriate to your course. Is there an opportunity for students to talk with each other in Spanish, as well as with you? Have you planned enough activities for the entire class hour? Many experienced instructors always have one extra exercise or activity prepared, just in case they finish a little early—a listening comprehension passage, a guessing game, a grammar review exercise, a conversation activity, and so on.

Remember to make an assignment for the next class. Many students appreciate being given very specific assignments, such as those listed in the sample lesson plans given in this section of the Manual. When clear, regular assignments are given along with frequent quizzes, students are more likely to keep up with their work on a day-to-day basis.

3. Prepare Your Materials

Some instructors write down every detail of their plans on index cards; others make most of their teaching notes in the margins of their books, and still others use a teaching notebook or a folder. After you have written down your plan, prepare the handouts, visuals, or transparencies you want to use, and then review your plan and materials one last time to make sure that everything fits together: Does every exercise have a purpose? Has anything important been omitted? How much time do you want to devote to each segment of the class? Have you planned a few minutes of review? Will most of the class hour be spent on the material you want to emphasize? Have you reserved a few minutes of the class for a preview of tomorrow's material? This kind of planning will help students learn and provide links between classes.

4. Evaluate Your Class Session

What went well? Why? What didn't go so well? Why not? Would a slight change improve an explanation or an activity? Should a particular activity be omitted? A few brief notations made on this term's plan will remind you to make the necessary changes next term or next year.

C. USING THE SUGGESTIONS IN THE *INSTRUCTOR'S EDITION*

The suggestions and supplementary exercises in the *Instructor's Edition* are intended to save you planning time. The sample lesson plans in this Manual will show you how to incorporate the suggestions and exercises into your lesson plans for the first chapters of the text. Suggestions and exercises fall into several categories and are labeled for easy use and application.

1. Suggestion

A suggestion presents one way to introduce material or use an exercise in class. It is by no means the only way to use text material, but it may give you some good ideas. For example, the suggestions on the first page of the bound-in supplementary materials of the *Instructor's Edition* give you a sequence to follow in presenting the first minidialogues in the text: introduction, modeling, choral repetition, individual repetition, and small groups.

2. Extension

An exercise extension provides several more items of the same type as the items in student text exercises. These extra items afford more practice than the student text provides. When an exercise has been assigned as homework, you may want to use only the first few items in the student text and then skip to the extension items in the *Instructor's Edition* to make sure that students have mastered the material.

Another advantage to the extension items is that they provide listening comprehension practice. An example is on page 155 of the *Instructor's Edition.*

3. Variation

This suggests use of exercises in a way that is different from the instructions given in the student text. An example is on page 151 of the *Instructor's Edition.*

4. Note

This information is intended for you. You may or may not want to pass it on to your students, depending on the information and your particular course goals. An example of this kind of additional information is on page 161 of the *Instructor's Edition.*

5. Follow-Up

These are additional exercises intended for use after related exercises in the student text. These include entirely new exercises, often personalized activities related to nonpersonalized ones or communicative activities related to precommunicative ones. An example is on page 33 of the *Instructor's Edition.*

6. Preliminary Exercises

This kind of very focused exercise usually precedes an exercise in the student text on a given grammar point. These are often mechanical verb drills, pattern practice, discrimination exercises, or listening exercises. For example, the preliminary exercises that precede the **-ar** verb exercises on page 42 of the *Instructor's Edition* give students focused practice with personal endings and listening comprehension.

7. *Reciclado*

This review exercise is intended to give students additional practice with material covered in earlier chapters. These are always preceded by the round recycling icon. An example is on page 38 of the *Instructor's Edition.*

D. SAMPLE LESSON PLANS

This section of the Instructor's Manual offers sample lesson plans for **Primeros pasos** and **Capítulo 1** for classes meeting five hours per week (six contact hours available per core chapter). These plans assume that instructors intend to devote only a minimal amount of class time to the optional **Paso 4: Un paso más** sections. Instructors who do not wish to cover **Paso 4: Un paso más** at all can simply expand the amount of time per section of the regular chapter. These plans also assume that instructors require students to use the Workbook. Assignments for the audio program are not given here.

LESSON PLANS: **PRIMEROS PASOS** (OVERVIEW)

First Day:	Introduction to the course Begin **Primeros pasos: Primer paso**
Second Day:	Main focus: **Primeros pasos: Primer paso** Preview aspects of **Primeros pasos: Segundo paso**
Third Day:	Finish **Primeros pasos: Primer paso** Main focus: **Primeros pasos: Segundo paso** Preview aspects of **Primeros pasos: Segundo paso, Tercer paso**
Fourth Day:	Main focus: **Primeros pasos: Segundo paso, Tercer paso** Finish **Primeros pasos: Segundo paso** Preview aspects of **Primeros pasos: Tercer paso**
Fifth Day:	Main focus: **Primeros pasos: Tercer paso** Finish **Primeros pasos: Tercer paso** Preview: Nothing (sixth day is review)
Sixth Day:	Main focus: Review of **Primeros pasos** test Preview aspects of **Capítulo 1**

The brief overview offered with each day's suggested lesson plan lists the major topics suggested for main focus on that day. You will note that, by and large, major sections of each chapter receive major in-class focus in the same sequence of presentation as in the textbook.

It is possible, of course, to cover materials in a different sequence, but you will find that adjustments in content may be needed. In particular, if you choose to introduce a section earlier than where it is presented in the text, it may be necessary to introduce some prerequisite knowledge for the section.

1. *Primeros pasos:* First Day

Overview: Introductions
Saludos y expresiones de cortesía

1. Greet students, saying **Buenos días/Buenas tardes/Buenas noches,** as appropriate, offering a handshake. Then have students greet other students who are sitting near them. (2 min.)
2. Introduce yourself and the course (see also "Teaching Techniques: The First Day of Class," Section III, this Manual). (5 min.)
3. Getting to know students (5 min.)
   Have students fill out information sheets: name, high school attended, local address and phone number; languages studied in high school or college and for how long; class rank and major; foreign study, work, or travel—where and for how long. Discuss some of the data, if appropriate.
4. **Primeros pasos: Primer paso: Saludos y expresiones de cortesía** (p. 2) (8 min.)
   a. Introduce the topic of the first **minidiálogo:** how to greet and take leave of friends.
   b. Point out: the English equivalents of minidialogues always appear at the bottom of the page.
   c. Model the minidialogue.
   d. Use multiple choral repetitions, followed by individual repetitions.
   e. Do a small-group practice: students pair off and practice the minidialogue, reverse roles, and then repeat the dialogue, using their own names.
5. **Saludos y expresiones de cortesía** (p. 2) (10 min.)
   a. Introduce the topic: how to greet and take leave of people you don't know well.
   b. Model the minidialogue.
   c. Discuss familiar (first-name basis) relationships versus formal (last-name) relationships.
   d. Do multiple choral repetitions followed by individual repetitions and pair practice.

6. **Saludos y expresiones de cortesía** (p. 2) (10 min.)
   a. Introduce the topic: one way to ask a person's name, and how to respond when meeting someone for the first time.
   b. Model, then do multiple choral repetitions, followed by individual repetitions.
   c. Ask several students: **¿Cómo se llama usted?** (formal) versus **¿Cómo te llamas?** (familiar). Have students use familiar form with each other, formal with you. Also point out the appropriate responses when meeting someone for the first time: **Mucho gusto. Encantado/a.** Possible rejoinder: **Igualmente.**
   d. Do a chain drill: The first student in the front row turns to the next student and asks: **¿Cómo te llamas?** Student answers: **Me llamo** _______. First student responds: **Mucho gusto (Encantado/a).** Second student then turns to the next student in the row and asks the same question. When students get to the end of the row, try to recall the names of the students.
7. Preview **El alfabeto español** (pp. 4–5) (5 min.)
   a. Point out: extra letters in the Spanish alphabet: **ñ, rr.**
   b. Model letters, followed by choral repetition and individual repetition.
8. Assignment (on board)
   a. Review: **Saludos y expresiones de cortesía 1, 2, 3** (p. 2).
   b. Read: **Los cognados** (pp. 6–7).

2. *Primeros pasos:* Second Day

Overview:	**Otros saludos y expresiones de cortesía**
	El alfabeto español
	Los cognados
	¿Cómo es usted?
	Spanish in the United States and in the World

1. Warm-up/Review (4 min.)
   a. Review greetings.
   b. Review **¿Cómo se llama usted?**
2. **Otros saludos y expresiones de cortesía/Nota comunicativa** (p. 3) (10 min.)
   a. Introduce the topic: variations of greetings already learned.
   b. Use model, choral repetition, individual repetition pattern.
   c. Point out mealtimes (optional note).
   d. Have students greet each other using **señor/señorita/señora** with last name and appropriate time expression: **Buenos días/Buenas tardes/Buenas noches.**
   e. Do **Conversación A** and **B** (p. 3).
3. **El alfabeto español** (pp. 4–5) (10 min.)
   a. Practice the alphabet.
   b. Practice pronunciation of names in list: model, choral repetition, individual repetition.
   c. Do a spelling dictation.
   d. Ask **¿Cómo se llama usted?** Have students answer and spell names: **Me llamo Juan: jota - u - a - ene.**
   e. Do **Práctica A** and **B** (pp. 5–6).
4. **Los cognados** (pp. 6–7) (5 min.)
   a. Present concept of cognates.
   b. Point out: spelling equivalents (**-ent** versus **-ente,** and so on), following examples in text.
   c. Model adjectives, followed by students' repetitions.
5. **¿Cómo es usted?** (p. 7) (10 min.)
   a. Model singular forms of **ser,** then do choral repetition, individual repetition.
   b. Point out: concept of familiar (**tú eres**) versus formal (**usted es**) already discussed in greetings.
   c. Do **Conversación A** (p. 7) using cognates presented on p. 6.

6. Spanish in the United States and the World (pp. 8–9) (6 min.)
   a. Ask: Where is Spanish spoken? Students answer using the names of Spanish-speaking countries from the map (p. 9). Write names of countries on the board as students give them.
   b. Point out: (1) There are more than twenty Spanish-speaking countries with 392 million speakers; (2) Spanish is the fifth most widely spoken language in the world.
   c. Model names of countries, followed by student repetition.
7. Assignment (on board)
   a. Review: **Otros saludos y expresiones de cortesía/Notas comunicativas** (pp. 2–3), **Los cognados** (pp. 6–7), and **¿Cómo es usted?** (p. 7).
   b. Read: **Más cognados** (p. 12), **Pronunciación: Las vocales** (pp. 12–13), and **Los números 0–30; hay** (p. 14).
   c. Write: the exercises for **Primeros pasos: Primer paso** in the Workbook (pp. 1–4).

3. *Primeros pasos:* Third Day

Overview: **Más cognados**
Pronunciación: Las vocales
Los números 0–30; hay

1. Warm-up/Review (7 min.)
   a. Greet students, using all expressions of courtesy and titles.
   b. Review **¿Cómo se llama... ?** and **Otros saludos y expresiones de cortesía.**
   c. Review the Spanish alphabet.
   d. Review **¿Cómo es usted?** and cognates. Ask, **¿La clase es interesante/importante/eficiente/terrible?,** using cognate adjectives from pp. 6–7.
2. **Primeros pasos: Segundo paso: Más cognados** (pp. 11–12) (10 min.)
   a. Point out: spelling equivalents (*-tion* versus **-ción,** *-ty* versus **-idad**).
   b. Read the cartoon on p. 11 and have students identify the cognate.
   c. Do **Práctica A** (p. 11). Point out words borrowed from English and adapted to the Spanish system: **líder, catcall, béisbol,** and so on.
   d. Do **Práctica B** (p. 12). Point out: Some Spanish words, in written form, look very much like English words, but they may not be so easy to recognize in speech.
3. **Pronunciación: Las vocales: a, e, i, o, u** (pp. 12–13) (8 min.)
   a. Introduce Spanish vowel sounds as compared to English vowel sounds (p. 13).
   b. Use model, choral repetition, individual repetition pattern.
   c. Do **Prácticas A, B, C,** and **D** (p. 13): model, choral repetition.
4. **Los números 0–30; hay** (pp. 14–15) (15 min.)
   a. Introduce the topic: a typical child's song from the Spanish-speaking world.
   b. **Canción infantil:** model, choral repetition, individual repetition.
   c. Present 0–30 with flash cards (5 x 8 file cards or half sheets of paper). Choral repetition as you point to numbers. Point out written accents on **dieciséis, veintidós, veintitrés, veintiséis,** and the change from final **-e** in **veinte** to **-i** (**veinti-**).
   d. Do **Prácticas A** and **B** (p. 15). Follow up with more math problems, given orally.
   e. Do **Conversación.**
5. Preview: **Gustos y preferencias** (pp. 15–17); **¿Qué hora es?** (pp. 19–21) (5 min.)
   a. **Gustar.** Preview **gustar** by using objects or drawings that you have brought to class.
   b. **¿Qué hora es?** Using a clock face on the board, model the question **¿Qué hora es?,** and the answer, **Son las dos (las tres,** and so on).
6. Assignment (on board)
   a. Review: **Más cognados** (pp. 11–12), **Pronunciación: Las vocales** (pp. 12–13), and **Los números 0–30; hay** (pp. 14–15).

b. Read: **Gustos y preferencias** (pp. 15–17), **El mundo hispánico (Parte 1)** (pp. 17–18), and **¿Qué hora es?** (pp. 19–21).
c. Write: the exercises for **Más cognados** and **Los números 0–30; hay** in the Workbook (pp. 5–7).

4. *Primeros pasos:* Fourth Day

Overview: **Gustos y preferencias**
¿Qué hora es?
El mundo hispánico (Parte 1)

1. Warm-up/Review (5 min.)
   a. Review **Más cognados** (pp. 11–12). Do **Conversación,** p. 12.
   b. Review numbers 0–30 and **hay.** Give math problems orally, as in **Práctica B,** p. 15. Ask, **¿Hay treinta días en una semana? ¿diecinueve, dieciocho, doce, veintisiete? ¿Hay veinticuatro estudiantes en la clase?**
2. **Gustos y preferencias** (pp. 15–17) (10 min.)
   a. Use objects or drawings that you have brought to class, in addition to those used when previewing **gustar** during the previous class session. Holding the appropriate item, say, **Me gusta el café. No me gusta la Coca-Cola.** Make appropriate facial expressions to accompany the model sentences. Use the question form (**¿Le gusta el cafe?**) to elicit full-sentence answers from several students.
   b. Present the concept of **gustar** (pp. 15–17). Write model sentences on the board as you give the explanation.
   c. Model **Me gusta la clase / No me gusta la clase** (and other appropriate cognates); do choral repetition.
   d. Do **Conversación A** on p. 16, asking questions of individual students while indicating possible model answers on the board.
   e. Working in pairs, have students do **Conversación B** (p. 17).
3. **A leer: El mundo hispánico (Parte 1)** (pp. 17–18) (10 min.)
   a. Point out: **Estrategia** sections precede reading passages in *¿Qué tal?* These sections will help students develop good reading skills in Spanish.
   b. Go over the **Estrategia** section for this reading.
   c. Use the reading as a guide for leading a discussion on the geography of the Hispanic world. Ask questions while students use maps to formulate answers.
   d. Have students do the reading out loud and help with pronunciation.
4. **Primeros pasos: Tercer paso: ¿Qué hora es?** (pp. 19–21) (15 min.)
   a. Introduce ways of telling time (pp. 19–20). Model pronunciation in examples, followed by student repetition.
   b. Introduce **Para expresar la hora/Nota comunicativa** (p. 20). Model expressions.
   c. Do **Práctica A** (p. 20).
   d. Do **Conversación A** (p. 21).
5. Preview: **Palabras interrogativas** (pp. 22–23) (5 min.)
   a. Preview the list of interrogative words by asking students such questions as **¿Cómo se llama usted? ¿A qué hora es la clase de español?,** etc.
   b. Point out the different interrogative phrases used to ask these questions.
6. Assignment (on board)
   a. Review: **Gustos y preferencias** (pp. 15–17) and **¿Qué hora es?** (pp. 19–21).
   b. Read: **Las palabras interrogativas** (pp. 22–23), **El mundo hispánico (Parte 2)** (pp. 24–26).
   c. Write: the exercises for **Gustos y preferencias, El mundo hispánico (Parte 1)**, and **¿Qué hora es?** in the Workbook (pp. 8–10).

5. *Primeros pasos:* Fifth Day

Overview: **Las palabras interrogativas**
El mundo hispánico (Parte 2)
Videoteca: En contexto

1. Warm-up/Review (8 min.)
   a. Review **gustar** and cognates. Ask individual students what they like or don't like, prompting them with cognates from pp. 6–7 and p. 11.
   b. Review **¿Qué hora es?** Do **Práctica B** (p. 20), and **Conversación B** (p. 21). Ask questions such as **¿A qué hora es la clase de español/historia/... ? ¿A qué hora es el programa de televisión** ***Los Simpson (Friends...)*?**
2. **Palabras interrogativas** (pp. 22–23) (12 min.)
   a. Model the interrogative phrases and ask the questions, with choral and individual repetition.
   b. Do **Práctica** and **Conversación** (p. 23).
3. **Lectura: El mundo hispánico (Parte 2)** (pp. 24–26) (15 min.)
   a. Go over **Estrategia.**
   b. Remind students about the significance of the underlined words. Go over the first such words with them.
   c. Go over the reading section by section, asking brief **sí/no** comprehension questions such as: **¿Hay pampas en la Argentina?**
   d. Do **Comprensión** (p. 26).
4. **Videoteca** (pp. 26–27) (10 min.)
   Note: The **Minidramas** vignettes are not referenced in the textbook, but are part of the *¿Qué tal?* Video Program. They also appear on the Video on CD packaged free with the textbook. See "Video Activities and Related Materials," Section X, **Capítulo 1,** this Manual for **Minidramas** activities.
   Point out: There is a **Videoteca** section in every chapter of *¿Qué tal?* It includes dialogues and activities related to the **En contexto** video. The conversation in the video segment resembles those in everyday situations. The segment that corresponds to **Primeros pasos** focuses on greetings and introductions.
   a. Review introductions and greetings.
   b. Model entire **En contexto** dialogue with choral repetitions for each line.
   c. Show **En contexto** video segment.
5. Assignment (on board)
   a. Review all of **Primeros pasos.**
   b. Complete Workbook for **Primeros pasos.**

6. *Primeros pasos:* Sixth Day

Overview: **Videoteca: En contexto**
Test
Preview of **Capítulo 1**

1. Warm-up/Review (5 min.)
   a. After greeting students, ask a variety of questions covering the different topics of **Primeros pasos,** such as: **¿Qué hora es? ¿A qué hora es la clase? ¿Te gusta la clase de español?**
   b. Offer students a chance to ask questions about material in **Primeros pasos.**
2. **En contexto** (10 min.)
   a. Do: **Lluvia de ideas.**
   b. Show video again. Have students complete **Dictado** section.

    c. Ask a few comprehension questions (see *Instructor's Edition* notes).
    d. Do: **Un diálogo original.**
3. Test (20–25 min.)
4. Preview: Overview of **Capítulo 1** (5–10 min.)
    a. Point out: *¿Qué tal?* has a regular chapter structure that begins with **Capítulo 1.**
    b. Introduce the theme and grammar structures of the chapter, focusing on opening page (p. 29).
5. Assignment (on board): Read **Paso 1: Vocabulario** (pp. 30–32).

LESSON PLANS: **CAPÍTULO 1** (OVERVIEW)

First Day:	Review **Primeros pasos** Main focus: **Paso 1: Vocabulario** Preview: **Paso 2: Gramática** (Grammar Section 1)
Second Day:	Review: **Paso 1: Vocabulario** Main focus: **Paso 2: Gramática,** GS 1 Preview: GS 2
Third Day:	Review: GS 1 Main focus: GS 2 Preview: **Paso 3: Gramática,** GS 3
Fourth Day:	Review: GS 2 Main focus: GS 3 Preview: **Un poco de todo, Paso 4: Un paso más: En contexto**
Fifth Day:	Review: GS 3 Main focus: **Un poco de todo, Paso 4: Un paso más: En contexto** Preview: **Paso 4: Un paso más: A leer** and **A escribir**
Sixth Day:	Test Main focus: **Paso 4: Un paso más: A leer** and **A escribir** Preview: **Paso 1: Vocabulario (Capítulo 2)**

7. *Capítulo 1:* First Day

Overview: **Paso 1: Vocabulario**

1. Warm-up/Review (10 min.)
    a. Greet students, using all expressions of courtesy and titles possible for the class.
    b. Review telling time, **gustar** questions, and questions with interrogatives.
2. **Vocabulario: Preparación** (pp. 30–32) (20 min.)
    a. **En la clase** (p. 30): Reenter vocabulary: model, choral repetition, individual repetition.
    b. Hold up classroom items, point to other items; use **¿Qué es esto? / ¿Quién es?,** as appropriate.
    c. Do **Conversación A, B** (p. 31).
    d. Introduce **Las materias** (p. 31): model, choral repetition, individual repetition.
    e. Do **Conversación A** (p. 32).
3. Preview: **Paso 2: Gramática** (GS 1): Singular Nouns: Gender and Articles (pp. 33–36) (15 min.).
    a. Introduce the topic.
    b. **Minidiálogo** (p. 35): model, choral repetition, one individual repetition.
    c. **¿Cómo se dice en inglés?** Items: **Aquí está; También hay; cuestan demasiado.**

d. Introduce the definite article (English *the*): **el hombre, la mujer, el libro, la mesa.**
e. Introduce the indefinite article (English *a, an*): **un hombre, una mujer, un libro, una mesa.**
f. Do the first few items in **Prácticas A, B** (p. 35).

4. Assignment (on board)
   a. Review: **Paso 1: Vocabulario: En la clase, Las materias** (p. 31).
   b. Read: GS 1: Singular Nouns: Gender and Articles (pp. 33–35). Prepare activities in book.
   c. Write: in Workbook, **Paso 1: Vocabulario, Las materias** (pp. 21–22); **Gramática:** GS 1. Singular Nouns: Gender and Articles (pp. 23–24); **Pronunciación:** Diphthongs and Linking (pp. 31–32).

8. *Capítulo 1:* Second Day

Overview: Grammar Section 1
Introduction of Grammar Section 2

1. Warm-up/Review (15 min.)
   a. Use visuals or objects and people to review **En la clase.**
   b. Review **Las materias,** practicing pronunciation (model/choral repetitions).
   c. Cognate recognition: use optional vocabulary. Expand with **¿Le gusta... ?** questions.
   d. Do **Conversación B** (p. 32).
2. GS 1: Singular Nouns: Gender and Articles (pp. 33–36) (15 min.)
   a. **Minidiálogo:** model, choral repetition.
   b. Students practice minidialogue in pairs; have one pair perform for the whole class.
   c. Do follow-up discussion exercises (p. 35, *Instructor's Edition*).
   d. Review concept of gender: not related to biological sex.
   e. Review definite article: **Dé el artículo definido. Items: libro, mesa, hombre, mujer, niño, consejero, niña, consejera.**
   f. Review indefinite article: **Dé el artículo indefinido.** Items: same as above.
   g. Ask: What gender are nouns that end in **-o,** usually? in **-a?** in **-ión?** in **-tad?** in **-dad?** the word **día?**
   h. Do **Prácticas A** (plus follow-up) and **B** (p. 35, student text and *Instructor's Edition*). Do **Conversación A, B** (p. 36).
3. Preview: GS 2: Nouns and Articles: Plural Forms (pp. 36–38) (15 min.)
   a. Introduce the topic.
   b. Realia: Ask students to identify plural nouns. Then do items in textbook.
   c. Introduce plural of nouns that end in a vowel: add **-s. Dé la forma plural.** Items: **el libro, el niño, el hombre, la mesa, la niña, la consejera.**
   d. Introduce plural of nouns that end in a consonant: add **-es. Dé la forma plural.** Items: **el papel, la universidad, la libertad, la mujer.**
   e. Present plural of articles. Do Preliminary Exercise (p. 37, *Instructor's Edition*).
   f. Do some items of **Prácticas A** and **B** (p. 37).
4. Assignment (on board)
   a. Review: GS 1.
   b. Read: GS 2. Prepare orally **Práctica** and **Conversación** activities (pp. 37–38).
   c. Read: **Enfoque cultural** (p. 39).
   d. Write: in Workbook, GS 2 (pp. 25–26).

9. *Capítulo 1:* Third Day

Overview:	Grammar Section 2
	Enfoque cultural
	Introduction of Grammar Section 3

1. Warm-up/Review: **Las materias,** GS 1: Singular Nouns: Gender and Articles (5 min.)
   a. Oral exercise: Conduct as choral or individual drill or mixture. Items: **Dé el femenino: el secretario, el consejero. Dé el masculino: la consejera, la profesora.** And so on.
   b. **¿Cómo se dice en español?** Give mix of masculine/feminine items and people.
2. GS 2: Nouns and Articles: Plural Forms (15 min.)
   a. Introduce the topic.
   b. Point out: plural of *a, an* → *some.* Review the plural form of nouns ending in a vowel (**-s**) and those ending in a consonant (**-es**).
   c. Do **Práctica A, B** (p. 37).
   d. Do **Conversación A, B** (plus **Paso 2**) (p. 38).
3. **Enfoque cultural** (p. 39) (10 min.)
   a. Introduce the section.
   b. **Datos esenciales:** Ask questions like **¿Cuál es el nombre oficial de México?**
   c. Practice reading out loud using the **¡Fíjese!** section.
   d. Do: Assign students **Conozca a...** section for reading in pairs. Follow up with comprehension questions.
4. Preview: GS 3: Subject Pronouns; Present Tense of **-ar** Verbs; Negation (pp. 40–45) (10 min.)
   a. Introduce the concept of the subject: a word or group of words about which something is said or asserted.
   b. Introduce subject pronouns in Spanish. Follow suggestions in *Instructor's Edition.*
   c. Call students' attention to brief discussion of use of subject pronouns (pp. 40–41).
   d. Introduce the concept of the infinitive.
   e. Introduce the concept of conjugation.
   f. Contrast English with Spanish: **yo hablo, tú hablas, él habla,** and so on. Emphasize how endings indicate the subject of the verb.
5. **En los Estados Unidos y el Canadá... Jaime Escalante** (p. 44) (5 min.).
   Discuss brief reading. See additional information in "Chapter-by-Chapter Supplementary Materials," Section IX, **Capítulo 1,** this Manual.
6. Assignment (on board)
   a. Review: GS 2.
   b. Read: GS 3 (explanation).
   c. Prepare orally: **Práctica** and **Conversación** (pp. 43, 45).
   d. Write: in Workbook, **Enfoque cultural** (p. 26), GS 3 (pp. 27–29).

10. *Capítulo 1:* Fourth Day

Overview:	Grammar Section 3
	Introduction of **Videoteca**

1. Warm-up/Review (10 min.)
   a. Practice conjugation of **estudiar** and **necesitar.**
   b. Hold up objects from **En la clase** vocabulary. Ask, **¿Necesita Ud. un(a) ________?**

c. Review: **Las materias.** Ask, **¿Estudia Ud. _______?**
d. Review: GS 1 and 2 as choral/individual drill, **Dé el plural: el libro, el consejero, la profesora, una mujer,** and so on. **Dé el singular: unos papeles, unos estudiantes, unas amigas,** and so on.

2. GS 3: Subject Pronouns; Present Tense of **-ar** Verbs; Negation (pp. 40–45) (30 min.)
   a. Introduce the topic: aspects of student life.
   b. **Minidiálogo** (p. 40): model, choral repetition, one individual repetition.
   c. Present infinitives of **-ar** verbs (pp. 41–42): model, choral repetition. Continue to follow *Instructor's Edition* suggestions.
   d. Model **Minidiálogo.** Do Suggestion and Follow-up (p. 40, *Instructor's Edition*).
   e. Ask: What is a pronoun? What are the subject pronouns in English? What are they in Spanish? What is the difference between **tú** and **Ud.**? between **vosotros/as** and **Uds.**?
   f. Do Preliminary Exercises (p. 42, *Instructor's Edition*).
   g. **¿Cómo se dice en inglés?** Items: **bailar, necesitar, pagar, trabajar, tomar, regresar, estudiar, desear, enseñar, buscar, comprar, cantar.**
   h. **¿Cómo se dice?** Items: *I dance, we dance,* and so on.
   i. Do **Prácticas A, B** (p. 43).
   j. Follow suggestions for Preliminary Exercises, (p. 44, *Instructor's Edition*).
   k. Do **Conversación A, B** (p. 45) plus **Note B** (p. 45, *Instructor's Edition*).
3. Preview: **Un poco de todo** and **Paso 4: Un paso más** (5 min.)
   a. **Un poco de todo** (p. 46).
   Point out: Purpose of this section is to provide a general review of grammar and vocabulary from this and preceding chapters.
   b. **Videoteca: En contexto** (pp. 47–48).
   The **En contexto** dialogue reviews greetings and introductions. It targets issues of time and schedule.
4. Assignment (on board)
   a. Review: GS 3.
   b. Prepare: **Un poco de todo** (p. 46).
   c. Read: **Lluvia de ideas** (p. 47).
   d. Write: in Workbook, **Un poco de todo** (pp. 29–30).

11. *Capítulo 1:* Fifth Day

Overview:	**Un poco de todo**
	Videoteca
	Introduction of **A leer**

1. Warm-up/Review (10 min.)
   a. Listening for structural cues—have students give the subject pronoun that corresponds to the verb in each sentence:
   1. **Hablas bien.** 2. **Compramos los libros.** 3. **Regreso mañana.** 4. **No trabajan aquí.** 5. **Cantan bien.** 6. **Enseñan historia.**
   b. Small-group activity: Conversation Cards. Students work in pairs, asking each other the following questions (from copies):
   1. **¿Hablas italiano?** 2. **¿Estudias en la biblioteca?** 3. **¿Bailas mucho?** 4. **¿Deseas bailar con (<u>estudiante</u>)?** 5. **¿Tomas cerveza? ¿Tomas cerveza en clase?** 6. **¿Necesitas dinero?** 7. **¿Trabajas?** 8. **¿Estudias historia? ¿sociología? ¿sicología? ¿matemáticas?**
   c. Whole-class follow-up: Ask individual students questions about the student(s) they talked with. For example, **Juan, ¿Susana habla italiano?,** and so on. Or ask questions such as **¿Quién habla italiano?** based on the copies. Students may answer only for the students they talked with, not for themselves. For example, Ana may answer, **Linda habla italiano,** and so on.

2. **Un poco de todo** (p. 46) (10 min.)
   Do Exercises **A** and **B.**
3. **Videoteca: En contexto** (p. 47–48) (20 min.)
   Note: See "Video Activities and Related Materials," Section X, **Capítulo 1,** this Manual.
   a. Do: **Lluvia de ideas**
   b. Show video; have students complete **Dictado.**
   c. Model entire dialogue, with choral repetitions after each line.
   d. Model dialogue with another student, substituting information with personal preferences, facts, and so on.
   e. Do **Un diálogo original** (p. 48).
   f. Discuss **Cultura en contexto.**
4. Preview: **A leer** and **A escribir** (pp. 48–50) (5 min.)
   a. Go over **Estrategia** section and introduce topic of reading.
   b. Discuss general purpose and scope of **A leer** and **A escribir** sections.
5. Assignment (on board)
   a. Read **A leer** and do **Comprensión** (p. 50).
   b. Review: **Capítulo 1.**
   c. Write: **A escribir** (p. 50); in Workbook, **Póngase a prueba** (pp. 35–36).

12. *Capítulo 1:* Sixth Day

Overview:	Test **A leer** **A escribir**

1. Warm-up/Review (5 min.)
   As needed, tailored to your class. Allow students to ask questions for review.
2. **A leer** (pp. 48–50) (15 min.)
   a. Do **Comprensión** (p. 50).
   b. Have students read out loud for pronunciation practice.
3. **A escribir** (p. 50) (10 min.)
   a. Take brief questions on assignment.
   b. Have students exchange and review each other's papers for content and errors.
4. Test (10–15 min.)
5. Preview: Overview of **Capítulo 2** (5 min.)
   Introduce the theme and grammar structures of the chapter, focusing on the opening page (p. 53).

VI. Using *¿Qué tal?* with the Video Program and Other Video Materials

The section called **Videoteca** includes activities to accompany the **En contexto** video segments. **En contexto** and a cultural segment about each of the countries highlighted in the **Enfoque cultural** section of the textbook, as well as the additional group of video vignettes called **Minidramas,** compose the Video Program for *¿Qué tal?*

The video to accompany *¿Qué tal?* incorporates appropriate grammar and vocabulary while maintaining authentic language in realistic cultural settings. The **En contexto** video segments offer functional vignettes that present individuals in familiar situations such as asking for directions or purchasing a train ticket. The **En contexto** vignettes were filmed on location in Peru, Mexico, and Costa Rica.

The cultural segments of the Video Program highlight the countries that are presented in the **Enfoque cultural** sections of the textbook. They include travelog-like footage about major cities, the geography and natural landmarks of the country, and its people, festivities, language, history, and traditions. A voice-over in Spanish describes the images in easily understood terms.

Minidramas is a fully integrated group of videos shot also on location in Mexico, Ecuador, and Spain. Each vignette features a cast of native speakers who interact in various contexts thematically tied to the chapters of the text.

In addition to providing contexts and formats designed to teach vocabulary and structures of foreign languages, materials prepared for language learners should also include authentic language whenever possible. The video to accompany *¿Qué tal?* is no exception. Many of the scripted scenes contain language particular to the country or region in which they were filmed, and many utterances by the actors, although not scripted, were left in the final cut in favor of authenticity. There are also instances on the video where the dialectical richness of the Spanish language is illustrated. Take, for example, the conversation between **Mariela** and **Amalia** in the **En contexto** segment for **Capítulo 9.** Here two Costa Rican young women use the grammatical structures unique to certain parts of Latin America. They address one another as **vos** and use language variants such as **sos, salís, querés,** and **tenés.**

Video is a fundamental component of the *¿Qué tal?* multimedia program. The activities of the **En contexto** section of **Videoteca** relate directly to their corresponding video segment. Included here is a **Dictado** that presents a portion of the dialogue from the video with blanks for students to fill in the missing words. Another activity encourages pairs of students to re-enact the chapter's video scene and then create and dramatize a similar one on their own. And, as described earlier, the **Enfoque cultural** video segment enhances the material presented in the **Enfoque cultural** section of the textbook.

Although **Minidramas** has no corresponding section in the textbook itself, first-viewing and subsequent-viewing activities for the **Minidramas** segments, as well as complete videoscripts, are included in "Video Activities and Related Materials," Section X, this Manual. This allows instructors flexibility to incorporate more exposure to spoken Spanish in class or in student laboratory situations.

The availability of facilities for videotape programs will vary from institution to institution, and individual instructors will have to determine how best to use these tapes. Some suggestions are as follows.

1. Play the scenes in class, asking students to listen and watch and then summarize what they understood. Because the vignettes often contain multiple scenes that deal with different situations,

including some that take place in a different location, you may also wish to stop each scene within a vignette and talk about it.

Focus on the goals of the speakers. Replay the scene, stopping the machine to clarify points in the dialogue. Focus on lexical items that the speakers use to make their needs and thoughts known. If there is time available after students have the basic idea of the scene, allow them to see it once more with the videoscript and ask them to role-play it, working in small groups.

2. Have the videocassettes available in the media center or language laboratory where students can view the tapes. Ask students to pay special attention to the video guide as she gives background information about each scene, to listen for the function that is being dramatized, and to understand the basic idea.
3. Stress to students that they will not understand every word—that they need only to get a sense for the action and goals of the speakers. Make clear to students that the point of the program is to stretch their language level and provide them with a view of native speakers acting out scenes.

Currently available for use with the Sixth Edition of *¿Qué tal?* are the *Destinos* Video Modules.

- The *Destinos* Video Modules are available for use with the Sixth Edition of *¿Qué tal?* The modules contain footage from the popular *Destinos* television series, as well as original footage shot on location for the modules in Spain, Mexico, Argentina, and Puerto Rico. Modules are divided into four 1-hour segments focusing on vocabulary, situational language, functional language, and culture. They are accompanied by an instructor's manual that offers suggestions for viewing, in-class activities, and complete scripts of the modules.

  The segments of the *Destinos* Video Modules coordinate with the chapters of *¿Qué tal?* in the following ways. (*Note:* This chart offers only the most obvious correlations with the chapters of *¿Qué tal?* Many segments of the *Destinos* Video Modules can be used with other chapters of *¿Qué tal?* as well. Instructors will also want to consider using the latter segments in each subsection as review/reentry of language functions and situations in particular later on in the term, after that material has been introduced.)

SEGMENT IN VIDEO MODULES	CHAPTER IN *¿QUÉ TAL?*
Module 1: Functional Language	
Greeting Others	**Primeros pasos**
Meeting Others	**Primeros pasos,** 2
Saying Good-bye	**Primeros pasos,** 8
Saying Thank You	**Primeros pasos**
Formal Versus Informal *You*	1
Asking/Telling the Time	**Primeros pasos**
Agreeing/Refusing to Do Something	9, 15
Asking for Directions	14
Excusing Oneself/Apologizing	**Primeros pasos,** 11
Using the Telephone	5
Showing Anger	11
Module 2: Situations	
Ordering a Meal	6
Checking into/out of a Hotel	7, 18
Traveling/Vacations	7, 18
Taking a Taxi	7, 14
Auto Repairs	14
Changing Money	16
Shopping	3, 12

Module 3:	Vocabulary	
	Los números	**Primeros pasos,** 2, 3
	Las materias	1
	Los colores	3
	La ropa	3
	El tiempo / Las estaciones	5
	La comida	6
	La familia	2
	Relaciones de la vida social	15
	Los deportes y los pasatiempos	9
	Las partes del cuerpo	10, 11
	La salud	10
	Las partes de una casa	4
	En una ciudad / las tiendas	3, 12
	El dinero	16
Module 4:	Culture	
	All segments	All segments

VII. Using *¿Qué tal?* with the CD-ROM and Other Multimedia Components

A. THE CD-ROM

The CD-ROM to accompany *¿Qué tal?* continues to be one of the most exciting and innovative components in the program. Completely revised for the Sixth Edition, this engaging and pedagogically sound language learning resource is the result of valuable feedback from instructors and students who used the CD-ROM that accompanied the previous edition of *¿Qué tal?* Corresponding to **Primeros pasos** and the 18 regular chapters of the textbook, the CD-ROM contains a variety of activities related to each chapter theme. Each lesson of CD-ROM is organized as follows.

1. *Vocabulario y gramática*

In this section students will find a set of engaging, interactive exercises and games that review and practice vocabulary and structures from the corresponding chapter of the textbook. Activities include "drag and drop," matching, completion, and so forth. Colorful art from the textbook adds to the beautiful design and also serves a pedagogical purpose.

2. *Videoteca*

This section corresponds to a section of the same name in the textbook. Here students have an opportunity to participate in a simulated video "interview" with characters that appear in the **En contexto** video segments and thus practice functional language. Students watch and listen to a series of questions on video and can record their responses to each. After answering all of the questions, they can watch and listen to the entire interview.

3. *Enfoque cultural*

In this section, students can watch a brief cultural video clip for each of the 21 Spanish-speaking countries covered in the textbook. In addition, a cultural note (**Nota cultural**) expands on a cultural point introduced in the text or in the video. A brief quiz (**¿Cuánto sabe Ud.?**) allows students to check their cultural comprehension in each lesson.

4. *Lectura y escritura*

This section gives students the opportunity to develop further their reading and writing skills in Spanish. Students work with a variety of texts, ranging from authentic realia pieces to longer passages. Writing tasks evolve from simple activities that involve filling out forms to longer essays appropriate for beginning students. An accent toolbar allows students to insert special characters. Save and print features allow students to print out their work to turn in to instructors.

5. *Prueba*

In this section, students have an opportunity to do a final review and self assessment of lesson content in three distinct areas. Students can check their vocabulary knowledge through a flashcard activity (**Vocabulario rápido**), complete additional vocabulary and grammar activities (**Actividades**), and do a final assessment of their cultural understanding (**Prueba cultural**).

Other special features of the CD-ROM include the following.

- W.W.W.: A link to the *¿Qué tal?* Online Learning Center Website offers a multitude of additional resources and activities for students and instructors and is accessed through the W.W.W. button at the bottom of each screen.
- Verbs: Students can access a complete set of verb charts, a valuable reference as they complete activities.
- Dictionary: A Spanish-English vocabulary of terms used in the CD-ROM provides another important reference for students. Students may click on main entries to hear them spoken in Spanish.
- Help: By clicking on Help at the bottom of each screen, information will appear that describes the functionality of each button on a given screen.
- Tracking System: Each time that students launch the CD-ROM, they are asked to input their name and course information. As they complete activities throughout each lesson, their progress is tracked and can be saved and printed out to be handed in as a way of holding students accountable for work completed.

The CD-ROM to accompany *¿Qué tal?* is offered to institutions (in a site-license laboratory pack version) and is also available for purchase by students. Because the availability of multimedia equipment will vary from institution to institution, individual instructors will have to determine how best to use the CD-ROM. Here are some possibilities.

1. One option is to demonstrate the first chapter of the CD-ROM in class or at the computer laboratory during the first weeks of class, then to assign each lesson (either officially or as an optional enrichment activity) for that chapter of the text thereafter.
2. As you complete each section in the textbook, you may wish to have all students hand in the corresponding progress report as recorded by the tracking feature. Alternatively, you may have students hand in only those activities that include a free-writing component (for example, **Escritura**).
3. Group or partner CD-ROM sessions in class or at the laboratory might be a regular part of your curriculum or an occasional motivating activity.

B. THE ONLINE LEARNING CENTER WEBSITE

The *¿Qué tal?* Online Learning Center Website, accessible at **www.mhhe.com/quetal,** offers a host of useful, engaging and interactive resources for students and instructors. Organized by chapter to correspond with the chapters of the textbook, these resources include the following.

1. For Students

- A list of learning objectives
- Self-correcting vocabulary and grammar practice exercises for each chapter
- Crossword puzzles that provide additional vocabulary review
- Cultural Internet activities and links to a variety of theme-based and culture-based websites
- Textbook-specific features that provide a strong integration between the textbook and the website
- Chapter quizzes, many with audio (listening-based) items

2. For Instructors

- Links to professional organizations and resources
- PowerPoint slides of the grammar sections in the textbook
- Digital transparencies of the vocabulary art from the textbook

3. General Resources

- Glossary of grammatical terms
- Verb charts
- Maps of the Spanish-speaking world

C. ELECTRONIC WORKBOOK AND LABORATORY MANUAL

With the publication of the Sixth Edition of *¿Qué tal?,* we are excited to offer an electronic version of the Workbook and Laboratory Manual. This exciting interactive ancillary provides the exact same content as is available in the traditional print version, though in an electronic medium. Benefits include automatic feedback and scoring, integration of the audio laboratory program, and a grading feature that allows students to print out their score to hand in.

D. THE MCGRAW-HILL ELECTRONIC LANGUAGE TUTOR (MHELT)

Developed by John Underwood (Western Washington University), the MHELT is a software program specifically created for the Sixth Edition of *¿Qué tal?* This tutorial software is free to adopting institutions.

E. SPANISH TUTOR

Developed at Vanderbilt University by Monica Morley and Karl Fisher and available for purchase by students, Spanish Tutor is a user-friendly program that helps students review and master vocabulary and grammar topics that all beginning students need to know. Students will also find the program to be of use for quick review if they continue with Spanish at the intermediate level.

VIII. Additional Resources for Use with the Sixth Edition

A. ACTIVE VERBS BY CHAPTER AND CATEGORY

The following table gives all of the verbs listed in the active chapter vocabulary lists of *¿Qué tal?* Verbs are shown by chapter number and by category (**-ar, -er, -ir,** irregular). Most idiomatic phrases given in the **Palabras adicionales** category of the chapter vocabulary lists are not given here.

Both stem changes are indicated for verbs throughout the chart, although the concept of the second stem change is not introduced in the student text until **Capítulo 4.**

CHAPTER	**-AR** VERBS	**-ER** VERBS	**-IR** VERBS	IRREGULAR VERBS, MISCELLANEOUS
Primeros pasos				está(s) es/son (*with time*) hay me/te/le gusta me llamo / te llamas / se llama nos vemos soy, eres, es
1	bailar buscar cantar comprar desear enseñar escuchar estudiar hablar necesitar pagar practicar regresar tocar tomar trabajar			estar
2	llegar mirar	aprender beber comer comprender creer deber leer vender	abrir asistir escribir recibir vivir	estoy (*with* de acuerdo) ser tengo/tienes/tiene (*for age*)

CHAPTER	**-AR** VERBS	**-ER** VERBS	**-IR** VERBS	IRREGULAR VERBS, MISCELLANEOUS
3	llevar regatear usar		preferir (ie, i)	cuesta ir tener poder (ue) querer (ie) venir
4	acostarse (ue) afeitarse almorzar (ue) bañarse cepillarse cerrar (ie) contestar despertarse (ie) ducharse empezar (ie) jugar (ue) levantarse llamarse peinarse pensar (ie) quitarse sentarse (ie)	entender (ie) perder (ie) volver (ue) volver a	divertirse (ie, i) dormir(se) (ue, u) pedir (i, i) servir (i, i) vestirse (i, i)	fue hacer hacer ejercicio hacer una pregunta hacer un viaje oír poner(se) salir traer ver
5	celebrar nevar (ie) pasar quedarse	llover (ue)		
6	acabar de ayudar cenar cocinar desayunar esperar invitar llamar preguntar preparar	conocer		saber

CHAPTER	**-AR** VERBS	**-ER** VERBS	**-IR** VERBS	IRREGULAR VERBS, MISCELLANEOUS
7	anunciar bajar contar (ue) encantar explicar facturar fumar guardar gustar mandar mostrar (ue) nadar odiar prestar recomendar (ie) regalar sacar (*to take* [*photos*]) viajar	ofrecer prometer	subir	dar decir estar de vacaciones hacer *camping* hacer cola hacer escalas/paradas hacer las maletas ir de vacaciones me gustaría
8	encontrar (ue) enfermarse enojarse faltar gastar llorar olvidar(se) portarse quejarse reaccionar recordar (ue)		conseguir (i, i) despedirse (i, i) discutir morir(se) (ue, u) reír(se) (i, i) reunirse sentirse (ie, i) sonreír(se) (i, i) sugerir (ie, i)	cumplir años dar/hacer una fiesta pasarlo bien/mal ponerse + *adj.*

CHAPTER	**-AR** VERBS	**-ER** VERBS	**-IR** VERBS	IRREGULAR VERBS, MISCELLANEOUS
9	dejar (en) entrenar esquiar ganar lavar limpiar montar a caballo pasar la aspiradora pasear en bicicleta patinar (en línea) pegar pelear pintar planchar la ropa quitar la mesa sacar la basura sonar (ue) tocarle a uno visitar	barrer correr	aburrirse sacudir	dar un paseo hacer la cama hacer un *picnic* hacer planes para poner la mesa ser aficionado/a
10	caminar cuidarse dejar de + *inf.* encontrarse (ue) examinar guardar cama internarse llevar una vida sana resfriarse respirar sacar (la lengua)	doler (ue) toser		hacer ejercicios aeróbicos ponerle una inyección tener dolor de
11	acabar acordarse (ue) entregar equivocarse estacionar pegarse quedar sacar	caer(se) recoger romper	pedir (i, i) disculpas sufrir presiones	darse con discúlpeme fue sin querer hace + *time* hace + *time* + que... hacerse daño levantarse con el pie izquierdo poner (*to turn on*) lo siento ser flexible

CHAPTER	**-AR** VERBS	**-ER** VERBS	**-IR** VERBS	IRREGULAR VERBS, MISCELLANEOUS
12	alegrarse alquilar arreglar cambiar copiar dudar esperar (*to hope*) fallar funcionar ganar grabar guardar mandar (*to order*) manejar navegar la red		imprimir permitir prohibir	haber hacer copia obtener
13	agradar apreciar crear desempeñar dibujar intentar negar (ie) representar tratar de + *inf.*	parecer tejer temer	aburrir esculpir sentir (ie, i)	es cierto (increíble, preferible, seguro, urgente, una lástima) hay que + *inf.* me (te, le,…) molesta me (te, le,…) sorprende
14	acabar arrancar conservar contaminar chocar (con) desarrollar desperdiciar doblar estacionar(se) evitar explotar gastar llenar parar reciclar revisar	obedecer proteger resolver (ue)	conducir construir cubrir descubrir destruir seguir (i, i) (*to continue*)	

CHAPTER	**-AR** VERBS	**-ER** VERBS	**-IR** VERBS	IRREGULAR VERBS, MISCELLANEOUS
15	amar casarse (con) divorciarse (de) enamorarse (de) llevarse bien/ mal (con) pasar tiempo (con) separarse (de)	crecer nacer romper (con)	salir (con)	querer (ie) (*to love*)
16	ahorrar cargar cobrar dejar (*to quit*) depositar economizar entrevistar escribir a máquina graduarse (en) jubilarse llenar (*to fill out*) mudarse renunciar sacar (el saldo)	caerle bien/mal devolver (ue)	pedir (i, i) prestado/a	
17	apoyar castigar comunicarse (con) durar enterarse (de) gobernar (ie) informar votar			
18	alojarse confirmar cruzar declarar registrar			

B. MOVEMENT OF MATERIAL AND CHAPTER NAME CHANGES FROM THE FIFTH TO THE SIXTH EDITION

The following chart shows vocabulary and grammar material that has moved in the current revision of *¿Qué tal?* Only Sixth Edition material that is now in a different chapter than it was in the Fifth Edition (or has been changed from being Vocabulary to an independent grammar section) is listed. References are not duplicated.

	¿QUÉ TAL?, 6TH ED.	*¿QUÉ TAL?*, 5TH ED.
Capítulo 2	Possessive Adjectives (Unstressed)	**Capítulo 3**
Capítulo 3	Demonstrative Adjectives	**Capítulo 4**
Capítulo 4	**Hacer, oír, poner, salir, traer,** and **ver**	**Capítulo 4** (as Vocab.)
Capítulo 6	Formal Commands	**Capítulo 7**

Note that the following chapters have new names in the Sixth Edition.

Capítulo 11	**Presiones de la vida moderna**	**Accidentes y presiones**
Capítulo 15	**La vida social y la vida afectiva**	**La vida social**
Capítulo 17	**En la actualidad**	**Las últimas novedades**

IX. Chapter-by-Chapter Supplementary Materials

A. OVERVIEW OF MATERIALS

The following section contains additional teaching strategies, comprehension questions, and information related to various sections in each chapter of the main text of *¿Qué tal?* It is suggested, however, that you first refer to the on-page annotations. This portion of the Manual includes chapter-by-chapter material such as the following:

- brief comprehension questions to accompany **Paso 1: Vocabulario** sections
- dialogues and additional activities to accompany **Videoteca**
- additional games and activities to reinforce vocabulary and grammar concepts

B. THE MASTER ORGANIZING DOCUMENT

The Sixth Edition of *¿Qué tal?* includes a Master Organizing Document (MOD). Each chapter's MOD displays the various resources (often with page numbers or other references) that are available to students and instructors. Many of the resources are further broken down in the MOD to show their contents and the types of items and exercises that users can expect to find in them. Although each chapter's MOD was created primarily to aid in lesson planning and construction of course syllabi, you may wish to photocopy it for student use.

C. PREFACE TO GAMES AND ACTIVITIES

Learning a second language is not an easy task. If students wish to attain more than mastery of a few key words and phrases, they will have to expend a great deal of effort over a long period of time in order to learn the language. Research demonstrates that such efforts are most fruitful when they are made in a low-anxiety environment.

Games of many kinds can provide such an environment because they are fun, motivating, and interesting. If structured properly, they are at a level appropriate for student comprehension. Games also encourage students to participate actively in the classroom interaction that is created when the focus of the class is on the game itself (and not on grammar rules and practice).

The games in this section of the manual were developed to reinforce vocabulary and grammar concepts for each chapter of the Sixth Edition of *¿Qué tal?* They also add humor and variety to the language classroom. Since the games include activities that are visual, auditory, and kinesthetic in nature, all students will find at least one that is appropriate for their individual learning styles. In addition to games for partner/pair work, there are games for small-group work, and whole-class activities.

Teachers in many settings have used games for instructional purposes for centuries. Our classroom experience with the games in this Manual validates their utility. All the games were field-tested with students at Citrus College. Their insights have been invaluable in the developmental process. In addition, we found that students of all ages enjoy playing games once they experience the benefits of doing so.

Following is a description of the types of games included in this section, along with a description of how to play them and suggestions for use.

Game/Activity: **¡A pescar!**

Goals: Skills: listening, speaking

Organization: Groups (four to five per group)

Time: 15 to 20 minutes

Materials/ Equipment: One deck of cards per group (thirteen different pictures; four of each)

Procedure: This card game is played like "Go Fish!"

Step 1: Each player is dealt five cards. The remainder of the deck is placed face down in the center of the group.

Step 2: Player 1 may ask any other player for a specific card, but Player 1 must have that card in his/her own hand. *Example:* **Susana, ¿tienes el sillón?**

Step 3: If Susana has one or more cards with the picture of the armchair, she must say, **Sí, tengo el sillón.** She then gives all her **sillón** cards to Player 1. If she has no **sillón** cards, she responds **No, no tengo el sillón. ¡A pescar!**

Step 4: Player 1 draws the top card from the deck. If she/he does not draw the card that she/he asked for, play passes to Player 2, and so on.

Step 5: As soon as any player has four of a kind, he/she should remove them from his/her hand and lay them on the table. The player who has the most sets of four cards wins the game.

Note: If a player runs out of cards before all the cards in the deck have been drawn, he/she should immediately draw one more card so that he/she can stay in the game.

Variations: Verbs are pictured on the **Capítulo 8 ¡A pescar!** activity cards; the letter in the corners of each card is the first letter of the infinitive. The players must formulate questions and answers with these verbs in the preterite. *Example:* **Raquel, ¿dormiste ocho horas anoche? —Sí, dormí ocho horas anoche.** (if she has one or more **Dormir** cards) or **—No, dormí solo seis horas anoche. ¡A pescar!** (if she has no **Dormir** cards).

Suggestions: Students should be encouraged to vary their questions, using as many different verbs as possible.

Students must communicate only in Spanish.

Cards should be duplicated on card stock, if possible. If items are colored, students can also practice color words and adjective agreement.

Before the cards are cut, each 8½" × 11" page may be backed with adhesive paper and laminated.

Game/Activity: **Arriésgate**

Goals: Skills: reading, speaking, simple translation

Organization: Groups (four to five students per group)

Time: 15 to 20 minutes

Materials/ Equipment: Overhead transparency of **Arriésgate** gameboard
Enough squares of opaque paper to cover each square on the gameboard
Overhead projector

Procedure: This game is similar to "Jeopardy."
In the **Vocabulario** category students identify the object(s) pictured, fill in the missing word, and so on.
In the **Verbos** category students produce the missing verb form or make a sentence describing the action pictured.
In the **Gramática** category students apply the grammatical structures learned in the chapter.
In the **Traducción** category students translate the sentences using the vocabulary and grammar of the chapter.

Step 1: Students are grouped. Designate Groups 1, 2, and so on.

Step 2: Group 1 chooses a category and the number of points they want to earn (e.g., **Verbos por 30 puntos**). The group then has one minute to produce the answer. Each student in the group should contribute.

Step 3: Group 1 answers the question. Accuracy is very important in this game. If there are any mistakes in the answer, the group loses the points. If the answer is wrong, Group 2 may answer the question, or it may pass.

Step 4: If Group 2 passes, Group 3 may answer, and so on.

Variations: Change the rules for passing or allowing a volunteer group to answer the question. For example, the next group may be required to attempt to answer the question.

Game/Activity: **Crucigramas**

Goals: Skills: speaking, listening, writing, paraphrasing

Organization: Partners

Time: 10 minutes

Materials/ Equipment: One **Crucigramas** game for each student (half the students receive the copy labeled "Partner A"; the other half receive the copy labeled "Partner B").

Procedure: Step 1: One partner's puzzle has only the answers for vertical spaces; the other has answers only for the horizontal spaces. Partner A starts the game by describing or defining the first word that appears on Puzzle A (1 across, for example). When Partner

B successfully fills in the word on Puzzle B, he/she then describes or defines the first word on Puzzle B (1 down, for example) to Partner A.

Step 2: Continue to alternate until both puzzles have been completed.

Suggestions: Students must communicate only in Spanish; they should not see each others' puzzles until the end of the activity.

Game/Activity: **¡Dígalo como pueda!**

Goals: Skills: listening, speaking, paraphrasing

Organization: Two groups

Time: 15 to 20 minutes

Materials/ Equipment: Lists of vocabulary words (may be mounted on index cards for the student describing the words)

Procedure: Step 1: A representative of Team A selects a word list, writes the name of the category on the board, and stands facing his/her team.

Step 2: The representative has one or two minutes (depending on student proficiency) to describe in Spanish the words on the list. He/She may also point at things, draw, or act out words. Synonyms, antonyms, or full sentence descriptions may be used. One point is earned for each word on the list said by any team member.

Step 3: This procedure is repeated by Team B, and so on. The team with the most points at the end wins the game.

Variations: For a simple review of vocabulary, the representative may be given one minute to describe the words in English.

Suggestions: The instructor should have copies of the word lists so that he/she can check off correct responses. Update the score on the board as each time period is completed.

Game/Activity: **La encuesta dice...**

Goals: Skills: writing, reading, speaking

Organization: Groups (four or five **familias**)

Time: 15 minutes, approximately

Materials/ Equipment: Transparency master of **La encuesta dice...**
One sheet of opaque paper to cover the answers
Overhead projector

Procedure: This game is similar to "Family Feud."

Step 1: Students are grouped into **familias.**

Step 2: Show students the question or incomplete statement (**Con frecuencia, durante los fines de semana los estudiantes van a...**).

Step 3: Teams go to the board and write their answers. Allow three to five minutes, depending on the number of answers they must produce.

Step 4: Uncover your answers one by one. The group that matches the largest number of items in your list wins.

Variations: The game may be played orally. Instead of having students write their answers, they may say them. The group that says something on your list gets a point. (You uncover the answer so that everyone can see it.)

Suggestions: Start the game by saying, "Last week, I asked 100 people to answer the following questions."

Play the three games for the chapter the same day.

Game/Activity: **La fotonovela**

Goals: Skills: writing, listening, narration

Organization: Groups (four to five per group)

Time: 15 to 20 minutes

Materials/ Equipment: Enough **Fotonovelas** to give at least two copies to each group

Procedure: Step 1: Students are grouped. This activity works best when the number of groups equals the number of students per group (e.g., four groups of four students).

Step 2: Give students ten minutes to write a story using only five pictures. The story must reflect the activities depicted in the pictures, not the characters shown. Encourage students to make the story as interesting as possible.

Step 3: One group is selected to read its story. All other groups send a **representante** to the board.

Step 4: Group 1 reads its story, and the **representantes** at the board write the letters of the pictures used by Group 1 in their story. Each **representante** who correctly writes the five letters used gets a point.

Step 5: Now Group 2 reads its story, and all other groups send a new **representante** to the board, and so on. All members of each group must go to the board at least once. The group with the most points wins.

Follow-up: Collect stories from all groups, and make copies for the whole class or have students write their stories on overhead transparencies. The next day different groups edit other groups' stories.

Game/Activity: **Frases ilustradas**

Goals: Skills: speaking, reading, listening, critical thinking

Organization: Partners

Time: 10 minutes

Materials/ Equipment: **Frases ilustradas** activity sheet for each student (half the students receive the copy labeled "Partner A"; the other half receive the copy labeled "Partner B"). Make double-sided copies to include the answers.

Procedure: Step 1: Partner A reads the first sentence aloud using the cues given on his/her paper. Partner B tells Partner A whether the sentence is correct or not. Partner A has three opportunities to exactly match the sentence that Partner B has on the back of his/her activity sheet.

Step 2: Students reverse roles.

Step 3: Students continue to alternate until the activity has been completed.

Variations: Students may be required to write the sentences in their notebooks.

Partner A may opt to complete all his/her sentences before partner B begins.

Suggestions: Students must communicate only in Spanish.

Activity sheets may be printed on different colored paper for Partner A and Partner B.

Game/Activity: **Juego de tablero I**

Goals: Skills: listening, speaking, reading

Organization: Groups (four to five per group)

Time: 15 minutes, approximately

Materials/ Equipment: One gameboard and set of cards per group
One marker per student
Dice
One answer sheet per group (to be left face down)

Procedure: Step 1: The first player in each group draws a card and reads it aloud. He/She then identifies the vocabulary item that corresponds to the definition or incomplete sentence on the card.

Step 2: If the player gives the correct answer (this may be verified with the answer sheet, if necessary), he/she throws a die or dice and advances his/her marker the designated number of spaces. If the player does not answer correctly, the card should be put at the bottom of the deck so that another player will have the opportunity to respond.

Step 3: Each player in the group repeats this procedure until all the correct answers have been given.

Step 4: The first player to reach the goal is the winner.

Variations: **Tablero** games may be played with the entire class, divided into two teams. Use an overhead projector to project a transparency of the gameboard and two markers. Read the cards aloud and call on students from alternate teams to respond. Students may be given the opportunity to author their own cards.

Game/Activity: **Juego de tablero II**

Goals: Skills: listening, speaking, reading, paraphrasing

Organization: Groups (four to five per group)

Time: 15 minutes, approximately

Materials/ Equipment:
One gameboard and set of situation cards per group
One marker per student, except for the student designated as the group leader
Dice
One answer sheet per group

Procedure: Step 1: The first player in each group draws a card and reads the instructions aloud in English. He/She follows the directions, communicating the ideas in Spanish.

Step 2: The group leader reads the correct answer aloud from the answer sheet and decides whether or not the player has given a satisfactory answer in Spanish. The leader then instructs the player to throw two dice (if the answer is correct or nearly correct), throw one die (if there are no more than a couple of errors), or return the card to the bottom of the deck without advancing the marker on the gameboard.

Step 3: Each player repeats this procedure until all the correct answers have been given.

Step 4: The first player to reach the goal is the winner.

Variations: Students may consult their textbooks but should then be permitted to throw only one die, even if their answers are correct. The group leader should set a time limit of one minute for students using textbooks to respond.

Game/Activity: **Lotería**

Goals: Skills: speaking, listening

Organization: Whole class

Time: 10 to 20 minutes

Materials/ Equipment: One copy of **Lotería** activity sheet for each student

Procedure: Step 1: Distribute questionnaires to students.

Step 2: Each student interviews as many classmates as possible. Students write the others' names as they find classmates who answer "yes, I do" to the questions. Students may not use any classmate's name more than once.

Step 3: When a student has any straight line filled with names, he/she wins. He/She then must report his/her findings to the class using the classmates' names: **Rosa comió pollo anoche.**

Suggestions: Have as many students as possible report their findings to the class.

Ask follow-up questions.

Game/Activity: **Memoria**

Goals: Skills: speaking, reading

Organization: Whole class, divided into two groups

Time: 10 minutes

Materials/ Equipment: Overhead transparency of gameboard
Enough squares of opaque paper to cover each square on the gameboard
Overhead projector

Procedure: This game is played like "Concentration."

Step 1: The first student of Team A says two numbers in Spanish, between 1 and 20 and 1 and 30.

Step 2: The instructor lifts the corresponding paper squares to reveal the contents of the two boxes. If the items match, word to picture, set the paper squares aside and give the team a point. If a match is not made, talk about each of the items by asking students questions in order to practice the vocabulary. Then put the paper squares back in place on the gameboard.

Step 3: The first player of Team B takes his/her turn, following the same procedure. Continue until all the boxes on the game are uncovered. The team with the most points wins the game.

Suggestions: Teammates may not help one another during play. Students should not be permitted to take notes.

Game/Activity: **Preguntas y respuestas**

Goals: Skills: reading, speaking, listening

Organization: Whole class

Time: 5 minutes

Materials/ Equipment: One copy of **Preguntas y respuestas** activity, cut into individual cards or strips

Procedure: Step 1: Distribute questions and answers to students.

Step 2: Each student must find the classmate who has the answer to his/her question or the question for his/her answer.

Step 3: Students line up with their partner as they find each other.

Step 4: Students read questions and answers to verify the match. (In **Capítulo 16,** questions must be asked by conjugating the verb in parentheses in the future tense. Questions must be answered by conjugating the verb in parentheses in the present subjunctive.)

Suggestions: Duplicate the questions and answers on card stock, if possible.

Game/Activity: **¿Quién lo tiene?**

Goals: Skills: reading, speaking, listening

Organization: Whole class

Time: 10 to 15 minutes

Materials/ Equipment: One copy of **¿Quién lo tiene?** activity, cut into individual cards

Procedure: Step 1: Have students form a circle.

Step 2: Distribute a question card and a picture card to each student, making sure that no student gets the picture card that corresponds to his/her question card.

Step 3: A student begins the activity by reading his/her question aloud.

Step 4: The student who has the picture of the object named in the question must respond to the question, using double object pronouns. *Example:* **Yo te (se) las compro.** He/She then gives his/her picture card to the student who asked the question.

Step 5: Continue this procedure until every student has the picture card that corresponds to his/her question card.

Suggestions: The question and picture cards should be duplicated on card stock, if possible.

As a follow-up activity, have students practice formal commands by each choosing an object on one of the picture cards and telling the classmate in possession of it to give it to him/her.

Game/Activity: **Videoteca**

Goals: Skills: writing, speaking, reading

Organization: Partners

Time: 10 to 15 minutes

Materials/ Equipment: Overhead transparency of **Videoteca**
Two sheets of opaque paper to cover answers
Overhead projector

Procedure: Step 1: Reveal illustration #1 and the English description of the situation.

Step 2: Read the situation aloud to students.

Step 3: Each pair of students has 30 to 60 seconds to write down, in Spanish, their response to the situation.

Step 4: Reveal the correct response and point value on the overhead. Students check their work and record one point for each underlined portion of the response that is correct.

Step 5: Repeat the procedure until the game is complete. The pair of students with the most points wins the game.

Variations: The game may be played by dividing the class into teams. One representative of each team goes to the board to write the response. The first student to write the correct answer earns the allotted points for his/her team.

Game/Activity: **Submarino**

Goals: Skills: speaking, listening

Organization: Partners

Time: 5 to 10 minutes

Materials/ Equipment: One **Submarino** game for each student

Procedure: This game is played like "Battleship."

Step 1: Students draw five submarines on their grid, making sure no one sees where.

Step 2: Students try to "sink" their partner's subs by asking yes/no questions using the actions and the pronouns depicted on the grid. Students respond **sí** or **no,** depending on whether they have a sub there or not.

Suggestions: The first time the game is played, it is best to demonstrate the procedure to the whole class using an overhead projector and a transparency of the game. Encourage students to keep track of their score by writing **sí** or **no** on their grid.

Game/Activity:	**Un viaje al extranjero**
Goals:	Skills: listening, speaking
Organization:	Entire class
Time:	15 to 20 minutes
Materials/ Equipment:	One set of **Un viaje al extranjero** game cards Large (8½" × 11") envelope or accordion file with title page glued to the front

Procedure:

Step 1: Have students form a circle.

Step 2: Distribute a picture card to each student.

Step 3: A student begins the activity by taking the "suitcase" and saying **Si yo hiciera un viaje al extranjero, en el equipaje llevaría...** (he/she names the object pictured on his/her card and explains why this item is necessary for the trip). The student should show the card to the class before putting it into the "suitcase." (*Note:* Some of the items are included only to add interest and humor to the game.)

Step 4: The "suitcase" is then passed to the next student. This student follows the same procedure, except that he/she must name the first student's item before identifying his/her own, telling its purpose for the trip and placing it in the "suitcase."

Step 5: Continue this procedure until each student has repeated, in order, the names of the items placed in the "suitcase" by his/her classmates, identified the item on his/her card, explained its purpose for the trip, and placed it in the "suitcase."

Step 6: The instructor should be the last one to play.

Suggestions: If possible, duplicate the cards on cardstock.

D. CHAPTER MATERIALS

PRIMEROS PASOS

Student Supplements

- Listening Comprehension Program CD, **Primeros pasos** (opening dialogues, selected word lists)
- Workbook/ Laboratory Manual, **Primeros pasos**
- Audio Program CD, **Primeros pasos**

Instructor Resources

- Instructor's Manual/IRK: Chapter-by-Chapter Supplementary Materials, **Primeros pasos**
  - **Primer paso**
    - **Saludos y expresiones de cortesía**
    - **Nota comunicativa**
    - **Los cognados**
    - Spanish in the United States and in the World
  - **Segundo paso**
    - **Más cognados**
    - **Pronunciación**
    - **Los numeros 0–30; Hay**
    - **Gustos y preferencias**
    - **A leer: El mundo hispánico (Parte 1)**
    - **A leer: El mundo hispánico (Parte 2)**
  - **Tercer paso**
    - **Videoteca**
  - Games and Activities
- Instructor's Manual/IRK: Video Activities and Related Materials
  - **A primera vista**
  - **A segunda vista**
  - Answers to Video Activities
  - Videoscripts
- Audioscript, **Primeros pasos**
- Transparencies 4–10
- Testing Program, **Primeros pasos**

Multimedia Resources

- Online Learning Center
- Electronic Workbook/Laboratory Manual
- Video, **Primeros pasos*** (cue 1:43)*; (cue 3:29)*
  - **En contexto** (0:56)†
  - **Minidramas** (1:54)
- Student CD-ROM, **Primeros pasos**
- Electronic Language Tutor, **Primeros pasos**

---

*Because the playback speeds of different machines vary, these and all subsequent times may not be exact for your classroom's VCR.

†The number in parentheses indicates the segment's running time in minutes.

Primer paso

SALUDOS Y EXPRESIONES DE CORTESÍA

Note: The word **usted** appears in its unabbreviated form in this chapter and at the beginning of **Capítulo 1.** After that, it will appear as **Ud.**

Suggestions:

- Model pronunciation for each dialogue. Use multiple choral repetitions followed by individual repetitions. See "Teaching Techniques: **Minidiálogos,**" in this Manual.
- Act out dialogues with several students.
- Have students use their own names in the exchanges. See "Teaching Techniques: Small Groups," in this Manual.
- Point out that English equivalents of **minidiálogos** will always appear at the foot of the page.
- Offer this optional vocabulary for **Minidiálogo 1: así así, más o menos, hasta pronto.**
- For **Minidiálogo 2,** discuss the use of courtesy titles and formal forms: first-name-basis vs. last-name-basis relationships.
- Point out that **buenas** and **muy buenas** can be used at any time of the day, instead of **buenos días, buenas tardes,** or **buenas noches.**
- For **Minidiálogo 3,** point out the formal **¿Cómo se llama usted?** vs. familiar **¿Cómo te llamas?** Have students use the familiar form with other students.
- Have students practice questions with a chain drill: Student 1 asks: **¿Cómo te llamas?** Student 2 answers and asks the same question of Student 3, and so on.
- Point out that **encantado** is used by males and **encantada** is used by females.
- Model **mucho gusto** and **encantado/a** in exchanges with several students, reversing roles. Have students practice the exchange.

Follow-up: Help students compare the **minidiálogos** and find patterns of formal vs. informal exchanges. Write on the board two columns, one for formal, the other for informal; list students' responses (**tú** vs. **usted; te** vs. **se; estás** vs. **está; hola** vs. **muy buenas;** and so on).

NOTA COMUNICATIVA

Point out:

- Lunchtime is often around 2 P.M.; the evening meal may be as late as 10 or 11 P.M. in Hispanic countries.
- Titles of respect are not capitalized when spelled out. When abbreviated, they are: **señor Sánchez; Sr. Sánchez.**
- **Don** and **doña** are titles of respect used only before the first name, as in **don Fernando** or **doña Flora.** These terms are not capitalized nor do they have standard abbreviations.

Heritage Speakers: Los títulos **don** y **doña** no tienen equivalente en inglés. Cuando se traduce, por ejemplo, **don Tomás,** se dice simplemente **Tomás** o **Mr. Tomás.** Pídales a los estudiantes hispanohablantes que le den ejemplos a la clase de algunas personas a las cuales ellos se refieren con estos títulos.

LOS COGNADOS

Notes:

- For easy access, sidebars in the text provide simplified versions of important examples and information described in the main body of the text.
- This section offers opportunities for pronunciation practice as well as being a vehicle to make students comfortable with Spanish and to encourage self-expression.
- Formal practice for **Los cognados** is found in the next section, **¿Cómo es usted?**

Suggestions:

- Point out that words in English and in Spanish may look alike but will not sound alike.
- Tell students that they need not try to memorize all words in this section.
- Model pronunciation of adjectives in brief sentences about yourself: **cruel... No soy cruel** (pointing to yourself), and so on.
- Think of a famous personality and have students describe her/him, using **es** or **no es.** Write the descriptions on the board with their translations.
- Provide optional vocabulary for pronunciation or listening practice, for example: **legal, superior, normal, diligente, excelente, natural, horrible, prudente, popular, inferior, intelectual, indiferente.**
- Present the vowel sounds and **soy, es** before beginning this section.
- Although **simpático/a** is not a cognate, students may recognize it and be able to use it in communicative activities.

SPANISH IN THE UNITED STATES AND IN THE WORLD

Point out: Top twelve world languages (source: World Almanac, 2000)

Chinese (Mandarin) 1,075 million
English 514 million
Hindi 496 million
Spanish 425 million
Russian 275 million
Arabic 256 million
Bengali 215 million
Portuguese 194 million
Malay Indonesian 176 million
French 129 million
German 128 million
Japanese 126 million

Segundo paso

MÁS COGNADOS: PRÁCTICA A

Suggestion: Have students express glossed categories in English before beginning pronunciation practice. Model the words.

Extension: Students give as many adjectives as they remember from **Los cognados.** Review the forms of **ser** by basing simple questions on adjectives they mention: **¿Es usted ______?**

PRONUNCIACIÓN: B

Extension: Present the last names in the following sentences; practice the phrases and then complete sentences. Emphasize clear diction and the use of mouth muscles.

a: Hasta mañana, señora Santana.
e: De nada, señora Pérez.
i: ¿Eres tímida, señorita Muñoz?
o: Con permiso, señor Ortega.
u: ¿Y usted, señora Cruz?

LOS NÚMEROS 0 – 30; HAY

Heritage Speakers: Recuérdeles a los estudiantes hispanohablantes que la forma **hay** es impersonal y que no cambia: **Hay un hombre; Hay dos libros.** Recuérdeles que, también en el pasado, **había** y **hubo** cuando expresan *there was/were* no cambian al aparecer ante un sustantivo plural: **Había muchos libros; Hubo varios problemas.**

Práctica B

Extension: **13.** 1 + 4 = ? **14.** 1 – 1 + 3 = ? **15.** 8 – 7 = ? **16.** 13 – 9 = ? **17.** 2 + 3 + 10 = ? **18.** 28 – 6 = ? **19.** 30 – 17 = ? **20.** 28 – 5 = ? **21.** 7 + 19 = ?

GUSTOS Y PREFERENCIAS

Suggestions:

- Encourage students to learn all of the **gustar** phrases as set expressions. There is no need to explain the **gustar** construction at this time; activities will not require students to produce **gustan** on their own.
- Students should relate **te/le gusta** to the informal/formal concept discussed in **Primeros pasos: Primer paso.**
- Contrast the indefinite articles practiced earlier and the definite articles practiced here, but do not require mastery of the concept at this time.

Note: Introduce **gustar** + infinitives to expand the communicative use of **gustar** phrases, as well as to introduce the concept of the infinitive.

A LEER: EL MUNDO HISPÁNICO (PARTE 1)

Suggestion **Estrategia.** Do the section in class the day before you intend to cover the reading in class. Emphasize the importance of guessing the meaning of words in context. Use additional examples for **¿dónde?** and **¿cuál?** if most students cannot immediately guess their meaning.

Optional: **Comprensión.** Students answer by giving only the name of the country.

1. **una república en el Mar Caribe**
2. **una nación comunista en el Mar Caribe**
3. **una nación muy grande al sur** (point) **de los Estados Unidos, en el continente de Norteamérica**
4. **una nación de habla portuguesa en Sudamérica**
5. **una parte de los Estados Unidos que está en el Mar Caribe**
6. **una nación de habla portuguesa en la Península Ibérica**

Suggestion: Students can find reference sources relating to Hispanic countries on the Internet. You may wish to expand this activity by having students find additional information and later ask questions similar to those presented here; for example: **¿Cuántos habitantes hay en la capital de Guatemala?** They can then write the correct answer on the board.

A LEER: EL MUNDO HISPÁNICO (PARTE 2)

Suggestion: **Estrategia.** Do the section in class the day before you intend to cover the reading. Remind students about the importance of guessing meaning from context, and explain the function of the underlined words (a feature that will continue throughout the text).

Suggestion: Go through the underlined words with students, asking several to explain how they guessed the meaning of the underlined words. There are many possibilities: cognates with English, context, clues from the photos, and so on. Hearing how other students guessed the meaning of words may help more timid students gain confidence in contextual guessing.

Comprensión: *Follow-up:*

- Ask students to give examples of geographical features from the Hispanic world that are not found in the reading. Accept answers in English, and give the Spanish equivalents if you know them.
- Additional association words (not all geographical features): **una ciudad, una nación, una capital, una república, una lengua, el sur, el oeste, una selva.**

Tercer paso

VIDEOTECA: MINIDRAMAS

The **Minidramas** vignettes are not referenced in the textbook, but are part of the *¿Qué tal?* Video Program. They also appear on the Video on CD packaged free with the textbook. If you show the **Minidramas** in class or have your students view them as homework, you might find the following suggestions helpful. You can also find blackline master activities in Section X of this Manual for **Minidramas.**

Comprensión: **¿Cierto o falso?**

1. **Diego es de México.**
2. **Diego es profesor.**
3. **Antonio es estudiante posgraduado.**

Suggestion: Encourage students to supply the correct answer to false statements by asking **¿quién? ¿qué? ¿dónde?** questions, followed by **sí/no** questions. *Modelo* (*for item 1*): **¿De dónde es Diego? ¿de España? ¿de California?**

Diálogo opcional: With help from two students, create a dialogue with personalized information similar to the following. The dialogue may be acted out, with students creating their own ending. You may wish to put the dialogue on the board to help students perform their parts.

ESTUDIANTE 1: **Perdón. ¿Es usted el profesor / la profesora ___________?**
PROFESOR(A): **Sí, soy yo.**
ESTUDIANTE 1: **Buenos días. / Buenas tardes (noches). Me llamo __________. Soy el/la __________ estudiante de __________ (estado).**
PROFESOR(A): **Ah, sí. Mucho gusto. / Encantado/a.**
ESTUDIANTE 1: **Igualmente.**
PROFESOR(A): **Bienvenido/a a Español __________ (número o título del curso). Él/Ella es __________ estudiante de español también.**
ESTUDIANTE 2: **¿Qué tal, __________?**
ESTUDIANTE 1: **Bien, gracias. ¿Y tú?**
ESTUDIANTE 2: **Muy bien. Mucho gusto.**
ESTUDIANTE 1: **Igualmente.**

ACTIVIDAD DE DESENLACE: A CONOCERNOS

Activity:	Students will create a skit in Spanish in which they meet, greet, and describe another person appropriately, and present it to the class.
Purpose:	To review and practice formal and informal verbal structures and expressions
Resources:	*¿Qué tal?* textbook, the Internet, and other sources as appropriate
Vocabulary:	Cordial expressions, cognates, numbers to 30, interrogative words, and the use of **te/me/le gusta,** and **hay**
Duration:	Out-of-class preparation time will vary. In-class time will be approximately 3 minutes per presentation.
Format:	Groups of 2–3 students

Games and Activities

Primeros pasos *Memoria*

1. (2 puntos)	You say good morning to your mother and you ask her what time it is. **Buenos días,** mamá. **¿Qué hora es?**
2. (4 puntos)	You tell her that Spanish class is at 9:00 a.m., and then you take your leave by saying . . . **La clase de español** es **a las nueve de la mañana. Adiós. (Hasta luego.)**
3. (1 punto)	At the college you want to get off the crowded bus. To the passengers blocking your exit, you say . . . **Con permiso.**
4. (2 puntos)	You see Ana, your good friend, on the way to class. You greet her and ask how she's doing. **Hola, Ana. ¿Qué tal?**
5. (1 punto)	When you enter the classroom, the professor asks you what your name is. You answer . . . **Me llamo...**
6. (1 punto)	As you go to take a seat in class, you accidentally step on a classmate's foot. You say . . . **Perdón.**

7. (1 punto)	The instructor mentions a number of important figures from the Spanish-speaking world. You raise your hand to ask who Diego Rivera is. **¿Quién es Diego Rivera?**
8. (1 punto)	After class you decide to go to the cafeteria to get something to eat. You ask the cashier how much the sandwich is. **¿Cuánto es el sándwich?**
9. (1 punto)	While you are eating your lunch, a friend stops by your table to introduce you to his cousin, Yolanda. You tell her that it is a pleasure to meet her. **Mucho gusto.** (Encantado/a.)
10. (3 puntos)	Later, you see your Spanish instructor on campus. You say good afternoon and ask her how she is. **Buenas tardes, profesora. ¿Cómo está usted?**
11. (3 puntos)	You tell the instructor that you like the Spanish class a lot. When she thanks you, you respond appropriately. **Me gusta mucho la clase de español. De nada.**
12. (1 punto)	After studying for several hours that evening, you say goodnight to the family. **Buenas noches.**

¿Qué hora es?	Son las cuatro de la tarde.
¿Quién es Antonio Banderas?	Es un actor español.
¿Cómo se llama usted?	Me llamo Teresa Sánchez.
¿Cómo está usted?	Muy bien, gracias. ¿Y usted?
¿Cómo es Gloria Estefan?	Es inteligente y generosa.
¿Qué es un elefante?	Es un animal.
¿Cuántos son siete y ocho?	Son quince.
¿Cuántas horas hay en un día?	Hay veinticuatro.

¿Qué es una guitarra?	Es un instrumento musical.
¿De dónde es usted?	Soy de los Estados Unidos.
¿Qué es el fútbol?	Es un deporte.
¿Cuál es la capital de España?	Es Madrid.
¿A qué hora es la clase de inglés?	A las diez de la mañana en punto.
¿Cuánto es el diccionario?	Es veintidós dólares.
¿Dónde está la profesora?	Ella está en la oficina.
¿Cuándo es la fiesta?	Es mañana por la noche.

CAPÍTULO 1 EN LA UNIVERSIDAD

Student Supplements

- Listening Comprehension Program CD, **Capítulo 1** (**Paso 1: Vocabulario** word lists)
- Workbook/Laboratory Manual, **Capítulo 1**
- Audio Program CD, **Capítulo 1**

Instructor Resources

- Instructor's Manual/IRK: Chapter-by-Chapter Supplementary Materials, **Capítulo 1**
  - **Paso 1: Vocabulario**
  - **Paso 2: Gramática**
    - Grammar Section 1
    - Grammar Section 2
    - **Enfoque cultural**
  - **Paso 3: Gramática**
    - Grammar Section 3
    - **Un poco de todo**
  - **Paso 4: Un paso más**
    - **Videoteca**
    - **A leer**
  - Games and Activities
- Instructor's Manual/IRK: Video Activities and Related Materials
  - **A primera vista**
  - **A segunda vista**
  - Answers to Video Activities
  - Videoscripts
- Audioscript, **Capítulo 1**
- Transparencies 11–16
- Testing Program, **Capítulo 1**

Multimedia Resources

- Online Learning Center
- Electronic Workbook/Laboratory Manual
- Video, **Capítulo 1** (cue 7:23)
  - **En contexto** (1:47)
  - **Minidramas** (4:19)
  - **Enfoque cultural: Los Estados Unidos** (1:00)
- Student CD-ROM, **Capítulo 1**
- Electronic Language Tutor, **Capítulo 1 (Vocabulario, Gramática)**

Paso 1: Vocabulario

EN LA CLASE

Preparation: Bring with you the objects listed in the vocabulary box, or know where you can find an example of each in the classroom. Have pictures for the rest of the items.

Presentation:

- Hold up objects or photographs, or point to class members; model pronunciation while students listen. Use both definite and indefinite articles.
- Pronounce seven or eight vocabulary words from this chapter. Encourage students to identify the "class" of the word, that is, whether it responds to **¿Dónde?, ¿Qué?,** or **¿Quién?**
- Identify and, at times, misidentify several objects or persons (point to them, show pictures, and so on). Have students respond **sí/no** or **correcto/incorrecto.**
- Indicate objects or persons and offer a choice: **¿Qué es esto, una mesa o una silla?** Have students answer in Spanish.
- Emphasize the difference between **librería** and **biblioteca.**
- Point out classroom objects, alternating the use of definite and indefinite articles. Students will learn the concept of gender later. For now, they should only listen to the words.
- Offer optional vocabulary: **el borrador, la carpeta, el estadio, el gimnasio, el laboratorio (de lenguas), el pupitre, el reloj, el sacapuntas, la tiza.**

Quick Comprehension Check: **¿Cierto o falso?**

1. **Una librería es un lugar. No es una persona.**
2. **La residencia es para los profesores.**
3. **Un consejero es una persona. No es un animal.**
4. **En la clase, son necesarios un libro, unos escritorios, papel y un secretario.**
5. **En la clase de español, hay** (*insert approximate number of students*) **estudiantes.**

LAS MATERIAS

Presentation: Have students skim the list of subjects as you pronounce each word out loud twice. This should take very little time. Then ask students to close their books.

- Model the names of academic subjects. Have students stand each time they hear the name of a subject that they are taking.
- Point out the many cognates that end in **-ía** and **-ción.**
- Explain that another word for **la computación** is **la informática.**
- Have students generate as many words as possible that they associate with the following categories: **las ciencias, la sicología, la biblioteca, el diccionario, el lápiz, el libro, el comercio.**
- Offer the following optional vocabulary: **la antropología, la biografía, la contabilidad** (accounting), **la geología, la geografía, la ingeniería, el mercadeo, el periodismo.**

Quick Comprehension Check: **¿Cierto o falso?**

1. **En una clase de historia, los libros no son muy importantes para los estudiantes.**
2. **Los números son muy importantes en una clase de matemáticas.**
3. **Es posible estudiar los animales en una clase de ciencias.**
4. **El comercio no es una materia popular en la universidad.**
5. **En una clase de literatura los estudiantes leen muchas novelas.**
6. **Es necesario participar mucho en una clase de español.**

Paso 2: Gramática

GRAMMAR SECTION 1: GENDER D

Suggestion: Emphasize that **la persona** is used whether the person talked about is male or female: **Ernesto es una buena persona.**

GENDER E

Suggestions:
- Point out that like **estudiante** some words refer to both men and women: **turista, artista, dentista.** The feminine of the word **poeta** is traditionally **poetisa,** but is often replaced today by **la poeta.**
- Explain that the "matching" between the article and the noun is called **la concordancia** (agreement).

Notes:
- Many Spanish speakers use **cliente / clienta, presidente / presidenta, dependiente / dependienta.**
- Some **-pa** and **-ta** words are also masculine: **el mapa, el cometa, el planeta.** Like the **-ma** words, they are of Greek origin.

ARTICLES B

Suggestions:
- Point out the words **un/una** can mean *one, a,* or *an.*
- Remind students that in English, too, the context in which we find a word can determine our understanding of it. Have students consider how they know what the word *will* means in the examples *Will you do this?, Will and I went to the park,* and *The lawyer wrote the will.*

CONVERSACIÓN

Optional: **A. Asociaciones.** Identifique dos cosas y dos personas que usted asocia con los siguientes lugares.

MODELO: la clase → la silla, el libro de texto
el profesor, el estudiante

1. **la biblioteca**
2. **la librería**
3. **una oficina**
4. **la residencia**
5. **el laboratorio de lenguas**
6. **la capital de los Estados Unidos (del Canadá)**
7. **la universidad**
8. **Puerto Rico**

Note: **Clase** means both *class* and *classroom.* The context of the sentence differentiates them.

Follow-up: Have students compare their lists. What items are similar? What items are different?

B. ¿Y ella? ¿Y él?

Give the male or female counterparts, as needed:

1. **Pablo Ortiz es consejero. ¿Y Paula Delibes?**
2. **Camilo es estudiante. ¿Y Conchita?**
3. **Carmen Leal es profesora. ¿Y Carlos Ortega?**
4. **Juan Luis es dependiente. ¿Y Juanita?**
5. **Josefina es una amiga de Luz. ¿Y José?**

GRAMMAR SECTION 2: PLURAL FORMS

Suggestions:
- Have them form small groups to translate the main points of the two ads.
- Have students read ads out loud to practice pronunciation of vowels.

Heritage Speakers:
- Anime a los estudiantes a ayudar a sus compañeros monolingües a traducir los anuncios.
- Invite a un estudiante hispanohablante a leer el anuncio en voz alta para que la clase oiga la pronunciación de las vocales.

PLURAL FORMS A

Suggestion: Point out that the stress does not shift when plurals are formed. Word stress and accentuation will not be formally presented until **Capítulo 3,** so you may prefer to discuss addition/deletion of accent marks in plurals now.

PLURAL FORMS C

Suggestion: Point out that even if a group includes only one male but many females, the masculine plural form is used. If the feminine plural is used, it excludes any male membership in the group: **los estudiantes** refers to males or females; **las estudiantes** includes only females.

ENFOQUE CULTURAL

DATOS ESENCIALES

Follow-up: After students review the **Datos esenciales** section, ask: **¿Es grande la población hispana en** ______ (name of your state)**? La mayoría de los hispanos de** ______ (name of your state), **¿son de origen mexicano (puertorriqueño/cubano** and so on)**?**

¡FÍJESE!

Follow-up: After students read the **¡Fíjese!** section, ask: **¿Conocen a un político hispano en** ______ (name of your state)**?** Point out that recent estimates project that Hispanics will be the largest minority group in the U.S. by the year 2050.

Point out:
- **Latinoamérica** means **Hispanoamérica** and **Iberoamérica.**
- Use **hispano/a** for people; **hispánico/a** as an adjective. This second word, in Spanish, refers to people from Spanish-speaking countries, and not to U.S. Hispanics. *Hispanic American* as a term for U.S. Hispanics cannot be translated as **hispanoamericano/a** or **latinoamericano/a.** The term **latino/a** is often used.

Note: **el idioma** means **la lengua.**

Suggestion: In order to engage students in a frank discussion of their own, possibly inaccurate, stereotypes, have them describe how they picture Hispanics physically (White, Indian, Mestizo, Black, and so on). Non-Hispanic (and even Hispanic) students from different regions of this country may have different images of Hispanics, according to the predominance of Hispanics of one origin or another in their area. Follow up by showing magazine (or family) pictures of very different-looking Hispanics.

CONOZCA A...

Note: For more information on the United Farm Workers students can visit the organization's Website.

Heritage Speakers: Pídales a los estudiantes hispanohablantes que investiguen más a fondo la vida y labor de César Chávez. Luego pueden preparar y presentarle a la clase un informe oral.

ENFOQUE CULTURAL: LOS HISPANOS EN LOS ESTADOS UNIDOS

A. Para completar (I). Complete el siguiente cuadro (*the following table*) con información en Datos esenciales y ¡Qué interesante!

Número	Información correspondiente (*corresponding*)
	el número de hispanos en el Congreso de los Estados Unidos en 1997
	el porcentaje (*percentage*) de personas de origen mexicano en los Estados Unidos
	el porcentaje de personas de origen cubano en los Estados Unidos
	año (*year*) de la fundación de Santa Fe, Nuevo México
	el porcentaje de personas de origen puertorriqueño en los Estados Unidos

B. Para completar (II). Las siguientes oraciones (*The following sentences*) son falsas. Corríjalas (*Correct them*) con información en Conozca a...

1. Ellen Ochoa tiene (*has*) un doctorado en ingeniería civil.

   Ellen Ochoa tiene un doctorado en ingeniería ________________.
2. En 1993, la Dra. Ochoa voló (*flew*) en Apollo XIII.

   En 1993, la Dra. Ochoa voló en ________________.
3. Ellen Ochoa estudió (*studied*) en la Universidad de Santa Fe.

   Ellen Ochoa estudió en la Universidad de ________________.
4. La Dra. Ochoa es la primera doctora hispánica.

   La Dra. Ochoa es la primera ________________ hispánica.

Paso 3: Gramática

GRAMMAR SECTION 3

Notes:

- The subject of a sentence is the word or group of words about which something is said or asserted. Usually the subject indicates who or what performs the action of the sentence: *The girl threw the ball.*
- A pronoun (**pronombre**) is a word used in place of a noun or to represent a person (*I, you*): *She (the girl) threw the ball.*

Suggestion: Have students indicate the subjects in the following sentences: 1. Olga is going to write a message. 2. The car ran off the road. 3. Have Jack and Joyce arrived yet? 4. Love conquers all.

SUBJECT PRONOUNS A

Suggestion: Point out that there is no Spanish equivalent for *it* as a subject.

SUBJECT PRONOUNS B

Suggestions:

- Emphasize the difference between **tú** and **Ud.,** explaining that the kind of relationship between two people determines the form they will use. Point out that the contexts for **tú** and **Ud.** are very different throughout the Spanish-speaking world, and they vary from country to country, and from one generation to another. In some countries (for example: Spain, Puerto Rico, and Cuba) people are much more liberal in the use of **tú** than others (for example: Colombia, Honduras, or Costa Rica).
- Remind students that people in some countries (among them, Argentina, Uruguay, and Costa Rica) use **vos** instead of **tú.** This form will not be presented formally in *¿Qué tal?* However, it appears in the **En contexto** video vignettes that take place in Costa Rica. You may wish to show these vignettes as an example.
- As you introduce **tú** and **Ud.,** review what students already know about formal and informal usages by asking them to address these questions to you or to another student, as appropriate. 1. **¿Cómo está?** 2. **¿Le gusta la universidad?** 3. **¿Te gusta la clase de español?** 4. **¿Cómo se llama Ud.?** 5. **¿Cómo te llamas?** 6. **¿Cómo estás?**

SUBJECT PRONOUNS C

Note: **Vosotros** will not be actively practiced in the regular activities and exercises of *¿Qué tal?*

VERBS: INFINITIVES AND PERSONAL ENDINGS

Suggestions:

- Model the pronunciation of each infinitive several times. Then use the **yo** form of each in a brief, simple sentence about yourself, repeating several times and pantomiming if necessary.
- Have students generate all forms of one verb, after you give the subject pronouns.
- Transform the base sentence into a simple **Ud.** question directed to a student, coaching him or her to answer using the **yo** form. Example: **bailar** → **Me gusta bailar. Bailo muy bien. Y Ud., ¿baila bien?**
- Ask students **¿Cómo se dice** *I / we dance, I / we sing, I / we buy*... **?**
- Emphasize **tocar** (music), and those infinitives that include prepositions in their meaning.
- Offer the following optional verbs: **caminar, fumar, hablar por teléfono, mirar (la televisión**).

VERBS C

Suggestion: Explain the use of present tense questions to indicate near-future actions: **¿Hablas con Juan mañana?** (*Will you speak to Juan tomorrow?*)

NEGATION

Suggestion: Point out that the second **no** = the English *not.*

CONVERSACIÓN

Optional: **Oraciones lógicas.** Form at least eight complete logical sentences by using one word or phrase from each column. The words and phrases may be used more than once, in many combinations. Be sure to use the correct form of the verbs. Make any of the sentences negative, if you wish.

MODELO: Yo no estudio francés.

yo		comprar	la guitarra, el piano, el violín
tú (estudiante)		regresar	el edificio de ciencias
nosotros (los miembros		buscar	en la cafetería, en la universidad
de esta clase)		trabajar	en una oficina, en una librería
los estudiantes de aquí		hablar	a casa por la noche
el extranjero		tocar	a la biblioteca a las dos
	(no)	enseñar	francés, alemán (*German*)
un secretario		pagar	bien el español
un profesor de español		tomar	los libros de texto con un cheque
un dependiente		estudiar	libros y cuadernos en la librería
		desear	tomar una clase de computación
		necesitar	hablar bien el español
			estudiar más (*more*)
			comprar una calculadora, una mochila
			pagar la matrícula (*tuition*) en septiembre

Note: This kind of activity is called a sentence builder. Each subject and verb can be used with more than one item from the right-hand column; many sentences are possible. The use of **no** is optional. Emphasize that forms of **desear** and **necesitar** must be followed by an infinitive. Also emphasize that verbs of motion, like **regresar,** are followed by **a.**

UN POCO DE TODO

Optional: **Conversaciones en la cafetería**

Paso 1. Form complete questions and answers based on the words given, in the order given. Conjugate the verbs and add other words if necessary. Do not use the subject pronouns in parentheses.

PREGUNTAS

1. ¿buscar (tú) / libro de español?
2. ¿no trabajar / Paco / aquí / en / cafetería?
3. ¿qué más / necesitar / Uds. / en / clase de cálculo?
4. ¿dónde / estar / Juanita?
5. ¿no desear (tú) / estudiar / minutos / más?

RESPUESTAS

1. no, / (yo) necesitar / regresar / a casa
2. no, / (yo) buscar / mochila

3. (nosotros) necesitar / calculadora / y / cuaderno
4. no, / él / trabajar / en / biblioteca
5. ella / trabajar / en / residencia / por / tardes

Paso 2. Now match the answers with the questions to form short conversational exchanges, or practice them with a partner, if you wish.

Suggestions:

- Explain that this type of exercise is called a "dehydrated sentence." Explain its purpose (see the "Drills," Section III "Teaching Techniques" in this Manual).
- Have students describe the following persons by telling what they do and, if possible, where they do it. 1. **un secretario** 2. **una profesora** 3. **un estudiante** 4. **una dependienta** 5. **Madonna** 6. **un bibliotecario**

Note: The subject pronouns in parentheses should not be used; they are cues only.

Variation: Have students work in pairs in which one student produces the question, the other, the answer. Emphasize that they should correct each other's mistakes. Finally, the whole class can go over all answers quickly.

Follow-up: **¿Qué busca en una librería? ¿Qué necesita para estudiar español? ¿Cuánto tiempo desea estudiar por la noche? ¿Trabaja? ¿Dónde? ¿Usa una mochila?**

UN POCO DE TODO A

Follow-up: Encourage students to form groups of three in which two students are journalists and one plays Ángela. The journalists interview Ángela for the school newspaper. They should ask all relevant and/or possible questions that can be answered using the letter's information.

Heritage Speakers: Pídales a los estudiantes hispanohablantes que mencionen otras palabras que tengan el mismo significado que **chévere.** Esta actividad puede ser el comienzo de una más extensa en la que estos estudiantes hacen una colección de variantes lingüísticas y entregan su lista al terminar el curso.

Paso 4: Un paso más

VIDEOTECA: EN CONTEXTO C

Suggestion: Give students five minutes to practice each of the **Pasos** in **Un diálogo original,** and then have some pairs act out the dialogue they have developed.

MINIDRAMAS

The **Minidramas** vignettes are not referenced in the textbook, but are part of the *¿Qué tal?* Video Program. They also appear on the Video on CD packaged free with the textbook. If you show the **Minidramas** in class or have your students view them as homework, you might find the following suggestions helpful. You can also find blackline master activities in Section X of this Manual for **Minidramas.**

Comprensión: **¿Cierto, falso o no se sabe** (*unknown*)**?**

1. **Lupe y Diego son estudiantes.**
2. **Lupe y Diego son compañeros de residencia.**
3. **A Diego no le gusta la antropología.**

4. **Lupe y Diego toman una clase con el profesor Salazar.**
5. **El profesor Salazar enseña sicología.**

Suggestion: Guide students through a possible dialogue by writing one on the board. Leave spaces blank for real students' answers. ***Modelo:***

ESTUDIANTE 1 (E1): **¡Huy, perdón! ¿Tú eres estudiante de Español ____?**
ESTUDIANTE 2 (E2): **Sí, soy estudiante de Español ____. Me llamo ____.**
E1: **Yo me llamo ____. Encantado/a.**
E2: **Igualmente.**
E1: **Busco un libro para la clase de ____.**
E2: **Yo necesito ____ (un libro / unos bolígrafos...). ¿Te gusta la clase de ____ / español?**
E1: **Sí, me gusta mucho. / No, no me gusta mucho. ¿Qué materias tomas?**
E2: **____.**
E1: **¿Cuál es tu materia favorita?**
E2: **Es ____. El profesor / La profesora es (muy) ____. La materia es (muy) ____. ¿Cuál es tu materia favorita?**
E1: **Es ____. El profesor / La profesora es (muy) ____. La materia es (muy) ____. Bueno, necesito pagar el libro.**
E2: **Muy bien. Nos vemos en clase.**
E1: **Sí, nos vemos.**

A LEER

Suggestion: **Estrategia.** Once again, do the section in class the day before you intend to cover the reading. Remind students to continue to practice this strategy actively as they read, as part of their homework assignment. Remember to follow up on underlined words the next day.

Optional: **Comprensión.**

- Write key words on the board. Using them, students create factual sentences based on the reading. 1. **residencias** 2. **casas particulares** 3. **autobús** 4. **zonas verdes** 5. **deportes** 6. **la música** 7. **otras diversiones**
- Students give two reasons why the Hispanic university campus is not **un centro de actividad social.**

Note: In the Hispanic world there is no tradition of going away to study, unless there is no university in one's hometown or in nearby cities. Most students live with their families throughout their education. The students who live in dormitories, pensions, and private homes are from out of town. However, an increasing number of these students rent and share their apartments with other students, like many American students.

Traditional, old universities are typically in the downtown area of large, important cities. Therefore, they are surrounded by the downtown life, with lots of bars and cafés. Many university buildings have their own **bar-cafetería.** Such bars and cafés are the equivalent of cafeterias and dining facilities in this country in that they bring students together outside the classroom. These bars and cafés have traditionally provided an intense university and intellectual life for students. It is normal for students to meet with each other and even with their professors after classes and chat over a beer or coffee.

Suggestions:

- Do the **Estrategia** section in class the day before you intend to cover the reading. Remind students to continue to practice this strategy actively as they read, as part of their homework assignment. Remember to follow up on the underlined words the next day.
- After students have completed the reading, check their comprehension by writing key words on the board. Then ask students to use the words to create factual sentences based on the reading. 1. **residencias** 2. **casas particulares** 3. **autobús** 4. **zonas verdes** 5. **deportes** 6. **la música** 7. **otras diversiones**
- Have students give two reasons why the Hispanic university campus is not **un centro de actividad social.**
- Encourage students to describe their own university by using adjectives taken from the text. They can also refer to some of the cognates presented in **Primeros pasos.** Ask: **¿Cómo es esta** (*this*) **universidad? ¿Es liberal? ¿grande? ¿privada?** and so on.
- Ask students what aspects of campus life are important to them. **¿Son importantes las actividades sociales en la universidad? ¿Y los deportes? ¿Qué más es importante?**

A ESCRIBIR

Suggestion: Go over the assignment orally in class to be sure that students understand the meaning of all suggested words and phrases. Assign the preparation of answers in writing as homework. The following day, use one student's answers as a model to form two coherent paragraphs, writing the sentences on the board. Then ask students to write paragraphs for the next day.

If students need more support, approach the assignment in this way:

In this exercise, you will write a description of your own **vida universitaria.** First, answer the following questions in short but complete sentences.

1. **¿Es grande o pequeña la universidad? (Mi universidad...)**
2. **¿Es pública or privada?**
3. **¿Cuántas residencias hay en el *campus*?**
4. **En general, ¿viven los estudiantes en residencias, en apartamentos o con su** (*their*) **familia?**
5. **¿Cuáles son los dos edificios más grandes** (*biggest*)**? ¿la biblioteca? ¿la administración? ¿la unión estudiantil?**
6. **¿Se da mucha importancia a los deportes? ¿a la música? ¿al teatro?**
7. **¿Dónde vive Ud.? (Yo vivo...)**
8. **¿Cómo llega Ud. al *campus*? ¿en coche o en autobús? ¿O camina Ud.?** (*Or do you walk?*)
9. **¿En qué edificios del *campus* estudia Ud.?**
10. **¿Qué materia le gusta más?**

Now take your individual answers and form two coherent paragraphs (using items 1–6 and 7–10) with them.

ACTIVIDAD DE DESENLACE: LOS NUEVOS AMIGOS

Activity: Students will create a skit in Spanish about new students getting acquainted, and present it to the class. They will ask and answer questions regarding their university classes, time schedules, and favorite activities.

Purpose: To create a context in which students can review and practice the grammar from **Capítulo 1** and vocabulary related to the university

Resources: *¿Qué tal?* textbook, the Internet, and other sources as appropriate

Vocabulary:	People and places in the university, classroom objects, time of day expressions, and course/subject areas
Grammar:	Principal grammar structures covered in **Capítulo 1** of the textbook, including articles, **-ar** verbs, and the verb **estar**
Recycled Content:	Numbers, time expressions, **me/te/le gusta,** cognates, and interrogatives
Duration:	Out-of-class preparation time will vary. In-class time will be approximately 5 minutes per presentation.
Format:	Groups of 3–4 students

Capítulo 1

Arriésgate

	Vocabulario	Verbos	Gramática	Traducción
10 pts	 (artículo definido)	La profesora de inglés _____ dos clases de literatura.	Sí, necesito el libro de texto.	There is a party in the dormitory tomorrow at 8:30 p.m.
20 pts	 (artículo indefinido)	Ud. _____ comprar un diccionario para la clase de español.	No, no cantamos en francés.	The classmates drink coffee in the cafeteria in the afternoon.
30 pts	 (forma plural)	Mis amigos y yo _____ la matrícula en el edificio de administración.	Los hombres compran cerveza alemana.	I want to study mathematics, psychology, and chemistry.
40 pts		¿Tú _____ en la biblioteca o _____ a casa ahora?	La secretaria busca papel en el escritorio.	The clerk works in the university bookstore every day.
50 pts		José _____ la guitarra, y Carlos y Luisa _____ el tango.	El profesor está en la oficina hasta las cuatro de la tarde.	The foreign student speaks with the counselor on the phone frequently.

Answer Key for *Arriésgate*

Capítulo 1

Vocabulario:	**10 pts**	la pizarra, el profesor, los estudiantes (la clase)
	20 pts	un bolígrafo, unos libros, una biblioteca
	30 pts	las mesas, los lápices, las mujeres
	40 pts	veintiocho cuadernos, diecinueve ventanas, once mochilas
	50 pts	veintiuna sillas, catorce calculadoras, treinta edificios
Verbos:	**10 pts**	enseña
	20 pts	necesita
	30 pts	pagamos
	40 pts	estudias, regresas
	50 pts	toca, bailan
Gramática:	**10 pts**	¿Necesitas (Necesita Ud.) el libro de texto?
	20 pts	¿Cantan Uds. en francés?
	30 pts	¿Qué compran los hombres? (¿Quiénes compran cerveza alemana?)
	40 pts	¿Qué busca la secretaria en el escritorio? (etcétera)
	50 pts	¿Dónde está el profesor? (etcétera)
Traducción:	**10 pts**	Hay una fiesta en la residencia mañana a las ocho y media de la noche.
	20 pts	Los compañeros de clase toman café en la cafetería por la tarde.
	30 pts	Deseo estudiar matemáticas, sicología y química.
	40 pts	El dependiente trabaja en la librería de la universidad todos los días.
	50 pts	El estudiante extranjero habla con el consejero por teléfono con frecuencia.

La fotonovela

Using six of the following pictures, write a short story about what a typical college student does every semester (**todos los semestres**). Include the expressions **por la mañana** (**tarde, noche**).

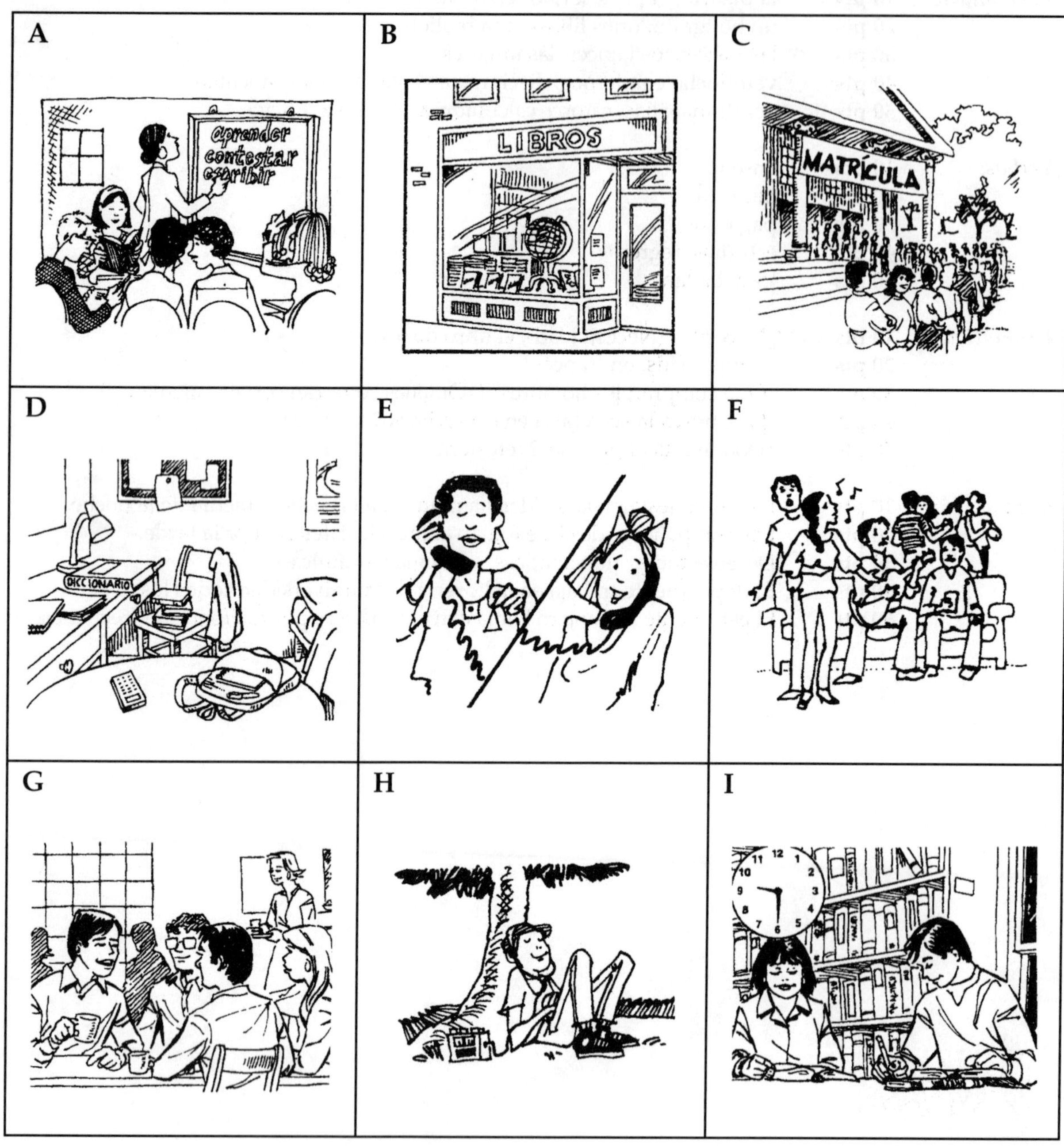

Capítulo 1 *Submarino*

This game is played like "Battleship." Place five submarines on the grid below. (Don't let your partner see where you have drawn your subs!) To win this game you need to sink your partner's submarines by asking questions such as:

TÚ: **¿Trabajan Uds. en una oficina?**
COMPAÑERO/A: **Sí, trabajamos en una oficina.** (*if there is a sub there*)
or **No, no trabajamos en una oficina.** (*if there is no sub there*)

 Uds.				
 el estudiante				
 tú				
 Lupe y Lola				

Student Supplements

- Listening Comprehension Program CD, **Capítulo 2** (**Paso 1: Vocabulario** word lists)
- Workbook/Laboratory Manual, **Capítulo 2**
- Audio Program CD, **Capítulo 2**

Instructor Resources

- Instructor's Manual/IRK: Chapter-by-Chapter Supplementary Materials, **Capítulo 2**
  - **Paso 1: Vocabulario**
  - **Paso 2: Gramática**
    - Grammar Section 4
    - Grammar Section 5
    - **Enfoque cultural**
  - **Paso 3: Gramática**
    - Grammar Section 6
    - Grammar Section 7
    - **En los Estados Unidos y el Canadá**
    - **Un poco de todo**
  - **Paso 4: Un paso más**
    - **Videoteca**
  - Games and Activities
- Instructor's Manual/IRK Video Activities and Related Materials
  - **A primera vista**
  - **A segunda vista**
  - Answers to Video Activities
  - Videoscripts
- Audioscript, **Capítulo 2**
- Transparencies 17–21
- Testing Program, **Capítulo 2**

Multimedia Resources

- Online Learning Center
- Electronic Workbook/Laboratory Manual
- Video, **Capítulo 2** (cue 13:30)
  - **En contexto** (1:14)
  - **Minidramas** (4:00)
  - **Enfoque cultural: México** (1:00)
- Student CD-ROM, **Capítulo 2**
- Electronic Language Tutor, **Capítulo 2** (**Vocabulario, Gramática**)

Paso 1: Vocabulario

LA FAMILIA Y LOS PARIENTES

Notes:

- Point out that **parientes** is a false cognate.
- Explain that **Manolo** is a nickname for **Manuel.**
- Point out the use of the masculine plural form—**el abuelo y la abuela** becomes **los abuelos,** and so on.

Suggestions:

- Have students give feminine equivalents of **el padre, el abuelo,** and so on; then give the masculine equivalents of **la tía, la esposa,** and so on.
- Have students identify relationships. 1. **Es el hijo de mis tíos.** 2. **Es la esposa de mi hermano.** 3. **Es la madre de mi padre.** 4. **Es el hijo de mi madrastra.** 5. **Es la hija de mi hermana.**
- Point out that many terms of endearment (**términos de cariño / afecto**) are used among Hispanic family members. **Los padres a los hijos: mi hijo (mi'jo), mi hija (mi'ja); nene/a; cielo** (lit. *heaven*); **corazón** (lit. *heart*); **mi vida** (lit. *my life*); **mi amor** (lit. *my love*). **Los hijos a los padres: papá, papi, papito, papaíto; mamá, mami, mamita, mamaíta.**
- Point out that diminutives are commonly used as terms of endearment: **abuelo** → **abuelito; hija** → **hijita; Juan** → **Juanito; Elena** → **Elenita.** Use diminutives freely, as appropriate, as you speak Spanish in class.

Preparation: Before class, draw your "own" family tree on the board. Include all family members you want to present and give them all first names.

Suggestion: Present a few family members in a conceptually related group, check comprehension, then present a few more, spiraling in vocabulary from the previous group, check comprehension, and so forth, finishing with a final review.

Sample Passage: (Always point to the person or persons you mention.) **En mi familia hay ______ personas. Es una familia grande/pequeña. Aquí estoy yo** (point). **Esta persona** (point) **es mi padre... mi padre. Esta persona es mi madre... mi madre. Mi padre y mi madre son mis padres** (point to both). **Todas las personas** (indicate entire tree) **son mis parientes, pero estas personas son mis padres. Yo soy la hija de mis padres... la hija. Esta persona es mi hermano...** (and so forth).

Quick Comprehension Check: Sample questions:
(pointing to parents) **¿Son mis padres o mis hermanos?**
(pointing to grandparents) **¿Son mis padres o mis abuelos?**
(pointing to brother) **¿Es mi abuelo o mi hermano?**

Final Review: Review all members, pointing to each one and asking **¿Quién es?** Students respond with the term that describes the relationship that the person indicated has with you. When you have finished this review, students will be ready to start the textbook activities.

ADJETIVOS

Suggestions:

- Present adjectives in pairs or semantic groups (as organized in the box), using magazine images, names of famous people, and people in class.
- Suggestions for negative adjectives: **feo** (Frankenstein, **un gorila**); **gordo** (Pavarotti, Dom DeLouis), **malo** (Dennis the Menace, Darth Vader), **tonto** (Jim Carrey, Steve Martin).
- Do several pairs; then check comprehension, offering students alternatives: **¿Es guapo o feo Ricky Martin?**
- Point out that **bajo/a** refers to height and **corto/a** to length. Also, explain that **joven** is used with people, **nuevo/a** with things, and that **guapo/a** refers to males and females whereas **bonito/a** usually only refers to females and things.
- Have students provide antonyms: **¿Cuál es el antónimo de rico? → pobre; ¿bajo? → alto;** and so on.
- Describe famous people or people in class using adjectives, sometimes incorrectly. Students respond **sí** or **no.**

LOS NÚMEROS 31–100

Suggestions:

- Ask **¿Cómo se dice** *thirty-one? ¿thirty-two?* Students produce numbers 31–39.
- Model 40, 50, . . . 100.
- Have class count in unison (40–49, 50–59). Then have students count in round robin (60–69, 70–79). Finally, have volunteers count (80–100). Count from 1 to 100 by 10s and 5s. Have volunteers count in reverse.
- Set up a bingo (**lotería**) game in which students fill out cards with numbers from 1–100 using digits and without repeating numbers. Call out numbers in Spanish. The winner (across, down, or diagonal) declares **¡Lotería!** and must read back winning numbers in Spanish.
- Remind students that from 30 on, numbers must be written as three words.
- Write on the board: **un coche, cuarenta y un coches; una mesa, sesenta y una mesas.** Point out similarities and emphasize ending of **un** and **una** for plural.
- Remind students that **ciento** is used for numbers greater than 100: **ciento uno, ciento dos,** and so on.
- Dictate cognate nouns and numbers with several students working on board: **100 estéreos, 76 trombones, 65 saxofones, 92 guitarras, 56 pianos,** and so on.
- Write the following series on the board and have volunteers state and complete them aloud: 1. 1, 4, 7, 10. ¿... ? 2. 0, 1, 10, 2, 3, 32, ¿... ? 3. 10, 15, 13, 18, 16, 21, ¿... ? 4. 2, 4, 3, 9, 4, 16, 5, 25, 6, ¿... ?

Paso 2: Gramática

GRAMMAR SECTION 4

Note: Students have already used forms of **estar** in **¿Cómo está(s)?** and for telling location. There is no need to go into more detail about **estar** at this time.

Suggestion: Ask the following questions about the **minidiálogo. ¿Qué es Manolo? ¿Es estudiante o profesor? ¿De dónde es? ¿Quién es Lola? ¿Cómo es Lola? ¿Y Manolo?**

Variation: Have students practice the **minidiálogo** in small groups, using information about themselves (Manolo's introduction) and about an important person in their lives (Lola's introduction).

PRESENT TENSE OF *SER* A

Suggestions:

- Most uses of **ser** in this section are a review of material formally presented or used in **Primeros pasos.** Other uses of **ser** will appear in the later chapters: in **Capítulo 3,** to tell what something is made of; in **Capítulo 5,** in contrast with **estar;** in **Capítulo 8,** to mean *to take place.*
- Telling time is not explicitly listed or reviewed in this section. You may wish to add it to your presentation or discussion.
- Point out that the indefinite article is not used after **ser** before unmodified (undescribed) nouns of profession. **Ella es profesora.**

PRESENT TENSE OF *SER* B

Suggestions:

- Practice possessive phrases to emphasize that there is no *'s* in Spanish: **Es el libro de Anita. Son los lápices de la profesora.**
- Point out the difference between **el** (article) and **él** (subject pronoun). Emphasize that **de** does not contract with **él.**

GRAMMAR SECTION 5

Suggestions:

- Present **mi(s), tu(s), su(s).** Students have seen **mi(s)** since the beginning of the chapter, and they may have been exposed to **tu(s)** and **su(s)** if you have used it in your input.
- Point out the formal vs. informal in **su** and **tu.**
- Have students identify the possessive forms that are the same for two different grammatical persons (**Ud.** and **él/ella**). Point out that the ambiguity of **su(s)** (**su hijo** = *your/his/her/their son*) can be clarified using **el hijo de él / de ella,** and so on.
- Remind students that **nuestro** and **vuestro,** like most **-o** adjectives, have four forms: **nuestro, nuestra, nuestros, nuestras; vuestro, vuestra, vuestros, vuestras.**

POSSESSIVE ADJECTIVES

Suggestion: Emphasize that possessive adjectives must agree with the noun they modify, that the choice between **mi/mis, tu/tus, su/sus,** and so on, depends on the number of the following noun, not on the number of possessors.

CONVERSACIÓN

Follow-up: Ask students what they associate with the following phrases: **su perro/gato, sus padres, la casa del presidente de los Estados Unidos / del primer ministro del Canadá, la casa del profesor / de la profesora.**

ENFOQUE CULTURAL: MÉXICO

A. Para completar Complete las siguientes oraciones con la información en Conozca a...

1. Las obras de muralistas decoran ________________________.
2. Los muralistas usan sus pinturas para enseñar la historia, ________________________.
3. José Clemente Orozco nació (*was born*) en ________________________.
4. Sus pinturas (*paintings*) se pueden ver (*can be seen*) en ________________________.

B. ¿Cierto o falso? (*True or false?*) Indique si las siguientes oraciones son ciertas (C) or falsas (F).

1. C F La UNAM es una de las universidades más grande (*largest*) del mundo.
2. C F La UNAM fue fundada (*was founded*) en 1551.
3. C F México no tiene (*doesn't have*) volcanes activos.
4. C F No hay mexicanos de origen indígena (*native*).

Suggestions:

- Bring or have students bring images of some of the murals by these artists to class. Have students compare the three artists.
- Point out that Rivera and Orozco created murals with social and political commentary. Siqueiros did not. What can they say about Rivera's and Orozco's personal opinions by studying the murals? Have students compare the social commentary of the two artists.
- Bring in images of the work of muralist Susan Cervantes (available on the Internet). Explain that many U.S. muralists have been influenced by their Mexican counterparts. Ask students whether they can see Rivera's influence in Cervantes' work.

Paso 3: Gramática

GRAMMAR SECTION 6

Suggestion: Read both versions of the poem. Point out that there is only one English equivalent given. Have the students note the differences between the two versions and who is described in each.

Follow-up:

- Have the students tell which adjectives could be used to describe themselves.
- Ask questions about the couple in the photo. **¿Quiénes son? ¿Dónde están? ¿De dónde son? ¿Son hermanos (amigos, estudiantes,** and so on)? **¿Qué hacen? ¿Cómo son? ¿Son** ______ (cue students with adjectives)? **¿Les gusta hablar (bailar, estudiar,** and so on**)?**

ADJECTIVES WITH *SER*

Suggestions:

- Alternative explanation: **ser** establishes the norm, what is considered to be basic reality: *snow is cold, water is wet.*
- Bring or have students bring magazine clippings of famous people. Have students identify and describe them.

FORMS OF ADJECTIVES

Note: Gender agreement with adjectives has been used by students since **Primeros pasos.** Handling of this grammar section will depend on how much you have stressed agreement.

Suggestions:

- Emphasize the concept of agreement.
- Point out that adjectives must agree with the gender of the noun they modify grammatically: **Pepe es una persona muy simpática.**
- Point out that adjectives of nationality can also be used as nouns: **el español** = *the Spaniard,* **los ingleses** = *the English,* and so on.

PLACEMENT OF ADJECTIVES

Suggestion: Ask students the following questions:

- **¿Cómo se dice en inglés... una ciudad grande / una gran ciudad; un estado grande / un gran estado?**
- **¿Cómo se dice en español...** *a large university / a great university; a large book / a great book?*

FORMS OF *THIS/THESE*

Note: Forms of **este** are not actively practiced in this section, but are included for recognition only, so that they may be used freely in direction lines and in reading passages. The complete set of demonstratives is introduced in **Capítulo 3.**

GRAMMAR SECTION 7

Suggestion: Read Diego's speech sentence by sentence. Ask students whether each sentence is true or false for them. Students correct each false sentence to make it true for them.

Note: **Gustar** appears in this narration. Students will learn more about the verb **gustar** and other verbs like **gustar** in **Capítulo 7.**

VERBS THAT END IN *-ER* AND *-IR*

Suggestions:

- Introduce **comer** as a model **-er** verb. Talk through the conjugation, using forms in complete sentences and questions, but writing only the verb forms on the board.
- Introduce meaning of **leer** and use forms in questions to students, writing only the verb forms on the board.
- Follow the same procedure with **escribir** and **vivir.**
- You may want to point out the emphatic phrases: *I do eat . . .* → **yo sí como...**

USE AND OMISSION OF SUBJECT PRONOUNS

Note: Emphasize that the omission of the subject pronouns is the norm in Spanish: **Bebemos café por la mañana.**

PRÁCTICA A

Preliminary exercise: **Paso 2.** Have students respond *sí* or *no* to the following sentences.

- **Los estudiantes de esta clase deben... comer durante la clase / asistir a clase todos los días / ir al laboratorio de lenguas con frecuencia / aprender muchas cosas nuevas todos los días.**
- **El profesor (La profesora) de español cree en... hablar español en clase / explicar toda la gramática / dar exámenes con frecuencia / llevar traje de baño para enseñar.**
- **¡Estos estudiantes son fantásticos!** Have students give sentences starting with **Debemos...** to show how good they are.

EN LOS ESTADOS UNIDOS Y EL CANADÁ... LOS SHEEN, FAMILIA DE ACTORES

Suggestions:

- Ask students if they know of the Sheen family and have them name some films and programs in which the actors have starred.
- Have students describe members of the Sheen family in Spanish.
- Ask students why they think Martin Sheen changed his name. Why do they think Emilio took the original family name? Point out that many Hispanic actors, especially those from earlier years, anglicized their names. Have students brainstorm names of other Hispanic actors.

UN POCO DE TODO

Paso 1. The following sentences will form a description of a family in which there is a new grandchild. The name of the person described is given in parentheses after each description when necessary. Form complete sentences based on the words given, in the order given. Conjugate the verbs and add other words if necessary. Be sure to pay close attention to adjective endings.

As you create the sentences, complete the family tree given below with the names of the family members. *Hint:* Hispanic families pass on first and middle names just as families in this country do.

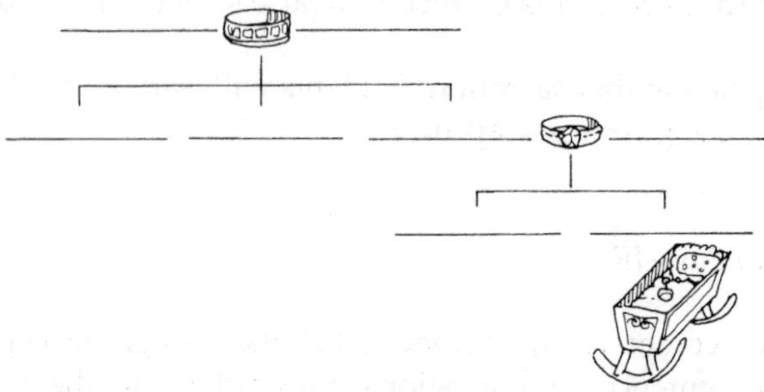

Suggestion: Draw the family tree on the board or overhead. Have students give invented last names to all the members of the family tree to practice last-name assignment in Spanish-speaking countries. Have the whole class make a list of Hispanic last names before starting the activity.

1. yo / ser / abuela / panameño (Anita)
2. nuevo / nieto / ser / de / Estados Unidos (Juan José)
3. Juan José / ser / padre / nieto
4. Juan José / también / ser / hijo / abuelo / panameño
5. uno / de / tías / de / nieto / ser / médico (Pilar)
6. otro / tía / ser / profesor / famoso (Julia)
7. madre / niño / ser / norteamericano (Paula)
8. hermana / niño / se llama / Concepción

Paso 2. Ahora conteste estas preguntas según la descripción de la familia.

1. ¿De dónde son los abuelos y tíos?
2. ¿De dónde es la madre del niño?
3. ¿Cómo se llama el abuelo de la familia?

Paso 4: Un paso más

VIDEOTECA

MINIDRAMAS

The **Minidramas** vignettes are not referenced in the textbook, but are part of the *¿Qué tal?* Video Program. They also appear on the Video on CD packaged free with the textbook. If you show the **Minidramas** in class or have your students view them as homework, you might find the following suggestions helpful. You can also find blackline master activities in Section X of this Manual for **Minidramas.**

Comprensión: **¿Formal o informal?**

1. **«Mucho gusto en conocerla, señora.»**
2. **«¿Qué tal?»**
3. **«Hola.»**
4. **«El gusto es mío, Gustavo.»**

Ask students how they can identify the degree of formality of the statements.

Variation: To stress the appropriate degree of formality according to situations, create situations that require either a formal or an informal introduction. It may be helpful to have students form groups of three to five and assign them roles. Provide each student with a situation card. Examples follow.

SITUACIÓN INFORMAL
Miguel
Introduce your friends Juan(a) and Pepe/a.
Juan(a) is your housemate.
Pepe/a is your classmate

SITUACIÓN FORMAL
Miguel Santana
Introduce your acquaintances (**conocidos**)
Ramón Vázquez and Ana Torres.
Ramón Vázquez works in the president's office (**la oficina de la presidenta**).
Ana Torres is a professor.

Point Out: In Spanish, titles are hardly ever used to introduce oneself or even people with whom one is on equal terms. Therefore, people in a formal situation like the one above may call each other by their first names, while using **usted** to acknowledge the formality of their acquaintance.

SITUACIÓN FORMAL
Miguel Santana
Introduce your mother and your professor.
Your mother is María Gutiérrez de Santana.
Your professor is Jaime Morales.

ACTIVIDAD DE DESENLACE: LA FAMILIA Y LOS PARIENTES

Activity:	Students will role-play the members of a five-member family from a Spanish-speaking country. They will give each member an authentic-sounding first and last name(s). Students will speak about their characters, and include nationality, appearance, personality, family relationship, age, habits, likes and dislikes, and family pets, and conclude by introducing another member of the family.
Purpose:	To create a context in which students can review and practice the grammar from **Capítulo 2** and vocabulary related to the family
Resources:	*¿Qué tal?* textbook, the Internet, and other sources as appropriate
Vocabulary:	Family and relatives, descriptive adjectives, numbers from 31–100, nationality and languages, and expressions of frequency
Grammar:	Principal grammar structures covered in **Capítulo 2** of the textbook, including articles, **-ar** verbs, and the verb **estar**
Recycled Content:	Numbers, time expressions, **me/te/le gusta,** cognates, and interrogatives
Duration:	Out-of-class preparation time will vary. In-class time will be approximately 5 minutes per presentation.
Format:	Groups of 5 students

Games and Activities

Capítulo 2: Partner A *Crucigrama*

You have the answers for half the puzzle, and your partner has those for the other half. Together you must complete the whole puzzle. You have to give clues to your partner so that he/she can guess the missing words. You *may not use the word itself.* Everything has to be done in Spanish.

Use definitions like: **Es lo opuesto de...**
Rosanne es...
Una persona de Portugal es...

Capítulo 2: Partner B *Crucigrama*

You have the answers for half the puzzle, and your partner has those for the other half. Together you must complete the whole puzzle. You have to give clues to your partner so that he/she can guess the missing words. You *may not use the word itself.* Everything has to be done in Spanish.

Use definitions like: **Es lo opuesto de...**
Rosanne es...
Una persona de Portugal es...

■	■	■	■	■	■	■	■	1 A			2 B			■	■	■	■	■	■	■
■	■	■	■	■	■	■	■	L	■	■	A	■	■	■	■	■	■	■	■	3 F
■	■	■	■	4	5 N			E		■	J	■	■	■	■	■	6 M	■	■	E
■	■	■	7 B	■	O	■	■	M	■	8	O				■	9	O			O
■	■	■	U	■	R	■	■	Á	■	■	■	■	■	■	■	■	R	■	■	■
■	■	■	E	■	T	■	10	N									E	■	■	■
11 G			N		E	■	■	■	■	■	■	■	■	■	■	■	N	■	12 B	■
O	■	■	O	■	13 A		14 T		15 P				16 C	■	■	■	O	■	O	■
R	■	■	■	■	M	■	R	■	E	■	■	■	A	■	17 F	■	■	■	N	■
D	■	■	■	■	E	■	A	■	Q	■	■	■	S	■	I	■	■	■	I	■
O	■	18 L	■	■	R	■	B	■	U	■	■	■	A	■	E	■	■	■	T	■
■	■	I	■	■	I	■	A	■	E	■	■	■	19 D		L	20 G			O	■
■	■	S	■	■	C	■	J	■	Ñ	■	■	■	O	■	■	U	■	■	■	■
■	■	T	■	■	A	■	A	■	O	■	■	■	■	■	21	A				■
■	22	O			N	■	D	■	■	■	■	■	■	■	■	P	■	■	■	■
■	■	■	■	■	O	■	O	■	■	■	23		24 R			O			■	■
■	■	■	■	■	■	■	25 R				■	■	U	■	■	■	■	■	■	■
■	■	■	■	■	■	■	■	■	■	■	■	■	B	■	■	■	■	■	■	■
■	■	■	■	■	■	■	■	■	■	■	■	26	I				■	■	■	■
■	■	■	■	■	■	■	■	■	■	■	■	■	O	■	■	■	■	■	■	■
■	■	■	■	■	■	■	■	■	■	■	■	■	■	■	■	■	■	■	■	■

Capítulo 2 *Submarino*

This game is played like "Battleship." Place five submarines on the grid below. (Don't let your partner see where you have drawn your subs!) To win this game you need to sink your partner's submarines by asking questions such as:

TÚ: **¿Son viejos tus abuelos?**
COMPAÑERO/A: **Sí, mis abuelos son viejos.** (*if there is a sub there*)
or **No, mis abuelos no son viejos.** (*if there is no sub there*)

viejo				
grande				
bueno				
español				

Arriésgate

	Vocabulario	Verbos	Gramática	Traducción
10 pts	Mi hermano es el ______ de mis padres.	—Yo ______ de España. ¿De dónde ______ Uds.? —Nosotros _____ de México.	La ciudad de Los Ángeles no es pequeña. Es ______.	Good students always attend Spanish class.
20 pts	Los primos de mis hijos son mis ______.	Mi hermano ______ un médico rico. El ______ una oficina nueva en Beverly Hills.	El actor Danny DeVito no es alto y rubio. Es ______ y ______.	I believe that they sell American, English, and German cars here.
30 pts	El padre de mis nietos es mi ______ y la madre de mis nietos es mi ______.	Si deseas ser una persona delgada, ¿por qué ______ pizza y _____ cerveza todos los días?	Tu perro no es listo, simpático y bonito. ¡Es ________, _______ y _______!	My grandfather reads the newspaper in the morning and watches T.V. in the afternoon.
40 pts	La hermana de mi padre es la madre de mis ______ y la ______ de mi tío.	¡El pájaro de la familia Gómez _____ a hablar! El _____ inglés y español.	Ana Ríos tiene noventa y dos años; su esposo se llama José. La señora Ríos es _____ y _____.	I ought to write a long letter to my French aunt who lives in Paris.
50 pts	Mi madre es la ______ de mi esposo y la ______ de mis hijos.	Muchos niños que ______ en los Estados Unidos _____ regalos de Santa Claus en la Navidad.	Mis mejores amigos son (*faithful*), (*young*), (*hardworking*) e (*intelligent*).	There are 31 lazy cats in Julia's house.

Answer Key for *Arriésgate*

Capítulo 2

Vocabulario:	**10 pts**	hijos
	20 pts	sobrinos
	30 pts	hijo (yerno), nuera (hija)
	40 pts	primos, esposa
	50 pts	suegra, abuela
Verbos:	**10 pts**	soy, son; somos
	20 pts	es, abre
	30 pts	comes, bebes
	40 pts	aprende, comprende
	50 pts	viven, reciben
Gramática:	**10 pts**	grande
	20 pts	bajo, moreno
	30 pts	tonto, antipático, feo
	40 pts	vieja, casada
	50 pts	fieles, jóvenes, trabajadores, inteligentes
Traducción:	**10 pts**	Los buenos estudiantes siempre asisten a la clase de español.
	20 pts	Creo que (ellos) venden coches norteamericanos, ingleses y alemanes aquí.
	30 pts	Mi abuelo lee el periódico por la mañana y mira la televisión por la tarde.
	40 pts	Debo escribir una carta larga a mi tía francesa que vive en Paris.
	50 pts	Hay treinta y un gatos perezosos en la casa de Julia.

Student Supplements

- Listening Comprehension Program CD, **Capítulo 3** (**Paso 1: Vocabulario** word lists)
- Workbook/Laboratory Manual, **Capítulo 3**
- Audio Program CD, **Capítulo 3**

Instructor Resources

- Instructor's Manual/IRK: Chapter-by-Chapter Supplementary Materials, **Capítulo 3**
  - **Paso 1: Vocabulario**
  - **Paso 2: Gramática**
    - Grammar Section 8
    - Grammar Section 9
    - **Enfoque cultural**
  - **Paso 3: Gramática**
    - Grammar Section 10
    - **En los Estados Unidos y el Canadá**
    - **Un poco de todo**
  - **Paso 4: Un paso más**
    - **Videoteca**
    - **A leer**
    - **A escribir**
    - Games and Activities
- Instructor's Manual/IRK: Video Activities and Related Materials
  - **A primera vista**
  - **A segunda vista**
  - Answers to Video Activities
  - Videoscripts
- Audioscript, **Capítulo 3**
- Transparencies 22–27
- Testing Program, **Capítulo 3**

Multimedia Resources

- Online Learning Center
- Electronic Workbook/Laboratory Manual
- Video, **Capítulo 3** (cue 19:20)
  - **En contexto** (1:41)
  - **Minidramas** (3:01)
  - **Enfoque cultural: Nicaragua** (1:00)
- Student CD-ROM, **Capítulo 3**
- Electronic Language Tutor, **Capítulo 3** (**Vocabulario, Gramática**)

Paso 1: Vocabulario

DE COMPRAS: LA ROPA

Note: In many Hispanic countries, store hours in the morning are similar to those in the United States and Canada; however, some shops close in the early afternoon until 4 P.M. and reopen until 9 or 10 P.M. All stores are generally closed on Sundays and holidays.

Suggestions:

- Model the pronunciation of clothing, pointing out items in the classroom or in photos. Stop after every three or four items to go back and review, indicating the item and asking students: **¿Es una blusa o una camisa? ¿Es una camisa o un suéter?** and so on.
- Offer additional vocabulary: **la gorra, los pantalones cortos, el anillo, los pendientes / los aretes, el collar, de cuero, a la medida.**
- Make statements about what students are wearing and have them respond **sí** or **no: Roberto lleva un abrigo.** → **No, Roberto lleva una chaqueta.** To follow-up, have students invent similar sentences about classmates.
- Discuss the concept of **mercado** vs. **tienda.** Point out the existence of large department stores and malls as well as small shops and open-air markets.
- To avoid stereotypes about bargaining (**regatear**) in Hispanic countries; point out situations in which one bargains in the U.S. and Canada: car sales, flea markets, and so on.
- Have students give words that they associate with **comprar, el almacén, el precio, la librería, pagar, el centro comercial, las rebajas.**
- Have students research clothing associated with different areas of the Hispanic world (for example, **sarapes** in Mexico, bowler and other kinds of hats in Bolivia). Remind them to note the materials used and suggest reasons for using these particular ones (for example, wool in the Andes for warmth and because it is an available resource).

Preliminary Exercises

- Have students give the words defined: 1. **el antónimo de** ***vender*** 2. **una tienda grande** 3. **la cantidad de dinero que es necesario pagar** 4. **un sinónimo de** ***llevar*** 5. **la parte céntrica de una ciudad** 6. **el antónimo de** ***tienda pequeña*** 7. **el antónimo de** ***vender muy poco*** 8. **el antónimo de** ***pagar el precio indicado*** 9. **el antónimo de** ***caro*** 10. **el antónimo de** ***estilos de los años setenta.***
- Point out a new use of **ser: ser + de** (*to be made of*). Write the following phrases on the board: **de metal, de papel, de plástico, de madera.** Point to objects and have students tell what they are made of. **¿De qué es esto** (point to a chair or another wooden object)**?** → **De madera.** 1. **el dinero** 2. **el lápiz** 3. **el libro** 4. **el cuaderno** 5. **el bolígrafo** 6. **la mesa** 7. **la foto**

Heritage Speakers: Pídales a sus estudiantes hispanohablantes que describan la ropa que llevan hoy mismo.

Preparation: Have students skim the vocabulary list quickly, then close books and listen to you, watching carefully. Each time you introduce a new word from the list, write it on the board. Use gestures and point when possible to items you are speaking of.

Sample Passage: **Hoy vamos a hablar de la ropa. Esto es la ropa** (indicate your own clothing). **Hay ropa para hombres y hay ropa para mujeres. También hay ropa «unisexo», para los dos sexos.**

¿Dónde compra Ud. la ropa? Hay dos lugares típicas para comprar ropa: el almacén y la tienda. Los almacenes son grandes (gesture) **y las tiendas son pequeñas. Penney's es un almacen y es grande, pero** (name of a local shop) **es una tienda y es pequeña. Los almacenes venden de todo... ropa, aparatos electrónicos y muchas otras cosas. Ud. compra muchas cosas en un almacén. Los almacenes venden cosas y Ud. compra cosas.** ***Vender*** **es el opuesto de** ***comprar...*** (and so forth, explaining terms through simple contexts).

Suggestion: To illustrate **regatear**, create and act out a brief dialogue, taking on both parts yourself. Sketch the faces of buyer and seller on the board, and point to the appropriate face as you say each one. Then summarize the transaction for further input.

Quick Comprehension Check: Sample questions.
¿Es cierto o falso?

1. **Los almacenes son grandes y las tiendas son pequeñas.**
2. **Sears sólo vende ropa de hombres.**
3. **Las tiendas venden de todo.**
4. **El opuesto de** ***comprar*** **es** ***vender.***

¿DE QUÉ COLOR ES?

Preparation: Wear items that represent some of the colors to be presented. Also bring magazine photos of familiar articles of clothing in all the colors, as well as in plaid, stripes, and polka-dots.

Presentation: Follow the model of the sample passage for **Capítulo 2.** Point to an article and discuss it, repeating its name and color at least twice, then go on to another item. After three or four items, go back and review. Check comprehension by pointing and asking either/or questions, such as **¿Es verde o es azul?**

Suggestions:

- Model words and phrases using clothing students are wearing. Verify student comprehension periodically with **¿sí o no?** questions.
- Emphasize gender and number agreement for colors. Remind students that gender is invariable for **azul, verde,** and **gris.**
- Offer these optional colors: **café** (or **de color café**) is a type of brown; **beige** (pronounced with English sound **j** at the end); **purpúreo** or **púrpura** = **morado.**
- Use nominalized forms as you review colors, for example, **La camisa de Janet es roja. ¿Y la de Susie?**
- Have students tell what colors they associate with the following: **¿Qué color asocia con... ? el mar Caribe, una cebra, un limón, el dinero, el café, una rosa, un gato, esta universidad, los Estados Unidos / el Canadá, una jirafa, un pingüino, un elefante, un teléfono.**
- Have students search for more information and images about Endara Crow on the Internet. Ask them to write sentences about the colors and designs in his works.

Final Review: Ask about items of clothing that students are wearing. **¿De qué color es la camiseta de Jorge? ¿Quién lleva una camisa de cuadros hoy?**, and so forth. When you have finished this review, students will be ready to start the textbook activities.

MÁS ALLÁ DEL NÚMERO 100

Suggestions:

- Model pronunciation of hundreds forms. Give addition and subtraction problems using hundreds (some incorrect) and have students respond **sí** or **no.** When a problem is incorrect, have them give the correct answer.
- Point out the following number facts: 1. 500, 700, 900 have irregular forms. 2. **un** is not used with **mil** (1000). 3. The hundreds must agree in gender; use **-cientas** before feminine nouns. 4. There is no **y** in **ciento uno,** and so on. 5. A period marks the thousands in Spanish, instead of a comma as in English.
- Write complex numbers on the board for students to read aloud, for example, 154, 672.
- Have students count by thousands (**mil, dos mil,...**) and then by millions (**un millón, dos millones,...**) to emphasize the singular **mil** and plural **millones.**
- Have students say the following in Spanish: 1. 500 men, 500 women, 700 male professors 2. 1,000 books, 2,000 friends, 3,000 universities 3. a million dollars; 3 million Americans; 7 million pesetas
- Students will get further practice in saying the years in **Capítulo 5.** Introduce this skill here by saying the current year in Spanish, and writing it on the board as you speak. Say a few more years, writing at the same time. Then begin to make mistakes as you write, asking students to verify the numbers as you write.

CONVERSACIÓN A

Heritage Speakers: Invite a sus estudiantes hispanohablantes a que lean en voz alta los nombres de los animales del anuncio y que la clase los repita.

Optional: **Compras personales**

Paso 1. With a classmate, determine how much the following items probably cost, using **¿Cuánto es... ?** or **¿Cuánto cuesta(n)... ?** Keep track of the prices that you decide on.

1. una calculadora pequeña
2. un coche nuevo/usado
3. una computadora Mac o IBM
4. un reloj Timex / de oro (*gold*)
5. unos zapatos de tenis
6. una casa en esta ciudad

Paso 2. Now compare the prices you selected with those of others in the class. What is the most expensive thing on the list? (**¿Cuál es la cosa más cara?**) What is the least expensive? (**¿Cuál es la cosa más barata?**)

Paso 2: Gramática

GRAMMAR SECTION 8

Suggestion: Have students act out the **minidiálogo** and try to define the italicized words before checking the translation below.

Follow-up: Give students the following information: **En los países hispánicos no es extraño ver vendedores en la calle. Algunos vendedores están siempre en el mismo lugar. Otros son ambulantes. ¿Es esto normal en su país? ¿En qué contextos?** (large cities, university centers, Girl Scouts, and so on)

Note: Although bartering is normally limited to flea markets (**rastros** or **pulguerías**) in this country, it is not uncommon to hear people bartering in most open-air markets of Latin America. Prices in Latin American malls or other commercial shopping centers, however, are not usually negotiable.

DEMONSTRATIVE ADJECTIVES

Suggestions:

- Hold up a book and say **este libro.** Place the book near a student and say **ese libro.** Place the book far from both yourself and the student and say **aquel libro.**
- Emphasize that the masculine singular forms do not end in **-o.**
- Point out that distance may be physical (**aquella casa que está lejos**) or temporal (**en aquella época**).
- In order to practice demonstrative adjectives, use real objects in the classroom: **este pupitre, esa pizarra, estos cuadernos.** You may also bring or have students bring in photographs or magazine clippings of buildings, houses, or city scenes to use in small group activities or to display in the classroom. Students can then describe the scenes: **Esta casa es bonita; Esta ciudad es moderna; Estos edificios son enormes.**

GRAMMAR SECTION 9

Follow-up: Ask for quick answers to the following questions. Have students start their responses with **prefiero: Para la ropa, ¿prefiere el azul o el negro? ¿el verde o el amarillo? ¿el anaranjado o el morado? ¿el rosado o el rojo? Para un coche, ¿prefiere colores oscuros** (write on board) **o claros?**

Suggestions:

- Model infinitives and talk through conjugations, using the forms in complete sentences and questions.
- Point out the similarities and differences among stem-changing verbs: some **yo** forms have a **-g-,** the **nosotros** and **vosotros** forms have the same stem as the infinitive; the stem becomes a diphthong (**e** → **ie** and **o** → **ue**) when stressed (with the exception of **tengo** and **vengo**).

SOME IDIOMS WITH *TENER*

Suggestions:

- Point out that there is generally no word-to-word correspondence of idioms between the two languages.
- Tell students some complete sentences about yourself that model the idioms.
- Give students these optional phrases: **mucha prisa, mucho miedo.**

Heritage Speakers: Pregúnteles a sus estudiantes hispanohablantes si se les ocurren otras expresiones con **tener.**

Note: Students will learn **tener calor / frío** in **Capítulo 5** with weather and **tener hambre / sed** in **Capítulo 6** with foods.

NOTA COMUNICATIVA

Optional: **Entrevista: Preferencias.** Try to predict the choices your instructor will make in each of the following cases. Then, using tag questions, find out if you are correct.

MODELO: El profesor / La profesora tiene...
(muchos libros) / pocos libros →
Ud. tiene muchos libros, ¿verdad?

1. El profesor / La profesora tiene...
   mucha ropa / poca ropa
   sólo un coche / varios coches
2. Prefiere...
   los gatos / los perros
   la ropa elegante / la ropa informal
3. Quiere comprar...
   un coche deportivo (*sports car*), por ejemplo, un Porsche / una camioneta (*station wagon*)
   un abrigo / un impermeable
4. Viene a la universidad...
   todos los días / sólo tres veces a la semana
   en coche / en autobús / en bicicleta / a pie (*on foot*)
5. Esta noche tiene muchas ganas de...
   mirar la televisión / leer
   comer en un restaurant / comer en casa
6. Su color favorito es...
   verde / rojo / amarillo
7. Prefiere usar...
   botas / zapatos / sandalias

Suggestions:

- Have students work in groups to compare notes. Then assign different areas of the board so that all groups make a short list of their conclusions. Compare all of the lists. Emphasize note taking.
- After students have used items to ask you questions, reverse the situation, using the same items or different ones.

ENFOQUE CULTURAL: NICARAGUA

Para completar. Use la información en Nota histórica y ¡Fíjese! para completar las siguientes oraciones.

1. En ____________________, Cristóbal Colón ____________________ las costas de Nicaragua.
2. Los Estados Unidos ha intervenida (*has intervened*) en la ____________________ del país.
3. William Walker fue ____________________ de Nicaragua.
4. El ____________________, con más de 300 ____________________, es el lago más ____________________ de ____________________.
5. La primera mujer presidenta de Centroamérica fue ____________________.

Suggestion: Have students look up additional information about Nicaragua's history, government, people, culture, geography, tourism, and media on the Internet. Encourage them to look for official government or tourism websites online for Nicaragua. You might assign specific topics and have students give brief oral reports about Nicaragua.

Point Out: Nicaragua declared its independence from Spain in 1821.

Paso 3: Gramática

GRAMMAR SECTION 10

Notes:

- **Ir** and **venir** are used somewhat differently than are their English equivalents. **Venir** means *to come to where* (*the speaker is*). **Ir** refers to some place other than where the speaker is. The speaker of **¿Vienes a mi casa?** is at his/her house when asking the question. Otherwise, he/she would ask **¿Vas a mi casa?**
- **¡Ya voy!** means *I'm coming,* not *I'm going.*

Follow-up: Ask students: **¿Qué voy a hacer yo mañana / esta tarde / noche?** Then give them sentences about things you may or may not do: **Voy a bailar en una fiesta esta noche.** Students guess if your sentences are true (**Es verdad**) or false (**No es cierto**).

Heritage Speakers: Los hispanohablantes tienden a usar la expresión **ir a** + infinitivo en vez del futuro. Por ejemplo, es más común oír **va a llamar** en vez de **llamará.** Pregúnteles a los hispanohablantes de la clase en qué situaciones usan el futuro en vez de **ir a** + infinitivo.

EN LOS ESTADOS UNIDOS Y EL CANADÁ... LOS HISPANOS EN EL MUNDO DE LA MODA

Suggestions:

- Bring a magazine clipping of Christy Turlington and have students describe her in Spanish. You might use a clipping of another model to compare and contrast the two.
- If possible, bring several clippings of Turlington wearing different kinds of clothing. Use the images for different activities: describe the clothing and have students identify which clipping you are describing; ask true/false or information questions about what she is wearing; have students describe what she is wearing.

Point Out: Remind students that some of the biggest names in fashion designers are Hispanic: Venezuelan Carolina Herrera, Dominican Óscar de la Renta, and Cuban-American Narciso Rodríguez, just to name a few.

UN POCO DE TODO

Optional: **A. ¿Qué prefieren?** Forme oraciones completas usando una palabra o frase de cada (*each*) columna. Si quiere, las oraciones pueden ser negativas también.

1. yo	(no) poder	estudiar en la biblioteca
2. mi mejor (*best*) amigo/a	tener que	visitar mi universidad
3. mis padres / hijos	tener ganas de	ir de compras en el centro
4. nuestro profesor / nuestra profesora	querer	comprar cuando hay rebajas
5. mi familia	preferir	escribir un informe (*report*) para la clase de ¿ ?
6. tú y yo	ir (a)	ir al cine (*movies*)
		llevar ropa informal
		leer novelas de ciencia ficción / terror / ¿ ?

Suggestion: Have each student make two or three statements about himself (herself), using verbs from the second column.

B. ¿Somos tan diferentes?

Paso 1. Answer the following questions. Then ask the same questions of other students in the class to try to find at least one person who answered a given question the way you did.

1. De la siguiente lista, ¿qué cosa tienes ganas de tener? ¿Por qué? (**¡OJO!** También es posible contestar: **No quiero tener ninguna.**)
   _____ un abrigo de pieles (*fur*)
   _____ unas botas de cuero (*leather*)
   _____ unos aretes de oro (*gold*)
   _____ un reloj de diamantes
2. ¿Cuál de las siguientes cosas que dicta la moda es la más tonta, en tu opinión?
   _____ llevar aretes en la nariz (*nose*)
   _____ llevar las gorras (*caps*) de atrás para delante (*backward*)
   _____ los *jeans* de los grandes diseñadores como Calvin Klein y Guess
   _____ la ropa de estilo rap
3. ¿Cierto o falso?
   _____ Las personas mayores (*older*) deben llevar siempre ropa de colores oscuros, como negro, gris, etcétera.
   _____ Una mujer que tiene más de 30 años nunca debe llevar minifalda.
   _____ Sólo las mujeres deben usar arete(s).
   _____ Cuando la moda cambia (*changes*), es necesario comprar mucha ropa nueva.

Suggestions:

- Most of the items in this activity lend themselves to follow-up discussion. Have students volunteer their answers. Try to get a sense for how the class as a whole answered, then ask students to explain their reasons.
- Have students work in pairs to create their own options for item 1. Encourage them to be creative and funny! As a follow-up, have students share some of their options and answers: **¿Qué prefieres (tener)? Prefiero (tener) _____ a _____. No quiero tener ninguno/a.** Students then elaborate on their answers.

Paso 2. Now ask a classmate his or her opinion about the following items. You can start your questions with the phrases **¿Qué opinas de... ?** or **¿Qué piensas de... ?** Your partner can begin his or her questions with **Creo que...** or **Pienso que...**

1. las personas que sólo llevan ropa oscura
2. las personas que llevan los *jeans* rotos en las rodillas (*torn at the knees*)
3. la ropa de los diseñadores famosos que vemos (*we see*) en las revistas como *Elle, Vogue,* etcétera
4. las personas que siempre visten formalmente
5. la ropa que llevan los artistas que van a la ceremonia del Óscar
6. los padres que escogen la ropa de sus hijos

Paso 4: Un paso más

VIDEOTECA

The **Minidramas** vignettes are not referenced in the textbook, but are part of the *¿Qué tal?* Video Program. They also appear on the Video on CD packaged free with the textbook. If you show the **Minidramas** in class or have your students view them as homework, you might find the following suggestions helpful. You can also find blackline master activities in Section X of this Manual for **Minidramas.**

Comprensión: **¿Cierto o falso? Corrija las respuestas falsas con la información correcta.**

1. **José Miguel está interesado en las chaquetas y los zapatos.**
2. **La dependienta saca** (*takes out*) **camisas de seda y de nilón.**
3. **Las camisas de algodón cuestan 60.500 sucres.**
4. **José Miguel desea comprar unos pantalones también.**

Variation: Have students complete the following matching activity. If this is done or corrected on the board, cues can be left there in case some students perform the dialogue in front of the class.

Paso 1. ¿Dependiente o cliente? Match the following parts of a dialogue with the appropriate speaker.

—Buenas. ¿Qué desea?
—¿Prefiere algún color o estilo en particular?
—Creo que sí. ¿Me lo/la puedo probar?
—Mire, este/a ____ es muy elegante, ¿no? ¿Le gusta?
—Busco un(a) ____ elegante: es para una ocasión especial.
—Sí. Quiero un(a) ____ de (*fabric*) **_____, de color ____.**
—¿Cuánto cuesta?
— ____ dólares.

Paso 2. Now put the sentences in order to form a logical dialogue.

A LEER

Suggestions: **Estrategia.** Do as an in-class activity the day before you intend to cover the reading. Bring in other magazine articles that have illustrations. Ask students to make predictions about their content based on the illustrations. Underscore the usefulness of approaching the reading task with some background knowledge about content, and note how illustrations and other visual clues can provide such knowledge.

A ESCRIBIR

Optional Follow-up: Working in pairs, students read paragraphs to each other. While one person reads the description of his/her favorite shoes, the other person draws them. (Note that this also functions as a listening comprehension activity.)

ACTIVIDAD DE DESENLACE: DE COMPRAS EN UN PAÍS HISPANOHABLANTE

Activity: Students will role-play a situation in a Hispanic shopping mall, between two clients and a clerk. They will prepare and present appropriate store objects, such as a poster board with the store's name and the discounted or sale items. They may also wish to bring in currency from the country.

Purpose: To create a context in which students can review and practice the grammar from **Capítulo 3** and vocabulary related to stores and shopping

Rsources: *¿Qué tal?* textbook, the Internet, and other sources as appropriate

Vocabulary: Clothing and accessories, and their cost; colors; numbers above 100

Grammar:	Principal grammar structures covered in **Capítulo 3** of the textbook, including demonstrative adjectives, the verb **ir** and **ir** + infinitive, the contraction **al**
Recycled Content:	Adjectives, gender and number, interrogatives, **me/te/le gusta(n), estar, ser,** and other verbs from previous chapters
Duration:	Out-of-class preparation time will vary. In-class time will be approximately 5 minutes per presentation.
Format:	Groups of 3–4 students
Comments:	You may wish to comment on difference/similarity of dress codes in the Spanish-speaking world and bring in examples of Latin American and Spanish currency.

Games and Activities

Capítulo 3 *La fotonovela*

Using six of the following pictures, write a short story about how these people spend their weekends (**los fines de semana**). Include the words **con frecuencia, a veces, casi nunca, nunca,** and **siempre.**

La encuesta dice...

Actividades que los estudiantes no hacen con mucha frecuencia.

Los estudiantes casi nunca:

1. **escriben cartas**
2. **leen novelas**
3. **estudian los viernes por la noche**
4. **llevan traje y corbata**
5. **descansan los fines de semana**

La encuesta dice...

Para asistir a la universidad los estudiantes prefieren llevar:

1. ***jeans***
2. **camiseta**
3. **zapatos deportivos (de tenis)**
4. **calcetines**
5. **chaqueta**

La encuesta dice...

Con frecuencia durante los fines de semana los estudiantes van:

1. **a las fiestas**
2. **al cine**
3. **a la casa de los amigos / al centro comercial**
4. **al trabajo**
5. **a la biblioteca**

¡A pescar!

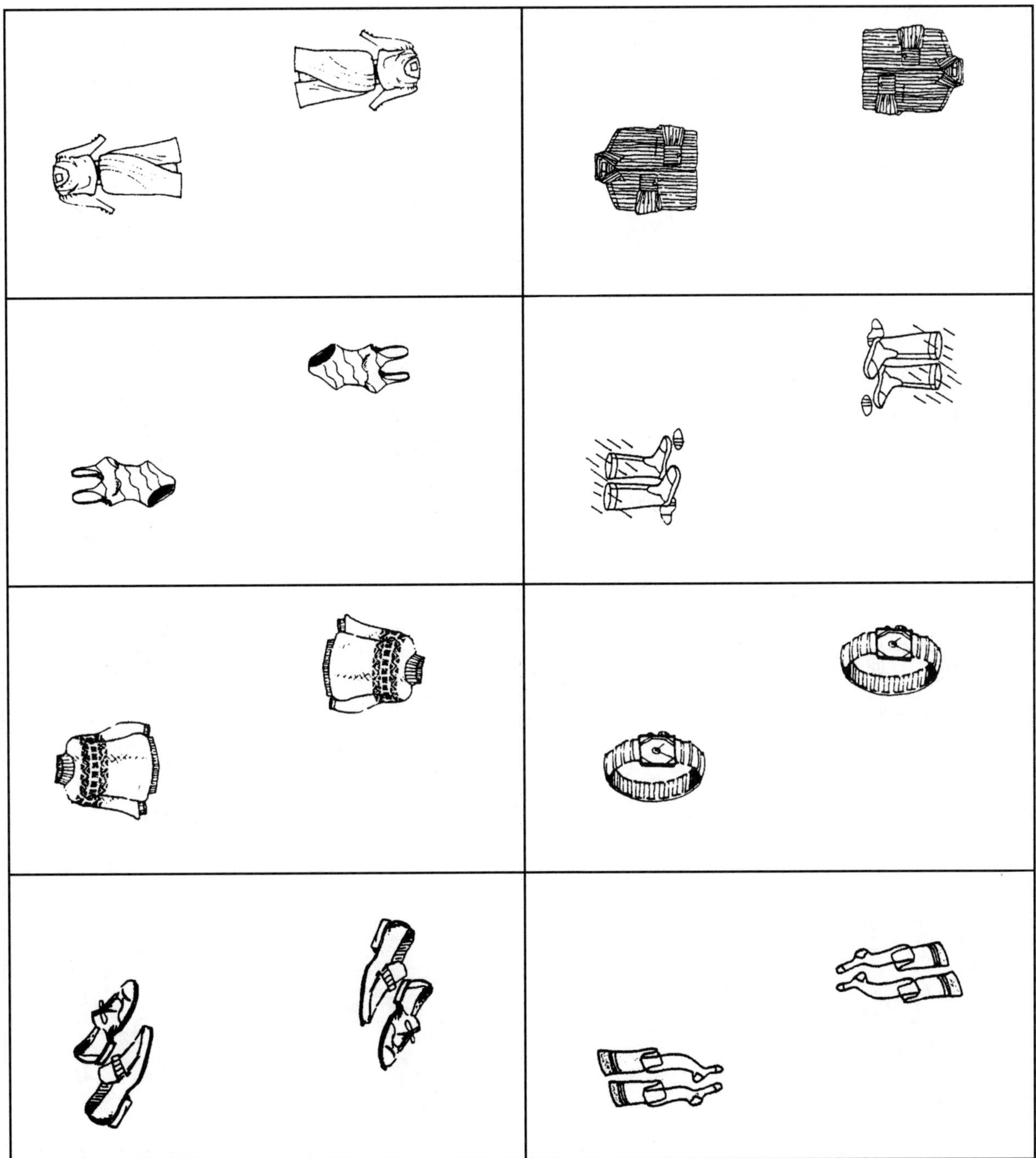

¡A pescar!

Arriésgate

	Vocabulario	Verbos	Gramática	Traducción
10 pts	**Voy a comprar...**	¿______ Ud. los exámenes largos o cortos?	Alicia y su esposo quieren comprar ropa interior nueva para (*their*) ______ hijo.	How much does the German watch cost? $2,400.00 dollars!
20 pts	**Ramón lleva...** 	¡Uds. no ______ regatear en un almacén porque hay precios fijos!	Alberto es chileno. Todos (*his*) ______ parientes viven en Sudamérica.	Where are you going, to the marketplace or to the shopping mall?
30 pts	**Prefiero...** 	Mis compañeros de clase ______ a mi residencia esta tarde para escuchar una cinta nueva.	¿Uds. compran (*your*) ______ libros en la librería de (*your*) ______ universidad?	There are many sales here! This ugly jacket is a bargain!
40 pts	**En esta tienda hay 534**  **y 869**	Tú no ______ razón. Yo no ______ miedo de los gatos negros.	(*Our*) ______ casa es blanca, pero (*our*) ______ coche es pardo.	I feel like resting, but I have to write many exercises for Spanish class.
50 pts	**El dependiente quiere vender 782** 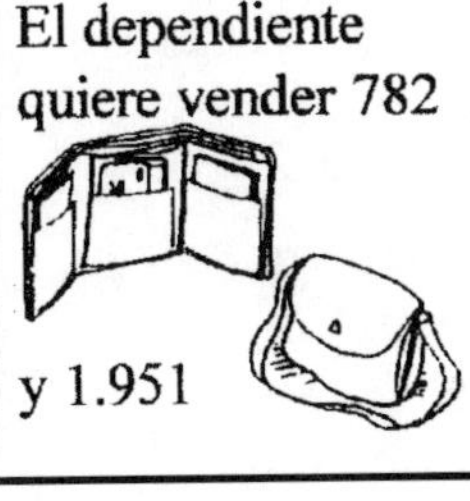 **y 1.951**	Eva y yo ______ de compras mañana. Yo ______ a comprar bluejeans.	(*My*) ______ gatos son blancos ¿De qué color es (*your*) ______ perro, amigo?	My daughter wants to wear clothing of the latest style, but it is very expensive!

Answer Key for *Arriésgate*

Capítulo 3

Vocabulario:	**10 pts**	Voy a comprar un sombrero verde, un traje de baño azul y un par de botas rojas.
	20 pts	Ramón lleva (a) una corbata, (b) un traje, (c) un abrigo y (d) un par de zapatos.
	30 pts	Prefiero los suéteres de lana, los vestidos de seda y los calcetines de algodón.
	40 pts	En esta tienda hay quinientos treinta y cuatro pantalones de cuadros y ochocientas sesenta y nueve camisas de rayas.
	50 pts	El dependiente quiere vender setecientas ochenta y dos carteras anaranjadas y mil novecientas cincuenta y una bolsas amarillas.
Verbos:	**10 pts**	Prefiere
	20 pts	pueden
	30 pts	vienen
	40 pts	tienes; tengo
	50 pts	vamos; voy
Gramática:	**10 pts**	su
	20 pts	sus
	30 pts	sus; su
	40 pts	Nuestra; nuestro
	50 pts	Mis; tu
Traducción:	**10 pts**	¿Cuánto cuesta el reloj alemán? ¡Dos mil cuatrocientos dólares!
	20 pts	¿Adónde vas, al mercado o al centro comercial?
	30 pts	¡Hay muchas rebajas aquí! ¡Esta chaqueta fea es una ganga!
	40 pts	Tengo ganas de descansar, pero tengo que escribir muchos ejercicios para la clase de español.
	50 pts	Mi hija quiere llevar (usar) ropa de última moda, pero ¡es muy cara!

ACCIONES

1. **comprar** to buy
2. **recibir** to receive
3. **escuchar** to listen (to)
4. **cantar** to sing
5. **abrir** to open
6. **tocar** to play (*a musical instrument*)
7. **leer** to read
8. **regresar** to return (*to a place*)
9. **aprender** to learn
10. **mirar** to look at, watch

***Dígalo como pueda,* Capítulos 1–3**

ACCIONES

1. **enseñar** to teach
2. **comprender** to understand
3. **trabajar** to work
4. **bailar** to dance
5. **vender** to sell
6. **tomar** to take; to drink
7. **ir** to go
8. **practicar** to practice
9. **escribir** to write
10. **buscar** to look for

***Dígalo como pueda,* Capítulos 1–3**

ADJETIVOS

1. **bajo/a** short (*in height*)
2. **joven** young
3. **pobre** poor
4. **amarillo/a** yellow
5. **amable** kind; nice
6. **guapo/a** handsome; good-looking
7. **pequeño/a** small
8. **azul** blue
9. **moreno/a** brunet(te)
10. **fiel** faithful

***Dígalo como pueda,* Capítulos 1–3**

ADJETIVOS

1. **corto/a** short (*in length*)
2. **perezoso/a** lazy
3. **malo/a** bad
4. **rosado/a** pink
5. **soltero/a** single (*not married*)
6. **inteligente** intelligent
7. **delgado/a** thin; slender
8. **verde** green
9. **rubio/a** blond(e)
10. **barato/a** inexpensive

***Dígalo como pueda,* Capítulos 1–3**

COSAS	*COSAS*
1. **la calculadora** calculator	1. **el diccionario** dictionary
2. **el dinero** money	2. **la mochila** backpack
3. **el reloj** clock; watch	3. **el cinturón** belt
4. **la puerta** door	4. **la silla** chair
5. **el bolígrafo** pen	5. **la pizarra** chalkboard
6. **los calcetines** socks	6. **la lana** wool
7. **la seda** silk	7. **la cartera** wallet
8. **le regalo** gift; present	8. **la chaqueta** jacket
9. **le coche** car	9. **el gato** cat
10. **la blusa** blouse	10. **la revista** magazine
***Dígalo como pueda,* Capítulos 1–3**	***Dígalo como pueda,* Capítulos 1–3**

COSAS	*COSAS*
1. **el cuaderno** notebook	1. **el libro de texto** textbook
2. **el escritorio** desk	2. **la mesa** table
3. **la camiseta** T-shirt	3. **el perro** dog
4. **el lápiz** pencil	4. **la carta** letter
5. **la ventana** window	5. **la ganga** bargain
6. **las medias** stockings	6. **el precio** price
7. **el pájaro** bird	7. **el algodón** cotton
8. **el vestido** dress	8. **el papel** paper
9. **los aretes** earrings	9. **las botas** boots
10. **el periódico** newspaper	10. **la corbata** tie
***Dígalo como pueda,* Capítulos 1–3**	***Dígalo como pueda,* Capítulos 1–3**

LUGARES	*LUGARES*
1. **la casa** house	1. **la ciudad** city
2. **el almacén** department store	2. **el mercado** market(place)
3. **la biblioteca** library	3. **la librería** bookstore
4. **la fiesta** party	4. **el edificio** building
5. **el país** country (*nation*)	5. **el apartamento** apartment
6. **la oficina** office	6. **el cuarto** room
7. **el centro** downtown	7. **los Estados Unidos** United States
8. **la tienda** shop, store	8. **la cafetería** cafeteria
9. **la clase** class	9. **la residencia** dormitory
10. **la universidad** university	10. **el centro comercial** shopping mall
Dígalo como pueda, **Capítulos 1–3**	*Dígalo como pueda,* **Capítulos 1–3**

PERSONAS	*PERSONAS*
1. **el/la secretario/a** secretary	1. **el/la extranjero/a** foreigner
2. **el/la dependiente/a** clerk	2. **el/la cliente** client, customer
3. **el/la compañero/a de clase** classmate	3. **el/la consejero/a** advisor
4. **el/la abuelo/a** grandfather/grandmother	4. **el/la primo/a** cousin
5. **el hombre** man	5. **la mujer** woman
6. **el/la tío/a** uncle/aunt	6. **el/la amigo/a** friend
7. **el/la bibliotecario/a** librarian	7. **el/la nieto/a** grandson/granddaughter
8. **el/la esposo/a** husband/wife	8. **el/la profesor(a)** professor
9. **el/la hijo/a** son/daughter	9. **el/la compañero/a de cuarto** roommate
10. **el/la estudiante** student	10. **el/la hermano/a** brother/sister
Dígalo como pueda, **Capítulos 1–3**	*Dígalo como pueda,* **Capítulos 1–3**

Student Supplements

- Listening Comprehension Program CD, **Capítulo 4** (**Paso 1: Vocabulario** word lists)
- Workbook/Laboratory Manual, **Capítulo 4**
- Audio Program CD, **Capítulo 4**

Instructor Resources

- Instructor's Manual/IRK: Chapter-by-Chapter Supplementary Materials, **Capítulo 4**
  - **Paso 1: Vocabulario**
  - **Paso 2: Gramática**
    - Grammar Section 11
    - Grammar Section 12
    - **Enfoque cultural**
  - **Paso 3: Gramática**
    - Grammar Section 13
    - **En los Estados Unidos y el Canadá**
  - **Paso 4: Un paso más**
    - **Videoteca**
  - Games and Activities
- Instructor's Manual/IRK: Video Activities and Related Materials
  - **A primera vista**
  - **A segunda vista**
  - Answers to Video Activities
  - Videoscripts
- Audioscript, **Capítulo 4**
- Transparencies 28–32
- Testing Program, **Capítulo 4**

Multimedia Resources

- Online Learning Center
- Electronic Workbook/Laboratory Manual
- Video, **Capítulo 4** (cue 23:44)
  - **En contexto** (1:34)
  - **Minidramas** (4:55)
  - **Enfoque cultural: Costa Rica** (1:00)
- Student CD-ROM, **Capítulo 4**
- Electronic Language Tutor, **Capítulo 4** (**Vocabulario, Gramática**)

Paso 1: Vocabulario

¿QUÉ DÍA ES HOY?

Preparation: It is optional for students to scan the vocabulary before you begin but recommended that they do not. Bring a large calendar to class, or draw one on the board. As you use new vocabulary from the list, write the word on the board or overhead.

Sample Passage: **¿Cuántos de Uds. tienen un calendario en la mochila? Levanta la mano si tienes un calendario en la mochila. Bueno. Para muchos estudiantes es importante tener un calendario. ¿Qué cosas indicamos en un calendario? Bueno, indicamos qué día son las fiestas, los partidos de fútbol y, por supuesto, las clases también. Hoy vamos a hablar sobre el calendario y los días de la semana. Uds. saben que una semana consiste en siete días. Sí, hay siete días en una semana. Hay cinco días de trabajo. Esto es la semana laboral. La semana laboral tiene cinco días: lunes, martes...** (and so forth). **También hay dos días para descansar. Esto es el fin de semana, el sábado y el domingo.** (Continue to discuss weekday vs. weekend activities, favorite days, first day of the week in United States/Canada vs. Hispanic countries, and so on.)

Quick Comprehension Check: Sample questions:
¿Cierto o falso?
1. **La semana consiste en siete días.**
2. **Tenemos la clase de español los sábados.**
3. **El día favorito de muchos estudiantes es el viernes.**
4. **El fin de semana consiste en dos días, jueves y sábado.**

Suggestions:
- Model the pronunciation of the words in the list.
- Give the day of the week and have students say the next day.
- Have students make associations: **¿Qué día de la semana asocia Ud. con... ? (las fiestas, la religión, el laboratorio de lenguas, la clase de español,** *Friends* **[el programa de la tele], el fin de semana, las elecciones).**
- Emphasize that *on Monday* is **el lunes;** and *on Mondays,* **los lunes.** Remind students that days of the week are not capitalized in Spanish and that **lunes** is the first day of the week on Hispanic calendars.
- Point out that a *week from today* can be expressed **de hoy en ocho días.**
- Have students respond **sí** or **no:** 1. **Hoy es ______.** 2. **Mañana es ______.** 3. **No tenemos clase el miércoles.** 4. **Los lunes siempre tenemos examen.**

Optional Activity: Draw a typical student's weekly schedule on the board, including weekday classes, with some quizzes (**pruebas**) and an exam. Add a dentist appointment (**cita con el dentista**) and a birthday (**cumpleaños de Marta**). First ask **cierto/falso** questions, then questions for specific information, such as **¿Qué día tiene que estudiar mucho? (examen) ¿Qué día va a una fiesta? (cumpleaños).**

LOS MUEBLES, LOS CUARTOS Y OTRAS PARTES DE UNA CASA

Suggestions:
- Offer optional vocabulary, such as **el balcón, la cama de matrimonio / sencilla, la entrada, el inodoro, la terraza.**
- Point out that **habitación** is used for rooms in general. Some other synonyms for **alcoba** are **cuarto** and **dormitorio.**

- Read through the list once while students listen and look at their books; they need not repeat. Then, with books open, have students give the correct words for the following definitions: 1. **Allí se duerme** (pantomime). 2. **Allí se nada** (pantomime). 3. **Los niños nadan allí.** 4. **Da iluminación.** 5. **Donde se prepara la comida.** 6. **La parte de una casa donde se pone el coche.** 7. **Allí se pone la ropa.**
- Have students tell what they associate with the following: **¿Qué palabras asocia Ud. con... ? el coche, los picnics o las barbacoas, la ropa, nadar, estudiar, una cena elegante, las mascotas, los libros.**
- Have students tell whether each of the following associations is **lógico** or **ilógico:** 1. **los platos y la cocina** 2. **el sofá y la piscina** 3. **el garaje y el coche** 4. **la alcoba y el armario** 5. **la cama y el comedor.**
- Have students draw a simple sketch of their bedroom, then describe it to a partner, who tries to draw it based on what he/she hears. Introduce the phrases: **a la derecha, a la izquierda.**
- Ask students the following questions: **En su casa o apartamento, ¿tiene Ud. un cuarto o mueble favorito? ¿Cuál es? ¿Por qué lo prefiere?**

Heritage Speakers: Explique a la clase que en algunos países hispanos se usa la palabra **tina** en vez de **baño.** Pregúnteles a los hispanohablantes de la clase cuál de las dos palabras usan, o si usan otra. ¿Qué otras variaciones saben o usan para las partes de la casa?

Notes:

- Traditional Spanish-style homes are built around an interior patio or courtyard where the family can enjoy the outdoor air while socializing.
- The word **casa** is also used in the sense of *home.* The word **casa** is frequently heard in reference to an apartment. A literal translation of *home* is **hogar.**

Preparation: Prepare a "floor plan" of your apartment/home to put on the board or for the overhead. It need not contain furniture, since you will add this during the presentation. As with family members, present a few items at a time in a conceptually related group, check comprehension, present a few more, and so forth.

Lead in by mentioning weekdays, when you work, and weekend days, when you enjoy being at home. Then tell students you are going to describe your home and have a floor plan (**planillo**). As you move from room to room, mention and draw in the furniture. Tell which rooms are your favorites and why, where you spend the most time, and so on. You might also mention items for your **casa ideal** that your present home does not have, such as **un patio** or **una piscina.**

Quick Comprehension Check: Sample questions:

¿Cierto o falso?

1. **No hay un sofá en la sala, sólo sillones.**
2. **Siempre como en el comedor.**
3. **Miro la televisión en la alcoba.**
4. **Tengo mis libros en la sala.**

Quick Comprehension Check: Variation:

1. **¿Dónde paso mucho tiempo, en la sala o en la cocina?**
2 **¿Cuántas cómodas tengo en mi alcoba, una o dos?**
3. **¿Dónde guardo mis camisetas, en el armario o en la cómoda?**

Optional Activity: Use your comments about your **casa ideal** to generate discussion about what the ideal house should have. Have the class brainstorm as you write rooms, items, and so forth on the board. Then have students draw a floor plan and write a brief paragraph about their ideal home (give them a time limit; avoid excessive detail). Then have students volunteer to present their floor plans and read their paragraphs.

¿CUÁNDO?: PREPOSICIONES

Suggestions:

- This is the first of two vocabulary sections on prepositions. The second, on spatial relationships, is in **Capítulo 5.**
- Model the pronunciation of the prepositions.
- Ask the following questions: 1. **¿Qué día viene después del miércoles (jueves / domingo)? ¿Qué día viene antes del martes (miércoles / viernes)?** 2. **¿Hasta qué hora mira Ud. la televisión los lunes? ¿y los viernes? ¿Hasta cuándo estudia cuando tiene un examen?** Point out the accent mark on the interrogative **cuándo** and the lack of one in the non-interrogative **cuando.**

NOTA CULTURAL

Suggestions:

- Ask students whether features mentioned in **Nota cultural** can also be found in the U.S. and Canada. Then ask what they consider typical of U.S. and Canadian housing.
- Point out that generalizations about housing in the Hispanic world are particularly difficult to make. Additional features of Hispanic housing in some parts of the world that seem different to some U.S. or Canadian residents include the presence of a room for a servant and the relatively plain exterior of many Hispanic homes, especially compared with their well-decorated interior. Some Hispanics note the following about the housing in this country: the reliance on air conditioning (compared with fresh air ventilation/cooling), and the lawn and extensive landscaping, especially in suburban areas.

Paso 2: Gramática

GRAMMAR SECTION 11

Suggestions:

- Point out that **hacer, oír, poner, salir,** and **traer** have the irregular **yo** form with a **-g-.**
- Contrast **oír** and **escuchar.**
- Emphasize the spelling change for the second and third person of **oír: i → y.**
- Point out that **traer** is an antonym of **llevar.** As with **ir** vs. **venir** (see note in Grammar 10), **traer** implies that the speaker is in the place to which something would be brought.
- Offer some optional phrases: **salir bien/mal en un examen; salir a (la calle, al patio,** and so on).
- Use the verbs in sentences about yourself, following up with questions about the students. For example, **Veo las noticias en la televisión antes de clase. ¿Ud. ve la televisión en la mañana?**

GRAMMAR SECTION 12

Follow-up: Ask students the following questions after reading the **minidiálogo: ¿Dónde compran Uds. sus libros y materiales? ¿Piensan que las compras son caras en esa tienda? ¿Piensan que pierden dinero allí? ¿Por qué vuelven a comprar en esa tienda?**

Suggestions:

- Model infinitives you have not yet presented, creating a brief conversational exchange with each.
- Emphasize the spelling differences between **perder** and **pedir.**
- Model verbs with infinitives to emphasize the use of prepositions with some, and not with others: **empezar a** + infinitive; **volver a** + infinitive; **pensar** + infinitive.
- Remind students that **volver** means *to return (to a place)* and **devolver** means *to return (something).*

Heritage Speakers: En México y en algunos dialectos del español del suroeste de los Estados Unidos, el verbo **almorzar** significa **desayunar.** Pregúnteles a los hispanohablantes de su clase qué palabras usan para expresar los nombres de las comidas del día.

ENFOQUE CULTURAL: COSTA RICA

A. ¿Cierto o falso? Indique si las siguientes oraciones son ciertas (C) o falsas (F) según (*according to*) la información en Datos esenciales y Conozca a... Corrija (*Correct*) las oraciones falsas.

1. C F Costa Rica tiene más (*more*) habitantes que (*than*) Nicaragua (**Enfoque cultural, Capítulo 3**).
2. C F Arias Sánchez fue (*was*) presidente de Costa Rica por seis años.
3. C F Arias Sánchez estudió (*studied*) en España.
4. C F Arias Sánchez recibió (*received*) el Premio Nobel de Literatura.
5. C F Recibió el Premio Nobel de la Paz en 1986.

B. Para investigar: Navegando por el Internet

Escoja (*Choose*) uno de los parques nacionales mencionados en **www.centralamerica.com/cr** y llene los espacios en blanco con información de la página.

1. Nombre del parque: ______________________
2. Tamaño (*Size*): ________ hectáreas
3. Distancia desde (*from*) San José al parque: ________ kilómetros
4. ¿Hay evidencia de civilizaciones indígenas (*native*) en el parque? Sí No
5. ¿Hay una playa (*beach*)? Sí No
6. ¿Hay animales o plantas interesantes en este parque? Sí No

Notes:

- Costa Rica was not developed as a Spanish colony to the same extent that other Central American countries were. A number of factors accounted for this. Costa Rica was geographically distant from Guatemala, the seat of Spanish government, and there were not the extensive mineral resources there, nor the abundant indigenous work force to develop those that were there. As a result, the few settlers that arrived turned to agriculture.
- Coffee became a primary agricultural product in the nineteenth century.
- In 1871 U.S. engineers recruited Chinese and Italian workers to build a railroad. Later Jamaican workers were used.
- The United Fruit Company, which developed with the coming of the railroad and which linked banana plantations to export centers, influenced national politics in Costa Rica. Labor disputes against the company began early in the twentieth century and continued into the 1930s.
- Costa Rica currently has a parliamentary democracy and an advanced social welfare system.

Paso 3: Gramática

GRAMMAR SECTION 13

Suggestions:

- Emphasize the change in meaning of some verbs: **dormir** (*to sleep*) vs. **dormirse** (*to fall asleep*); **poner** (*to put, place*) vs. **ponerse** (*to put on*).
- Model verbs from the chart in a conversational setting, saying sentences about yourself and following up with questions to students: **Generalmente me acuesto a las once. Y Ud., ¿a qué hora se acuesta?**
- Rapid response drill. Ask students short, yes/no questions: **¿Se baña?** → **Sí, me baño. ¿Se bañan?** → **Sí, nos bañamos.** Use all of the verbs in the chart.
- Point out that other verbs can change meaning in the reflexive. Write the following examples on the board:

NON-REFLEXIVE	MEANING
caer	*to fall*
comer	*to eat*
decidir	*to decide*
ir	*to go*

REFLEXIVE	MEANING
caerse	*to fall down*
comerse	*to eat (something) up*
decidirse	*to make up one's mind*
irse	*to go away*

Optional Activities:

Un día típico

Paso 1. Complete las siguientes oraciones lógicamente para describir su rutina diaria. Use el pronombre reflexivo cuando sea necesario. **¡OJO!** Use el infinitivo después de las preposiciones.

1. **Me levanto después de ________.**
2. **Primero (yo) ________ y luego ________.**
3. **Me visto antes de / después de ________.**
4. **Luego me siento a la mesa para ________.**
5. **Me gusta estudiar antes de ________ o después de ________.**
6. **Por la noche me divierto un poco y luego ________.**
7. **Me acuesto antes de / después de ________ y finalmente ________.**

Paso 2. Con las oraciones del **Paso 1,** describa los hábitos de su esposo/a, su compañero/a de cuarto/casa, sus hijos...

Entrevista: ¿Cómo es tu rutina diaria?

Paso 1. Ahora, con un compañero / una compañera, hagan y contestan preguntas breves sobre su rutina diaria. Anote (*Jot down*) las respuestas de su compañero/a.

1. **Los días de semana** (*weekdays*), **¿te levantas temprano? ¿antes de las siete de la mañana? ¿A qué hora te levantas los sábados?**
2. **¿Te bañas o te duchas? ¿Cuándo lo haces** (*do you do it*), **por la mañana o por la noche?**
3. **¿Te afeitas todos los días? ¿Usas una afeitadora eléctrica? ¿Prefieres no afeitarte los fines de semana?**

4. **Por lo general, ¿te vistes con elegancia o informalmente? ¿Qué ropa te pones cuando quieres estar elegante? ¿cuando quieres estar muy cómodo/a** (*comfortable*)**? ¿Qué te pones para ir a la universidad?**
5. **¿A qué hora vuelves a casa, generalmente? ¿Qué haces cuando regresas? ¿Te quitas los zapatos? ¿Te pones ropa más cómoda? ¿Estudias? ¿Miras la televisión? ¿Preparas la cena** (*dinner*)**?**
6. **¿A qué hora te acuestas? ¿Cuál es la última** (*last*) **cosa que haces antes de acostarte? ¿Cuál es la última cosa o persona en que piensas antes de dormirte?**

Paso 2. Ahora, describa la rutina de su compañero/a a la clase, usando las respuestas del **Paso 1.** ¿Cuántos estudiantes de la clase tienen rutinas parecidas (*similar*)?

EN LOS ESTADOS UNIDOS Y EL CANADÁ: VICENTE WOLF

Note: Vicente Wolf believes that in an interior, as in nature, balancing color tones is very important. He likes to use colors that change as the light of day changes. He feels that some colors, such as light-greyish seafoam and pale robin's-egg blue, take on different personalities with the changing light of day, thus creating a balanced, inviting, and relaxed environment.

Paso 4: Un paso más

VIDEOTECA

MINIDRAMAS

The **Minidramas** vignettes are not referenced in the textbook, but are part of the *¿Qué tal?* Video Program. They also appear on the Video on CD packaged free with the textbook. If you show the **Minidramas** in class or have your students view them as homework, you might find the following suggestions helpful. You can also find blackline master activities in Section X of this Manual for **Minidramas.**

Comprensión:

1. **¿Quién es el nuevo compañero de cuarto?**
2. **¿Quién se levanta antes? ¿Quién es el último en levantarse?**
3. **¿Quién come con su novia?**
4. **¿Quién come en casa al menos** (*at least*) **tres días por semana?**

Suggestions: Brainstorm with class about possible questions and topics they would likely cover in a conversation regarding personal routines. Possible questions: **¿A qué hora te levantas? ¿Qué haces por la mañana antes de ir a clase? ¿Cuáles son los días ocupados? ¿Por qué? Por lo general, ¿puedes volver a casa a mediodía para almorzar? ¿y por la noche para cenar** (have dinner)**? Si no comes en casa, ¿dónde comes? ¿Dónde vives? ¿Tienes compañeros de casa/cuarto?**

ACTIVIDAD DE DESENLACE: PROBLEMAS DE VIVIENDA

Activity: Students will role-play situations between:

- a renting agent and two would-be renters who identify their preferences and daily routines
- roommates renting a room to another student. They must decide what rooms they will use, identify their daily schedules, and negotiate house rules.
- roommates the day after a party, who argue about cleaning the house

Purpose:	To create a context in which students can review and practice the grammar from **Capítulo 4** and vocabulary related to the parts and furnishings of a house
Resources:	*¿Qué tal?* textbook, the Internet, and other sources as appropriate
Vocabulary:	The house and furniture
Grammar:	Principal grammar structures covered in **Capítulo 4** of the textbook, including the verbs **hacer, oír, poner, salir, traer,** and **ver,** stem-changing verbs, and reflexive pronouns
Optional Writing:	Students write a newspaper announcement that describes a housing situation, for example, looking for a house/apartment or looking for roommates.
Recycled Content:	Grammar structures and vocabulary from previous chapters
Duration:	Out-of-class preparation time will vary. In-class time will be approximately five minutes per presentation.
Format:	Groups of three to four students

Capítulo 4: *Memoria*

1. 
2. 
3. 
4. Los estudiantes se divierten mucho los fines de semana.
5. 
6. 
7. Me peino antes de salir para la universidad.
8. Verónica se acuesta a las once y media de la noche.
9. 
10. Nos ponemos los vestidos elegantes.
11. 
12. Me llamo Pedro Martínez. ¿Cómo se llama Ud.?
13. La profesora se quita los zapatos después de la clase.
14. 
15. ¿Te cepillas los dientes tres veces al día?
16. Me levanto tarde los sábados.
17. 
18. A mi papá le gusta afeitarse todas las mañanas.
19. Mercedes se sienta en el laboratorio de lenguas para hacer la tarea.
20.

Capítulo 4: Partner A *Frases ilustradas*

Read each sentence to your partner using the cues given. Your partner will tell you if your sentences are correct or not. You have three chances to guess correctly.

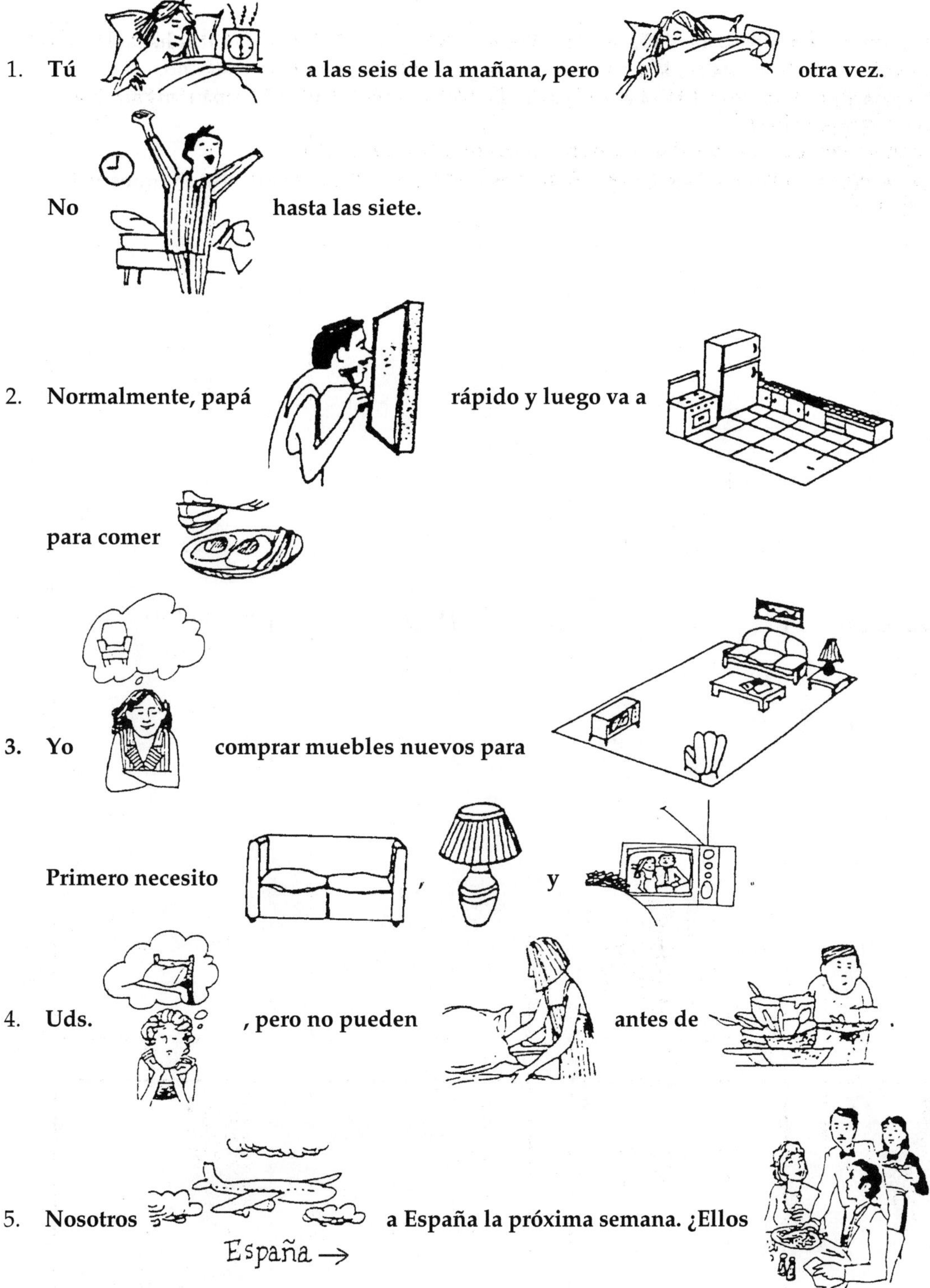

1. **Tú ______ a las seis de la mañana, pero ______ otra vez.**

   No ______ hasta las siete.

2. **Normalmente, papá ______ rápido y luego va a ______**

   para comer ______

3. **Yo ______ comprar muebles nuevos para ______**

   Primero necesito ______, ______ y ______.

4. **Uds. ______, pero no pueden ______ antes de ______.**

5. **Nosotros ______ a España la próxima semana. ¿Ellos ______**

   paella en todos los restaurantes?

Capítulo 4: Partner B *Frases ilustradas*

These are your partner's answers. Listen to what your partner tells you. If the answer is not exactly what you have, just tell him/her: **No está bien. Trata de hacerlo otra vez.** Give your partner three opportunities to guess correctly.

1. **Tú te despiertas a las seis de la mañana, pero te duermes otra vez. No te levantas hasta las siete.**
2. **Normalmente, papá se afeita rápido y luego va a la cocina para comer el desayuno.**
3. **Yo pienso comprar muebles nuevos para la sala. Primero necesito un sofá, una lámpara y un televisor (una televisión).**
4. **Uds. tienen sueño, pero no pueden acostarse antes de lavar los platos.**
5. **Nosotros hacemos un viaje a España la próxima semana. ¿(Ellos) Sirven paella en todos los restaurantes?**

Capítulo 4: Partner B *Frases ilustradas*

Read each sentence to your partner using the cues given. Your partner will tell you if your sentences are correct or not. You have three chances to guess correctly.

1. **Elena ______ en la cafetería a las doce. De beber, ella ______ ______ ______ de naranja, ______ o un ______.**

2. **Después de ______, Adriana ______ para ir al trabajo.**

3. **Los ______, papá ______ con sus amigos. Los domingos por la noche, ______ en un sillón cómodo para leer.**

4. **Para ______, necesito ______, ______ y ______.**

5. **¿Tú vuelves a nadar en ______ o prefieres ir al cine para ver ______?**

Capítulo 4: Partner A *Frases ilustradas*

These are your partner's answers. Listen to what your partner tells you. If the answer is not exactly what you have, just tell him/her: **No está bien. Trata de hacerlo otra vez.** Give your partner three opportunities to guess correctly.

1. **Elena almuerza en la cafetería a las doce. De beber, ella pide jugo de naranja, leche o un refresco.**
2. **Después de ducharse, Adriana se viste para ir al trabajo.**
3. **Los fines de semana, papá juega al tenis con sus amigos. Los domingos por la noche, se sienta en un sillón cómodo para leer.**
4. **Para la alcoba, necesito una cama, una cómoda y un estante.**
5. **¿Tú vuelves a nadar en la piscina o prefieres ir al cine para ver una película?**

¡A pescar!

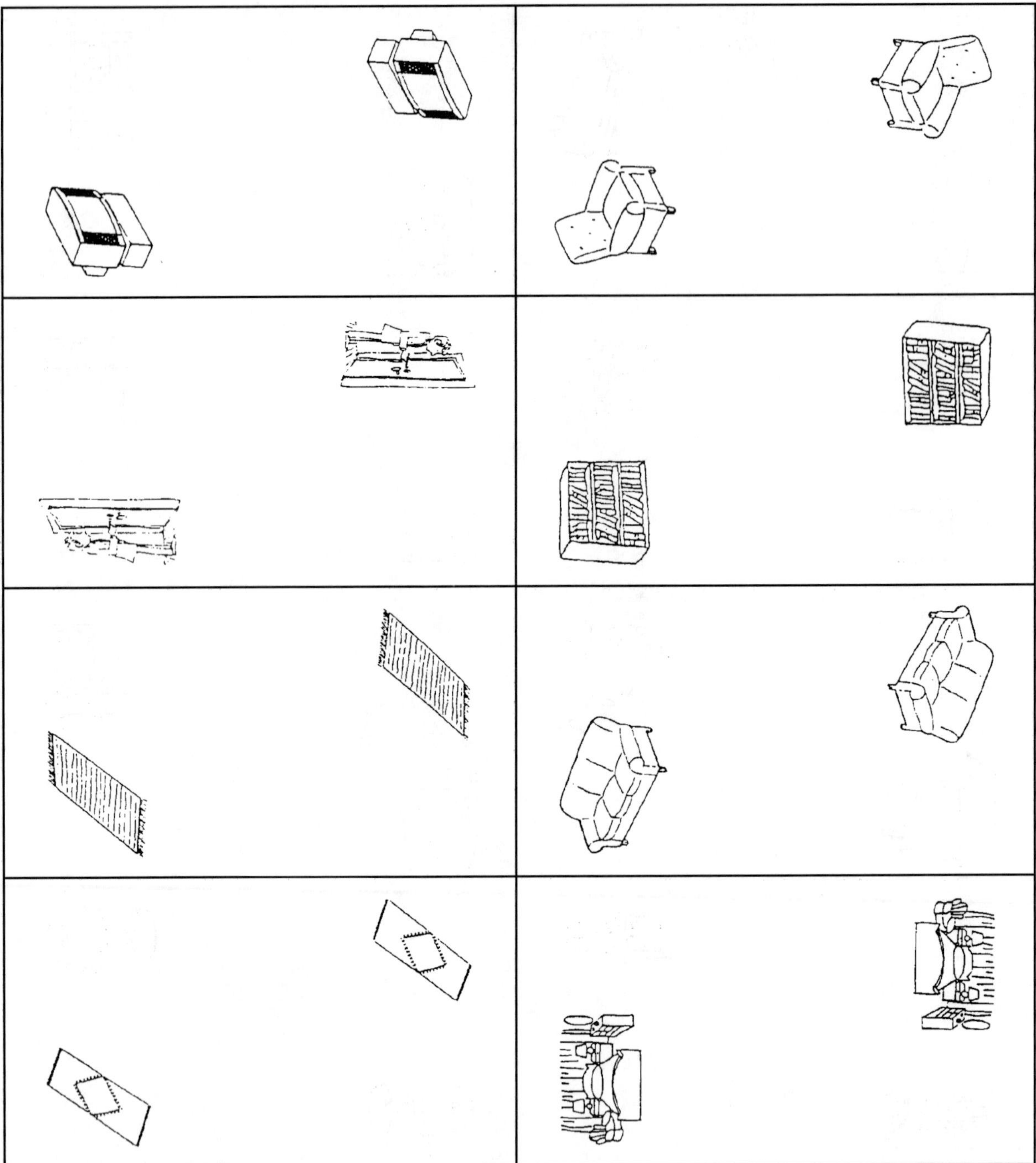

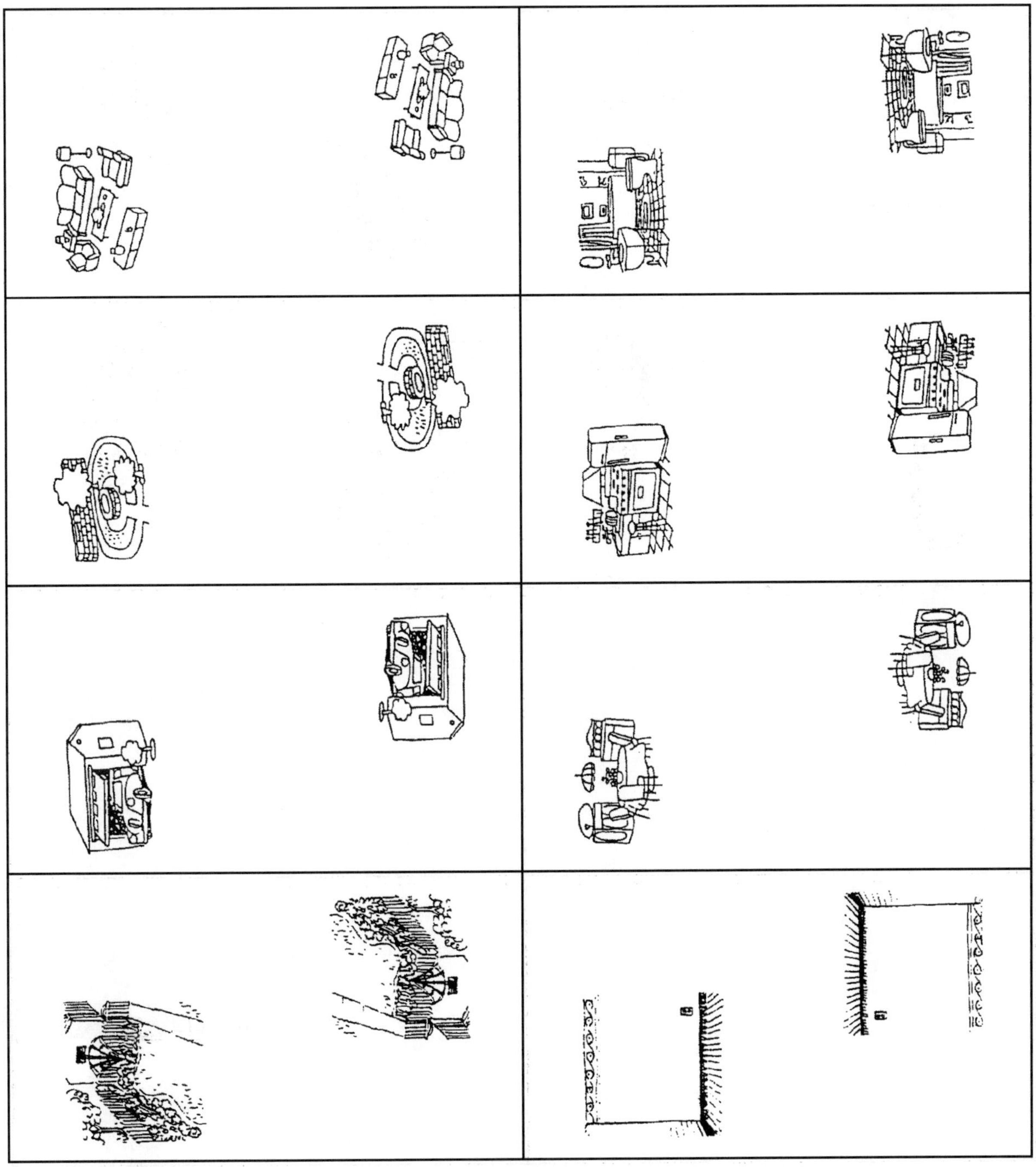

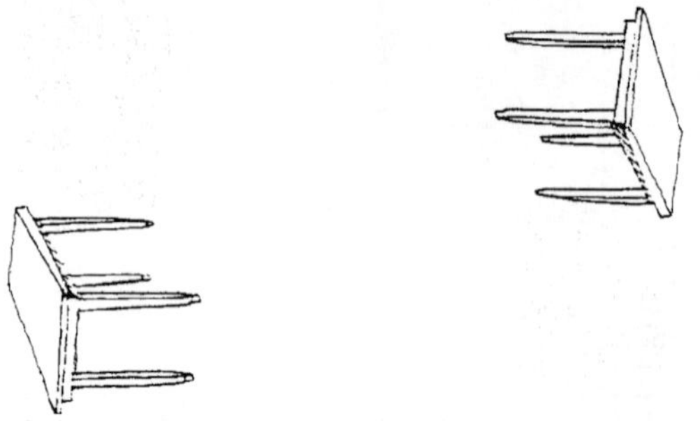

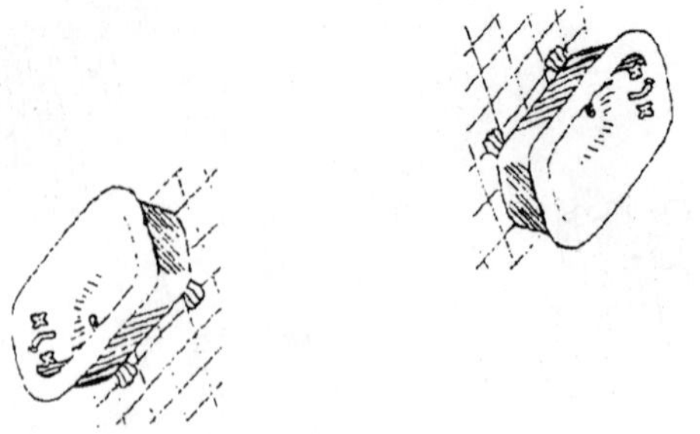

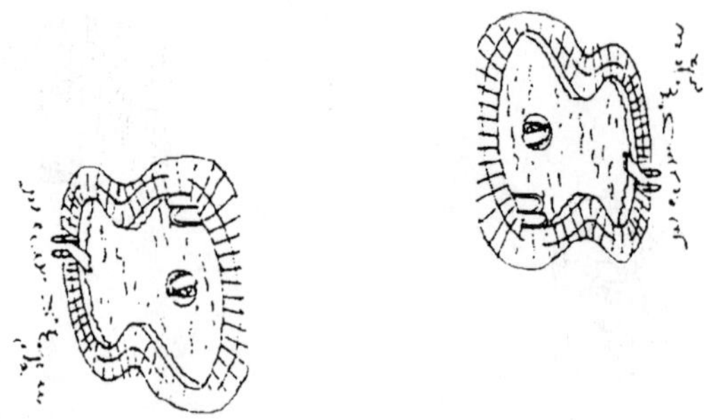

Arriésgate

	Vocabulario	Verbos	Gramática	Traducción
10 pts			Hay mucho ruido en (*this*) _______ residencia. No puedo oír (*these*) _______ cintas.	On Mondays I leave for the university at 7:30 a.m.
20 pts			(*Those*) _______ patios españoles son muy bonitos. Quiero volver a verlos algún día.	Dad feels like taking a nap after having lunch.
30 pts			¿Qué es (*this*) _______? ¡Pienso que hay un insecto en mi sopa!	Next Saturday my family is going to eat breakfast at Denny's.
40 pts	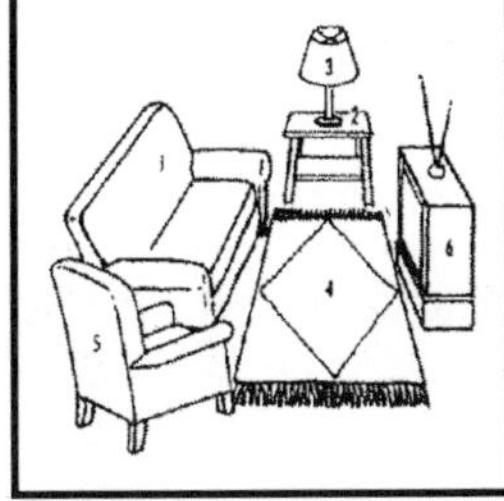		Jaime, (*that*) _______ corbata que llevas hoy no hace juego con (*those*) _______ calcetines.	This old bathtub is not comfortable. I prefer to take a shower.
50 pts			¡(*This*) _______ película es tonta! Vamos a (*that*) _______ cine que está en el centro.	On Saturdays we have to work in the yard before playing in the swimming pool.

Answer Key for *Arriésgate*

Capítulo 4

Vocabulario:	**10 pts**	el baño: el lavabo, la bañera
	20 pts	el comedor: la mesa, las sillas, los platos
	30 pts	el patio, la piscina, el jardín
	40 pts	la sala: el sofá, la mesita, la lámpara, la alfombra, el sillón, el televisor
	50 pts	la alcoba: la cama, la cómoda, el escritorio, la silla, el estante, el armario
Verbos:	(Ejemplos: hay que usar verbos del **Capítulo 4**)	
	10 pts	En el restaurante... los Sres. Ramírez **piden** hamburguesas y José **sirve** la comida.
	20 pts	En la clase de español... Carmen **hace** una pregunta, Gloria **se sienta** en una silla y Anita **cierra** el libro.
	30 pts	Patricia **se levanta** a las seis de la mañana. **Se cepilla** los dientes y **se viste** antes de salir para la escuela.
	40 pts	Mi tío **se despierta** temprano, y luego **se afeita** y **se ducha.**
	50 pts	Mi hermana **vuelve** a casa y **se quita** los zapatos. Normalmente, ella **se acuesta** a las diez de la noche.
Gramática:	**10 pts**	esta, estas
	20 pts	Aquellos
	30 pts	esto
	40 pts	esa, esos
	50 pts	Esta, aquel
Traducción:	**10 pts**	Los lunes salgo para la universidad a las siete y media de la mañana.
	20 pts	Papá tiene ganas de dormir la siesta después de almorzar.
	30 pts	El próximo sábado mi familia va a comer el desayuno en Denny's.
	40 pts	Esta bañera vieja no es cómoda. Prefiero ducharme.
	50 pts	Los sábados tenemos que trabajar en el jardín antes de jugar en la piscina.

CAPÍTULO 5 LAS ESTACIONES, EL TIEMPO Y UN POCO DE GEOGRAFÍA

Student Supplements

- Listening Comprehension Program CD, **Capítulo 5** (**Paso 1: Vocabulario:** word lists)
- Workbook/Laboratory Manual, **Capítulo 5**
- Audio Program CD, **Capítulo 5**

Instructor Resources

- Instructor's Manual/IRK: Chapter-by-Chapter Supplementary Materials, **Capítulo 5**
  - **Paso 1: Vocabulario**
  - **Paso 2: Gramática**
    - Grammar Section 14
    - Grammar Section 15
    - **En los Estados Unidos y el Canadá...**
    - **Enfoque cultural**
  - **Paso 3: Gramática**
    - Grammar Section 16
    - **Un poco de todo**
  - **Paso 4: Un paso más**
    - **Videoteca**
    - **A leer**
    - **A escribir**
  - Games and Activities
- Instructor's Manual/IRK: Video Activities and Related Materials
  - **A primera vista**
  - **A segunda vista**
  - Answers to Video Activities
  - Videoscripts
- Audioscript, **Capítulo 5**
- Transparencies 33–40
- Testing Program, **Capítulo 5**

Multimedia Resources

- Online Learning Center
- Electronic Workbook/Laboratory Manual
- Video, **Capítulo 5** (cue 30:35)
  - **En contexto** (2:08)
  - **Minidramas** (4:50)
  - **Enfoque cultural: Guatemala** (1:00)
- Student CD-ROM, **Capítulo 5**
- Electronic Language Tutor, **Capítulo 5** (**Vocabulario, Gramática**)

Paso 1: Vocabulario

¿QUÉ TIEMPO HACE HOY?

Suggestions:

- Model weather expressions. As you present each, have students tell you what kind of clothing is worn for that weather condition. Also, you may want to review all weather expressions, asking, **¿Cómo está Ud. cuando... (hace frío, calor,** and so on)**? ¿Qué tiene ganas de hacer cuando... (llueve, nieva,** and so on)**?**
- Point out the pronunciation of **llueve.** The pronunciation of **ll** and consonantal **y** is identical in most parts of the Spanish-speaking world. Therefore, the difference in spelling is not accompanied by a difference in pronunciation. In some areas of Spain, **ll** is a sound made with the tongue against the palate, resembling the sound in the English word *million.*
- Point out that **tiempo** means both *weather* and *time.* **Tiempo** should not be confused with **hora** as in **¿Qué hora es?**
- Contrast **hacer, tener, estar,** and **ser.** Discuss the differences among the following expressions: **Hace frío/calor** for weather, **tener frío/calor** for people, and **estar frío/caliente** to indicate the condition of things.
- Optional vocabulary: **Hay mucha humedad; está húmedo.**

LOS MESES Y LAS ESTACIONES DEL AÑO

Preparation: On the board before you begin, draw a blank one-year calendar, divided into 12 months. As you use target vocabulary items, repeat them and write them on the board. Use sketches to aid comprehension.

Sample Passage: **¿Qué es un año? ¿Es más grande o menos grande que una semana? Sí, es más grande. ¿Cuántas semanas hay en un año? Sí,...**

El año está dividido también en doce meses... doce meses. Un mes consiste en treinta o treinta y un días, con la excepción de febrero. Febrero...

Entonces, hay doce meses en un año. El primer mes (hold up one finger) **es enero... enero** (write into blank calendar). (Present all the months.) **¿Cuántos días tiene noviembre?** And so on. **¿Qué personas famosas tienen el cumpleaños en febrero?** And so forth.

El año está dividido en cuatro estaciones... cuatro estaciones: el otoño, el invierno, la primavera y el verano. El otoño consiste en tres meses: septiembre, octubre y noviembre. Oficialmente, el otoño comienza el 21 de septiembre... (write and repeat) **21 de septiembre. Muchos estudiantes regresan a clases en el otoño. También...** (Mention other things associated with autumn, including weather. Continue with other seasons.)

Quick Comprehension Check: Sample items:

¿A qué estación corresponden estas palabras y frases?

el béisbol	**las flores** (mimic as smelling them)
hace mucho frío	**el fútbol**
verde	**amarillo y rojo**

¿Cierto o falso?

1. **Hay trece meses en un año.**
2. **Todas las estaciones tienen tres meses.**
3. **Todos los meses tienen treinta días.**
4. **En abril llueve y hace fresco.**

Suggestions:

- Model months of the year, linking them to seasons: **Los meses de otoño son septiembre, octubre y noviembre, ¿verdad? Los meses de verano son mayo, junio y julio, ¿no?,** and so on. Then ask students what the weather is like in each season: **En muchas partes de los Estados Unidos hace frío en enero, ¿cierto o falso? También nieva mucho en julio, ¿cierto o falso?,** and so on.
- Point out that September has two accepted spellings: **septiembre** and **setiembre.**
- Remind students that months are not capitalized.
- Ask students what they prefer: **¿Prefiere Ud... ?** 1. **¿los días cortos del invierno o los días largos del verano?** 2. **¿el tiempo del otoño o el de la primavera?** 3. **¿las actividades de verano o las de invierno?**

Reciclado: Review numbers and years with the following questions: **¿En qué año estamos? ¿En qué año nació Ud.? ¿En qué año nació su padre (madre, abuela,** and so on)? **¿En qué año piensa graduarse?**

Heritage Speakers: Pregúnteles a los hispanohablantes de su clase qué días festivos celebran. Pídales que describan las celebraciones.

¿DÓNDE ESTÁ? LAS PREPOSICIONES

Point out: The Iberian Peninsula is occupied by Spain, Portugal, and the smallest independent country in the world, Andorra. The peninsula's name is derived from its ancient inhabitants, whom the Greeks called Iberians. This name probably comes from the Ebro (Iberus), the peninsula's second longest river after the Tajo.

Paso 2: Gramática

GRAMMAR SECTION 14

Follow-up: After covering the **minidiálogo,** ask students the following question: **¿Cuáles son algunas actividades que Ud. puede hacer pero que no está haciendo en este momento?** Coach students, based on activities they mentioned in the previous class discussion: **Carlos, ¿estás mirando la televisión en este momento?**

USES OF THE PROGRESSIVE

Suggestions:

- Use visuals to teach the concept of the progressive; students should be able to produce progressive forms by following the models given.
- Emphasize that the Spanish progressive is used only for describing actions actually in progress. Ask which of the following sentences would be expressed with progressive forms in Spanish: 1. *They are reading the newspaper now.* 2. *Mary is typing all her homework this year.* 3. *I'm speaking English now.* 4. *We're going to San Francisco next summer.*

EN LOS ESTADOS UNIDOS Y EL CANADÁ: ALFREDO JAAR

Emphasize: In Spanish usage, **América** refers to all of North and South America. Spanish speakers throughout the Western Hemisphere consider themselves **americanos.** Jaar objected to being classified only as "Hispanic" or "Latino," because the "American" aspect of his identity was thereby completely unacknowledged. This exclusionary usage of the term "American" in the United States affects many people's attitudes.

Suggestion: Ask students what power relationships are implied by (1) monopolizing the term "American" to the exclusion of other North Americans (e.g., Canadians, Mexicans) and all Central and South Americans and (2) referring to Mexico, Nicaragua, or Grenada as "America's backyard."

Heritage Speakers:

- Pídales a los estudiantes hispanohablantes que hagan una lista de términos como **chicano, boricua** y **pachuco.** Pídales que le expliquen al resto de la clase el sentido de estos términos.
- Invite a los estudiantes hispanohablantes a investigar entre sus familiares cuál es su opinión con respecto al término **americano** cuando sólo es empleado para referirse a los ciudadanos de los Estados Unidos. Pídales que compartan estas opiniones con el resto de la clase.

GRAMMAR SECTION 15

SER AND *ESTAR* WITH ADJECTIVES

Suggestions:

- Point out that **ser** + adjective represents the norm; **estar** + adjective represents a change from the norm.
- Point out that **estar** is used to express an unexpected quality: **¡Qué fría está el agua!** To express what is expected, **ser** is used: **El agua es fría.** (The speaker expects the water to be cold.)
- Offer the following additional vocabulary: **de buen humor, de mal humor, enojado/a, enfadado/a, roto/a.** Point out that **estar alegre** can be used to mean *to be tipsy.*
- Point out that to express how something looks, tastes, feels, or appears, **estar** is used. Contrast pairs of sentences and meanings found in this section.

Notes:

- **Práctica C** in this section explicitly practices new adjectives from the list.
- Point out that **Daniel está muy guapo esta noche** does not imply that he is by nature ugly, but rather comments on his appearance at a given point in time (he is especially handsome) or expresses the surprise of the speaker at how handsome he is tonight.

Optional Activity: Write **la computadora es / está...** on the board and have students form sentences with the following cues.

1. **en la mesa del comedor**
2. **un regalo de cumpleaños**
3. **para mi compañero de cuarto**
4. **de la tienda Computec**
5. **en una caja** (*box*) **verde**
6. **de los padres de mi compañero**
7. **un regalo muy caro pero estupendo**
8. **de metal y plástico gris**
9. **una IBM, el último** (*latest*) **modelo**
10. **muy fácil** (*easy*) **de usar**

PRÁCTICA B

Variation: **La pandilla**[a]

Ahora en el mundo hispánico no (ser/estar[1]) necesario tener chaperona. Muchas de las actividades sociales se dan[b] en grupos. Si Ud. (ser/estar[2]) miembro de una pandilla, sus amigos (ser/estar[3]) el centro de su vida social y Ud. y su novio[c] o novia salen frecuentemente con otras parejas[d] o personas del grupo.

[a]*group of friends* [b]**se...** *occur* [c]*boyfriend* [d]*couples*

Heritage Speakers: El término **pandilla** (**Práctica C**) tiene connotaciones negativas para algunos hispanohablantes.

CONVERSACIÓN

Comprensión: **¿Sí o no?** ¿Son estas las opiniones de un joven hispano?

1. **Es necesario salir con chaperona.**
2. **La pandilla tiene poca importancia para mí.**

Suggestion: Have students prepare descriptions of famous people, using a minimum of five sentences. Then have volunteers present their descriptions to the class. For example: **Elizabeth Taylor → Es una actriz. Es morena. Es muy rica. Tiene muchos diamantes. Tiene muchos ex esposos.**

Optional Activities: **Sentimientos.** Complete the following sentences by telling how you feel in the situations described. Then ask questions of other students in the class to find at least one person who completed a given sentence the way you did.

MODELO: **Cuando saco** (*I get*) **una «A» en un examen, estoy** *alegre.* →
¿Cómo te sientes (*do you feel*) **cuando sacas una «A» en un examen?**

1. **Cuando el profesor da una tarea difícil, estoy _______.**
2. **Cuando tengo mucho trabajo, estoy _______.**
3. **En otoño generalmente estoy _______ porque _______.**
4. **En verano estoy _______ porque _______.**
5. **Cuando llueve (nieva), estoy _______ porque _______.**
6. **Los lunes por la mañana estoy _______.**
7. **Los viernes por la noche estoy _______.**
8. **Cuando me acuesto muy tarde, estoy _______ al día siguiente** (*the next day*).
9. **Cuando otra persona habla y habla y habla, _______.**
10. **Cuando estoy con mi familia, _______.**
11. **Cuando estoy de vacaciones, _______.**
12. **Cuando tengo problemas con mi coche, _______.**
13. **Cuando voy al consultorio del dentista, _______.**

¿Qué haces? Tell what you are usually doing if you are . . .

1. **Estoy preocupado/a cuando _______.**
2. **Estoy aburrido/a cuando _______.**
3. **Estoy furioso/a cuando _______.**
4. **Estoy de buen/mal humor cuando _______.**

Variation: Read the following places aloud and have students tell where they are:

1. **Madrid, Barcelona, Toledo, Segovia**
2. **Bolivia, Colombia, el Paraguay, el Brasil**
3. **Acapulco, Cancún, Puerto Vallarta**
4. **Costa Rica, Guatemala, Nicaragua, Panamá**
5. **Amarillo, Toledo, Santa Cruz, San Agustín**

ENFOQUE CULTURAL: GUATEMALA

A. ¿Cierto o falso? Indique si las siguientes oraciones son ciertas (C) o falsas (F), según la información en Nota histórica y Datos esenciales. Corrija las oraciones falsas.

1. C F Más de (*More than*) 5.500 de los habitantes de Guatemala son de origen maya.
2. C F La ciudad de Tikal es famosa por su ropa artística.
3. C F El calendario azteca es más antiguo que (*older than*) el calendario maya.
4. C F El sistema político de los mayas era (*was*) muy desorganizado.
5. C F Las ruinas de Tikal son un lugar turístico muy popular.

B. Para contestar. Conteste las siguientes preguntas con la información en Conozca a...

1. ¿Cómo se llama el período entre 1978 y 1985 en Guatemala?

   ____

2. ¿De qué grupo étnico es Rigoberta Menchú?

   ____

3. ¿Qué temas presenta en su autobiografía?

   ____

4. ¿En qué año recibió (*did she receive*) el Premio Nobel de la Paz?

   ____

Suggestion: Encourage students to research the following topics and report to the class:

- the colonial history of Guatemala, especially the figures of Pedro de Alvarado and his wife
- the twin volcanoes of the first Spanish capital, Antigua
- the U.S. involvement in Guatemala in the latter part of the twentieth century
- the controversies surrounding Rigoberta Menchú's book in the 1990s.

Paso 3: Gramática

GRAMMAR SECTION 16

PRÁCTICA A

Note:

- Antonio Banderas was introduced to U.S. audiences in the film *The Mambo Kings.* Banderas won two 2000 ALMA awards (American Latino Media Arts awards): one for directing *Crazy in Alabama* and another for his part in *13th Warrior*.

- Jennifer Lynn López's parents came to New York from Ponce, Puerto Rico. At the age of 16, Jennifer had a bit part in the film *My Little Girl* (starring Mary Stuart Masterson). Later, Jennifer was chosen to play Selena Quintanilla Pérez, in the official biographical film of this popular Tejana singer. This film gave Jennifer a jumpstart in the film and music industries.
- Carlos Santana was born July 20, 1947, in Autlán, Mexico. His band, Santana, is one of the most influential bands in rock music. In 1969 Santana performed at Woodstock, reaching new audiences outside the Mission district of San Francisco. Santana's combination of rock and Latin music was completely new, powerful, and riveting. Santana continues to break through genres and generations: his comeback CD *Supernatural* won several Grammys.

UN POCO DE TODO

Optional Activity: **Las comparaciones son odiosas** (*despicable*)**... ¡pero interesantes!**

Paso 1. Complete estas oraciones con información verdadera (*true*) para Ud.

1. **Tomo _______ cursos, que hacen un total de _______ créditos.**
2. **Generalmente, me levanto a las _______ y me acuesto a las _______.** **Duermo _______ horas diarias, aproximadamente.**
3. **Tengo _______ años.**
4. **Tengo _______ hermanos. (No tengo hermanos. Soy hijo único / hija única** [*only child*].)
5. **Trabajo _______ horas a la semana, en _______.**

Paso 2. Usando las oraciones de arriba (*above*) como guía (*as a guide*), haga preguntas a uno o dos compañeros. Anote (*Jot down*) sus respuestas.

MODELO: **¿Cuántos cursos tomas?**

Paso 3. Ahora haga comparaciones entre sus compañeros y Ud.

MODELOS: Mike toma más cursos que yo, pero yo tomo más cursos que Susie.

Variation: Assume the identity of a famous person (actor, artist, singer, athlete, and so on). Have students ask you yes/no questions in order to determine your identity. They may ask about your place of origin, your personality traits, your nationality, your profession, and so on. Model questions to get them started:

1. **¿Es Ud. hombre? (mujer / niño / animal)**
2. **¿Es Ud. viejo? (joven / guapo / rubio / moreno)**
3. **¿Es de los Estados Unidos? (del Canadá / de México)**
4. **¿Es casado? (soltero / viudo)**
5. **¿Está en (lugar) hoy?**
6. **¿Está muy ocupado con su vida estos días? (contento)**
7. **¿Está en (programa de televisión / película)?**

Paso 4: Un paso más

VIDEOTECA

MINIDRAMAS

The **Minidramas** vignettes are not referenced in the textbook, but are part of the *¿Qué tal?* Video Program. They also appear on the Video on CD packaged free with the textbook. If you show the **Minidramas** in class or have your students view them as homework, you might find the following suggestions helpful. You can also find blackline master activities in Section X of this Manual for **Minidramas.**

Comprensión:
1. **¿Dónde está Marta?**
2. **¿Por qué llama Carolina?**
3. **¿Qué debe hacer Manolo, el papá de Marta?**

Suggestion: Using two columns on board, review basic exchanges of a typical phone call.

Persona que recibe la llamada	***Persona que llama***
(1) Saludo telefónico **—¿Diga? (España)** **(—¿Aló? / —¿Bueno? en Latinoamérica)**	**(2) Saludo/identificación/pregunta** **—Buenos días. Soy ____. ¿Está ____?**
(3) Respuesta **—No, no está. / Sí, un momento, por favor. Voy a llamarlo/a.**	**(4) Mensaje y gracias** **—¿Puedo dejar un mensaje para ____? Favor de decirle...** **—Gracias. Adiós.**

A LEER

Suggestions: **Comprensión.** Since this is the longest reading that students have had so far, it is important to go over the comprehension questions in class. Accept different answers for **Comprensión B** and encourage students to explain why they answered as they did.

A ESCRIBIR

Suggestion: Have several students read their written descriptions. Ask the entire class two or three comprehension questions after each description, to encourage students to listen to one another.

ACTIVIDAD DE DESENLACE: ¿DÓNDE EN LATINOAMERICA ESTÁ LA PATAGONIA?

Activity: Teams of students will participate in a game in which they identify Spanish-speaking countries, their weather, and their geography.

Purpose: To create a context in which students can review and practice the grammar from **Capítulo 5** and vocabulary related to geography, climate, and weather

Resources: *¿Qué tal?* textbook, the Internet, and other sources as appropriate

Vocabulary: Weather and climate, months and seasons of the year

Grammar:	Principal grammatical structures covered in **Capítulo 5** of the textbook, including the present progressive using **estar** + **-ndo, ser** and **estar,** comparisons
Recycled Content:	Grammar structures and vocabulary from previous chapters
Duration:	Out-of-class preparation time will vary. In-class time will be approximately 25 minutes.
Format:	Two teams, each one composed of half the members of the class
Comments:	You may wish to have students prepare (as an assignment) four to five questions about the weather, climate, or geography of Spanish-speaking countries. Examples:

- **Cuando en Toronto es primavera, en Chile es __________.**
- **¿Qué país suramericano tiene la costa más larga?**
- **¿Qué dos países se encuentran al sur del Perú?**
- **Es julio. Me gusta esquiar y ver ejemplos de fauna exótica —como, por ejemplo, los pingüinos. Por eso, voy de vacaciones a ____________.**
- **¿Cómo es el clima de ____________?**

In class, have teams take turns answering the questions. Give extra credit for using **estar** + the present progressive correctly and for using prepositions that indicate location. The team that answers the most questions correctly wins the game.

Games and Activities

Capítulo 5: Partner A *Crucigrama*

You have the answers for half the puzzle, and your partner has those for the other half. Together you must complete the whole puzzle. You have to give clues to your partner so that he/she can guess the missing words. You *may not use the word itself*. Everything has to be done in Spanish.

Give clues and definitions such as: **Cuando una persona trabaja mucho, está...**
Lo opuesto de limpio es...

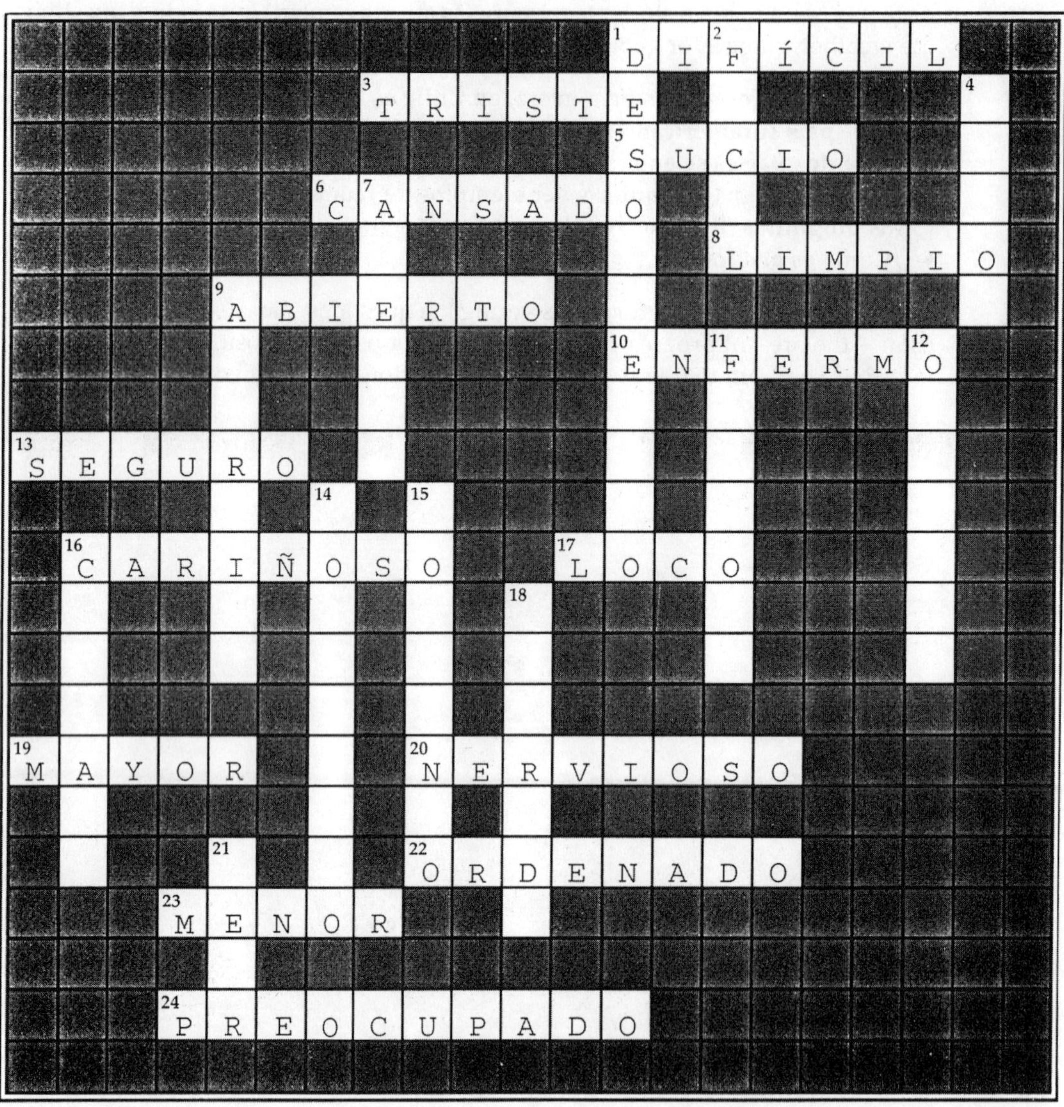

Capítulo 5: Partner B *Crucigrama*

You have the answers for half the puzzle, and your partner has those for the other half. Together you must complete the whole puzzle. You have to give clues to your partner so that he/she can guess the missing words. You *may not use the word itself.* Everything has to be done in Spanish.

Give clues and definitions such as: **Cuando una persona trabaja mucho, está...**
Lo opuesto de limpio es...

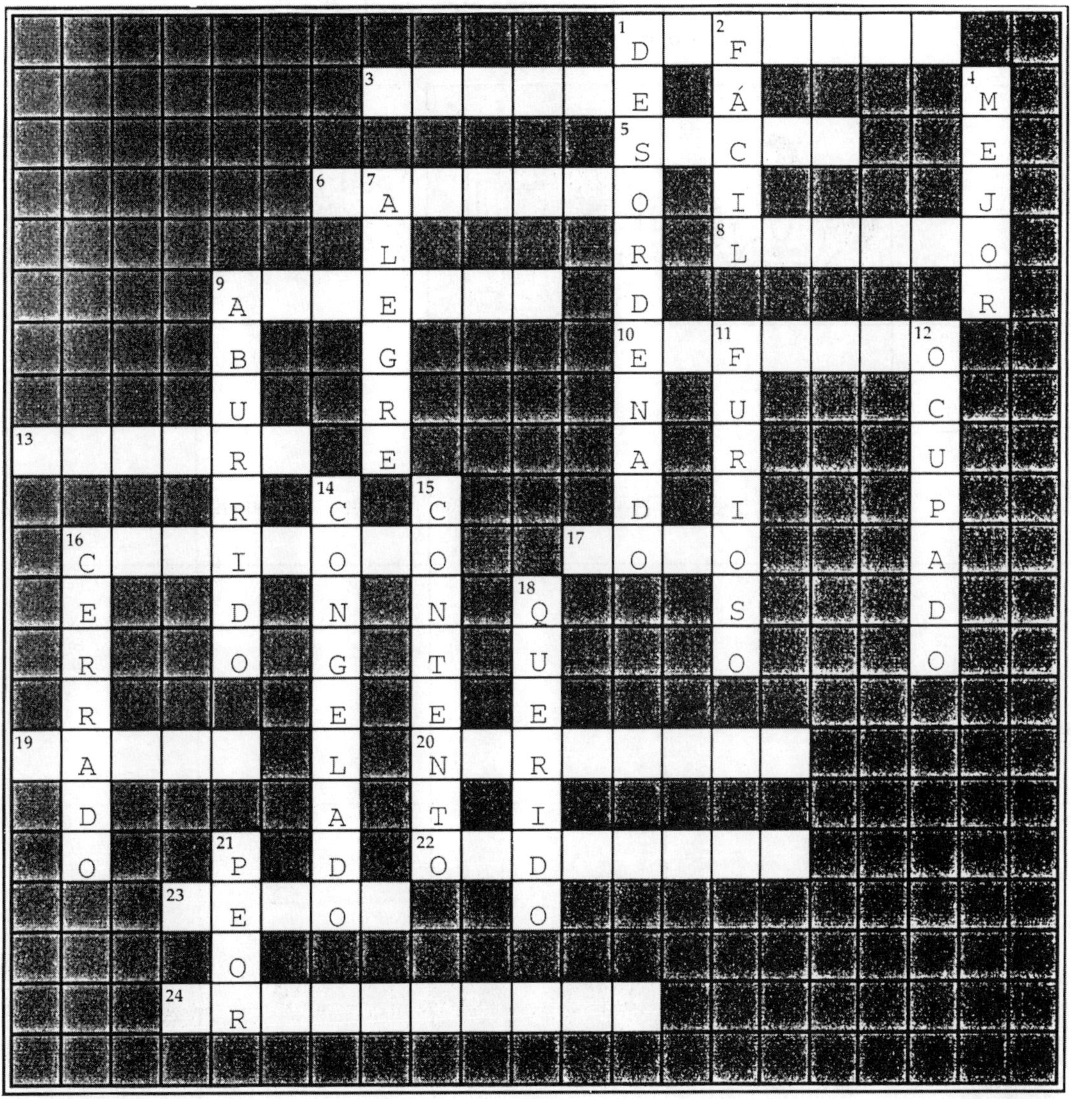

Capítulo 5 *Submarino*

This game is played like "Battleship." Draw a submarine in any five squares on your gameboard without letting your partner see your paper. You and your partner will ask each other questions to try to locate (and sink) the other players' submarines. This time your questions and answers should demonstrate the correct use of present progressive verb forms.

MODELO: TÚ: **¿Tú estás haciendo ejercicio?**
COMPAÑERO/A: **Sí, estoy haciendo ejercicio.** (*if there is a sub in that square*)
or **No, no estoy haciendo ejercicio.** (*if there is no sub in that square*)

(Draw your partner.) **Tú**				
El estudiante				
(Draw your partner and another classmate.) **Uds.**				
Felicia y Elena				

Arriésgate

	Vocabulario	Verbos	Gramática	Traducción
10 pts		Mis abuelos _____ de Cuba. Ellos _____ cubanos.	**Pepe**  **Lola**	The bookshelf is to the left of the desk.
20 pts		Mi esposa y yo _____ muy preocupados porque nuestros hijos _____ enfermos.	**Ana** 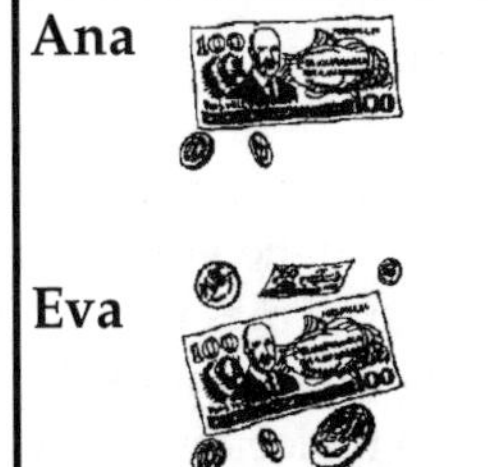 **Eva**	The capital city is close to the beach.
30 pts		El País Vasco _____ en España y _____ muy interesante.	**Tito** **Luis** 	The dog's house is outdoors, close to the garage.
40 pts		¡Qué guapo _____ José esta noche! Lleva un traje nuevo.	**Inés** 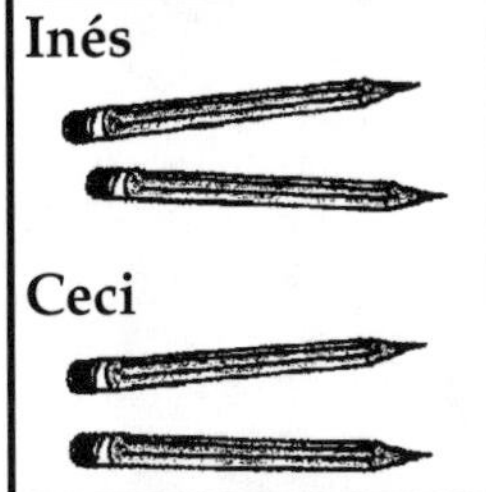 **Ceci**	The dirty socks are under the bed, beside the shoes.
50 pts		Mi novio _____ mayor que yo. Él _____ estudiante universitario.	**Mi tía**  **Mamá**	Tonight I am going to celebrate my birthday far from my family.

Answer Key for *Arriésgate*

Capítulo 5

Vocabulario:	**10 pts**	Mi cumpleaños es el trece de octubre.
	20 pts	el otoño; se(p)tiembre, octubre, noviembre; hace viento
	30 pts	el verano; junio, julio, agosto; hace mucho calor
	40 pts	el invierno; diciembre, enero, febrero; nieva
	50 pts	la primavera; marzo, abril, mayo; hace buen tiempo
Verbos:	**10 pts**	son; son
	20 pts	estamos; están
	30 pts	está; es
	40 pts	está
	50 pts	es; es
Gramática:	**10 pts**	Pepe tiene **más** cuadernos **que** Lola.
	20 pts	Ana tiene **menos** dinero **que** Eva.
	30 pts	Tito es **más** bajo **que** Luis.
	40 pts	Inés tiene **tantos** lápices **como** Ceci.
	50 pts	Mi tía lee **tanto como** mamá.
Traducción:	**10 pts**	El estante está a la izquierda del escritorio.
	20 pts	La capital está cerca de la playa.
	30 pts	La casa del perro está afuera, cerca del garaje.
	40 pts	Los calcetines sucios están debajo de la cama, al lado de los zapatos.
	50 pts	Esta noche voy a celebrar mi cumpleaños lejos de mi familia.

Student Supplements

Listening Comprehension Program CD, **Capítulo 6** (**Paso 1: Vocabulario:** word lists)

Workbook/Laboratory Manual, **Capítulo 6**

Audio Program CD, **Capítulo 6**

Instructor Resources

Instructor's Manual/IRK: Chapter-by-Chapter Supplementary Materials, **Capítulo 6**

Paso 1: Vocabulario

Paso 2: Gramática

Grammar Section 17

Grammar Section 18

Enfoque cultural

Paso 3: Gramática

Grammar Section 19

En los Estados Unidos y el Canadá...

Paso 4: Un paso más

Videoteca

Games and Activities

Instructor's Manual/IRK: Video Activities and Related Materials

A primera vista

A segunda vista

Answers to Video Activities

Videoscripts

Audioscript, **Capítulo 6**

Transparencies 41–45

Testing Program, **Capítulo 6**

Multimedia Resources

Online Learning Center

Electronic Workbook/Laboratory Manual

Video, **Capítulo 6** (cue 37:30)

En contexto (1:44)

Minidramas (3:53)

Enfoque cultural: Panamá (1:00)

Student CD-ROM, **Capítulo 6**

Electronic Language Tutor, **Capítulo 6** (**Vocabulario, Gramática**)

Paso 1: Vocabulario

LA COMIDA

Preparation: It's helpful to have pictures of food items large enough to see easily. As you say each new target vocabulary item, write it on the board. As with family members, present foods a few at a time by food groups, check comprehension, present another group, check, and so forth.

Sample Passage: **Hoy vamos a hablar de la comida. La palabra *comida* se relaciona con la palabra *comer.*** (Write both words.) ***Comer* es la acción; la *comida* es el objeto de la acción. Entonces, ¡Ud. come comida! Hay varios grupos importantes de comida.** (Write each category name as you introduce those items.) **Primero, las carnes. ¿Qué es una carne? Bueno, el jamón es carne. El jamón viene del cerdo** (draw pig with curly tail). **El jamón es muy popular en los sándwiches. También hay chuletas de cerdo** (draw a chop). **Otra clase de carne es el bistec.** (And so forth.)

Quick Comprehension Check: Sample items.

¿Cierto o falso?

1. **El bistec viene del cerdo.**
2. **El bistec es más caro que la hamburguesa.**
3. **Son populares los sándwiches de jamón.**

¿Cuál es correcto?

1. **En Nebraska, ¿sirven mucho el bistec o muchos mariscos frescos?**
2. **¿Cuál es más barata, la hamburguesa o la langosta?**
3. **¿Se usa *Shake 'n' Bake* con los mariscos o con el pollo?**

Suggestions:

- Work with half of the vocabulary one day (up to and including **Otras verduras**) and the other half on the second day.
- Use magazine clippings or other visuals to present words from the vocabulary. Model pronunciation and ask **sí/no** questions.
- Have students complete the following sentences: 1. **Los niños beben ______.** 2. **Se comen ______ y ______ en McDonald's.** 3. **Con el desayuno se bebe ______.** 4. **Los conejos** (draw on the board) **comen ______.** 5. **Un almuerzo sencillo incluye sopa y ______.** 6. **Generalmente se come ______ para el desayuno.** 7. **Los Oreos son un tipo de ______.**
- Offer students the following optional vocabulary: **el cubierto (el tenedor, la cuchara, el cuchillo, la servilleta, el vaso, la copa, la taza), merendar, la merienda, las uvas, la toronja, el helado de fresa (vainilla, chocolate), los caramelos.**
- Discuss the variety of words for names of food in the Spanish-speaking world. For example: **papas** (L.A.) vs. **patatas** (Sp.), **banana** (L.A.) vs. **plátano** (Sp.) or **guineo** (P. Rico), **frijoles** (L.A.) vs. **judías** (Sp.), **camarones** (L.A.) vs. **gambas** (Sp.), **arvejas** (L.A.) vs. **guisantes** (Sp.), **tortilla** (flat corn meal or flour pancake, L.A.) vs. **tortilla** (potato and onion omelet, Sp.), **sándwich** (with **pan de molde,** like the U.S. loaf) vs. **bocadillo** (with **pan de barra,** like French bread).

Heritage Speakers: Algunos mexicanos y mexicoamericanos dicen **guajolote** en vez de **pavo.** Pregúnteles a los hispanohablantes de la clase qué otras variaciones usan para referirse a la comida.

Optional Activity: **Preferencias gastronómicas**

Paso 1. Haga una lista de sus tres platos favoritos y de sus tres lugares preferidos para comer en la ciudad donde Ud. vive.

Paso 2. Entreviste (*Interview*) a cinco compañeros de clase para averiguar (*find out*) cuáles son sus platos y lugares favoritos para comer.

MODELO: ¿Cuáles son tus tres lugares favoritos para comer?

Paso 3. Estudie los resultados de su encuesta (*survey*) para averiguar si hay gustos comunes entre todos de la clase. Después, comparta (*share*) con el resto de la clase sus observaciones.

¿QUÉ SABE UD. Y A QUIÉN CONOCE? SABER AND *CONOCER*

Suggestions:

- Model pronunciation and go over the statements in class.
- Ask the following questions to practice usage: 1. **¿Qué restaurantes conoce Ud. muy bien?** 2. **¿Es excelente la comida allí?** 3. **¿Come Ud. allí con frecuencia?** 4. **¿Cuántos platos sabe Ud. preparar?** 5. **¿Cuál es su favorito?**
- Emphasize that the **yo** forms are irregular: **sé** and **conozco.**

Note: The uses of **saber** and **conocer** are not always exact. There exist gray areas (knowing a language, history, or poetry, for example), where only context and the speaker's meaning determine whether **saber** or **conocer** is appropriate.

PERSONAL *A*

Suggestions:

- Illustrate the concept of direct objects by tapping someone on the shoulder, tossing an eraser to a student, breaking a piece of chalk. Ask: Who/What is first affected by the action? → person, eraser, chalk.
- Point out that the direct object answers the question *what?* or *whom?* after the verb.

Notes:

- The personal **a** has been used passively in the text for some time.
- Pets are often treated like people and take a personal **a: Veo un perro allí** but **Veo a Bear, mi perro, allí.**

Preliminary Exercise: Have students say the following in Spanish: 1. *I'm looking at the TV (at María).* 2. *We're listening to the radio (to the professor).* 3. *She's looking for her pen (for her brother).* 4. *They're waiting for the bus (for the doctor).*

Paso 2: Gramática

GRAMMAR SECTION 17

Suggestions:

- Introduce third-person direct object pronouns first. Put a number of objects on the desk (**un libro, una flor, un coche** [toy car]) and model sentences with a noun-to-pronoun transformation: **Miro el libro.** → **Lo miro.**
- Follow a similar sequence with feminine singular nouns, then plural masculine and feminine nouns.
- After presenting third-person object pronouns with visuals, expand their use to include the meaning of *you.* Have students stand up as appropriate: **Yo lo/la veo (a Ud., Roberto,** and so on). **¿Ud. me ve (a mí)?** → **Sí, profesor(a), lo/la veo.**

- Point out that, like the subject pronoun **ellos,** the direct object pronoun **los** can refer to either a masculine group or a combination of masculine and feminine nouns.
- Point out that like direct object nouns, direct object pronouns answer the question *what?* or *whom?* after the verb.
- Stress the position of the object pronoun.
- Use the following question to practice new words. Write a model answer on the board. **Ud. prepara un pastel. ¿Necesita las siguientes cosas? los huevos, la leche, el azúcar** (*sugar*), **el chocolate, la vainilla, la sal, la harina** (*flour*)... Students respond: **Claro que (no) lo necesito.**
- Explicit practice with reflexive verbs used with direct objects is offered in **Práctica C.** Have students note the verbs **despertar, sentar, afeitar, acostar,** and **bañar.**

Reciclado: Review clothing vocabulary. Have students answer the following questions using direct object pronouns. Write a model answer on the board: **Claro que [no] lo necesito. Ud. hace la maleta** (*you are packing*) **para un viaje a Acapulco. ¿Necesita las siguientes cosas? el traje de baño, las sandalias, las gafas de sol, el libro de español, el libro de sicología, los pantalones cortos, las camisetas, la crema bronceadora, el reloj**

Heritage Speakers: En España y en algunos países de Latinoamérica, a veces se usa **le** en vez de **lo.** Este fenómeno se llama **leísmo.** Por ejemplo, **Raquel lo/le conoció en Sevilla. Ella lo/le vio en el tren.** Aunque la mayoría de los españoles prefiere usar **le** en estos casos, la Real Academia Española y la mayoría de los latinoamericanos prefieren el uso de **lo.**

GRAMMAR SECTION 18

Suggestions:

- Act out models for using indefinite and negative words. To show comprehension, have students produce sentences that describe the situations you are setting up. Hints: place one book on one desk, several on another, and none on a third to show some books vs. one book vs. no book (something vs. nothing) or point to a chair where no one is sitting, and so on.
- Alternatively, use the drawing in **Práctica B** on page 160 as a vehicle for introducing these words.
- Offer optional vocabulary: **o... o...** and **ni... ni...**

Note: The plural forms **ningunos/as** are rarely used. As in the example, indefinite questions with plural **algunos/as** frequently require singular **ningún/ninguna** in the negative answers. The exceptions would be nouns usually used in plural in Spanish, for example, **pantalones, medias, vacaciones,** and so on.

PRÁCTICA A

Follow-up: **Ahora imagine las preguntas que hace Lola, según las respuestas de Manolo.**

MODELO: MANOLO: **No, no hay nada interesante en el periódico.**
LOLA: **¿Hay *algo* interesante en el periódico?**

MANOLO:

1. **No, no hay nada interesante en la tele esta noche.**
2. **No, no hay nadie cómico en el programa.**
3. **No, no hay ninguna película buena en el cine esta semana.**
4. **No, no como nunca en la facultad.**
5. **Tampoco almuerzo entre clases.**

ENFOQUE CULTURAL: PANAMÁ

A. **Para completar.** Complete las siguientes oraciones con información en Fíjese.

1. **Panamá** significa ____________________.
2. El sistema de carreteras que va de Alaska a Sudamérica se llama ____________________.
3. Este sistema se interrumpe en la selva ____________________.
4. Es necesario tomar un ____________________ a ____________________ para continuar en la carretera.
5. La primera mujer en asumir la presidencia panameña se llama ____________________.

B. **¿Cierto o falso?** Indique si las siguientes oraciones son ciertas (C) o falsas (F) según la información en Conozca a... Corrija las oraciones falsas.

1. C F La idea de construir un canal a través de (*through*) Panamá es una idea reciente.
2. C F El viaje por el Canal de Panamá es muy corto.
3. C F Antes del canal, era imposible ir del Atlántico al Pacífico.
4. C F El canal está a cargo de los Estados Unidos.

Paso 3: Gramática

GRAMMAR SECTION 19

Note: Commands are strong forms, even when they are formal. They show power or control on the part of the person who says them. Encourage students to use **por favor** whenever possible to soften their requests, particularly until they learn more polite forms. Also make them aware of the importance of tone: a command uttered with a soft tone will not sound like a command but rather communicate a request.

FORMAL COMMAND FORMS

Suggestions:

- Explain that formal command forms use the "opposite" vowel: **-ar → -e; -er/-ir → -a.**
- Present the regular command forms.
- Use the following rapid response drill: **¿Cuál es el mandato formal (Ud.) de ______? cierro, recomiendo, vuelvo, duermo, prefiero, sirvo, pido.**
- Present commands with spelling changes, including these verbs: **tocar, llegar, jugar, almorzar.**
- Present irregular commands. Review irregular **yo** forms. Give students the **Ud.** command form and have students give the infinitive, then give students the infinitive and have them respond with the **Ud.** command form.
- Point out that there are only five irregular commands. The accent is needed on **dé** to distinguish it from the preposition **de,** but not on **den.** Remind students that **esté** and **estén** both require accents.

EN LOS ESTADOS UNIDOS Y EL CANADÁ... GOYA FOODS

Suggestions: Use the Goya Foods website on the Internet in English or in Spanish to develop the following activities.

- Have students browse the recipes in Spanish and pick one they like. They can share the recipe in class, explaining why they chose it.
- Print out some recipes from the website in Spanish, and have students read and review them in class, voting for a favorite. Have students highlight words and phrases they understand and work with a partner to try to understand the rest.
- Have students "shop" at the Goya website and list the products they would buy. Ask if they have tried them before, how would they use the products, and so on.

POSITION OF PRONOUNS WITH FORMAL COMMANDS

Suggestion: Stress the use of written accents in command forms with attached direct object and reflexive pronouns.

Optional Activity: **Una cena en casa.** Los siguientes mandatos describen las acciones posibles cuando se prepara una cena elegante en casa. Póngalos en orden cronológico, del 1 al 8.

a. _______ **Vaya a la tienda para comprar comida y bebidas.**

b. _______ **Abra la puerta cuando lleguen los invitados.**

c. _______ **Prepare algunos platos especiales.**

d. _______ **Haga una lista de invitados.**

e. _______ **Diviértase con sus amigos.**

f. _______ **Ponga** (*Set*) **la mesa.**

g. _______ **Llame a los amigos para invitarlos.**

h. _______ **Póngase ropa elegante.**

Extension: Change the commands to plural forms.

Suggestion: Have students add more possible commands to the list and insert them in the proper order.

Paso 4: Un paso más

VIDEOTECA

MINIDRAMAS

The **Minidramas** vignettes are not referenced in the textbook, but are part of the *¿Qué tal?* Video Program. They also appear on the Video on CD packaged free with the textbook. If you show the **Minidramas** in class or have your students view them as homework, you might find the following suggestions helpful. You can also find blackline master activities in Section X of this Manual for **Minidramas.**

Comprensión:

1. **¿Cuántos platos piden Manolo y Lola?**
2. **¿Qué plato no han pedido** (*have not ordered*) **todavía?**
3. **Antes de pedir la comida, ya** (*already*) **hay vino en la mesa. ¿Es eso lo normal en un restaurante de los Estados Unidos?**

Variation: **Paso 1.** Brainstorm for problems that may occur while dining out. Examples: **no tener dinero; la comida está fría; no hay pan en la mesa; algo está sucio;...**

Optional Vocabulary: **la cuchara** (*spoon*); **la cucharilla** (*teaspoon*); **el cuchillo** (*knife*); **el tenedor** (*fork*).

Paso 2. Students negotiate a problem with the waiter/waitress, played by you for the first exchange. The following cards can be assigned to the participants in the dialogue.

YOU ARE THE WAITER/WAITRESS

There is a problem with your customer. Try to solve it as best you can.

- Be very polite: Be sure to apologize if something goes wrong.
  —Lo siento mucho. —Disculpe.
  —No se preocupe. Ahora mismo le traigo otro/a _______.
- Ask customer if he or she needs anything else before you leave.
  —¿Desea algo más?
- If the problem gets out of hand, tell customer he or she had better speak to your boss.
  —Perdone, pero yo no puedo ayudarle. Es mejor que Ud. hable con el jefe / la jefa.
  —Un momento, por favor. Voy a llamar al jefe / a la jefa.

YOU ARE THE CUSTOMER

You are dining in a restaurant, and there is a problem. Choose among the following.

A. Your soup is cold.
B. The fork is dirty.
C. You forgot your wallet.

- If you choose A or B, ask your waiter to take care of the problem. Be polite but firm.
  —La sopa está fría. Me gusta la sopa muy caliente.
  —Necesito otro tenedor, por favor. Este está sucio.
- If you choose C, try to explain your problem to the waiter as well as you can. Show that you´re very sorry and embarrassed.
  —Lo siento muchísimo.
  —Estoy muy avergonzado/a.

ACTIVIDAD DE DESENLACE: ¿QUÉ VAMOS A COMER?

Activity:	Students will create a skit that takes place in the following places: • a restaurant • a market • a cooking show They will make any necessary props, and bring a prepared food dish (if possible, from a Spanish-speaking country) to share with the class.
Purpose:	To create a context in which students can review and practice the grammar from **Capítulo 6** and vocabulary related to food
Resources:	*¿Qué tal?* textbook, the Internet, and other sources as appropriate
Vocabulary:	Food, drinks, serving and eating utensils, and expressions for commenting on the food
Grammar:	Principal grammatical structures covered in **Capítulo 6** of the textbook, including direct object pronouns, indefinite and negative words, and formal commands
Optional Writing:	Students may wish to distribute copies of the recipe for the dish they bring in.
Recycled Content:	Grammar structures and vocabulary from previous chapters
Duration:	Out-of-class preparation time will vary. In-class time will be approximately 5 minutes per presentation.
Format:	Groups of three to four students

Games and Activities

Capítulo 6 *Juego de tablero: ¿A qué hora vamos a comer? I*

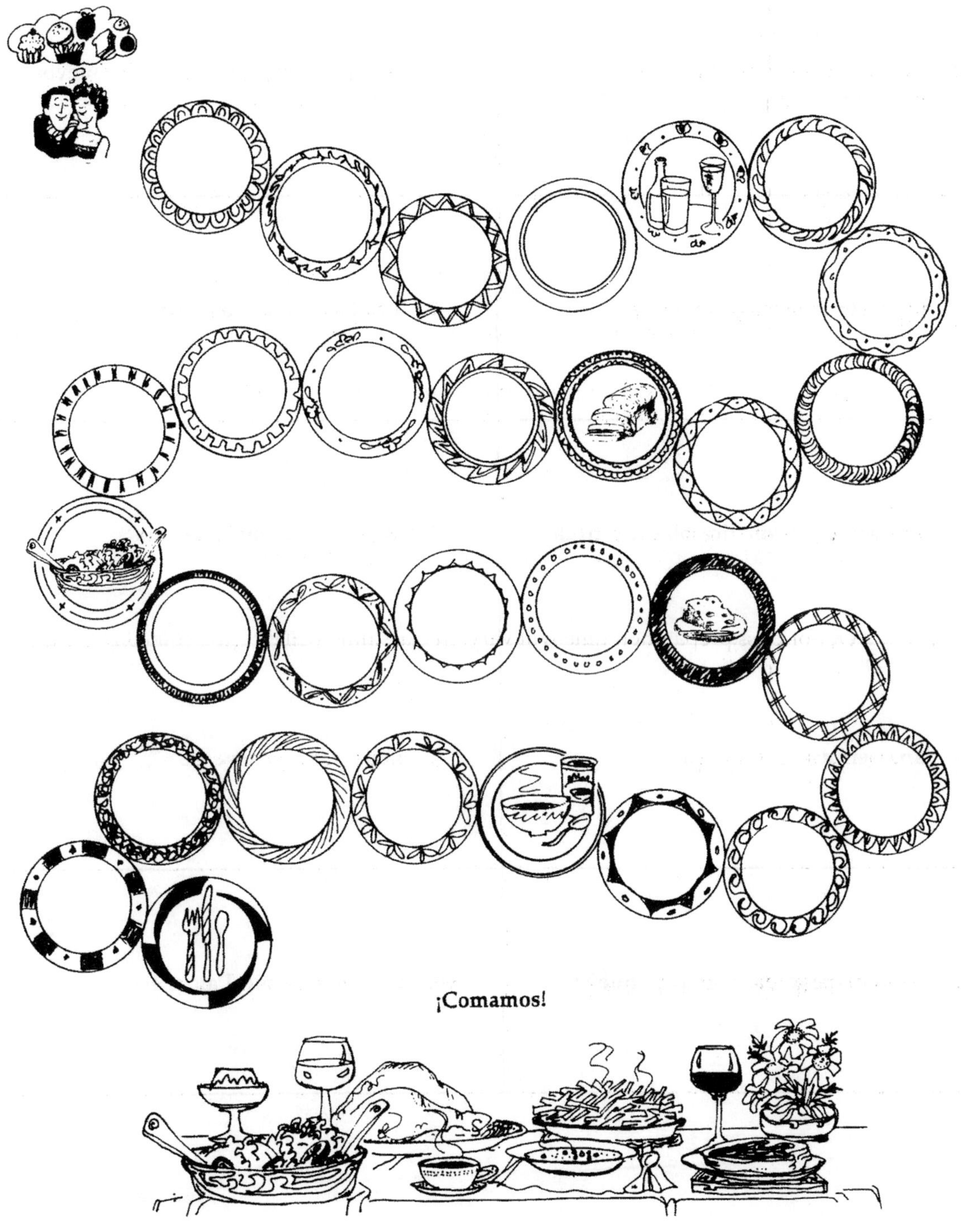

¡Comamos!

1. un líquido caliente que se toma con cuchara (*spoon*)	**6. un postre español hecho de huevos, leche y azúcar**
2. un plato de lechuga y tomate	**7. una carne que no es roja**
3. una bebida alcohólica blanca o tinta	**8. la primera comida del día**
4. una verdura anaranjada	**9. una fruta roja o verde**
5. verduras redondas y muy pequeñas	**10. una fruta tropical amarilla**

11. un líquido de color blanco que se sirve especialmente a los niños	**16. alimento rico en colesterol que tiene el centro amarillo y el resto blanco**
12. la bebida tradicional de los ingleses	**17. la carne roja que por tradición se usa para la barbacoa en los Estados Unidos**
13. se necesita para preparar sándwiches	**18. un plato muy común en la China y en el Japón**
14. un postre muy frío	**19. la comida favorita de los ratones**
15. un postre que se sirve en las fiestas de cumpleaños	**20. una verdura que se come frita con las hamburguesas**

21. **mariscos más pequeños y más baratos que la langosta**	**26.** **el plato tradicional que se sirve para el Día de Gracias en los Estados Unidos**
22. **Coca-Cola, Pepsi-Cola y Sprite**	**27.** **legumbres de color café que se sirven con los platos mexicanos**
23. **un pescado que se usa mucho para hacer sándwiches**	**28.** **el bistec, el jamón y las chuletas de cerdo**
24. **una bebida hecha de frutas o verduras**	**29.** **marisco más grande y más caro que los camarones**
25. **el agua que se vende en botella**	**30.** **merienda (*snack*) dulce que los niños toman con leche después de la escuela**

Answer Key for *Juego de tablero: ¿A qué hora vamos a comer? I*

Capítulo 6

1. **la sopa**
2. **la ensalada**
3. **el vino**
4. **la zanahoria**
5. **las arvejas**
6. **el flan**
7. **el pollo (el pavo)**
8. **el desayuno**
9. **la manzana**
10. **la banana**
11. **la leche**
12. **el té**
13. **el pan**
14. **el helado**
15. **el pastel**
16. **el huevo**
17. **el bistec**
18. **el arroz**
19. **el queso**
20. **la patata (la papa)**
21. **los camarones**
22. **los refrescos**
23. **el atún**
24. **el jugo**
25. **el agua mineral**
26. **el pavo**
27. **los frijoles**
28. **la carne**
29. **la langosta**
30. **las galletas**

Juego de tablero: ¿A qué hora vamos a comer? II

1. Tell your dinner companions that you want to eat something light because you are not hungry.	**5. Explain that you are always on a diet, and you never eat cookies, cake, or ice cream.**
2. Tell your friends that you know how to prepare some Spanish dishes.	**6. Tell the group that Mexican beer is pleasing to you, but you don't drink it frequently.**
3. Ask the waiter if you can pay the bill with a credit card.	**7. Say that you know a good restaurant close to the beach where they serve fish and shellfish.**
4. Say that you have just ordered mineral water because you are very thirsty.	

8. Ask why that waiter does not bring the menu. Say that you want to see it.	**12. Tell the maid to buy apples, oranges, and bananas and prepare a fruit salad. (Use formal commands.)**
9. Ask a classmate if he/she eats lunch in the cafeteria from time to time.	**13. Say that you prefer toast and juice for breakfast, but you have to prepare eggs and ham for the family every Saturday.**
10. Politely tell the waiter to bring more bread and butter. (Use a formal command.)	**14. Say that you feel like eating chicken soup, but they don't have it today.**
11. Politely tell the waiter to serve white wine before dinner and coffee after dessert. (Use a formal command.)	

Answer Key for *Juego de tablero: ¿A qué hora vamos a comer? II*

Capítulo 6

1. **Quiero comer algo ligero porque no tengo hambre.**
2. **Sé preparar algunos platos españoles.**
3. **¿Puedo pagar la cuenta con tarjeta de crédito?**
4. **Acabo de pedir agua mineral porque tengo mucha sed.**
5. **Siempre estoy a dieta y nunca como galletas, pastel ni helado.**
6. **Me gusta la cerveza mexicana, pero no la bebo (tomo) con frecuencia.**
7. **Conozco un buen restaurante cerca de la playa donde sirven pescado y mariscos.**
8. **¿Por qué no trae el menú ese camarero? Quiero verlo.**
9. **¿Almuerzas en la cafetería de vez en cuando?**
10. **Traiga Ud. más pan y mantequilla, por favor.**
11. **Por favor, sirva Ud. vino blanco antes de la cena y café después del postre.**
12. **Por favor, compre Ud. manzanas, naranjas y bananas, y prepare una ensalada de fruta.**
13. **Prefiero pan tostado y jugo para el desayuno, pero tengo que preparar huevos y jamón para la familia todos los sábados.**
14. **Tengo ganas de comer sopa de pollo, pero no la tienen hoy.**

La encuesta dice...

Los estudiantes universitarios prefieren comer...

1. **hamburguesas**
2. **patatas fritas**
3. **sándwiches**
4. **ensaladas**
5. **helado**
6. **pizza**

La encuesta dice...

¿Qué hacemos con las galletas?

1. **Las miramos en el supermercado.**
2. **Las compramos.**
3. **A veces las preparamos en la cocina.**
4. **Las servimos después del almuerzo.**
5. **Las comemos con leche.**
6. **Si no nos gustan, se las damos al perro.**

La encuesta dice...

Un grupo de estudiantes va a hacer un viaje a Madrid. No saben nada de las costumbres ni de la comida de España. ¿Qué consejos les da la profesora de español?

1. **Coman Uds. la comida principal a las dos de la tarde.**
2. **No vayan Uds. a un restaurante de comida rápida.**
3. **Pidan agua mineral u otra bebida embotellada.**
4. **Hablen español con el camarero.**
5. **Pidan Uds. un plato típico de España (paella, gazpacho, flan, etcétera).**
6. **Usen pesetas o una trajeta de crédito para pagar la cuenta.**

	Vocabulario	Verbos	Gramática	Traducción
10 pts		¿Me (tú) ______ por teléfono este fin de semana?	¿Ves algo debajo de la mesa? No,...	I am very thirsty. I want to drink fruit juice.
20 pts		Mamá _______ de preparar chuletas de cerdo.	¿Hay algunos platos ligeros en el menú? No,...	The cookies? Put them on the table beside the cake.
30 pts	el desayuno	Me gusta _____ a cocinar la comida para el Día de Gracias.	¿Siempre pide Ud. el pescado en este restaurante? No,...	Do you see the dirty dishes? Bring them to the kitchen, please.
40 pts	el almuerzo	¿______ Ud. el nombre del dueño?	¿Ellos van a servir los mariscos a alguien? No,...	(The) Lobster? Order it in Mexico. It is very inexpensive there.
50 pts	la cena	Yo _______ a ese camarero, pero no _______ de dónde es.	Ellos no me invitan a cenar. ¿Y Uds.? No,...	Don't go to the store tonight. Wait until tomorrow.

Answer Key for *Arriésgate*

Capítulo 6

Vocabulario:	**10 pts**	la ensalada + 2 ingredientes
	20 pts	el sándwich + 3 ingredientes
	30 pts	(4 cosas que se sirven)
	40 pts	(5 cosas que se sirven)
	50 pts	(5 cosas que se sirven)
		¡OJO! Hay que contestar con palabras diferentes cada vez.
Verbos:	**10 pts**	llamas
	20 pts	acaba
	30 pts	ayudar
	40 pts	Sabe
	50 pts	conozco; sé
Gramática:	**10 pts**	No, no veo **nada** debajo de la mesa.
	20 pts	No, no hay **ningún** plato ligero en el menú.
	30 pts	No, **nunca lo** pido. (No, **no lo** pido **nunca.**)
	40 pts	No, ellos **no los** van a servir a **nadie.** (No, **no** van a servir**los** a **nadie.**)
	50 pts	**No te (lo, la)** invitamos a cenar **tampoco.**
Traducción:	**10 pts**	Tengo mucha sed. Quiero beber (tomar) jugo de fruta.
	20 pts	¿Las galletas? Póngalas en la mesa, al lado del pastel. (... Pónganlas...)
	30 pts	¿Ve Ud. los platos sucios? Tráigalos a la cocina, por favor. (¿Ven Uds.... ? Tráiganlos...)
	40 pts	¿La langosta? Pídanla en México, es muy barata allí. (... Pídala...)
	50 pts	No vayan Uds. a la tienda esta noche. Esperen hasta mañana. (No vaya Ud.... Espere...)

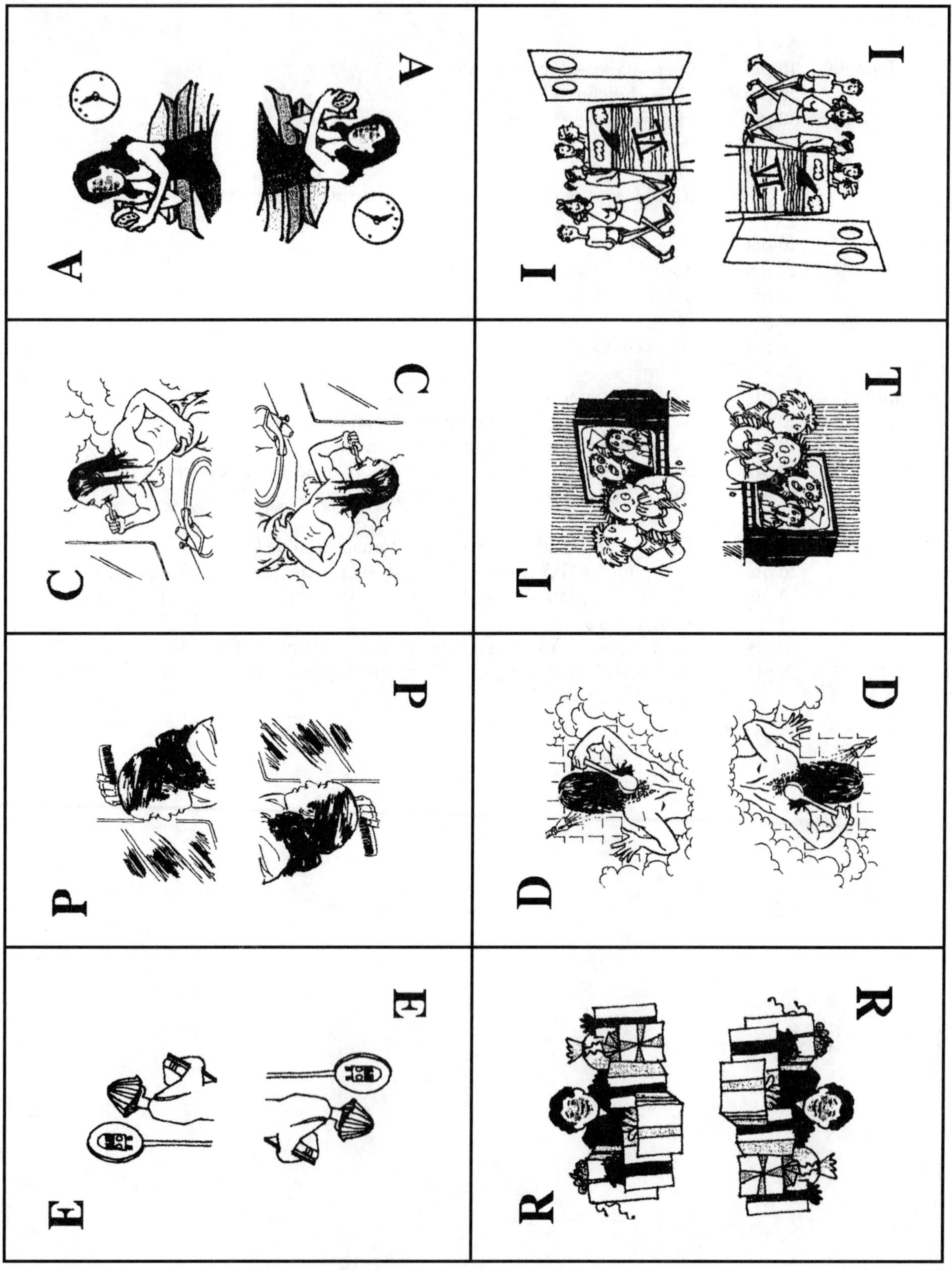
A
A
C
C
P
P
E
E
I
I
T
T
D
D
R
R

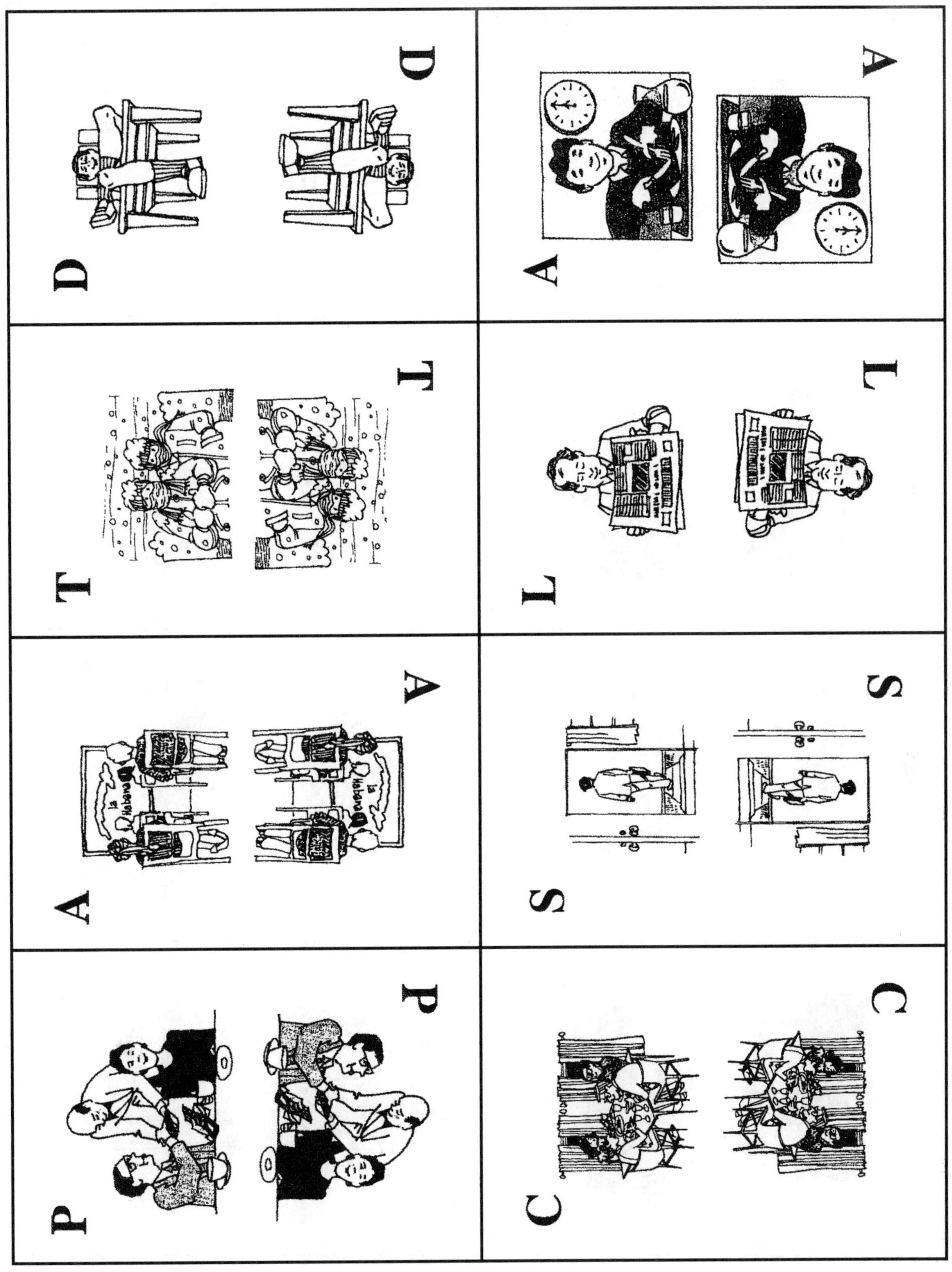
D
T
A
P
A
L
S
C

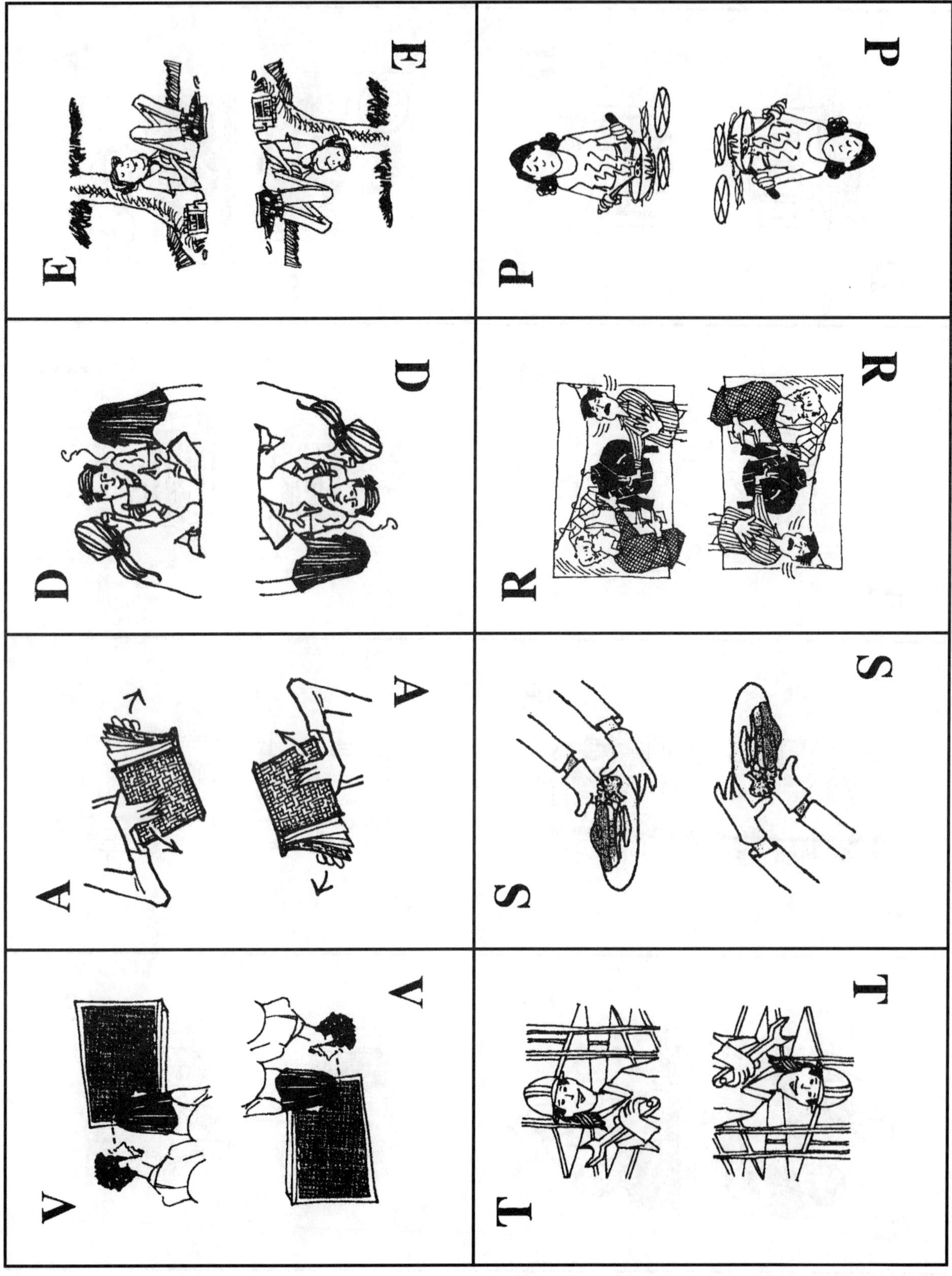
E
D
A
V
P
R
S
T

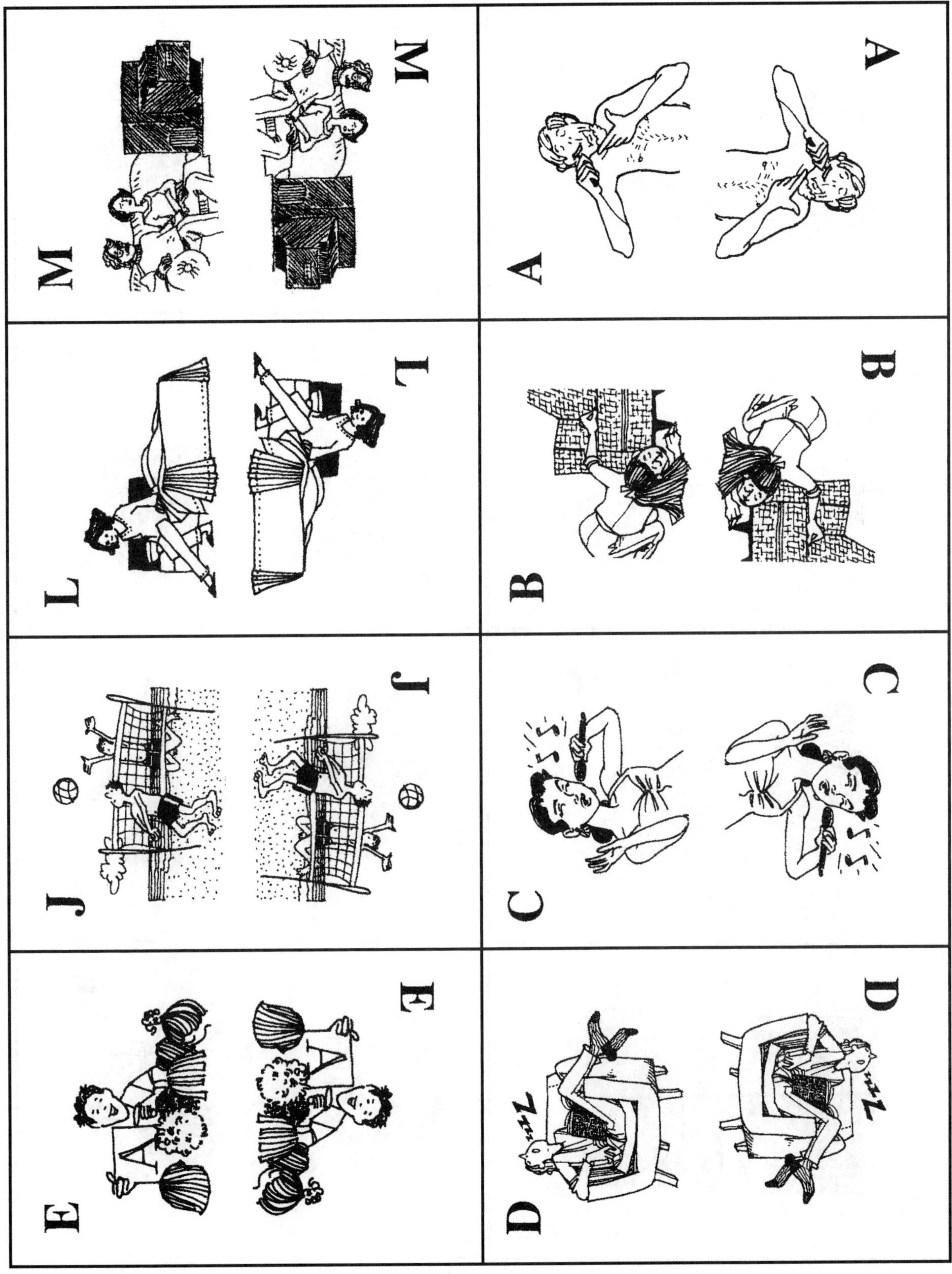
M
M
L
L
J
J
E
E
A
A
B
B
C
C
D
D

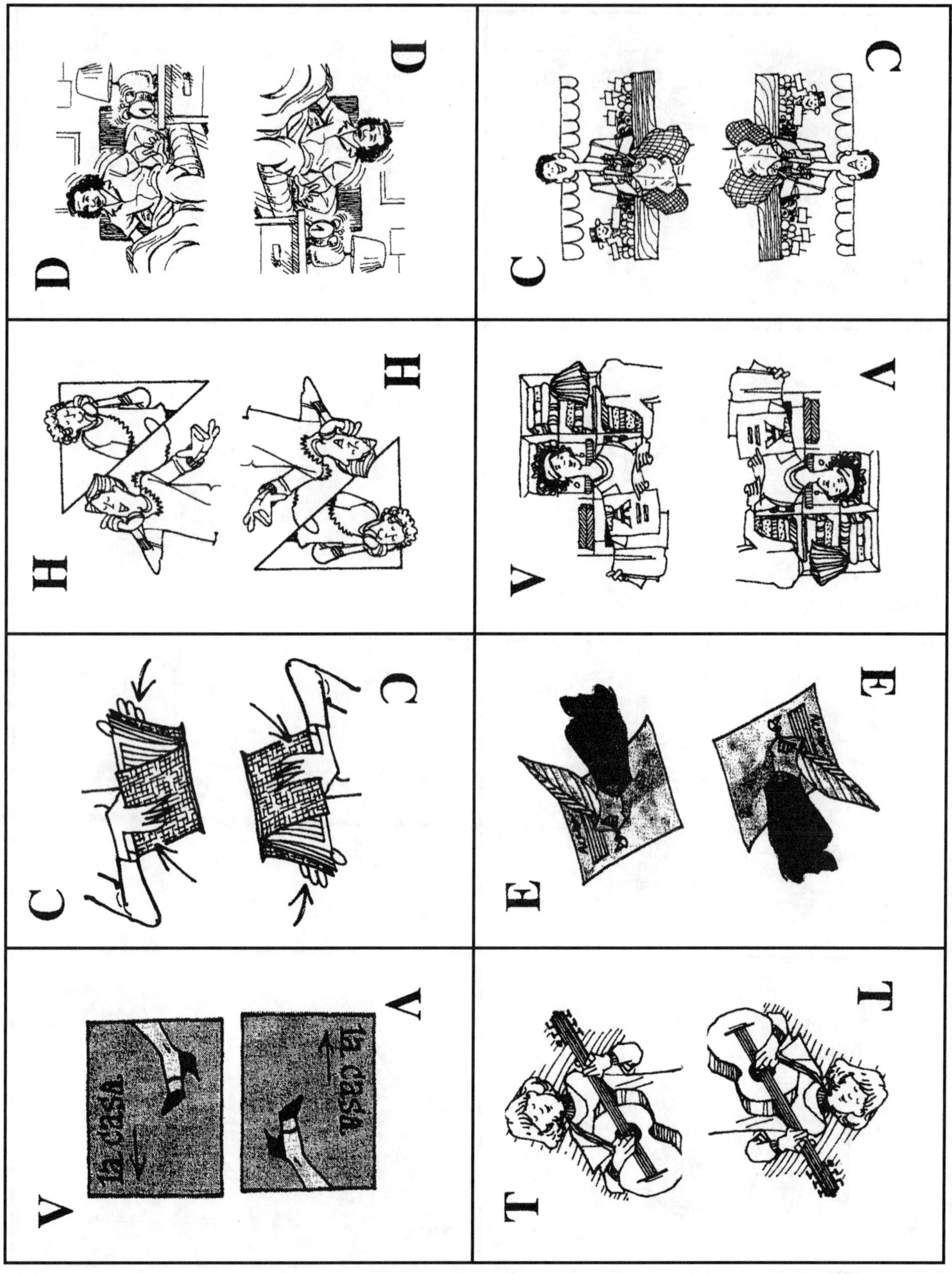
V
la casa
la casa
C
H
D
T
E
V
C

Student Supplements

- Listening Comprehension Program CD, **Capítulo 7** (**Paso 1: Vocabulario:** word lists)
- Workbook/Laboratory Manual, **Capítulo 7**
- Audio Program CD, **Capítulo 7**

Instructor Resources

- Instructor's Manual/IRK: Chapter-by-Chapter Supplementary Materials, **Capítulo 7**
  - **Paso 1: Vocabulario**
  - **Paso 2: Gramática**
    - Grammar Section 20
    - Grammar Section 21
    - **Enfoque cultural**
  - **Paso 3: Gramática**
    - Grammar Section 22
    - **En los Estados Unidos y el Canadá...**
  - **Paso 4: Un paso más**
    - **Videoteca**
    - **A leer**
    - **A escribir**
  - Games and Activities
- Instructor's Manual/IRK: Video Activities and Related Materials
  - **A primera vista**
  - **A segunda vista**
  - Answers to Video Activities
  - Videoscripts
- Audioscript, **Capítulo 7**
- Transparencies 46–50
- Testing Program, **Capítulo 7**

Multimedia Resources

- Online Learning Center
- Electronic Workbook/Laboratory Manual
- Video, **Capítulo 7** (cue 43:05)
  - **En contexto** (2:11)
  - **Minidramas** (2:54)
  - **Enfoque cultural: Honduras, El Salvador** (2:00)
- Student CD-ROM, **Capítulo 7**
- Electronic Language Tutor, **Capítulo 7** (**Vocabulario, Gramática**)

Paso 1: Vocabulario

¡BUEN VIAJE!

Preparation: No materials are necessary, although pictures of any of the items or actions mentioned will facilitate comprehension. Write new target vocabulary on the board as you talk.

Sample Passage: **Hoy vamos a hablar de las vacaciones y los viajes. Para hacer un viaje, Ud. puede manejar un automóvil** (show picture), **tomar un autobús** (picture), **tomar un tren o tomar un avión. Si es un viaje largo, de mucha distancia, ¿es mejor tomar el tren o el avión?**

En el avión hay varias personas importantes. Primero está el piloto. El piloto es muy importante porque conduce el avión. Luego están los asistentes de vuelo. Los asistentes llevan uniforme. Ellos ayudan a los pasajeros y sirven las bebidas y las comidas. Otro nombre para un asistente de vuelo es *camarero*, si es hombre, o *camarera*, si es mujer.

El vuelo es un viaje en avión. Por ejemplo, hay vuelos de Detroit a Nueva York. (Give other examples.) **No se habla de un vuelo en tren, no, sólo hay vuelos en avión. Los vuelos siempre tienen números. El vuelo de Detroit a Cincinnati en la compañía Delta es el vuelo número 83.**

Quick Comprehension Check: Sample items.

1. **¿Quién sirve la comida en el avión, el piloto o el asistente de vuelo?**
2. **Si una persona toma el vuelo número 60, ¿viaja en tren o en avión?**
3. **¿Hay camareros en los autobuses?**

Variation.

¿Probable o improbable?

1. **Los pasajeros sirven las bebidas.**
2. **Los asistentes de vuelo compran un pasaje para el viaje.**
3. **El piloto lleva uniforme.**

¿Posible o imposible?

4. **Unos pasajeros llevan uniforme.**
5. **Hay un vuelo en tren de Filadelfia a Boston.**
6. **Si Ud. no tiene mucho tiempo, se puede comprar el pasaje en el avión.**

Suggestions:

- Model each word then ask questions to contextualize it. 1. ***El aeropuerto:* ¿Es una persona o un lugar? ¿Qué tipo de transporte hay allí, un tren o un avión?** 2. ***La asistente de vuelo:* ¿Es una persona o un lugar? ¿Trabaja en el aeropuerto o en el avión?** 3. ***El vuelo:* ¿Es una persona o una actividad? Generalmente, ¿tienen letras o números los vuelos? ¿Hay vuelos en tren?** 4. ***El boleto:* ¿Es un lugar o un objeto? ¿Se necesitan los boletos sólo para los vuelos en avión?** 5. ***La playa:* ¿Es una persona o un lugar? ¿Qué hacen las personas allí? ¿Toman el sol? ¿Nadan? ¿Qué más hacen?**
- Point out that **vacaciones** is always plural. Also note the meanings of the verbs **bajar** and **subir: bajar** = *to get down* vs. **bajar de** = *to get out of (a vehicle)* and **subir** = *to go up* vs. **subir a** = *to get in/on (a vehicle).* Point out the spelling change for **sacar** in the formal command: **saque.** They will see this change for the preterite as well.
- Have students name items and activities they associate with the following: **¿Qué asocia Ud. con... un avión, una asistente de vuelo, el equipaje, la sala de espera, la sección de fumar, las maletas, un boleto?**

- Offer additional vocabulary for communication: **el/la viajero/a, el cheque de viajero, la cola** (*line, cue*)
- Ask the following questions to personalize and contextualize vocabulary: 1. **¿Quiere Ud. viajar en sus próximas vacaciones? ¿Adónde? ¿Con quién? ¿Cree que es posible que esa persona vaya con Ud.?** 2. **Cuando Ud. viaja en avión, ¿es importante que haga buen tiempo? ¿Le molesta mucho cuando hay demora?** 3. **Cuando mi esposo/a (hijo/a) viaja solo/a, yo siempre le pido que me llame cuando llegue a su destino. ¿Llama Ud. siempre a sus padres (su esposo/a) cuando llega a su destino?**
- Use the impersonal **se** in input or questions to prepare students for the **Nota comunicativa** of this section, for example: **¿Dónde se compran pasajes de avión?** or **En muchos casos se hace cola para facturar el equipaje.**
- Read the following sentences as a **dictado** or as listening comprehension. In either case, have students correct false statements: 1. **Si hay una demora, el avión llega temprano.** 2. **Los pasajeros hacen las maletas después de hacer un viaje.** 3. **El avión está atrasado; no tenemos que esperarlo.** 4. **Hay mucha gente en la sala de espera; no hay ningún asiento desocupado.** 5. **El asistente de vuelo nos sirve la comida durante el vuelo.** 6. **Cuando se hace cola, generalmente es necesario esperar un poco.** 7. **No quiero subir las maletas al avión; voy a facturarlas.** 8. **El maletero es un objeto en que se pone la ropa.** 9. **Los billetes sólo pueden ser de ida y vuelta.** 10. **Al final de un vuelo, se baja del avión; no se sube.**
- Read the following definitions and have students give the corresponding words: 1. **La persona que nos ayuda con el equipaje en la estación de trenes.** 2. **La cosa que se compra antes de hacer un viaje.** 3. **El antónimo de subir a.** 4. **Se va allí cuando se hace un viaje en avión.** 5. **Se va allí cuando se hace un viaje en tren.** 6. **La persona que nos ayuda durante un vuelo.**

Optional Activities: **¡Seamos** (*Let's be*) **lógicos!** ¿Qué va a hacer Ud. en estas situaciones? [The situations in this activity may be used as springboards for mini-role-playing.]

1. **Ud. no tiene mucho dinero. Si tiene que viajar, ¿qué clase de pasaje va a comprar?**
   a. **clase turística**
   b. **primera clase**
   c. **un pasaje en la sección de fumar**
2. **Ud. es una persona muy nerviosa y tiene miedo de viajar en avión. Necesita ir desde Nueva York a Madrid. ¿Qué pide Ud.?**
   a. **una cabina en un barco**
   b. **un vuelo sin escalas**
   c. **un boleta de tren**
3. **Ud. viaja en tren y tiene muchas maletas. Pesan** (*They weigh*) **mucho y no puede cargarlas** (*carry them*). **¿Qué hace Ud.?**
   a. **Compro boletos.**
   b. **Guardo un asiento.**
   c. **Facturo el equipaje.**
4. **Su vuelo está atrasado, pero Ud. está tranquilo/a. ¿Qué dice Ud.** (*do you say*)?
   a. **Señorita, insisto en hablar con el capitán.**
   b. **Una demora más... no importa.**
   c. **Si no salimos dentro de** (*within*) **diez minutos, bajo del avión.**
5. **Ud. quiere pedir dos asientos juntos, uno para Ud., el otro para su amigo/a. Él/Ella tiene alergia a los cigarrillos. ¿Qué pide Ud.?**
   a. **Dos boletos, sección de fumar, por favor.**
   b. **Dos pasajes, sin escala, por favor.**
   c. **Dos asientos, sección de no fumar, por favor.**

Prueba (*Quiz*) **cultural.** ¿Cierto o falso? Corrija (*Correct*) las oraciones falsas.

1. **Se habla español en el Brasil.**
2. **Se comen tacos en México.**
3. **Se puede esquiar en Chile en junio.**
4. **En España a veces se cena a las diez de la noche.**
5. **La paella se prepara con lechuga.**
6. **Se dice «chau» en la Argentina.**
7. **Se habla español en Miami.**
8. **En este país se puede votar a los dieciocho años.**

Paso 2: Gramática

GRAMMAR SECTION 20

INDIRECT OBJECT PRONOUNS

Note: Direct and indirect object pronouns are not used together until *Grammar Section 25* in **Capítulo 8.**

Suggestions:

- Point out that indirect object pronouns have the same form as direct object pronouns except in the third-person singular and plural: **le** and **les.** Gender is not reflected in third-person indirect object pronouns.
- Illustrate the concept of the indirect object by suggesting that a student has asked you to get another student's attention for him/her. Tap the student: I tapped John for Tom. Ask: Who is directly affected? Students should answer: John, the direct object. Ask: Who was indirectly affected (second recipient of the action)? Students should answer: Tom, the indirect object.
- Point out that the use of the seemingly redundant **le(s)** with **a** + noun / pronoun is normal, not the exception. In general, the **le(s)** is obligatory and **a** + noun / pronoun is optional, even if it conveys more information than **le(s).**
- Offer these additional verbs to practice indirect objects: **contar (ue), permitir.**
- Point out that the indirect object for verbs of separation, such as **comprar** and **quitar** is also expressed with **a** in Spanish, whereas in English *from,* not *to* or *for,* is used: **Le quito el bolígrafo al niño** (from the child); **Le compra un periódico al vendedor** (from the salesperson). Native English speakers have a tendency to say **del niño** and **del vendedor.**

DAR AND *DECIR*

Note: The introduction of **dar** and **decir** has been delayed so that they could be used naturally.

Suggestions:

- Point out the irregular **yo** form of **dar.** Also, review the forms of **decir:** the **-g-** in the first-person singular (**yo**) and the **e** → **i** stem-changing pattern.
- Model the differences between **dar** vs. **regalar** and **decir** vs. **hablar (charlar).**

GRAMMAR SECTION 21

CONSTRUCTIONS WITH *GUSTAR*

Note: Spanish constructions with **gustar** are similar to some English ones: *The very idea disgusts me.*

Suggestions:
- Remind students to use the definite article when referring to something in general: *I like tacos.* = **Me gustan *los* tacos.**
- Point out that in Spanish there is no need to use a pronoun to identify the thing or things liked: *I like it.* = **Me gusta.** and *I don't like them.* = **No me gustan.**

WOULD LIKE/WOULDN'T LIKE

Note: **Gustaría** will be used only with infinitives until all forms of the conditional are presented (**Capítulo 18**).

Suggestion: Introduce verbs that are similar to **gustar: encantar, faltar, importar, interesar, parecer, quedar.**

ENFOQUE CULTURAL: HONDURAS Y EL SALVADOR

A. Para completar. Complete las siguientes oraciones con información en ¡Qué interesante!

1. En ____________________ se encuentran ruinas de la civilización ____________________.
2. Otra palabra para **jefe** o **líder** es ____________________.
3. El Volcán de Izalco tuvo (*had*) erupciones constantes por casi (*almost*) ____________________ años.
4. El Volcán de Izalco se conoce como «el faro del Pacífico» porque sirvió de ____________________.
5. El nombre español de Honduras se refiere a (*refers to*) la ____________________ de sus aguas de la costa.

B. Para completar. Complete el siguiente cuadro (*table*) usando la información de los Enfoques culturales de los Capítulos 5 a 7.

El país (Los países) con el mayor número de habitantes:	
El país (Los países) en el/los que se habla otro idioma además del español (mencione el país/los países y el edioma/los idiomas):	
El país con menos habitantes:	

Notes: **Honduras**
- Copán, founded by Mayan groups that reached the western part of Honduras in the fifth century A.D., developed over a period of 350 years. Copán was an important center for astronomy and art, as well as trade. Copán was apparently abandoned at the height of Mayan civilization; the last hieroglyph in the city is dated in the year 800. Although much of the population remained, there is no trace of the artists and priest astronomer/mathematicians who were previously so active.

- Much of Honduras has always been underdeveloped, due to geography and topography, as well as to historical experience. Honduras' lack of access to good ports and its high central mountains have kept the country isolated. Additionally, the repeated intervention by outsiders in the country's political and economic life have kept Hondurans from seeking out strong external ties. The United Fruit Company and the Standard Fruit Company, for example, were powerful political forces in the country during the first part of the twentieth century.
- The Peace Corps' presence in Honduras in the early 1960s was the largest in the world. Presently there are approximately 200 volunteers in country.

El Salvador

- Spain established its first settlements in El Salvador in 1524, and the country remained a colony until 1821, when it declared its independence. For two years after that, it was part of the Mexican Empire and then formed part of the Central American Federation, along with other Central American countries.
- Poor economic conditions and the failure of land reform plans of the 1970s resulted in guerrilla warfare and a 12-year civil war, which lasted until 1992.

Paso 3: Gramática

GRAMMAR SECTION 22

PRETERITE OF REGULAR VERBS

Note: There will be opportunities to practice the preterite and the imperfect in **Capítulos 7–10,** and throughout the rest of the text.

Suggestions:

- Model the pronunciation of regular forms, emphasizing the stress on **yo** and **Ud.** forms.
- Point out that the **nosotros** preterite forms of **-ar** and **-ir** verbs are identical to present tense forms. Context will clarify the meaning.
- Use **llamar, aprender,** and **recibir** in brief conversational exchanges with students, first in a sentence about yourself, then asking **Ud./Uds.** questions of the students.
- Point out the importance of word stress to distinguish some verbal forms, such as **hablo** (*I speak*) vs. **habló** (*he/she/you spoke*); **hable** (*speak,* **Ud.** command) vs. **hablé** (*I spoke*).
- Say the following word pairs and have students identify the preterite form: **hable, hablé; hablo, habló; bailé, baile; busqué, busque; estudio, estudió; tomó, tomo.**
- Say the following verbs and have students give the corresponding subject pronoun. Singular forms: **pregunté, bajó, ayudaste, fumé, llamé, anunció, mandaste, bebió, aprendí, comiste, contesté, ayudó.** Plural forms: **escuchamos, terminaron, mirasteis, estudiamos, bailaron, regresaron, pagamos, bebieron, comimos, aprendisteis.**
- Say the following verbs and have students tell whether each could be present, past, or both: **miró, mandé, escuché, escucha, escribimos, fumaste, bebió, ayudamos, vive, volvió, creo, empiezan, leyó, pagáis, buscaste.**
- Say the following verbs and have students tell whether each is a command or a form of the preterite: **estudie, estudié, fumé, fumen, ayudé, busque, leyó, hablé, pagué, lleve, decidí.**

- Point out that no written accent is needed for the **yo** and **Ud.** forms of **ver** because they are single syllables: **vi, vio.** Other single-syllable forms also will not require an accent (**dar, ir, ser**).
- Write some formal commands using **-gar, -car,** and **-zar** verbs on the board (**toque, llegue, comience**) to emphasize that these are the same spelling changes they use in the preterite.

IRREGULAR PRETERITE FORMS

Suggestions:

- Present some sentences using the preterite of **ser** and **ir** to show that context clarifies the meaning.
- Remind students that single-syllable forms such as the **yo** and **Ud.** forms of **dar** and **ver** do not require an accent: **di, dio; vi, vio.**

Optional Activities:

Un semestre en México. Cuente la siguiente historia desde el punto de vista de la persona indicada, usando el pretérito de los verbos.

1. **(yo) pasar un semestre an México**
2. **mis padres: pagarme el vuelo...**
3. **...pero (yo) trabajar para ganar el dinero para la matrícula y los otros gastos** (*expenses*)
4. **vivir con una familia mexicana encantadora** (*enchanting*)
5. **aprendar mucho sobre la vida y la cultura mexicanas**
6. **visitar muchos sitios de interés turístico e histórico**
7. **mis amigos: escribirme muchas cartas**
8. **(yo) mandarles muchas tarjetas postales**
9. **comprarles recuerdos** (*souvenirs*) **a todos**
10. **volver a los Estados Unidos al final de agosto**

Suggestions for Optional Activity:

- Vary the subject of items as appropriate.
- Have students read through the list before starting the activity.
- Read the sentences using the present tense, and have students write them as dictation, changing all the verbs to the preterite.

EN LOS ESTADOS UNIDOS Y EL CANADÁ... ELLEN OCHOA, UNA VIAJERA ESPACIAL

Suggestion:

Have students respond to **cierto/falso** statements about Ellen Ochoa.

1. **La Dra. Ochoa es norteamericana.**
2. **Tiene su doctorado en astrofísica de la Universidad de Stanford.**
3. **Es la única mujer hispana astronauta.**
4. **Hay unos veinte astronautas hispanos en NASA.**

Have students look up the biographies of different Hispanic astronauts at the NASA website. They can work in pairs to look up different astronauts, and give brief presentations in Spanish about each one.

Paso 4: Un paso más

VIDEOTECA

MINIDRAMAS

The **Minidramas** vignettes are not referenced in the textbook, but are part of the *¿Qué tal?* Video Program. They also appear on the Video on CD packaged free with the textbook. If you show the **Minidramas** in class or have your students view them as homework, you might find the following suggestions helpful. You can also find blackline master activities in Section X of this Manual for **Minidramas.**

Comprensión:
1. **¿Adónde desea ir Elisa?**
2. **¿Cómo va a llegar allí?**
3. **¿Cuánto tiempo va a pasar allí?**
4. **¿Cuánto cuesta un boleto de ida y vuelta?**

A LEER

Note: San Miguel de Allende, a colonial Mexican town nestled in a beautiful valley, is a national monument, which has allowed the town to preserve its character, beautiful Spanish architecture, and cobblestone streets from the colonial period. The charm and pleasant climate have attracted many visitors, who sometimes become permanent residents. San Miguel de Allende, population 50,000, is a center of intellectual and artistic life. Its schools and universities, which teach painting, sculpture, music, literature, language, and drama, attract many artists.

Suggestions: Encourage students to look for websites where they can listen to samples of **mariachi** music. Have students search the Internet for information on assigned areas or topics related to Mexico (Chiapas, Jalisco, Pacific Coast, Caribbean, or pyramids, pottery, indigenous languages). Have them make oral/visual presentations based on their findings.

Suggestions: **Estrategia.** Do in class the day you assign the reading as homework. Bring in titles of articles from several different magazines and have students match each article with the magazine it came from. This will further demonstrate how we associate certain types of feature with specific magazines.

Optional: **Comprensión B.** Have students write a short statement about which place mentioned in the article they would like to visit and why. Then read the statements without identifying the authors; the class must try to determine who wrote each. See how well the class members know each other!

A ESCRIBIR

Suggestion: Have several students read their paragraphs aloud. Ask several comprehension questions about each, encouraging students to listen to one another.

ACTIVIDAD DE DESENLACE: DE TURISTA EN UN PAÍS HISPANOHABLANTE

Activity: Students will research tourist sites in a Spanish-speaking city, region, or country, and create a travelogue for the class.

Purpose:	To create a context in which students can review and practice the grammar from **Capítulo 7** and vocabulary related to vacation and travel
Resources:	*¿Qué tal?* textbook, the Internet, and other sources as appropriate
Vocabulary:	Modes of transport, travel, and vacations
Grammar:	Principal grammatical structures covered in **Capítulo 7** of the textbook, including indirect object pronouns, the preterite, and the use of the verb **gustar** to express likes and dislikes
Recycled Content:	The weather, clothing, interrogatives, and greetings
Duration:	Out-of-class preparation time will vary. In-class time will be approximately five minutes per presentation.
Format:	Groups of three to four students
Comments:	Students may wish to prepare slides, transparencies, posters, or other visuals in the multimedia laboratory and use them as part of their presentation.

Games and Activities

Capítulo 7: Partner A *Crucigrama*

You have the answers for half the puzzle, and your partner has those for the other half. Together you must complete the whole puzzle. You have to give clues to your partner so that he/she can guess the missing words. You *may not use the word itself.* Everything has to be done in Spanish.

Give clues and definitions such as: **Lo que necesitamos cuando...**
El lugar donde...
La persona que...
La cosa que...

Capítulo 7: Partner B

Crucigrama

You have the answers for half the puzzle, and your partner has those for the other half. Together you must complete the whole puzzle. You have to give clues to your partner so that he/she can guess the missing words. You *may not use the word itself.* Everything has to be done in Spanish.

Give clues and definitions such as: **Lo que necesitamos cuando...**
El lugar donde...
La persona que...
La cosa que...

		1 S		2 M		3 B														
	4	A		A		I														
		L		N		L								5 V						
		I		D		6 L								U			7 F			
		D		A		E								8 E			A			
		A		R		T								L			C			
					9 A	E		O			10 E		11 T	O			T			
					V						Q		A			12	U			
		13			I						U		R				R			
					Ó						I		J				A			
14	15 O				N						16 P		E				R			
	C										A		T						17 A	
	É										J		18 A		19 T		20 B		S	
21	A						22				E				R		A		I	
	N														E		R		E	
23	O														N		C		N	
																	O		T	
																			O	

Capítulo 7 *Lotería*

Ud. debe encontrar a una persona que conteste *sí* a las siguientes preguntas.

¿Viajaste a otro país alguna vez?	**¿Te levantaste tarde esta mañana?**	**¿Fuiste al cine el fin de semana pasado?**	**¿Hiciste la tarea anoche?**
¿Jugaste a algún deporte en la escuela secundaria?	**¿Compraste muebles nuevos recientemente?**	**¿Dormiste ocho horas anoche?**	**¿Celebraste tu cumpleaños con tus amigos el año pasado?**
¿Te cepillaste los dientes anoche antes de acostarte?	**¿Nadaste en el océano el verano pasado?**	**¿Leíste el periódico esta mañana?**	**¿Miraste la televisión por más de una hora ayer?**
¿Llegaste a la clase de español a tiempo hoy?	**¿Desayunaste esta mañana antes de salir?**	**¿Pagaste los libros con tarjeta de crédito este semestre?**	**¿Le diste un regalo a alguien para el Día de San Valentín (el 14 de febrero)?**

Arriésgate

<table>
<tr><th></th><th>Vocabulario</th><th>Verbos</th><th>Gramática</th><th>Traducción</th></tr>
<tr><td>10 pts</td><td></td><td></td><td>La asistente de vuelo ______ (ofrecer) ______ bebidas a los pasajeros.</td><td>Did you all check your baggage, or did the porter check it?</td></tr>
<tr><td>20 pts</td><td></td><td></td><td>Yo ______ (mandar) ______ una tarjeta postal de Cancún, profesora.</td><td>They have just announced the arrival of flight 747.</td></tr>
<tr><td>30 pts</td><td></td><td></td><td>Mi tía ______ (prestar) ______ dos maletas a mi hermana y a mí.</td><td>The last time you traveled to Europe, did you buy a first-class ticket?</td></tr>
<tr><td>40 pts</td><td></td><td></td><td>Tu padre y yo (guardar) ______ un puesto en la cola, hijita.</td><td>I didn't get on the bus on time because I took so many photos in the airport.</td></tr>
<tr><td>50 pts</td><td></td><td></td><td>A mí no ______ (gustar) ______ las demoras.</td><td>We are late because the plane made stops in Dallas and Miami.</td></tr>
</table>

Answer Key for *Arriésgate*

Capítulo 7

Vocabulario:	*Ejemplos:*	
	10 pts	(una cosa) el autobús
	20 pts	(dos cosas) las tiendas de campaña, la montaña, la camioneta
	30 pts	(tres cosas) la sala de espera, la sección de no fumar, las maletas
	40 pts	(cuatro cosas) los asistentes de vuelo (los pasajeros, los asientos, la clase turística), el barco, el avión, el tren
	50 pts	(cinco cosas) los pasajeros, los billetes (boletos, pasajes), el aeropuerto, la asistente de vuelo, el avión, la puerta de salida

¡OJO! Los estudiantes deben contestar sin repetir vocabulario ya mencionado.

Verbos:	*¿Qué hicieron estas personas ayer? Ejemplos:*	
	10 pts	(una acción) Los pasajeros subieron al avión.
	20 pts	(dos acciones) Mamá fue de compras ayer. El dependiente le mostró una blusa y una falda.
	30 pts	(tres acciones) Roberto celebró su cumpleaños anoche. Sus amigos le dieron (hicieron) una fiesta sorpresa. Ellos le regalaron muchas cosas bonitas.
	40 pts	(cuatro acciones) Los Sres. Gómez fueron a una agencia de viajes y le hicieron muchas preguntas a la agente de viajes. La agente de viajes les recomendó un viaje a España. Los Sres. Gómez compraron dos boletos para Barcelona.
	50 pts	(cinco acciones) Andrés, Margarita y Luis hicieron cola para el baño. Esperaron por más de veinte minutos. Cuando yo por fin salí, Andrés se cepilló los dientes, Margarita se duchó y Luis se afeitó.

¡OJO! Los estudiantes deben contestar en el pretérito sin repetir verbos ya mencionados.

Gramática:	*Pronombres de complemento indirecto; verbos*	
	10 pts	La asistente de vuelo **les ofrece** (**ofreció**) bebidas a los pasajeros.
	20 pts	Yo **le mando** (**mandé**) una tarjeta postal de Cancún, profesora.
	30 pts	Mi tía **nos presta** (**prestó**) dos maletas a mi hermana y a mí.
	40 pts	Tu padre y yo **te guardamos** (**guardamos**) un puesto en la cola, hijita.
	50 pts	A mí no **me gustan** (**gustaron**) las demoras.
Traducción:	**10 pts**	¿Facturaron Uds. el equipaje o lo facturó el maletero?
	20 pts	Acaban de anunciar la llegada del vuelo 747.
	30 pts	La última vez que viajaste a Europa, ¿compraste un boleto de primera clase?
	40 pts	Yo no subí al autobús a tiempo porque saqué tantas fotos en el aeropuerto.
	50 pts	Estamos atrasados porque el avión hizo escalas en Dallas y Miami.

CAPÍTULO 8 LOS DÍAS FESTIVOS

Student Supplements

Listening Comprehension Program CD, **Capítulo 8** (**Paso 1: Vocabulario:** word lists)

Workbook/Laboratory Manual, **Capítulo 8**

Audio Program CD, **Capítulo 8**

Instructor Resources

Instructor's Manual/IRK: Chapter-by-Chapter Supplementary Materials, **Capítulo 8**

Paso 1: Vocabulario

Paso 2: Gramática

Grammar Section 23

Grammar Section 24

Enfoque cultural

Paso 3: Gramática

Grammar Section 25

En los Estados Unidos y el Canadá...

Un poco de todo

Paso 4: Un paso más

Videoteca

Games and Activities

Instructor's Manual/IRK: Video Activities and Related Materials

A primera vista

A segunda vista

Answers to Video Activities

Videoscripts

Audioscript, **Capítulo 8**

Transparencies 51–55

Testing Program, **Capítulo 8**

Multimedia Resources

Online Learning Center

Electronic Workbook/Laboratory Manual

Video, **Capítulo 8** (cue 72:78)

En contexto (1:32)

Minidramas (4:18)

Enfoque cultural: Cuba (1:00)

Student CD-ROM, **Capítulo 8**

Electronic Language Tutor, **Capítulo 8** (**Vocabulario, Gramática**)

Paso 1: Vocabulario

LOS DÍAS FESTIVOS Y LAS FIESTAS

Suggestions:

- Model vocabulary in short sentences and questions, for example: **Cuando hago una fiesta en mi casa, siempre sirvo entremeses y refrescos. ¿Qué tipo de entremeses le gusta a Ud.? ¿En qué tipo de fiesta se divierte Ud. más?**
- Ask students the following questions about the class: **De los miembros de su clase de español, ¿quién... ?** 1. **¿falta a clase con frecuencia?** 2. **¿nunca falta a clase?** 3. **¿nunca se divierte?** 4. **¿siempre lo pasa bien?**
- When introducing **ser** + **en** + place, review the difference between **ser** (to take place) and **estar** (to be located).
- Bring greeting cards in Spanish to class and have students read the different kinds of expressions used. Students may wish to find examples of Spanish-language virtual greeting cards on the Internet and send them to classmates and friends. Encourage them to design greeting cards of their own and include appropriate sentiments in Spanish.
- Use a calendar and present the holidays month-by-month. Emphasize and explain holidays of importance to Hispanics: **el Cinco de Mayo, el Día de los Reyes Magos.** If you know when your saint's day is, point it out and explain its relevance. At the end, review by asking questions such as **¿Qué día festivo se celebra en febrero? ¿en octubre? ¿en marzo?,** and so on.
- Present vocabulary or draw symbols for particular holidays on the board, for example, **El corazón es un símbolo que todos asociamos con el Día de San Valentín. ¿Qué más asocian Uds. con ese día? ¿el amor? ¿el color rojo? ¿las tarjetas? ¿las flores? ¿Cupido?,** and so on. Have students tell what holidays they associate with the following: **los irlandeses, el champán, los regalos, las flores y los bombones.**
- Have students respond to the following statements with **cierto** or **falso:** 1. **Hoy es el cumpleaños de ______; vamos a darle una fiesta.** 2. **La Noche Vieja se celebra en octubre.** 3. **La Nochebuena viene después de la Navidad.**
- Point out that there are variations of names for some holidays. Although **Navidad** is the word for *Christmas,* you can express *Merry Christmas* as **¡Felices Pascuas!** or **¡Feliz Navidad! Pascua** is used in the singular and plural, and the expression **Felices Pascuas** can express *Happy Holidays* in a sense that includes other religious holidays. Point out the difference between the U.S. secular holiday, Halloween, and the religious holiday **el Día de los Muertos** (November 2).

Point Out:

Holidays vary widely from one country to another in the Hispanic world, sometimes, even from region to region. The following popular Hispanic holidays are not generally celebrated among non-Hispanic groups in the U.S. or Canada.

- **Las Misas de Aguinaldo** (*Christmas gift*) is celebrated in Mexico, El Salvador, and in some states in the U.S. with a high percentage of Mexicans. This holiday is celebrated during the **novena** (nine days before Christmas Eve).
- **La Gritería** is a celebration that occurs in Nicaragua and Colombia on December 7th, the day the Roman Catholic Church recognizes as the eve of the Immaculate Conception. **Gritería** refers to the shouting from door to door of **¿Quién causa tanta alegría? ¡La Concepción de María!**
- **El Velorio** (*Gathering*) **de Reyes** is a solemn tradition among rural people of the west coast of Puerto Rico. It is usually sponsored by a family that has made a **promesa** to the Magi and wishes to thank them for a special blessing they have received. To celebrate an altar is set up in the home on the night of the 5th of January and decorated with flowers and three boughs. Neighbors visit and a trained singer makes up impromptu **décimas,** very formal poems on topical and religious themes.

EMOCIONES Y CONDICIONES

Preparation: Ask students to skim both vocabulary lists and the **Vocabulario útil.** It is helpful to use pictures representing any of the actions, emotions, or conditions, if you have any. Continue to write target vocabulary on the board as you talk.

Sample Passage: **Hoy vamos a hablar de algo muy importante a los estudiantes... ¡las fiestas! También vamos a hablar de los días festivos, los días especiales del año. A veces celebramos los días festivos con fiestas, a veces con tarjetas y regalos y a veces con decoraciones. Muchas veces no trabajamos los días festivos. Un día festivo muy importante para muchas personas es la Navidad, el 25 de diciembre. ¿Cómo celebramos la Navidad? Sí, con decoraciones... y tarjetas... y también con regalos y fiestas. Y ¿qué es la Navidad? ¿Es una fiesta de cumpleaños? Sí, es el cumpleaños de...** (see whether students supply the answer) **el niño Jesús (Cristo, Jesucristo).** (Present other holidays.)

Generalmente, pasamos los días festivos bien... estamos alegres con los amigos, nos divertimos y nos reímos. Sí, lo pasamos bien, estamos contentos. Pero a veces alguien lo pasa mal. Se siente triste, no se divierte, posiblemente llora. ¿Por qué lo pasa mal? ¿Cuándo se pasa mal un día festivo? (Encourage suggestions.) **Sí, cuando está solo, cuando no está con la familia, cuando no está con los amigos. Sí, también cuando tiene problemas con el novio o con la novia...**

Quick Comprehension Check: Sample items. **¿En qué días festivos mandamos tarjetas?**

1. **la Navidad**
2. **el Cuatro de Julio**
3. **el Día de San Valentín**
4. **el cumpleaños**

¿Qué colores asociamos con estos días festivos?

5. **la Pascua Florida**
6. **la Navidad**
7. **el Cuatro de Julio**
8. **el Día de San Patricio**

Variation: **¿Probable o improbable?**

1. **Se siente triste si los amigos se olviden del cumpleaños.**
2. **Se ríe si su novio/a sale con otra persona.**
3. **El profesor se enoja si los estudiantes se portan bien.**

Suggestions:

- Ask students the following questions: 1. **¿Se ríe Ud. con frecuencia? ¿fácilmente? ¿Sonríe fácilmente? Dé un ejemplo de una situación en que Ud. sonríe. ¿Sonríe cuando está nervioso/a? ¿Cuándo no se debe sonreír? ¿Cuándo es necesario sonreír?** 2. **¿Cuándo fue la última vez que Ud. se sintió muy feliz? ¿Qué pasó ese día? ¿Alguien le mandó dinero?** 3. **¿Llora Ud. mucho? ¿Quiénes lloran más, los niños o los adultos? ¿las mujeres o los hombres? ¿En qué situaciones es común que lloren las personas? ¿Es bueno que los hombres no lloren con frecuencia? Cuando alguien llora, ¿qué indica?** 4. **¿Se enoja Ud. fácilmente? ¿Discute con frecuencia con alguien? ¿Se pone contento/a fácilmente? ¿nervioso/a? ¿Cuándo se pone Ud. nervioso/a? ¿durante un examen? ¿cuando habla español? ¿durante una entrevista?** 5. **¿Tiene Ud. hoy todas las cosas necesarias para la clase? ¿Se olvidó de traer algo? ¿Se olvidó alguna vez de un examen?** 6. **¿Recuerda Ud. fácilmente los nombres? ¿los números? ¿los números de teléfono? ¿el vocabulario nuevo? ¿Qué números es muy necesario que uno recuerde?**
- Offer the following optional vocabulary: **enojado/a, enojarse, llegar a ser, hacerse, acordarse de.**
- Point out that the following adjectives are frequently used with **ponerse** (*to become*): **alegre, triste, rojo, contento.** *To become* can also be expressed with reflexive forms: **enojarse, alegrarse, enrojecerse, entristecerse,** and so on. Contrast the following words: **olvidar, olvidarse de, recordar.**

Paso 2: Gramática

GRAMMAR SECTION 23

Suggestions:

- Point out that the third-person singular of irregular forms has no accent on the **-o.** For example, students should not confuse this with the present indicative **yo** form.
- Emphasize and model verbs that change meaning in the preterite.

Preliminary Exercises:

- Write the following sentences on the board and have students complete each sentence with the **yo** form of the most appropriate verb: 1. ______ **un examen ayer. (Tuve)** 2. ______ **enfermo/a la semana pasada. (Estuve)** 3. ______ **a clase todos los días el semestre/trimestre pasado. (Vine)** 4. ______ **hacer todo el trabajo. (No pude)** 5. **Les** ______ **varios chistes a mis amigos. (Dije)** 6. ______ **la radio. (Puse)** 7. ______ **un viaje. (Hice)** 8. ______ **razón. (Tuve)** 9. ______ **los libros a clase. (Traje)**
- Use the following chain drill to practice the preterite forms. **¿Qué pasó en la fiesta del Día del Año Nuevo?** 1. **Todos estuvieron unas horas en casa de Mario. (yo, Raúl, Uds., tú, nosotros, vosotras)** 2. **Muchos trajeron comida y bebidas. (Ud., nosotros, tú, Rosalba, Uds., vosotros)** 3. **Todos dijeron que la fiesta estuvo estupenda. (tú, Anita, Uds., yo, ellas, vosotros)**

Optional Activity:

Hechos históricos. Describa Ud. algunos hechos históricos, usando una palabra o frase de cada grupo. Use el pretérito de los verbos.

en 1957 los rusos	traer	en Valley Forge con sus soldados
en 1969 los estadounidenses	saber	un hombre en la luna
Adán y Eva	conocer	un satélite en el espacio por primera vez
George Washington	decir	«que coman (*let them eat*) pasteles»
los europeos	estar	el significado (*meaning*) de un árbol especial
los aztecas	poner	a Livingston en África
Stanley		el caballo (*horse*) al Nuevo Mundo
María Antonieta		a Hernán Cortés en Tenochtitlán

Note:

- **Marie Antoinette** (1755–1793): At the age of 15, Marie was wed to Louis XVI, heir to the French throne. When the French monarchy fell, the royal family was imprisoned for suspicion of treason. Marie was tried by the Revolutionary Tribunal, convicted of treason, and beheaded on Oct. 16, 1793.
- **Hernán Cortés** (1485–1547): Spanish explorer and conqueror of the Aztec Empire of Mexico, Cortés was born in Medellín, Extremadura. He studied law at the University of Salamanca but cut short his university career in 1501 and decided to try his fortune in the Americas. Head of the Spanish forces, he entered the Aztec capital in 1519.
- **The Aztecs and Tenochtitlán:** The Aztecs built a great empire and developed a complex social, political, and religious structure. Their capital, Tenochtitlán, in central Mexico, was possibly the largest city in the world at the time of the Spanish conquest.
- **Dr. David Livingston** (1813–1873): Scottish explorer and medical missionary in today's Botswana, Africa, who discovered Victoria Falls. While searching for the source of the Nile River, he disappeared.
- **Sir Henry Morton Stanley** (1841–1904): British journalist and explorer. In 1871 he was sent to Africa by the New York *Herald* to find David Livingston. He succeeded.

Suggestion: Talk about recent current events and/or people in the news.

GRAMMAR SECTION 24

Suggestions:

- Emphasize and model the **-ar** and **-er** verbs that do not have stem changes in the preterite (as they do in the present indicative).
- Have students give the third-person singular and plural of the following verbs:
  1. **(ue): contar, recordar, encontrar, jugar, volver, llover** (third-person singular only)
  2. **(ie): empezar, recomendar, cerrar, despertarse, nevar** (third-person singular only)
- Remind students that the second stem change indicated in word lists—**(ie, i)**, **(i, i)**, **(ue, u)**—occurs in the third-person singular and plural of the preterite. These changes only occur in **-ir** verbs. The changes appear in the first- and second-person plural of the subjunctive as well. Model these verbs: ***dormir:*** **durmió, durmieron (durmiendo, durmamos, durmáis),** ***preferir:*** **prefirió, prefirieron (prefiriendo, prefiramos, prefiráis),** ***repetir:*** **repitió, repitieron (repitiendo, repitamos, repitáis).**

PRÁCTICA B

Follow-up: Ask the following questions after completing the activity: 1. **¿Dónde almorzó Ud. ayer? ¿Qué pidió? ¿Quién se lo sirvió? ¿Quién pagó la cuenta? ¿Cuánto dejó Ud. de propina? La última vez que cenó en un restaurante, ¿qué pidió? ¿Prefiere Ud. que otra persona pague en un restaurante elegante?** 2. **¿A qué hora se acostó Ud. anoche? ¿Cuántas horas durmió? ¿Durmió bien? ¿Se sintió descansado/a cuando se despertó? ¿Cómo se vistió esta mañana, elegante o informalmente?** 3. **¿Qué película o programa de televisión lo/la divirtió más el año pasado? ¿Se rió Ud. mucho cuando vio... ? ¿Les gustó también a sus amigos? ¿Qué película quiere ver este mes?**

Optional Activity: **Las historias que todos conocemos.** Cuente algunos detalles de unas historias tradicionales, usando una palabra o frase de cada grupo y el pretérito de los verbos.

la Bella Durmiente (*Sleeping Beauty*)	conseguir	en un baile
el lobo (*wolf*)	perder	encontrar (*to find*) a la mujer misteriosa
Rip Van Winkle	divertirse	(por) muchos años
Romeo	preferir	entrar en la chimenea de los Tres Cochinitos (*Little Pigs*)
la Cenicienta (*Cinderella*)	morirse	por el amor de Julieta
el Príncipe	sentir	hasta que el príncipe la besó (*kissed*)
las hermanastras de la Cenicienta	vestirse	de (*as a*) abuela
	dormir	un zapato
		la envidia (*envy*) de su hermanastra

Suggestions for Optional Activity:

- Start the activity by giving students true/false statements with the characters mentioned. Then let them form their own sentences.
- For homework have each student write six trivia questions on 3×5 index cards. The questions should be in the preterite, with answers on the back. In class divide the students into groups of two to four to form an even number of teams (four teams, six teams, eight teams). Each team gets together to select the ten best questions and to correct the Spanish. The teams should write the selected questions individually, without answers, on 3x5 cards. Have pairs of teams compete against each other by taking turns asking and responding to questions. Members from each team take turns selecting a card from the opposing team and answering the question.
- Have students add their own details when possible. **¡OJO!** Tell them to limit themselves to actions only, not descriptions or background information, which would be expressed in the imperfect.

Note:

- ***Rip Van Winkle:*** Rip Van Winkle, a character in Washington Irving's novel, is a henpecked husband who sleeps for twenty years and wakes as an old man to find his wife dead, his daughter happily married, and America now an independent country.
- ***Romeo and Juliet:*** This tragedy by William Shakespeare was probably written in 1595. It is the story of two feuding noble families (the Capulets and the Montagues) whose children meet and fall in love.
- ***Cinderella:*** Cinderella (**la Cenicienta**) is the heroine of a European folktale, the theme of which appears in numerous stories worldwide. More than 500 versions of the story have been recorded in Europe alone. Its essential features include a youngest daughter who is mistreated by her jealous stepmother and elder stepsisters or a cruel father, the intervention of a supernatural helper on her behalf, and a prince who falls in love with her and marries her. One of the oldest known literary renderings of the theme is a Chinese version recorded in the 9th century A.D.

Optional Activity:

Una entrevista indiscreta

Paso 1. Lea las siguientes preguntas y piense en cómo va a contestarlas. Debe contestar algunas preguntas con información verdadera. Para otras, debe inventar una respuesta.

1. **¿A qué hora se durmió anoche?**
2. **En alguna ocasión, ¿perdió Ud. mucho dinero?**
3. **¿Cuánto dejó de propina** (*tip*) **la última vez que comió en un restaurante?**
4. **Alguna vez, ¿se despidió Ud. de alguien tardísimo?**
5. **¿Se rió alguna vez al oír una noticia** (*piece of news*) **trágica?**
6. **¿Con qué programa de televisión se divirtió mucho el año pasado / la semana pasada... pero se avergüenza** (*you're ashamed*) **de admitirlo?**

Paso 2. Ahora use las preguntas para entrevistar a un compañero / una compañera de clase. Luego Ud. va a decirles a todos algunas de las respuestas de su compañero/a. La clase va a decidir si la información es cierta o falsa.

MODELO:
E1: **¿A qué hora te dormiste anoche?**
E2: **Me dormí a las tres de la mañana... y me levanté a las siete.**
E1: **Alicia se durmió a las tres... y se levantó a las siete.**
CLASE: **No es cierto.**
E2: **¡Sí, es cierto! (Tienes razón. / No es cierto.)**

ENFOQUE CULTURAL: CUBA

A. ¿Cierto o falso? Indique si las siguientes oraciones son ciertas (C) o falsas (F) según la información en ¡Fíjese! y Conozca a... Si la información no se presenta en estas secciones, escoja ND (No lo dice). Corrija las oraciones falsas.

1. C F ND Cuba queda unas 145 millas de Florida.
2. C F ND Cuba obtuvo su independencia de España en 1959.
3. C F ND La tasa de analfabetismo (*illiteracy rate*) en Cuba sobrepasa (*surpasses*) el 95 por ciento.
4. C F ND Cuba dependía de los fondos que recibía de la Unión Soviética.
5. C F ND Nicolás Guillén estudió ciencias naturales en la universidad.

6. C F ND Uno de los temas principales de la poesía de Guillén es la experiencia afro-cubano en los Estados Unidos.

7. C F ND Nicolás Guillén publicó muchas de sus obras en Cuba.

B. Para investigar: Navegando por el Internet (www.cubaweb.cu). En la página principal, en la sección de Arte y Cultura, seleccione **Museos.** Allí hay una lista de museos organizada por las ciudades en las que (*in which*) se encuentran. Escoja dos de los museos que a Ud. le interesen y complete el siguiente cuadro. ¡OJO! Es posible que no se presente toda la información para cada museo. Escriba sus respuestas en español.

Nombre del museo:		
Ciudad en que se encuentra:		
Dirección:		
Horas de operación:		
¿En qué consiste la colección?		
Otros datos:		

Paso 3: Gramática

GRAMMAR SECTION 25

Suggestions:

- Emphasize and model that the indirect object pronoun goes before the direct object pronoun.
- Remind students that most verbs require an accent mark after object pronouns are attached to the end of infinitives, commands, and gerunds

LE(S) → SE

Suggestions:

- Emphasize and model the change of **le(s)** → **se** before **lo/la/los/las.**
- In sentences with both direct and indirect third-person object pronouns, students should focus only on the gender of the direct object pronoun, since indirect object pronouns will always be **se.**
- To emphasize the need for written accents on affirmative commands with pronouns, give the following dictation: **démelo, cómpramelo, pídaselo, tómenselo, dénselo.**

Optional Activity: **En la mesa.** Imagine que Ud. acaba de comer pero todavía tiene hambre. Pida más comida, según el modelo. Fíjese en el uso del tiempo presente como sustituto para el mandato.

MODELO: ensalada → ¿Hay más **ensalada**? ¿Me **la** pasas, por favor?

1. **pan** 2. **tortillas** 3. **tomates** 4. **fruta** 5. **vino** 6. **jamón**

Suggestions:

- Have students toss a ball or toy (or any other small object). Have each student give a command or a sentence about what the recipient should do with the object once he/she gets it. Write the following verbs on the board: **tirar, pasar, traer, dar, llevar.** Model the following sentences to set up the activity: **Désela a la profesora. Tíresela a Manuel. Tráigamela.**
- Tell students that you are supposed to throw a party this evening but that you have the following problems. Have them give you advice to help you out, for example, **No hay refrescos en casa.** → **No se preocupe. Yo se los compro.** 1. **No hay leche en casa.** 2. **No tengo suficiente champán para la fiesta.** 3. **Me olvidé de mandar las invitaciones para la fiesta de cumpleaños.** 4. **No recordé preparar un pastel.**

EN LOS ESTADOS UNIDOS Y EL CANADÁ... EL DÍA DE CÉSAR CHÁVEZ

Note: Senator Richard Polanco, who authored the César Chávez Day legislation, attended Garfield High School in East Los Angeles, the school that became famous for Jaime Escalante and the achievements of his low-income Hispanic students. Jaime Escalante was featured in **En los Estados Unidos y el Canadá... Capítulo 1.**

Point Out: César Chávez was born on March 31, therefore the holiday is always as close to that date as possible.

Suggestion: Ask students short-answer questions about the reading: **¿En qué día se celebra el Día de César Chávez? ¿Quién inició la legislación para declarar el Día de César Chávez? ¿Qué gobernador firmó la legislación? ¿En qué año?** and so on.

UN POCO DE TODO

Optional Activities: **Un día en la vida de...** [Use this as a class activity. Have students narrate in round-robin the progression of a typical day for Antonio. Students should try to keep the narration going at a good pace. You might record the narration or have a volunteer take notes.]

Paso 1. Antonio Sifuentes, el compañero de casa de Diego Gonzáles, es estudiante posgraduado en la UNAM. Los siguientes verbos sirven de base para hacer una descripción de un día típico de la vida de Antonio. Úselos para describir lo que él hizo ayer.

POR LA MAÑANA

despertarse a las siete
levantarse en seguida
ducharse
afeitarse
vestirse
peinarse
desayunar
tomar sólo un café con leche
ir a la universidad
asistir a clases toda la mañana

POR LA TARDE

almorzar con unos amigos en la cafetería
divertirse hablando con ellos
despedirse de ellos
ir a la biblioteca
quedarse allí estudiando hasta las cuatro y media
volver a casa después
ayudar a Diego a preparar la cena

POR LA NOCHE

cenar con Diego y Lupe
querer estudiar por una hora
no poder (estudiar)
mirar la televisión con sus amigos
darles las buenas noches (a sus amigos)
salir a reunirse con otros amigos en un bar
volver a casa a las dos de la mañana
quitarse la ropa
acostarse
leer por cinco minutos para poder dormirse
dormirse

Paso 2. Use los verbos del **Paso 1** para describir lo que Ud. hizo ayer. Cambie los detalles necesarios para dar la información correcta. Añada (*Add*) verbos si es necesario.

Situaciones y reacciones

Paso 1. Imagine que ocurrieron las siguientes situaciones en algún momento en el pasado. ¿Cómo reaccionó Ud.? ¿Sonrió? ¿Lloró? ¿Rió? ¿Se enojó? ¿Se puso triste, contento/a, furioso/a? ¿Qué hizo?

MODELO: Su compañero de cuarto hizo mucho ruido a las cuatro de la mañana. ¿Cómo reaccionó Ud.? →
Me enojé.
(Me puse furiosísimo/a.)
(Salí de casa y fui a dormir en casa de un amigo.)
(Hablé con él).

SITUACIONES

1. El profesor le dijo que no va a haber clase mañana.
2. Ud. rompió el reloj que era de su abuelo.
3. Su hermano perdió el disco compacto que a Ud. más le gusta.
4. Su mejor amigo lo/la llamó a las seis de la mañana el día de su cumpleaños.
5. Nevó muchísimo y Ud. tuvo que hacer un viaje en auto.
6. Ud. recibió el aumento de sueldo (*raise*) más grande de la oficina.

Paso 2. Ahora pregúntele a un compañero / una compañera si se le ocurrieron algunos de esas cosas y cuáles fueron sus reacciones.

Paso 4: Un paso más

VIDEOTECA

MINIDRAMAS

The **Minidramas** vignettes are not referenced in the textbook, but are part of the *¿Qué tal?* Video Program. They also appear on the Video on CD packaged free with the textbook. If you show the **Minidramas** in class or have your students view them as homework, you might find the following suggestions helpful. You can also find blackline master activities in Section X of this Manual for **Minidramas.**

Follow-up:

1. **Busque en el diálogo frases similares a** «See you (soon)».
2. **Haga una lista de otras frases en el diálogo que le parezcan** (*seem to you*) **típicas de las despedidas** (*good-byes*). **¿Son similares a ciertas frases que se dicen en inglés?**
3. **¿Qué otras frases se dicen en inglés cuando uno se despide de amigos o parientes? Su profesor(a) puede enseñarle las frases equivalentes en español.**

Optional Vocabulary: **decir adiós = despedirse** (**de alguien**); **echar de menos/añorar** (*to miss*)

Optional Follow-up: **Preguntas.**

1. **Para Ud., ¿es fácil o difícil despedirse? ¿De quién le es más difícil despedirse?**
2. **¿Recuerda Ud. la despedida más triste de su vida? ¿Por qué fue tan triste?**
3. **¿Llora Ud. fácilmente en las despedidas? ¿Quién de su familia llora más?**

ACTIVIDAD DE DESENLACE: LAS CELEBRACIONES EN EL MUNDO HISPANO

Activity: Students will research a holiday or festival from a Spanish-speaking country and recreate in the classroom some of its activities and traditions.

Purpose: To investigate and discuss holidays and festive traditions in the Spanish-speaking world; to create a context in which students can review and practice the grammar from **Capítulo 8** and vocabulary related to celebrations and feelings

Resources: *¿Qué tal?* textbook, the Internet, and other sources as appropriate

Vocabulary: Festivities and emotions

Grammar: Principal grammatical structures covered in **Capítulo 8** of the textbook, including irregular preterites and stem-changing verbs, and double object pronouns

Optional Writing: Students may include a short paper comparing their own cultural tradition to those of their selected country.

Duration: Out-of-class preparation time will vary. In-class time will be approximately seven minutes per presentation.

Format: Groups of three to four students. One student will present the basic information about the festival and the others will create a dialogue or skit related to its events.

Comments: The chapter's **Nota cultural** and the **A leer** can serve as guides and provide information.

Games and Activities

Capítulo 8 *¿Quién lo tiene?*

¿Quién me presta los lápices?	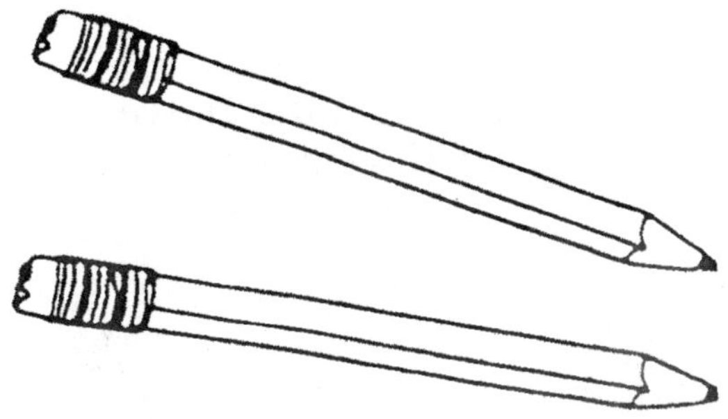
¿Quién me quiere vender la camisa?	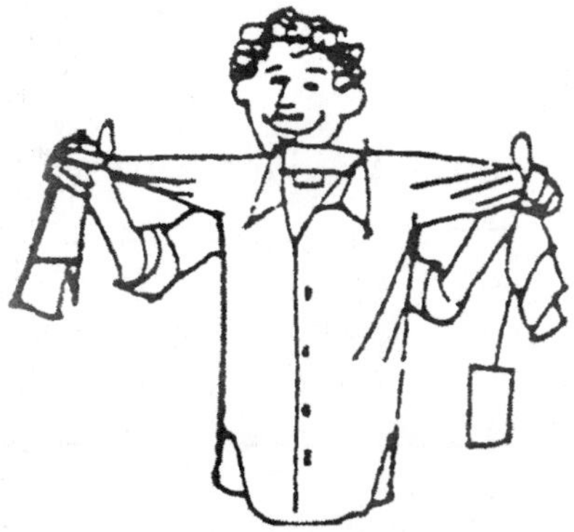
¿Quién me preparó el pastel de cumpleaños?	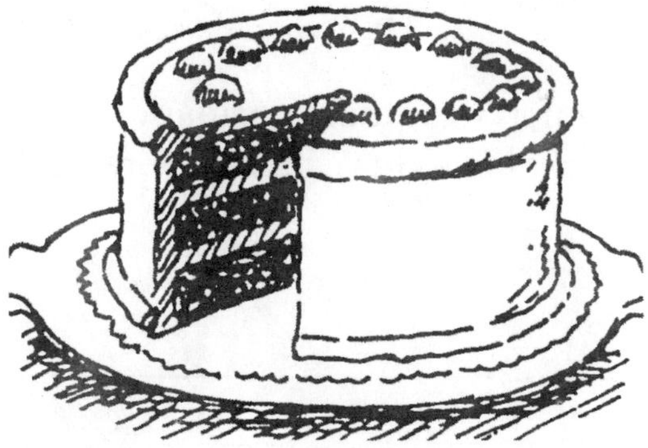
¿Quién me recomienda un buen restaurante italiano?	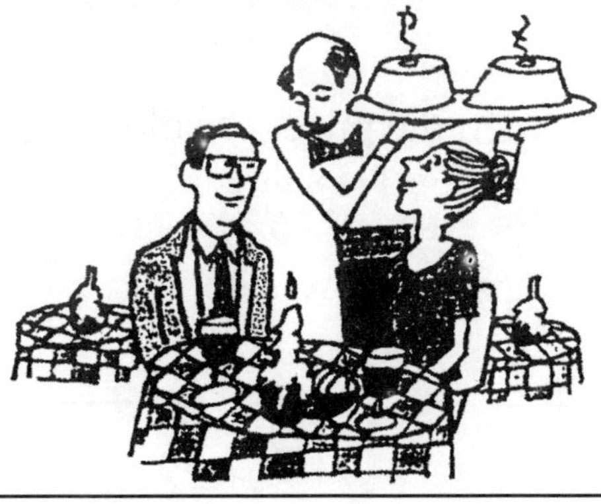

¿Quién me ayuda a buscar la mochila?	
¿Quién me trajo los refrescos?	
¿Quién me quiere cocinar el pavo para el Día de Acción de Gracias?	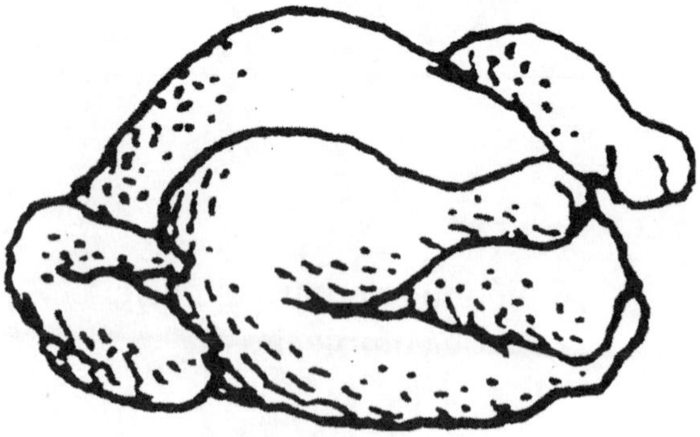
¿Quién me puso los sillones en la sala?	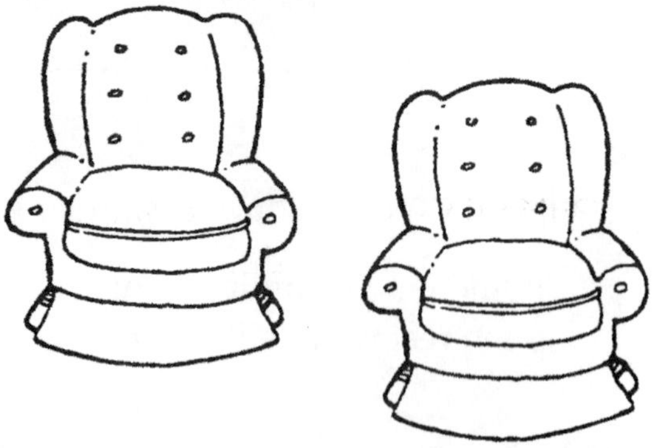

¿Quién me encontró el coche de segunda mano?	
¿Quién insiste en regalarme estos sombreros?	
¿Quién me abre la puerta?	 DAMAS
¿Quién tiene ganas de prepararme la ensalada?	

¿Quién me mandó dinero para mi viaje a Acapulco?	
¿Quién me va a explicar este menú?	
¿Quién me va a dar el sofá viejo?	
¿Quién me ofreció un suéter para el frío?	

Capítulo 8

¿Quién lo tiene?

¿Quién me compra el traje de baño?	
¿Quién me escribió las tarjetas postales?	
¿Quién me puede decir el precio de la alfombra?	
¿Quién me sirvió los entremeses?	

¿Quién me buscó la casa ideal?	
¿Quién me está guardando el asiento?	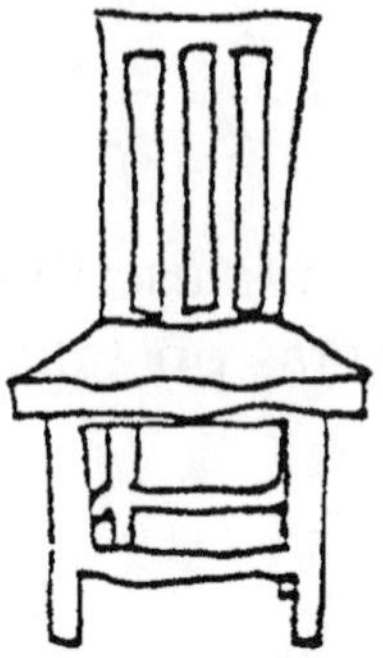
¿Quién me consiguió estas lámparas para mi casa nueva?	
¿Quién me prometió dar un pájaro exótico?	

¿Quién me cuenta lo que dice el periódico?

¿Quién me regaló estas corbatas feas?

¿Quién me está pagando los boletos para el concierto?

¿Quién me consiguió los diccionarios?

¿Quién me sugirió el viaje a España?	
¿Quién me baña el perro?	
¿Quién me va a hacer una fiesta?	
¿Quién me piensa enseñar la playa más bonita de California?	

¿Quién me quiere facturar el equipaje?	
¿Quién me paga la ventana rota?	
¿Quién me toca mi canción favorita en la guitarra?	

Capítulo 8 *Nuestras tradiciones*

Primero conteste cada pregunta. Después busque a una persona que tenga respuestas iguales a las que Ud. dio y escriba su nombre.

MODELO: ***El año pasado yo fui al Desfile de las Rosas el Día del Año Nuevo. ¿Y tú?***

		Yo	**Compañero/a**
1	¿Qué hiciste el Día del Año Nuevo?		
2	¿Qué te regalaron el Día de San Valentín?		
3	¿Adónde fuiste durante las vacaciones de primavera?		
4	¿Cómo celebraste el Cuatro de Julio?		
5	¿Quién sirvió la cena el Día de Acción de Gracias?		
6	¿Con quiénes celebraste tu cumpleaños?		
7	¿Cuántos regalos de Navidad pusiste debajo del árbol?		
8	¿Dónde pasaste la Noche Vieja?		
9	¿Cuál es el día festivo más interesante para ti?		
10	¿Quién te regaló algo bonito el día de tu santo?		

Arriésgate

	Vocabulario	Verbos	Gramática	Traducción
10 pts	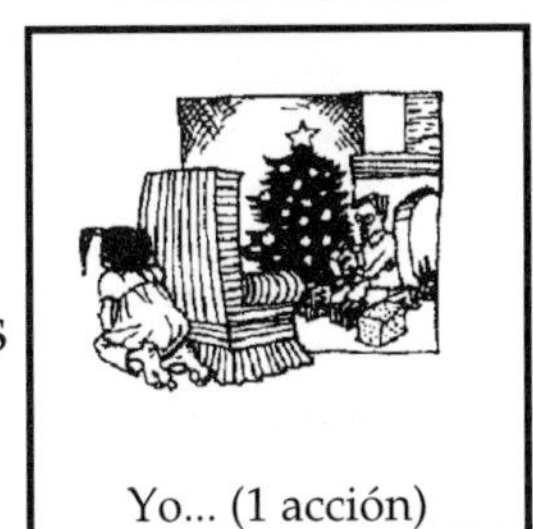 Yo... (1 acción)		Te presté mi libro de texto, ¿verdad? No,...	The hostess served hors d´oeuvres and refreshments, and all the guests had a good time.
20 pts	 Nosotros... (2 acciones)		¿Los abuelos te mandaron esas tarjetas postales? Sí,...	The whole family felt sad and cried when their old pet died.
30 pts	 Los novios... (3 acciones)		¿Le contaste el chiste al profesor? No,...	Last night my friends and I got together and didn´t say goodbye until midnight.
40 pts	 La viuda... (4 acciones)		¿Ud. me regaló la piñata? Sí,...	When Lupe turned 21, we gave her a great surprise party. No one was absent!
50 pts	 Tú... (5 acciones)		¿Uds. nos consiguieron los boletos? Sí,...	The children complained, argued, and behaved badly in the car until their parents got angry with them.

Answer Key for *Arriésgate*

Capítulo 8

Vocabulario:	**10 pts**	**la Nochebuena (la Navidad)** *Ejemplo:* **Yo puse** muchos regalos debajo del árbol.
	20 pts	**el Cuatro de Julio** *Ejemplo:* **Vimos** fuegos artificiales **e hicimos** un *picnic* en el parque.
	30 pts	**el Día de los Enamorados (San Valentín)** *Ejemplo:* Los novios **se dieron** regalos, **se besaron** y **cenaron** en un restaurante elegante.
	40 pts	**el Día de Todos los Santos** y **el Día de los Muertos** *Ejemplo*: La viuda **compró** flores, **visitó** el cementerio, **preparó** una cena grande y **fue** a misa.
	50 pts	**la Noche Vieja** y **el Día del Año Nuevo** *Ejemplo*: **Tú tomaste** champán, **bailaste**, **escuchaste** música, **comiste** entremeses y **te divertiste** mucho.
Verbos:		*¿Qué pasó ayer? Ejemplos:*
	10 pts	Elena **se enfermó.**
	20 pts	A Arturo **se le olvidó** el dinero.
	30 pts	El señor Gómez **se quejó** de la comida
	40 pts	Mamá y el vendedor **discutieron** por media hora.
	50 pts	La familia Ramírez **sonrió.**
Gramática:	**10 pts**	No, no **me lo** prestaste.
	20 pts	Sí, **me las** mandaron.
	30 pts	No, no **se lo** conté.
	40 pts	Sí, **se la** regalé.
	50 pts	Sí, **se los** conseguimos.
Traducción:	**10 pts**	La anfitriona sirvió entremeses y refrescos, y todos los invitados lo pasaron bien (se divirtieron).
	20 pts	Toda la familia se sintió triste y lloró cuando su mascota vieja (se) murió.
	30 pts	Anoche mis amigos y yo nos reunimos y no nos despedimos hasta la medianoche.
	40 pts	Cuando Lupe cumplió (los) ventiún años, le hicimos (dimos) una gran fiesta sorpresa. ¡No faltó nadie!
	50 pts	Los niños se quejaron, discutieron y se portaron mal en el coche hasta que sus padres se enojaron con ellos.

Student Supplements

- Listening Comprehension Program CD, **Capítulo 9** (**Paso 1: Vocabulario:** word lists)
- Workbook/Laboratory Manual, **Capítulo 9**
- Audio Program CD, **Capítulo 9**

Instructor Resources

- Instructor's Manual/IRK: Chapter-by-Chapter Supplementary Materials, **Capítulo 9**
  - **Paso 1: Vocabulario**
    - **Nota comunicativa**
  - **Paso 2: Gramática**
    - Grammar Section 26
    - Grammar Section 27
    - **Enfoque cultural**
  - **Paso 3: Gramática**
    - Grammar Section 28
    - **En los Estados Unidos y el Canadá...**
    - **Un poco de todo**
  - **Paso 4: Un paso más**
    - **Videoteca: Minidramas**
    - **A leer**
    - **A escribir**
  - Games and Activities
- Instructor's Manual/IRK: Video Activities and Related Materials
  - **A primera vista**
  - **A segunda vista**
  - Answers to Video Activities
  - Videoscripts
- Audioscript, **Capítulo 9**
- Transparencies 56–62
- Testing Program, **Capítulo 9**

Multimedia Resources

- Online Learning Center
- Electronic Workbook/Laboratory Manual
- Video, **Capítulo 9** (cue 54:49)
  - **En contexto** (1:59)
  - **Minidramas** (5:02)
  - **Enfoque cultural: Colombia** (1:00)
- Student CD-ROM, **Capítulo 9**
- Electronic Language Tutor, **Capítulo 9** (**Vocabulario, Gramática**)

Paso 1: Vocabulario

PASATIEMPOS, DIVERSIONES Y AFICIONES

Preparation: Ask students to skim the vocabulary before you begin. It is helpful to show pictures of each activity as you mention it, in addition to writing target vocabulary on the board.

Sample Passage: **Hoy vamos a hablar de un tema muy popular entre los estudiantes: el tiempo libre. El tiempo libre es importante para descansar, para divertirse y también para cuidar la casa. Hoy día los estudiantes no tienen mucho tiempo libre. Los profesores no tienen mucho tiempo libre. Todos estamos muy ocupados. Pero, ¿qué hacemos en los ratos libres... los ratos libres, cuando no tenemos clases, cuando no estamos muy ocupados, cuando tenemos tiempo? Primero voy a hablar un poco sobre las actividades físicas. Sabemos que los médicos dicen que el ejercicio físico es importante tanto para el cuerpo** (indicate body) **como para la salud mental** (indicate head). **¿Hacen Uds. mucho ejercicio? Si les gusta estar con los amigos, pueden jugar al fútbol, al basquetbol, al tenis,** (and so forth). **Estos son deportes muy divertidos. Pero, también hay muchas actividades para las personas que prefieren los deportes con menos contacto físico o los deportes que se pueden practicar solo. Por ejemplo, pueden jugar al golf, pasear en bicicleta, correr** (pantomime), **nadar** (pantomime), (and so forth).

Quick Comprehension Check: **¿Sí o no?**

1. **El béisbol requiere la participación de varias personas.**
2. **El ejercicio es importante para la salud mental.**
3. **Si le gusta estar entre mucha gente, la natación es el deporte perfecto.**
4. **¿Dónde se puede escuchar música, en un concierto o en un museo?**
5. **¿Cuál es una actividad cultural, hacer *camping* o ir al teatro?**
6. **¿Dónde se puede ver a su actor favorito, en un bar o en el cine?**

Suggestions:

- Introduce part of the vocabulary by telling students what your plans are for the upcoming weekend, for example, **Bueno, tengo muchos planes para este fin de semana. El viernes pienso ir al teatro con un amigo y después vamos a cenar fuera. El sábado voy a dar un paseo por la mañana, trabajar un poco en mi oficina y jugar al golf por la tarde. Por la noche, voy al cine para ver la nueva película de Almodóvar. Y el domingo creo que voy a descansar, o tal vez visitar un museo y trabajar un poco más.**
- Read statements about what you told the students and have them respond **cierto** or **falso** to check comprehension, for example: 1. **El viernes voy al cine.** 2. **El domingo voy a visitar un museo.** 3. **Voy al cine solo/a.** 4. **El sábado voy a jugar al tenis.** 5. **El domingo tengo que trabajar.** 6. **El sábado voy a dar un paseo.**
- Present additional expressions using magazine clippings of sports and pastimes. Use the images to go back and ask questions such as **¿A qué juega el hombre, al fútbol o al hockey?**
- Have students tell what sport or activity they associate with the following people and things by asking: **¿Con qué deporte o actividad asocia Ud. ...? Arantxa Sánchez Vicario, Sammy Sosa, Shaquille O'Neal, Ricky Martin, el verano, el otoño, el invierno, la primavera, una cita especial, un día de lluvia.**
- Point out the following variations in expressions and additional vocabulary: **hacer camping = hacer acampada; pasear en bicicleta = montar en bicicleta = andar en bicicleta, el atletismo / carreras y saltos** (*track*), **ir de copas** (*to go to the bars*), **el patinaje** (*skating*).

TRABAJANDO EN CASA

Suggestions:

- Offer the following optional vocabulary: **la licuadora** (*blender*), **limpiar toda la casa = limpiar la casa entera, barrer el piso = barrer el suelo.**
- Point out and model the difference between **dejar** and **salir.**
- Have students tell what words or expressions they associate with the following things: **¿Qué palabras o frases asocia Ud. con... ? ¿el aire acondicionado? ¿la cafetera? ¿la estufa? ¿la secadora? ¿el refrigerador? ¿cocinar? ¿limpiar la casa? ¿el congelador? ¿la tostadora?**

Optional:

Read the following information to the class, and use it as a springboard for discussing domestic services.

Las criadas. Muchas familias hispánicas de la clase media y alta tienen una criada que vive en casa. La criada, o «la muchacha del servicio», como la llaman en algunas partes, siempre tiene su propia alcoba y también su propio baño. Ella prepara las comidas, cuida a (*takes care of*) **los niños, lava la ropa y ayuda a mantener la casa limpia. Muchas veces la criada parece ser de la misma familia.**

Si Ud. visita una casa hispánica que tiene una criada, acuérdese de (*remember*) **que ella tiene mucho trabajo. No le cause mucho trabajo extra. Si Ud. va a pasar una o varias noches en la casa, pregúntele a la señora de la casa qué gesto de agradecimiento** (*thanks*) **debe darle a la criada antes de salir. En algunas casas es costumbre dejarle una propina** (*tip*)**; en otras, un regalito. A veces no se le deja nada** (*one doesn't leave her anything*)**, pero siempre se le debe dar las gracias.**

Optional Vocabulary:

Here are some alternative phrases related to household chores and appliances that are used in some parts of the Spanish-speaking world. This vocabulary will not be actively practiced in *¿Qué tal?*

hacer la cama → tender (ie) la cama
lavar los platos → fregar los platos
sacar la basura → tirar la basura
sacudir los muebles → quitar el polvo (literally, *to remove the dust*)
el congelador → la nevera
la estufa → la cocina (**el horno** is generally used for *oven*)
el refrigerador → el frigorífico, la refrigeradora

Suggestion:

Remind students that the ability to express meaning though gestures and circumlocution is important when speaking a second language. Do an item or two yourself to model the task of the first Optional Activity: **Windex es un producto líquido que se usa para limpiar las ventanas; Mr. Coffee es un aparato para hacer café.** Then, to follow up and to practice circumlocution give pairs of students cards with words they have not studied yet. Emphasize that the point, in this case, is to communicate, not to know the word in Spanish. Some possible words: tape, clip, scissors, backgammon, diary, address book, car wash, surge protector plug.

Optional Activities:

Las marcas (*Brand names*)**. ¿Para qué se usan los siguientes productos? Explíqueselo a su amigo Arturo, que acaba de llegar de la Argentina y no conoce las marcas estadounidenses.**

1. Windex
2. Mr. Coffee
3. Endust
4. Glad Bags
5. Joy
6. Cascade
7. Tide
8. Lysol

¿En qué consiste un fin de semana? El concepto del «fin de semana» es diferente para cada individuo según su horario personal... y también según dónde vive y la vida que lleva.

Paso 1. Piense en las siguientes preguntas y organice sus respuestas.

1. **Para Ud., ¿cuándo comienza «oficialmente» el fin de semana? (día y hora)**
2. **¿Qué hace Ud. para celebrar la llegada del fin de semana?**
3. **¿Cuándo termina su fin de semana? (día y hora)**
4. **¿Qué hace, generalmente, los días de su fin de semana?**

Paso 2. Ahora use las mismas preguntas para entrevistar a un compañero / una compañera para saber algo sobre su fin de semana.

Paso 3. Compare las respuestas de todos los compañeros de clase. ¿Son muy variadas sus respuestas?

NOTA COMUNICATIVA

Suggestions:

- Remind students that they know several ways to express obligation: **Tengo que...**, **Necesito...**, **Debo...** Remind them that **tener que** + infinitive is the strongest of the three expressions.
- Ask students the following questions: 1. **¿Qué tiene que hacer Ud. esta tarde? ¿mañana? ¿Tiene que hacer alguna tarea? ¿para qué clase?** 2. **¿Cómo debe ser una persona para ser un buen amigo / una buena amiga (un buen padre / una buena madre; un buen estudiante / una buena estudiante)?** 3. **¿Necesita ir al médico pronto? ¿al dentista? ¿a la oficina de matriculación? ¿a la oficina de su consejero/a?** 4. **En su casa / apartamento, ¿a quién le toca barrer esta semana? ¿ir de compras al supermercado? ¿lavar la ropa?** 5. **Por lo general, en una familia típica ¿a quién le toca lavar la ropa, al esposo o a la esposa? ¿hacer la comida? ¿hacer una barbacoa? ¿arreglar el coche? ¿poner y quitar la mesa?**
- Have students interview each other in order to find out what they have to do (**¿qué tienen que hacer?**), need to do (**¿qué necesitan hacer?**), or should do (**¿qué deben hacer?**) at home or during their free time. Have students report their findings to the class and use follow-up questions to make general observations: **¿Quién tiene que lavar ventanas, tender las camas, poner la mesa?**, and so on.

Paso 2: Gramática

GRAMMAR SECTION 26

Note: The Aztecs dominated central and southern Mexico from the 14th to the 16th centuries through military alliances with other groups. Moctezuma II died in 1520, and the Spanish conquistadors, led by Hernán Cortés, defeated the Aztecs easily in 1521. Their victory was facilitated by the divisions and internal strife among the 38 tributary provinces and the fiercely independent peoples who lived at the fringes of the Aztec Empire.

The name Aztec is derived from a mythical homeland to the north called **Aztlán;** the Aztecs also called themselves the Mexica. Their language belongs to the Nahuatl branch of the Uto-Aztec language family.

FORMS OF THE IMPERFECT

Suggestions:

- Point out that the imperfect is the second of two simple past tenses. This section presents and practices only the imperfect. Grammar 29 of **Capítulo 10** contrasts the two tenses, but some activities before that section will combine the two tenses in controlled situations.
- Use the regular imperfect forms of **trabajar, beber,** and **vivir** in conversational exchanges with students.
- Emphasize that *would* can imply both conditional and habitual actions in the past. Only the latter (habit) is expressed by the imperfect.
- Point out that the **yo** form is identical to the **Ud./él/ella** form. Context will often make the meaning clear, but the subject pronouns are more frequently used with the imperfect forms in order to clarify the meaning.
- Point out that there are no stem changes in the imperfect.
- Present and model the irregular forms of **ir, ser,** and **ver.**

USES OF THE IMPERFECT

Suggestions:

- Emphasize that the preterite and imperfect are both equally "past" tenses. Their use depends on which aspect of a past action the user focuses on (completion or development of an action).
- Have students give the Spanish equivalents for some expressions: *I always used to stay... Every summer we used to go...,* and so on. Vary the subjects in your sentences.
- Emphasize the English "cues" associated with the imperfect: *used to, would* (habitual action), *every day* (*month,* and so on), *was/were ______-ing.*
- Emphasize that **mientras** and **mientras que** indicate simultaneous actions.
- Point out that in the imperfect, unlike in the preterite, **saber, conocer, querer,** and **poder** retain the base meaning of their infinitives. See Grammar 29 for more details.
- Contrast an action in progress and the past progressive. Reenter the contrast between the simple present tense and the present progressive.
- Point out that the imperfect is used to project into the future from a specific point in the past. Contrast: **Va a ser una noche de lluvia. Sabíamos que iba a ser una noche de lluvia.**

PRÁCTICA B

Follow-up: Ask students the following questions after completing the activity: **En la escuela primaria:** 1. **¿Cantaba / Jugaba Ud. mucho en la primaria?** 2. **De niño/a, ¿bebía mucha leche / Coca-Cola? ¿Dormía la siesta? ¿De qué hora a qué hora?** 3. **¿Veía Ud. programas interesantes en la televisión cuando era niño/a? ¿Cuáles le gustaban más?** 4. **¿A qué hora se acostaba Ud. cuando tenía 3 (7, 12) años? ¿Le gustaba acostarse tan temprano / tarde? ¿Leía Ud. a veces en la cama?**

PRÁCTICA C

Follow-up: **Paso 2.** Using verbs in the imperfect, personalize the sequences given. 1. **El semestre/trimestre pasado, ¿venía Ud. a la universidad todos los días? ¿Asistía a todas sus clases? ¿Hacía muchas preguntas?** 2. **En la secundaria, ¿trabajaba Ud. después de las clases? ¿los fines de semana? ¿durante las vacaciones? ¿Dónde? ¿Cómo se llamaba su jefe? ¿Cuántas horas trabajaba por semana?** 3. **De niño/a, ¿dónde vivía Ud.? ¿Llovía mucho allí? ¿Le gustaba el clima?**

GRAMMAR SECTION 27

Suggestions:

- Review the comparative forms and structures before presenting the superlatives. **¿Cómo se dice?** 1. *taller than John* 2. *bigger than an apple* 3. *better than Susie* 4. *easier than Spanish* 5. *older than my grandmother*
- Emphasize the importance of the definite article. Remind students to use **de,** not **en** (for the English *in*).

PRÁCTICA A

Note: ***El Ingenioso Hidalgo Don Quijote de la Mancha*** (*The Ingenious Knight Don Quijote of la Mancha*), better known simply as *Don Quijote,* was written by Miguel de Cervantes Saavedra and is by far the best-known Spanish literary piece of all time. Some critics consider it the first modern novel. It has been translated, fully or in parts, into more than 60 languages. This novel, written and published in two parts (1605 and 1615), was originally conceived as a comic satire against the chivalric romances that were in literary vogue in the 17th century. It is the story of the adventures of Alonso Quijano, who names himself Don Quijote de la Mancha and goes forth to right wrongs and rescue damsels in distress on his nag, Rocinante, and with his shrewd squire, Sancho Panza. The novel presents the conflict between the ideal and the real.

ENFOQUE CULTURAL: COLOMBIA

A. Para contestar. Conteste las siguientes preguntas con la información en ¡Fíjese! y Conozca a...

1. ¿Quién fue el primer presidente de la República de la Gran Colombia?

   ____

2. ¿Quién es Gabriel García Márquez?

   ____

3. ¿En qué año ganó el Premio Nóbel de Literatura?

   ____

4. ¿Cuál es la novela más importante del siglo XX?

   ____

5. ¿Qué es el *realismo mágico?*

   ____

6. ¿Cuáles son tres de los productos importantes colombianos?

   ____

7. ¿De qué siglo datan (*date back to*) las estatuas de piedra de San Agustín?

   ____

8. ¿Qué porcentaje de la población colombiana es de origen africano?

   ____

B. Para investigar: Navegando por el Internet. Visite la página principal de la Embajada de Colombia y de allí seleccione *For Kids.* Complete las siguientes oraciones en español con la información que hay en esa página.

VOCABULARIO ÚTIL:

andino/a Andean	**la orquídea**
el árbol tree	**el/la patriota**
el carbón coal	**el recurso** resource
derramado/a spilled, shed	**el río** river
la lucha fight	**la riqueza** wealth
el océano	**la sangre** blood

1. ¿Qué representan los colores de la bandera (*flag*) colombiana?

   ____

2. La fecha en que Colombia se independizó de España: ____________________

3. La flor nacional: ______________; el árbol nacional: ______________; el animal nacional: ______________

4. Colombia está dividida en ______________ estados y ______________ regiones geográficas.

5. Mencione tres de los productos importantes, aparte de los que se mencionaron en ¡Qué interesante!

   ______________, ______________ y ______________.

Suggestions:

- Ask students to research Simón Bolívar's place in Latin American history, and present short reports to the class. You may wish to have teams of students work together to report on Bolívar's contribution to the status of different countries.
- Have students do further research on the mysterious stone figures, and do presentations on these and other unattributable structures in Latin America, such as the statues on Easter Island.
- Ask students who have read short stories or novels by García Márquez, to talk to the class about them, perhaps describing incidents of magical realism.
- A number of films have been made of García Márquez' short stories and novels, most recently of *El coronel no tiene quien le escriba.* This last film, directed by Mexican Arturo Ripstein, won the Latin American Cinema Award of the Sundance Film Festival 2000 as well as other prizes. You may wish to show this film to the class.
- Have students research the history of magical realism from its beginnings in the works of Alejo Carpentier in Cuba to the present.

Paso 3: Gramática

GRAMMAR SECTION 28

Notes:

- Students have actively used all of the interrogatives in this section. Treat this section as a summary, using it to emphasize variations of the interrogative forms, for example, **¿dónde?** vs. **¿de dónde?** vs. **¿adónde?**
- In Latin America, **¿cuál?** and **¿cuáles?** may be used as adjectives, for example, **¿Cuál libro quieres?** In Spain, they are used only as pronouns.

Suggestions:

- Point out the plural forms of **¿cuál?** and **¿quién?** Point out the difference in meaning in English between **¿cuánto/a?** and **¿cuántos/as?**
- Point out that **¿Cómo?** is used to request repetition or clarification in communicative exchanges.

Optional Activity:

Una encuesta

Paso 1. ¿Cuáles son las preferencias de su compañero/a con respecto a las siguientes categorías? Hágale preguntas, empezándolas con **¿Qué... ?**

MODELO: estaciones del año →
¿Qué estación del año prefieres (entre todas)?

1. tipos de música
2. pasatiempos o deportes
3. programas de televisión
4. materias este semestre/trimestre
5. colores
6. tipos de comida

Paso 2. Ahora use las mismas frases para hacerle preguntas a su compañero/a sobre lo que prefería de niño/a. También trate de (*try to*) sacarle algunos detalles a su compañero/a.

MODELO: estaciones del año →
E1: ¿Qué estación preferías (entre todas) de niño/a?
E2: Prefería el invierno.
E1: ¿Por qué?
E2: Porque me gustaba jugar en la nieve.

EN LOS ESTADOS UNIDOS Y EL CANADÁ... LA IMPRESIONANTE VARIEDAD DE MÚSICA LATINA

Point Out: Although salsa and similar music are styles most associated with Hispanic music in this country, there are many Hispanic classical composers as well. Like the salsa tradition, the classical compositions of Hispanics often reflect different cultures that have contributed to the Hispanic music, including Greek, Roman, medieval, Arabic, and later, Afro-Caribbean traditions. One of the distinguishing elements of some of the compositions especially by the Spanish composers is the use of the guitar as a feature instrument. Juan del Encina, Cristóbal de Morales, Luis de Narváez, Enríquez de Valderrábano, Diego Pisador, Antonio de Cabezón, Diego Ortiz, Francisco Guerrero, Alonso Mudarra, Tomás Luis de Victoria, and Francisco Correa de Arauxo are just a few of the Hispanic classical composers.

Heritage Speakers: Pídales a los hispanohablantes que mencionen o describan la música española y latinoamericana que conozcan, como el flamenco, el tango, la cumbia, la salsa o la música mariachi. Puede pedirles que traigan ejemplos de música grabada a la clase.

UN POCO DE TODO

Optional Activity: **¿De verdad estudia mucho los fines de semana?**

Paso 1. Muchos estudiantes se quejan de tener mucha tarea los fines de semana. Calcule cuántas horas pasó el pasado (*last*) fin de semana con sus libros, con sus amigos... y con su almohada (*pillow*). ¡Diga la verdad!

	LIBROS	AMIGOS	ALMOHADA
el viernes	______	______	______
el sábado	______	______	______
el domingo	______	______	______
TOTAL	______	______	______

Paso 2. Ahora compare sus listas con las de sus compañeros de clase para contestar las siguientes preguntas.

¿Quién es la persona... ?
1. más estudiosa de la clase
2. más parrandera (*party-loving*)
3. más perezosa

Follow-up: **Paso 2.** Try to determine if there is any correlation between students' answers and their majors.

Paso 4: Un paso más

VIDEOTECA

MINIDRAMAS

The **Minidramas** vignettes are not referenced in the textbook, but are part of the *¿Qué tal?* Video Program. They also appear on the Video on CD packaged free with the textbook. If you show the **Minidramas** in class or have your students view them as homework, you might find the following suggestions helpful. You can also find blackline master activities in Section X of this Manual for **Minidramas.**

Comprensión:
1. **¿Quién va a cumplir años?**
2. **¿Quién quiere dar una fiesta?**
3. **¿Qué tipo de fiesta va a ser?**
4. **¿Quién no puede ir a la fiesta?**

Suggestion: Have students brainstorm useful phrases for extending and accepting or declining invitations. Provide some examples.

INVITING
¿Estás libre a... (time)?
¿Te gustaría... (verb) **conmigo / con nosotros?**

ACCEPTING
Claro. Me encantaría.

DECLINING
Lo siento, pero...
Es una lástima, pero...

Me encantaría, pero...
tengo que...
ya tengo planes.
estoy invitado/a a (comer en casa de unos amigos, pasar el día en la playa...).

A LEER

Follow-up: **Comprensión.** Have students research theme parks on the Internet. You might assign different countries. Information on parks in Argentina, Colombia, Mexico, Spain, Uruguay, and Venezuela can be found on the Internet. Brazil also has several theme parks, many of which post information in Spanish. Have them print out the home page of the park and compare the themes, attractions, prices, and so on.

A ESCRIBIR

Follow-up: Have volunteers read their essays to the class. You might also have students work in groups to compare the attractions they included (or did not include) in their essays.

ACTIVIDAD DE DESENLACE: ¡FIESTA!

Activity: Students will plan and hold a party in the classroom or at another venue. Party small-talk will include the past semester's highlights and conversation about changing school traditions, and about sports and cultural events on campus.

Purpose: To create a context in which students can review and practice the grammar from **Capítulo 9** and vocabulary related to leisure time activities

Resources: *¿Qué tal?* textbook, the Internet, and other sources as appropriate

Vocabulary: Sports and leisure, chores

Grammar: Principal grammatical structures covered in **Capítulo 9** of the textbook, including the imperfect, superlatives, and interrogatory words

Duration: Out-of-class preparation time will vary. In-class time will be approximately five minutes per presentation.

Format: Groups of three to four students. One student will present the basic information about the festival and the others will create a dialogue or skit related to its events.

Comments: While in the planning stage, encourage the use of questions to determine the preparatory tasks that students will need to accomplish. Ask: **¿Qué preguntas debemos hacer al planear la fiesta?** Students may suggest such questions as: **¿Qué día vamos a tener la fiesta? ¿Cuáles de ustedes van a limpiar el lugar después de la fiesta?**

Games and Activities

Capítulo 9: Partner A *Crucigrama*

You have the answers for half the puzzle, and your partner has those for the other half. Together you must complete the whole puzzle. You have to give clues to your partner so that he/she can guess the missing words. You *may not use the word itself.* Everything has to be done in Spanish.

Use clues such as: **Lo que usamos para...**
El deporte que...
El lugar donde...
La cosa que...

Capítulo 9: Partner B *Crucigrama*

You have the answers for half the puzzle, and your partner has those for the other half. Together you must complete the whole puzzle. You have to give clues to your partner so that he/she can guess the missing words. You *may not use the word itself.* Everything has to be done in Spanish.

Use clues such as: **Lo que usamos para...**
El deporte que...
El lugar donde...
La cosa que...

	1 L		2 P				3 C										4 C		5 P	
	I		A				O									6	A		E	
	7 M		S				N			8 F							F		L	
	P		E				C			Ú							E		E	
	I		O			9	I			T							T		A	
	A						E			B							E		R	
	R						R			O			10 B				R			
					11 A		T			12 L			A				A			
13			14 L		S		O						S							
			A		P							15	U		16 B		17 E			
			V		I								R		A		S			
	18 E		A		R								A		R		Q			
	S		19 P		A										R		U			
	T		L		D										E		I			
20	U		A		O										R		A			
	F		T		R					21 H				22 C			R			
	A		O		23 A					O				O						
			S							R				R						
										N				R						
24										O			25	E						
														R						

Capítulo 9 *Nuestra niñez*

Primero conteste cada pregunta. Después busque a una persona que tenga respuestas iguales a las que Ud. dio y escriba su nombre.

MODELO: **Cuando yo era niño/a, iba al parque los domingos. ¿Y tú?**

		Yo	**Compañero/a**
1	¿Cuál era tu comida favorita?		
2	¿Dónde preferías jugar con tus amigos?		
3	¿Qué quehaceres domésticos tenías que hacer los sábados? (2)		
4	¿Cómo llegabas a la escuela?		
5	¿A qué hora te acostabas los viernes?		
6	¿Qué perdías con frecuencia?		
7	¿Adónde ibas los domingos?		
8	¿Qué hacías los veranos?		
9	¿Quién se enojaba contigo a menudo?		
10	¿Qué te regalaban el día de tu cumpleaños?		

Arriésgate

	Vocabulario	Verbos	Gramática	Traducción
10 pts		 Nosotros	What is the happiest place on earth?	Every spring my family and I used to clean the entire house.
20 pts			Who is the tallest basketball player in the United States?	As a youth, my mother would make me visit her cousins in Puerto Rico every summer.
30 pts	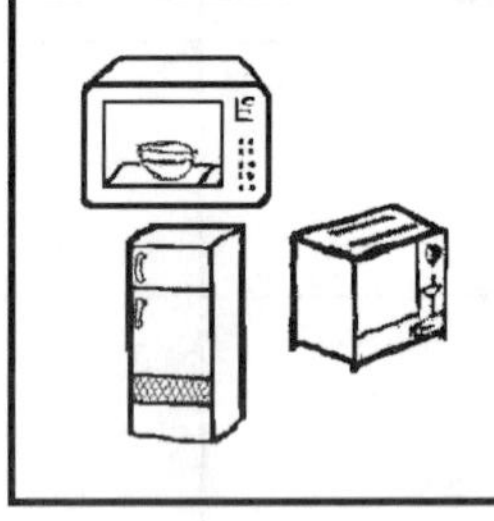	 La profesora	What is the most enjoyable holiday in Mexico?	When you were living in N.Y., did you always ski and skate during your winter vacations?
40 pts		 Yo	What is the most difficult sport in the Olympics (*los Juegos Olímpicos*)?	Mom swept the floor, dusted the furniture, and ironed the clothing every Friday.
50 pts		 Tú	What is the most boring household chore?	In that era, the people would have a picnic or take a walk on Sunday afternoons.

Answer Key for *Arriésgate*

Capítulo 9

Vocabulario:	**10 pts**	la aspiradora
	20 pts	la cafetera, el lavaplatos
	30 pts	el horno de microondas, la tostadora, el refrigerador
	40 pts	sacar la basura, lavar la ropa, jugar al fútbol, andar en bicicleta
	50 pts	jugar a las cartas, practicar la natación (nadar), poner la mesa, lavar las ventanas
Verbos:	*Cuando eran jóvenes, ¿adónde iban y qué hacían estas personas en sus ratos libres?*	
	10 pts	Nosotros íbamos a las montañas; hacíamos *camping*.
	20 pts	Nadia y Guadalupe iban al cine; veían una película.
	30 pts	La profesora iba a las discotecas; se divertía (bailaba) mucho.
	40 pts	Yo iba a la playa; tomaba el sol.
	50 pts	Tú ibas al parque (a las montañas, etcétera); montabas a caballo.
Gramática:	**¡OJO!** *Las respuestas varían, pero los estudiantes deben usar el superlativo.* *Ejemplos:*	
	10 pts	Disneylandia es el lugar más feliz del mundo.
	20 pts	Shaquille O'Neal es el jugador de básquetbol más alto de los Estados Unidos.
	30 pts	El día festivo más divertido de México es el 16 de septiembre, el Día de la Independencia.
	40 pts	El deporte más difícil de los Juegos Olímpicos es la natación.
	50 pts	El quehacer doméstico más aburrido es hacer la cama.
Traducción:	**10 pts**	Todas las primaveras mi familia y yo limpiábamos la casa entera.
	20 pts	De joven, mi madre hacía planes para visitar a sus primos en Puerto Rico todos los veranos.
	30 pts	Cuando tú vivías en Nueva York, ¿siempre esquiabas y patinabas durante tus vacaciones de invierno?
	40 pts	Mamá barría el piso, sacudía los muebles y planchaba la ropa todos los viernes.
	50 pts	En aquella época, la gente hacía un *picnic* o daba un paseo los domingos por la tarde.

CAPÍTULO 10 LA SALUD

Student Supplements

Listening Comprehension Program CD, **Capítulo 10** (**Paso 1: Vocabulario:** word lists)

Workbook/Laboratory Manual, **Capítulo 10**

Audio Program CD, **Capítulo 10**

Instructor Resources

Instructor's Manual/IRK: Chapter-by-Chapter Supplementary Materials, **Capítulo 10**

- **Paso 1: Vocabulario**
- **Paso 2: Gramática**
  - Grammar Section 29
  - **Enfoque cultural**
- **Paso 3: Gramática**
  - Grammar Section 30
  - **En los Estados Unidos y el Canadá...**
  - **Un poco de todo**
- **Paso 4: Un paso más**
  - **Videoteca: Minidramas**
- Games and Activities

Instructor's Manual/IRK: Video Activities and Related Materials

- **A primera vista**
- **A segunda vista**
- Answers to Video Activities
- Videoscripts

Audioscript, **Capítulo 10**

Transparencies 63–66

Testing Program, **Capítulo 10**

Multimedia Resources

Online Learning Center

Electronic Workbook/Laboratory Manual

Video, **Capítulo 10** (cue 1:02:04)

- **En contexto** (1:35)
- **Minidramas** (3:40)
- **Enfoque cultural: Venezuela** (1:00)

Student CD-ROM, **Capítulo 10**

Electronic Language Tutor, **Capítulo 10** (**Vocabulario, Gramática**)

Paso 1: Vocabulario

LA SALUD Y EL BIENESTAR

Suggestions

- Offer optional vocabulary: **la cara y el cuerpo: la barbilla, las cejas, el frente, la mejilla, las muelas, el pecho, las pestañas; actividades: hacer footing, jugar a los bolos (al tenis, al ráquetbol), levantar pesas, montar en bicicleta, nadar.**
- Ask students the following questions to check comprehension and personalize: 1. **¿Hace Ud. algún ejercicio físico? ¿Camina? ¿Corre? ¿Juega al ráquetbol? ¿No hace nada?** 2. **En su opinión, ¿qué tipo de ejercicio es el mejor de todos? ¿Por qué?** 3. **¿Lleva Ud. una vida sana? ¿Qué hace Ud. para cuidarse? ¿Come equilibradamente? ¿Duerme lo suficiente? ¿Practica algún deporte?**
- Read the following Spanish proverbs related to health, medicine, and doctors. Have students tell whether they agree or disagree: 1. **Músculos de Sansón** (*Samson*) **con cerebro de mosquito.** 2. **Si quieres vivir sano, acuéstate y levántate temprano.** 3. **Para enfermedad de años, no hay medicina.** 4. **De médico, poeta y loco, todos tenemos un poco.** 5. **La salud no se compra, no tiene precio.**
- Point out that **sano/a** (*healthy*) is a false cognate.
- Ask students in Spanish how their diets have changed since they began their studies at the university. Younger students' diets tend to change radically once they leave home. Ask students if they eat more junk food than they did when they lived at home and whether or not they follow the recommended guidelines for proper nutrition. Discuss in Spanish what the guidelines are, perhaps drawing a food pyramid or a chart on the board.

Optional Activity:

Para la salud

¿Hace Ud. las siguientes cosas para mantener la salud y el bienestar?

	SÍ	NO
1. comer una dieta equilibrada	☐	☐
2. no comer muchos dulces	☐	☐
3. caminar por lo menos (*at least*) dos millas por día	☐	☐
4. correr	☐	☐
5. hacer ejercicios aeróbicos	☐	☐
6. dormir por lo menos ocho horas por día	☐	☐
7. tomar bebidas alcohólicas en moderación	☐	☐
8. no tomar bebidas alcohólicas en absoluto (*at all*)	☐	☐
9. no fumar ni cigarrillos ni puros (*cigars*)	☐	☐
10. llevar ropa adecuada (abrigo, suéter, etcétera) cuando hace frío	☐	☐

Variation: Have students give the answers in the form of **Ud.** commands.

EN EL CONSULTORIO

Preparation: Ask students to skim the vocabulary before you begin. It is helpful to show pictures of parts of the body, activities, and concepts (such as **mareado**) as you mention them, in addition to writing target vocabulary on the board.

Sample Passage: **Hoy vamos a hablar del cuerpo** (point to the body) **y de la salud física** (inhale and pat your chest with palm of hand).

Para tener buena salud, es necesario comer equilibradamente. Es decir, comer una variedad de comidas como cereales, frutas, verduras... No es bueno comer sólo

pizza o sólo hamburguesas con queso. Hay una relación directa entre la comida y la salud. También es buena idea hacer ejercicio... hacer ejercicio. Muchas personas corren para hacer ejercicio. El correr es bueno para el corazón (point, draw, or show) **y para los pulmones** (point, draw, or show). **El correr es un ejercicio aeróbico. Muchas personas famosas corren. Carl Lewis corre; el presidente de los Estados Unidos corre. Pero, ¡atención! Si Ud. tiene algo malo en el corazón, necesita consultar con el médico. Si el médico cree que Ud. no debe correr, entonces Ud. puede caminar. El caminar es también un buen ejercicio. Muchas personas viejas caminan porque no pueden correr.**

Hay otras cosas que son importantes para la salud (and so forth).

Quick Comprehension Check:

Sample items.

1. **Una persona come hamburguesas y toma Coca-Cola todo el tiempo. ¿Come bien o come mal?**
2. **Si se tiene problemas del corazón, ¿se debe caminar o correr para hacer ejercicio?**
3. **Si se duerme siete horas y media cada noche, ¿duerme lo suficiente o necesita dormir más? (lo suficiente)**

Variation:

4. **¿Con qué órgano o parte del cuerpo se asocian estas cosas?**

la comida	**el oxígeno**	**el amor**
la música	**las películas**	**el cálculo**

5. **¿Se refiere a la médica o al paciente?**

Examina los ojos.	**Escribe recetas.**
Tiene fiebre.	**Le duele la garganta.**
Saca la lengua.	**Recomienda un jarabe.**

Suggestions:

- Model vocabulary and ask questions during your presentation: 1. **¿Se necesita receta para comprar un jarabe para la tos? ¿para comprar pastillas para rebajar de peso** (*lose weight*)**? ¿para comprar medicinas para diabéticos?** 2. **¿Qué hace Ud. cuando le duele la cabeza / la garganta?** 3. **¿Se enferma Ud. con frecuencia? De niño/a, ¿se enfermaba Ud. fácilmente? ¿Cuántas veces al año se resfría Ud.? ¿Cuántas veces, más o menos** (*do the hand gesture*), **se resfrió Ud. el año pasado? ¿Qué puede hacer una persona para no resfriarse?** 4. **¿Por qué nos piden los médicos que saquemos la lengua? ¿Qué significa cuando una persona le saca la lengua a otra persona que no es un médico?**
- Offer the following optional alternate expressions and vocabulary: **constipado** = **resfriado** (Sp.); **operarse; la consulta** = **el consultorio; ponerse enfermo** = **enfermarse; la cita.** Point out that **cita** is the term for both *appointment* and *date.*
- Point out the difference between **ponerse enfermo / enfermarse** (*to get / become sick*) and **estar enfermo** (*to be sick*).
- Point out that the construction with **doler** is similar to **gustar.**

Heritage Speakers:

Hay varios sinónimos para la palabra **resfriado,** por ejemplo, **catarro** y **constipado. La gripe** o **la gripa** significa **influenza.** Pregúnteles a los hispanohablantes de la clase qué expresiones prefieren usar.

Paso 2: Gramática

GRAMMAR SECTION 29

Suggestions:

- Emphasize the importance of the speaker's perspective. Many sentences are equally correct in either the imperfect or the preterite, but they will mean something different.
- Point out that every action or state can be seen as having three phases or aspects: a beginning, a middle, and an end. When the focus is on an action's beginning or ending, the preterite is used. When the focus is on the middle, or on the repetitive nature of an action, the imperfect is used.
- Offer students these examples.

  Two preterite actions occurring either sequentially or simultaneously in the past.
  Me puse los zapatos y me levanté. Elena se fue cuando yo entré.

  Two on-going actions occurring simultaneously in the past.
  Hacía mi tarea mientras veía las noticias.

  One on-going action in the past when another interrupts.
  Yo estudiaba cuando llegó Juan.

- Read the following to continue a discussion of the preterite and imperfect in Spanish: **Estos dos tiempos dan imágenes muy diferentes de una acción. Si Ud. dice, por ejemplo, «Cuando visité a mi tío, salí de casa a las seis de la mañana», yo entiendo que Ud. lo visitó solamente una vez. En cambio, si Ud. dice: «Cuando visitaba a mi tío, salía de casa a las seis de la mañana», entiendo que iba a visitar a su tío con cierta frecuencia y que habla de algo rutinario que ocurría en todas sus visitas. Las dos oraciones están correctas gramaticalmente, pero sólo Ud. puede saber cuál comunica la «verdad». Si Ud. dice, «Ayer por la tarde íbamos a la tienda», su oyente espera que Ud. siga hablando, que le cuente qué pasó mientras iban. Normalmente no lo va a interrumpir con un comentario. En cambio, si Ud. dice, «Ayer fuimos a la tienda por la tarde», su oyente puede interrumpirlo con una pregunta porque él va a creer que Ud. ya acabó una parte de su narración. Otra vez, las dos oraciones están «correctas». El uso del imperfecto o del pretérito depende totalmente de lo que Ud. quiere expresar.**

PRÁCTICA B

Extension:

estaba leyendo	salí
había	se apagaron[b]
estaban apagadas[a]	me levanté
tenía	

Eran las once de la noche cuando ¡de repente ______[1] todas las luces[c] de la casa! Puse el libro que ______[2] en la mesa y ______[3] para investigar la causa del incidente. La verdad es que ______[4] mucho miedo. ______[5] a la calle y vi que ______[6] las luces de todo el barrio.[d] En ese momento me di cuenta[e] que ______[7] un problema con la electricidad en toda la ciudad.

[a]*out* [b]se... *went out* [c]*lights* [d]*neighborhood* [e]me... *I realized*

A. ¿Cierto o falso? Indique si las siguientes oraciones son ciertas (C) o falsas (F) según la información en Conozco a... y Pasatiempos y diversiones. Si la información no se presenta en estas secciones, escoja ND (No lo dice). Corrija las oraciones falsas.

1. C F ND Simón Bolívar es de origen europeo.
2. C F ND Bolívar ayudó (*helped*) en la independencia de varios países sudamericanos.
3. C F ND «El Libertador» quería realizar (*wanted to carry out*) una unión de países hispánicos.
4. C F ND El clima venezolano es muy severo (*harsh*).
5. C F ND Hay pocas atracciones turísticas en Venezuela.
6. C F ND Hay muchos hoteles en la Isla Margarita.

B. Para investigar: Navegando por el Internet. En la página principal de EscapeArtist, seleccione *Travel Tourism and Resorts in Venezuela.* De aquí, escoja *Guamanchi Expeditions.* Llene los espacios en blanco o escoja la palabra apropiada según la información de la página principal de *Guamanchi Expeditions.*

1. Guamanchi Expeditions está en la ciudad de ______________________________.
2. Al norte de la ciudad, se encuentran las montañas llamadas ______________________________.
   La Sierra Nevada está al ______________________________.
3. Guamanchi Expeditions sólo ofrece excursiones a las montañas. Sí No
4. En Mérida, la estación seca dura (*lasts*) del mes de ______________________________ hasta el mes de ______________________________.
5. Si un turista llega a Mérida y quiere practicar el alpinismo, Guamanchi Expeditions puede prestarle todo el equipo necesario. Sí No
6. En Mérida hay una heladería (*ice cream parlor*) muy popular que se llama ______________________________. ¡Tienen más de ______________________________ sabores (*flavors*) en total!
7. ______________________________ puede llevar a los pasajeros a regiones de más altura (elevación).

Notes:

- Christopher Columbus first sighted what is now Venezuela in 1498. It was the home of Caribs and Arawaks, indigenous peoples who also populated the Antilles.
- The Spanish explorer named the country Venezuela, "little Venice," because the villages, built on pilings on Lake Maracaibo, reminded him of the European city. In 1567, Diego de Losada founded the city of "Caracus" in the **tierra templada** more than half a mile above sea level. Colonization of the country continued rapidly in the next century, with Caracas as its urban center.
- With the help of Simón Bolívar, Venezuela remained under Spanish rule until 1821, although it had declared itself a republic in 1811. For ten years it was a part of **Gran Colombia,** which also included Colombia and Ecuador.
- The Venezuelan Andes run east-west, although elsewhere in South America they run north-south. Other geographical regions include the Guiana Plateau southeast of the Orinoco, the Orinoco **Llanos** south of the Andes, and the Maracaibo Basin.
- Petroleum provides almost half of Venezuela's revenues and constitutes 85 percent of its exports.

- Writer Rómulo Gallegos (1884–1969) was president of Venezuela from February 1948 until November of the same year, when he was overthrown by the military. He was the author of ***Doña Bárbara,*** the story of a ruthless woman who runs an **hacienda** and defends it against a number of villains. It focuses on the exploitation of the land by outsiders, a popular theme of the period.

Paso 3: Gramática

GRAMMAR SECTION 30

Suggestions:

- Review the use of **nos, os,** and **se** in reflexive verbs from **Capítulo 4.**
- Compare reflexive actions to reciprocal actions: **nos lavamos** vs. **nos queremos.** Point out the importance of context.
- Point out that reciprocal pronouns work as either direct or indirect object pronouns. In the sentences, **Se quieren** (*They love each other*) and **Nos llamamos** (*We call each other*), the reciprocal pronouns indicate persons directly affected by the action. In the sentences **Uds. se mandaron cartas** (*You sent each other letters*) and **Nos compramos regalos** (*We bought each other gifts*), the reciprocal pronouns indicate persons indirectly affected by the action.
- Emphasize that not all verbs can be made reciprocal, as not all verbs can be reflexive. Model some examples of intransitive verbs in exchanges with students: **¿Adónde se van Uds. después de clase?** vs. **¿Uds. se ven después de clase?**

EN LOS ESTADOS UNIDOS Y EL CANADÁ... EDWARD JAMES OLMOS: ACTOR Y ACTIVISTA DE LA COMUNIDAD

Point Out: Jaime Escalante was featured in the **En los Estados Unidos y el Canadá... Capítulo 1.**

Note: Hispanics in television and cinema have struggled for years to have more and better parts that do not portray a stereotypical image of their culture. Have students discuss the different characters that Olmos has portrayed and decide which successfully avoid stereotyping.

UN POCO DE TODO

Optional Activity: **Un accidente tragicómico.** Complete the following paragraphs with the correct form of the words in parentheses—for verbs, the present, preterite, or imperfect—as suggested by the context. When two possibilities are given in parentheses, select the correct word.

Cuando mi hermana y yo (tener[1]) 9 y 7 años respectivamente, (nuestro[2]) madre (tener[3]) un pequeño accidente. Papá (tener[4]) que pasar unos días fuera a causa del trabajo. (Por/Para[5]) eso, (*nosotras:* ir[6]) a despedirlo al aeropuerto.

Cuando (*nosotras:* salir[7]), vimos un perrito (que/quien[8]) tenía la pata[a] atrapada[b] en una puerta. Las tres (correr[9]) a ayudarlo. Mamá (tomar[10]) al perrito en sus brazos y lo estaba (examinar[11]) mientras (*nosotras:* caminar[12]). Íbamos (tan/tanto[13]) preocupadas por la patita del perro que no (*nosotras:* ver[14]) un escalón.[c] (*Nosotras:* Caerse[15])[d] las tres... bueno, los cuatro. La situación (ser[16]) algo cómica. (*Nosotros:* Levantarse[17]) muertas de risa[e] y un poco avergonzadas.

Por fin (*nosotras:* dejar[18]) al perrito con (su[19]) dueños y (decidir[20]) irnos a casa. Nuestra madre (cojear[21])[f] un poco. Esa misma tarde (*nosotras:* ir[22]) al hospital porque le (doler[23]) mucho todavía la pierna.[g] No (haber[24]) duda.

[a]*paw* [b]*trapped* [c]*step* [d]*To fall down* [e]muertas... *dying of laughter* [f]*to limp* [g]*leg*

(*Ella:* Tener[25]) el tobillo roto.[h] Le escayolaron[i] la pierna y le (*ellos:* dar[26]) un par de muletas.[j] Además le (*ellos:* recomendar[27]) reposo absoluto.

Todavía hoy mi hermana y yo (acordarse[28]) de lo bien que (*nosotras:* pasarlo[29]) jugando a ser las enfermeras de mamá. Afortunadamente los abuelos (venir[30]) a ayudarnos.

[h]el... *a broken ankle* [i]Le... *They put a cast on* [j]*crutches*

Comprensión: ¿Quién lo dijo?

1. Tenemos que ir a ayudar a las chicas. No pueden cuidar a Marisa a solas (*alone*).
2. ¿Dónde está el perro? No lo veo en ningún sitio.
3. Siento (*I'm sorry*) decirle, señora, que tiene el tobillo fracturado.
4. ¡Qué torpes (*clumsy*) somos!, ¿verdad?
5. ¿Por qué no te llevamos a la sala de urgencia?

Paso 4: Un paso más

VIDEOTECA

MINIDRAMAS

The **Minidramas** vignettes are not referenced in the textbook, but are part of the *¿Qué tal?* Video Program. They also appear on the Video on CD packaged free with the textbook. If you show the **Minidramas** in class or have your students view them as homework, you might find the following suggestions helpful. You can also find blackline master activities in Section X of this Manual for **Minidramas.**

Comprensión:
1. **¿Quién está enferma?**
2. **¿Cuáles son los síntomas?**
3. **¿Cuál es el diagnóstico?**
4. **¿Cómo contrajo Marta la enfermedad?**

Variation: **Paso 1. Imagínese que Ud. tiene la gripe. ¿Cuáles son sus síntomas? Haga una lista de estos síntomas para poder hablar con el médico.**
Paso 2. Con su profesor(a) o un compañero / una compañera, hagan los papeles de médico/a y paciente. El paciente tiene la gripe. ¡OJO! El médico debe hacer todas las preguntas necesarias para estar seguro de que es una gripe y no algo más grave o menos grave.

ACTIVIDAD DE DESENLACE: UNA VISITA AL MÉDICO

Activity: Students will create a skit in which a patient, a doctor, and a nurse interact in a doctor's office.

Purpose: To create a context in which students can review and practice the grammar from **Capítulo 10** and vocabulary related to health and the human body

Resources: *¿Qué tal?* textbook, the Internet, and other sources as appropriate

Vocabulary: Health and well-being, the doctor's office

Grammar:	Principal grammatical structures covered in **Capítulo 10** of the textbook, including the use of the preterite and the imperfect, relative pronouns, and reciprocal actions with reflexive pronouns
Recycled Content:	Preterite, imperfect, formal commands
Duration:	Out-of-class preparation time will vary. In-class time will be approximately 5 minutes per presentation
Format:	Groups of three to four students. One student will present the basic information about the festival and the others will create a dialogue or skit related to its events.
Comments:	You may wish to comment about the health systems of the Spanish-speaking world, for example, the role of the pharmacy and the different ways of taking someone's temperature.

Capítulo 10 *Submarino*

This game is played like "Battleship." Draw a submarine in any five squares on your gameboard without letting your partner see your paper. You and your partner will ask each other questions to try to locate (and sink) the other players' submarines. This time your questions and answers should demonstrate the correct use of imperfect and preterite verb forms.

MODELO: TÚ: **¿Llovía mucho cuando Uds. se enfermaron?**
COMPAÑERO/A: **Sí, llovía mucho cuando nos enfermamos.** (if there is a sub there)
or **No, no. llovía mucho cuando nos enfermamos.** (if there is no sub)

	(poner)	(enfermarse)	(dejar)	(traer)
(llover)				
(dormir)				
(ser)				
(correr)				

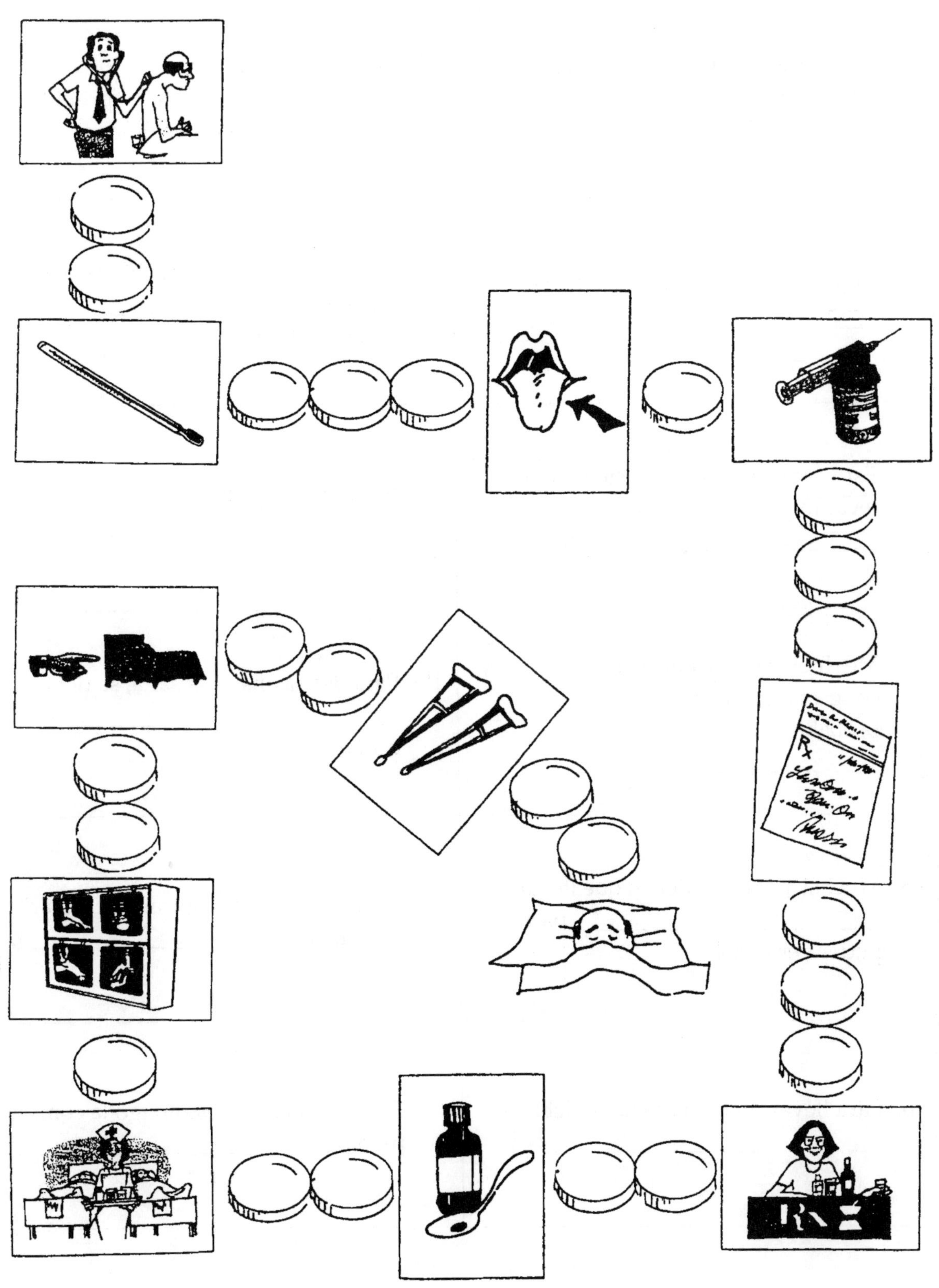

1. Se puede comprar varias medicinas en forma de líquido o ________________________.	7. Alguien que se siente __________________ tiene problemas con el oído o con el estómago.
2. El médico examina al paciente en su ________________________.	8. Si una persona tose mucho, es porque tiene los ____________________ congestionados.
3. Estoy enfermo. Me acuesto y no me levanto por varios días. ______________________ cama.	9. Se habla y se come con la __________________________.
4. Me duele la garganta, estoy congestionado y toso mucho. Es probable que tenga un ________________________.	10. Para llevar una vida sana, se debe __________________________ de fumar.
5. Muchas personas tienen que llevar ________________________ para poder ver mejor.	11. Si uno no puede respirar por la nariz, tiene la nariz ____________________.
6. Para llevar una vida sana, se debe ________________________.	12. Entre la boca y el estómago la comida pasa por _______________________.

13. Es necesario ____________ la lengua para que el médico pueda mirar la garganta.	19. Si uno no se cuida bien, probablemente va a ____________.
14. Se usan los pulmones y la nariz para ____________.	20. Un ataque al ____________ puede causar la muerte.
15. La digestión se asocia con ____________.	21. La persona que ayuda a los médicos y cuida a los pacientes en el hospital es ____________.
16. Para curar la tos, se toma ____________.	22. Si uno lee con poco luz, puede arruinarse ____________.
17. Alguien que toma aspirinas probablemente tiene ____________.	23. ____________ es una medicina para combatir una infección.
18. Para comprar algunas medicinas en una farmacia en los Estados Unidos, se necesita ____________.	24. El termómetro sirve para tomarle la temperatura a una persona que tiene ____________.

Answer Key for *Juego de tablero: ¡Ay doctor, qué dolor! I*

Capítulo 10

1. **pastilla**
2. **consultorio**
3. **Guardo**
4. **resfriado**
5. **lentes de contacto (gafas)**
6. (*Answers will vary.*)
7. **mareado**
8. **pulmones**
9. **boca**
10. **dejar**
11. **congestionada (tapada)**
12. **la garganta**
13. **sacar**
14. **respirar**
15. **el estómago**
16. **(un) jarabe**
17. **dolor (fiebre)**
18. **una receta**
19. **enfermarse (resfriarse)**
20. **corazón**
21. **el enfermero (la enfermera)**
22. **los ojos**
23. **El antibiótico**
24. **fiebre**

Capítulo 10 *Juego de tablero: ¡Ay doctor, qué dolor! II*

1. Tell the doctor that you caught a cold three times last year.
2. Say that you wanted a prescription, but the doctor gave you an injection.
3. Explain that you went to the emergency room because you had a sore throat.
4. Tell the group that when you were a child, you used to go to the medical office two times a year.
5. Explain that you were doing aerobics when suddenly you began to cough.
6. Say that the nurse was taking your temperature while you were waiting for the doctor.
7. Tell the group that, during your childhood, you and your dentist did not see each other frequently.
8. Tell the doctor that you couldn't sleep last night because your nose and lungs were congested.
9. Say that when you were ten years old, the good thing about being sick was that your mom always prepared chicken soup for you.
10. Tell your doctor that last month you stopped smoking and began to jog; now you can breathe better.
11. You are the doctor. Tell your patient to eat in a balanced way, sleep enough, and exercise.
12. You are the doctor. Tell your patient to stay in bed, take these antibiotics, and take care of himself/herself.
13. You are the doctor. Tell your staff that the patient who you have just examined should check into a hospital.
14. Tell your son/daughter that you went to the pharmacy and bought him/her cough syrup for (**para**) his/her cough.
15. Tell your parents that the doctor examined your eyes and inner ears, and then she listened to your heart and lungs.
16. You own and operate a health food store. Tell your customers that the pills that you sell are good for (**para**) the blood and the brain.
17. You are the star of an "infomercial." Convince the audience that, in order to (**para**) lead a healthy life, they need to buy your new book for (**por**) only $39.95.
18. Tell the doctor that glasses are not pleasing to you. Tell him/her that you want to discuss the advantages and disadvantages of contact lenses.

Answer Key for *Juego de tablero: ¡Ay doctor, qué dolor! II*

Capítulo 10

1. **Me resfrié tres veces el año pasado.**
2. **Quería una receta, pero el doctor me puso una inyección.**
3. **Fui a la sala de emergencias (urgencia) porque me dolía la garganta.**
4. **Cuando yo era niño/a, iba al consultorio dos veces al año.**
5. **Yo hacía ejercicios aeróbicos cuando de repente empecé a toser.**
6. **El enfermero / La enfermera me tomaba la temperatura mientras esperaba al médico / a la médica.**
7. **En mi niñez, mi dentista y yo no nos veíamos con frecuencia.**
8. **Yo no podía (pude) dormir anoche porque la nariz y los pulmones estaban congestionados.**
9. **Cuando yo tenía diez años, lo bueno de estar enfermo/a era que mi mamá siempre me preparaba sopa de pollo.**
10. **El mes pasado, dejé de fumar y empecé a correr; ahora puedo respirar mejor.**
11. **Coma Ud. equilibradamente, duerma lo suficiente y haga ejercicio.**
12. **Guarde Ud. cama, tome estos antibióticos y cuídese.**
13. **El/La paciente a quien acabo de examinar debe internarse en un hospital.**
14. **Hijo/a, fui a la farmacia y te compré un jarabe para la tos.**
15. **La médica me examinó los ojos y los oídos, y luego me escuchó el corazón y los pulmones.**
16. **Señores, las pastillas que vendo son buenas para la sangre y el cerebro.**
17. **Amigos, para llevar una vida sana, Uds. necesitan comprar mi libro nuevo por sólo treinta y nueve dólares y noventa y cinco centavos.**
18. **No me gustan las gafas. Quiero discutir las ventajas y desventajas de los lentes de contacto.**

La encuesta dice...

Voy a ver al médico cuando...

1. **necesito un chequeo.**
2. **tengo fiebre.**
3. **necesito una receta / una inyección.**
4. **me duele la garganta.**
5. **me resfrío.**
6. **estoy mareado/a.**

La encuesta dice...

La enfermera le dice al paciente en el consultorio:

1. **«Quítese la ropa.»**
2. **«Póngase esta bata.»**
3. **«Dígame sus síntomas.»**
4. **«Abra la boca para que yo le tome la temperatura.»**
5. **«Siéntese aquí.»**
6. **«Espere al doctor.»**

La encuesta dice...

El doctor le da estos consejos a su paciente:

1. **«Coma equilibradamente.»**
2. **«Haga ejercicio por lo menos tres veces a la semana.»**
3. **«Duerma lo suficiente.»**
4. **«No tome mucha cafeína.»**
5. **«No fume.»**
6. **«Beba mucha agua.»**

Student Supplements

- Listening Comprehension Program CD, **Capítulo 11** (**Paso 1: Vocabulario:** word lists)
- Workbook/Laboratory Manual, **Capítulo 11**
- Audio Program CD, **Capítulo 11**

Instructor Resources

- Instructor's Manual/IRK: Chapter-by-Chapter Supplementary Materials, **Capítulo 11**
  - **Paso 1: Vocabulario**
  - **Paso 2: Gramática**
    - Grammar Section 31
    - **Nota comunicativa**
    - **Enfoque cultural**
  - **Paso 3: Gramática**
    - Grammar Section 32
    - **Un poco de todo**
    - **En los Estados Unidos y el Canadá...**
  - **Paso 4: Un paso más**
    - **Videoteca: Minidramas**
    - **A leer**
    - **A escribir**
  - Games and Activities
- Instructor's Manual/IRK: Video Activities and Related Materials
  - **A primera vista**
  - **A segunda vista**
  - Answers to Video Activities
  - Videoscripts
- Audioscript, **Capítulo 11**
- Transparencies 67–68
- Testing Program, **Capítulo 11**

Multimedia Resources

- Online Learning Center
- Electronic Workbook/Laboratory Manual
- Video, **Capítulo 11** (cue 1:07:34)
  - **En contexto** (1:45)
  - **Minidramas** (3:14)
  - **Enfoque cultural: Puerto Rico** (1:00)
- Student CD-ROM, **Capítulo 11**
- Electronic Language Tutor, **Capítulo 11** (**Vocabulario, Gramática**)

Paso 1: Vocabulario

LAS PRESIONES DE LA VIDA ESTUDIANTIL

Preparation: Ask students to skim the vocabulary list.

Sample Passage: **Las presiones son situaciones que causan estrés. La palabra *estrés* es idéntica en inglés y en español, ¿verdad?, pero en español empieza con la letra «e» y no con la letra «s». Escuchen: *estrés* y *stress.***

La vida estudiantil, la vida de los estudiantes, tiene muchas presiones y, por eso, muchos estudiantes sufren estrés. ¿Cuáles son algunas de estas presiones? Probablemente la mayor presión es la de sacar buenas notas o calificaciones. Las mejores calificaciones son las As **y las peores son las** Fs (you can let students fill in the best and worst grades). **Otra causa de estrés es, por ejemplo, la necesidad de acordarse de entregar todas las tareas a tiempo.**

***Acordarse de* es sinónimo de *recordar.* Para entregar las tareas y los informes a tiempo es necesario saber la fecha límite para entregarlos. La fecha límite es el último momento en que podemos hacer algo. Afortunadamente, hay cosas que nos ayudan a acordarnos de nuestras fechas límites: los calendarios y las agendas. Pero, con frecuencia, el problema es acordarse de mirar el calendario, ¿no?**

Hay otras cosas que los estudiantes no se acuerdan de hacer con frecuencia: se les olvida que tienen algunas pruebas, poner el despertador, tomar la llave antes de salir de casa, recordar donde pusieron la tarjeta de identificación de la universidad,...

Quick Comprehension Check:

1. **¿Con qué letra empieza la palabra «estrés»?**
2. **¿Cuál es la causa más importante del estrés para los estudiantes?**
3. **Un sinónimo de «acordarse de».**
4. **¿Cuál es la fecha límite para entregar las hojas del Workbook de *¿Qué tal?* para este capítulo?**
5. **¿Cuál es la diferencia entre una prueba y un examen?**

Suggestions:

- Point out that **estudiantil** is an adjective derived from **estudiante.**
- Indicate that the first-person singular of **recoger** is **recojo.**
- Provide the following alternate and optional vocabulary: **estacionar(se) = aparcar** (Sp.) = **parquear** (Mex.); **notas = calificaciones; la tranquilidad** (the opposite of **el estrés**); **estar tranquilo/a.**
- Model vocabulary using it in sentences about yourself and in exchanges with the students. Explain some expressions in Spanish: 1. ***Acordarse* es un verbo reflexivo. Uds. conocen un verbo sinónimo, ¿verdad? ¿Cuál es? (*recordar,* del Capítulo 8) ¿Cuál es un antónimo? El verbo *acordarse,* como *recordar,* tiene un cambio en la radical (o → ue): *me acuerdo, te acuerdas, nos acordamos.* ¿Se acuerda Ud. de quién era el presidente de los Estados Unidos en 1995?** 2. **El verbo *entregar* es sinónimo de ______** (students answer). **¿Qué se puede entregar? ¿Entregaron alguna tarea ayer para alguna clase?** 3. **Estacionar el coche es un gran problema en muchas ciudades (en esta universidad). ¿Uds. tienen problemas cuando necesitan estacionar su coche? ¿Dónde? ¿Cuándo?**
- Read the following definitions and descriptions and have students give the correct words: 1. **Muchos estudiantes sufren esto.** 2. **Es una prueba que se hace para demostrar la comprensión de los estudios que se han hecho.** 3. **Es un aparato que nos despierta por la mañana.** 4. **Es una cosa que sirve para abrir puertas.** 5. **Estas dos expresiones se usan para pedir disculpas.** 6. **Uno escribe esto para planear las cosas que tiene que hacer cada día (clases, citas, otras actividades, etcétera).**

7. Es poner el coche en un lugar cuando no lo conducimos. 8. **Es sinónimo de** ***dar,*** **en el sentido de** ***darle una tarea al profesor.***

- Point out that **acordarse (de)** and **olvidarse (de)** are antonyms.
- Ask students the following questions to personalize the vocabulary: 1. **¿Está Ud. contento/a con su horario de este semestre/trimestre? ¿Por qué? ¿Tiene Ud. que entregar algún informe esta semana? ¿Cuál es la fecha límite? ¿Tiene pruebas o exámenes? ¿Tuvo algún examen o informe importante la semana pasada?** 2. **¿Viene Ud. en coche a la universidad? ¿Tiene problemas para estacionar? ¿Dónde estaciona?** 3. **¿Está sacando Ud. buenas notas este semestre? ¿Son mejores o peores que las del semestre pasado?** 4. **¿Le gusta el calendario de esta universidad (cuando empieza y termina el semestre [trimestre], / cuando hay vacaciones)? ¿Por qué?** 5. **Normalmente, ¿es Ud. una persona que llega tarde o temprano a las citas / las clases? ¿Necesita un despertador por la mañana o puede Ud. despertarse solo/a?** 6. **¿Se acuerda Ud. de sus citas sin mirar la agenda? ¿Se acuerda Ud. de escribir sus citas en la agenda y de mirarla después?**
- Remind students that **lunes** is the first day of the week on Hispanic calendars.

Heritage Speakers:

- Por la influencia del inglés en algunos dialectos del español del suroeste de los Estados Unidos, se oye decir **grado** en vez de **calificación.** Las palabras aceptadas, sin embargo, son **nota** y **calificación.** Otra expresión influida por el inglés es la palabra **notas** para expresar **apuntes.**
- Algunos hispanohablantes de los Estados Unidos usan la palabra **alarma** para referirse al **despertador.**
- El término **parquear (estacionar)** que se oye en México también se usa en algunos países latinoamericanos y en los Estados Unidos. Algunas derivaciones son **el parqueadero (estacionamiento)**. En España, donde dicen **aparcar,** usan la palabra **aparcamiento.**

Optional Activity:

Asociaciones

Paso 1. ¿Qué palabras asocia Ud. con estos verbos? Pueden ser sustantivos, antónimos o sinónimos.

1. estacionar
2. recoger
3. acordarse
4, entregar
5. sacar
6. abrir
7. perder
8. estar feliz
9. llegar a tiempo
10. ser flexible

Paso 2. ¿Qué palabras y/o situaciones asocia Ud. con los siguientes sustantivos?

1. el calendario
2. el despertador
3. las calificaciones
4. el estrés
5. la fecha límite
6. el horario
7. los informes
8. la llave
9. la tarjeta de identificación
10. la tranquilidad

Variation: Use a game format to get synonyms and antonyms. Divide the class into teams. Allow teams to work on each word for only one minute; the team with the most associations wins the round.

LA PROFESORA MARTÍNEZ SE LEVANTÓ CON EL PIE IZQUIERDO

Preparation: Ask students to skim the vocabulary list.

Sample Passage: **Algunas personas tienen más accidentes que otras porque son personas distraídas o torpes. Una persona distraída es una persona que no está pensando en lo que está pasando en este momento y su mente está en las nubes** (gesticulate like looking up to the air). **Las personas torpes son personas que rompen las cosas con facilidad o se dan contra otras cosas** (act out both actions). **El problema con ser torpe es que una persona puede hacerse daño o lastimarse o puede hacerle daño o lastimar a otra persona. Por ejemplo si Ud. se da contra una persona mayor (vieja) en la calle, es probable que la persona mayor vaya a hacerse más daño que Ud., es decir, algo le va a doler. «Doler » es como gustar. También se puede caer** (act out). **Si le hacemos daño a alguien es necesario decir inmediatamente «Perdón, fue sin querer». Esto significa que su acción no tenía la intención de hacer daño.**

Quick Comprehension Check: Sample items:

1. **Si un estudiante se olvida de entregar su trabajo a tiempo, ¿es distraído o torpe?**
2. **Si una profesora se da contra el estudiante que está enfrente de la mesa, ¿es distraída o torpe?**
3. **¿Qué se dice cuando se lastima o otra persona?**

Suggestions:

- Model vocabulary in sentences about yourself and in communicative exchanges with the students.
- Point out to students the toes of the professor in the illustration. Highlight the difference between **dedos del pie** and **dedos de la mano.**
- Explain to students that the first-person singular of **caerse** is **me caigo.**
- Have students give the corresponding word: 1. **Es sinónimo de tener razón.** 2. **Tomo esto cuando me duele la cabeza.** 3. **Es sinónimo de hacerse daño.** 4. **Es un adjetivo que significa no estar atento a lo que pasa.** 5. **Es una persona que tiene muchos accidentes.**
- Remind students again that the structure for **doler** is like **gustar.**
- Have students respond **cierto or falso:** 1. **Tenemos tres cabezas (diez piernas, dos ojos,...)** 2. **La pierna entra en el zapato.** 3. **Escribimos con el pie.** 4. **Pensamos con la cabeza.**
- Ask students the following questions to personalize the vocabulary: 1. **¿Le duele la cabeza con frecuencia? ¿Qué hace cuando le duele? ¿En qué situaciones es común que a una persona le duela la cabeza?** (Point out: subjunctive) 2. **Las personas distraídas, ¿se olvidan o se acuerdan de muchas cosas? ¿Pierden objetos? ¿Qué tipo de objetos? ¿Es Ud. distraído/a? ¿Por qué? Dé algunos ejemplos.** 3. **¿Es Ud. torpe? ¿Se da con los muebles con frecuencia? ¿con los pies de otras personas? ¿Deja caer** (*to drop*) **cosas? ¿Qué personas son típicamente torpes? ¿los futbolistas? ¿los payasos** (*clowns*)**?**

TALKING ABOUT HOW THINGS ARE DONE: ADVERBS

Suggestions:

- Point out that when two **-mente** adverbs are used together, joined by a conjunction in a single sentence, the first adverb is shortened to the feminine singular adjective and only the second adverb includes the **-mente** suffix: **Carlos hizo la lección rápida- y fácilmente.**
- Remind students that **mucho** and **poco** are invariable when used as adverbs: **Isabel tiene muchas** (adjective) **clases, por eso estudia mucho** (adverb).
- Point out that when an adjective does not end in **-o,** there is no **-a** before **-mente** to form the adverb: **fácilmente, totalmente.**

Paso 2: Gramática

GRAMMAR SECTION 31

Suggestions:

- Point out that the subject of the English sentence becomes the indirect object pronoun in the Spanish equivalent.: I = **se *me;*** Antonio = **se *le.*** The structure is similar to that of **gustar.**
- Point out the option of emphasizing or clarifying the indirect object with the corresponding prepositional phrase: **a mí, a Antonio.**
- Point out that the use of the singular vs. the plural verb depends on the direct object from the English sentence.
- This section concentrates on the use of this structure with **me, te,** and **le.** You might expand the activities in this section to cover **nos, os,** and **les.**

CONVERSACIÓN B

Note:

- **Gloria Estefan:** Gloria was born in 1957 in Havana, Cuba, but her family fled to Miami before she was two. At 21, she married Emilio Estefan, the bandleader of The Miami Sound Machine.
- **Sammy Sosa:** Born November 12, 1968, in San Pedro de Macoris in the Dominican Republic. Sosa is a player for the Chicago Cubs baseball team.
- **Antonio Banderas:** Native of Spain who worked with the renowned Pedro Almódovar. Antonio's first film in 1982 was *Laberinto de pasiones.* He went on to make a total of five Almodóvar films before bowing out of a contract for a sixth movie when he came to the U.S. to film *The Mambo Kings.*
- **John Grisham:** Born February 8, 1955, in Jonesboro, Arkansas, to a construction worker and a homemaker. His works include: *A Time to Kill, The Firm,* and *The Pelican Brief.*
- **Cristóbal Colón:** (1451–1506), born in Genoa, Italy. **Colón** (**Cristoforo Colombo,** in Italian) was a navigator who sailed west across the Atlantic Ocean in search of a route to Asia. **Colón** achieved fame by making landfall, instead, on a Caribbean island.
- **John Lennon:** (1940–1980), born in England. Lennon was a British singer and songwriter, and a member of the Beatles. He was murdered in 1980.

NOTA COMUNICATIVA

Optional Activity:

Entrevista

Paso 1. Find out from a classmate how long he or she has been . . .

1. living in this state
2. attending this university
3. living in his or her house (apartment, dorm, . . .)
4. studying Spanish

Paso 2. Now find out how long ago he or she . . .

1. last visited his or her parents (grandparents, children, . . .)
2. met his or her best friend
3. learned to drive (**manejar**)
4. handed in his or her last major assignment

Suggestion: Go through the items with the class as a whole before students work on their own.

ENFOQUE CULTURAL: PUERTO RICO

A. Para contestar. Conteste las siguientes preguntas con información de ¡Fíjese! y Conozco a...

1. ¿En qué año perdió España sus últimas colonias de su imperio? ¿Qué impacto tuvo esto en las relaciones entre Puerto Rico y los Estados Unidos?

____

2. ¿Qué otro nombre se usa para referirse a Puerto Rico? ¿y a los puertorriqueños? ¿De qué idioma originaron?

____

3. ¿Cómo se llama el único bosque tropical del sistema de Bosques Nacionales de los Estados Unidos? ¿Dónde está?

____

4. ¿Quién es Alonso Ramírez?

____

B. Para completar. Complete el siguiente cuadro usando la información de los Enfoques culturales de los Capítulos 8 a 11.

El país (Los países) con el mayor número de habitantes:	
El país (Los países) en el/los que se habla otro idioma además del español (mencione el país/los países y el idioma/los idiomas):	
El país con menos habitantes:	

Notes:

- The Igneri culture appeared in Puerto Rico about 25 A.D. and remained until the fifth century. Another indigenous group, now called the Pre-Taino culture, later populated the same area. These groups left a ceremonial complex, complete with nine ball courts and three ceremonial plazas. The rains of hurricane Eloisa in 1975 unearthed the remnants of this complex, Tibes, and in the following years the site has become an important archeological center, perhaps the most important of its kind in the Antilles.
- Vieques, a small island to the south of Puerto Rico, has recently been the focus of much international attention because of its population's resistance to the U.S. Navy presence. As early as 1947, the Navy had attempted to appropriate the island by sending the entire population of Vieques to the Virgin Islands. Although the attempt was not successful, nevertheless the Navy took over 72% of the island for military maneuvers, bombing practice, and storage of military explosives. In May 2000,

protesters, who had been demonstrating for over a year against the Navy's use of a bombing range, were forcibly removed from the front gates of the Navy base.

- Sila María Calderón was elected in November 2000 as Puerto Rico's first woman governor. The mother of eight children and ex-mayor of the city of San Juan, had been a prominent public figure for many years before her election to the post.
- Doña Felisa Rincón de Gautier was another woman mayor of the capital city. A beloved figure, known for her extravagant hairdos as much as for her highly developed political sense, she ran San Juan from 1946 to 1968. Today a museum in the old city is dedicated to her life and work.

Paso 3: Gramática

GRAMMAR SECTION 32

POR

Suggestions:

- Have students say the following in Spanish (the numbers are coordinated with the presentation of the uses of **por**): 1. by train / plane; by phone / letter 2. through the campus / plaza; along the river / street 3. in the afternoon / evening; at 2:00 in the afternoon (**¡OJO! de la tarde**) 4. because of the test / accident 5. Thanks for the book / pen / money. 6. I'm doing it for you / him / us. 7. I studied for four hours / two days.
- Point out that *in order to get* or *in search of* is expressed with **por: Van por pan.**
- Have students use fixed expressions with **por** to respond to these questions or comments: 1. **¿Es necesario estudiar treinta minutos cada día para la clase de español?** 2. **Parece que va a llover hoy. ¿Debo llevar impermeable?** 3. **¿Le paso la carne? ¿la ensalada?** 4. **Me dicen que Ud. toma ocho clases este semestre.** 5. **Empecé a leer este libro el año pasado; lo terminé esta mañana.** 6. **¡Me robaron el coche anoche!** 7. **¿Le gusta viajar?** 8. **¿Por qué llegué tarde? Pues hay mil razones.**

PARA

Suggestions:

- Emphasize that **para** is *for* with the concept of destination. a. Destined for whom? → **para su hijo** b. Destined for what point in time? → **para mañana** c. Geographical destination, in space? → **Salieron para Lima.** d. Destined for what use? → **un vaso para agua.**
- Have students give the English equivalents (the numbers are coordinated with the order of presentation of the uses of **para**): 1. They came back to eat lunch / to rest. 2. It's for her / me. 3. The exercise is for Monday / Friday. 4. They left for Bolivia / Costa Rica. 5. It's a wine / beer glass. 6. For an American / German, he speaks French well. 7. She works for Ramón / Mr. Jiménez. (**¡OJO!** ***el señor Jiménez***)

Optional Activity:

Situaciones. Escoja una respuesta para cada pregunta o situación. Luego invente un contexto para cada diálogo. ¿Dónde están las personas que hablan? ¿Quiénes son? ¿Por qué dicen lo que dicen?

1. ______ ¡Huy! Acabo de jugar al basquetbol por dos horas.
2. ______ ¿Por qué quieres que llame a Pili y Adolfo? Nunca están en casa por la noche, sobre todo (*especially*) a estas horas.
3. ______ ¿No vas a comer nada? ¿Por lo menos un sándwich?
4. ______ ¡Cuánto lo siento, don Javier! Sé que llegué tarde a la cita (*appointment*). No fue mi intención hacerlo esperar.
5. ______ Es imposible que tome el examen hoy, por muchas razones.

6. ______ ¿No oíste? Juana acaba de tener un accidente horrible.
7. ______ ¡Pero, papá, quiero ir!
8. ______ Ay, Mariana, ¿no sabías que hubo un terremoto (*earthquake*)? Murieron más de cien personas.

a. ¡Por Dios! ¡Qué desgracia!
b. Te digo que no, por última vez.
c. No se preocupe. Lo importante es que por fin está aquí.
d. ¡Por Dios! ¿Qué le pasó?
e. No, gracias. No tengo mucha hambre y además tengo que salir en seguida.
f. ¿Por ejemplo? Dígame...
g. Ah, por eso tienes tanto calor.
h. Llámalos de todas formas, por si acaso...

PRÁCTICA

Note: Most older people in the Hispanic world end up living with their grown-up children and their grandchildren when they can no longer take care of themselves. At this point family members will take care of them until they die. Being too old or sick is not the only reason for older people to live with their children. This may also happen after the loss of a spouse. In any case, grandparents have an important role in the upbringing of their grandchildren, often taking care of them while the parents work. For this reason, there are very few **residencias para ancianos** (nursing homes) in Hispanic countries.

Optional Activities:

Causa y efecto

Paso 1. Form complete sentences with the cues given. Pay attention to the various clues given to decide whether you will need to use the present, the preterite, or the imperfect in your sentences. Change words and add additional words when necessary. You will use these sentences again in **Paso 2.**

1. anoche / Sra. Ortega / poner / trajes de baño / y / toallas (*towels*) / en / bolsa
2. cuando / ser / pequeño / Cecilia / acostarse / temprano / todo / noches
3. este / mañana / a Lorenzo / perder / llaves / y caer / taza de café
4. esta noche / estudiantes / clase de historia / no / ir a dormir / mucho
5. ahora / Amalia / estar / contento

Paso 2. Now match the sentences above, followed by **porque,** with the phrases below. (The first one is done for you.) Conjugate the verbs below as needed to complete your new sentences. There is more than one possible answer in most cases.

MODELO: querer ir hoy a la playa →
1. Anoche la Sra. Ortega puso los trajes de baño y las toallas en la bolsa porque quería ir hoy a la playa.

estar nervioso/a por su boda (*wedding*) mañana
tener un examen final
encontrar su cartera
ser la fecha límite para un informe
empezar la clase de natación hoy
estar distraído/a
celebrar el cumpleaños de su esposo/a en la playa
ver la tele hasta muy tarde todas las noches
haber una fiesta grande en casa de la profesora

UN POCO DE TODO

Follow-up: **Paso 1.** Have students give sentences about themselves using the same time markers: 1. **anoche** 2. **cuando era pequeño/a** 3. **esta mañana** 4. **esta noche** 5. **ahora**
Paso 2. Have students give a reason (**porque...**) for each of their sentences.

¡Qué desastre!

Paso 1. Indique todas las opciones verdaderas para Ud. Haga las modificaciones necesarias de acuerdo con sus experiencias.

Una vez...

1. ☐ se me perdió la tarjeta de identificación de la universidad.
2. ☐ se me cayó un vaso de vino tinto en la ropa.
3. ☐ se me perdieron los lentes de contacto.
4. ☐ se me rompió un objeto caro.
5. ☐ se me quedó en casa un trabajo para la clase.
6. ☐ ¿ ?

Paso 2. Con un compañero / una compañera, expliquen qué problemas tuvieron Uds. a consecuencia de esos accidentes y cómo los resolvieron (*you solved*).

EN LOS ESTADOS UNIDOS Y EL CANADÁ... RICKY MARTIN

Point Out: Menudo is a pop group that began in 1977. Members were rotated out of the group as they got older and their voices changed. In 1997 they changed the name to MDO. There are more than thirty Menudo/MDO alumni, and in 1998 many of them had a reunion. Six of the past members from different Menudo years put together a new album and a round of musical tours.

Suggestion: Ask questions about Ricky Martin in Spanish. Because Ricky Martin is well known in the U.S. and Canada, you might include questions about things not presented in the reading.

Paso 4: Un paso más

VIDEOTECA

MINIDRAMAS

The **Minidramas** vignettes are not referenced in the textbook, but are part of the *¿Qué tal?* Video Program. They also appear on the Video on CD packaged free with the textbook. If you show the **Minidramas** in class or have your students view them as homework, you might find the following suggestions helpful. You can also find blackline master activities in Section X of this Manual for **Minidramas.**

Comprensión:

1. **¿Cómo expresa José Miguel que hoy tiene un mal día?**
2. **¿Cómo expresa Elisa que los incidentes de hoy no son serios?**

Variation: Have students act out the following scenes.

EN UNA MESA
PERSONA A: **¡Ay! Discúlpeme. ¿Permítame que le limpie la camisa?**
PERSONA B: **No se preocupe. No es nada.**
PERSONA A: **Lo siento muchísimo.**

EN EL METRO

JOVEN: **Sígueme, hay un asiento en el fondo.**
AMIGO/A: **Hombre, es imposible llegar allí.**
JOVEN: **¿Sí? Mira... Con permiso... Perdón...**
MUJER: **¡Ay! ¡Cuidado! ¡No ve que no hay por donde pasar!**
JOVEN: **Disculpe, señora, fue sin querer...**
MUJER: **La gente joven siempre tiene prisa...**

EN LA UNIVERSIDAD

E1: **Oye, ¿trajiste los apuntes que te presté** (*lent*)**?**
E2: **¿Qué apuntes? ¡Ay! Se me olvidaron por completo. Ahora mismo vuelvo a casa para traértelos.**
E1: **No, no los necesito ahora. Me los traes mañana, ¿eh?**

A LEER

Suggestion: **Estrategia.** Practice this strategy by making up titles of textbook chapters and readings. For example, **Capítulo 2 La familia, A leer: El amor y la disciplina.**

Follow-up: **Comprensión.** Have students discuss in Spanish modern-life problems that they have or that concern them. You might model and initiate the discussion with a brief description of a concern or problem you have.

A ESCRIBIR

Optional: List each item named as the biggest source of pressure for students. Group similar, though not identical, items under an inclusive category. See which was named most often. Have groups debate to defend different sources.

ACTIVIDAD DE DESENLACE: ¡UN DÍA HORRIBLE!

Activity: Students will create a skit that presents a humorous character having a horrible day.

Purpose: To create a context in which students can review and practice the grammar from **Capítulo 11** and vocabulary related to the pressures of student life and to accidents

Resources: *¿Qué tal?* textbook, the Internet, and other sources as appropriate

Vocabulary: Pressures of human life, accidental events

Grammar: Principal grammatical structures covered in **Capítulo 11** of the textbook, including **se** to express unexpected or unplanned events and **por** and **para**

Recycled Content: The human body, emotions, reflexive verbs

Duration: Out-of-class preparation time will vary. In-class time will be approximately five minutes per presentation.

Format: Groups of three to four students

Capítulo 11 *Lotería*

Para cada pregunta, escriba el nombre de un compañero / una compañera de clase que conteste «sí» a la pregunta. **¡OJO!** No escriba el mismo nombre más de una vez.

MODELO: ESTUDIANTE 1: **¿Se te rompió el brazo o la pierna alguna vez?**
ESTUDIANTE 2: **Sí, se me rompió el brazo cuando tenía siete años.**

¿Se te rompió el brazo o la pierna alguna vez?	**¿Apagaste la luz anoche antes de las diez?**	**Cuando eras niño/a, ¿caminabas a la escuela todos los días?**	**En tu niñez, ¿siempre te pegaba algún muchacho antipático / alguna muchacha antipática?**
Cuando eras niño/a, ¿siempre ponías el televisor los sábados por la mañana?	**¿Te levantaste con el pie izquierdo esta mañana?**	**Por lo general, ¿eres una persona distraída?**	**¿Eras un(a) niño/a torpe?**
¿Se te perdieron las llaves de la casa alguna vez?	**¿Tienes un horario difícil este semestre?**	**¿Le pediste disculpas a un profesor / una profesora de esta universidad alguna vez?**	**¿Se te acabó la gasolina de tu carro alguna vez?**
¿Siempre entregas la tarea a tiempo?	**¿Te acordaste de asistir al laboratorio de lenguas la semana pasada?**	**¿Sufres muchas presiones en la clase de español?**	**Por lo general, ¿tienes buena suerte?**

	Vocabulario	Verbos	Gramática	Traducción
10 pts		 A mí...	_______ lo general, ¿a qué hora sales _______ la universidad?	That child falls down frequently and cries constantly.
20 pts		 A nosotros	Busqué _______ todas partes pero no encontré aspirinas _______ mi jefe.	In order to lead a life without stress, it is necessary to be flexible.
30 pts	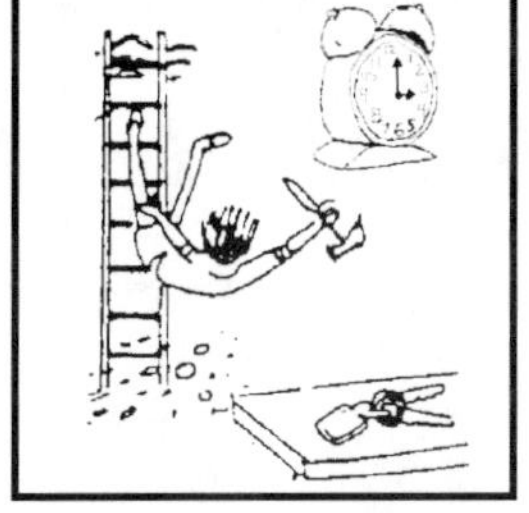	 A mi tío distraído...	Mi hermana trabaja _______ un médico _______ la mañana.	We were wrong (made a mistake). It was unintentional. We apologize to all of you.
40 pts		 A mis hermanos...	_____ extranjera, Beatriz habla inglés muy bien. Tomó clases ______ sólo dos años en su patria.	I have been under a lot of pressure at work for ten months. I need to go on a vacation immediately.
50 pts		 A tí...	Vamos a España _______ la Semana Santa. Viajamos de Madrid a Sevilla _______ tren.	You bumped into that door a week ago. Does your head still hurt?

Answer Key for *Arriésgate*

Capítulo 11

Vocabulario: *¿Cómo se llaman estas cosas? ¿Con qué acciones se asocian? Se debe contestar sin repetir ningún verbo ya mencionado. Ejemplos:*

10 pts Pensamos con la cabeza; escribimos con la mano; jugamos al tenis con el brazo.

20 pts Tocamos el piano con los dedos; bailamos con las piernas; caminamos con los pies.

Los dibujos que siguen representan palabras de vocabulario de este capítulo. Hagan oraciones con estas palabras que demuestren su significado. Ejemplos:

30 pts Ponemos el despertador si queremos levantarnos temprano; necesitamos una llave si queremos abrir una puerta; usamos una escalera para lavar las ventanas del segundo piso.

40 pts Necesitamos la luz de una lámpara para leer por la noche; mi jefe antipático insiste en que yo trabaje durante los fines de semana; tengo una cita con mi novio esta noche para ir al cine.

Hoy el señor Delgado se levantó con el pie izquierdo. ¿Qué accidentes tuvo?

50 pts El señor Delgado se dio con una puerta, se equivocó (y entró en el servicio para damas), y se hizo daño en el pie.

Verbos: *¿Qué les pasó a estas pobres personas? Hay que contestar en el pretérito sin repetir verbos ya mencionados. Ejemplos:*

10 pts A mí se me perdió el libro.

20 pts A nosotros se nos acabó la leche.

30 pts A mi tío distraído se le cayó una taza de café.

40 pts A mis hermanos se les rompió una ventana.

50 pts A ti se te olvidó la llave.

Gramática: *¿Por o para?*

10 pts Por lo general, ¿a qué hora sales para la universidad?

20 pts Busqué por todas partes pero no encontré aspirinas para mi jefe.

30 pts Mi hermana trabaja para un médico por la mañana.

40 pts Para extranjera, Beatriz habla inglés muy bien. Tomó clases por sólo dos años en su patria.

50 pts Vamos a España para la Semana Santa. Viajamos de Madrid a Sevilla por tren.

Traducción:

10 pts Ese niño / Esa niña se cae frecuentemente y llora constantemente.

20 pts Para llevar una vida sin estrés (tensión), es necesario ser flexible.

30 pts Nos equivocamos. Fue sin querer. Les pedimos disculpas a Uds.

40 pts Hace diez meses que sufro muchas presiones en el trabajo. Necesito ir de vacaciones inmediatamente.

50 pts Hace una semana que te diste (Ud. se dio) con esa puerta. ¿Todavía te (le) duele la cabeza?

Capítulo 11 *Juego de tablero: ¡Vamos a viajar por Latinoamérica!*

Escoja una carta y léala en voz alta, llenando el espacio en blanco con **por** o **para**. Si su respuesta es correcta, tire un dado para ver cuántos países puede recorrer. **¡OJO!** Si el jugador no puede identificar el país en el cual se encuentra, debe regresar a los Estados Unidos y empezar su viaje de nuevo.

Capítulo 11 *Juego de tablero: ¡Vamos a viajar por Latinoamérica!*

1. El verano pasado viajamos a Lima ____________ avión.
2. Este regalo de cumpleaños es ____________ mi madre.
3. Los domingos nos gusta dar un paseo ____________ la plaza.
4. El pobre estudiante tuvo que pagar más de ochenta dólares ____________ el libro de texto.
5. Romeo murió ____________ el amor de Julieta.
6. Viví en Madrid ____________ un año.
7. Hablas inglés muy bien ____________ extranjero.
8. Esta alfombra nueva es ____________ la sala.
9. Hace diez años que la profesora de español trabaja ____________ esta universidad.
10. ____________ mí, Plácido Domingo es el mejor cantante del mundo.
11. No dejes ____________ mañana lo que puedas hacer hoy.
12. El límite de velocidad es 65 millas ____________ hora.

13. Páseme la mantequilla, ____________ favor.	19. Íbamos a hacer un *picnic* pero no fuimos al parque ____________ la lluvia.
14. Muchos estudiantes universitarios trabajan ____________ la tarde ____________ pagar la matrícula.	20. Gracias ____________ todo.
15. Esta composición es ____________ el miércoles.	21. ¡ ____________ Dios, hijo, limpia tu alcoba!
16. Mis tíos salieron ____________ Nueva York ayer.	22. Se usa una aspiradora ____________ limpiar la alfombra.
17. Si estás enfermo, puedo trabajar ____________ ti mañana.	23. Mi hermana estudia ____________ doctora.
18. Necesito comprar unas copas de cristal ____________ vino.	24. Se puede comprar muchas frutas en el invierno, ____________ ejemplo naranjas y manzanas.

Answer Key for *Juego de tablero: ¡Vamos a viajar por Latinoamérica!*

Capítulo 11

Países de Latinoamérica

1. México
2. Guatemala
3. El Salvador
4. Honduras
5. Nicaragua
6. Costa Rica
7. Panamá
8. Cuba
9. Haití
10. República Dominicana
11. Puerto Rico
12. Venezuela
13. Colombia
14. Ecuador
15. Perú
16. Bolivia
17. Chile
18. Argentina
19. Uruguay
20. Paraguay
21. Brasil

¿POR o PARA?

1. por
2. para
3. por
4. por
5. por
6. por
7. para
8. para
9. para
10. Para
11. para
12. por
13. por
14. por; para
15. para
16. para
17. por
18. para
19. por
20. por
21. Por
22. para
23. para
24. por

Student Supplements

- Listening Comprehension Program CD, **Capítulo 12** (**Paso 1: Vocabulario:** word lists)
- Workbook/Laboratory Manual, **Capítulo 12**
- Audio Program CD, **Capítulo 12**

Instructor Resources

- Instructor's Manual/IRK: Chapter-by-Chapter Supplementary Materials, **Capítulo 12**
    - **Paso 1: Vocabulario**
    - **Paso 2: Gramática**
        - Grammar Section 33
        - **Nota comunicativa**
        - Grammar Section 34
        - **Enfoque cultural**
    - **Paso 3: Gramática**
        - Grammar Section 35
        - **En los Estados Unidos y el Canadá...**
        - **Un poco de todo**
    - **Paso 4: Un paso más**
        - **Videoteca: Minidramas**
    - Games and Activities
- Instructor's Manual/IRK: Video Activities and Related Materials
    - **A primera vista**
    - **A segunda vista**
    - Answers to Video Activities
    - Videoscripts
- Audioscript, **Capítulo 12**
- Transparencies 69–72
- Testing Program, **Capítulo 12**

Multimedia Resources

- Online Learning Center
- Electronic Workbook/Laboratory Manual
- Video, **Capítulo 12** (cue 1:12:50)
    - **En contexto** (2:04)
    - **Minidramas** (4:07)
    - **Enfoque cultural: Perú** (1:00)
- Student CD-ROM, **Capítulo 12**
- Electronic Language Tutor, **Capítulo 12** (**Vocabulario, Gramática**)

Paso 1: Vocabulario

TENGO... NECESITO... QUIERO...

Preparation: Pictures of any of the items would be useful, although they are not necessary.

Sample Passage: **En español hay un dicho, una expresión, que dice que el mundo es un pañuelo** (bring a handkerchief or tissue to class). **Esta expresión quiere decir que el mundo es muy pequeño. Con los modernos avances tecnológicos y científicos, es verdad que el mundo es muy pequeño. Por ejemplo, si Ud. quiere comunicarse con un amigo en Australia o en Italia, puede usar el teléfono. Y si anda en su carro, puede usar el teléfono del carro. O, si Ud. toma el sol en el patio de su casa** (pantomime), **puede usar el teléfono celular. Pero el teléfono no es el único medio de comunicarse con el mundo. Otro medio es el *fax*. Si Ud. necesita mandar un documento importante a una persona en Los Ángeles (Nueva York), sólo tiene que insertar el documento en la máquina y marcar el número... el documento se transmite inmediatamente. O, si Ud. tiene computadora, puede comunicarse con los amigos por correo electrónico. Sólo necesita la «dirección» de la otra persona. La dirección es una serie de números y letras. Es posible mandar documentos entre dos computadoras o tener una conversación electrónica. Realmente el mundo es un pañuelo porque es posible estar en contacto con todo el mundo a cualquier hora del día.**

Quick Comprehension Check: Sample items:

1. **Además del teléfono tradicional, ¿qué otros tipos de teléfono hay?**
2. **Para mandar documentos, fotografías, etcétera, ¿qué aparato resulta muy rápido?**
3. **¿Qué se necesita para comunicarse por correo electrónico?**

Notes: This section expands students' vocabulary for describing personal possessions and introduces the topic of the working world. Students will learn more about the working world and talking about career choices and job interviews in **Capítulo 16.** In this chapter, the conceptual link between the two topics is working to earn money to buy the things we want or need. In addition, adults (vs. typically college-age students) should find the working-world vocabulary useful for self-expression.

Suggestions:

- Model vocabulary in sentences about yourself and communicative exchanges with the students.
- Have students give sentences about the kinds of vehicles or the kinds of uses of vehicles they associate with the following circumstances or people: 1. **una persona muy deportista** 2. **un joven que vive en Miami** 3. **una tarde de verano** 4. **un hombre joven soltero que gana mucho dinero y vive en el sur de California** 5. **adolescentes urbanos**
- Bring and/or have students bring mounted photos from magazines related to the chapter topic. Present as many items as possible. Periodically go back to a photo and ask questions such as: **¿Qué es esto, una grabadora o un contestador automático?**
- Display images of **aparatos** around the room. Have students stand and identify objects, for example, **Mark, levántese y señale** (*gesture*) **la foto del televisor.**
- Point out additional terms related to the Internet: **la autopista de la información** (*information superhighway*), **la telaraña mundial** (*World Wide Web*).
- Point out that **conseguir (consigo)** is conjugated like **seguir.** Explain that **el televisor** is the apparatus and that **la televisión** refers to the event or broadcasting of programs. Remind students that **la moto** and **la foto** are short for (and more commonly used than) **la motocicleta** and **la fotografía.**

- Introduce other computer-related vocabulary: **buscador** (*search engine*), **el ciberespacio** (*cyberspace*), **cliquear / hacer clic / clicar** (*to click on the mouse*), **la contraseña** (*password*), **escanear** (*to scan*), **la memoria virtual** (*virtual memory*), **la página Web** (*Web page*), **el sitio Web** (*Web site*). Write the words **el buscapersonas** and **el localizador.** Tell students they mean the same thing and have them try to guess the meaning (*beeper*). Point out that in some areas of the U.S., Spanish speakers might call it **el bíper.**
- Point out that **el trabajo** has several meanings: *work; job* (position); *schoolwork* (such as a written report or term paper). Explain that **el puesto** is another word for *job* or *position.*
- Ask students the following questions to personalize the vocabulary: 1. **¿Trabaja Ud. ahora o sólo estudia? ¿Dónde trabaja? ¿Recibe un buen sueldo? ¿Le gustaría cambiar de puesto? ¿Por qué?** 2. **¿Es un buen empleado / una buena empleada o es perezoso/a?** 3. **¿Cómo es su jefe/a? ¿Es comprensivo/a y simpático/a o es muy mandón/mandona** (act out)**? Descríbalo/la. ¿Hay muchas diferencias entre su jefe/a y un profesor / una profesora? ¿En qué son similares / diferentes?**

Suggestions:

- Offer the following optional vocabulary: **el ascensor** (*elevator*), **el piso** (*floor of a building or floor that one sweeps*) vs. **la planta.**
- Read the following definitions and have students give the words defined. 1. **la persona que vive al lado** 2. **el número y la calle donde Ud. vive** 3. **la cantidad de dinero que Ud. paga cada mes para vivir en su apartamento** 4. **la parte principal de una ciudad, donde hay muchos edificios altos** 5. **el antónimo de *centro*** 6. **la persona que alquila un apartamento**
- Have students restate the following sentences to make them reflect their own situations: 1. **Vivo en el centro.** 2. **Mis vecinos son muy simpáticos.** 3. **Tengo una vista magnífica de la ciudad.** 4. **Alquilo un apartamento cerca de la universidad.** 5. **El dueño de la casa de apartamentos paga la luz y el gas.** 6. **Hay portero en mi casa de apartamentos 7. Hay portería automática** (*security system*).
- Take a poll of students to see how many live in a house, in an apartment, in the dorm, or in a fraternity or sorority house. Keep track of findings on the board. Discuss the results and have students compare the advantages and disadvantages of living in the different places: **¿Cuáles son las ventajas / desventajas de vivir... ?**
- Have students work in pairs to interview each other about where their girlfriend / boyfriend (husband / wife or best friend) lives: 1. **¿Dónde vive su pareja / su mejor amigo/a?** 2. **¿Qué gastos paga (gas, luz...)?** 3. **¿Tiene vista?** 4. **¿Hay portero? ¿Cómo es?** 5. **¿Tiene Ud. companero/a? ¿Cómo es?** After the interview, have some students report the information they learned to the class. Alternatively, students can write up the information in a brief paragraph.

Paso 2: Gramática

GRAMMAR SECTION 33

NEGATIVE *TÚ* COMMANDS

Suggestions:

- Point out to students that they already know all of the forms involved in this tense, and that the position of the object pronouns is identical to the pronoun position used in formal (**Ud.** and **Uds.**) commands.
- You may wish to treat the material in this section for passive recognition only. Have students learn only high-frequency irregular **tú** commands.

- Explain to students that the command system in Spanish (although easy to understand when someone gives you a command) is difficult to master in speaking. They should not be discouraged if using the system correctly does not come easily.

AFFIRMATIVE *TÚ* COMMANDS

Suggestion: Remind students of the impoliteness implied in any command, particularly with **tú.** Even with friends, they should use questions instead of commands: **¿Me pasas la sal, por favor? ¿Me prestas tu suéter? ¿Me cierras la puerta?** Then, have students give affirmative commands to a friend who says he/she should do the following things. Write the following example on the board, then give the additional statements: **Debo hacer la cama. → Haz la cama. (Hazla.) Debo decir la verdad / hacer más tacos / ir a la biblioteca / poner los libros en la mesa / salir ahora / tener más paciencia / venir a clase todos los días / ser buen(a) estudiante.**

PRELIMINARY EXERCISES

- Have students make the following commands or questions more polite: 1. To the teacher: **Repita.** 2. To a classmate: **Repite lo que dijo la profesora.** 3. To a housemate: **Lava los platos. / Compra leche de camino a casa.** 4. To a middle-aged woman in the street: **¿Dónde está la parada** (*stop*) **del autobús?** 5. To a young man in the street: **¿Qué hora es?**
- Have students work in groups to get advice from each other, for example, what kind of computer to buy, which kind of exercise to do to lose weight, where to study, what movie to see, and so on. Students should try to use as many commands as possible.

NOTA COMUNICATIVA

Heritage Speakers: Pregúnteles a los hispanohablantes de la clase si saben usar o si usan las formas de **vosotros/as.** También es posible que haya hispanohablantes en su clase que usen el **voseo,** que se oye en Colombia, el Ecuador, Costa Rica, la Argentina y el Uruguay. Revise con la clase los mandatos con **vos:**

Hablá vos.
Acostate vos.
No hablés vos.
No te acostés vos.

Optional Activity: **Recuerdos de la niñez**

Paso 1. Indique los mandatos afirmativos que Ud. oía con frecuencia cuando era niño/a. Después de leerlos todos, indique los dos que oía más. ¿Hay entre estos algún mandato que Ud. no oyó nunca?

1. ______ Limpia tu cuarto.
2. ______ Cómete el desayuno.
3. ______ Haz la tarea.
4. ______ Cierra la puerta.
5. ______ Bébete la leche.
6. ______ Lávate las manos.
7. ______ Díme la verdad.
8. ______ Quítate el *walkman.*
9. ______ Guarda tu bicicleta en el garaje.

Paso 2. Ahora indique los mandatos negativos que escuchaba con frecuencia. Debe indicar también los dos que oía más. ¿Hay alguno que no oyó nunca?

1. ______ No cruces la calle solo/a.
2. ______ No jueges con cerillas (*matches*).
3. ______ No comas dulces antes de cenar.
4. ______ No me digas mentiras (*lies*).
5. ______ No les des tanta comida a los peces.
6. ______ No hables con desconocidos.
7. ______ No dejes el monopatín en el jardín.
8. ______ No cambies los canales tanto.
9. ______ No digas tonterías (*silly things*).

Point Out: Note in this Optional Activity the use of the reflexive pronoun with the verbs **comer** and **beber.** This use of the reflexive means *to eat up* and *to drink up,* respectively.

Cómete las zanahorias.
Eat up your carrots.

No **te bebas** la leche tan rápido.
Don't drink up your milk so fast.

GRAMMAR SECTION 34

Note: The subjunctive is a difficult concept for native speakers of English, and most will need years of practice and immersion to master it. Aim at conceptual awareness and partial control at the elementary level. Partial control means that students are aware of the existence of subjunctive and know the rules of use and the forms, but that they only produce it in well-guided contexts.

PRESENT SUBJUNCTIVE: AN INTRODUCTION

Note: Students were introduced to the subjunctive for passive recognition in **Capítulo 6,** along with formal commands.

Suggestions:

- Point out that the subjunctive also exists in English, although it is less conspicuous because its forms are not exclusively subjunctive, for example, *God bless you, I suggest you be there at one, If I were a rich man, . . .*
- Point out that in English, the conjunction *that* is often optional, but **que** is required in Spanish.
- Emphasize the syntactic requirements for the subjunctive: 1. two clauses 2. a different subject in each clause.
- Provide a diagram to illustrate the structure of a sentence that points out the different subjects and their corresponding verbs in the indicative and subjunctive.

FORMS OF THE PRESENT SUBJUNCTIVE

Note: Emphasize the forms of the subjunctive only for student production, but use full syntax in your input.

Suggestions:

- Emphasize the relationship of the **Ud.** commands to the subjunctive.
- Emphasize that the personal endings in this tense are the same as those of the present indicative (**-s, -mos,** and so on).

- Using brief sentences, present the subjunctive forms of **trabajar.** Write the forms on the board as they are produced. **Yo quiero que Uds. trabajen mucho. ¿Quieren Uds. que yo trabaje mucho? ¿Quiero que John trabaje mucho?,** and so on. Present additional sentences with **beber** and **recibir.**
- Provide some common expressions with the subjunctive: **Que te vaya bien; Que Dios te bendiga.**
- Briefly present the verbs with spelling changes, pointing out that the spelling changes occur in all persons of the subjunctive.
- Briefly model the subjunctive forms of irregular verbs in communicative exchanges with students, asking one or two questions using each verb. Continue to use only **Quiero que...** as the semantic cue or introduce **Ojalá que.**
- Point out that the subjunctive of **hay** is **haya.**
- Introduce the subjunctive forms of stem-changing verbs. Emphasize the second stem-change and its connection to the preterite forms.

Optional Activities:

La vida tecnológica. Indique si está de acuerdo o no con las siguientes oraciones.

1. En la vida actual es absolutamente necesario tener una computadora.
2. Yo quiero comprarme una computadora nueva, pero no creo que pueda comprármela inmediatamente.
3. Hoy día (*These days*) es posible comprar una buena computadora portátil por $1.000.
4. Es horrible que la tecnología cambie tan rápidamente; nadie puede aprender a este ritmo.
5. Prefiero que la gente no dependa tanto de la tecnología.
6. Es ridículo que tantas personas usen un teléfono celular.
7. Dudo que el precio de las llamadas de los teléfonos celulares baje más en los próximos dos años.
8. Espero que mi compañero/a de casa (esposo/a, hijo/a) cambie el mensaje del contestador automático.

¿Puede Ud. substituir en la ausencia de su profesor(a)? Demuéstrele a su profesor(a) que Ud. lo/la conoce bien, formando oraciones como las que dice él/ella en clase. (Sólo tiene que cambiar el infinitivo.)

Quiero que	(nombre de un[a] estudiante)	estudiar
Espero que	todos Uds.	llegar a tiempo
Prohíbo (*I forbid*) que	nadie	copiar en un examen
Dudo que	alguien de la clase	saber el subjuntivo
Es necesario que	yo	sacar notas mejores
Me alegro de que		entender esto
No creo que		navegar por la red
Recomiendo que		dormirse
		hacer la tarea
		¿ ?

ENFOQUE CULTURAL: EL PERÚ

A. Para contestar. Conteste las siguientes preguntas con información en ¡Fíjese! y Conozca...

1. ¿Cuál es el lago más grande de Sudamérica?

___

2. ¿Qué método de agricultura usaban los antiguos indígenas del Perú?

____

3. ¿Qué cultivo que subsiste en las altitudes de más de 13.000 pies fue importante para los incas?

____

4. ¿Cuál es una de las lenguas que hablaban los antiguos habitantes del Perú?

____

5. ¿Por qué «tecnologías» se destacaron los incas?

____

B. Para investigar: Navegando por el Internet. En la página principal de la red científica peruana (**ekeko.rcp.net.pe**), seleccione **Perú.** De allí, escoja **Símbolos populares—Tradición.** Luego, seleccione **Festival de la Marinera.** Use la información de esta última página para completar las siguientes oraciones.

1. La ciudad en la cual se celebra el Festival de la Marinera: _______________
2. La frecuencia con la cual se celebra este festival: cada mes / cada año / cada dos años
3. La región geográfica en la que se encuentra esta ciudad: _______________
4. La distancia de esta ciudad a Lima: _______________
5. El nombre de la persona que fundó (*founded*) la ciudad de Trujillo: _______________
6. Otro nombre que tiene la ciudad de Trujillo: _______________
7. El nombre de las ruinas de barro (*mud*) que se encuentran en Trujillo: _______________

Notes:

- The most important chronicler of the Incan presence in Peru, "El Inca" Garcilaso, was related to some of the outstanding literary figures of Spain, including the brilliant Spanish lyric poet, soldier, and courtier Garcilaso de la Vega, who died in 1536. Thus the need to use "El Inca" with his name, a distinction he was justly proud of, as his mother was descended from a brother of the Incan ruler, Huayna Capac, the last of the great Incan emperors (d. 1525).
- Alberto Fujimori (1938–), the son of Japanese immigrants to Peru, became the country's president in 1990, after a hard-fought run-off election against novelist Mario Vargas Llosa. Initially he was considered an enlightened leader, who had campaigned on issues of improving the economy and controlling the twin rebel organizations, the Maoist **Sendero Luminoso** and the Túpac Amaru Revolutionary Movement. By 1992 however, he had imposed press censorship, suspended some parts of the constitution, and dissolved the legislature. His regime continued to be controversial, and he resigned in November 2000, months before another run-off election scheduled for June 2001.
- César Vallejo (1892–1938) is possibly the greatest South American poet after Neruda, and certainly one of its most original voices. Born in Santiago de Chuco, in the **zona andina,** he published his first poems before arriving in Lima in 1917. His first book of poems, *Los heraldos negros,* a collection that is clearly representative of the **posmodernismo** of the period, was published the following year. *Trilce* (1922), a brilliant and experimentative book, reflects its author's emotional turmoil after several years of leftist political activity that included several months in jail. In 1927, he declared himself a Marxist and during the Spanish Civil War worked as a

correspondent in Spain. He disappeared the day Franco's forces entered Madrid. A posthumous collection, *Poemas humanos,* was published in 1939.

Paso 3: Gramática

GRAMMAR SECTION 35

Suggestions:

- Point out that when an expression of influence is followed by a subject change, the subjunctive is required: **La jefa quiere que los empleados estén contentos.** Ask who wants (→ **la jefa**). Ask who should be happy (→ **los empleados**).
- Point out that when there is no subject change, the infinitive is used, just as in English: **Quiero estar contento.** Ask who wants (→ **yo**). Ask who would like to be happy (→ **yo**).
- Point out that influence implies that the speaker wants (expects / hopes / dreams) to affect somebody's behavior or even his/her own. The influence can be exerted from a power position (using verbs such as **ordenar, insistir en, pedir, mandar, exigir,** and **prohibir**) to the humblest position (**suplicar** [*to beg*] and **desear**).
- Point out that **decir** and **insistir en** are both information and influence verbs, depending on the context.
- When the verbs are informative, they trigger the indicative in dependent clauses: **Carolina nos dice que llegamos a las siete.** = *Carolina tells* (informs) *us that we will arrive at 7:00.* **Insisto en que son amigos.** = *I insist that they are friends* (not something else).
- When verbs imply influence, they trigger the subjunctive: **Carolina nos dice que lleguemos a las siete.** = *Carolina tells us to arrive at 7:00.* **Insisto en que sean amigos.** = *I insist that they be(come) friends.*
- Have students work in groups to make a list of five things that they would like other people to do. Then, have them present requests to someone in class, who must either do it or give a good excuse for not doing it, for example, **Queremos que Roberto nos traiga donuts mañana.** → **Lo siento. No les puedo traer donuts porque no tengo dinero.**

Optional Activity:

El día de la mudanza (*moving*). Imagine que Ud., su esposo/a y sus hijos acaban de llegar, con todas sus cosas, a un nuevo apartamento. ¿Dónde quieren Uds. que se pongan los siguientes muebles? Siga el modelo. Luego explique por qué quiere que cada cosa esté en el sitio indicado. Empiece la primera oración con frases como: **Queremos que... , Preferimos que... , Es necesario que... , Es buena idea que...** Use el verbo **gustar** en la segunda oración.

MODELO:	LOS MUEBLES	LA EXPLICACIÓN
	los trofeos de Julio / la sala	mirarlos todos los días →

Queremos que los trofeos de Julio estén en la sala. ¡Nos gusta mirarlos todos los días!

	LOS MUEBLES	LA EXPLICACIÓN
1.	el nuevo televisor / la sala	ver la tele todos juntos
2.	el televisor portátil / la cocina	ver la tele al cocinar (*while cooking*)
3.	el equipo estereofónico / la alcoba de Julio	escuchar música al estudiar
4.	el sillón grande / la sala	leer el periódico allí
5.	los monopatines de los niños / la patio	jugar allí
6.	la computadora / la oficina	hacer las cuentas allí
7.	el acuario / la alcoba de Anita	mirar los peces

Suggestions:

- Do this as a whole-class activity, or have students do the first sentence working individually, then work as a class to come up with explanations.
- Tell students to imagine that their family friend, don Carlos, gave them the following commands, and have them report what their friend wants them to do, for example, **¡No fume Ud.! → Carlos no quiere que yo fume.** 1. **Grabe el programa.** 2. **No crea eso.** 3. **No cambie de canal.** 4. **Tráigame el control remoto.** 5. **No diga eso.** 6. **No me llame.** 7. **Escúchela.** 8. **Espérelo.** 9. **No nos busque.** 10. **Sírvalos.**

EN LOS ESTADOS UNIDOS Y EL CANADÁ... LAS COMPUTADORAS Y LA COMUNIDAD HISPANA

Suggestion: Assign different countries to students and have them look up online newspapers for their countries. Have them print the front page for at least one newspaper, preferably all students printing the same day, and compare the front pages in class. What can students infer about the different papers based on the front page? Does the paper have a political bias? What are the big stories of the day? And so on.

UN POCO DE TODO

Optional Activities:

Dos diablitos (*little devils*)

Paso 1. Alberto y Eduardo Suárez son dos niños que siempre hacen lo que no deben. Para cada par de oraciones, lea el mandato que les da su madre en la primera oración. Luego, complete la segunda oración con el mandato opuesto.

MODELO: Alberto, siéntate en la silla. No ______ (sentarte) en el suelo. →
No *te sientes* en el suelo.

1. Alberto, no escuches la radio ahora. ______ (Escucharme) a mí.
2. Eduardo, haz tu tarea. No ______ (hacer) eso.
3. Eduardo, no juegues con la pelota en casa. ______ (Jugar) afuera.
4. Alberto, no cantes en la mesa. ______ (Cantar) después de cenar.
5. Alberto, dame tu almuerzo a mí. No ______ (dárselo) al perro.
6. Eduardo, pon los pies en el suelo. No ______ (ponerlos) en el sofá.

Paso 2. ¿Qué quiere la Sra. Suárez que hagan los dos niños? ¿Qué prefiere que *no* hagan? Indique sus deseos con oraciones completas.

MODELO: La Sra. Suárez prefiere que Alberto se siente en la silla. No quiere que se siente en el suelo.

Palabras útiles: querer, desear, esperar, insistir en, preferir, permitir, prohibir

Follow-up: **Paso 2.** Ask students: **¿Qué cosas quieren sus padres, sus hijos o sus amigos que Ud. haga esto año? Explique por qué y si piensa hacerlo o no.**

Una carta al presidente

Paso 1. Divídanse en grupos de tres personas. Cada miembro del grupo va a completar dos de las siguientes oraciones. **¡OJO!** La palabra **presidente** se refiere al presidente de los Estados Unidos. En español, **el rector / la rectora** = *university president.*

Queremos que el presidente (primer ministro) / el rector (la rectora)...
Recomendamos que el presidente (primer ministro) / el rector (la rectora)...
Es importante que el presidente (primer ministro) / el rector (la rectora)...
Sugerimos que el presidente (primer ministro) / el rector (la rectora)...

Paso 2. Ahora los miembros del grupo deben seleccionar las tres mejores oraciones. Una persona de cada grupo las va a escribir en la pizarra.

Paso 3. Lea las oraciones que están en la pizarra y use algunas para escribir una breve carta al presidente de los Estados Unidos, al primer ministro del Canadá o al rector / a la rectora de la universidad. Añada (*Add*) otra información y use **Ud.** en vez de (*instead of*) **el presidente (primer ministro) / el rector (la rectora).**

Suggestion: Encourage students to suggest corrections for what is being written on the board.

Follow-up:
- Have the class vote for the best letter.
- The final version can be assigned as homework. For the next day, have them exchange and correct each other's letters.

Paso 4: Un paso más

VIDEOTECA

MINIDRAMAS

The **Minidramas** vignettes are not referenced in the textbook, but are part of the *¿Qué tal?* Video Program. They also appear on the Video on CD packaged free with the textbook. If you show the **Minidramas** in class or have your students view them as homework, you might find the following suggestions helpful. You can also find blackline master activities in Section X of this Manual for **Minidramas.**

Comprensión:
1. **¿Piensa Ud. que José Miguel y Gustavo entienden bastante de computadoras? ¿Por qué?**
2. **¿Cree Ud. que el inglés tiene influencia en el español en el campo de la tecnología? ¿Puede Ud. dar algunos ejemplos?**

Variation: **Problemas con la computadora.**

A. **En una tienda de computadoras. Complete el diálogo con las frases siguientes:**
póngala allí **que hacer un trabajo urgente** **voy a ver** **¿qué desea?**

DEPENDIENTE: **Buenas, ____________**
CLIENTE: **Necesito que me arreglen esta impresora.**
DEPENDIENTE: **Bien, _____. Alguien la va a arreglar mañana o pasado mañana.**
CLIENTE: **Pero... tengo ___________. ¿No podrían arreglarla hoy mismo?**
DEPENDIENTE: **La verdad es que tenemos mucho trabajo. ¿Ud. la compró aquí?**
CLIENTE: **Sí, aquí está el recibo.**
DEPENDIENTE: **Bueno, ____________ si alguien puede ayudarlo ahora mismo.**

B. **En la residencia. Ponga en orden las partes del diálogo.**

____ ANITA: **Sí, cómo no. Sólo te pido que tengas un poco de cuidado.**
____ ANITA: **Claro. Es la época de los parciales** (*midterms*).
____ MARIBEL: **Necesito trabajar con la computadora y todos los terminales del *campus* están ocupados.**
____ MARIBEL: **Oye, si tú no tienes que usarla esta noche, ¿me permites que use tu computadora? Tengo que entregar este trabajo mañana a las nueve.**

ACTIVIDAD DE DESENLACE: ¡EL CONCURSO SENSACIONAL!

Activity:	Groups of students will recreate television programs in the classroom. They may, for example, choose among the following: • **¡Ese es el precio!** (*The Price is Right*)**:** The master/mistress of ceremonies (alternating team members) describes vehicles and electronic equipment and the class tries to guess their price. • **Los sobrevivientes** (*Survivors*)**:** Students set up the rules for winning items they can use on a desert island. These rules are expressed as **tú** commands. The class plays the game, with the group members acting as "hosts." • **¡Arriésgate!** (*Jeopardy*)**:** A team makes up answers and classmates try to guess the questions. The topics are those presented in the **Vocabulario** sections of the chapter.
Purpose:	To create a context in which students can review and practice the grammar from **Capítulo 12** and vocabulary related to consumer items (vehicles and electronic equipment) and housing
Resources:	*¿Qué tal?* textbook, the Internet, and other sources as appropriate
Vocabulary:	Vehicles and electronic equipment, housing
Grammar:	Principal grammatical structures covered in **Capítulo 12** of the textbook, including the use of informal commands, and the subjunctive to express actions or states and desires and requests
Duration:	Out-of-class preparation time will vary. In-class time will be approximately seven minutes per presentation.
Format:	Groups of three to four students

La encuesta dice...

Una novia muy enamorada le dice a su novio:

1. **Invítame a cenar.**
2. **Tráeme flores (y otros regalos).**
3. **Dime que me quieres.**
4. **No mires a otras mujeres.**
5. **Llámame por teléfono todos los días.**
6. **No salgas tanto con tus amigos.**
7. **No veas tantos partidos en la televisión.**

La encuesta dice...

El padre le dice a su hija de quince años:

1. **No hables mucho por teléfono.**
2. **No veas televisón toda la tarde.**
3. **No uses faldas muy cortas.**
4. **No fumes.**
5. **No tomes cerveza.**
6. **No llegues tarde a casa.**
7. **No salgas con los muchachos.**

La encuesta dice...

Una jefa muy antipática le dice a su secretario:

1. **Llega a tiempo todos los días.**
2. **Haz todo tu trabajo.**
3. **No me pidas aumentos de sueldo.**
4. **Sírveme café.**
5. **Dame mis mensajes inmediatamente.**
6. **Maneja la computadora (la impresora, el *fax*, etcétera) con cuidado.**
7. **No uses el teléfono para llamarles a tus amigos.**

La encuesta dice...

El dueño antipático de una casa de apartamentos le dice a su nuevo inquilino joven:

1. **Paga el alquiler a tiempo.**
2. **No des fiestas en el apartamento.**
3. **Limpia tu apartamento.**
4. **Bájale el volumen al equipo estereofónico.**
5. **No gastes mucha agua.**
6. **No traigas animales a casa.**
7. **Apaga las luces y el gas.**

Capítulo 12: Partner A *Frases ilustradas*

Read each sentence to your partner using the cues given. Your partner will tell you if your sentences are correct or not. You have three chances to respond correctly.

1. **Queremos que tú a_______________ el**  **que no funciona bien.**

2. **Recomiendo que Uds. a_______________ un apartamento en el** 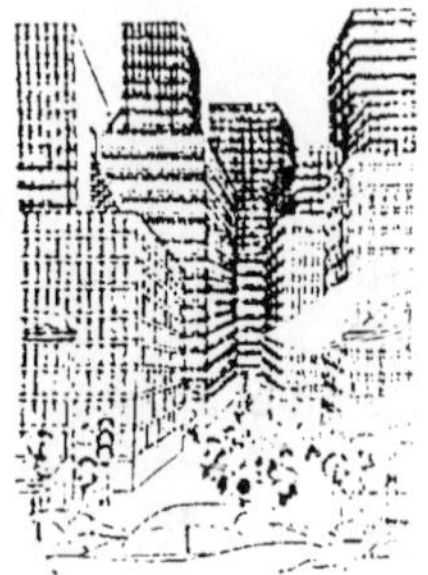

3. **Es necesario que la jefa le d_______________ una** 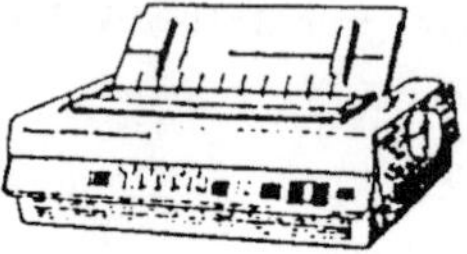 **nueva a su secretario.**

4. **El dueño pide que yo s_______________ unas**  **en la fiesta de Navidad.**

5. **El profesor manda que nosotros v_______________ la**  **de Picasso en ese museo.**

6. **Sus padres prohíben que Guillermo g_______________ su**  **en la casa.**

7. **Es bueno que los niños c____________________ el agua del**  **frecuentemente.**

8. **Si necesitas dinero, sugiero que tú c_______________ un**  **de tiempo parcial.**

Capítulo 12: Partner A *Frases ilustradas*

These are your partner's answers. Listen to what your partner tells you. If his/her answer is not exactly what you have, just tell him/her: **No está bien. Trata de hacerlo otra vez.** Give your partner three opportunities to respond correctly.

1. **Esperamos que tú ganes un trofeo esta vez.**
2. **Mi padre no permite que yo maneje su motocicleta.**
3. **¿Prefieres que yo grabe este programa en la videocasetera?**
4. **Los vecinos dudan que un coche descapotable cueste más de veinte y cinco mil dólares.**
5. **Me alegro de que haya una casa en esta vecindad que tiene una vista bonita. Quiero comprarla.**
6. **Es importante que esta computadora no falle constantemente. ¿Puedes arreglarla?**
7. **Mamá insiste en que nosotros pongamos el contestador automático si vamos a salir.**
8. **Es mejor que las personas perezosas tengan un televisor con control remoto.**

Capítulo 12: Partner B *Frases ilustradas*

Read each sentence to your partner using the cues given. Your partner will tell you if your sentences are correct or not. You have three chances to respond correctly.

1. **Esperamos que tú g______________ un**  **esta vez.**

2. **Mi padre no permite que yo m______________ su**  **.**

3. **¿Prefieres que yo g______________ este programa en la**  **?**

4. **Los vecinos dudan que un**  **c____________ más de veinte y cinco mil dólares.**

5. **Me alegro de que h______________ una**  **en esta vecindad que tiene una vista bonita. Quiero comprarla.**

6. **Es importante que esta**  **no f__________ constantemente. ¿Puedes arreglarla?**

7. **Mamá insiste en que nosotros p______________ el**  **si vamos a salir.**

8. **Es mejor que las personas perezosas t______________ un**  **con control remoto.**

Capítulo 12: Partner B *Frases ilustradas*

These are your partner's answers. Listen to what your partner tells you. If his/her answer is not exactly what you have, just tell him/her: **No está bien. Trata de hacerlo otra vez.** Give your partner three opportunities to respond correctly.

1. **Queremos que tú arregles el radio portátil que no funciona bien.**
2. **Recomiendo que Uds. alquilen un apartamento en el centro.**
3. **Es necesario que la jefa le dé una impresora nueva a su secretario.**
4. **El dueño pide que yo saque unas fotos en la fiesta de Navidad.**
5. **El profesor manda que nosotros veamos la pintura de Picasso en ese museo.**
6. **Sus padres prohíben que Guillermo guarde su bicicleta en la casa.**
7. **Es bueno que los niños cambien el agua del acuario frecuentemente.**
8. **Si necesitas dinero, sugiero que tú consigas un trabajo de tiempo parcial.**

¡A pescar!

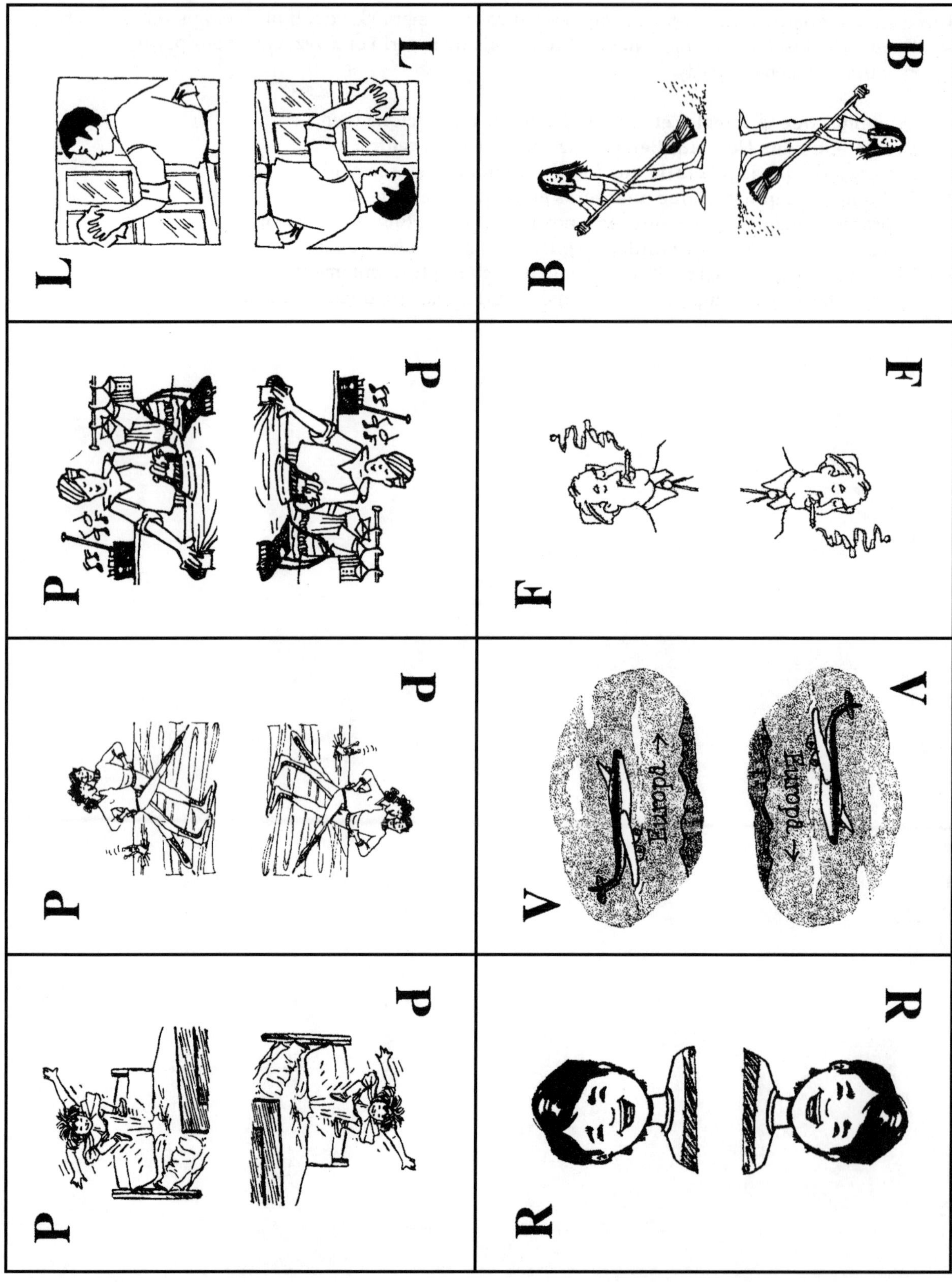

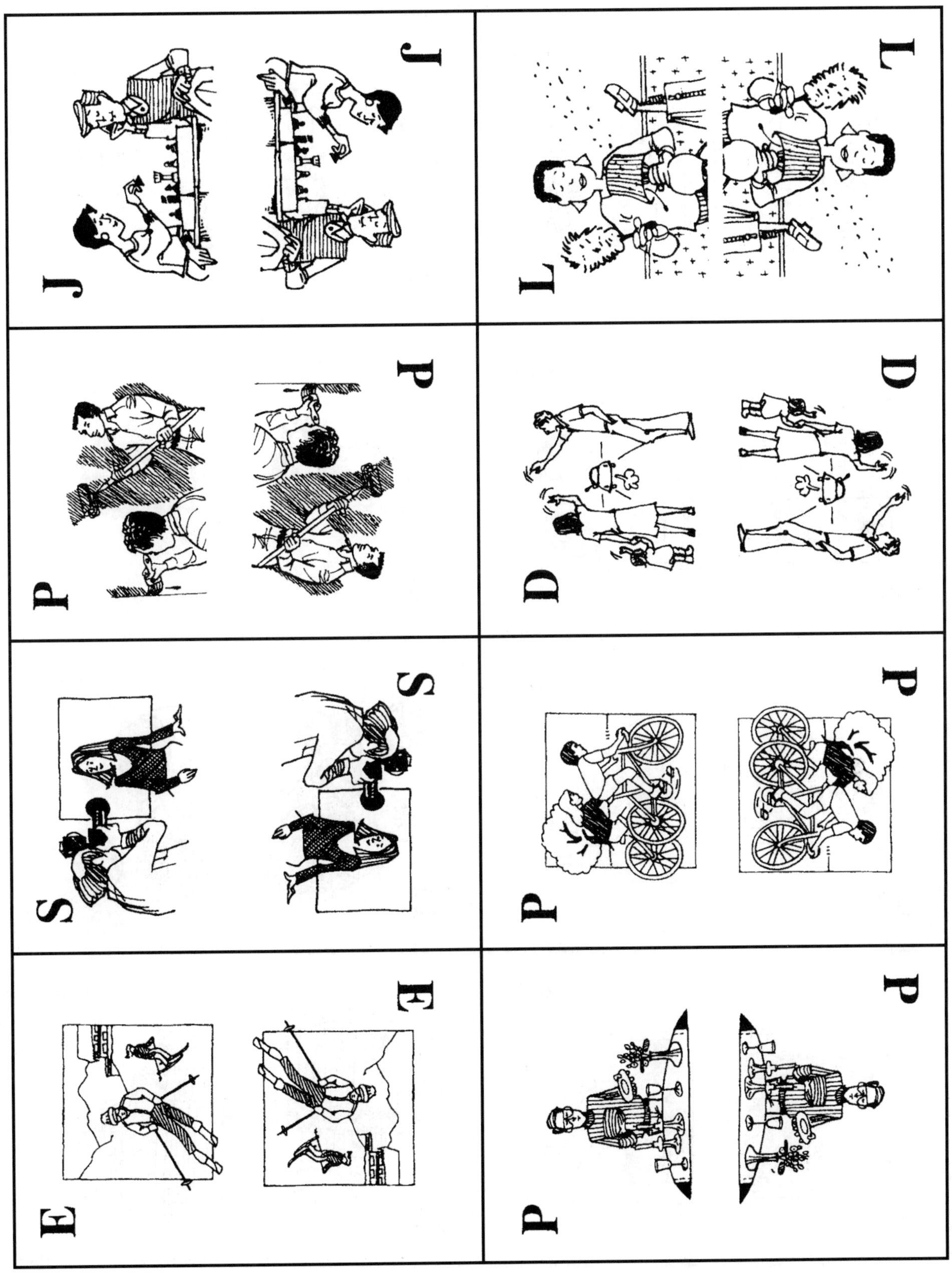
J
J
L
L
P
P
D
D
S
S
P
P
E
E
P
P

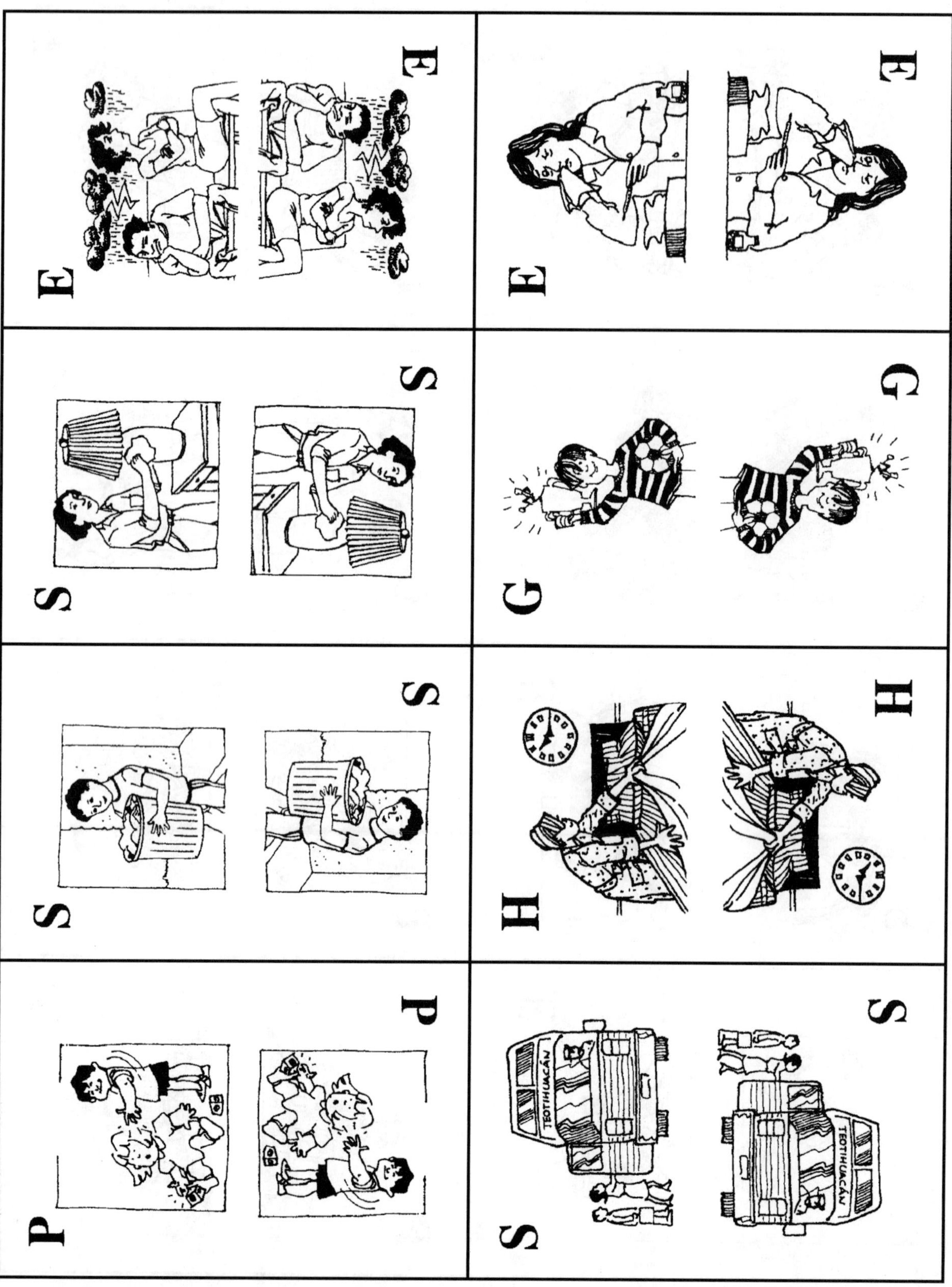
E
E
S
S
S
S
P
P
E
E
G
G
H
H
S
S
TEOTIHUACÁN
TEOTIHUACÁN

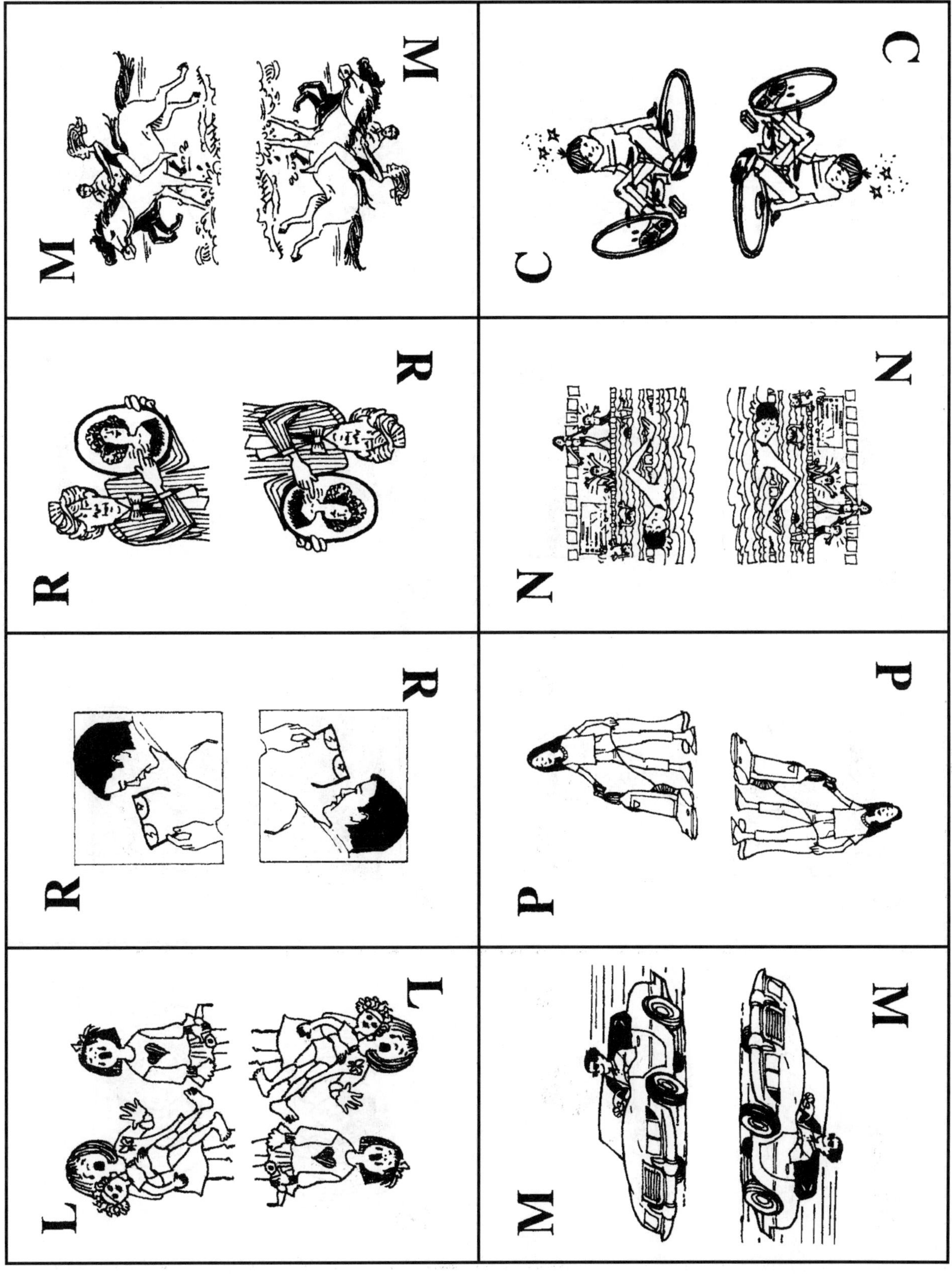
M
M
C
C
R
R
N
N
R
R
P
P
L
L
M
M

¡A pescar!

CAPÍTULO 13 EL ARTE Y LA CULTURA

Student Supplements

- Listening Comprehension Program CD, **Capítulo 13** (**Paso 1: Vocabulario:** word lists)
- Workbook/Laboratory Manual, **Capítulo 13**
- Audio Program CD, **Capítulo 13**

Instructor Resources

- Instructor's Manual/IRK: Chapter-by-Chapter Supplementary Materials, **Capítulo 13**
  - **Paso 1: Vocabulario**
  - **Paso 2: Gramática**
    - Grammar Section 36
    - **Enfoque cultural**
  - **Paso 3: Gramática**
    - Grammar Section 37
    - **En los Estados Unidos y el Canadá...**
    - **Un poco de todo**
  - **Paso 4: Un paso más**
    - **Videoteca: Minidramas**
  - Games and Activities
- Instructor's Manual/IRK: Video Activities and Related Materials
  - **A primera vista**
  - **A segunda vista**
  - Answers to Video Activities
  - Videoscripts
- Audioscript, **Capítulo 13**
- Transparencies 73–75
- Testing Program, **Capítulo 13**

Multimedia Resources

- Online Learning Center
- Electronic Workbook/Laboratory Manual
- Video, **Capítulo 13** (cue 1:19:02)
  - **En contexto** (2:49)
  - **Minidramas** (4:32)
  - **Enfoque cultural: Bolivia, Ecuador** (2:00)
- Student CD-ROM, **Capítulo 13**
- Electronic Language Tutor, **Capítulo 13** (**Vocabulario, Gramática**)

Paso 1: Vocabulario

LAS ARTES

Preparation: It is helpful, but not essential, to bring pictures representing as many of the arts and artists as possible. Have students skim the vocabulary before you begin.

Suggestion: After presenting the main categories of art, expand on each, presenting vocabulary in word families, for example, **la escultura, el/la escultor(a), esculpir,** when possible.

Sample Passage: **Hoy vamos a hablar de las artes. Cuando oyen la palabra «arte», muchas personas piensan inmediatamente en la pintura** (show a painting). **Pero, la pintura es solamente una forma de expresión artística. ¿Qué otras formas de expresión artística hay? Bueno, la música es un arte importante y muy popular. ¿Qué más... ? El baile** (pantomime or show picture) **es otro arte. Y el drama... ¿Se considera el drama como un arte? Sí, claro que sí. Bueno, tenemos la pintura, la música, el baile, el drama y ¿qué más... ? La literatura: las novelas, los cuentos y la poesía... la literatura es un arte también. La escultura es otro y también la arquitectura.**

Hablamos de la música. ¿Cómo se llama una persona que escribe música? Se llama el compositor o la compositora. Mozart es un compositor famosísimo. Aaron Copland es un compositor de los Estados Unidos y Manuel de Falla es un compositor español. De Falla compuso música española tradicional y música para el ballet también.

Las personas que tocan la música son músicos. ¿Quiénes son algunos músicos famosos? (Accept names.) **Isaac Stern, sí, es un músico que toca el violín. ¿Quién más? Ah, sí, George Winston... él toca el piano** (and so forth).

Quick Comprehension Check: Sample items:

1. **¿Es cierto que Frank Lloyd Wright fue compositor? (arquitecto)**
2. **La ópera es una combinación de dos artes. ¿Cuáles son? (la música y el drama)**
3. **¿La *Mona Lisa* es un ejemplo de qué tipo de arte? (la pintura)**
4. **¿Saben Uds. quién fue pintor de la Mona Lisa? (Leonardo da Vinci)**

Suggestions:

- Emphasize the dual gender of the following words: **el/la artista, el/la cantante, el/la guía, el/la poeta.** Point out that **la guía** can refer to a guidebook or a female guide.
- Point out the spelling differences between English and Spanish: **escultura** vs. *sculpture,* **arquitectura** vs. *architecture.*
- Help students relate the following words: *scene* → **escena** → **escenario.**
- Point out that a play is called **una obra de teatro.** Offer additional vocabulary such as **artesanal** and **artístico.**
- Have students look at the art and vocabulary for one or two minutes. Then describe the art scene using as many words from the list as possible, and have students repeat them.
- Write a column on the board for each of the different types of art. Have students supply words from the vocabulary that belong to each art form. Repeat and model the pronunciation of the words added to the columns.
- Read the following definitions and have students give the words defined: 1. **Es una actividad artística en la que unas personas representan la vida de otras personas imaginarias o reales.** 2. **Picasso, O'Keeffe y Van Gogh formaban parte de este tipo de artistas.** 3. **Esta persona diseña y dibuja casas o edificios.** 4. **En este lugar se representan obras de teatro.** 5. **Gloria Estefan y Julio Iglesias tienen esta profesión.** 6. **El sinónimo de crear una escultura.** 7. **Los artistas hacen esto antes de pintar un cuadro, generalmente.**

- Have students tell whether the following sentences about traditional culture are **cierto** or **falso:** 1. **Se puede comprar artesanías en un supermercado.** 2. **La cerámica es una de las artes más conocidas de este país.** 3. **En este país no hay ningún tipo de ruinas de civilizaciones anteriores a la nuestra.** 4. **Los tejidos** (*woven goods*) **no son una forma de producción artística.** 5. **Cada región de este país tiene sus canciones típicas. (Dé ejemplos.)**
- Have students answer the following questions: 1. **¿Tiene Ud. algún tipo de talento artístico? ¿Cuál es? ¿Cuándo desarrolla** (*develop*) **Ud. su talento?** 2. **¿Tiene un pintor favorito / una pintora favorita? ¿Quién es? ¿Le gusta la pintura abstracta o figurativa?** 3. **Para Ud., ¿qué es más importante, que un edificio sea elegante o práctico? ¿Qué tipo de arquitectura le gusta más? ¿Le gusta la arquitectura de su universidad? ¿Por qué sí o por qué no?** 4. **Para Ud., ¿qué es más importante en una película, el guión, la dirección o la actuación? ¿Quiénes son sus actores favoritos? ¿Tiene algún director favorito o alguna directora favorita? ¿Quién es?**
- Present the following questions to establish a class discussion: **¿Cree que todas las personas son artistas de alguna manera? Si una persona tiene mucho talento, ¿cree que es fácil que pueda vivir de su arte y su producción artística?**

CONVERSACIÓN A

Notes:

- **Diego Rivera** (1886–1957), Mexico's foremost muralist, was inspired by the pre-Columbian history of his native land. He captured the images and spirit of Mexico in his murals with a direct, realist style.
- ***El lago de los Cisnes*** (1877) a ballet set to music by Peter Ilyich Tchaikovsky (Russia, 1840–1893), tells the story of a woman who turns into a swan. It is an important part of the repertoire of all of the major classical ballet companies in the world.
- ***El amor brujo*** is a ballet written in 1915 by the Spanish composer Manual de Falla (1876–1946).
- ***El ciudadano Kane*** (*Citizen Kane,* 1941) is a classic masterpiece considered by many to be the best American film ever. Making his film debut at the age of 25, Orson Welles was at once the actor, co-writer, and director.
- ***El mago de Oz*** (*The Wonderful Wizard of Oz,* 1900) is a favorite American classic written by L. Frank Baum (1856–1919), an American journalist, playwright, and author of juvenile stories. The novel was made into a movie in 1938.
- ***La Bohème,*** first produced in 1896, was the first of three operas that Puccini wrote with the librettists Illica and Giacosa (the others were *Madama Butterfly* and *Tosca*). Based on Murger's autobiographical *Scènes de la vie de Bohème,* this opera depicts the lives of artists living in Paris during the mid-1800s.
- ***La Traviata*** is an opera written by Giuseppi Verdi (1813–1901), which mounts a romantic attack on conventional bourgeois morality. The story argues that a good heart is more important than propriety and that true love must triumph over all.

RANKING THINGS: ORDINALS

Suggestions:

- Select a row of students and identify the first ten using ordinal numbers, for example, **Juan es el primer estudiante, Isabel es la segunda estudiante, Susana** es **la tercera,** and so on.
- Remind students that they have used **el primero** with dates, and in **Capítulo 12** they used ordinal numbers to refer to floors of a building.
- Point out that cardinal numbers are more commonly used than ordinal numbers above tenth: **Alfonso XIII (trece).**

Paso 2: Gramática

GRAMMAR SECTION 36

Suggestions:

- Point out that a change of subject is required for the subjunctive with emotional statements, just as with expressions of influence.
- Emphasize the use of the infinitive, not the subjunctive, after expressions and generalizations of emotion when there is no change of subject, for example, **Siento estar tan cansado** vs. **Siento que estés tan cansado;** and **Es mejor esperar** vs. **Es mejor que esperen.**
- Many of these verbs and generalizations are also value judgments (**es bueno / malo / necesario / extraño**). They are reactions that imply a personal opinion, which may differ from one person to another.

Optional Activities:

Comentarios. Complete las oraciones con la forma apropiada del verbo entre paréntesis.

1. **Dicen en la tienda que esta videocasetera es fácil de usar. Por eso me sorprende que no (funcionar) bien. Temo que (ser) muy complicada. Me sorprende que ni** (*not even*) **mi compañera (entenderla).**
2. **¡Qué desastre! El profesor dice que nos va a dar un examen. ¡Es increíble que (darnos) otro examen tan pronto! Es terrible que yo (tener) que estudiar este fin de semana. Espero que el profesor (cambiar) de idea.**
3. **Este año sólo tengo dos semanas de vacaciones. Es ridículo que sólo (tener) dos semanas. No me gusta que las vacaciones (ser) tan breves. Es una lástima que yo no (poder) ir a ningún sitio.**

Suggestions:

- Have students invent similar situations and present them to the class.
- Have students explain the choice of mood in all the sentences in the activity.

Los valores de nuestra sociedad. Express your feelings about the following situations by restating the situations, beginning with one of the following phrases or any others you can think of: **es bueno/malo que, es extraño/increíble que, es una lástima que.**

1. **Muchas personas viven para trabajar. No saben descansar.**
2. **Somos una sociedad de consumidores.**
3. **Muchas personas no asisten a las funciones teatrales.**
4. **Juzgamos** (*We judge*) **a los otros por las cosas materiales que tienen.**
5. **Las personas ricas tienen mucho prestigio en esta sociedad.**
6. **Las mujeres generalmente no ganan tanto como los hombres cuando hacen el mismo trabajo.**
7. **Los jugadores profesionales de fútbol norteamericano ganan sueldos fenomenales.**
8. **Para la gente joven, la televisión es más popular que los libros.**
9. **Los hombres generalmente no reciben** *paternity leave* **después del nacimiento de un bebé.**
10. **Hay discriminación contra la gente mayor para ciertas profesiones.**

Follow-up:

Follow up with a similar activity that uses real-world statements related to students: 1. **(Estudiante) está enfermo/a.** 2. **No tenemos clase el sábado.** 3. **(Estudiante) se gradúa en junio.** 4. **El coche de ______ no funciona bien.** 5. **Los profesores (no) reciben un sueldo muy alto.** 6. **Llueve mucho/poco este año.**

ENFOQUE CULTURAL: BOLIVIA Y EL ECUADOR

A. ¿Cierto o falso? Indique si las siguientes oraciones son ciertas (C) o falsas (F) según la información en Datos esenciales y ¡Fíjese! Si la información no se presenta en estas secciones, escoja ND (No lo dice). Corrija las oraciones falsas.

1. C F ND El Ecuador y Bolivia tienen más de un idioma en común.
2. C F ND El Ecuador tiene menos habitantes que Bolivia.
3. C F ND Hay una gran influencia indígena en la cultura boliviana.
4. C F ND La ciudad capital más alta del mundo está en el Perú.
5. C F ND Las islas Galápagos están rodeadas por (*surrounded by*) corrientes (*currents*) marinas muy fuertes.

B. Para completar. Complete el siguiente cuadro usando información de los Enfoques culturales de los Capítulos 12 y 13.

El país (Los países) con el mayor número de habitantes:	
El país (Los países) en el/los que se habla otro idioma además del español (mencione el país/los países y el idioma/los idiomas):	
El país con menos habitantes:	

Suggestions:

- Bring in examples of Bolivian music (many samples can be downloaded from the Internet), then have students compare this music to other versions of Andean music they may have heard. Ask, for example, what differences they hear between the Simon and Garfunkle song "**El condor pasa**" and its Quechua counterpart. Students may enjoy seeing the Quechua lyrics to the song, which can also be found on the Internet.
- Show the Bolivian film *Cuestión de fe* (1998) in class. Directed by Paolo Agazzi, it tells the story about a **santero** (a sculptor of wooden images of saints) and an atheist who carry an image of the Virgin in a truck through the Bolivian jungle to a lost village. This film has won numerous European, North and South American, and Caribbean awards.
- Tell students that Ecuador replaced its currency, the **sucre,** in favor of the U.S. dollar in the year 2000. Have them check the Internet for the present status of the currency, and talk with them about the meaning of the change.
- Challenge students to an Ecuador food and beverage scavenger hunt (and join them!) by asking them to find the answers to the following questions on the Internet. The winner is the one who can provide the most, and the most thorough, answers. 1. How is **chicha** made? 2. Where can you find a good plate of **encocados**? 3. How do you make **pollo sin pollo**? 4. What is most commonly served with Ecuadorian **ceviche**? What is the main ingredient in **caldo de pata**? In **tronquito**? What is **yaguarlocho**?

Paso 3: Gramática

GRAMMAR SECTION 37

Suggestions:

- Point out the similarity of this pattern (two verbs, a second subject) to that of the subjunctive after expressions of influence / emotion.
- Point out that when there is no subject change, Spanish uses either the subjunctive or the infinitive after expressions of doubt or denial. Generalizations are followed by the infinitive only when there is no subject change. **Dudo que tenga el dinero. / Dudo tener el dinero.** = *I doubt that I have the money.* **Es imposible tener el dinero para mañana.** vs. **Es imposible que yo tenga el dinero para mañana.**
- Contrast and model **no creer** and **dudar** (subjunctive) with **creer,** which usually implies affirmation and is therefore followed by the indicative.
- Point out that an easy rule is that *all* negated verbs take subjunctive in the dependent clause. **No niego** and **no dudo** are the only exceptions. They can take either the subjunctive or the indicative, depending on the meaning the speaker wishes to convey. Most students are not ready for these subtleties, and the use of **no niego** and **no dudo** should be restricted for now.
- In questions with **creer,** the use of the indicative or subjunctive in dependent clauses reflects the opinion of the person asking the question. Indicative: **¿Crees que los Ramírez son ricos?** (The speaker believes they are.) Subjunctive: **¿Crees que los Ramírez sean ricos?** (The speaker doubts that they are.)

Preliminary exercise: Have students express the following ideas in Spanish: 1. I doubt that they are rich / that they are coming. 2. I don't believe that they are rich / that they are coming. 3. I believe that they are rich / that they are coming.

EN LOS ESTADOS UNIDOS Y EL CANADÁ... CARLOS SANTANA

Suggestions:

- Ask questions about Santana. Because Santana is well known in the U.S. and Canada, you might include questions about information not presented in the reading.
- If you have students over the age of 35 who listened to Santana when they were younger, compare their experience with his music with that of younger students who may not have listened to Santana before the release of *Supernatural.* How many younger students bought older Santana albums after listening to *Supernatural*?

UN POCO DE TODO

Optional Activity:

Reacciones

Paso 1. Las siguientes oraciones mencionan temas de vital importancia en el mundo de hoy. ¿Qué cree Ud.? Reaccione Ud. a estas oraciones, empezando con una de estas expresiones.

Dudo que...	Es bueno/malo que...
(No) Es verdad que...	Es una lástima que...
No hay duda que...	Es increíble que...
Es probable que...	(No) Me gusta que...

1. Los niños miran la televisión seis horas al día.
2. Hay mucha pobreza (*poverty*) en el mundo.
3. En este país gastamos mucha energía.
4. Hay mucho sexo y violencia en la televisión y en el cine.
5. Se come poco y mal en muchas partes del mundo.

6. Los temas de la música *rap* son demasiado violentos.
7. Hay mucho interés en la exploración del espacio.
8. El fumar no es malo para la salud.
9. Los deportes para las mujeres no reciben tanto apoyo (*support*) financiero como los de los hombres.
10. No se permite el uso de la marihuana.

Paso 2. Indique Ud. soluciones para algunos de los problemas que se mencionan en el **Paso 1.** Empiece las soluciones con estas frases.

Es urgente que...	Es necesario que...
Es preferible que...	Es importante que...
Quiero que...	Insisto en que...

Suggestions:

- Assign this in groups of five to six students so they can have a discussion. Remind them to be polite in their disagreement.
- Use the following transformation drill to review the subjunctive structure. Write the following model on the board: **Marcos nunca llega a casa temprano. Dudo que...** → **Dudo que Marcos llegue a casa temprano hoy.** 1. **Marcos nunca ayuda a limpiar la casa. Dudo que...** 2. **Nunca se acuesta temprano. Es probable...** 3. **Casi nunca hace su cama por la mañana. No creo que...** 4. **Con frecuencia no se despierta hasta las once. Dudo que...** 5. **Usa mi coche y lo deja sin gasolina. Estoy seguro que...**

Variations:

- Make up statements about yourself, your family, or class members to which students can react using the phrases provided in the Optional Activity. Some statements should be false, even outrageous.
- Substitute more controversial statements for those given in the text, for example, **Creo que el aborto debe ser legal. Creo que no se debe fumar marihuana.**

Paso 4: Un paso más

VIDEOTECA

MINIDRAMAS

The **Minidramas** vignettes are not referenced in the textbook, but are part of the *¿Qué tal?* Video Program. They also appear on the Video on CD packaged free with the textbook. If you show the **Minidramas** in class or have your students view them as homework, you might find the following suggestions helpful. You can also find blackline master activities in Section X of this Manual for **Minidramas.**

Comprensión:

1. **¿De quiénes hablan Lupe y Diego?**
2. **¿Qué tipo de cuadros pintaban estos artistas?**
3. **¿Qué aspectos de la vida de Frida Kahlo se pueden destacar?**

Suggestion: Review and expand on board verbs and expressions that express likes and dislikes. Ask students which ones express stronger preferences.

POSITIVO	**NEGATIVO**
me gusta	**no me gusta**
me agrada	**no me agrada**
aprecio	**no sé apreciar**
me interesa	**me aburre**
me encanta	**odio**
prefiero	**detesto**

Students should keep this gradation in mind in their dialogues since, generally, expressing a strong negative reaction to another person's taste implies great familiarity.

A LEER

Suggestion: **Estrategia.** Have students share their predictions about verb forms and infinitives. Then, ask them how they think these verb forms translate into English.

Suggestion: **Comprensión.** Ask students to identify the passages that contain the information referred to in these questions.

A ESCRIBIR

Suggestion: **Paso 1.** Have students connect their responses in writing to form a short composition.

ACTIVIDAD DE DESENLACE: EL ARTE Y LA CULTURA DEL MUNDO HISPANO

Activity: Students will research a famous Spanish or Latin American artist and do a class presentation with accompanying visuals.

Purpose: To explore the artistic heritage of the Spanish-speaking world; to create a context in which students can review and practice the grammar from **Capítulo 13** and vocabulary related to the arts.

Resources: *¿Qué tal?* textbook, the Internet, and other sources as appropriate

Vocabulary: The visual and plastic arts, ordinals

Grammar: Principal grammatical structures covered in **Capítulo 13** of the textbook, including the use of the subjunctive to express emotion, uncertainty and emotion, doubt, and denial

Duration: Out-of-class preparation time will vary. In-class time will be approximately five minutes per presentation.

Format: Individually or in groups of two to three students

Comments: Encourage students to create posters, show pictures of their artists' works, or play videos or music.

Capítulo 13

Memoria

1	2	3	4
(el compositor)	(los actores)	Cantan temas tradicionales o populares.	Dirige dramas.
5	**6**	**7**	**8**
Pinta cuadros.	(los músicos)	Escribe novelas, cuentos, ensayos y libros de texto.	(la pintora)
9	**10**	**11**	**12**
(el escritor)	Esculpe estatuas en piedra, bronce o mármol.	Hace composiciones musicales.	Baila el flamenco.
13	**14**	**15**	**16**
Desempeñan papeles en la televisión, en las películas o en el teatro.	(los cantantes)	(el escultor)	(el director)
17	**18**	**19**	**20**
Tocan los instrumentos musicales.	(el arquitecto)	Diseña edificios.	(la bailarina)

Capítulo 13 *Lotería*

Para cada pregunta a continuación, busque una persona de la clase que conteste «sí» y escriba su nombre. **¡OJO!** No escriba el mismo nombre más de una vez. Cuando alguien conteste en el afirmativo, es necesario pedirle más información. Si Ud. gana el juego de «Lotería», tiene que reportar esta información a la clase antes de recibir un premio.

En tu niñez, ¿asistías a clases de ballet? ¿Eras un bailarín / una bailarina torpe?	**¿Sabes el nombre de algún cantante hispano? ¿Cuál es?**	**¿Te gusta la ópera? ¿En qué lengua se canta tu ópera preferida?**	**Cuando vas al teatro, ¿prefieres sentarte cerca del escenario? Por lo general, ¿cuánto pagas por un boleto?**
¿Fuiste al cine el fin de semana pasado? ¿Qué película(s) viste?	**¿Visitaste un museo recientemente? ¿Cuál?**	**En la escuela secundaria, ¿desempeñaste un papel en una obra de teatro? ¿Cómo se llamaba la obra?**	**¿Visitaste las ruinas de alguna civilización precolombina? ¿Dónde estaban?**
¿Fuiste a un concierto de música clásica el año pasado? ¿Dónde? ¿Quienes eran los compositores cuya música oíste?	**¿Pintaste algún cuadro en el primer grado? ¿Qué pasó con tu «obra de arte»?**	**¿Conoces personalmente a algún actor, cantante o músico famoso? ¿Cómo se llama?**	**¿Tienes un pintor preferido? ¿Cómo se llama? ¿Cuál es su nacionalidad?**
¿Sabes cantar alguna canción en español? ¿Cómo se llama la canción?	**¿Tienes algún objeto de cerámica en tu casa o apartamento? ¿Qué es?**	**¿Eres escritor(a)? ¿Qué escribes?**	**¿Hiciste algún objeto de artesanía a mano? ¿Qué era?**

Capítulo 13: Partner A *Frases ilustradas*

Read each sentence to your partner using the cues given. Your partner will tell you if your sentences are correct or not. You have three chances to guess correctly.

1. **Es probable que el guía nos (decir) ________ el nombre del mejor mercado de**  **.**

2. **Es necesario que tú (ir) ________ al Palacio de Bellas Artes para ver las**  **del Ballet Folklórico de México.**

3. **Ojalá que (haber) ________ un**  **de Miró en este** 

.

4. **Es cierto que ese grupo de mariachis sólo (tocar) ________**  **ranchera.**

5. **Es triste que el público norteamericano no (apreciar) ________ más la** 

española. Por ejemplo, todos deben leer *Don Quijote de la Mancha*.

6. **Estoy seguro/a que a los niños les (interesar) ________ el**  **más que el teatro.**

7. Es terrible que ese actor todavía no (saber) __________ su papel. ¿Quién le da una copia del  ?

8. Profesor, ¿Ud. insiste en que los estudiantes de  (hacer) __________ varios dibujos antes de empezar a esculpir?

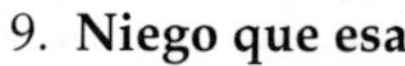

9. Niego que esa  (ser) __________ Gloria Estefan.

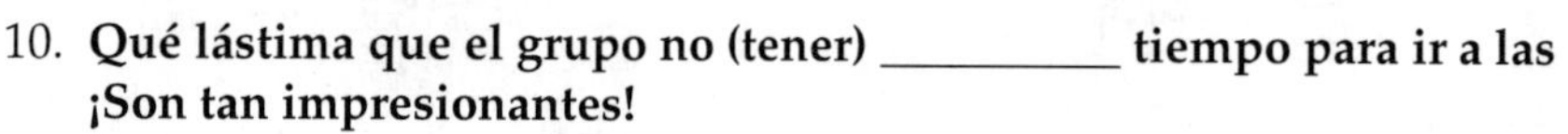

10. Qué lástima que el grupo no (tener) __________ tiempo para ir a las 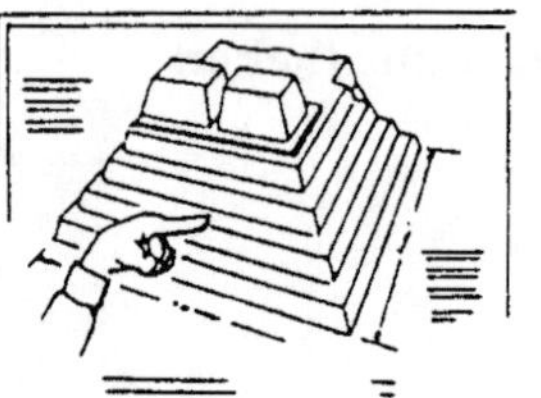 . ¡Son tan impresionantes!

Capítulo 13: Partner A *Frases ilustradas*

These are your partner's answers. Listen to what your partner tells you. If his/her answer is not exactly what you have, just tell him/her: **No está bien. Trata de hacerlo otra vez.** Give your partner three opportunities to respond correctly.

1. **Es posible que tú conozcas a ese pintor. Hubo una exposición de sus cuadros en nuestro café preferido.**

2. **El artesano pobre espera que los turistas le compren la cerámica y los tejidos.**

3. **¿Recomiendas que nosotros veamos las ruinas de la civilización azteca?**

4. **Creo que muchos escritores vienen a nuestra tertulia literaria** (*literary gathering*) **esta noche.**

5. **A algunos aficionados al cine no les gusta que la actriz Demi Moore desempeñe el papel de una bailarina exótica.**

6. **Tememos que ese actor famoso no vuelva a actuar en las películas porque es muy viejo y enfermo.**

7. **Los extranjeros se alegran de que el guía les dé suficiente tiempo para ver la pintura de Velázquez en el Museo del Prado.**

8. **Me sorprende que a Uds. no les agrade esta canción de Julio Iglesias. ¡Es muy romántica!**

9. **Es importante que tú trates de ver la Iglesia de la Sagrada Familia en Barcelona. Es un buen ejemplo de la arquitectura de Gaudí.**

10. **Es verdad que nosotros nos sentamos cerca del escenario esta noche. Compré los boletos más caros.**

Capítulo 13: Partner B *Frases ilustradas*

Read each sentence to your partner using the cues given. Your partner will tell you if your sentences are correct or not. You have three chances to guess correctly.

1. **Es posible que tú (conocer) ___________ a ese**  **. Hubo una exposición de sus cuadros en nuestro café preferido.**

2. **El artesano pobre espera que los turistas le (comprar) ___________**  .

3. **¿Recomiendas que nosotros (ver)___________ las**  **de la civilización azteca?**

4. **Creo que muchos** 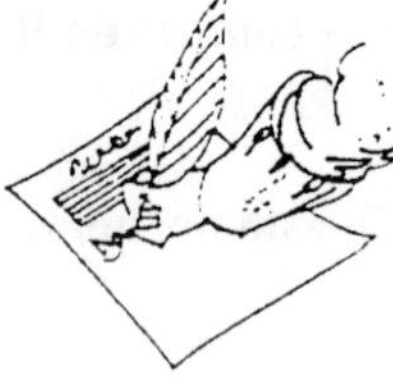 **(venir) ___________ a nuestra tertulia literaria** (*literary gathering*) **esta noche.**

5. **A algunos aficionados al cine no les gusta que la actriz Demi Moore (desempeñar) ___________ el papel de una**  **exótica.**

6. **Tememos que ese**  **famoso no (volver) ________ a actuar en las películas porque es muy viejo y enfermo.**

7. **Los extranjeros se alegran de que el guía les (dar) ___________ suficiente tiempo para ver la** Sala de Velázquez **de Velázquez en el Museo del Prado.**

8. **Me sorprende que a Uds. no les (agradar) ___________ esta** **de Julio Iglesias. ¡Es muy romántica!**

9. **Es importante que tú (tratar) ___________ de ver la Iglesia de la Sagrada Familia en Barcelona. Es un buen ejemplo de la** **de Gaudí.**

10. **Es verdad que nosotros (sentarse) ___________cerca del** **esta noche. Compré los boletos más caros.**

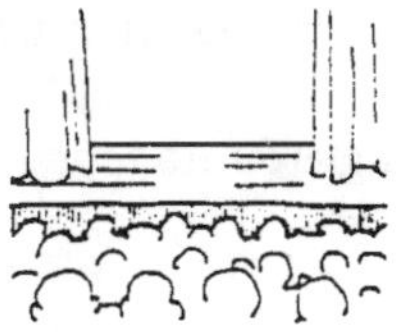

Capítulo 13: Partner B *Frases ilustradas*

These are your partner's answers. Listen to what your partner tells you. If his/her answer is not exactly what you have, just tell him/her: **No está bien. Trata de hacerlo otra vez.** Give your partner three opportunities to respond correctly.

1. **Es probable que el guía nos diga el nombre del mejor mercado de artesanía.**
2. **Es necesario que tú vayas al Palacio de Bellas Artes para ver las danzas del Ballet Folklórico de México.**
3. **Ojalá que haya un cuadro de Miró en este museo.**
4. **Es cierto que ese grupo de mariachis sólo toca música ranchera.**
5. **Es triste que el público norteamericano no aprecie más la literatura española. Por ejemplo, todos deben leer *Don Quijote de la Mancha.***
6. **Estoy seguro/a que a los niños les interesa el cine más que el teatro.**
7. **Es terrible que ese actor todavía no sepa su papel. ¿Quién le da una copia del guión?**
8. **Profesor, ¿Ud. insiste en que los estudiantes de escultura hagan varios dibujos antes de empezar a esculpir?**
9. **Niego que esa cantante sea Gloria Estefan.**
10. **Qué lástima que el grupo no tenga tiempo para ir a las ruinas. ¡Son tan impresionantes!**

	Vocabulario	Verbos	Gramática	Traducción
10 pts		Ojalá que _____ (haber) un buen arquitecto en esta ciudad.	Dudo que tú ________ (saber) el nombre de esa danza.	The actors are reading the scripts on the stage for the first time.
20 pts	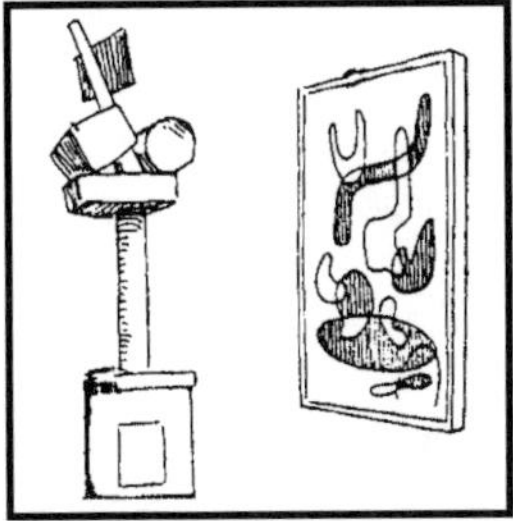	Me sorprende que el ballet clásico no me ________ (aburrir).	No es verdad que el compositor norteamericano ________ (tratar) de escribir música latina.	In my free time I like to draw and sculpt.
30 pts		Tememos que los niños no ________ (apreciar) el arte.	El guía niega que la artesanía que se vende aquí ________ (ser) auténtica.	The favorite actors of my grandparents were dancers and singers also.
40 pts		Es lástima que ese cantante no ________ (desempeñar) un papel en esta ópera.	Es posible que yo _______ (tocar) la guitarra para Uds., pero es improbable que ________ (cantar).	In the fifth Spanish literature class I took in college, I studied the modern playwrights.
50 pts		Es ridículo que ese poeta mexicano ________ (negar) que ________ (ir) a inmigrar a los EE.UU.	Es cierto que tú ________ (tener) talento artístico, pero no creo que el público _______ (entender) tu obra.	The ninth musician in the mariachi group plays the guitar, and the tenth plays the violin.

Answer Key for *Arriésgate*

Capítulo 13

Vocabulario:	**10 pts**	las ruinas
	20 pts	la escultura, el cuadro
	30 pts	el tejido, la cerámica, la canción
	40 pts	los actores, la directora, el guión
	50 pts	los músicos, el compositor, el escenario
Verbos:	**10 pts**	haya
	20 pts	aburra
	30 pts	aprecien
	40 pts	desempeñe
	50 pts	niegue, vaya
Gramática:	**10 pts**	sepas
	20 pts	trate
	30 pts	sea
	40 pts	toque, cante
	50 pts	tienes, entienda
Traducción:	**10 pts**	Los actores están leyendo los guiones en el escenario por primera vez.
	20 pts	En mis ratos libres, me gusta dibujar y esculpir.
	30 pts	Los actores favoritos de mis abuelos eran bailarines y cantantes también.
	40 pts	En la quinta clase de literatura española que tomé en la universidad, estudié los dramaturgos modernos.
	50 pts	El noveno músico del grupo de mariachi toca la guitarra, y el décimo toca el violín.

CAPÍTULO 14 EL MEDIO AMBIENTE

Student Supplements

- Listening Comprehension Program CD, **Capítulo 14** (**Paso 1: Vocabulario:** word lists)
- Workbook/Laboratory Manual, **Capítulo 14**
- Audio Program CD, **Capítulo 14**

Instructor Resources

- Instructor's Manual/IRK: Chapter-by-Chapter Supplementary Materials, **Capítulo 14**
  - **Paso 1: Vocabulario**
  - **Paso 2: Gramática**
    - Grammar Section 38
    - **Enfoque cultural**
  - **Paso 3: Gramática**
    - Grammar Section 39
    - **En los Estados Unidos y el Canadá**
    - **Un poco de todo**
  - **Paso 4: Un paso más**
    - **Videoteca: Minidramas**
  - Games and Activities
- Instructor's Manual/IRK: Video Activities and Related Materials
  - **A primera vista**
  - **A segunda vista**
  - Answers to Video Activities
  - Videoscripts
- Audioscript, **Capítulo 14**
- Transparencies 76–78
- Testing Program, **Capítulo 14**

Multimedia Resources

- Online Learning Center
- Electronic Workbook/Laboratory Manual
- Video, **Capítulo 14** (cue 1:24:49)
  - **En contexto** (1:51)
  - **Minidramas** (4:49)
  - **Enfoque cultural: Argentina** (1:00)
- Student CD-ROM, **Capítulo 14**
- Electronic Language Tutor, **Capítulo 14** (**Vocabulario, Gramática**)

Paso 1: Vocabulario

EL MEDIO AMBIENTE

Suggestions:

- Point out that **el delito** = *crime,* and that for most Spanish speakers, **el crimen** = *murder.* Also have students note that **la fábrica** and **la falta** are false cognates.
- Emphasize the spelling changes in the conjugations of **destruir** and **construir: destruyo, destruyes,...** and **construyo, construyes,...** Also point out the first-person singular of **proteger: protejo.** Model the structure with **acabar** in **se nos acabó** and **se nos acabaron.**
- Provide the following optional vocabulary: **lento/a, tener la culpa, echarle la culpa (a alguien).**
- Model the pronunciation of the words as well as the use of selected words. Integrate them in statements about yourself, your community, and/or the university.

Preliminary Exercises:

- Read the following definitions and have students give the corresponding word from the vocabulary: 1. **bonito o hermoso, no feo** 2. **cuando no hay suficiente cantidad de algo** 3. **lo opuesto de destruir** 4. **puede ser de varios tipos, depende de si viene del aire, del agua, del sol, etcétera** 5. **un sistema político** 6. **el grupo de personas que vive en una ciudad o un estado.**
- Have students imagine that they have a Hispanic friend who does not know what the following are. Have them explain the meaning of each: 1. the EPA 2. the Secretary of the Interior 3. the welfare system 4. the National Parks system and park rangers 5. a parole officer 6. the inner city
- Ask students the following questions to personalize the vocabulary: 1. **¿Hay mucha contaminación en esta ciudad?** 2. **¿Cómo es el ritmo de vida en (ciudad), acelerado o lento? ¿Qué ritmo de vida prefiere Ud.? ¿Le gusta caminar por la ciudad durante la noche?** 3. **¿Trata Ud. de conservar la energía? ¿Hay ahora una escasez de energía? Si una persona realmente quiere conservar energía, ¿qué puede hacer?** 4. **¿Hay muchos delitos y crímenes en esta ciudad? ¿Qué lugares son famosos por la frecuencia de sus delitos? ¿Tiene Ud. miedo de visitar estos lugares?** 5. **¿Va Ud. al campo con frecuencia? ¿Tiene su familia una finca en el campo? ¿La visita Ud.? ¿Cuándo? Descríbala. ¿Le gustaría vivir en una finca? ¿Cómo es el ritmo de vida en una finca típica?**

Optional Activities:

Problemas del mundo. Los siguientes problemas afectan en cierta medida (*in some measure*) a los habitantes de nuestro planeta. ¿Cuáles le afectan más a Ud. en este momento de su vida? Póngalos en orden, del 1 al 10, según la importancia que tienen para Ud. ¡No va a ser fácil!

______ la contaminación del aire
______ la destrucción de la capa de ozono
______ la escasez de petróleo
______ la deforestación de la selva (jungla) de Amazonas
______ la falta de viviendas (*housing*) para todos
______ el ritmo acelerado de la vida moderna
______ el uso de drogas ilegales
______ el abuso de los recursos naturales
______ la sobrepoblación (*overpopulation*) del mundo
______ el crimen y la violencia en el país

Definiciones. Dé Ud. una definición de estas palabras.

MODELO: el agricultor → Es el dueño de una finca.

1. la fábrica
2. el campesino
3. el delito
4. la finca
5. la naturaleza
6. la población
7. el aislamiento
8. el rascacielos

LOS COCHES

Preparation: It is helpful to bring pictures that illustrate the things and concepts you wish to present. Ask students to skim the vocabulary lists before you begin.

Sample Passage: **Hoy vamos a hablar del medio ambiente. ¿Saben Uds. lo que es el medio ambiente? Pues, el medio ambiente es donde vivimos. Es decir, es el aire, el agua, la tierra — todos los elementos que nos rodean, que están alrededor de nosotros** (gesture). **Vamos a hablar de la importancia de cuidar nuestro medio ambiente.**

Hoy día hay problemas con la contaminación del aire, es decir que el aire está sucio, no es tan puro como antes. ¿De dónde viene la contaminación del aire? Pues, viene de las fábricas... las fábricas, que hacen muchos productos. También viene de las plantas de energía, donde producen electricidad, la luz eléctrica. En la ciudad, los coches y los autobuses también contaminan el aire. Pero en el campo el aire es muy puro. No hay contaminación allí, ¿verdad? No, no es verdad. También hay cosas que contaminan el aire en el campo. ¿Qué son? Sí, los tractores, los camiones y los coches también son una fuente de contaminación en el campo. (Continue with water and soil pollution, diminishing resources, and so on, then actions to mitigate environmental impacts. Follow with car vocabulary.)

Quick Comprehension Check: **¿Cierto o falso?**

1. **La contaminación no es un problema en el campo. (F)**
2. **Los coches contaminan el aire, el agua y la tierra. (C)**
3. **No es posible usar menos agua para bañarnos. (F)**

Variation:

4. **¿La capa del ozono nos protege de la lluvia ácida o del sol? (del sol)**
5. **¿Están los rascacielos en la finca o en la ciudad? (en la ciudad)**
6. **¿Cuáles de estas dos cosas producen el oxígeno que respiramos, las plantas o los animales? (las plantas)**

Suggestions:

- Ask students what vocabulary words they associate with the following: **¿Con qué asocia Ud... ?** 1. **¿ los colores rojo, amarillo y verde?** 2. **¿los mecánicos?** 3. **¿la contaminación?** 4. **¿parar?** 5. **¿una llanta?** 6. **¿arrancar?** 7. **¿la carretera?** 8. **¿doblar?**
- Point out that **gastar dinero** means *to spend money.*
- Provide the following optional vocabulary: **una llanta desinflada, un pinchazo.** Point out the difference between **la llanta** and **la rueda.** Explain that **el chófer** is a synonym of **el conductor.**
- Point out the spelling changes in **conducir (zc), arrancar (qu), chocar (qu), obedecer (zc),** and **seguir (g).**

Preliminary Exercises:

- Read the following statements and have students respond **cierto** or **falso:** 1. **El tanque del coche contiene aceite.** 2. **Si el semáforo está rojo, es necesario parar.** 3. **Un Cadillac gasta poca gasolina.** 4. **Es necesario tener una licencia para conducir.** 5. **Si Ud. no dobla, Ud. sigue todo derecho.**
- Ask students the following questions: 1. **En esta clase, ¿cuántos tienen coche? ¿Es viejo o nuevo su coche? ¿grande o pequeño? ¿Gasta mucha o poca gasolina? ¿mucho o poco aceite? ¿Cuánto le cuesta llenar el tanque?** 2. **En general, ¿funciona bien su coche? Cuando no funciona, ¿lo arregla Ud. o se lo arregla un mecánico? ¿un amigo? ¿Es vieja o nueva la batería? ¿Le es difícil hacer arrancar el coche por la mañana? ¿Le es difícil arrancar cuando hace frío?** 3. **¿Tuvo Ud. alguna vez una llanta desinflada** (pantomime)**? ¿Dónde y cómo ocurrió? ¿Quién la cambió? ¿Tuvo Ud. que llamar para pedir ayuda? ¿Siempre lleva Ud. una llanta de repuesto (una quita llanta)?** 4. **¿Maneja Ud. para venir al campus? ¿Es fácil estacionarse aquí? ¿Es necesario pagar para poder estacionarse en el campus? ¿Cuánto? ¿Quiénes encuentran un estacionamiento con más facilidad, los profesores o los estudiantes?** 5. **¿Sabe Ud. manejar? ¿Cuántos años hace que aprendió a manejar? ¿Cuántos años tenía? ¿Quién le enseñó a manejar? ¿Tuvo Ud. algún accidente mientras aprendía? ¿Qué es lo mejor de manejar? ¿y lo peor?**
- Read the following narration to the class, then discuss car ownership, car problems, and auto mechanics.

  En este país, cuando algo le pasa al coche, automáticamente lo llevamos a un mecánico. ¿Y qué hace el mecánico? Si tiene suerte, encuentra la parte dañada (*damaged*) **y la cambia por otra nueva. En realidad, hay mecánicos que no reparan nada o que reparan partes que no tienen problema. Si un mecánico no puede arreglar un coche, es muy probable que el dueño norteamericano decida por comprarse un coche nuevo en vez de gastar dinero en reparaciones. En cambio, en América Latina y en España, un coche nuevo cuesta relativamente mucho dinero y en algunos países hasta un dineral** (*fortune*). **Además, los repuestos** (*spare parts*) **son costosos y los mecánicos intentan reparar verdaderamente las partes que no funcionan. Por eso es común ver coches viejos que después de 15 ó 20 años de uso diario todavía funcionan.**

Paso 2: Gramática

GRAMMAR SECTION 38

FORMS OF THE PAST PARTICIPLE

Note: Students have been using a number of past participles, especially with **estar,** since the early chapters: **casado, cansado, ocupado, aburrido, preocupado, abierto, cerrado,** and so on.

Suggestions:

- Model the past participle forms as you present them, for example, **cerrar, cerrado** → **La puerta está cerrada.**
- Use the following rapid response drill to practice the forms. Have students give the past participle for each verb you say: **comprar, pagar, mandar, terminar, preparar, llamar, recomendar, invitar, arreglar, visitar, vender, conocer, leer, llover, perder, comer, recibir, pedir, dormir, seguir.**
- Model the pronunciation of irregular past participles. Say the participle and have students give the corresponding infinitive. Then, reverse the procedure.
- Have students express the following in Spanish: *broken, seen, covered, discovered, returned, written, said, dead, made, done, open(ed), put.*

THE PAST PARTICIPLE USED AS AN ADJECTIVE

Suggestion: Emphasize that the past participle used as an adjective must agree in gender and number with the noun it modifies.

Preliminary Exercise: Use the following rapid response drill to practice agreement. Have students change the participle to agree with the nouns indicated: 1. **hecho: bolsas, vestidos, camisa** 2. **escrito: carta, ejercicio, libros** 3. **roto: tazas, silla, disco.**

Suggestions:

- Emphasize the use of the past participle with **estar** to describe resulting conditions. Point out that they learned this in **Capítulo 5** with **estar** expressions.
- Provide additional examples to contrast the English simple past and past participle with the Spanish, for example, **Hice la tarea. La tarea está hecha.** vs. *I did the homework. The homework is done.*
- Point out that **estar** + past participle would be used to express *The door was open (when I arrived)* but not *The door was opened (by the porter).* The second example implies action (passive voice construction), whereas the first implies the result of a previous action.
- Explain that another common structure with the past participle is **tener** + object + past participle: **Tengo los ejercicios preparados.** This construction is equivalent to the present perfect (**He preparado los ejercicios.**) but emphasizes the completion and recentness of the action. Notice that **estar** + past participle is impersonal. The **tener** + object + past participle is personal, that is, it tells who did the action.
- Point out that compound verbs that have an irregular root verb, with few exceptions, have the same irregularity as the root verb in the past participle: **decir** → **pre*decir*: pre*dicho*; poner** → **com*poner*: com*puesto*; hacer** → **satisf*acer*: satisf*echo*** (some words that now have the letter **h** at one time were written with **f**). Have students give the past participle for the following verbs: **revolver, exponer, prescribir, prever, recubrir, imponer, suponer, rehacer, deponer, describir, reponer, envolver, oponer, premorir, presuponer, rever, encubrir, redecir, subscribir.**

Optional Activity: **Comentarios sobre el mundo de hoy.** Complete cada párrafo con los participios pasados de los verbos apropiados de la lista.

Información sobre el reciclaje: desperdiciar (*to waste*), destruir, hacer, reciclar

Todos los días, Ud. tira en el basurero[a] aproximadamente media libra[b] de papel. Si Ud. trabaja en un banco, en una compañía de seguros[c] o en una agencia del gobierno, el promedio[d] se eleva a tres cuartos de libra al día. Todo ese papel ______[1] constituye un gran número de árboles ______.[2] Esto es un buen motivo para que Ud. comience un proyecto de recuperación de papeles hoy en su oficina. Ud. puede completar el ciclo del reciclaje únicamente si compra productos ______[3] con materiales ______.[4]

[a]*wastebasket* [b]media... *half a pound* [c]*insurance* [d]*average*

La conservación de la energía: acostumbrar, agotar (*to use up*), apagar (*to turn off*), bajar, cerrar, limitar

Las fuentes[a] de energía no están ______[5] todavía. Pero estas fuentes son ______.[6] Desgraciadamente, todavía no estamos ______[7] a conservar energía diariamente. ¿Qué podemos hacer? Cuando nos servimos la comida, la puerta del refrigerador debe estar ______.[8] Cuando miramos la televisión, algunas luces de la casa deben estar ______.[9] El regulador termómetro debe estar ______[10] cuando nos acostamos.

[a]*sources*

Note: These passages are adapted, slightly simplified, from authentic materials from Mexico and Spain. Have students read completely through each paragraph before completing it.

Suggestion: Have students mark all the words they do not know during the first reading, then try to guess the meaning. Have students share the strategies they used to complete the reading successfully.

Heritage Speakers: En los países hispanohablantes, se usa el sistema internacional (SI), es decir, métrico, para medir. Pregúnteles a los hispanohablantes de la clase si saben usar SI. Pídales a ellos o a otros estudiantes que sepan usar SI que den algunas medidas comunes, por ejemplo, una temperatura climática moderada (70° F) o un peso posible (común) de una mujer (110–140 lbs.) o de un hombre (175–215 lbs.). Hablen de las ventajas y desventajas de SI y del sistema usado en los Estados Unidos.

ENFOQUE CULTURAL: LA ARGENTINA

A. Para contestar. Conteste las siguientes preguntas con la información en Datos esenciales, ¡Fíjese! y Conozca ...

1. ¿Cuántos habitantes tiene la Argentina?

   ____

2. ¿En qué año fue fundada la ciudad de Buenos Aires?

   ____

3. ¿Cómo es la capital?

   ____

4. ¿De qué país era la mitad de los inmigrantes a la Argentina entre los años 1856 y 1930?

   ____

5. El gobierno argentino dio la bienvenida a los inmigrantes, porque quería poblar la Pampa. ¿Por qué no se pobló?

   ____

6. ¿Cuándo y en qué parte de Buenos Aires se originó el tango?

   ____

B. Para investigar: Navegando por el Internet. En la página principal de Latinworld—Argentina, seleccione *Travel*/**Viajes.** De allí escoja *Argentine Ranches* / **Estancias argentinas.** Escoja dos de las estancias que le parecen interesantes y complete el siguiente cuadro con la información de la página principal de cada estancia.

Nombre:	
Ubicación (¿Dónde está?):	
Distancia desde Buenos Aires:	
Habitaciones:	
Escoja dos actividades que le interesarían a Ud. (*would interest you*):	

Suggestions:

- Have students gather information on Evita Perón and on the Perón regime on the Internet and then show the film *Evita* (1997). Have students compare the historical figures and events with those in the film.
- Give students background information about Astor Piazzola (1921–1986). The Argentine musician and composer influenced by Carlos Gardel and trained in Paris by Nadia Boulanger, used the tango as the inspiration for his classical compositions. Play some Gardel tangos and some Piazzola pieces for students and ask them to compare the two.
- Show Carlos Saura's 1999 film *Tango* in class. You may wish to show the 1933 film of the same name, which stars Argentine actress Libertad Lamarque as the tango singer, as a comparison.
- Ask whether any of the students have read any of the stories of Jorge Luis Borges (1899–1986), and, if some have, encourage them to tell the class about them. Some students may wish to read one or several of the stories and report on them for extra credit. You may wish to tell them that the author of noted collections such as *Ficciones* (1945), *El Aleph* (1949) and *El libro de los seres imaginarios* wrote highly learned, ironic narratives in which the reader's sense of reality is transmuted and a fantastic, sometimes metaphysical world replaces the familiar one.

Paso 3: Gramática

GRAMMAR SECTION 39

PRESENT PERFECT INDICATIVE

Suggestions:

- Review the present tense of **haber** and the formation of the present perfect.
- Emphasize that only the masculine singular of the past participle is used in the present perfect tense. In this construction, the past participle is not an adjective.
- Point out that the object pronouns must precede the conjugated **haber** form; they are never placed after the conjugated form of **haber** nor attached to the end of the participle: **Ya la he llamado. (a María) Ya se lo he dado. (el trabajo a María)**

- Emphasize and model that **hay** is a special third-person (impersonal) form of **haber** meaning *there is/are*. Only **ha** and **han** are used as helping verbs for third-person conjugations of the present perfect tense.
- Read the following phrases and have students give the corresponding subject pronoun: **he corrido, hemos caminado, han perdido, has dormido, habéis dicho, ha visto.**
- Have students express the following ideas in Spanish: **¿Cómo se dice en español?** 1. *I have studied / eaten / read / gotten up.* 2. *He/She has answered / promised / lived / opened.* 3. *We have called / lost / written.* 4. *They have traveled / run / discovered.*
- Point out that both in English and Spanish the present perfect is often used as an alternative for the simple past tense, especially when the action has just taken place: **¿Leíste / Has leído el periódico?**

PRESENT PERFECT SUBJUNCTIVE

Suggestions:

- Review the basic concept and uses of the subjunctive before beginning: 1. influence 2. emotion 3. doubt.
- Review the subjunctive forms of **haber.**
- Emphasize that these forms are the subjunctive counterparts of the present indicative (**he hablado, has hablado, ha hablado,** and so on).
- Point out that the first- and third-person forms (**yo, Ud./él/ella**) are the same.
- Read the following phrases and have students give the corresponding subject pronouns: ***haya dicho, hayamos perdido, hayan escuchado, hayáis llamado.***

PRÁCTICA B

Heritage Speakers: También se dice **echar dedo** para expresar **hacer autostop.** Pregúnteles a los hispanohablantes de la clase qué expresión usan. Si son de un país hispanohablante, pregúnteles si es común que la gente haga autostop en su país y qué tipo de persona lo haría.

Optional Activity: **El pasado y el futuro**

Paso 1. Indique las actividades que Ud. ha hecho en el pasado.

1. ______ He hecho un viaje a Europa.
2. ______ He montado a camello (*camel*).
3. ______ He tomado una clase de informática.
4. ______ He buceado (*gone scuba diving*).
5. ______ He ido de safari a África.
6. ______ He comprado un coche.
7. ______ He preparado una comida italiana.
8. ______ He ocupado un puesto (*position*) político.
9. ______ He tenido una mascota.
10. ______ He escrito un poema.

Paso 2. Ahora, entre las cosas que Ud. no ha hecho, ¿cuáles le gustaría hacer? Conteste, siguiendo los modelos.

MODELOS: Nunca he montado a camello, pero me gustaría hacerlo.
(Nunca he montado a camello y no me interesa hacerlo.)

Suggestion: Have students report what they have done or not done by saying **ya lo he hecho** or **no lo he hecho todavía.**

EN LOS ESTADOS UNIDOS Y EL CANADÁ... CHI CHI RODRÍGUEZ

Suggestions:

- Ask comprehension questions in Spanish: **¿Dónde nació Chi Chi Rodríguez? ¿Qué deporte juega? ¿Quién invitó a Rodríguez a trabajar con jóvenes en peligro? ¿Qué hace la Fundación Chi Chi Rodríguez para ayudar a esos jóvenes?** And so on.
- Have students who are golf fans provide other information they may know about Chi Chi Rodríguez.
- Have students name and talk about other Hispanic athletes in the U.S. and Canada. Ask questions in Spanish: **¿Qué deporte juega? ¿Son originalmente de este país o inmigraron?** And so on.

UN POCO DE TODO

Optional Activity: **¿Ya lo has hecho?** Con un compañero / una compañera, háganse preguntas y contéstenlas, según el modelo.

MODELO: escribir la carta →
E1: ¿Ya *está escrita* la carta?
E2: No, no la *he escrito.*
E1: ¡Hombre! Es imposible que no la *hayas escrito* todavía.

1. **hacer las maletas**
2. **comprar los boletos**
3. **preparar la cena**
4. **facturar el equipaje**
5. **sacudir los muebles**
6. **poner la mesa**
7. **comprar el fax**
8. **salvar la información en la computadora**
9. **apagar la computadora**
10. **darle el trabajo al profesor / a la profesora**

Paso 4: Un paso más

VIDEOTECA

MINIDRAMAS

The **Minidramas** vignettes are not referenced in the textbook, but are part of the *¿Qué tal?* Video Program. They also appear on the Video on CD packaged free with the textbook. If you show the **Minidramas** in class or have your students view them as homework, you might find the following suggestions helpful. You can also find blackline master activities in Section X of this Manual for **Minidramas.**

Comprensión: **¿Cierto o falso? Corrija las oraciones falsas.**

1. **La conductora se ha perdido.**
2. **Es muy probable que en el pueblo más cercano no haya un taller.**
3. **Es posible que haya un taller en otro pueblo en la carretera de Quito.**
4. **La mujer decide abandonar su coche en la carretera y se va con Elisa.**

Suggestion: Optional.

Paso 1. Repase las frases y los verbos que se usan con más frecuencia cuando se piden y se dan direcciones.

Perdón, ¿puede/podría decirme
dónde queda / está... ?
a cuánto queda / está... ?

Doble a la derecha / a la izquierda
Siga todo derecho = sin doblar

¿Cómo se usan estos verbos con un amigo? ¿y con una persona mayor que Ud. no conoce?

Paso 2. Practique cómo dar direcciones explicando cómo se llega a algún sitio del *campus* desde la sala de clase. Sus compañeros tienen que adivinar (*guess*) qué lugar es ese.

ACTIVIDAD DE DESENLACE: LOS PROBLEMAS ECOLÓGICOS DEL MUNDO

Activity: Students will research a Spanish-speaking country with ecological and /or conservational concerns, and prepare visual materials (such as poster boards) to present their findings to the class.

Purpose: To explore the artistic heritage of the Spanish-speaking world; to create a context in which students can review and practice the grammar from **Capítulo 14** and vocabulary related to the environment and automobiles.

Resources: *¿Qué tal?* textbook, the Internet, and other sources as appropriate

Vocabulary: The environment, the gas station

Grammar: Principal grammatical structures covered in **Capítulo 14** of the textbook, including the past participle used as an adjective, and perfect forms (present perfect indicative and present perfect subjunctive)

Duration: Out-of-class preparation time will vary. In-class time will be approximately five minutes per presentation.

Format: Groups of three to four students

Comments: You may wish to display the materials that students prepare in the classroom or a Spanish department commons area.

Games and Activities

Capítulo 14: Partner A *Crucigrama*

You have the answers for half the puzzle, and your partner has those for the other half. Together you must complete the whole puzzle. You have to give clues to your partner so that he/she can guess the missing words. You *may not use the word itself*. Everything has to be done in Spanish.

Use clues such as: **Lo que usamos para...**
La persona que...
El lugar donde...
La cosa que...
Lo que se hace cuando...

Capítulo 14: Partner B

Crucigrama

You have the answers for half the puzzle, and your partner has those for the other half. Together you must complete the whole puzzle. You have to give clues to your partner so that he/she can guess the missing words. You *may not use the word itself.* Everything has to be done in Spanish.

Use clues such as: **Lo que usamos para...**
La persona que...
El lugar donde...
La cosa que...
Lo que se hace cuando...

Capítulo 14 *Lotería*

Para cada pregunta a continuación, busque una persona de la clase que conteste «sí» y escriba su nombre. **¡OJO!** No escriba el mismo nombre más de una vez.

¿Has comprado zapatos nuevos este mes?	**¿Ha estado enfermo algún miembro de tu familia últimamente?**	**¿Has comido langosta alguna vez?**	**¿Has visitado a tus abuelos este mes?**
¿Has hecho la tarea todos los días?	**¿Te has roto el brazo o la pierna alguna vez?**	**¿Has ido con tu familia a un parque de diversionas este año?**	**(escribe una pregunta)**
¿Te has mudado este año?	**(escribe una pregunta)**	**¿Has tomado cerveza mexicana?**	**¿Has vivido en alguna finca o rancho alguna vez?**
¿Has visitado algún país latino?	**¿Has leído *Don Quijote de la Mancha*?**	**¿Has trabajado en alguna fábrica?**	**¿Has perdido algo de valor alguna vez?**

	Vocabulario	Verbos	Gramática	Traducción
10 pts	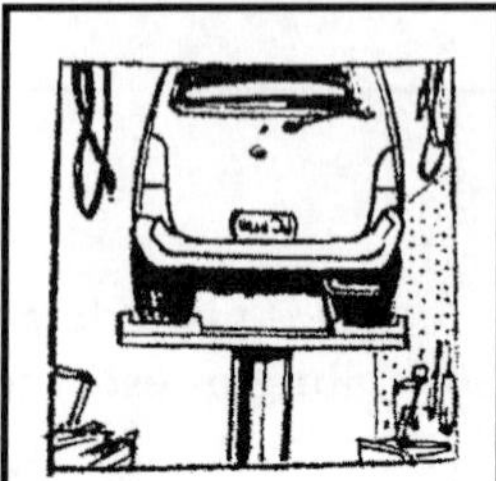	La policía (*has said*) que hay menos violencia en esta ciudad ahora que en 1990.		There is a lack of housing, transportation, and public services.
20 pts		La población (*has wasted*) la energía y (*has exploited*) los recursos naturales de su país.		The farmer prefers the clean air, the pure water, and the isolation of his farm.
 30 pts		No creo que los científicos (*have resolved*) el problema de la destrucción de la capa del ozono.		The mechanic checked the oil, cleaned the windshield, and filled the tank.
 40 pts		(*I have discovered*) un camino donde no hay mucho tráfico. Ojalá que tú (*have not seen it*).		After running into the tree, the young driver turned the corner, parked the car, and gave the keys to his father.
 50 pts		El gobierno (*has constructed*) una carretera nueva. Es lástima que (*we have not obeyed*) el límite de velocidad.		I forgot to stop at the gas station yesterday, and I ran out of gas on the 210 freeway.

Answer Key for *Arriésgate*

Capítulo 14

Vocabulario:	**10 pts**	el taller
	20 pts	el delito, el policía
	30 pts	las llantas, los frenos, el semáforo
	40 pts	las fábricas, la contaminación, los rascacielos
	50 pts	el bosque, los árboles, el conductor, el tráfico (la circulación)
Verbos:	**10 pts**	ha dicho
	20 pts	has desperdiciado, ha explotado
	30 pts	hayan resuelto
	40 pts	He descubierto, no lo hayas visto
	50 pts	ha construido, no hayamos obedecido
Gramática:	**10 pts**	(un continente nuevo) **descubierto**
	20 pts	(el vidrio) **reciclado,** (la llanta) **desinflada**
	30 pts	(la ventana) **rota,** (la cama) **hecha,** (la revista) **abierta**
	40 pts	(el coche) **arreglado,** (la calle) **cubierta,** (la estudiante) **sentada**
	50 pts	(la mesa) **puesta,** (las cartas) **escritas,** (los parientes) **muertos**
Traducción:	**10 pts**	Hay una falta (escasez) de viviendas, transporte y servicios públicos.
	20 pts	El agricultor prefiere el aire limpio, el agua pura y el aislamiento de su finca.
	30 pts	El mecánico revisó el aceite, limpió el parabrisas y llenó el tanque.
	40 pts	Después de chocar con el árbol, el conductor joven dobló la esquina, se estacionó y le dio las llaves a su padre.
	50 pts	Se me olvidó parar en la gasolinera (estación de gasolina) ayer, y se me acabó la gasolina en la autopista 210.

Juego de tablero: ¡Manejen con cuidado!

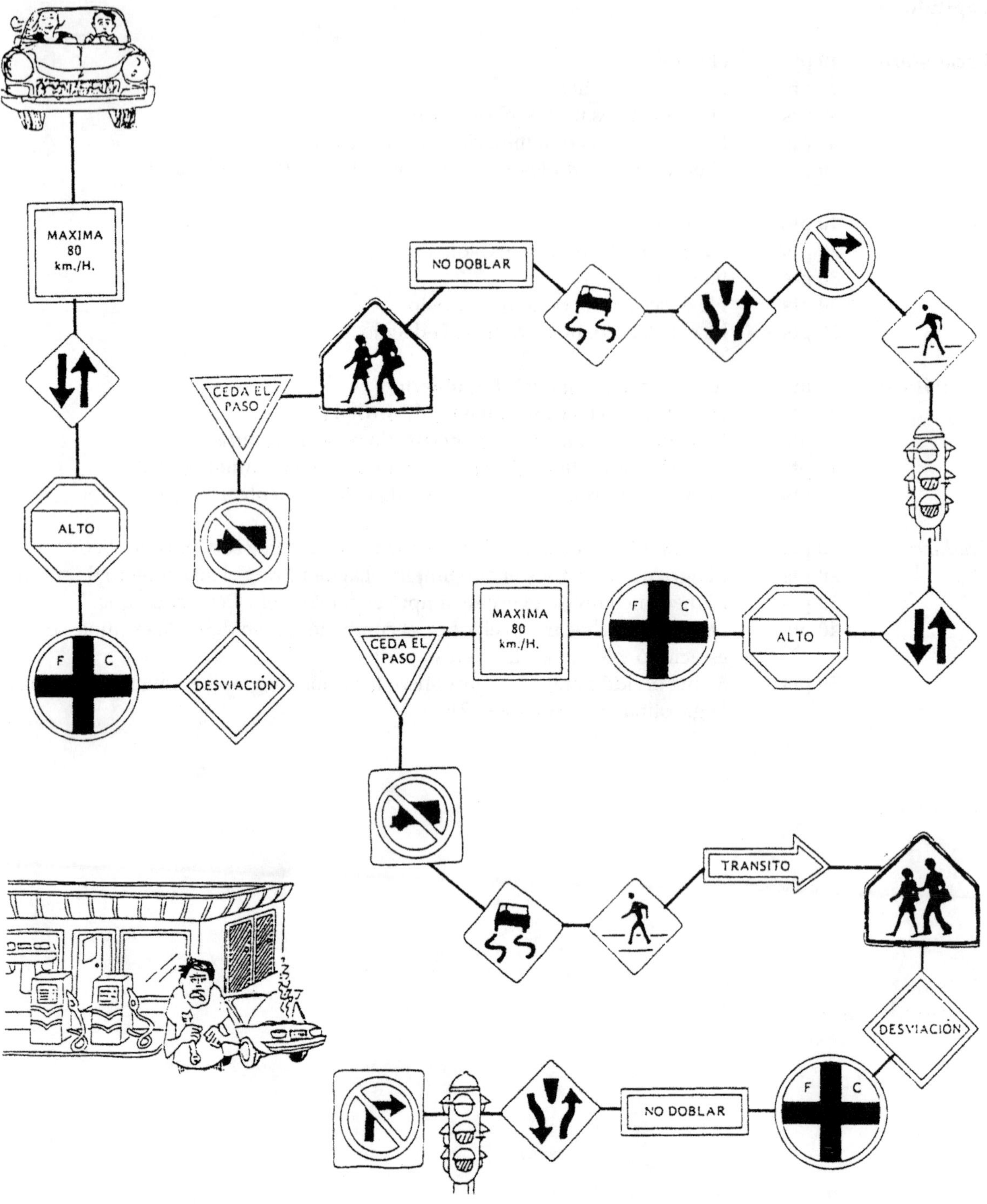

1. En los Estados Unidos, si se maneja en el lado izquierdo de la calle, se va a ________________ con otro coche.	7. Los ________________ revisan y arreglan los coches.
2. Si los conductores no obedecen a los semáforos, ________________ los va a parar.	8. Al conductor se le olvidaron las llaves. Ahora es imposible ________________ el motor del coche.
3. El límite de ________________ en las carreteras de los Estados Unidos es 70 millas por hora.	9. Se pone ________________ en el tanque del coche.
4. En la actualidad, hay pocas ________________ que dan servicio completo; el conductor tiene que llenar el tanque de su coche.	10. Se llenan las ________________ de aire.
5. Es importante que el ________________ esté limpio para que el conductor pueda ver el camino.	11. Se pone ________________ en el motor para lubricarlo.
6. ________________ es un sinónimo de «manejar».	12. Si el coche no funciona, hay que dejarlo en un ________________.

13. Se encuentran los ________________ en las esquinas de la ciudad. Tienen luces rojas, amarillas y verdes.	19. La ________________ identifica al conductor. Incluye una foto fea y esta información: la dirección, el color de los ojos y del pelo, la estatura, el peso y el cumpleaños.
14. La ________________ es un sinónimo de la palabra «tráfico».	20. No se puede arrancar el coche si la ________________ no está cargada.
15. Cuando se deja el coche en la calle o en el garaje, hay que ________________ lo con mucho cuidado.	21. La persona que maneja un coche es el ________________.
16. En Los Ángeles hay muchas ________________: la 210, la 110, la 605... Y siempre están llenas de coches que contaminan el aire.	22. Es necesario cambiar una llanta cuando está ________________.
17. Si los ________________ no funcionan bien, es difícil para el coche.	23. En la intersección de dos calles hay cuatro ________________.
18. Un coche económico ________________ poca gasolina.	24. Si el conductor no quiere seguir todo derecho, tiene que ________________.

Answer Key for *Juego de tablero: ¡Manejen con cuidado!*

Capítulo 14

1. **chocar**
2. **la policía (un[a] policía)**
3. **velocidad**
4. **estaciones de gasolina (gasolineras)**
5. **parabrisas**
6. **Conducir**
7. **mecánicos**
8. **arrancar**
9. **gasolina**
10. **llantas**
11. **aceite**
12. **taller**
13. **semáforos**
14. **circulación**
15. **estacionar**
16. **autopistas**
17. **frenos**
18. **gasta**
19. **licencia**
20. **batería**
21. **conductor**
22. **desinflada**
23. **esquinas**
24. **doblar**

Student Supplements

- Listening Comprehension Program CD, **Capítulo 15** (**Paso 1: Vocabulario:** word lists)
- Workbook/Laboratory Manual, **Capítulo 15**
- Audio Program CD, **Capítulo 15**

Instructor Resources

- Instructor's Manual/IRK: Chapter-by-Chapter Supplementary Materials, **Capítulo 15**
  - **Paso 1: Vocabulario**
  - **Paso 2: Gramática**
    - Grammar Section 40
    - **Enfoque cultural**
  - **Paso 3: Gramática**
    - Grammar Section 41
    - **En los Estados Unidos y el Canadá...**
    - **Un poco de todo**
  - **Paso 4: Un paso más**
    - **Videoteca: Minidramas**
    - **A leer**
    - **A escribir**
  - Games and Activities
- Instructor's Manual/IRK: Video Activities and Related Materials
  - **A primera vista**
  - **A segunda vista**
  - Answers to Video Activities
  - Videoscripts
- Audioscript, **Capítulo 15**
- Transparencies 79–81
- Testing Program, **Capítulo 15**

Multimedia Resources

- Online Learning Center
- Electronic Workbook/Laboratory Manual
- Video, **Capítulo 15** (cue 1:31:39)
  - **En contexto** (1:58)
  - **Minidramas** (3:43)
  - **Enfoque cultural: Chile** (1:00)
- Student CD-ROM, **Capítulo 15**
- Electronic Language Tutor, **Capítulo 15** (**Vocabulario, Gramática**)

Paso 1: Vocabulario

LAS RELACIONES SENTIMENTALES

Preparation: Bring in a large photo or photos of a young man and a young woman. Display on the board and write the names **Mario** and **Ángela.**

Sample Passage: **Hoy les voy a contar la historia de Mario y Ángela** (point to pictures). **Mario es estudiante de biología en la Universidad Nacional. Es muy inteligente y quiere ser médico. También es muy simpático y se lleva bien con todos. Por eso es muy popular y tiene muchos amigos, pero no tiene novia. Un día en la cafetería, un amigo de Mario le presenta a Ángela. Ángela estudia antropología y le interesa la cultura azteca. Resulta que a Mario también le interesa ese tema. Entonces invita a Ángela a tomar un café y los dos se ponen a hablar de los aztecas y de muchas otras cosas.**

Mario y Ángela pasan mucho tiempo juntos. Son grandes amigos y casi inseparables (link two fingers). **Es decir que tienen una amistad muy fuerte. Pero poco a poco sus relaciones cambian de amistosas a cariñosas. Empiezan a salir en citas románticas. Pronto se enamoran y ya son novios, además que amigos** (draw linked hearts). **Deciden que quieren casarse, que quieren pasar la vida como pareja** (show two fingers). **Pero saben que el matrimonio es difícil cuando uno es estudiante. Por eso deciden no casarse hasta terminar los estudios.**

Los padres de Mario son pesimistas. No quieren que Ángela sea la esposa de Mario. No se llevan bien con ella. En realidad, ellos creen que no hay ninguna mujer apropiada para su hijo. Le dicen a Mario: «Si te casas con Ángela, Uds. se van a divorciar. No será un matrimonio amistoso y cariñoso.» (Continue with story of successful marriage, family, and in-laws' change of heart, etc.)

Quick Comprehension Check: Sample items. **¿Cierto o falso?**

1. **Mario y Ángela se enamoran a primera vista.**
2. **Piensan terminar los estudios antes de casarse.**
3. **Los padres de Mario quieren que rompa con Ángela.**
4. **Ángela se divorcia de Mario a causa de sus suegros.**

Suggestions:

- Use definitions as in **Conversación A** to present the vocabulary. Model some words in sentences about yourself and in communicative exchanges with the students: **Yo estoy casado. Me casé en... Mi esposa...**
- Offer the following optional vocabulary: **el compromiso matrimonial, separado/a, divorciado/a.** Point out that **separado/a** and **divorciado/a** are used with **estar,** not **ser.**
- Note that **un matrimonio** means *a married couple* as well as *a marriage.*
- Point out that **novio/a** connotes a more serious relationship in Hispanic culture than implied by the English words *boyfriend/girlfriend.* See the **Nota cultural** after **Conversación B.** Emphasize and model the multiple meanings of **novio/a.**
- Words for in-laws were introduced in a **Vocabulario útil** section in **Capítulo 2.** Reenter those now. Use the Durán family tree in that chapter to help model them. Draw the tree on the board and read the following paragraph:
  Luisa García Romero es la suegra de Lola Benítez Guzmán. En cambio, Lola es la nuera de Luisa y Manuel Durán Parrado. Manuel es el esposo de Luisa. Jaime Vargas Arias es el cuñado de Manolo Durán García. Jaime está casado con Elena Durán García, la hermana de Manolo. Jaime y Elena también son los cuñados de Lola, la esposa de Manolo.

- Have students write down four adjectives to describe their ideal mate. Then, on the board, write the adjectives in separate columns, one for **el esposo ideal** and the other for **la esposa ideal.** Use this information as a springboard for a class discussion. Are there apparent differences in the columns? Do men look for certain qualities and women others? Which is more important: physical beauty or inner beauty (personality, sense of humor, and so on)?

Heritage Speakers: Si hay hispanohablantes en su clase, pídales que hablen de sus familias y de la importancia de las relaciones entre familiares y amigos. Anime a los otros estudiantes a hacerles preguntas sobre sus familias y las diferencias y las semejanzas entre los hispanos y los no-hispanos en cuanto a la familia.

ETAPAS DE LA VIDA

Suggestions:

- Offer the following optional vocabulary: **la pubertad, la tercera edad, criar.** Point out and model the difference between **crecer** (*to grow up*) and **criar** (*to raise*).
- Emphasize and model the conjugation of **nacer** and **crecer,** which is similar to **conocer: nazco, crezco, conozco.**
- Have students make associations with stages of life: **¿Qué colores / estaciones del año asocia Ud. con cada una de las etapas de la vida? ¿Qué actividades asocia con ellas?**
- Ask students the following questions to personalize the vocabulary: 1. **¿Cuál es su fecha de nacimiento? ¿Dónde creció Ud.? ¿Quién lo/la crió?** 2. **En su opinión, ¿cuál es la mejor/peor etapa de la vida de una persona? ¿Por qué?** 3. **¿Tiene Ud. miedo a la muerte? ¿Cree Ud. que hay otra vida después de esta?**

Heritage Speakers: Pídales a los hispanohablantes que nombren otras expresiones de cariño que usan. Pregúnteles con quién(es) las usan y en qué circunstancias.

Paso 2: Gramática

GRAMMAR SECTION 40

Follow-up:

- Have students complete the following sentences: 1. **Mi pareja ideal es una persona que tenga / sea...** 2. **Mi casa ideal es una que tenga / sea / esté...** 3. **Mis vacaciones ideales son unas en las que yo (no) tenga / esté...** 4. **Mi coche ideal es uno que tenga / sea...**
- As a follow-up activity, you may want to have your students interview each other about their own special person. For those students who do not have a significant other, what type of person would be their ideal?

Suggestions:

- Review noun clauses and the use of the subjunctive in them before introducing adjective clauses.
- Emphasize and model the relationship between adjectives and adjective clauses (to modify a noun), for example, **Veo una casa blanca / que tiene ventanas.** Draw parallels with noun clauses and their relationship to nouns.
- Give students the following formulas and models to help them conceptualize the use of subjunctive with adjective clauses: 1. experience = knowledge of the existence of the object qualified 2. + subjunctive = – experience: **Quiero salir con un muchacho que tenga interés en la política internacional. (No lo conozco todavía.)** 3. –subjunctive = + experience: **Quiero salir con un muchacho que tiene interés en la política internacional. (Ya lo conozco.)**

- Relate the uses of the subjunctive in adjective clauses to the general use of the subjunctive to express conceptualized states / actions.
- Emphasize and model the use of *donde* to introduce the adjective clause: **Queremos trabajar en una ciudad donde haya una comunidad intercultural. Viven en un barrio donde los niños pueden jugar en la calle.**
- Model, in brief exchanges with students, more examples of the question/answer series noted in the first **¡OJO!** box, for example, **¿Hay estudiantes en esta clase que tengan hijos? → No, no hay ningún estudiante en esta clase que tenga hijos. / Sí, hay un (dos) estudiante(s) en esta clase que tienen hijos. ¿Hay profesores en esta universidad que vivan en residencias estudiantiles? → No, no hay ningún profesor en esta universidad que viva en una residencia estudiantil. / Sí, hay profesores en esta universidad que viven en residencias estudiantiles.**

ENFOQUE CULTURAL: CHILE

Oraciones. Complete las oraciones con palabras de la lista.

abandono	literatura	nieves	tierra
chilli	maestra	quechua	valles
desierto	mapuche	selva	vinos
economías	maternidad	suicidio	viñedos
hispanoamericana			

1. El español es la lengua oficial de Chile, pero también se hablan ______________ y ______________.
2. La palabra ______________ significa «lugar donde termina la ______________».
3. La geografía de Chile incluye una ______________ tropical, un ______________ en el norte, fértiles ______________ y zonas de ______________ perpetuas en el extremo sur.
4. Chile tiene una de las ______________ más fuertes de Sudamérica.
5. Chile tiene una región con muchos ______________ y hoy es un importante productor de ______________ que se consumen en los Estados Unidos y Europa.
6. Gabriela Mistral fue la primera ______________ en ganar el premio Nóbel de ______________.
7. Además de poeta, Mistral fue ______________.
8. Los momentos tristes de la vida de Mistral incluyen el ______________ de su padre, el ______________ de su prometido y su ______________ frustrada.

Suggestions:

- Point out the Mistral poem strategies of contrasting disparate but not quite opposite elements (**fiel / perdida; rosa / espina; púrpura / melancolía; amada / amante; desposeída / rica**) and then uniting the elements by calling them **frutas mellizas.**
- Also point out the frequent use of repetition, and have students find examples in the poem. Ask students what effect the repetition has on them.
- Explain that in Spanish poetry it is possible to rhyme words that end in similar vowels but dissimilar consonants (**rima asonante**). Have students find the **i / a** rhymes in this poem (**perdida / espina / mellizas**). Point out that **desposeída,** because of its accent on the **i,** and **melancolía,** because the **lía** is two syllables rather than one, are assonant rhymes. Discuss inexact rhyme and the similarly inexact comparisons of the poem.

- Bring in copies of poems by other Chilean poets and work with the class to translate and interpret them. Poems you might choose include Pablo Neruda's "**Oda a la alcachofa,**" the "antipoet" Nicanor Parra's "**Un hombre,**" or Vicente Huidobro's "**Ella.**"

Paso 3: Gramática

GRAMMAR SECTION 41

Follow-up: Have students complete the following sentences with their own ideas: 1. **En una fiesta, nunca bailo a menos que...** 2. **Cuando salgo con mis amigos siempre tengo mi licencia de conducir en caso de que...** 3. **No me voy a casar a menos que...** 4. **Tengo planes hechos en caso de que...** 5. **Voy a estudiar ______ para que...**

Suggestions:

- Present the following initial pattern to help students remember the five conjunctions that are always followed by the subjunctive:
  A PACE:

  ***A* menos que**
  ***P*ara que**
  ***A*ntes (de) que**
  ***C*on tal (de) que**
  ***E*n caso de que**

- Include the lower frequency **sin que** in your presentation of the always subjunctive conjunctions (A SPACE).
- Emphasize and model the relationship of the adverbial clauses to adverbs (they function as an adverb): **Llega mañana / antes de que salgamos.**

Optional Activity: **Un fin de semana en las montañas**

Paso 1. Hablan Manolo y Lola. Use la conjunción entre paréntesis para unir las oraciones, haciendo todos los cambios necesarios.

1. No voy. Dejamos a la niña con los abuelos. (a menos que)
2. Vamos solos. Pasamos un fin de semana romántico. (para que)
3. Esta vez voy a aprender a esquiar. Tú me enseñas. (con tal de que)
4. Vamos a salir temprano por la mañana. Nos acostamos tarde la noche anterior. (a menos que)
5. Es importante que lleguemos a la estación (*resort*) de esquí. Empieza a nevar. (antes de que)
6. Deja la dirección y el teléfono del hotel. Tus padres nos necesitan. (en caso de que)

Paso 2. ¿Cierto, falso o no lo dice?

1. Manolo y Lola acaban de casarse.
2. Casi siempre van de vacaciones con su hija.
3. Los dos son excelentes esquiadores.
4. Van a dejar a la niña con los abuelos.

EN LOS ESTADOS UNIDOS Y EL CANADÁ... ISABEL ALLENDE

Suggestion: Isabel Allende's uncle, Salvador Allende, was elected to the Chilean presidency in 1970, during the Richard Nixon years in the United States. He was a physician and socialist politician representing the Unidad Popular, a leftist political party. Have students look up information on Allende, U.S. involvement in the military coup opposing Allende, and U.S. support of Augusto Pinochet, the general who would become the dictator of Chile from 1973 to 1990.

UN POCO DE TODO

Optional Activities: **Situaciones de la vida.** Con un compañero / una compañera, háganse preguntas y contéstenlas, según el modelo. Deben justificar sus respuestas.

MODELOS: compañero/a de cuarto // tener coche →
E1: ¿Buscas un compañero de cuarto que tenga coche?
E2: No, ya tengo coche.
(Sí, para que yo no tenga que manejar tanto.)
(Sí, en caso de que mi coche viejo no funcione.)

1. marido/mujer // ser médico/a
2. amigo/a // no haber roto recientemente con su pareja
3. casa // estar lejos de la ciudad
4. ciudad // haber un buen sistema de transporte público
5. amistad // estar basada en la confianza (*trust*)
6. coche // arrancar inmediatamente, sin problemas

Reciclado: Recycle the weekend activities vocabulary. Have students express the following ideas in Spanish: 1. We go there to have fun. 2. We also go so that the kids can play baseball. 3. They're going to swim before eating (they eat). 4. Are they going to swim before we eat? 5. Don't go without talking to your mother. 6. And don't leave without your father giving you money.

¿Qué prefiere Ud.? ¿Qué espera? Complete las siguientes oraciones con información verdadera.

1. Prefiero comer en restaurantes donde ______.
2. No me gusta que los programas de televisión ______.
3. Voy a graduarme en ______ a menos que ______.
4. Me gusta que los profesores ______.
5. Algún día deseo tener un coche que ______.
6. Este verano voy a ______ a menos que ______.
7. Me gustan las personas que ______.
8. En el futuro, quiero tener ______ hijos, con tal de que ______.

Suggestion: Assign this activity as homework and use the topics for discussions during the next class period.

Paso 4: Un paso más

VIDEOTECA

MINIDRAMAS

The **Minidramas** vignettes are not referenced in the textbook, but are part of the *¿Qué tal?* Video Program. They also appear on the Video on CD packaged free with the textbook. If you show the **Minidramas** in class or have your students view them as homework, you might find the following suggestions helpful. You can also find blackline master activities in Section X of this Manual for **Minidramas.**

Comprensión: 1. **¿Por qué no pueden verse Lola y Eva durante el fin de semana?**
2. **¿Cuándo deciden verse?**
3. **¿Qué les gustaría hacer?**

Variation: Have students work in pairs to complete the following dialogue with information they invent. Then have them practice and act it out.

E1: **¡Por fin es _____________!**
E2: **¡Qué alegría! ¿Qué vas a hacer este fin de semana?**
E1: **El sábado voy a pasar el día en __________ (con __________). ¿Quieres venir?**
E2: **Gracias, me encantaría pero no puedo. Tengo que _____________.**
E1: **Pues, ¿por qué no _____________ conmigo (y con _____________) esta noche?**
E2: **¡Qué buena idea! ¿A qué hora?**
E1: **_____________.**
E2: **[Cierra la conversación y se despide.]**
E1: **[Se despide.]**

A LEER

Follow-up: **Comprensión.** Have students compare the information in the graph to what they think the divorce/separation situation in this country is. If possible, bring statistical data showing the same or similar information in this country. This information can be found on the Internet. Students can create charts based on that data, translating the information into Spanish.

A ESCRIBIR

Optional: Have students write a how-to article on divorce and the family. Suggest several possible angles, for example, ways to maintain stability and well-being for children, dealing fairly with finances, forming new families (step-parents and step-siblings), and so on. Have students imagine they are writing the how-to article for a column. Have volunteers read their articles to the class.

ACTIVIDAD DE DESENLACE: LAS RELACIONES SENTIMENTALES

Activity: Students will prepare a skit that idealizes or satirizes a stage of life such as childhood, adolescence, or marriage.

Purpose: To create a context in which students can review and practice the grammar from **Capítulo 15** and vocabulary related to relationships and marriage, and to stages of life.

Resources: *¿Qué tal?* textbook, the Internet, and other sources as appropriate

Vocabulary: Stages in relationships, life stages

Grammar: Principal grammatical structures covered in **Capítulo 15** of the textbook, including the past participle used as an adjective, and perfect forms (present perfect indicative and present perfect subjunctive)

Optional Writing:	Students may wish to write and read an original poem about the stage of life that they've chosen to enact. Remind them to use the vocabulary and grammar from the chapter.
Recycled Content:	The present perfect, the present subjunctive to express emotion, and the preterite and imperfect.
Duration:	Out-of-class preparation time will vary. In-class time will be approximately five minutes per presentation.
Format:	Groups of three to four students

Games and Activities

Capítulo 15 *La fotonovela*

Usando seis dibujos, escriba la historia de amor de Paco y Lucía. Empiece su historia así: **Un día de primavera...**

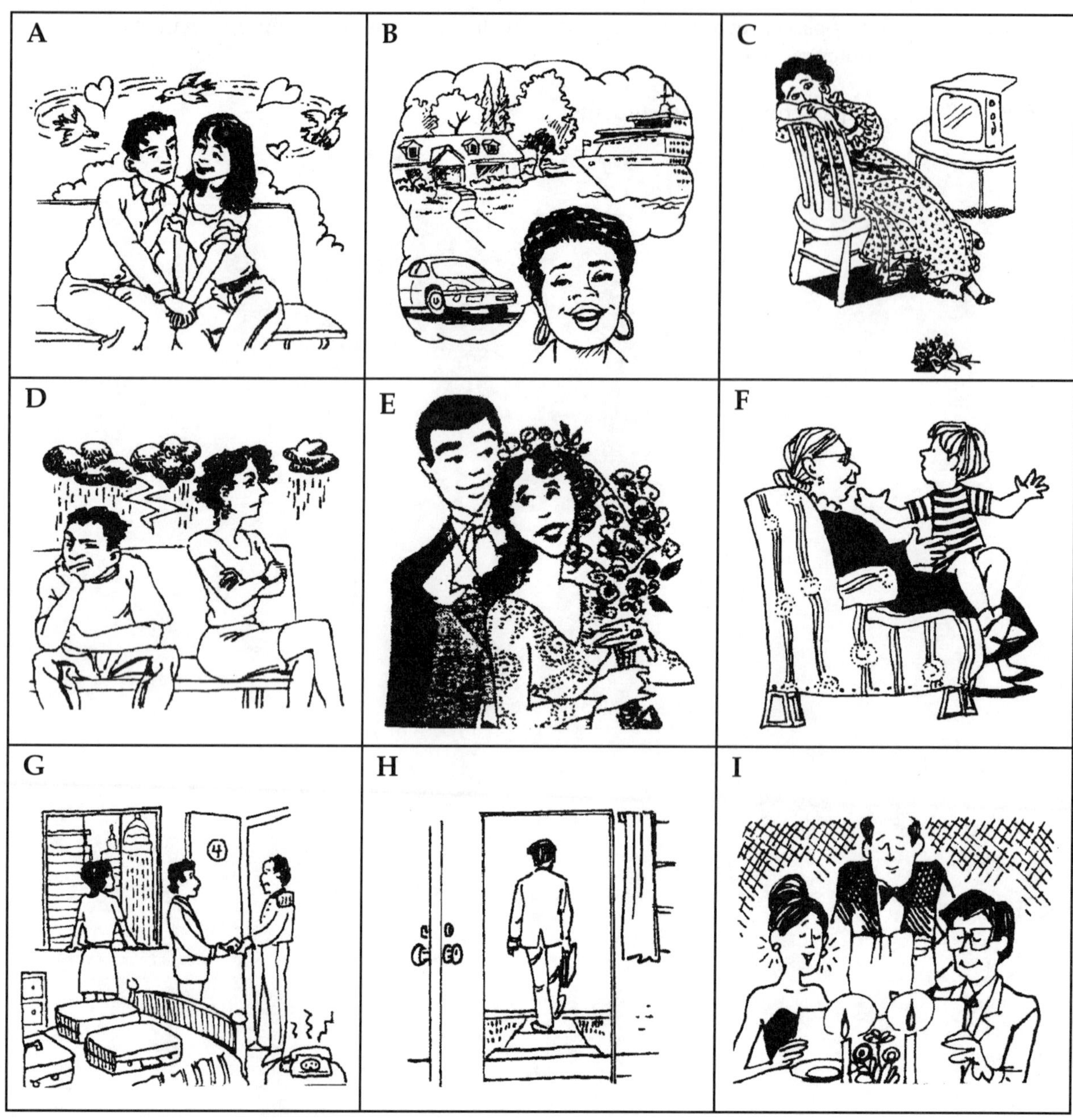

La encuesta dice...

¿De qué se queja el hombre recién casado? Les dice a sus amigos...

1. ¡Mi esposa no sabe cocinar!

2. ¡Mi suegra no nos deja en paz!

3. ¡Mi esposa está muy fea por la mañana!

4. ¡Ella siempre quiere gastar dinero que no tenemos!

5. ¡Mi mujer habla por teléfono con sus amigas constantemente!

6. ¡No hay espacio en el armario ni en la cómoda para mi ropa!

¡La luna de miel se acabó!

La encuesta dice...

¿De qué se queja el mujer recién casada? Les dice a sus amigas...

1. ¡Mi esposo pasa demasiado tiempo fuera de casa!
2. ¡Él no quiere perder ningún partido en la televisión!
3. ¡Mi suegra no nos deja en paz!
4. ¡Mi marido siempre deja la ropa en el suelo después de quitársela!
5. ¡Él siempre deja el baño sucio y desordenado!
6. ¡Mi esposo ya no me manda cartas de amor ni flores!

¡La luna de miel se acabó!

La encuesta dice...

¿Cómo quieres pasar la vejez? Ojalá que yo...

1. pueda vivir en un lugar donde haga buen tiempo todo el año.
2. lleve una vida sana y activa.
3. vea a la familia y los amigos con frecuencia.
4. tenga la oportunidad de hacer viajes y excursiones.
5. tenga tiempo para leer muchos libros, periódicos y revistas.
6. no repita los errores de mi juventud.

Si la juventud supiera y la vejez pudiera.

Arriésgate

	Vocabulario	Verbos	Gramática	Traducción
10 pts	la madurez / la vejez	Busco una universidad que (ofrecer) cursos en mi especialización.	Corazón, tienes que decirme que me quieres (*before*) nosotros (tener) otra cita.	The newlyweds love each other a lot.
20 pts	la infancia / la niñez	Vamos a hacer planes para una luna de miel que (ser) larga y romántica.	Querido, rompo contigo (*unless*) tú me (traer) flores y bombones de vez en cuando.	Lola's fiancé is affectionate, generous, hardworking, intelligent . . . and he is still single!
30 pts	la amistad / el noviazgo	Hay muchas mujeres que (gastar) más de mil dólares en el vestido de novia.	Amor mío, me caso contigo (*provided that*) tú me (regalar) un coche de lujo antes de la boda.	My father fell in love with my mother at first sight!
40 pts	separarse / divorciarse	Llame al sicólogo del radio que (dar) consejos sobre la relaciones sentimentales.	Cielo, firma este contrato prenupcial (*in case*) nosotros (divorciarse).	The married couple gave a big party to celebrate the birth of their first child.
50 pts	la boda / el matrimonio	No conozco a nadie que (creer) que la adolescencia es la etapa más agradable de la vida.	Mi vida, pasa más tiempo con tu suegra (so that) ella nos (ayudar) a comprar nuestra propia casa.	After the death of her husband, my grandmother met a younger man with whom she gets along well.

Answer Key for *Arriésgate*

Capítulo 15

Vocabulario: *¿Cuál es la diferencia? Las repuestas varían.*

Verbos:

10 pts	ofrezca
20 pts	sea
30 pts	gastan
40 pts	da
50 pts	crea

Gramática: *¿Qué le dice Ramona a su futuro esposo?*

10 pts	antes (de) que; tengamos
20 pts	a menos que; traigas
30 pts	con tal (de) que; regales
40 pts	en caso de que; nos divorciemos
50 pts	para que; ayude

Traducción:

10 pts	Los recién casados se quieren mucho.
20 pts	El novio de Lola es cariñoso, generoso, trabajador, inteligente... ¡y todavía es soltero!
30 pts	Mi padre se enamoró de mi madre a primera vista.
40 pts	La pareja dio (hizo) una fiesta grande para celebrar el nacimiento de su primer hijo.
50 pts	Después de la muerte de su esposo (marido), mi abuela conoció a un hombre más joven con quien ella se lleva bien.

Student Supplements
- Listening Comprehension Program CD, **Capítulo 16** (**Paso 1: Vocabulario:** word lists)
- Workbook/Laboratory Manual, **Capítulo 16**
- Audio Program CD, **Capítulo 16**

Instructor Resources
- Instructor's Manual/IRK: Chapter-by-Chapter Supplementary Materials, **Capítulo 16**
  - **Paso 1: Vocabulario**
  - **Paso 2: Gramática**
    - Grammar Section 42
    - **Enfoque cultural**
  - **Paso 3: Gramática**
    - Grammar Section 43
    - **En los Estados Unidos y el Canadá...**
    - **Un poco de todo**
  - **Paso 4: Un paso más**
    - **Videoteca: Minidramas**
  - Games and Activities
- Instructor's Manual/IRK: Video Activities and Related Materials
  - **A primera vista**
  - **A segunda vista**
  - Answers to Video Activities
  - Videoscripts
- Audioscript, **Capítulo 16**
- Transparencies 82–87
- Testing Program, **Capítulo 16**

Multimedia Resources
- Online Learning Center
- Electronic Workbook/Laboratory Manual
- Video, **Capítulo 16** (cue 1:37:44)
  - **En contexto** (2:10)
  - **Minidramas** (5:20)
  - **Enfoque cultural: Paraguay, Uruguay** (2:00)
- Student CD-ROM, **Capítulo 16**
- Electronic Language Tutor, **Capítulo 16** (**Vocabulario, Gramática**)

Paso 1: Vocabulario

PROFESIONES Y OFICIOS

Preparation: It is helpful to bring pictures that illustrate the professions and trades you wish to present. Allow students to skim the vocabulary list for about two minutes before you begin.

Sample Passage: **De niño o niña, ¿qué quería ser Ud. en la vida? ¿Sabe Ud. ahora la profesión u oficio que quiere ejercer? ¿Es lo mismo? Hoy vamos a hablar de algunas personas famosas y de lo que fueron o lo que son. Uds. van a ver que esas personas han tenido otra carrera o que tienen una profesión «secreta».**

Vamos a comenzar con una persona fácil: Abraham Lincoln. Todos sabemos que Lincoln era presidente de los Estados Unidos durante la Guerra Civil. Pero, ¿qué fue antes de ser presidente? ¿Siempre fue político? (See whether anyone responds.) **No. Lincoln fue abogado. Fue abogado en Illinois; ejerció su profesión en Springfield.**

Y Paul Newman. Es actor, pero ¿qué otra fama tiene? (Racecar driver is correct, but not primary.) **Newman tiene gran fama de cocinero, una persona que prepara comida. Claro, él no es cocinero en un restaurante, pero en Hollywood es uno de los cocineros más respetados entre los actores. Y varios productos comerciales llevan su nombre.**

Ahora, una persona difícil. Jon Peters es un productor de Hollywood muy conocido. Pero antes tuvo otra ocupación. ¿Cuál era? (Wait.) **Bueno, fue peluquero. Fue peluquero de los actores. Un peluquero le corta y arregla el pelo a otra persona. Vidal Sassoon es un peluquero famoso. Jon Peters dejó de ser peluquero cuando él y Barbra Streisand se hicieron novios y se convirtió en productor para la película *A Star Is Born* (*Nace una estrella*).**

(After checking comprehension, continue with a game in which you describe a famous member of a given profession, and students guess whom you have described.)

Quick Comprehension Check: Sample items.
¿Cuál es la palabra que se asocia con la primera profesión o la profesión «secreta» de la persona?

1. Lincoln: **la Casa Blanca, el congreso, *la ley*, el teatro**
2. Newman: **la oficina, *la comida*, las novelas, los periódicos**
3. Peters: ***el pelo*, la radio, la educación, los animales**

Continuation: **Ahora les doy la profesión y Uds. deben decirme la palabra asociada.**

4. **la siquiatra: *la mente*** (point), **las manos** (show), **el corazón** (point)
5. **el periodista: los discos compactos, los coches, *la computadora***

Suggestions:

- Offer the following optional vocabulary: **el/la cirujano/a, el/la cocinero/a, el/la gerente, el/la astronauta, el/la piloto/a, el/la atleta profesional.**
- Use the following questions to check comprehension: 1. **¿Quién gana más dinero, un plomero o un enfermero? ¿un obrero o un siquiatra?** 2. **¿Quién tiene el trabajo más aburrido, un siquiatra o un peluquero? ¿un comerciante o un abogado? ¿un plomero o un vendedor?** 3. **¿Quién tiene más responsabilidades, un maestro o un ingeniero? ¿un abogado o un comerciante?** 4. **¿Para qué profesiones es necesario asistir a la universidad? ¿Por cuántos años?** 5. **¿Cuál de estos trabajos le gusta más/menos? Explique por qué, dando las ventajas y desventajas.**
- Point out that there is little consensus in the Spanish-speaking world about words used for females practicing certain professions. Names given here should be

acceptable to most Spanish speakers, but there is considerable discussion about terms such as **la pilota, la médica,** and so on. Have students review the **Nota cultural** on page 363.

Optional Activity:

¿A quién necesita Ud.? ¿A quién debe llamar o con quién debe consultar en estas situaciones? Hay más de una respuesta posible en algunos casos.

1. La tubería (*plumbing*) de la cocina no funciona bien.
2. Ud. acaba de tener un accidente automovilístico; el otro conductor dice que Ud. tuvo la culpa (*blame*).
3. Por las muchas tensiones y presiones de su vida profesional y personal, Ud. tiene serios problemas afectivos (*emotional*).
4. Ud. está en el hospital y quiere que alguien le dé una aspirina.
5. Ud. quiere que alguien lo/la ayude con las tareas domésticas porque no tiene mucho tiempo para hacerlas.
6. Ud. quiere que alguien le construya un muro (*wall*) en el jardín.
7. Ud. conoce todos los detalles de un escándalo en el gobierno de su ciudad y quiere divulgarlos.

Suggestion: Do as a listening comprehension activity.

EL MUNDO DEL TRABAJO

Suggestions:

- Have students respond **cierto** or **falso** to the following sentences: 1. **Una persona que busca un puesto se llama *un aspirante.*** 2. **Si a Ud. no le gusta su trabajo, debe despedirlo.** 3. **Si a Ud. le gustaría renunciar su trabajo, debe conseguir una solicitud.** 4. **Para llenar una solicitud, es necesario tener bolígrafo o lápiz.** Have students correct the false statements.
- Point out that **compañía** is frequently used in company names, but **empresa** is the general word for *corporation* and *company.* **Caerle bien/mal** is used like **gustar** to refer to people. **Renunciar** and **dimitir** mean *to resign* from a job. **Resignar** is a false cognate and is never used to express that.
- Point out that **cobrar un cheque** means *to cash a check,* but for cashing traveler's checks **cambiar un cheque de viajero** is used. Explain and model the differences between **ahorrar** (*to save* money or time), guardar (*to save, keep* something), and **salvar** (*to save, rescue* someone). Contrast and model the difference between **gastar** (*to spend* money) and **pasar** (*to spend* time).
- Explain that vocabulary for financial and banking transactions varies a good deal in the Spanish-speaking world. Introduce other terms you might prefer or hear, for example, **depositar** vs. **ingresar** and **libreta (de ahorros)** vs. **cartilla.**
- Offer the following optional vocabulary: **los ingresos** (*income*), **hacer una transferencia / un giro.**

Preliminary Exercises:

Ask students the following questions to personalize the vocabulary: 1. **¿Tiene Ud. una cuenta de ahorros? ¿En qué banco? ¿Ha ahorrado mucho dinero este año? ¿Es posible que ahorre más el año que viene? ¿Tiene también una cuenta corriente? ¿Escribe muchos cheques? ¿Hay siempre suficiente dinero en su cuenta? ¿Qué ocurre si no hay suficientes fondos en su cuenta?** 2. **En esta clase, ¿cuántos de Uds. tienen tarjetas de crédito?** (to one student) **¿Son tarjetas nacionales como Visa o son tarjetas para tiendas locales? ¿Las usa con mucha frecuencia? ¿Las usa demasiado? ¿Tiene muchas facturas que pagar ahora?** 3. **En general, ¿tienen muchas facturas los estudiantes? ¿Cuáles son los gastos típicos de un estudiante? ¿Tiene Ud. todos estos gastos? ¿Tiene también un presupuesto? ¿Qué porcentaje de su presupuesto es para el**

alquiler? 4. **¿Cuánto paga de alquiler? ¿Lo paga siempre el primero del mes o a veces lo paga más tarde? ¿Qué pasa si lo paga tarde?** 5. **¿Gasta Ud. mucho dinero en ropa? ¿Cómo la paga, con tarjetas de crédito, al contado o con cheque? ¿Se queja Ud. del precio de la ropa?**

CONVERSACIÓN

Follow-up: Have students work in groups to write brief dialogues that illustrate the different parts of the sequence. Then have them present their sections to the class.

Optional Activity: **El mes pasado.** Piense en sus finanzas personales del mes pasado. ¿Fue un mes típico? ¿Tuvo dificultades al final del mes o todo le salió bien?

Paso 1. Indique las respuestas apropiadas para Ud.

	¡CLARO QUE SÍ!	¡CLARO QUE NO!
1. Hice un presupuesto al principio del mes.	☐	☐
2. Deposité más dinero en el banco del que (*than what*) saqué.	☐	☐
3. Saqué dinero del cajero automático sin apuntar (*writing down*) la cantidad.	☐	☐
4. Pagué todas mis cuentas a tiempo.	☐	☐
5. Saqué un préstamo (Le pedí dinero prestado al banco) para pagar mis cuentas.	☐	☐
6. Tomé el autobús en vez de (*instead of*) usar el coche, para economizar un poco	☐	☐
7. Gasté mucho dinero en diversiones.	☐	☐
8. Saqué el saldo (*I balanced*) de mi cuenta de cheques (*checkbook*) sin dificultades.	☐	☐
9. Le presté dinero a un amigo.	☐	☐
10. Usé mis tarjetas de crédito sólo en casos de urgencia.	☐	☐

Paso 2. Vuelva a mirar sus respuestas. ¿Fue el mes pasado un mes típico? Pensando todavía en sus respuestas, sugiera tres cosas que Ud. debe hacer para mejorar su situación económica.

MODELO: Debo hacer un presupuesto mensual.

Suggestion: Have students complete this as a pair activity, turning the items into questions.

Paso 2: Gramática

GRAMMAR SECTION 42

Suggestions:

- Model the future of regular verbs.
- Ask students brief questions using the future of **comprar, beber,** and **escribir.**
- Read the following forms and have students give the corresponding subject pronoun: **tomaré, regresarán, mandará, necesitarás, llevarán, viajaremos, entrará, compraré, celebraremos, aprenderán, comprenderás, leeré, creerán, vivirá.**
- Model the irregular futures and **habrá** in sentences about yourself and in brief communicative exchanges with the students.

- Point out the similarities among irregular stems: 1. drop a vowel: **haber, poder, querer, saber** 2. drop two letters: **decir, hacer** 3. replace the theme vowel with **–d-: poner, salir, tener, venir.**
- Emphasize that in Spanish and English the future is most often expressed with present indicative and subjunctive rather than with the future tense. The future tense implies strong intention: *I'm going to study tonight* vs. *I will study tonight,* and **Voy a estudiar esta noche** vs. **Estudiaré esta noche.** Future can also be used to command: **No matarás** (the Ten Commandments, **los Diez Mandamientos**).
- Model the difference between the English *will* for future versus *will* for expressing willingness. **Querer** is used for willingness, but makes very strong requests. Point out that other verbs such as **poder** and **importar** can be used to soften the request: **¿Podrías cerrar la puerta, por favor?** (*Could you please close the door?*) and **¿Te importa cerrar la puerta, por favor?** (*Do you mind closing the door, please?*).

ENFOQUE CULTURAL: URUGUAY Y PARAGUAY

A. Para contestar. Conteste las siguientes preguntas con la información en Datos esenciales, ¡Fíjese! y Conozca...

1. ¿Qué países latinoamericanos no tienen costa en el mar?

____

2. ¿Qué porcentaje de la población uruguaya vive en Montevideo?

____

3. ¿En qué año se fundó la ciudad de Asunción?

____

4. ¿Cuál es la represa hidroeléctrica más grande del mundo?

____

5. ¿Qué país recibe energía de la represa?

____

B. ¿Cierto o falso? Indique si las siguientes oraciones son ciertas (C) o falsas (F) según la información en ¡Fíjese! y Conozca... Corrija las oraciones falsas.

1. C F Los uruguayos tienen que pagar su educación universitaria.
2. C F Más de la mitad de los uruguayos vive en Montevideo.
3. C F El analfabetismo (*illiteracy*) es un gran problema para el Uruguay.
4. C F Asunción fue la primera ciudad permanente en Sudamérica.
5. C F Paraguay tiene dos lenguas oficiales.
6. C F Itaipú está en la frontera del Paraguay, la Argentina y Bolivia.
7. C F Guaraní significa *guerrero.*

Suggestion: Have students form teams to research the following topics and report on their significance to Uruguay or Paraguay. Uruguay: Eduardo Galeano, Mario Benedetti, Delmira Agustini, Juana de Ibarbourou, Julio Herrera y Reussig, Juan Díaz de Solís,

Ferdinand Magellan, the Charrúas, José Gervasio Artigas and the Battle of **Las Piedras,** the Tupamaros. Paraguay: Sebastian Cabot, *el rey blanco* and the discovery of Iguazú Falls, José Arturo Rodríguez Francia, Arturo Stroessner, Raúl Cubas Grau, Augusto Roa Bastos and **Yo, el supremo.**

Paso 3: Gramática

GRAMMAR SECTION 43

Suggestions:

- Remind students that they learned certain conjunctions that always require the subjunctive in Grammar 41 (conjunctions of contingency and purpose). Point out that with conjunctions of time (with the exception of **antes de que**), the subjunctive is used only when they introduce future, uncompleted actions or states.
- Model and contrast a future action, a habitual action, and a past action.
- Emphasize that the subjunctive is always used after **antes de que,** even though it is a time conjunction. **(¡OJO!).** Due to its meaning, it is always followed by a future uncompleted action.
- Point out that the subjunctive is used with most time conjunctions even without a change of subject in the dependent clause: **Vamos a salir tan pronto como terminemos. Después de** and **hasta,** however, are followed by an infinitive when there is no change in subject: **Saldremos después de comer. No vamos a salir hasta terminar la tarea.**

EN LOS ESTADOS UNIDOS Y EL CANADÁ... EL CRECIENTE MERCADO HISPANO

Point Out: Remind students that the Hispanic population in the country is not at all a homogenous group. They come from a wide variety of racial and ethnic backgrounds, regional cultures, and experiences. Some families have lived in regions of the United States since before those regions became part of the United States. Others have recently immigrated from not only Mexico, but Central and South America as well.

Suggestions: Have students explore the difficulties that marketers will have targeting this diverse group. Point out the dangers of alienating large portions of the group by stereotyping what *Hispanic* means. Ask students what some of the biggest pitfalls might be. Have them consider physical features, dialects, music, food, religion, and dress.

UN POCO DE TODO

Optional Activities: **Los planes de la familia Alonso**

Paso 1. Forme oraciones completas, según las indicaciones. Use el futuro donde sea posible.

1. ser / necesario / que / (nosotros) ahorrar / más
2. yo / no / usar / tanto / tarjetas / crédito
3. mamá / buscar / trabajo / donde / (ellos) pagarle / más
4. (nosotros) pedir / préstamo / en / banco
5. nos / lo / (ellos) dar, / ¿no / creer (tú)?
6. papá / estar / tranquilo / cuando / todos / empezar / economizar
7. (tú) deber / pagar / siempre / al contado
8. no / (nosotros) poder / irse / de vacaciones / este verano

Paso 2. Según los comentarios de las personas en el **Paso 1,** ¿cree Ud. que la familia Alonso está muy bien económicamente o no? Explique.

Follow-up: **Paso 1.** Have students indicate if the sentences are **cierto** or **falso** for them and their families. When a statement is not true for them, have them correct it.

Planes para una boda. Use las conjunciones entre paréntesis para unir cada oración con la frase que la sigue. Haga todos los cambios necesarios. **¡OJO!** No se usa el subjuntivo en todos los casos. Tenga cuidado con las formas verbales.

MODELO: Miguel quiere casarse con Carmen./él: conseguir un trabajo (tan pronto como) → Miguel quiere casarse con Carmen tan pronto como él consiga un trabajo.

1. Carmen quiere esperar. / ella: graduarse en la universidad (hasta que)
2. Miguel se lo va a decir a los padres de Carmen. / ellos: llegar a la ciudad (tan pronto como)
3. Los padres de Carmen siempre quieren ver a Miguel. / él visitar a su hija (cuando)
4. Los padres se van a alegrar. / (ellos) oír las noticias (en cuanto)
5. Miguel y Carmen van a Acapulco en su luna de miel. / (ellos) tener dinero (cuando)

Paso 4: Un paso más

VIDEOTECA

MINIDRAMAS

The **Minidramas** vignettes are not referenced in the textbook, but are part of the *¿Qué tal?* Video Program. They also appear on the Video on CD packaged free with the textbook. If you show the **Minidramas** in class or have your students view them as homework, you might find the following suggestions helpful. You can also find blackline master activities in Section X of this Manual for **Minidramas.**

Comprensión: **¿Cierto o falso? Corrija las oraciones falsas.**

1. **Lupe tiene el currículum más interesante entre todos los aspirantes.**
2. **A Lupe no le gustaba su trabajo anterior.**
3. **En la oficina del abogado, Lupe contestaba el teléfono y escribía informes.**
4. **Lupe debe pasar seis horas aprendiendo su trabajo.**

Suggestion:

1. Ask students what questions they were asked when interviewed for their current or last job.
2. Ask students what questions they would consider unacceptable during a job interview.

ACTIVIDAD DE DESENLACE: MI FUTURO

Activity: Students will prepare and give an oral presentation in which they talk about the future that they envision for themselves, and in which they talk about their profession, family, hobbies, travel, investments, and property.

Purpose: To create a context in which students can review and practice the grammar from **Capítulo 16** and vocabulary related to the world of work and personal finances

Resources:	*¿Qué tal?* textbook, the Internet, and other sources as appropriate
Vocabulary:	Professions and trades, the work world
Grammar:	Principal grammatical structures covered in **Capítulo 16** of the textbook, including future verb forms, and the indicative and subjunctive after conjunctions of time
Duration:	Out-of-class preparation time will vary. In-class time will be approximately five minutes per presentation.
Format:	Groups of three to four students

Games and Activities

Capítulo 16: Partner A

Crucigrama

You have the answers for half the puzzle, and your partner has those for the other half. Together you must complete the whole puzzle. You have to give clues to your partner so that he/she can guess the missing words. You *may not use the word itself.* Everything has to be done in Spanish.

Use clues such as: **La persona que...**
El lugar donde...
La cosa que...
Lo que se hace cuando...

Capítulo 16: Partner B *Crucigrama*

You have the answers for half the puzzle, and your partner has those for the other half. Together you must complete the whole puzzle. You have to give clues to your partner so that he/she can guess the missing words. You *may not use the word itself.* Everything has to be done in Spanish.

Use clues such as: **La persona que...**
El lugar donde...
La cosa que...
Lo que se hace cuando...

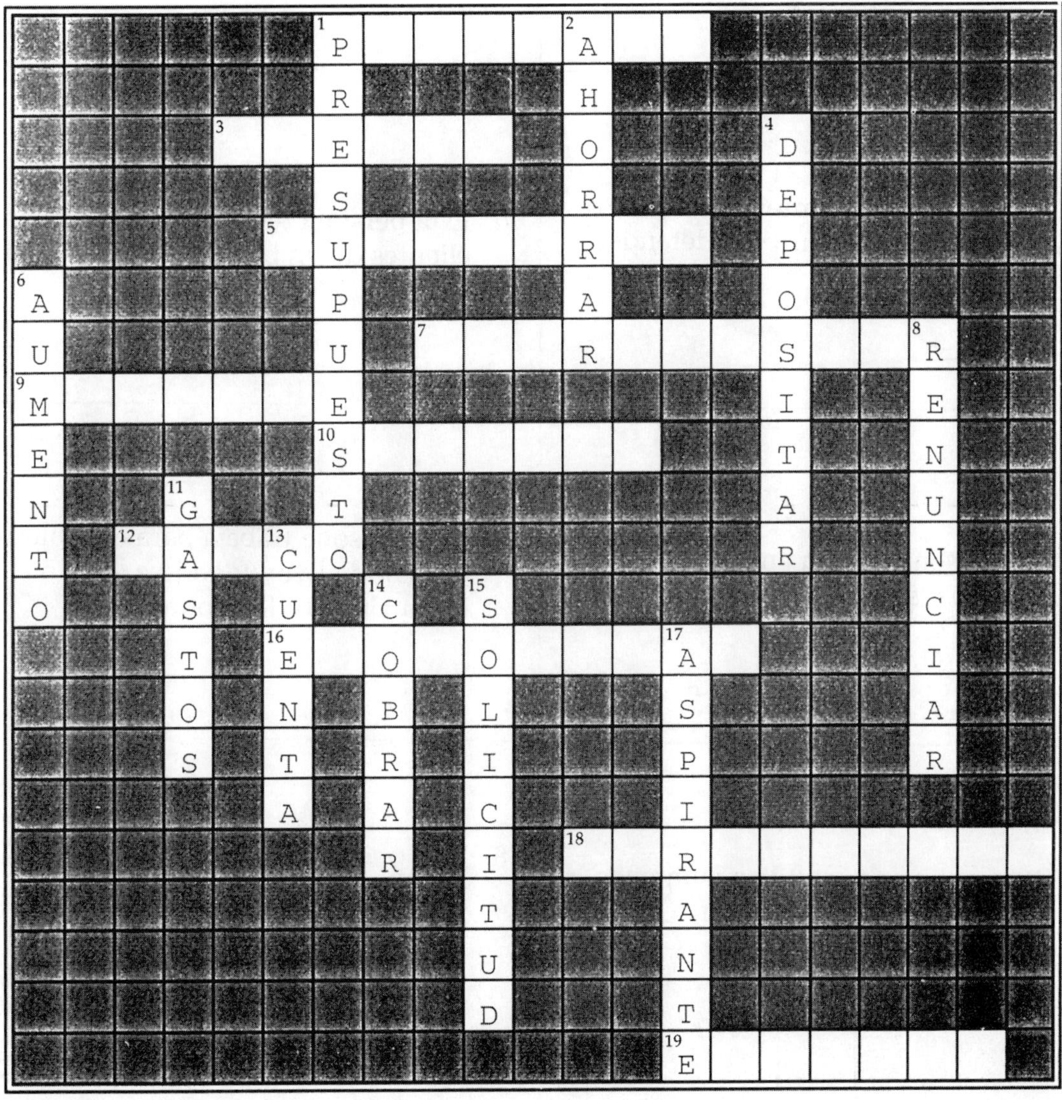

1. Esta persona trabaja en fábricas y normalmente gana poco dinero.	5. Esta persona arregla las tuberías de la cocina o el baño.
2. Esta persona es miembro del ejército y a veces debe luchar para defender a su patria.	6. Esta persona recibe el dinero de los clientes de un banco o de una tienda.
3. Esta persona enseña en una escuela primaria o secundaria.	7. Esta persona trabaja para el gobierno o el condado ayudando a los niños, los ancianos o los pobres.
4. Esta persona nos ayuda a mantener buena salud y cura nuestras enfermedades.	8. Esta persona habla varios idiomas y nos ayuda a comunicarnos con personas que no hablen nuestro idioma.

9. Esta persona es experta en leyes.	13. Esta persona diseña computadoras.
10. Esta persona selecciona y organiza los libros. Trabaja en un edificio donde no se puede hablar en voz alta.	14. Esta persona está a cargo de las cuentas bancarias, el presupuesto y el pago de los impuestos de una compañía.
11. Esta persona se asegura de que sus pacientes tengan una bella sonrisa.	15. Esta persona ayuda a los doctores y cuida a los enfermos.
12. Esta persona puede especializarse en la electrónica, la mecánica, la construcción de sistemas de transporte.	16. Esta persona trabaja en un taller arreglando motores.

17. Esta persona informa al público sobre los eventos importantes en el mundo.	21. Esta persona enseña en una universidad.
18. Esta persona diseña programas para las computadoras.	22. Esta persona cuida y cura las enfermedades de los animales.
19. Esta persona prepara la comida en los restaurantes.	23. Esta persona tiene pacientes que necesitan ayuda para resolver problemas personales.
20. Este médico ayuda a las personas que tienen dificultades con la realidad.	24. Esta persona corta y arregla el pelo y hace permanentes y tintes. Trabaja en un salón de belleza.

Answer Key for *Quiero llegar a ser...*

Capítulo 16

1. **el obrero / la obrera**
2. **el soldado / la mujer soldado**
3. **el maestro / la maestra**
4. **el médico / la médica**
5. **el plomero / la plomera**
6. **el cajero / la cajera**
7. **el trabajador / la trabajadora social**
8. **el traductor / la traductora**
9. **el abogado / la abogada**
10. **el bibliotecario / la bibliotecaria**
11. **el/la dentista**
12. **el ingeniero / la ingeniera**
13. **el/la analista de sistemas**
14. **el contador / la contadora**
15. **el enfermero / le enfermera**
16. **el mecánico / la mecánica**
17. **el/la periodista**
18. **el programador / la programadora**
19. **el cocinero / la cocinera**
20. **el/la siquiatra**
21. **el profesor / la profesora**
22. **el veterinario / la veterinaria**
23. **el sicólogo / la sicóloga**
24. **el peluquero / la peluquera**

¿__________ (Ganar) mi equipo de fútbol el año que viene?

Sí, tu equipo ganará todos los partidos en cuanto un joven jugador mexicano __________ (ser) parte del equipo.

¿__________ (Cambiar) yo el futuro del mundo?

Sí, cambiarás el futuro del mundo tan pronto como __________ (enseñar) tu primera clase en la escuela primaria.

En la madurez, ¿__________ (estar) yo en buenas condiciones físicas?

No, no estarás en buenas condiciones físicas a menos que __________ (seguir) los consejos de tu médico.

Ahora vivo en el campo y trabajo en la ciudad. ¿__________ (Mudarse) a la ciudad o __________ (encontrar) trabajo en el campo?

Te mudarás a la ciudad tan pronto como __________ (alquilar) un apartamento en el centro.

¿__________ (Cantar) en un bar musical en el futuro?

Sí, cantarás en un bar musical en cuanto tus amigos te __________ (llevar) a un bar donde se toque música «Karaoke».

¿__________ (Llevarse) bien con mis compañeros de cuarto?

Sí, te llevarás bien con tus compañeros de cuarto hasta que tú __________ (perder) la paciencia.

¿__________ (Casarse) con el hombre / la mujer ideal algún día?

Sí, te casarás con el hombre / la mujer ideal después de que tu futura suegra les __________ (dar) su permiso.

¿__________ (Tener) algún problema con la policía en el futuro?

Sí, tendrás muchos problemas con la policía hasta que tú __________ (aprender) a obedecer el límite de velocidad en las autopistas.

¿__________ (Regresar) a la universidad después de tener hijos?

No, no regresarás a la universidad antes de que tu hijo menor __________ (empezar) a asistir a la escuela todo el día.

Si tengo una hija algún día, ¿ella __________ (comportarse) bien?

Sí, ella se comportará bien hasta que tú __________ (estar) ocupado/a en otra parte de la casa.

¿Siempre me __________ (gustar) divertirme al aire libre?

Sí, sobre todo te gustará divertirte en las montañas hasta que tú __________ (hacer) *camping* con un grupo de «Boy Scouts».

¿__________ (Graduarse) en esta universidad?

Sí, te graduarás después de que tú __________ (escribir) los trabajos y los exámenes finales.

¿__________ (Conocer) el maravilloso país de España pronto?

Sí, conocerás España tan pronto como tú __________ (ahorrar) el dinero para comprar el boleto.

¿__________ (Haber) muchas riquezas en mi vida?

Sí, habrá riquezas en tu vida en cuanto tú __________ (ir) al banco la próxima vez.

¿__________ (Aprender) a cocinar bien algún día?

No, no aprenderás a cocinar hasta que tú __________ (asistir) a la escuela culinaria de Julia Child.

¿__________ (Servir) a la humanidad?

Sí, servirás a la humanidad tan pronto como tú __________ (conseguir) trabajo de camarero.

¿__________ (Poder) comprar un coche descapotable en el futuro?

Sí, podrás comprar un coche descapotable tan pronto como tu jefe te __________ (dar) un aumento de sueldo.

¿__________ (Hacer) un viaje en barco algún día?

Sí, harás un viaje en barco después de que __________ (jubilarse).

¿__________ (Perder) algo de valor en el futuro?

Sí, seguramente perderás algo de valor después de que tú __________ (olvidar) de cerrar la puerta.

¿__________ (Ser) el dueño / la dueña de una casa grande y lujosa algún día?

Sí, serás el dueño / la dueña de una mansión en cuanto __________ (morir) un tío abuelo muy viejo a quien no conoces.

¿__________ (Esquiar) más rápido que mis hermanos y amigos algún día?

Sí, esquiarás más rápido que todos los demás hasta que se te __________ (romper) la pierna.

¿__________ (Pasar) las vacaciones de primavera en el Caribe?

Sí, pasarás las vacaciones de primavera en el Caribe antes de que __________ (haber) otro huracán.

¿Mi familia y yo __________ (vivir) en un barrio tranquilo?

Sí, Uds. vivirán en un barrio tranquilo hasta que su perro __________ (conocer) al gato de los vecinos.

¿Mis amigos me __________ (dar) una fiesta sorpresa para mi cumpleaños?

Sí, te darán una fiesta sorpresa en cuanto tú __________ (cumplir) los cuarenta años.

¿Mi amigo __________ (dejar) de fumar cigarrillos algún día?

Sí, tu amigo dejará de fumar cigarrillos en cuanto __________ (conocer) a una extranjera que lleva uniforme.

Necesito hacer más ejercicio. ¿__________ (Practicar) algún deporte?

Sí, practicarás la natación después de que tú __________ (construir) una piscina.

Acabo de gastar más de mil dólares en una computadora nueva. ¿__________ (Saber) manejarla en el futuro?

No, no sabrás manejar tu computadora nueva antes de que __________ (asistir) a clases de informática.

¿__________ (Trabajar) para un jefe simpático en una oficina moderna y bonita?

No, trabajarás para el jefe más antipático del mundo en una oficina horrible hasta que tú __________ (mandar) tu currículum a otras empresas.

	Vocabulario	Verbos	Gramática	Traducción
10 pts	Con esta máquina se puede depositar o sacar dinero de una cuenta bancaria sin hablar con un empleado del banco.	En dos años (*I will graduate*) en la universidad y (*I will be able to*) buscar un puesto.	Tan pronto como yo _________ (recibir) la factura, la pagaré.	When they give me a raise in salary, I'll open a savings account.
20 pts	El plan que se desarrolla para limitar los gastos.	En cinco años mis abuelos (*will retire*) y (*will move*) a la Florida.	No te presto más dinero hasta que me _________ (devolver) el dinero que me debes.	Sir, you can pay for the car in installments or ask for a loan at the bank.
30 pts	Un resumen de los títulos, honores y trabajos realizados que califican a una persona.	Primero, tú (*will fill out*) la solicitud y luego la directora de personal (*will interview you*).	Uds. querrán economizar en cuanto _________ (oír) el informe de su contador.	That electrician does not make a good impression on us because he always charges too much.
40 pts	Muchas empresas mantienen estas oficinas en varias ciudades, estados o países.	La plomera (*will put on*) su mejor vestido para su cita esta noche y (*will enjoy herself*) mucho.	Antes de que Ud. _________ (renunciar), hable con la directora de personal.	If the bill is not paid by check or with a credit card, it has to be paid in cash.
50 pts		Mañana mi marido y yo (*will balance*) el talonario de cheques y (*will spend*) cada centavo en un viaje a Europa.	Cuando nosotros _________ (ser) ancianos, tendremos buenos recuerdos de nuestra juventud.	Computers interest me so much that my major is computer science. Will I be a programmer or a systems analyst?

Answer Key for *Arriésgate*

Capítulo 16

Vocabulario:	**10 pts**	el cajero automático
	20 pts	el presupuesto
	30 pts	el currículum
	40 pts	el sucursal
	50 pts	el peluquero, el cocinero, la criada, la abogada
Verbos:	**10 pts**	me graduaré; podré
	20 pts	se jubilarán; se mudarán
	30 pts	llenarás; te entrevistará
	40 pts	se pondrá; se divertirá
	50 pts	balancearemos; gastaremos
Gramática:	**10 pts**	reciba
	20 pts	devuelvas
	30 pts	oigan
	40 pts	renuncie
	50 pts	seamos
Traducción:	**10 pts**	Cuando me den un aumento de sueldo, abriré una cuenta de ahorros.
	20 pts	Señor, Ud. puede pagar el coche a plazos o pedir un préstamo en el banco.
	30 pts	Ese electricista no nos cae bien porque siempre cobra demasiado.
	40 pts	Si no se paga la cuenta con cheque ni con tarjeta de crédito, hay que pagarla en efectivo (al contado).
	50 pts	Me interesan tanto las computadoras que mi especialización es la computación. ¿Seré programador(a) o analista de sistemas?

Student Supplements
- Listening Comprehension Program CD, **Capítulo 17** (**Paso 1: Vocabulario:** word lists)
- Workbook/Laboratory Manual, **Capítulo 17**
- Audio Program CD, **Capítulo 17**

Instructor Resources
- Instructor's Manual/IRK: Chapter-by-Chapter Supplementary Materials, **Capítulo 17**
  - **Paso 1: Vocabulario**
  - **Paso 2: Gramática**
    - Grammar Section 44
    - **En los Estados Unidos y el Canadá...**
    - **Enfoque cultural**
  - **Paso 3: Gramática**
    - **Un poco de todo**
  - **Paso 4: Un paso más**
    - **Videoteca: Minidramas**
    - **A leer**
    - **A escribir**
  - Games and Activities
- Instructor's Manual/IRK: Video Activities and Related Materials
  - **A primera vista**
  - **A segunda vista**
  - Answers to Video Activities
  - Videoscripts
- Audioscript, **Capítulo 17**
- Transparency 88
- Testing Program, **Capítulo 17**

Multimedia Resources
- Online Learning Center
- Electronic Workbook/Laboratory Manual
- Video, **Capítulo 17** (cue 1:44:58)
  - **En contexto** (1:57)
  - **Minidramas** (4:49)
  - **Enfoque cultural: República Dominicana** (1:00)
- Student CD-ROM, **Capítulo 17**
- Electronic Language Tutor, **Capítulo 17** (**Vocabulario, Gramática**)

Paso 1: Vocabulario

LAS NOTICIAS

Suggestions:

- Remind students that the first-person singular of **ofrecer** is **ofrezco.**
- Read the following definitions and have students give the corresponding words from the vocabulary: 1. **cuando una persona asesina a alguien** 2. **cuando un grupo de obreros o empleados deja de trabajar como protesta** 3. **cuando se sabe algo por primera vez** 4. **las formas en que se da la información al mundo 5. antónimo de la guerra**
- Have students provide names from current events that correspond to the following categories: **¿Está Ud. bien informado/a? Dé un nombre de la vida real para cada una de las siguientes categorías.** 1. **un reportero famoso que informe en la tele** 2. **una guerra que esté ocurriendo ahora mismo** 3. **un desastre actual en el que Ud. piense con frecuencia** 4. **un acuerdo de paz que se haya firmado recientemente** 5. **un asesinato reciente que haya sido enfatizado en los medios de comunicación**
- Point out that **testigo** does not change the ending for the feminine form: **el testigo** and **la testigo.**
- Give students the following **dictado:** 1. **Merecemos sueldos más altos, pero el jefe no quiere darnos un aumento.** 2. **Es necesario que nos declaremos en huelga.** 3. **Pero el jefe va a despedir a todos los obreros que protesten.** 4. **No te preocupes: todos juntos podemos hacer cambios positivos.**
- Ask students the following questions to personalize the vocabulary: 1. **¿Cómo se entera Ud. de las noticias? ¿Lee el periódico o mira el noticiero en la tele o escucha las noticias en la radio?** 2. **¿Cree todo lo que lee en la prensa? ¿Cree que los medios de información informan bien al público, por lo general?**

EL GOBIERNO Y LA RESPONSABILIDAD CÍVICA

Preparation: Give students about four minutes to skim the vocabulary lists before you begin.

Suggestion: Present target vocabulary from both lists at once for a smoother presentation.

Sample Passage: **En el siglo XVIII** (write **siglo XVIII = 1701–1800** on board**) hubo dos acontecimientos políticos muy importantes. Pues, estos dos acontecimientos fueron las revoluciones norteamericana (1776) y francesa (1789). Los revolucionarios querían ciertos derechos civiles. El concepto de derechos es abstracto. Un derecho es algo que todo ser humano debe tener sólo por ser humano. El derecho es similar al privilegio, pero se puede revocar un privilegio. Teóricamente, no se puede un derecho.**

Un derecho deseado por los colonos norteamericanos y los ciudadanos franceses era el derecho a votar. Votar es participar en una elección. En una elección, los ciudadanos hacen decisiones sobre el gobierno. Si no tienen el derecho de votar, no tienen el poder de influir en el gobierno. En 1776 y 1789, los norteamericanos y los franceses vivieron bajo sistemas monárquicas. En esas monarquías, el rey tenía todo el poder y control. La gente no tenía el derecho de votar. El rey o la reina es un monarca. Unos reyes muy famosos son Enrique VIII de Inglaterra, Luis XIV de Francia y Fernando de Aragón de España; las reinas más famosas son Elizabeth I y Victoria de Inglaterra, María Antonieta de Francia e Isabel de Castilla de España. Ahora España tiene un rey, Juan Carlos I de Borbón, pero él no es un monarca absoluto. España es una monarquía democrática o parlamentaria. Bajo este sistema de gobierno, hay un presidente elegido por el pueblo. La esposa de Juan Carlos es la reina Sofía.

Quick Comprehension Check: Sample items.

1. **¿Cuál de estos es un acontecimiento, *una revolución* o el derecho de votar?**
2. **¿Qué ocurrió primero, *la revolución norteamericana* o la revolución francesa?**
3. **¿Quién es el rey actual de España? (*Juan Carlos I de Borbón*)**

Variations: **¿Es una ley o simplemente un deber?**

4. **pagar los impuestos**
5. **dejar una propina en un restaurante**

¿Asocia Ud. estos conceptos con una dictadura o no?

6. **derechos** 7. **obedecer** 8. **reina** 9. **militar**

Optional: **¿Cuáles de estas naciones han tenido una dictadura?**

1. **Francia** (*no*) 3. **Italia** (*sí*) 5. **México** (*sí*)
2. **Alemania** (*sí*) 4. **Japón** (*no*) 6. **EE.UU.** (*no*)

Suggestions:

- Remind students that the first-person singular of **obedecer** is **obedezco.**
- Read the following definitions and have students give the corresponding word from the vocabulary: 1. **las otras personas de nuestra comunidad** 2. **la acción de aceptar una ley, regla o mandato** 3. **una responsabilidad** 4. **una persona que representa a un país de forma hereditaria, no por votación** 5. **el grupo de personas que defiende a un país en caso de guerra**
- Point out the difference in meaning between **el derecho** (*right; law*) and **la derecha** (*the conservative right, right-hand side*). Review other meanings of **derecho,** for example, **todo derecho** (*straight ahead*).
- Ask students the following questions to personalize the vocabulary: 1. **En este país, ¿hay una ley que proteja la libertad de prensa? ¿Existe tal ley en otros países también? ¿Qué derechos individuales se garantizan en la constitución?** (Write **la libertad de ______** on the board.) 2. **¿Vota Ud. en todas las elecciones? ¿Votó en las últimas elecciones para presidente o primer ministro? ¿en las últimas elecciones municipales? ¿Cree Ud. que el votar es un deber? ¿Bajo qué tipo de gobierno no es posible votar con libertad?** 3. **¿Cree Ud. que siempre debemos obedecer la ley? ¿Hay leyes que sean más importantes que otras? ¿Siempre obedece Ud. las leyes de tránsito? ¿Qué castigos** (*punishments*) **hay para los delitos menores? ¿y para los delitos más graves?**
- Point out that having rights also means respecting others' rights and liberties. Others are entitled to the same rights that you enjoy, and their needs and priorities may be quite different from your own. Have students list on the board the responsibilities that also imply rights. Discuss specific rights that have led to conflicts, for example, freedom of speech and flag burning or musical expression.

CONVERSACIÓN B

Note: Offer the following background information about items 1 and 5 in **Conversación B.**

- Juan Domingo Perón (1895–1974) was the president of Argentina (1946–1955, 1973–1974). He brought long-lasting changes to national Argentine policies and is considered one of the most remarkable Latin American figures of the twentieth century.
- In Spain, all males are required to take part in military service (**el servicio militar**). The Spanish government contacts all males after their seventeenth birthday and their military service begins after they turn 18. Students can find out more about this topic online at the official Spanish government Website.

Paso 2: Gramática

GRAMMAR SECTION 44

FORMS OF THE PAST SUBJUNCTIVE

Note: The pluperfect subjunctive is not presented in *¿Qué tal?*, since it is beyond the expectations and ability of beginning students for control and production. If you wish to present this grammar point, you can introduce it in this section and reintroduce it in **Capítulo 18** with the **si** clauses.

Suggestions:

- Have students give the third-person plural preterite forms of **caminar, terminar, usar, pensar, esperar, cerrar, nadar, ofrecer, resolver, correr, prometer, volver, leer, creer, abrir, escribir, subir, admitir.**
- Present the formation of the past subjunctive and emphasize that all forms, without exception, are based on the third-person plural of the preterite.
- Model the past subjunctive in sentences about yourself or communicative exchanges. Use the verbs **trabajar, volver,** and **abrir.**
- Have students give the third-person plural preterite forms of **dar, hacer, ser, ir, decir, estar, poder, poner, querer, saber, tener, traer, venir, divertirse, servir, dormir, jugar,** and **pedir.**
- Model the past subjunctive forms of **servir, sentir, dar, decir, hacer, ir,** and **venir** in sentences about yourself and communicative exchanges with the students.

Heritage Speakers: Pregúnteles a los hispanohablantes de la clase si usan o no las terminaciones en **-se, -ses, -se, -semos, -seis, -sen** del pasado de subjuntivo. Si las usan, pregúnteles cuándo y por qué.

USES OF THE PAST SUBJUNCTIVE

Suggestions:

- Point out that the past subjunctive is used to describe past events in grammatical contexts that require the subjunctive.
- Emphasize that when a verb in the main clause is in the past, the past (never the present) subjunctive is used in the subordinate clause (past → past).
- Remind students that when the verb in the main clause is in the present, the verb in the dependent can be in the past: **Siento que no pudieran estar allí. Sé que no estaban allí.** Help students develop simple logic about time sequence (I'm sorry now about something that happened yesterday).
- Emphasize that this tense is used to form polite requests. This is similar to the English *really should* and *would like you to* softened requests.
- Point out that the verbs **deber** and **poder** are used by some Spanish speakers in softened requests: **Debieras estudiar más. ¿Pudieras darme el libro?**
- Remind students of the importance of tone whenever requests of any kind are made. The most polite words can be said in a harsh way.

EN LOS ESTADOS UNIDOS Y EL CANADÁ... TRES HISPANOS EN EL MUNDO DE LA TELEVISIÓN

Suggestions: Have students design and write resumés for Ray Rodríguez, María Hinojosa, and Jim Ávila. They can use information from the reading, but should also include additional information by researching these three people on the Internet or in printed sources. Compare the different resumés in class. You might have the class pool information to put together more complete resumés.

ENFOQUE CULTURAL: REPÚBLICA DOMINICANA

A. Para completar. Complete las siguientes oraciones con información de Datos esenciales, ¡Fíjese! y Conozca a...

1. La capital de la República Dominicana, ________________, fue fundada en 1496 por el ________________ de Cristóbal Colón.
2. Los dominicanos hablan español y ________________.
3. Los bucaneros ________________ fundaron la colonia de Sant Domingue en el oeste de la isla.
4. Algunos de los beisbolistas que han tenido éxito en las Grandes Ligas de los Estados Unidos incluyen ________________, ________________ y los hermanos ________________ y ________________ Alomar.
5. Julia Álvarez nació en ________________ pero pasó su niñez en ________________.
6. Julia Álvarez escribe ________________ y ________________.

B. Para completar. Complete el siguiente cuadro usando información de los Enfoques culturales de los Capítulos 14 a 17.

El país (Los países) con el mayor número de habitantes:	
El país (Los países) en el/los que se habla otro idioma además del español (mencione el país/los países y el idioma/los idiomas):	
El país con menos habitantes:	

Suggestions:

- Bring in and play examples of traditional and contemporary **merengue** music.
- Have students listen to Dominican news reports online and write a paragraph on what they hear.
- Have students find recipes from the Dominican Republic online and bring them to class. You may wish to make or have students make some of these for students to taste.
- Invite a student or member of the community from the Dominican Republic to come to class and talk to the students about his or her country.
- Have students research Taíno art and culture and prepare short written reports for extra credit.

Paso 3: Gramática

UN POCO DE TODO

Optional Activities:

¡No es justo (*fair*)!

Paso 1. Complete las siguientes oraciones, según las indicaciones, para enterarse de lo que le pasó a Pepe Ramírez ayer. Añada otras palabras cuando sea necesario. **¡OJO!** Va a usar el imperfecto del subjuntivo en algunos casos.

1. ayer / (yo) ver / mi / nota / en / último / examen
2. no / poder / creer / que / nota / ser / tan / bajo
3. no / ser / posible / que / yo / hacer / examen / tan / mal
4. por eso / (yo) hablar / con / profesor / para que / (él) explicarme / causa / de / nota
5. (él) decirme / que / haber / errores / importante / pero / que / haber / partes / bueno / también
6. (él) pedirme / que / leer / examen / otro / vez
7. ser / verdad / que / haber / errores / en / examen
8. pero / ¡no / ser / justo / que / profesor / darme / nota / tan / bajo!

Paso 2. Con un compañero / una compañera, háganse las siguientes preguntas y contéstenlas.

1. ¿Te ha ocurrido algo similar?
2. ¿Qué hiciste? ¿Te cambió la nota tu profesor(a) o no?
3. ¿Piensas que muchos profesores son injustos? ¿Por qué?

Escenas históricas

Paso 1. La gente emigra por varias razones. Complete las siguientes oraciones con la forma correcta del infinitivo. Luego, si puede, nombre un grupo que emigró por la razón citada.

1. Las leyes de su país de origen no permitían que este grupo (practicar) libremente su religión.
2. Algunas personas esperaban que (haber) oro y plata en América.
3. El rey no quería que estos criminales (seguir) viviendo en su país.
4. Estos inmigrantes buscaban un país donde (haber) paz y esperanza y seguridad (*safety*) personal.
5. Los miembros de este grupo buscaban un país donde no (tener) que pasar hambre.

Paso 2. Dé una breve descripción del pasado histórico de los Estados Unidos, haciendo oraciones según las indicaciones. Empiece en el pasado. Desde el número 8, las oraciones se refieren al presente.

1. indios / temer / que / colonos / quitarles / toda la tierra
2. colonos / no / gustar / que / ser necesario / pagarle / impuestos / rey
3. parecía imposible / que / joven república / tener éxito (*success*)
4. los del sur / no / gustar / que / gobernarlos / los del norte
5. abolicionistas / no / gustar / que / algunos / no / tener / mismo / libertades
6. era necesario / que / declararse / en huelga / obreros / para / obtener / alguno / derechos
7. era terrible / que / haber / dos / guerra / mundial
8. para que / nosotros / vivir / en paz / es cuestión de / aprender / comunicarse
9. también / es necesario / que / haber / leyes / que / garantizar / derechos

Suggestions:

- **Paso 1.** The following are some possible answers: 1. **los Pilgrims, los Quakers** 2. **los españoles, los portugueses** 3. **los primeros colonos de Australia** 4. **muchos grupos orientales y del Medio Oriente** 5. **los irlandeses, algunos grupos de África y de Asia**
- **Paso 2.** Expand each item with questions about the historical situation in the question. Focus on the imperfect / preterite in the questions, not necessarily on the use of the imperfect subjunctive. For example, for item 1 you might ask: **¿En qué año llegaron al Nuevo Mundo los primeros colonos? ¿Había muchos indios aquí en aquel entonces** (*back then*)? **¿Qué hicieron los colonos tan pronto como llegaron? ¿Tenían miedo de los indios?**

Note: Use the theme of immigration to discuss Hispanics in the U.S. and the history of their presence. The majority of Hispanics in the U.S. are found in three geographical areas: 1. south Florida (Cubans), 2. the Southwest: Texas, New Mexico, Arizona, and California (Mexicans), and 3. New York (Puerto Ricans). Although we can generalize in terms of which Hispanics are located in a particular region of the U.S., Hispanics from all areas of Spain and Latin America live in every major metropolitan city throughout the U.S.

Paso 4: Un paso más

VIDEOTECA

MINIDRAMAS

The **Minidramas** vignettes are not referenced in the textbook, but are part of the *¿Qué tal?* Video Program. They also appear on the Video on CD packaged free with the textbook. If you show the **Minidramas** in class or have your students view them as homework, you might find the following suggestions helpful. You can also find blackline master activities in Section X of this Manual for **Minidramas.**

Comprensión: **¿Cierto o falso?**

1. **Estas personas hablan del tiempo.**
2. **Estas personas tienen opiniones políticas distintas.**
3. **Manolo es escéptico con respecto a las noticias de la televisión.**

Suggestion: Ask students to list all the expressions that show disagreement in the dialogue. They should be aware that these expressions are quite strong, because the participants are friends and feel secure not to offend anyone by disagreeing. Have students brainstorm other, more polite forms of disagreement that they might use with people who are not close friends.

A LEER

Suggestions:

- Have students list words in the poem in categories. Compare the different categories that students come up with and explore how the poet uses these words in the poem.
- Point out that the poet invented words for this poem. Have students find those words (**descubanizada, recubanizar**) and talk about their connotations and their function in the poem.

A ESCRIBIR

Suggestion: After students have completed the assignment, divide the class into two groups and debate the immigration issue they explored.

ACTIVIDAD DE DESENLACE: EL NOTICIERO HISPANO

Activity: Students will research news programs in a Spanish-speaking country of their choosing (maybe Hispanic programs in the U.S. or Canada) and create a news program to broadcast the news. The program could involve an interview with a person from the country and timely information.

Purpose: To create a context in which students can review and practice the grammar from **Capítulo 17** and vocabulary related to news and government

Resources: *¿Qué tal?* textbook, the Internet, and other sources as appropriate

Vocabulary: The news, the government, civic responsibilities

Grammar: Principal grammatical structures covered in **Capítulo 17** of the textbook, including past subjunctive, and stressed possessives

Duration: Out-of-class preparation time will vary. In-class time will be approximately five minutes per presentation.

Format: Groups of three to four students

Comments:

1. If there is a student radio station on campus, you may wish to make arrangements to have it broadcast students' news reports.
2. You may prefer to have students choose interesting dates in history and create news reports as if they were present when the important event(s) occurred.

Games and Activities

Capítulo 17 *Submarino*

This game is played like "Battleship." Place five submarines on the grid below. (Don't let your partner see where you have drawn your subs!) To win this game you need to "sink" your partner's submarines by asking questions like:

TÚ: **¿Quería papá que tú pusieras la mesa?**
COMPAÑERO/A: **Sí, él quería que yo la pusiera.** (*if there is a sub there*)
or **No, él no quería que yo la pusiera.** (*if there is no sub there*)

	Tú (Luis, Paula)	Nosotros	Anito	Ellos
Papá quería que...				
La profesora insistía en que...				
Mis tíos recomendaba que...				
La abuela prefería que...				

Primero, conteste cada pregunta. Después busque a una persona que haya tenido las mismas experiencias que Ud. y escriba su nombre.

MODELO: **Cuando yo estaba en la escuela secundaria, mis padres prohibían que yo fumara. ¿Y a ti?**

		Yo	Compañero/a
1	¿Qué prohibían tus padres que hicieras?		
2	¿Qué querías que tus padres dejaran de hacer?		
3	¿Qué esperabas que te regalaran para tu cumpleaños?		
4	¿Qué pedían tus amigos que les prestaras?		
5	¿Adónde era importante a tus padres que fueras?		
6	¿Qué temías que pasara cuando te portabas mal?		
7	¿En qué insistían tus maestros?		
8	¿Qué necesitabas que te dieran tus padres?		
9	¿Cómo preferías que fueran tus amigos?		
10	¿Qué no te gustaba que hicieran tus hermanos/as?		

Capítulo 17: Partner A *Crucigrama*

You have the answers for half the puzzle, and your partner has those for the other half. Together you must complete the whole puzzle. You have to give clues to your partner so that he/she can guess the missing words. You *may not use the word itself*. Everything has to be done in Spanish.

Use clues such as: **Lo que usamos para...**
La persona que...
El lugar donde...
La cosa que...
Lo que se hace cuando...

Capítulo 17: Partner B *Crucigrama*

You have the answers for half the puzzle, and your partner has those for the other half. Together you must complete the whole puzzle. You have to give clues to your partner so that he/she can guess the missing words. You *may not use the word itself.* Everything has to be done in Spanish.

Use clues such as: **Lo que usamos para...**
La persona que...
El lugar donde...
La cosa que...
Lo que se hace cuando...

Student Supplements

- Listening Comprehension Program CD, **Capítulo 18** (**Paso 1: Vocabulario:** word lists)
- Workbook/Laboratory Manual, **Capítulo 18**
- Audio Program CD, **Capítulo 18**

Instructor Resources

- Instructor's Manual/IRK: Chapter-by-Chapter Supplementary Materials, **Capítulo 18**
  - **Paso 1: Vocabulario**
  - **Paso 2: Gramática**
    - Grammar Section 45
    - **En los Estados Unidos y el Canadá...**
    - **Enfoque cultural**
  - **Paso 3: Gramática**
    - **Un poco de todo**
  - **Paso 4: Un paso más**
    - **Videoteca: Minidramas**
  - Games and Activities
- Instructor's Manual/IRK: Video Activities and Related Materials
  - **A primera vista**
  - **A segunda vista**
  - Answers to Video Activities
  - Videoscripts
- Audioscript, **Capítulo 18**
- Transparencies 89–92
- Testing Program, **Capítulo 18**

Multimedia Resources

- Online Learning Center
- Electronic Workbook/Laboratory Manual
- Video, **Capítulo 18** (cue 1:51:54)
  - **En contexto** (2:09)
  - **Minidramas** (5:34)
  - **Enfoque cultural: España** (1:00)
- Student CD-ROM, **Capítulo 18**
- Electronic Language Tutor, **Capítulo 18** (**Vocabulario, Gramática**)

Paso 1: Vocabulario

LUGARES Y COSAS EN EL EXTRANJERO

Suggestions:

- Have students identify the places where the following activities take place. 1. **Se compran y se venden medicamentos aquí.** 2. **Aquí se puede tomar algo de beber y mirar pasar a la gente.** 3. **Aquí se esperan los autobuses.** 4. **Se compran cigarrillos y fósforos aquí.** 5. **Se compran sellos y se mandan cartas y paquetes aquí.** 6. **Si se tiene ganas de comer un pastel, se puede ir a este sitio.**
- Point out that **el correo** means *mail* or *post office,* but the plural **los correos** means *postal service.* Tell students there are several words for stamps: **el sello, el timbre, la estampilla.**
- Ask students the following questions to personalize the vocabulary: 1. **¿Adónde va Ud. si quiere tomar una copa / un trago con los amigos? ¿Le gustan los batidos? ¿Dónde se toma un buen batido en esta ciudad? En general, ¿es necesario preparar los batidos con puro helado o se puede sustituir los ingredientes artificiales?** 2. **¿Está bien situado el lugar donde Ud. vive? ¿Hay un correo cerca? ¿una parada de autobús? ¿Adónde va Ud. para comprar artículos de uso personal (el champú, la pasta dental, etcétera)? ¿Hay una tienda de comestibles cerca de donde Ud. vive?** 3. **¿Hay quioscos en este país? ¿Qué cosa espera Ud. comprar en un quiosco?** 4. **¿Cuánto vale un sello para mandar una carta de primera clase? ¿Se puede usar un sello de primera clase para mandar una carta a México? ¿a España? ¿a Puerto Rico?**

EN UN VIAJE AL EXTRANJERO

Preparation: Bring in props or pictures of the items that are difficult to explain. The travel concepts are grounded in common experience. Give students two minutes to skim the vocabulary lists.

Sample Passage: **¿Adónde va Ud. si necesita comprar champú para lavarse el pelo? ¿al supermercado? ¿Adónde va si necesita comprar una revista? ¿También al supermercado? Pues, si Ud. hace la mayoría de las compras en el supermercado, Ud. es típicamente norteamericano. Pero, ¿es igual en otros países? ¿Adónde va Ud. en España, por ejemplo, si necesita comprar champú? ¿al supermercado? No, porque en España y en muchos países latinos y europeos, las compras se hacen en varias tiendas pequeñas.**

Primero, si Ud. necesita comprar champú, o jabón (hold up), **pasta dental, o cualquier otro producto de «uso personal», necesita ir a una farmacia. En las farmacias se venden champú, jabón y otros productos similares. Pero, ¿se puede comprar papel para escribir y sobres** (hold up) **en una farmacia? No.**

Para comprar papel para escribir, sobres, lápices y cuadernos, se necesita una papelería. En las papelerías se venden todos los productos de papel. Pero, ¿qué pasa si Ud. necesita comprar cigarrillos o necesita fósforos (hold up)**? Pues si Ud. necesita cigarrillos y fósforos, tiene que buscar un estanco. Un estanco es una tienda que se especializa en vender tabaco y los productos relacionados con el tabaco.**

Quick Comprehension Check: Sample items.

1. **¿Se puede comprar pasta dental en un quiosco o en *una farmacia*?**
2. **Si Ud. quiere papel para cartas, ¿va a *una papelería* o a un estanco?**
3. **Para comprar sellos para su carta, ¿debe ir Ud. a la papelería o *al estanco*?**

Sample Items for ***En un viaje extranjero:***

1. **¿Cómo se llama la línea política entre dos países, una aduana o *una frontera*?**
2. **¿Qué paga Ud. si lleva más de la cantidad permitida de un producto, la propina o *una multa*?**
3. **En la aduana, ¿qué hacen los inspectores, cruzan la frontera o *registran las maletas*?**

Suggestions:

- Read the following statements and have students respond **cierto** or **falso.** Help students correct false statements. 1. **Por lo general, cuando uno cruza una frontera, tiene que pasar por la aduana también.** 2. **En la aduana se registran los derechos.** 3. **El pasaporte indica la nacionalidad de uno.** 4. **Las multas son un tipo de castigo.** 5. **En este país, no es necesario llevar pasaporte a menos que uno viaje al extranjero.** 6. **En muchos moteles u hoteles, hay ducha pero no hay baño en los cuartos.** 7. **Si Ud. quiere confirmar una reservación, hay que llamar al huésped.** 8. **En los hoteles de lujo hay botones que ayudan con las maletas.** 9. **Propina es un sinónimo de cuenta.** 10. **Si Ud. no ha hecho una reservación, el hotel no le puede garantizar un cuarto desocupado.** 11. **Un cuarto en un hotel de lujo cuesta mucho dinero.**
- Point out that **derechos de aduana** is always expressed in the plural.
- Ask students the following questions to personalize the vocabulary: 1. **¿Ha viajado Ud. por el extranjero? ¿Qué país(es) ha visitado? ¿Cuánto tiempo estuvo en... ? ¿Tiene ganas de volver? ¿Qué hizo allí? ¿Trabajó? ¿Estudió? ¿Visitó a sus parientes o a sus amigos?** 2. **En esta clase, ¿cuántos tienen pasaporte? ¿Les fue difícil conseguirlo? ¿Qué hizo Ud. para conseguirlo? ¿Tuvo que pagar algo? ¿Salió Ud. bien en la foto o no le gusta como salió?** 3. **¿Ha cruzado Ud. alguna vez la frontera entre el Canadá y los Estados Unidos? ¿la frontera entre México y los Estados Unidos? ¿Tuvo problemas al cruzar? ¿Qué le pidió el inspector? ¿el pasaporte? ¿una visa? ¿Qué le preguntó? ¿Estaba Ud. nervioso/a? ¿Tenía algo que declarar que no declarara antes?** 4. **¿Siempre declara la gente lo que tiene cuando pasa por la aduana?**
- Have students use the **alojamiento** vocabulary to describe their last stay in a (luxury) hotel or motel. They should give as many details as possible, using new vocabulary whenever possible.

Paso 2: Gramática

GRAMMAR SECTION 45

Suggestions:

- Point out that the infinitive is used as the stem, as with the future.
- Remind students that context and pronouns will distinguish the **yo** and **Ud./él/ella** forms (which are the same).
- Present the **-ía** endings for infinitives to enable students to complete the **minidiálogo** follow-up.
- Help students identify the endings for the conditional: they are the same as the imperfect indicative endings for **-er** and **-ir** verbs.
- Model conditional forms in brief communicative exchanges with students. Try to use high frequency verbs: **comprar, beber, escribir, decir, hacer, salir,** and **tener.**
- Emphasize that the future and conditional have the same set of irregular verbs.
- Remind students that when *would* refers to a habitual action (*I would study in the library every afternoon.*), the imperfect indicative, not the conditional, is required.
- Model the use of future vs. conditional in quoting people: **Estela dice que vendrá** vs. **Estela dijo que vendría.**

EN LOS ESTADOS UNIDOS Y EL CANADÁ...
MANJARES HISPANOCANADIENSES

Suggestion: Have students look up the Canadian restaurant guide on the Internet that lists restaurants by city, cuisine, price, and so on. Have them find out what different Hispanic cuisines are offered (Spanish, Caribbean, Latin American, and so on), how prices compare from cuisine to cuisine, which cities offer more variety, and so on . You might assign specific cities or topics to different students and compare their findings in class. Some restaurants have their own websites on which students can view menus and photos of the establishments.

ENFOQUE CULTURAL: ESPAÑA

¿Cierto o falso? Indique si las siguientes oraciones son ciertas (C) o falsas (F) según la información en Datos esenciales, ¡Fíjese! y Conozca a... Corrija las oraciones falsas.

1. C F El nombre oficial de España es la República de España.
2. C F El único idioma en España es el español.
3. C F La cultura romana marcó el principio de la historia de España más que ninguna otra.
4. C F Los romanos dominaron la península Ibérica entre el año 200 a.C. y 1492 d.C.
5. C F España no se unificó como un solo país hasta el siglo XV cuando los Reyes Católicos se casaron.
6. C F Pedro Almodóvar es un actor español famoso.
7. C F La película *Todos sobre mi madre* de Almodóvar ganó el Óscar para la mejor película extranjera de 1999.

Extension: Make copies of the following paragraph, and have students discuss it in class.

Conozca a... Miguel de Cervantes Saavedra

El escritor más célebre de España nace en Alcalá de Henares en 1547. A los veinticuatro años, ya miembro de las fuerzas armadas españolas, toma parte en la batalla de Lepanto en contra de los turcos. En esta batalla pierde una mano y, de ahí en adelante, lleva el nombre de «el manco[a] de Lepanto». Sigue en el servicio del rey hasta que, en el año 1575 es tomado prisionero. Pasa cinco años en una carcel[b] en Argelia.

Al volver a España empieza a escribir y a publicar sus obras. A la vez, trabaja de recaudador de impuestos.[c] En 1601, publica su obra más famosa, *El ingenioso hidalgo[d] don Quijote de la Mancha*. La figura central de esta novela es un idealista que se cree caballero errante[e] y trata de corregir todos los problemas a los cuales se enfrenta. Cervantes muere el 23 de abril de 1616, el mismo día en que muere Shakespeare.

[a]*one-handed man* [b]*jail* [c]**recaudador...** *tax collector* [d]**ingenioso...** *clever nobleman*
[e]**caballero...** *knight errant*

Paso 3: Gramática

UN POCO DE TODO

Optional Activities: **¡Entendiste mal!** Con un compañero / una compañera, háganse preguntas y contéstenlas según el modelo.

MODELO: llegar el trece de junio / tres →
E1: Llegaré el trece de junio.
E2: ¿No dijiste que llegarías el tres?
E1: ¡Que no! Te dije que llegaría el trece. Entendiste mal.

1. estar en el café a las dos / doce
2. estudiar con Juan / Juana
3. ir de vacaciones en julio / junio
4. verte en casa / en clase
5. comprar la blusa rosada / roja
6. haber un examen el viernes / la semana que viene
7. ser el examen en el laboratorio /en la clase
8. costar el libro $20 / $30

Si el mundo fuera diferente... Adaptarse a un nuevo país o a nuevas circunstancias es difícil, pero también es una aventura interesante. ¿Qué ocurriría si el mundo fuera diferente?

MODELO: Si yo fuera la última persona en el mundo... →
- tendría que aprender a hacer muchas cosas.
- sería la persona más importante —y más ignorante— del mundo.
- me adaptaría fácilmente/difícilmente.
- los animales y yo nos haríamos buenos amigos.

1. Si yo pudiera tener solamente un amigo / una amiga, ______.
2. Si yo tuviera que pasar un año en una isla desierta, ______.
3. Si yo fuera (otro persona), ______.
4. Si el president**e** fuera president**a**, ______.
5. Si yo viviera en Puerto Rico, ______.

Suggestion: Have students write their own **si** clauses for classmates to complete. Encourage creativity and humor.

Paso 4: Un paso más

VIDEOTECA

MINIDRAMAS

The **Minidramas** vignettes are not referenced in the textbook, but are part of the *¿Qué tal?* Video Program. They also appear on the Video on CD packaged free with the textbook. If you show the **Minidramas** in class or have your students view them as homework, you might find the following suggestions helpful. You can also find blackline master activities in Section X of this Manual for **Minidramas.**

Comprensión:

1. **¿Adónde van Diego y Lupe y por cuánto tiempo?**
2. **¿Qué tipo de hotel buscan Diego y Lupe?**
3. **¿Por qué deciden cambiar la fecha de su viaje?**

Variation: Have students pretend they are making the reservations on the phone. They should sit back to back so they cannot see each other when they talk.

ACTIVIDAD DE DESENLACE: FERIA HISPANOAMERICANA

Activity: Students will prepare booths and exhibits about Spanish-speaking countries, which highlight such elements as

- geography
- culture and the arts
- history
- food and drink
- economy
- ethnic groups and minorities
- government and politics

They will hold a **Conozca Latinoamérica** fair, which they will publicize.

Purpose: To create a context in which students can review and practice the grammar from **Capítulo 18** and vocabulary related to travel abroad

Resources: *¿Qué tal?* textbook, the Internet, and other sources as appropriate

Vocabulary: Places and things the traveler might encounter during a trip abroad

Grammar: Principal grammatical structures covered in **Capítulo 18** of the textbook, including the conditional, and **si** clause sentences

Duration: Out-of-class preparation time will vary. In-class time will be approximately five minutes per presentation.

Format: Groups of three to four students

Comments: Students may wish to use the cultural footage from the *¿Qué tal?* video at the booths.

La encuesta dice...

¿Qué planes haría Ud. para su primer viaje a Madrid?

1. **Yo llamaría a un agente de viajes.**
2. **Haría y confirmaría las reservas con anticipación.**
3. **Conseguiría un pasaporte.**
4. **Compraría los boletos de ida y vuelta con anticipación.**
5. **Compraría cheques de viajero.**
6. **Iría de compras.**

La encuesta dice...

Si Ud. fuera agente de viajes y sus clientes viajaran por primera vez en avión, ¿qué consejos les daría?

1. **Insistiría en que llegaran temprano al aeropuerto.**
2. **Yo les aconsejaría que no llevaran muchas maletas.**
3. **Les recomendaría que facturaran el equipaje.**
4. **Les sugeriría que compraran un libro o unas revistas en al aeropuerto para leer en el avión.**
5. **Les diría que no tomaran bebidas alcohólicas durante el vuelo.**
6. **Les pediría que confirmaran el vuelo.**

Capítulo 18: Partner A

Crucigrama

You have the answers for half the puzzle, and your partner has those for the other half. Together you must complete the whole puzzle. You have to give clues to your partner so that he/she can guess the missing words. You *may not use the word itself.* Everything has to be done in Spanish.

Use clues such as: **Lo que usamos para...**
La persona que...
El lugar donde...
La cosa que...
Lo que se hace cuando...

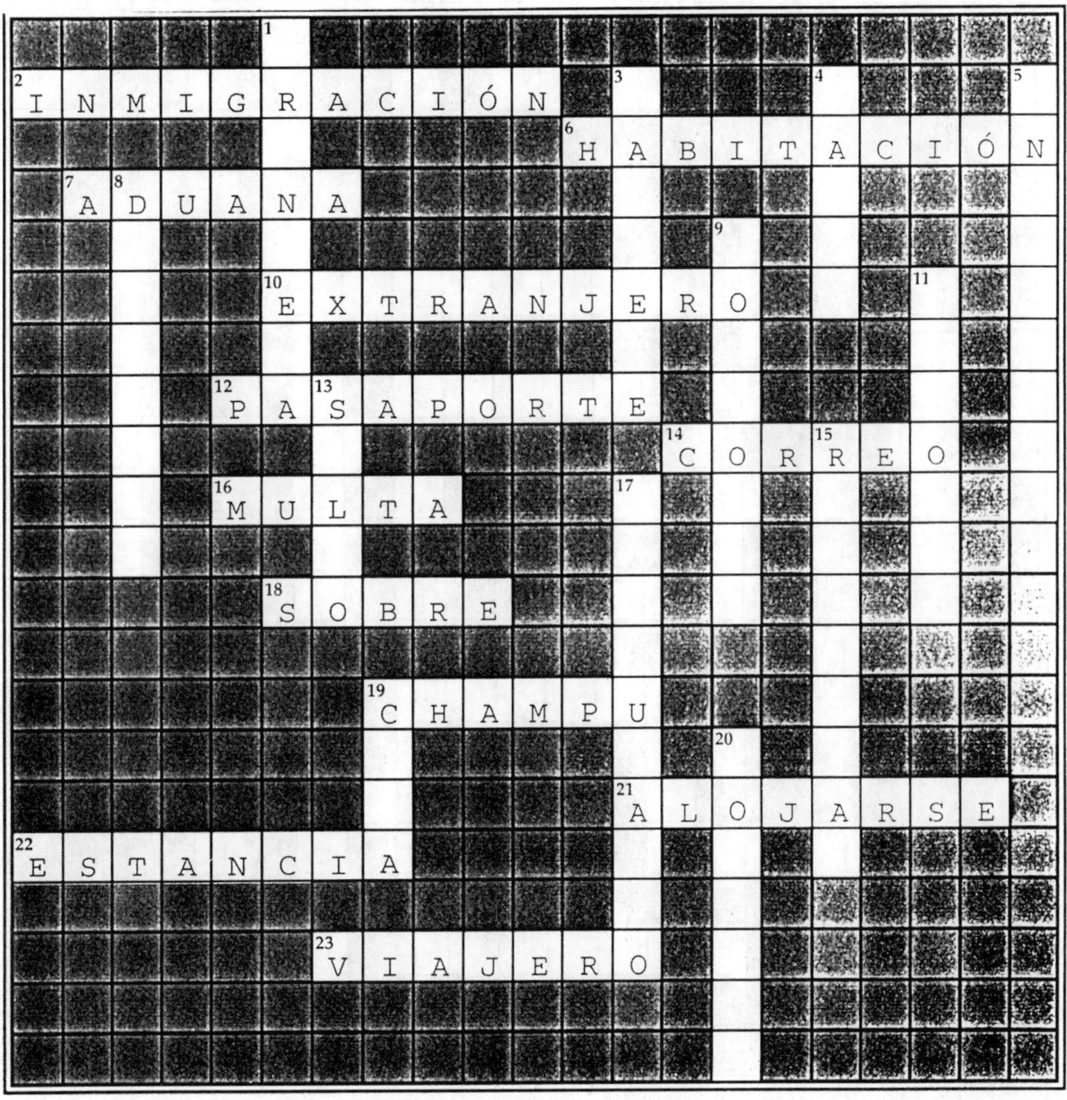

Capítulo 18: Partner B

Crucigrama

You have the answers for half the puzzle, and your partner has those for the other half. Together you must complete the whole puzzle. You have to give clues to your partner so that he/she can guess the missing words. You *may not use the word itself.* Everything has to be done in Spanish.

Use clues such as: **Lo que usamos para...**
La persona que...
El lugar donde...
La cosa que...
Lo que se hace cuando...

					1 F															
2					R							3 P				4 J				5 I
					O						6	A				A				N
	7	8 D			N							Q				B				S
		E			T							U		9 F		O				P
		C			10 E							E		O		N		11 Q		E
		L			R							T		S				U		C
		A		12	A	13 S						E		F				I		T
		R				E							14	O		15 R		O		O
		A		16		L						17 F		R		E		S		R
		R				L						O		O		G		C		
					18	O						R		S		I		O		
												M				S				
							19 C					U				T				
							O					L		20 B		R				
							P					21 A		O		A				
22							A					R		T		R				
												I		O						
						23						O		N						
														E						
														S						

Dígalo como pueda

A

1. **el arte** – *art*
2. **el aumento de sueldo** – *raise*
3. **el aire** – *air*
4. **el aceite** – *oil*
5. **el aislamiento** – *isolation*
6. **el arquitecto** – *architect*
7. **el amor** – *love*
8. **el agricultor** – *farmer*
9. **la autopista** – *freeway*
10. **la artesanía** – *arts and crafts*

B

1. **el bailarín** – *dancer*
2. **la boda** – *wedding*
3. **el banco** – *bank*
4. **el bosque** – *forest*
5. **el botones** – *bellhop*
6. **la batería** – *battery*
7. **el bibliotecario** – *librarian*
8. **el ballet** – *ballet*
9. **el batido** – *milkshake*
10. **balancear** – *to balance*

A

1. **la amistad** – *friendship*
2. **el árbol** – *tree*
3. **el abogado** – *lawyer*
4. **la adolescencia** – *adolescence*
5. **el analista de sistemas** – *systems analyst*
6. **el asesinato** – *assassination*
7. **el aspirante** – *candidate*
8. **la aduana** – *customs*
9. **el acontecimiento** – *event, happening*
10. **la arquitectura** – *architecture*

C

1. **el cantante** – *singer*
2. **la contaminación** – *pollution*
3. **el cuadro** – *painting*
4. **la cuenta de ahorros** – *savings account*
5. **el compositor** – *composer*
6. **el cajero automático** – *automatic teller machine*
7. **la cerámica** – *pottery, ceramics*
8. **el camino** – *street, road*
9. **el criado** – *servant*
10. **la capa de ozono** – *ozone layer*

C

1. **el campesino** – *farm worker; peasant*
2. **la calle** – *street*
3. **la cuenta corriente** – *checking account*
4. **el cocinero** – *cook, chef*
5. **la canción** – *song*
6. **el currículum** – *résumé*
7. **el ciudadano** – *citizen*
8. **la carretera** – *highway*
9. **el café** – *café*
10. **la copa** – (*alcoholic*) *drink*

D

1. **el director** – *director*
2. **el divorcio** – *divorce*
3. **el dramaturgo** – *playwright*
4. **el desastre** – *disaster*
5. **el delito** – *crime*
6. **la desigualdad** – *inequality*
7. **el deber** – *responsibility*
8. **los demás** – *others, other people*
9. **el dictador** – *dictator*
10. **la discriminación** – *discrimination*

C

1. **la circulación** – *traffic*
2. **el comerciante** – *merchant, shopkeeper*
3. **el canal** – *channel*
4. **el conductor** – *conductor*
5. **las compras** – *purchases*
6. **el correo** – *post office*
7. **el cine** – *movie theater*
8. **el contador** – *accountant*
9. **el coche** – *car*
10. **la cita** – *date*

E

1. **la escultura** – *sculpture*
2. **el efectivo** – *cash*
3. **la especialización** – (*academic*) *major*
4. **el escenario** – *stage*
5. **el electricista** – *electrician*
6. **la energía** – *energy*
7. **la empresa** – *corporation, business*
8. **el esquina** – *street corner*
9. **la escasez** – *lack, shortage*
10. **la estación de gasolina** – *gas station*

E

1. **el entrevistador** – *interviewer*
2. **la esperanza** – *hope, wish*
3. **el ejército** – *army*
4. **el extranjero** – *foreigner*
5. **la estancia** – *stay* (*in a hotel*)
6. **el escultor** – *sculptor*
7. **el esposo** – *husband*
8. **el estanco** – *tobacco stand or shop*
9. **el escritor** – *writer*
10. **la estación del metro** – *subway stop*

F

1. **la fábrica** – *factory*
2. **la factura** – *bill*
3. **el fotógrafo** – *photographer*
4. **la falta** – *lack, absence*
5. **la farmacia** – *pharmacy, drugstore*
6. **la finca** – *farm*
7. **el formulario** – *form* (*to fill out*)
8. **la frontera** – *border*
9. **los frenos** – *brakes*
10. **los fósforos** – *matches*

L

1. **la literatura** – *literature*
2. **la llanta** – *tire*
3. **la ley** – *law*
4. **el lujo** – *luxury*
5. **la licencia** – *license*
6. **la lástima** – *shame*
7. **el lugar** – *place*
8. **el límite de velocidad** – *speed limit*
9. **la luna de miel** – *honeymoon*
10. **la libertad** – *liberty, freedom*

M

1. **el músico** – *musician*
2. **el matrimonio** – *marriage; married couple*
3. **el museo** – *museum*
4. **el mecánico** – *mechanic*
5. **el marido** – *husband*
6. **la muerte** – *death*
7. **el maestro** – *schoolteacher*
8. **la madurez** – *middle age*
9. **la mujer de negocios** – *businesswoman*
10. **la multa** – *fine*

P

1. **la pastelería** – *pastry shop*
2. **la prensa**– *press*
3. **el parabrisas** – *windshield*
4. **el préstamo** – *loan*
5. **la papelería** – *stationery store*
6. **el peluquero** – *hairstylist*
7. **la pareja** – *married couple; partner*
8. **el presupuesto** – *budget*
9. **el paquete** – *package*
10. **el pasaporte** – *passport*

R

1. **las ruinas** – *ruins*
2. **los recursos naturales** – *natural resources*
3. **el rey** – *king*
4. **los recién casados** – *newlyweds*
5. **la reserva** – *reservation*
6. **el rascacielos** – *skyscraper*
7. **la revista** – *magazine*
8. **el reportero** – *reporter*
9. **la recepción** – *front desk*
10. **el ritmo** – *rhythm, pace*

P

1. **el periodista** – *journalist*
2. **la paz** – *peace*
3. **la pasta dental** – *toothpaste*
4. **el plomero** – *plumber*
5. **la parada del autobús** – *bus stop*
6. **la política** – *politics*
7. **la pensión** – *boardinghouse*
8. **el papel para cartas** – *stationery*
9. **la población** – *population*
10. **la propina** – *tip*

S

1. **el servicio militar** – *military service*
2. **el salario** – *salary*
3. **el semáforo** – *traffic signal*
4. **el sobre** – *envelope*
5. **el soltero** – *unmarried man*
6. **el siquiatra** – *psychiatrist*
7. **la solicitud** – *application (form)*
8. **el sello** – *stamp*
9. **el soldado** – *soldier*
10. **el sicólogo** – *psychologist*

T

1. **los tejidos** – *woven goods*
2. **el teatro** – *theater*
3. **el transporte** – (*means of*) *transportation*
4. **la tarjeta de crédito** – *credit card*
5. **el taller** – *repair shop*
6. **el traductor** – *translator*
7. **el terrorista** – *terrorist*
8. **el testigo** – *witness*
9. **el trabajador social** – *social worker*
10. **la tarjeta postal** – *postcard*

V

1. **la violencia** – *violence*
2. **la vejez** – *old age*
3. **la vivienda** – *housing*
4. **el vendedor** – *salesperson*
5. **el viajero** – *traveler*
6. **la velocidad** – *speed*
7. **el veterinario** – *veterinarian*
8. **la vista** – *sight*
9. **votar** – *to vote*
10. **la vida** – *life*

X. Video Activities and Related Materials

Each *¿Qué tal?* chapter has a corresponding video section, composed of two vignettes: **En contexto** and a cultural segment that relates to the chapter's country of focus. The **En contexto** vignettes were filmed in Peru, Mexico, and Costa Rica, and correspond to each chapter.

Also available as part of the *¿Qué tal?* Video Program, although not referenced in the textbook, are the **Minidramas** vignettes. The **Minidramas** vignettes were filmed in Mexico, Ecuador, and Spain, and are thematically linked to the chapters. Should you choose to use them, the following worksheets contain activities to guide students through the process of listening and viewing the **Minidramas** segment. They may be photocopied for distribution to students. There are two sections of video activities: **A primera vista** (activities that students do after a first viewing of the particular segment) and **A segunda vista** (review activities).

A primera vista activities contain the following components: **Antes de ver** (pre-viewing activities), **Palabras y expresiones útiles** (useful words found in the video segments that accompany most **Antes de ver** sections), and **Después de ver** (post-viewing activities).

A segunda vista activities can be done later on in the semester, after a given chapter has been covered in class, as review. At that point, students will understand the segments much more than they did upon the first viewing. **A segunda vista** activities also contain the **Antes de ver** and **Despúes de ver** sections, but they do not contain the **Palabras y expresiones útiles** features.

Following the video activities are answers to many of the activities, as well as videoscripts to accompany each vignette found on the video.

A. *A primera vista*

Primeros pasos

A PRIMERA VISTA

Antes de ver *(Before Watching)*

A. Write **S** (**saludo**) by the expressions you would use when meeting or greeting someone and **D** (**despedida**) by those you would use when saying good-bye.

1. ____ ¿Qué tal?
2. ____ Hasta mañana.
3. ____ Hola.
4. ____ Hasta luego.
5. ____ Buenas noches.
6. ____ Adiós.

B. Below are several answers. What were the questions? Choose from the list at the right.

1. ____ Es a las diez en punto de la mañana.
2. ____ Es la Sra. Martínez.
3. ____ Hay cuatro.
4. ____ Es Buenos Aires.
5. ____ Es muy paciente y generosa.
6. ____ Está en México.

a. ¿Cuál es la capital de la Argentina?
b. ¿Dónde está Guadalajara?
c. ¿A qué hora es la clase de español?
d. ¿Cuántas clases de español hay en una semana?
e. ¿Quién es la profesora de español?
f. ¿Cómo es la profesora?

PALABRAS Y EXPRESIONES ÚTILES

The useful words and expressions in this section will help to improve your understanding of the video scene and to complete the activities.

cómo no *of course*
se dice *one says / you say*
significa *means*
te presento *I'd like to introduce you*
tu país *your country*

- Quickly scan **Actividad A** of **Después de ver** before you watch the video segment.

Después de ver *(After Watching)*

A. In this scene Diego introduces himself to a professor, and the professor introduces Diego to another student. Answer the following questions about information found in the video segment.

1. ¿Cuál es el apellido (*last name*) del profesor?
   a. González   b. Salazar   c. Sifuentes

2. ¿Cuál es el apellido de Diego?
   a. González   b. Salazar   c. Sifuentes

3. ¿Cuál es el apellido de Antonio, el estudiante posgraduado?
   a. González   b. Salazar   c. Sifuentes

4. ¿De dónde es Diego?
   a. México   b. Texas   c. California

5. ¿De dónde es Antonio?
   a. México   b. Texas   c. California

6. Según (*According to*) Antonio, ¿cómo se llama también la Ciudad de México?
   a. México   b. la capital   c. el D. F.

B. Paso 1. Working with a classmate, introduce yourself and ask questions in Spanish. Find out your classmate's name, how he or she is, and what he or she is like. You should also respond to your classmate's introduction and questions.

Paso 2. Now, with your partner, join one of the other pairs of classmates. Introduce your partner to them and let him or her introduce you. Respond to the introductions and questions the other pair of classmates ask you.

Capítulo 1

A PRIMERA VISTA

Antes de ver

A. Which of the following is true for you? Check off the appropriate box.

	SÍ	NO
¿Necesita Ud...		
comprar más libros para la clase de español?	❑	❑
buscar palabras en un diccionario bilingüe?	❑	❑
practicar el español con otro/a estudiante?	❑	❑
trabajar?	❑	❑
¿Le gusta...		
estudiar con un amigo / una amiga?	❑	❑
cantar y bailar en las fiestas?	❑	❑
hablar con los estudiantes extranjeros?	❑	❑
tomar café con los amigos por la tarde?	❑	❑

PALABRAS Y EXPRESIONES ÚTILES

sobre todo	*especially*
debo	*I should*
¿Me acompañas?	*Will you accompany me?*
tenemos el mismo curso	*we have the same class*

- Quickly scan **Actividad A** of **Después de ver** before you watch the video segment.

Después de ver

A. Lupe Carrasco and Diego González meet again in this scene. Answer the questions about their meeting.

1. ¿Dónde están Lupe y Diego?

   a. en la biblioteca b. en una librería c. en una oficina

2. Lupe necesita comprar libros para sus (*her*) clases. ¿Cuáles son tres de las clases que menciona (*she mentions*)?

   a. ______________________________

   b. ______________________________

   c. ______________________________

3. ¿Qué clase tienen (*do they have*) en común Diego y Lupe?

   a. el español b. el arte c. la antropología

4. Diego invita a Lupe a tomar _____.

   a. una cerveza b. un café c. un té (*tea*)

5. En su (*your*) opinión, ¿cómo es Diego? ¿Cuáles de estos adjetivos lo describen (*describe him*)?

   a. extrovertido c. inteligente e. generoso g. arrogante i. sincero
   b. impulsivo d. tímido f. romántico h. serio

6. Y Lupe, ¿cómo es?

   a. extrovertida c. inteligente e. generosa g. arrogante i. sincera
   b. impulsiva d. tímida f. romántica h. seria

B. Lupe and Diego found that they are taking the same class. Work with a classmate to find out some of the things the two of you have in common.

Paso 1. Write your classmate's answers to the following questions. Ask at least one original question of your own. Then answer the questions your classmate asks you.

1. ¿Qué tipo de música te gusta? ¿la música clásica? ¿la latina? ¿el jazz? ¿el rock?

   ____

2. ¿Cuál es tu (*your*) programa de televisión favorito?

   ____

3. ¿Trabajas mientras (*while*) estudias en la universidad? ¿Dónde?

   ____

4. ¿Cuál es tu clase favorita?

   ____

5. ¿Qué aspecto de la universidad te gusta mucho?

   ____

6. ¿Qué aspecto de la universidad *no* te gusta mucho?

   ____

7. ¿ ?

   ____

Paso 2. Share the items you both have in common with the rest of the class. Are there some things that almost everybody shares? Some things that almost nobody likes?

Capítulo 2

A PRIMERA VISTA

Antes de ver

Write the answers to the clues in the appropriate spaces to complete this crossword puzzle about the family.

HORIZONTALES

2. Los otros hijos de mis padres son mis ____.
6. La esposa de mi padre es mi ____.
7. Las hijas de los hijos de mis abuelos son sus ____.
9. El padre de mi madre es mi ____.
10. Mi padre es el ____ de mi madre. (**¡OJO!** No es **marido.**)

VERTICALES

1. El hijo de uno de mis hermanos es mi ____.
3. Mi madre es la ____ de mi padre.
4. Otro nombre, muy familiar, para **madre** es ____.
5. El hijo de uno de los hermanos de mi madre o de mi padre es mi ____.
8. El hermano de mi padre o de mi madre es mi ____.

PALABRAS Y EXPRESIONES ÚTILES	
oye	*listen, hey*
antiguas	**viejas**
se ve tan joven	*he looks so young*
oscuro	**moreno**
debe de tener... años	*he's probably . . . years old*
No regresen muy tarde.	*Don't come home very late.*

- Quickly scan **Actividad A** of **Después de ver** before you watch the video segment.

Después de ver

A. In this scene José Miguel helps his mother sort family photos, then leaves to go to a movie with Paloma and Gustavo. How much do you remember?

1. La madre de José Miguel, Elisa Velasco, tiene el pelo (*hair*) ____.
   a. rubio b. moreno c. blanco
2. Paloma es la ____ de José Miguel.
   a. hermana b. sobrina c. prima
3. José Miguel es ____.
   a. bajo b. gordo c. joven
4. Según la Sra. Velasco, hay por lo menos (*at least*) ____ fotos que tiene que ordenar.
   a. cien b. cincuenta c. sesenta y seis
5. Cuando Paloma y Gustavo llegan a la casa de los Velasco, la Sra. Velasco les dice (*says to them*) «¡Adelante!». ¿Qué cree Ud. que significa (*means*) **¡Adelante!**?
   a. *Oh, its you!* b. *Come in!* c. *Stop right there!*

B. Interview a classmate to find out the following information about him or her and his or her family. Also, answer the questions your classmate asks you.

PADRE

Nombre: ______________________________

Edad (*age*): ______________________________

¿Cómo es? ______________________________

MADRE

Nombre: ______________________________

Edad: ______________________________

¿Cómo es? ______________________________

HERMANOS

¿Cuántos? ________________________

Edad del mayor (*eldest*): ________________

¿Cómo es? ________________________

Edad del menor (*youngest*): ______________

¿Cómo es? ________________________

Número de

solteros: ____ casados: ____

EL COMPAÑERO / LA COMPAÑERA DE CLASE

¿Es soltero/a? ❑ sí ❑ no
¿Está casado/a? ❑ sí ❑ no

Nombre del esposo / de la esposa: ________

____

(Número de) Años de casados: ___________

Número de hijos: ____________________

Capítulo 3

A PRIMERA VISTA

Antes de ver

A. There's a Spanish saying that goes: «**La ropa hace** (*makes*) **al hombre**.» Do you think this is true? Answer the following questions about your clothing preferences.

1. ¿Es importante para Ud. la ropa? ❑ sí ❑ no
2. ¿Ya tiene Ud. toda la ropa que necesita para este año? Indique la ropa que piensa comprar dentro de poco (*soon*).

a. suéter	e. abrigo	i. *bluejeans*
b. camisa	f. blusa	j. zapatos
c. camiseta	g. sombrero	k. vestido
d. botas	h. pantalones	l. chaqueta

3. Por lo general (*Usually*), ¿dónde compra Ud. la ropa?

a. en un almacén	c. en un centro comercial	e. por catálogo
b. en una tienda pequeña	d. en el centro de la ciudad	

4. ¿Cuáles son sus colores favoritos? ________________
5. ¿Qué dice de su personalidad la ropa que Ud. lleva? ________________

B. Did you dress up this morning or did you dress casually? Describe in Spanish the clothes you're wearing right now.

____

____

PALABRAS Y EXPRESIONES ÚTILES	
un rato	*a little while*
¿Qué talla usa?	*What size do you wear?*
por lo general	*usually*
Sí, cómo no.	*Yes, of course.*

- Quickly scan **Actividad A** of **Después de ver** before you watch the video segment.

Después de ver

A. Answer the following questions about the video episode.

1. En este episodio, ¿qué lleva José Miguel (**JM**)? ¿Qué lleva Paloma (**P**)? **¡OJO!** Algunos (*Some*) artículos de ropa no aparecen (*appear*) en el episodio.

a. ____ sombrero azul

b. ____ pantalones de color caqui

c. ____ chaqueta morada

d. ____ camisa de manga larga (*long-sleeved shirt*)

e. ____ camisa oscura (*dark*)

f. ____ suéter pardo

g. ____ *bluejeans*

2. ¿De qué colores son las camisas que mira José Miguel en la tienda?
   a. verde   b. azul   c. rojo   d. morado   e. negro   f. amarillo

3. ¿Cuánto cuestan las camisas? ________ mil sucres.

4. ¿Qué talla de camisa lleva José Miguel, por lo general? La ________.

5. ¿Qué compra Paloma? ________________________________

6. ¿Qué tipo de camiseta no le gusta a Paloma? ________________________________

7. ¿Quién tiene prisa por ir a sus clases? ________________________________

B. Paso 1. Imagine that the exchange students, a man and woman, are in your Spanish class. They just arrived in this country and would like to buy some new clothes. What would you recommend? Working with a partner, make a list of at least five articles of women's clothing and five articles of men's clothing. Include colors in your lists whenever possible.

MUJER	HOMBRE
1. ________________	1. ________________
2. ________________	2. ________________
3. ________________	3. ________________
4. ________________	4. ________________
5. ________________	5. ________________

Paso 2. Now compare your lists with those of the rest of the class. What items appear on most of the lists? Which are unique?

Capítulo 4

A PRIMERA VISTA

Antes de ver

A. What is your daily routine like? Put the following activities in order according to your schedule. (Some of these activities may not apply to you. You may leave those spaces blank.)

_____ Me acuesto.

_____ Me afeito.

_____ Me baño.

_____ Me cepillo los dientes.

_____ Me ducho.

_____ Me despierto.

_____ Me duermo.

_____ Me levanto.

_____ Me visto.

PALABRAS Y EXPRESIONES ÚTILES	
ya no puedo más	*I can't take it anymore*
la recámara (*Méx.*)	*la alcoba*
mientras	*while*

- Quickly scan **Actividad A** of **Después de ver** before you watch the video segment.

Después de ver

A. How much do you remember about the episode? Match the sentence beginnings on the left with the sentence endings on the right.

1. ____ La tía Matilde siempre despierta a Diego...
2. ____ Diego no quiere hacer ruido por la noche porque...
3. ____ Los lunes, miércoles y viernes, Antonio vuelve a casa para almorzar porque...
4. ____ Antonio le promete (*promises*) a Diego que...
5. ____ Normalmente, Antonio se levanta a las siete y...
6. ____ La tía Matilde llama a Diego para preguntarle (*ask him*)...

a. si necesita vitaminas.
b. nadie (*nobody*) en la casa se levanta a las cinco.
c. Juan se levanta a las seis y media.
d. a las cinco de la mañana porque canta mientras se baña.
e. la tía Matilde se acuesta a las nueve de la noche.
f. no tiene clases por la tarde.

B. Paso 1. What's your life like? Complete the following survey about some aspects of your daily life.

	CON FRECUENCIA	A VECES	NUNCA
Me acuesto tarde.	❑	❑	❑
Me despierto tarde.	❑	❑	❑
Escucho música cuando estudio.	❑	❑	❑
Prefiero el silencio para estudiar.	❑	❑	❑
Paso mucho tiempo en el baño por la mañana.	❑	❑	❑
Salgo con los amigos los fines de semana.	❑	❑	❑
Salgo las noches de entre semana (*weeknights*).	❑	❑	❑
Invito a los amigos a casa.	❑	❑	❑
Veo la televisión.	❑	❑	❑

Paso 2. Now that you have listed your preferences, look for classmates who have a similar way of life. Be sure to ask them questions in Spanish only.

Capítulo 5

A PRIMERA VISTA

Antes de ver

A. What season do you associate with the following activities? Write **P (primavera)**, **V (verano)**, **O (otoño)**, or **I (invierno)**. Some activities may be associated with more than one season.

1. ____ esquiar en las montañas (*mountains*)
2. ____ mirar la serie mundial (*world*) de béisbol
3. ____ celebrar las fiestas de Año Nuevo
4. ____ celebrar el Día de la Independencia de los Estados Unidos
5. ____ descansar de los estudios e ir a lugares como Ft. Lauderdale y Palm Springs
6. ____ regresar a las clases
7. ____ esquiar en el agua

EXPRESIÓN ÚTIL

está lloviendo a cántaros — *it's raining cats and dogs*

- Quickly scan **Actividad A** of **Después de ver** before you watch the video segment.

Después de ver

A. Indicate which of the following statements about the episode are **ciertas (C)** and which are **falsas (F).**

	C	F
1. Hace muy mal tiempo en Sevilla para el mes de abril.	❑	❑
2. En Sevilla está lloviendo a cántaros.	❑	❑
3. Lola es profesora en la universidad y tiene unos estudiantes magníficos.	❑	❑
4. Manolo no encuentra sus exámenes.	❑	❑
5. Carolina Díaz llama a Marta para preguntarle (*ask her*) si quiere jugar esta tarde.	❑	❑
6. Carlos Suárez va a estar en La Coruña mañana y quiere ver a Manolo y Lola.	❑	❑
7. Lola encontró (*found*) los exámenes debajo de la cama.	❑	❑

B. Are your moods affected by the weather? How do you react to the following weather conditions? Write how you feel in complete sentences, using **estar** and one of the following adjectives or any other, if you like.

MODELO: Hace sol. → Estoy muy contento cuando hace sol.

aburrido/a	enfermo/a	preocupado/a
alegre	furioso/a	triste
congelado/a	nervioso/a	¿ ?
contento/a		

1. Hace mucho frío. ________________
2. Llueve por una semana entera (*whole*). ________________
3. Hace mucho viento. ________________
4. Hace sol, pero hace fresco. ________________
5. Hace calor y hay mucha contaminación. ________________

Capítulo 6

A PRIMERA VISTA

Antes de ver

A. Do you know what's in your refrigerator right now? Write down everything you can remember.

CARNES	VERDURAS Y FRUTAS
____________	____________
____________	____________
____________	____________

BEBIDAS	¿ ?
____________	____________
____________	____________
____________	____________

B. Which of the following specialties from Hispanic countries have you tried? Did you like them?

	ME GUSTÓ.	NO ME GUSTÓ.
❑ el arroz con pollo	❑	❑
❑ el mole poblano	❑	❑
❑ la pasta de guayaba	❑	❑
❑ la ropa vieja	❑	❑
❑ el flan	❑	❑
❑ el cebiche	❑	❑
❑ la paella valenciana	❑	❑
❑ el gazpacho	❑	❑
❑ el arroz con habichuelas	❑	❑
❑ el café cubano	❑	❑

- Quickly scan **Actividad A** of **Después de ver** before you watch the video segment.

Después de ver

A. In this scene, Manolo and Lola are talking in their kitchen, and then they go out to dinner. Answer the following questions about the episode.

1. Lola dice que nunca hay comida en la casa. ¿Cuáles de las siguientes comidas menciona?
   a. carne c. huevos e. agua mineral g. patatas i. leche
   b. atún d. manzanas f. queso h. lechuga

2. Manolo le dice (*tells*) a Lola que no se preocupe (*not to worry*). Esta noche van a cenar afuera porque hoy es un día especial. ¿Cuál es la ocasión?
   a. el cumpleaños de Lola b. el aniversario de bodas c. el Año Nuevo

3. Según Manolo, ¿cómo es el restaurante donde van a cenar?
   a. nuevo b. exótico c. excelente d. muy típico e. muy romántico f. viejo

4. ¿Qué platos comieron (*ate*) Lola y Manolo? Indique quién comió (*ate*) qué. Escriba **L** (**Lola**), **M** (**Manolo**), **A** (**ambos**) o **N** (**ninguno**) al lado de los siguientes platos.

   a. ____ bistec estilo argentino

   b. ____ calamares a la gallega

   c. ____ gambas al limón con arroz

   d. ____ paella valenciana

   e. ____ sopa de ajo

   f. ____ tortilla de patatas

   g. ____ una ensalada mixta

   h. ____ vino tinto y agua mineral

B. Paso 1. With a classmate, take turns interviewing each other to find out the following information.

1. ¿Dónde comes, por lo general, las siguientes comidas?

a. el desayuno	❑ en casa	❑ en un restaurante	❑ en la cafetería
b. el almuerzo	❑ en casa	❑ en un restaurante	❑ en la cafetería
c. la cena	❑ en casa	❑ en un restaurante	❑ en la cafetería

2. ¿Cuál es la comida que, por lo general, te saltas (*skip*)?
   a. el desayuno   b. el almuerzo   c. la cena   d. ninguna

3. ¿Cuáles son tus preferencias en cuanto a (*regarding*) la comida?
   ❑ la comida rápida (sándwiches, hamburguesas, patatas fritas, refrescos, etcétera)
   ❑ una dieta equilibrada (preferencia por los cereales, verduras y frutas)
   ❑ los dulces (pasteles, helados, refrescos, chocolate, galletas, etcétera)
   ❑ la comida vegetariana
   ❑ ¿ ? ______________________________

4. ¿Cuál es una comida que no te gusta para nada? ______________________________

Paso 2. Now compare your results with those of the rest of the class. Can you make any generalizations about the food preferences of the class as a whole?

Capítulo 7

A PRIMERA VISTA

Antes de ver

Write the answers to the clues in the appropriate spaces of this crossword puzzle about traveling.

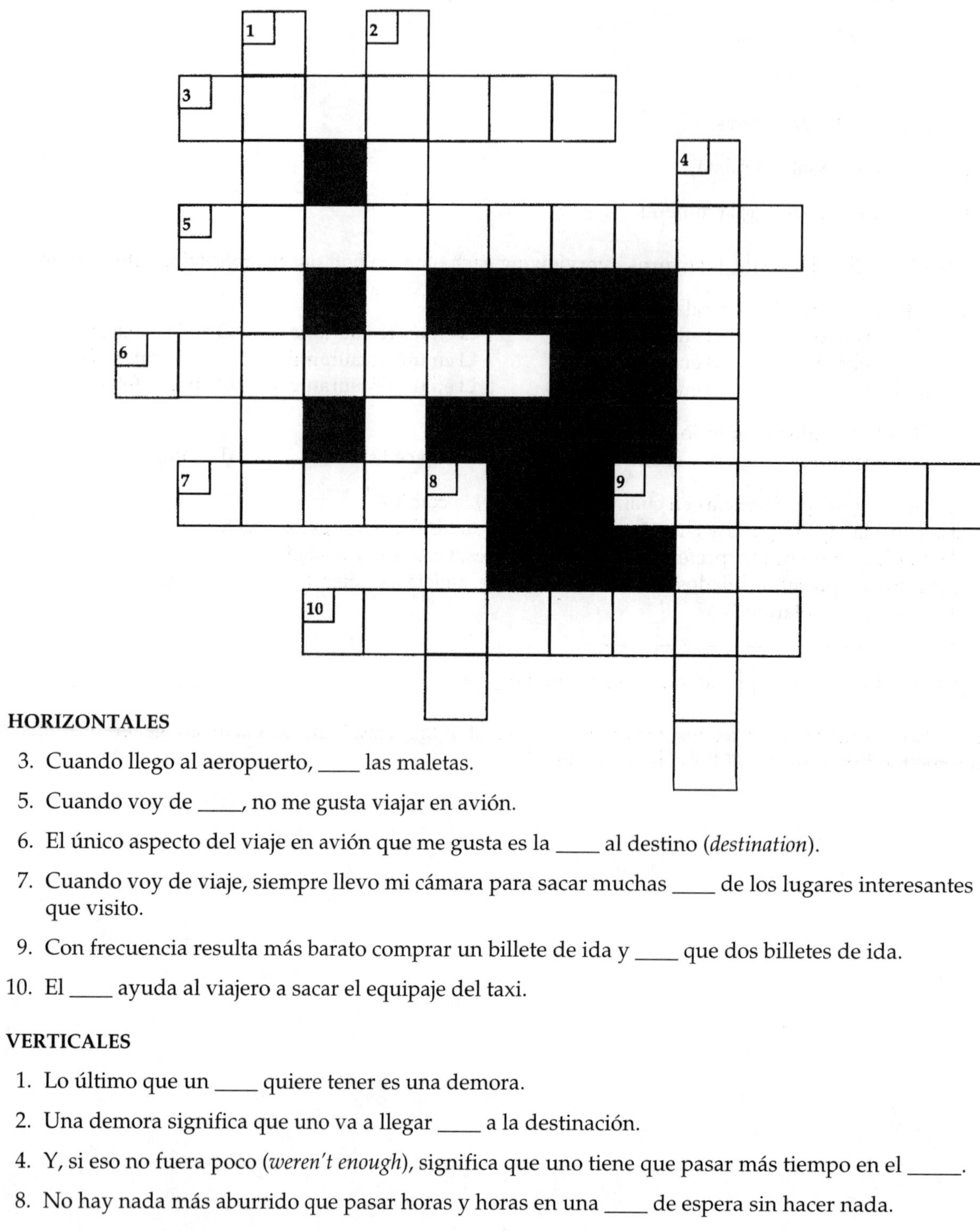

HORIZONTALES

3. Cuando llego al aeropuerto, ____ las maletas.
5. Cuando voy de ____, no me gusta viajar en avión.
6. El único aspecto del viaje en avión que me gusta es la ____ al destino (*destination*).
7. Cuando voy de viaje, siempre llevo mi cámara para sacar muchas ____ de los lugares interesantes que visito.
9. Con frecuencia resulta más barato comprar un billete de ida y ____ que dos billetes de ida.
10. El ____ ayuda al viajero a sacar el equipaje del taxi.

VERTICALES

1. Lo último que un ____ quiere tener es una demora.
2. Una demora significa que uno va a llegar ____ a la destinación.
4. Y, si eso no fuera poco (*weren't enough*), significa que uno tiene que pasar más tiempo en el _____.
8. No hay nada más aburrido que pasar horas y horas en una ____ de espera sin hacer nada.

- Quickly scan **Actividad A** of **Después de ver** before you watch the video segment.

Después de ver

A. In this scene, Elisa Velasco goes to the travel agency. Answer the following questions about the episode.

1. ¿Cuál es la profesión de Elisa?
   a. profesora b. periodista c. dentista
2. ¿Adónde va de viaje?
   a. Puerto Rico b. las Islas Galápagos c. Hawai
3. ¿Cuánto tiempo piensa quedarse allí?
   a. un fin de semana b. una semana c. dos semanas
4. ¿Cuánto cuesta un boleto de ida y vuelta en avión?
   a. 615.000 sucres b. 750.000 sucres c. 715.000 mil sucres
5. ¿Cómo paga Elisa los pasajes y la reservación?
   a. con tarjeta de crédito b. en efectivo (*cash*) c. con cheque

B. Paso 1. In groups of three, plan a vacation to one of the following Hispanic regions. Think about what you already know about the region and what you would like to learn. Decide on the places your group wants to see and why you think they are noteworthy.

Chile, la Argentina y el Uruguay
Colombia y Venezuela
Cuba, Puerto Rico, la República Dominicana
el Ecuador, el Perú y Bolivia
España y las Islas Canarias
México y Centroamérica

Paso 2. Share your vacation itinerary with the rest of the class. Invite the class to contribute suggestions about things to see and do that your group might have overlooked.

Capítulo 8

A PRIMERA VISTA

Antes de ver

Conteste las siguientes preguntas sobre los días festivos que celebran Ud. y su familia.

1. A veces los miembros de una familia viven en ciudades distantes y no pueden reunirse con frecuencia. ¿En qué ocasiones suele (*tends to*) reunirse su familia?

❑ un aniversario de bodas	❑ el Día de Acción de Gracias	❑ la Pascua Florida
❑ un bar/bas mitzvah	❑ un cumpleaños	❑ una primera comunión
❑ el Día de la Independencia	❑ la Fiesta de las Luces	❑ una reunión familiar
❑ el Día del Trabajo	❑ la Navidad	❑ otra ________________

2. ¿Hay un lugar en particular en donde la familia se reúne? ¿Cuál es?

   ____

3. ¿Siempre lo pasa Ud. bien en las reuniones familiares? ❑ sí ❑ más o menos ❑ no

4. En una reunión familiar con frecuencia hay situaciones en que alguien expresa sus sentimientos positivos o negativos, ¿no? Indique lo que pasa en las reuniones de su familia.

   __________ discute sobre __________________ con __________________.

   __________ se enoja con __________________.

   __________ se pone ❑ triste ❑ contento/a ❑ enojado/a ❑ animado/a.

   __________ siempre recuerda __________________.

   __________ se porta(n) ❑ bien ❑ mal.

   __________ siempre se queja de __________________.

PALABRAS Y EXPRESIONES ÚTILES

me di cuenta	*I realized*
la iglesia	*church*
no te enfades	*don't get annoyed*
la peluca	*wig*
la mala educación	*rude behavior*
el árbol navideño	*Christmas tree*

- Quickly scan **Actividad A** of **Después de ver** before you watch the video segment.

Después de ver

A. ¿Cuánto recuerda Ud. de la reunión familiar de Lola y Manolo? Empareje frases de las dos columnas para formar oraciones completas.

1. ____ Los parientes de Lola y Manolo se reunieron...
2. ____ Después de la ceremonia,...
3. ____ El día de su primera comunión...
4. ____ Lola y el muchacho a su lado...
5. ____ Había (*There was*) una señora cerca de ellos...
6. ____ De repente, a esa señora dormida,...
7. ____ Según la madre de Lola,...

a. comenzaron a reírse de una señora.
b. con ocasión de la primera comunión de Marta.
c. es un acto de mala educación reírse en la iglesia de una señora.
d. la familia fue al parque María Luisa para almorzar.
e. Lola se portó bastante mal.
f. que se durmió durante la ceremonia y roncaba (*was snoring*).
g. se le cayó (*fell*) la peluca.

B. Paso 1. Con un compañero / una compañera de clase, háganse y contesten preguntas para saber la siguiente información sobre los días festivos.

1. ¿Cuál es tu día festivo favorito? ______________________________
2. ¿Por qué es tu favorito? ______________________________
3. ¿Con quiénes te reúnes? ¿Con tu familia nuclear? ¿tu familia extendida? ¿tus amigos?

   ____
4. ¿Dónde celebras esa ocasión, por lo general? ______________________________
5. ¿Preparas alguna comida especial? ¿Qué preparas? ______________________________
6. ¿Participas en actividades especiales? ¿Cuáles son? ______________________________

Paso 2. Ahora comparen los resultados de su entrevista con los de los demás. ¿Cuál es el día festivo más popular? ¿Hay actividades similares en las que todos participan? ¿Cuáles son?

Capítulo 9

A PRIMERA VISTA

Antes de ver

¿Cómo pasa Ud. los fines de semana? ¿Ofrece muchas diversiones la ciudad en que Ud. vive?

1. ¿En cuáles de las siguientes actividades ha participado Ud. (*have you participated in*)? Para cada actividad a continuación, escriba **A** (**aficionado**) o **P** (**participante**) en el espacio en blanco. Puede escribir **A** y **P** si las dos categorías son aplicables a Ud.

ACTIVIDADES CULTURALES	ACTIVIDADES SOCIALES	ACTIVIDADES FÍSICAS
____ un concierto	____ el ajedrez	____ el basquetbol
____ una conferencia (*lecture*) pública	____ un bar musical	____ el *camping*
____ una exposición de arte	____ las cartas	____ el ciclismo
____ un museo	____ el cine	____ el correr
____ una obra de teatro (*play*)	____ una discoteca	____ el fútbol
____ una ópera	____ una fiesta	____ el fútbol (norte)americano
____ un recital de poesía	____ un *picnic*	____ la natación
____ ¿ ?	____ ¿ ?	____ el patinaje en línea
		____ el tenis
		____ ¿ ?

2. ¿Cuál es su pasatiempo favorito? ____

3. ¿Hay algún pasatiempo en que a Ud. le gustaría participar pero que todavía no ha probado (*haven't tried*)? ¿Cuál es?____

PALABRAS Y EXPRESIONES ÚTILES

¿Qué onda? (Méx.) *Whats happening?*
¡Qué casualidad! *What a coincidence!*

- Quickly scan **Actividad A** of **Después de ver** before you watch the video segment.

Después de ver

A. ¿Cuánto recuerda Ud. del episodio?

1. Lupe quiere ____ a Diego este fin de semana porque es su cumpleaños.
   a. comprarle un regalo b. hacerle una fiesta sorpresa c. darle un pastel
2. Rocío ya tiene planes para el fin de semana. Ella y sus padres van ____.
   a. al Ballet Folklórico b. al Bosque (*Park*) de Chapultepec c. al Museo de Antropología
3. En este momento, Rocío y Juan salen para ____.
   a. comer a un restaurante japonés b. estudiar en la biblioteca c. ver una película
4. Según Lupe, ¿cuáles son algunas de las cosas que Diego y ella tienen en común?
   a. estudian música
   b. les gusta viajar
   c. tenían un perro negro
   d. les gusta bailar y escuchar música
   e. practican un deporte
   f. son de una familia grande
   g. les gustan los animales
   h. son aficionados al fútbol
   i. vivían en el campo
5. Diego quiere invitar a Lupe a un concierto ____.
   a. de guitarra clásica b. de baile flamenco c. de Luis Miguel

B. Paso 1. Piense en un día típico para Ud. ¿A cuáles de las siguientes actividades le dedica Ud. más tiempo? Indique el promedio (*average*) de minutos diarios que le dedica a cada actividad.

conversar con los amigos ________

escuchar la radio ________

escuchar música ________

practicar un deporte o hacer ejercicio ________

leer el periódico ________

leer libros ________

pasear ________

tomar copas ________

ver la televisión ________

¿ ? ________

Paso 2. Compare sus resultados con los del resto de la clase. ¿Se parecen (*Are similar*) las cantidades de tiempo dedicadas a cada actividad o hay mucha variación? ¿Cuál es la actividad favorita entre todos? ¿Cuál es la actividad menos favorita?

Capítulo 10

A PRIMERA VISTA

Antes de ver

Hay ciertas enfermedades asociadas con la niñez. ¿Se acuerda Ud. de las enfermedades que contrajo (*you caught*)?

1. Indique las enfermedades que Ud. contrajo de niño/a.
   a. la amigdalitis (*tonsilitis*)
   b. la gripe (*flu*)
   c. las paperas (*mumps*)
   d. el resfriado
   e. el sarampión (*measles*)
   f. la varicela (*chicken pox*)
2. ¿Cuáles de los siguientes síntomas sufrió?
   a. el cansancio
   b. la congestión
   c. dificultad en respirar
   d. dolor de cabeza
   e. dolor de estómago
   f. dolor de garganta
   g. los estornudos (*sneezing*)
   h. la fiebre
   i. la tos
3. De niño/a, ¿tuvo que guardar cama cuando se enfermaba? ❑ sí ❑ no
4. Para un niño / una niña, ¿qué es lo mejor de tener que guardar cama? ________________________

   ____
5. ¿Qué es lo peor? ________________________________

PALABRAS Y EXPRESIONES ÚTILES

embarazada	*pregnant*
los pañales	*diapers*
dar de comer	*to feed*

- Quickly scan **Actividad A** of **Después de ver** before you watch the video segment.

Después de ver

A. ¿Cuánto recuerdas de este episodio? Empareje frases de las dos columnas para formar oraciones completas.

1. ____ A Marta le dolían mucho...
2. ____ Marta se puso contenta cuando supo que...
3. ____ Lola sospechaba (*suspected*) que...
4. ____ Manolo recordó que, cuando Marta era pequeña,...
5. ____ Cuando regresaron del hospital con Marta,...
6. ____ Manolo se llevó una sorpresa cuando...

a. el estómago y la garganta.
b. él y Lola se levantaban mucho por la noche.
c. estaba embarazada.
d. Lola entró en la tienda de maternidad.
e. Lola tenía miedo de cada estornudo.
f. tenía que quedarse en casa.

B. Paso 1. Un refrán español dice: «Abogado, juez (*judge*) y doctor, cuanto más lejos mejor.» ¿Qué significa para Ud. este refrán? ¿Está de acuerdo? ¿Qué hace para mantenerse lejos del doctor? Llene el siguiente formulario sobre sus actitudes y hábitos con respecto a la salud.

EJERCICIO

1. Sigo un programa de ejercicio ❑ sí ❑ no
2. ¿Qué hago?

❑ calistenia ❑ natación ❑ ejercicios aeróbicos ❑ correr ❑ yoga

❑ otro ________________

ALIMENTACIÓN

1. Como una dieta equilibrada. ❑ sí ❑ no
2. Los aspectos de la dieta que me importan:

la reducción de la cantidad ingerida (*ingested*)

❑ de grasa (*fat*) ❑ de sal ❑ de azúcar

el aumento de la cantidad ingerida

❑ de frutas ❑ de verduras ❑ de cereales

VICIOS

1. Fumo. ❑ sí ❑ no Número de cigarrillos al día: ____
2. Bebo café. ❑ sí ❑ no Número de tazas al día: ____
3. Tomo bebidas alcohólicas. ❑ sí ❑ no

Consumo diario ❑ 0 ó 1 copa ❑ 1 ó 2 ❑ 3 ó 4 ❑ más de 4

4. Me acuesto ❑ temprano ❑ tarde

Promedio (*Average*) de horas dormidas por noche: _____

Me siento cansado/a durante el día. ❑ sí ❑ no

Paso 2. Ahora entreviste a un compañero / una compañera de clase para ver cuáles son sus actitudes y hábitos. ¿Coinciden con los de Ud.? ¿Tiene Ud. alguna sugerencia para que él/ella pueda cuidar mejor de su salud?

Capítulo 11

A PRIMERA VISTA

Antes de ver

A. En su opinión, ¿cuáles son las presiones de la vida moderna que más afectan a los estudiantes universitarios?

- ❑ el costo alto de la educación
- ❑ las crisis de la vida personal
- ❑ el racismo
- ❑ el sexismo
- ❑ la homofobia
- ❑ la falta de empleo después de graduarse
- ❑ mantenerse al tanto de los avances tecnológicos
- ❑ las presiones para consumir bebidas alcohólicas o drogas
- ❑ el riesgo de contraer el SIDA
- ❑ otra ____________________________

B. Hay días en que todo parece salirnos mal. Por lo general esos incidentes irritantes parecen chistosos (*funny*) al recordarlos después. ¿Le pasó a Ud. alguna vez uno de los siguientes incidentes? Escriba sobre el incidente más irritante que le pasó a Ud.

- ❑ Se me olvidó la cartera y lo descubrí cuando iba a pagar en una tienda.
- ❑ Se me olvidó quitarme las gafas antes de entrar en la ducha.
- ❑ Se me quedaron las llaves dentro del coche (apartamento).
- ❑ Se me cayó un cartón de huevos y todos se me rompieron sobre los pies.
- ❑ Se me rompió una bolsa llena de comestibles y todo se me cayó al suelo.

El incidente más irritante: ____

____

EXPRESIÓN ÚTIL	
la vecina	*the neighbor*

- Quickly scan **Actividad A** of **Después de ver** before you watch the video segment.

Después de ver

A. Ponga en orden los sucesos del «día horrible» que tuvo José Miguel.

____ Al salir del mercado la bolsa se le rompió a José Miguel y todas las compras se le cayeron al suelo.

____ José Miguel andaba muy distraído y se dio con una señora en la calle.

____ La nueva bolsa se le rompió cuando la puso en la mesa de la cocina.

____ También se le perdieron las llaves y tuvo que tocar a la puerta.

B. Paso 1. Piense en las presiones de la vida que Ud. indicó en **Antes de ver.** Ahora entreviste a un compañero / una compañera de clase para ver cuáles son sus opiniones al respecto.

Paso 2. Todo el mundo (*Everybody*) tiene su propia manera de relajarse (*relaxing*). ¿Cuáles son algunas de las cosas que Ud. le recomendaría (*would recommend*) a un amigo / una amiga para reducir los efectos del estrés diario? Explique por qué le recomendaría cierto método.

- ❑ dejar de tomar café
- ❑ tomar una infusión de plantas (*herbal tea*)
- ❑ bailar o hacer ejercicios
- ❑ salir con los amigos
- ❑ practicar la meditación
- ❑ tomar un baño o una ducha caliente
- ❑ tomar un martini
- ❑ recibir un masaje
- ❑ otro ____________

Capítulo 12

A PRIMERA VISTA

Antes de ver

A. ¿Qué aparatos electrónicos tiene Ud.? ¿Cuáles le gustaría adquirir algún día? Escriba **T** (**tengo**) al lado de los que ya tiene, **Q** (**quiero**) al lado de los que quiere adquirir y **¡ !** al lado del aparato que quiere adquirir más urgentemente.

____ una cámara de video
____ un disco compacto portátil
____ una computadora
____ una computadora portátil
____ un contestador automático
____ equipo estereofónico
____ equipo fotográfico
____ un lector de CD-ROM
____ un módem
____ un telefax
____ un teléfono celular
____ un videocasetera
____ un *walkman*
____ otro: ________________

¿En qué manera cree Ud. que la adquisición de algunos de estos aparatos va a mejorar la calidad de su vida? ____

B. ¿Cuál es su participación en el Internet?

1. Navego la red con frecuencia. ❑ sí ❑ no
2. Uso la información que saco del Internet para ayudarme con mis clases. ❑ sí ❑ no
3. Me adentro en (*I access*) las páginas web en español. ❑ sí ❑ no
4. Intercambio correo electrónico con personas de habla española. ❑ sí ❑ no

PALABRAS Y EXPRESIONES ÚTILES

oferta	*bargain, sale*
pagar a plazos	*to pay in installments*

- Quickly scan **Actividad A** of **Después de ver** before you watch the video segment.

Después de ver

A. ¿Cuánto recuerda Ud. del episodio? Indique la palabra o frase correcta para completar cada oración.

1. Gustavo leyó el anuncio de una tienda de ____ que tiene una oferta especial.
   a. equipo electrónico b. equipo estereofónico c. equipo fotográfico
2. La tienda está ____ y está abierta ahora.
   a. en un mercado b. en el centro comercial c. cerca de la casa

3. Gustavo le dice a Paloma: «Quiero que ____ tu *walkman*.»
   a. me prestes b. dejes aquí c. lleves contigo

4. José Miguel dice que quiere una computadora con ____.
   a. lector de CD-ROM interno b. ratón ergonómico c. disco duro interno

5. También dice que quiere un modelo con el que pueda ____ y usar programas de multimedia.
   a. diseñar gráficos b. jugar a los vídeojuegos (*video games*) c. navegar la red

B. Paso 1. En este país hay varias revistas dedicadas al modo de vivir de una región determinada como, por ejemplo, el de California, del Sur, del Suroeste y de Nueva Inglaterra. ¿Tiene la región donde Ud. vive un modo de vivir distintivo? Con un compañero / una compañera de clase, indiquen si en su región hay algo distintivo respecto a las siguientes categorías. Pueden añadir cualquier categoría que les parezca apropiada. Añadan detalles específicos sobre cada categoría que marquen con «sí».

comida ❑ sí ❑ no

Detalles ____________________

arquitectura ❑ sí ❑ no

Detalles ____________________

actividades/deportes/pasatiempos ❑ sí ❑ no

Detalles ____________________

condiciones geográficas y climáticas ❑ sí ❑ no

Detalles ____________________

composición étnica / carácter histórico ❑ sí ❑ no

Detalles ____________________

otra categoría: ____________________

Detalles ____________________

Paso 2. Ahora comparen sus resultados con los del resto de la clase para crear un perfil (*profile*) del modo de vivir de su región. ¿Indicaron todos las mismas características? ¿Apuntaron detalles diferentes varias parejas?

Capítulo 13

A PRIMERA VISTA

Antes de ver

Paso 1. ¿Cuáles de estas afirmaciones le describen a Ud.?

	SÍ	NO
1. Me gusta mucho mirar la tele. Lo hago cada noche.	❑	❑
2. Prefiero ir a un museo de arte o a una exposición en una galería.	❑	❑
3. Me gustan mucho la ópera y el ballet. Asisto a las presentaciones cuando puedo.	❑	❑
4. Para mí, no hay nada más aburrido que ver un espectáculo de baile.	❑	❑
5. No entiendo el arte moderno. No me gusta porque casi nunca representa formas que uno puede reconocer (*recognize*).	❑	❑
6. Me gusta mucho ir al cine. Veo por lo menos tres películas al mes.	❑	❑
7. Me gusta mucho leer, especialmente los libros «clásicos». Soy gran aficionado/a a la literatura.	❑	❑
8. Me encanta la artesanía, especialmente los tejidos y la cerámica.	❑	❑

Paso 2. Ahora mire los resultados del **Paso 1.** ¿Qué revelan de Ud. sus selecciones? ¿Le gustan más los espectáculos populares o los «culturales»?

EXPRESIÓN ÚTIL

saqué una buena nota *I got a good grade*

- Quickly scan **Actividad A** of **Después de ver** before you watch the video segment.

Después de ver

A. ¿Cuánto recuerda Ud. de la conversación entre Diego y Lupe? Empareje frases de las dos columnas para formar oraciones completas.

1. ____ Diego está estudiando para un examen...
2. ____ Lupe va a escribir un trabajo...
3. ____ A Lupe le gustan mucho los murales...
4. ____ A Diego le impresionan más los murales...
5. ____ Lupe invita a Diego a...
6. ____ Diego no puede ir, pero sugiere que...
7. ____ Al final del episodio, Diego invita a Lupe a...

a. de Diego Rivera.
b. para la clase del profesor Ramírez.
c. ir al Museo de Arte Moderno en el Bosque de Chapultepec.
d. de José Clemente Orozco.
e. los dos vayan al Museo de Arte Moderno el próximo sábado.
f. sobre el arte y la vida de Frida Kahlo.
g. tomar un cafecito.

B. Paso 1. Entreviste a un compañero / una compañera de clase para ver cuáles son sus gustos artísticos y culturales.

1. ¿En cuáles de las siguientes actividades culturales has participado (*have you participated*) durante el último semestre?

- ❑ asistir a un concierto
- ❑ asistir a un ballet
- ❑ ir a la ópera
- ❑ ir al teatro
- ❑ estudiar modelos de arquitectura
- ❑ ver una exposición de arte
- ❑ ver una película
- ❑ visitar un museo

2. ¿Tienes artistas preferidos? Indica tus preferencias en cada categoría.

Actor / Actriz: ______________________________

Cantante: ______________________________

Compositor(a): ______________________________

Director(a): ______________________________

Dramaturgo/a: ______________________________

Escritor(a): ______________________________

Pintor(a): ______________________________

Poeta: ______________________________

Paso 2. Ahora comparen sus gustos con los del resto de la clase. ¿Cuáles son las artes más populares entre Uds.? ¿Por qué? ¿Hay algún /alguna artista que sea admirado/a por la mayoría de la clase? ¿Tienen muchos de Uds. gustos parecidos (*similar*) o hay variedad de gustos?

Capítulo 14

A PRIMERA VISTA

Antes de ver

A. Ponga en orden de urgencia, de esta lista de problemas del mundo de hoy, los cinco problemas que Ud. considera más urgentes.

____ el agotamiento (*depletion*) de los recursos naturales

____ el calentamiento (*warming*) global

____ la contaminación del medio ambiente

____ el crecimiento (*growth*) no controlado de las ciudades

____ la destrucción de la capa del ozono

____ la violencia y el crimen

____ la destrucción de los bosques

____ la drogadicción

____ la escasez de viviendas adecuadas

____ la extinción de especies de animales y plantas

____ el subempleo (*underemployment*)

B. Conteste las siguientes preguntas sobre Ud. y el uso del automóvil.

1. ¿Tiene Ud. coche u otro vehículo motorizado? ❑ sí ❑ no
2. ¿Cuál es el promedio (*average*) de millas a la semana que Ud. maneja el coche? ____________________
3. ¿En pos de (*In pursuit of*) qué actividad conduce la mayor parte de estas millas?

❑ viajar de la casa a la universidad y viceversa

❑ salir con los amigos

❑ ir a lugares de recreación

❑ ir de compras

❑ llevar a los hijos a la escuela

❑ otra: ____________________

- Quickly scan **Actividad A** of **Después de ver** before you watch the video segment.

Después de ver

A. ¿Cuánto recuerda Ud. del episodio? Complete las siguientes oraciones con la frase apropiada.

1. Mientras Elisa ____, José Miguel explora el cráter.
   a. escribe su artículo b. mira las nubes (*clouds*) c. observa los pájaros
2. Elisa se interesa mucho por ____.
   a. las industrias del Ecuador
   b. los problemas del medio ambiente en el Ecuador
   c. varios lugares bellos que visitan los turistas
3. Una automovilista le pide a la Sra. Velasco direcciones ____.
   a. al pueblo más cercano b. a Quito c. al cráter del Pululahua

4. El carro de la automovilista ha comenzado a hacer un ruido muy extraño, y ella quiere que ____.
   a. un agricultor lo compre
   b. Elisa y José Miguel la lleven a la población más cercana
   c. un mecánico lo revise
5. La Sra. Velasco invita a la automovilista a acompañarlos a ella y a José Miguel porque ____.
   a. ellos se sienten solos en un lugar tan remoto
   b. no le gusta que la automovilista se quede sola con un carro que no funciona
   c. quiere entrevistarle para su artículo

B. Paso 1. Con cuatro compañeros de clase, repasen las respuestas que dieron en la **Actividad A** en **Antes de ver**. ¿Coinciden Uds. en sus opiniones sobre los problemas más urgentes?

Paso 2. Ahora piensen en un problema que los estudiantes universitarios tienen más posibilidad de ayudar a resolver. Escriban tres o más cosas que los estudiantes pueden hacer para solucionar ese problema.

Paso 3. Comparen las conclusiones a las que llegó su grupo con las de los otros grupos. ¿Son parecidas (*similar*) las soluciones? ¿Creen Uds. que hay mucho que los estudiantes pueden hacer para solucionar los problemas del mundo de hoy?

Capítulo 15

A PRIMERA VISTA

Antes de ver

A. Ponga las siguientes etapas de la vida humana en el orden natural.

a. ____ la adolescencia
b. ____ la infancia
c. ____ la juventud
d. ____ la madurez
e. ____ la muerte
f. ____ el nacimiento
g. ____ la niñez
h. ____ la vejez

B. ¿Cuál es el orden en que, por lo general, ocurren las siguientes etapas en las relaciones entre una pareja?

a. ____ la amistad
b. ____ el matrimonio
c. ____ la comprensión
d. ____ el noviazgo
e. ____ el conocimiento mutuo
f. ____ el deterioro de las relaciones
g. ____ la luna de miel
h. ____ la separación
i. ____ el divorcio

PALABRAS Y EXPRESIONES ÚTILES

el Príncipe Azul	*Prince Charming* (lit. *Blue Prince)*
si no me meta en líos con	*if it doesn't get me into trouble with*
¡Vaya sorpresa!	*What a surprise!*
los padrinos	*the godparents*
los compadres	*co-parents (i.e., the godparents of a child)*
¡Enhorabuena!	*Congratulations!*

- Quickly scan **Actividad A** of **Después de ver** before you watch the video segment.

Después de ver

A. ¿Cuánto recuerda Ud. de la conversación entre Lola y Eva? Empareje frases de las dos columnas para formar oraciones completas.

1. ____ Lola y Eva piensan salir a cenar e ir al cine esta noche a menos que...
2. ____ Eva le cuenta a Lola que su amiga Susana...
3. ____ Susana cree que su novio es la persona más cariñosa y dulce en todo el mundo, pero...
4. ____ Eva dice que puede guardar el secreto de Lola con tal de que...
5. ____ El secreto que Lola le cuenta a Eva es que...
6. ____ Lola le pide a Eva que...

a. ella y Jesús sean los padrinos del nuevo bebé.
b. ella y Manolo están esperando otro hijo.
c. Lola cree que no hay nadie que sea tan perfecto.
d. no la meta en líos con su marido.
e. sus maridos hayan hecho otros planes.
f. tiene un nuevo novio y que está totalmente enamorada de él.

B. Paso 1. Un dicho (*saying*) español dice: «Cuando te cases, mira bien lo que haces.» ¿Ha considerado Ud. lo que implica el matrimonio? Con dos compañeros de clase, túrnense (*take turns*) para comentar las siguientes afirmaciones.

Escala: 4 = Estoy totalmente de acuerdo.
3 = Me inclino a pensar lo mismo.
2 = No estoy totalmente de acuerdo.
1 = No estoy de acuerdo para nada.

1. ____ El matrimonio es para siempre. Una vez casada, una pareja no debe separarse por ninguna razón. Las leyes (*laws*) deben ser modificadas para que el divorcio sea más difícil de obtener.
2. ____ El matrimonio debe ser para siempre —especialmente cuando hay niños—, pero se debe permitir el divorcio en casos de mal tratamiento o de abuso físico.
3. ____ El divorcio es un hecho (*fact*) establecido de la vida moderna y no se debe ni considerarlo como algo malo ni cambiar las leyes sobre el mismo.
4. ____ El divorcio es preferible a la continuación de un matrimonio cuando la pareja es muy infeliz y no ve ninguna otra manera de mejorar la situación.
5. ____ El matrimonio no es nada más que un estado legal promovido (*promoted*) por la religión y el gobierno para regular y controlar las relaciones socioeconómicas de la familia.

Paso 2. Elijan a un miembro de su grupo para compartir la conclusión del grupo con el resto de la clase. Comenten las conclusiones de los otros grupos también.

Capítulo 16

A PRIMERA VISTA

Antes de ver

¿Ha pensado Ud. en su futura profesión? Conteste las siguientes preguntas sobre sus planes. Si Ud. ya ejerce una profesión, haga comentarios sobre qué hace y cómo llegó a hacerlo.

1. ¿Qué profesión piensa seguir después de graduarse en la universidad? (Puede mencionar más de una opción.) ______________________________
2. ¿Es necesario conseguir formación profesional después de graduarse? ❑ sí ❑ no

   ¿Qué tipo de formación es? ______________________________

   ¿Por cuánto tiempo dura (*lasts*)? ______________________________
3. ¿Ha preparado ya su currículum? ❑ sí ❑ no
4. ¿Ha pensado Ud. en...
   a. cómo serán las entrevistas? ❑ sí ❑ no
   b. el tipo de preguntas que le harán los entrevistadores? ❑ sí ❑ no
   c. las mejores respuestas que Ud. puede darles? ❑ sí ❑ no

- Quickly scan **Actividad A** of **Después de ver** before you watch the video segment.

Después de ver

A. ¿Cuánto recuerda Ud. del episodio? Complete las siguientes oraciones con la frase apropiada.

1. Lupe busca un trabajo o de (*either as a*) ____ porque ese puesto ofrecerá horas flexibles.
   a. bibliotecaria o de peluquera
   b. mecánica o de fisioterapeuta
   c. vendedora o de recepcionista
2. Una de las responsabilidades que tendrá Lupe si consigue el puesto en el banco será la de ____.
   a. contestar preguntas sobre todos los servicios del banco
   b. servirles café de vez en cuando a los gerentes (*managers*) del banco
   c. llevar las cuentas en caso de urgencia
3. A Lupe le gustaba mucho su puesto en la oficina del abogado, pero lo dejó porque allí querían que ella ____.
   a. estudiara en la facultad de derecho
   b. trabajara la jornada completa
   c. trabajara los sábados
4. Según la Sra. Ibáñez, el banco busca a una persona que ____.
   a. tenga interés en trabajar todos los sábados en una sucursal en las afueras del D.F.
   b. tenga ambiciones de adelantarse (*getting ahead*) dentro del banco hasta llegar a ser gerenta
   c. sea amable, que aprenda rápido y que sepa escribir a máquina y usar una computadora

B. **Paso 1.** Con un compañero / una compañera de clase, hagan el papel de entrevistado/a y director(a) de personal de una compañía. Escojan el campo (*field*) de negocios a que se dedica la compañía y cuál es el puesto que se ofrece. Piensen también en las responsibilidades del puesto y en los requisitos necesarios que deben tener los/las aspirantes. Preparen las preguntas y respuestas apropiadas.

Paso 2. Ahora presenten la entrevista ante la clase. Cuando todos hayan presentado sus entrevistas, la clase debe decidir cuál fue la mejor entrevista y quién obtendrá el puesto solicitado.

Capítulo 17

A PRIMERA VISTA

Antes de ver

A. ¿Cómo se mantiene Ud. al tanto de (*up-to-date on*) las noticias? Marque cada medio de comunicación que utiliza y el número de veces a la semana que lo usa.

	0	1–2	3–5	6–7
1. un periódico nacional	❑	❑	❑	❑
2. un periódico local	❑	❑	❑	❑
3. una revista de noticias	❑	❑	❑	❑
4. un noticiero nacional televisivo	❑	❑	❑	❑
5. un noticiero local televisivo	❑	❑	❑	❑
6. un programa de noticias locales de la radio	❑	❑	❑	❑
7. un programa de noticias nacionales de la radio	❑	❑	❑	❑
8. el Internet	❑	❑	❑	❑

B. Conteste las siguientes preguntas sobre cómo Ud. y sus amigos comentan los temas actuales.

1. ¿Es Ud. miembro de un grupo que se reúne regularmente para comentar temas de interés para los miembros? ❑ sí ❑ no

2. ¿Cuáles son los temas de conversación preferidos cuando Ud. se reúne con los amigos?
   - ❑ las bellas artes
   - ❑ los chismes (*gossip*)
   - ❑ los deportes
   - ❑ la ecología
   - ❑ la política internacional
   - ❑ la política nacional
   - ❑ la literatura
   - ❑ otro: ________________

3. ¿Dónde se reúnen Ud. y sus amigos?
   - ❑ un bar
   - ❑ un café
   - ❑ una casa o un apartamento
   - ❑ un restaurante
   - ❑ la unión estudiantil
   - ❑ otro lugar: ________________

PALABRAS Y EXPRESIONES ÚTILES

echar de menos	*to miss* (*the presence of someone or something*)
cuanto antes	**lo más rápido posible**

- Quickly scan **Actividad A** of **Después de ver** before you watch the video segment.

Después de ver

A. Complete las siguientes oraciones con la frase apropiada.

1. Lola no puede participar en la tertulia con Manolo porque ____.
   a. no se siente muy bien
   b. tiene muchos exámenes que corregir
   c. tiene que escribir una crítica para el lunes

2. Cuando Manolo llega al bar, Maricarmen y Paco ya están discutiendo sobre ____.
   a. la política b. la literatura c. quién pagará las tapas

3. Según Maricarmen, los líderes del partido de Paco creen que ____.
   a. no se puede creer todo lo que se lee en la prensa
   b. tienen soluciones razonables a problemas graves
   c. tienen el derecho de dictar cómo viven los demás

4. Según Paco, durante los últimos años del gobierno del anterior presidente, ____.
   a. había huelgas, desempleo y desastres económicos
   b. aprobaron (*they passed*) varias leyes laborales desastrosas
   c. la prensa distorsionó las actividades del gobierno

5. La única cosa en que Paco, Maricarmen y Manolo están de acuerdo es en que ____.
   a. no están de acuerdo
   b. las gambas del bar son enormes
   c. el camarero está de huelga

B. Paso 1. Con cuatro compañeros de clase, refiéranse a las respuestas que dieron en **la Actividad B** de **Antes de ver.** ¿Cuáles son los medios de información más utilizados por el grupo? (Mencionen medios *específicos* en su región.) En la opinión del grupo, ¿cuáles son los medios de información más imparciales? ¿Y los que tienen la cobertura (*coverage*) más amplia? ¿Y los que son más útiles para el público cuando toma decisiones?

Paso 2. Elijan a un miembro del grupo para que presente las conclusiones al resto de la clase. Comenten las conclusiones de los otros grupos.

Capítulo 18

A PRIMERA VISTA

Antes de ver

HORIZONTALES

1. El ____ se usa para lavarse el pelo.
2. Cuando no hay ninguna habitación desocupada se dice que el hotel está ____.
6. El viajero va a un hotel o una pensión para buscar ____.
8. La viajera que se aloja en un hotel es la ____ del hotel.
9. El documento que, por lo general, un viajero necesita para poder cruzar una frontera internacional es el ___.
10. El ____ ayuda a los viajeros a llevar sus maletas a la habitación.

VERTICALES

1. Algunos toman una ____ de whisky durante un vuelo para calmar los nervios.
3. Es siempre buena idea darle una ____ al camarero, taxista o botones.
4. En la recepción del hotel, un viajero tiene que llenar un ____ con algunos datos personales.
5. Los turistas y las personas de negocios son los ____ más frecuentes.
7. En ciertos países, solamente se puede comprar sellos, tabaco y fósforos en un ____.

- Quickly scan **Actividad A** of **Después de ver** before you watch the video segment.

Después de ver

A. ¿Cuánto recuerda Ud. del episodio? Empareje frases de las dos columnas para formar oraciones completas.

1. ____ Diego invita a Lupe a acompañarlo a la península de Yucatán...
2. ____ También quiere que Lupe lo acompañe a...
3. ____ En la agencia de viajes, Lupe y Diego quieren saber...
4. ____ No quieren viajar en avión porque el autobús...
5. ____ Los jóvenes quieren un hotel que sea decente...
6. ____ Quieren pasar una semana en Yucatán...
7. ____ Es probable que Diego pase por la aduana de los Estados Unidos...

a. California para conocer a los padres de él.
b. cuánto cuesta el pasaje a Mérida, Yucatán, en autobús.
c. donde él piensa visitar las ruinas de Chichén Itzá.
d. más rápidamente que Lupe porque él es ciudadano de los Estados Unidos.
e. pero no muy caro, no tienen dinero para pagar un hotel de lujo.
f. sale más barato y también porque pueden ver el paisaje (*countryside*).
g. y dos en California.

B. Paso 1. Con dos compañeros de clase, hagan planes para un viaje a un destino (*destination*) que Uds. creen que será una verdadera aventura. Expliquen por qué consideran que será una aventura. Incluyan detalles como:

- cómo llegarán a ese destino
- el tipo de alojamiento que tendrán allí
- lo que harán
- los problemas que enfrentarán (*you will face*)
- qué es lo extraordinario de ese lugar

Paso 2. Compartan sus planes con el resto de la clase. La clase debe escoger el destino 1) lleno de más aventuras, 2) que no representa una verdadera aventura, 3) más divertido y 4) que a la mayoría le gustaría visitar.

B. *A segunda vista*

Primeros pasos

A SEGUNDA VISTA

Antes de ver

Conteste las siguientes preguntas personales.

1. ¿Cómo se llama Ud.? ______
2. ¿Cuántos años tiene? ______
3. ¿Qué materias estudia? ______
4. ¿De dónde es? ______
5. ¿Cuántas clases tiene cada semana? ______
6. ¿A qué hora es la clase de español? ______
7. ¿Cómo se llama el profesor / la profesora? ______
8. ¿Cómo es? ______

¿Hay alguna pregunta que desea hacerle al profesor / a la profesora? Escríbala aquí.

______

Después de ver

A. Llene cada espacio en blanco con la forma correcta de una de las palabras y expresiones a continuación. **¡OJO!** Dos de las palabras se usan más de una vez.

estar	llamar	ser
gracias	mucho gusto	tres menos cuarto
gustar	qué tal	

DIEGO: Perdón. ¿Es usted el profesor Salazar?

PROFESOR: Sí, yo ______.[1]

DIEGO: Buenas tardes. Me ______[2] Diego González. Soy el estudiante de la Universidad de California.

PROFESOR: Ah, sí. El estudiante de Los Ángeles. ______.[3]

DIEGO: Igualmente.

PROFESOR: ¡Bienvenido a México! Él es Antonio Sifuentes. Es estudiante posgraduado en la facultad.

ANTONIO: ¿ ______,[4] Diego?

DIEGO: Muy bien, ______.[5] ¿Y tú?

ANTONIO: Muy bien. Mucho gusto.

DIEGO: Igualmente, Antonio.

PROFESOR: ¡Ay! ¡Es tarde! Son las ____________,[6] y tengo una reunión con el director del Museo de Antropología a las tres. Con permiso.

ANTONIO: Cómo no, profesor. (...) Bueno, Diego, ¿te ____________[7] México?

DIEGO: Sí, mucho. ¿Tú eres de la Ciudad de México?

ANTONIO: Sí, ____________[8] de aquí. (...) Mira, allí ____________[9] una amiga mía. Se ____________[10] Lupe Carrasco. Vamos, te presento.

DIEGO: ¡Vamos!

B. ¿Cómo es usted? Escriba tres oraciones en las que describa su aspecto físico y su personalidad.

____

____

____

____

Capítulo 1

A SEGUNDA VISTA

Antes de ver

1. ¿Cuáles son tres de los aspectos que *más* le gustan de la vida universitaria?

   a. ______________________________

   b. ______________________________

   c. ______________________________

2. ¿Cuales son tres de los aspectos que *menos* le gustan?

   a. ______________________________

   b. ______________________________

   c. ______________________________

3. ¿Cuáles son algunos buenos lugares en su universidad para conocer a (*to meet*) otras personas?

   ____

Después de ver

A. En el episodio previo, Diego iba a conocer a (*was going to meet*) Lupe Carrasco. Ahora los dos se encuentran (*meet*) en la librería. Llene cada espacio en blanco con la forma correcta de una de las palabras a continuación.

antropología	estudiar	ser
buscar	favorito	sicología
cantar	librería	tomar
estar		

Un día, Diego y Lupe se encuentran tres veces en la ______________[1] de la universidad. Los dos ______________[2] libros para sus clases. Es obvio que Diego ______________[3] un poco tímido, y se despide de[a] Lupe en seguida.[b] Unos momentos después, se encuentran otra vez. Ahora Lupe busca un libro para su clase de ______________[4] precolombina, una de sus clases ______________.[5] Después de hablar un poco más, se despiden otra vez.

Bueno, la tercera es la vencida.[c] Cuando se encuentran esta vez, Lupe busca un libro de ______________[6] y uno para su clase de arte. A Diego le gusta el arte y especialmente la música. Resulta que a él le gusta ______________[7] y bailar. Pues, a Lupe también le gusta bailar. Por fin, Diego invita a Lupe a ______________[8] un café. Ella acepta y, además, le dice:[d] «Como tenemos el mismo curso de antropología, ¿por qué no ______________[9] juntos?» Parece que[e] por fin van a conocerse mejor.[f]

[a]se... *says good-bye to* [b]en... *right away* [c]la... *the third time's the charm* [d]le... *she says to him*
[e]Parece... *It seems that* [f]van... *they're going to get to know one another better*

B. Para Diego y Lupe, es un poco difícil dar el primer paso (*to take the first step*) para llegar a conocerse mejor. Muchas personas tienen dificultades en esta situación, pero otras personas no. ¿Cómo es Ud. en esas situaciones?

❑ un poco tímido/a ❑ moderado/a ❑ un poco atrevido/a (*forward*)

En su opinión, ¿cuál es la mejor manera de presentarse a una persona que Ud. no conoce?

____

____

Capítulo 2

A SEGUNDA VISTA

Antes de ver

¿Es muy unida su familia? Indique la frecuencia con que Ud. hace las siguientes cosas.

3 = con frecuencia 2 = a veces 1 = casi nunca

	3	**2**	**1**
1. Les pido consejos a (*I ask for advice from*) mis padres/hijos.	❑	❑	❑
2. Les pido consejos a mis hermanos.	❑	❑	❑
3. Mis hermanos me piden consejos a mí.	❑	❑	❑
4. Invito a mis parientes a mis fiestas.	❑	❑	❑
5. Asisto a las fiestas que hacen mis parientes.	❑	❑	❑
6. Visito a mi familia los fines de semana.	❑	❑	❑
7. Les presento mis amigos a mis padres/hijos.	❑	❑	❑

Total: ______

1–7 Parece que Ud. no se siente muy unido/a a su familia.
7–14 Parece que Ud. no se siente ni muy unido/a a su familia ni muy distante de ella.
14–21 Parece que Ud. se siente muy unido/a a su familia.

Después de ver

A. En este episodio, Ud. conoce a varias personas en Quito, Ecuador. Llene cada espacio en blanco con la forma correcta de una de las palabras a continuación. **¡OJO!** Una de las palabras se usa dos veces.

hermano	novio	tener
hijo	pariente	tío
joven	primo	viejo

Elisa Velasco está ordenando fotos para su nuevo álbum. Suena[a] el teléfono y su ______________,[1] José Miguel, lo contesta.[b] Es su ______________[2] Paloma, que lo invita a ver una película con ella y su nuevo ______________,[3] Gustavo. José Miguel acepta y, luego, ayuda a[c] su mamá. Los dos separan las fotos en dos grupos: uno, de fotos ______________[4] y otro, de las recientes.

José Miguel no reconoce a algunos de sus ______________[5] que aparecen en las fotos viejas. El ______________[6] Ernesto, por ejemplo, tiene el pelo blanco ahora, lo cual[d] es diferente de su imagen en la foto. Tampoco[e] reconoce a Miguel, el ______________[7] de su mamá y padre de Paloma. En la foto ______________[8] sólo tres o cuatro años.

Cuando Paloma llega, presenta a Gustavo a su ______________[9] Elisa. José Miguel y Gustavo ya se conocen. Después de las presentaciones, los ______________[10] salen para ir al cine.

[a]*Rings* [b]lo... *answers it* [c]ayuda... *helps* [d]lo... *which* [e]*Neither*

B. ¿Puede Ud. hacer una foto con palabras? Escoja a un miembro de su familia y describa su aspecto físico. ¿Cómo es? ¿Es alta o baja esta persona? ¿Se ve joven o vieja? ¿Tiene el pelo moreno, negro o rubio? Conteste estas preguntas y agregue más información.

____

____

____

____

Capítulo 3

A SEGUNDA VISTA

Antes de ver

¿Qué ropa está de moda este año? Dé una ojeada por (*Glance around*) la sala de clase y escriba tres prendas de ropa y dos colores que están de moda ahora. ¿Recuerda dos prendas y colores que estaban de moda (*were in style*) el año pasado (o antes) y que ahora no están de moda? Escríbalos aquí también.

Ropa que está de moda este año	Ropa que no está de moda este año
1. __________	1. __________
2. __________	2. __________
3. __________	3. __________

Colores que están de moda	Colores que ahora no están de moda
1. __________	1. __________
2. __________	2. __________

Después de ver

A. En este episodio, José Miguel y su prima Paloma caminan por las calles de Quito, Ecuador. Llene cada espacio en blanco con la forma correcta de los siguientes verbos.

ir	querer	venir
preferir	tener	

Una mañana, rumbo a[a] la universidad, José Miguel le pregunta a Paloma[b] si __________[1] a la fiesta de Eduardo. Ella le dice[c] que no, que __________[2] ir al cine con Gustavo. Al contrario, José Miguel __________[3] ganas de ir porque le gustan las fiestas de Eduardo. Entonces pasan por una tienda que __________[4] en el escaparate[d] un letrero[e] que anuncia: «¡GRANDES REBAJAS!»

—¿Entramos? —le pregunta Paloma—. __________[5] que comprar *bluejeans*, y si hay rebajas, mejor.

José Miguel no __________[6] entrar porque no __________[7] ganas de ir de compras. Pero, al ver[f] la ropa en la tienda, cambia de idea.[g] La empleada __________[8] a ayudarlo[h] y él decide probarse[i] una camisa y un par de pantalones. Así que, cuando Paloma está lista[j] para salir, él *no* está listo.

Entonces Paloma está un poco enojada. —«¡Ay! Ahora que __________[9] con los *bluejeans*, lista para salir, *él* decide que sí __________[10] ir de compras. ¡¿Quién comprende a los hombres?!»

[a]rumbo... *on their way to* [b]le... *asks Paloma* [c]le... *tells him* [d]*display window* [e]*sign* [f]al... *upon seeing* [g]cambia... *he changes his mind* [h]*help him* [i]*to try on* [j]*ready*

B. ¿Qué tipo de ropa prefiere Ud. llevar? ¿Depende de qué hace y dónde está? Haga una breve descripción de lo que lleva los días de entresemana (*weekdays*) y los fines de semana. ¿Hay mucha diferencia entre la ropa que lleva esos días?

Capítulo 4

A SEGUNDA VISTA

Antes de ver

¿Cómo es la situación en que Ud. vive? ¿Vive con sus padres o hijos? ¿en una residencia estudiantil? ¿en un apartamento con amigos? Escriba tres de las cosas que a Ud. le gustan de esa situación y tres de las que no le gustan.

Lo que me gusta	Lo que no me gusta
1. ____________________	1. ____________________
2. ____________________	2. ____________________
3. ____________________	3. ____________________

Después de ver

A. Paso 1. ¿Cuánto recuerda Ud. de este episodio? Todas las siguientes afirmaciones sobre el episodio son falsas. Corríjalas, escribiendo oraciones completas.

1. Es obvio que a la tía Matilde no le importa mucho qué ropa lleva Diego cuando habla con su profesor.

   ____

   ____

2. Para Diego, es muy satisfactorio vivir en casa de su tía Matilde.

   ____

   ____

3. En la alcoba del apartamento que Diego va a compartir (*share*) con Antonio y Juan no hay ni cama ni donde poner la ropa.

   ____

   ____

4. El horario de Antonio es perfecto porque puede despertar a Diego a las cinco de la mañana todos los días de la semana.

   ____

   ____

Paso 2. Escriba dos de las cualidades o costumbres de la tía Matilde que a Diego le gustan y dos de las que no le gustan.

Cualidades o costumbres agradables	Cualidades o costumbres desagradables
1. ____________________	1. ____________________
2. ____________________	2. ____________________

B. Aunque la tía Matilde es una buena persona, también le gusta meterse (*get involved*) en la vida de su sobrino Diego. ¿Conoce Ud. a una persona parecida (*similar*) a ella? ¿Quién es? ¿Qué hace? ¿Qué hace Ud. para no molestarse (*bother yourself*) con esta persona? Escríbalo en un párrafo corto.

____

____

____

____

____

Capítulo 5

A SEGUNDA VISTA

Antes de ver

Gracias a la tecnología, es posible nadar en pleno invierno y jugar al hockey durante el verano. Sin embargo (*Nevertheless*), todavía hay actividades que hacemos durante determinadas estaciones. ¿Cuál es su estación favorita? ¿Por qué le gusta tanto? ¿Qué tiempo hace en la región donde vive Ud. durante esta estación? ¿Qué actividades hace Ud. durante esta estación?

Estación favorita: ________________ Tiempo que hace normalmente: ______________________________

____

Por qué me gusta: ____

Mis actividades durante esta estación:

____

Después de ver

A. Paso 1. En este episodio Ud. conoce a algunos personajes de Sevilla, España. Todas las siguientes afirmaciones sobre el episodio son falsas. Corríjalas, escribiendo oraciones completas.

1. Manolo quiere quedarse en casa mañana porque el pronóstico del tiempo dice que va a hacer muy mal tiempo.

   ____

   ____

2. Carolina Díaz llama por teléfono para estudiar con Marta esta tarde.

   ____

   ____

3. En Sevilla está lloviendo a cántaros (*it's raining cats and dogs*) mientras que en La Coruña hace buen tiempo.

   ____

   ____

4. Lola está preocupada por sus clases en la universidad porque los estudiantes son perezosos y antipáticos.

   ____

   ____

5. Carlos Suárez invita a Manolo y a su familia a visitarlo en La Coruña al día siguiente.

   ____

   ____

Paso 2. Llene los espacios en blanco con los adjetivos que mejor describen a Lola y a Manolo.

cariñoso/a	desorganizado/a	preocupado/a
contento/a	juguetón/juguetona (*playful*)	simpático/a

1. En su opinión, ¿cómo son Lola y Manolo como pareja (*couple*), normalmente?

____

____

2. Y esta mañana, ¿cómo está Manolo?

____

____

3. Y Lola, ¿cómo está?

____

____

B. El clima de la región de Castilla-La Mancha, donde se encuentra Madrid, España, queda descrito (*is described*) irónicamente en un dicho (*saying*): «Hay tres meses de invierno y nueve de infierno (*hell*).» ¿Es así el clima donde vive Ud.? Descríbalo brevemente. ¿Preferiría Ud. (*Would you prefer*) vivir en un lugar donde el clima es diferente?

____

____

____

____

Capítulo 6

A SEGUNDA VISTA

Antes de ver

¿Qué hace Ud. para celebrar las ocasiones especiales de su vida? ¿Cena en un restaurante elegante? ¿Hace una fiesta? ¿Va de vacaciones? En un párrafo corto, describa lo que le gusta hacer para celebrar una ocasión especial.

Ocasión: ____________________

____

____

____

Después de ver

A. ¿Recuerda Ud. lo que pidieron (*ordered*) Lola y Manolo en el restaurante? Llene cada espacio en blanco con la forma correcta de una de las siguientes palabras para completar el diálogo.

asado	decir	recomendar
atún	ensalada	rico
bistec	plato	sopa

CAMARERO: ¿Ya saben lo que desean de comer los señores?

MANOLO: Creo que sí, pero, ¿qué ____________[1] Ud.?

CAMARERO: Hoy tenemos un ____________[2] especial: gambas al limón con arroz, un plato ligero y delicioso. Y también tenemos un salmón buenísimo que acaba de llegar esta tarde.

LOLA: ¡Qué ____________![3] Yo quiero las gambas, por favor.

MANOLO: Eh, para mí, el ____________[4] estilo argentino, poco ____________.[5] Y una ____________[6] mixta para dos.

CAMARERO: ¿Y para empezar? Tenemos una ____________[7] de ajo muy rica.

LOLA: Para mí, una sopa, por favor.

MANOLO: Y para mí, también. Y le ____________[8] al chef que por favor le ponga un poco de ____________[9] a la ensalada.

CAMARERO: Muy bien, señor.

B. A continuación hay algunas adivinanzas (*riddles*) españolas relacionadas con la comida y la acción de comer. Con un compañero / una compañera de clase, traten de adivinarlas (*guess them*).

1. A pesar de[a] tener patas[b]
yo no me puedo mover;
llevo encima la comida
y no la puedo comer.

Respuesta: ______________________________

2. Me cuentan por docenas
y me guardan en las alacenas.[c]

Respuesta: ______________________________

3. Blanca nací,[d] blanca fui;[e]
pobres y ricos comen de mí.

Respuesta: ______________________________

4. Llenos de agua, llenos de vino;
sobre la mesa están y son de cristal fino.

Respuesta: ______________________________

5. Blanca por dentro y verde por fuera,
si no lo adivinas, espera.

Respuesta: ______________________________

[a]A... *Despite* [b]*legs* [c]*cupboards* [d]*I was born* [e]*I was*

Capítulo 7

A SEGUNDA VISTA

Antes de ver

¿Hizo Ud. un viaje en los últimos años? Llene el siguiente cuestionario sobre ese viaje.

CUESTIONARIO

Destino (*Destination*): ______________________________

Medio(s) de transporte: ______________________________

Donde se alojó: ______________________________

Actividades en que participó: ______________

¿Llevó ropa apropiada? ❑ sí ❑ no

¿ropa suficiente? ❑ sí ❑ no

Si contesta que no, explique. ______________________________

Recuerdos (*souvenirs*) que compró: ______________________________

____

Después de ver

A. Ud. ya sabe que Elisa Velasco escribe artículos sobre los viajes. ¿Cuánto recuerda de su última visita a la agencia de viajes? Todas las siguientes afirmaciones sobre el episodio son falsas. Corríjalas, escribiendo oraciones completas.

1. Elisa viajó a las Galápagos el año pasado.

____

____

2. A Elisa le gustaría ir de Guayaquil a las Galápagos en barco y quedarse allí dos semanas.

____

____

3. Naturalmente, Elisa prefiere pagar en efectivo (*in cash*).

____

____

4. Cuando el Sr. Gómez y su esposa estuvieron en las islas Galápagos, cazaron (*hunted*) animales exóticos.

____

____

B. Imagínese que Ud. está de vacaciones en que, en su opinión, es el lugar más exótico del mundo. Quiere escribirles una tarjeta postal a sus compañeros de clase. Dígales dónde está, qué está haciendo y otros datos (*information*) interesantes.

Queridos (Dear) *compañeros de clase,*

____

____

____

____

____

Reciban un abrazo (hug) *de*

____

Capítulo 8

A SEGUNDA VISTA

Antes de ver

1. Piense en los días festivos. ¿Cuáles son los días festivos más importantes para Ud.?

   ______________________________ ______________________________

2. ¿Por qué son tan importantes?

   ____

3. ¿Qué día festivo le gusta menos?

   ____

4. ¿Por qué?

   ____

5. Hay días festivos para conmemorar sucesos religiosos y seculares importantes. Ahora, piense en algo (serio o no) que Ud. cree que merece (*deserves*) ser conmemorado con un día festivo. ¿Qué es?

   ____

6. ¿En qué consistirían (*would consist*) esas festividades?

   ____

Después de ver

A. En las reuniones familiares suele haber (*there is usually*) alguien que vuelve a contar las cosas graciosas, y por lo general ya bien conocidas, que algunos miembros de la familia hicieron alguna vez. Cuente brevemente cómo Lola se portó el día de su primera comunión y cómo los padres de Lola tuvieron dos árboles navideños el mismo año.

LA PRIMERA COMUNIÓN DE LOLA	LOS DOS ÁRBOLES NAVIDEÑOS
______________________________	______________________________
______________________________	______________________________
______________________________	______________________________
______________________________	______________________________
______________________________	______________________________
______________________________	______________________________
______________________________	______________________________

B. ¿Ha presenciado (*Have you witnessed*) un incidente en que alguien, en una ocasión solemne, hizo algo ridículo que causó mucha risa (*laughter*)? Narre el incidente.

____

____

____

____

Capítulo 9

A SEGUNDA VISTA

Antes de ver

Escriba, en orden de preferencia para Ud., los seis pasatiempos que más le gustan para los fines de semana.

1. ______________________ 4. ______________________

2. ______________________ 5. ______________________

3. ______________________ 6. ______________________

¿Varían los pasatiempos de estación a estación? ❑ sí ❑ no
Explique:

____

____

Después de ver

A. Llene cada espacio en blanco con una forma del imperfecto o el pretérito de uno de los siguientes verbos, según el contexto. **¡OJO!** Uno de los verbos se usa más de una vez.

aceptar	invitar	prometer	ser
entrar	ir	querer	tener
estar	preguntar	salir	

Una tarde, Lupe ______________[1] a casa de Diego a invitar a los compañeros de casa de Diego a una fiesta sorpresa para él. Todos estaban de acuerdo en que ______________[2] una idea fantástica y ______________[3] la invitación, con excepción de Rocio. A ella no le era posible asistir ya que[a] ______________[4] planes para ese día. Sus padres iban a venir al D. F. y ella ______________[5] al Ballet Folklórico con ellos esa noche. Todos ______________[6] no decirle nada a Diego.

Después de que Rocio y Juan ______________[7] para el cine a ver una película, Antonio le confió[b] a Lupe que Diego ______________[8] invitarla a un concierto. Pero, justo en el momento en que Antonio le ______________[9] a Lupe si le gustaría ir, ______________[10] Diego. —¿Van Uds. al concierto? —les preguntó. Antonio, divertido,[c] le explicó que *él* no ______________[11] invitando a Lupe. Lupe le explicó todo a Diego y le preguntó si él iba a invitarla al concierto o no. Diego, por supuesto, la ______________[12] y ella —por supuesto— aceptó.

[a]ya... *since* [b]*confided* [c]*amused*

B. ¿Qué hizo Ud. el pasado fin de semana? Escriba un párrafo corto en el que describa cómo se divirtió. Escriba qué hizo, con quién(es) estuvo, adónde fue y otros datos relevantes.

____

____

____

____

____

____

Capítulo 10

A SEGUNDA VISTA

Antes de ver

Hay un dicho (*saying*) español que dice: «Más vale prevenir que curar.» Escriba tres cosas que Ud. no hace porque son dañosas (*harmful*) a la salud y tres cosas que sí hace porque son buenas para la salud.

Cosas dañosas que evito (*I avoid*)	Cosas buenas que hago
1. ______________________	4. ______________________
2. ______________________	5. ______________________
3. ______________________	6. ______________________

Después de ver

A. ¿Qué pasó en el consultorio de la Dra. Méndez? Indique cuáles de las siguientes afirmaciones son ciertas y cuáles son falsas. Corrija las falsas.

	CIERTO	FALSO
1. La enfermedad de Marta no es muy seria. ______________________	❑	❑
2. Marta se va a sentir mejor y puede volver a la escuela mañana. ______________________	❑	❑
3. Esta mañana Lola se sentía muy bien. ______________________	❑	❑
4. Manolo se acuerda de lo preciosa que era Marta cuando era pequeña. ______________________	❑	❑
5. Manolo no se lleva la menor sorpresa (*is not the least bit surprised*) cuando Lola lo invita a entrar en la tienda de ropa de maternidad. ______________________ ______________________	❑	❑

B. ¿Se llevó Ud. una gran sorpresa alguna vez? ¿Cuál fue? ¿Fue una sorpresa buena o mala? ¿Cómo afectó su vida? ¿Afectó también la vida de sus amigos? ¿de su familia? Escriba un párrafo corto que describe lo que le pasó.

____

____

____

____

____

Capítulo 11

A SEGUNDA VISTA

Antes de ver

¿Cuáles son las principales causas del estrés en su vida? ¿Qué hace Ud. para reducir los efectos del estrés?

Causas del estrés	Maneras de reducir los efectos del estrés
1. ______________________	4. ______________________
2. ______________________	5. ______________________
3. ______________________	6. ______________________

¿Cree Ud. que reacciona bien en situaciones que le causan estrés o no? ❑ sí ❑ no

Explique: ____

____

Después de ver

A. Llene los espacios en blanco con palabras y expresiones de la lista a continuación.

caérsele   levantarse   rompérsele
darse con   perdérsele

ELISA: ¿Qué te pasa, hijo?

JOSÉ MIGUEL: ¡Qué horrible día! Tuve muy mala suerte hoy.

MARÍA: ¿Cómo? Cuéntanos cómo fue.

JOSÉ MIGUEL: No sé... Es que todo me salió mal. Fui al mercado esta mañana. Como iba muy distraído, ______________[1] una señora en el camino. ¡Qué vergüenza! Estaba a punto de regresar a casa cuando ______________[2] la bolsa. ¡Qué lío! Gracias a Dios, una señora me dio otra bolsa. También ______________[3] las llaves. No las pude encontrar. Por eso toqué a la puerta. ¿Ven? No sé qué me pasó hoy, pero tuve un día horrible. Bueno, mamá, aquí están las compras del mercado.

ELISA: ¡Ay! ¡José Miguel! ¡______________[4] todo! (...)

JOSÉ MIGUEL: Parece que ______________[5] con el pie izquierdo hoy. ¡Qué lata! (...)

MARÍA: Bueno, pero hay algo bueno en todo esto.

ELISA: ¿Qué es?

MARÍA: ¡Que no llevamos una vida aburrida!

B. Todo el mundo tiene, de vez en cuando, un día horrible. Piense en un día horrible que tuvo Ud. y haga una lista de las cosas que le salieron mal. ¿Realmente le salió mal *todo*?

1. ______________________________
2. ______________________________
3. ______________________________
4. ______________________________

Capítulo 12

A SEGUNDA VISTA

Antes de ver

Conteste las siguientes preguntas sobre Ud. y las computadoras.

1. ¿Tiene Ud. computadora? ❑ sí ❑ no
   Si no tiene una, ¿utiliza Ud. la computadora de un amigo / una amiga o una de la universidad? ❑ sí ❑ no
   ¿Le gustaría tener una? ❑ sí ❑ no
2. ¿Para qué aprovecha (*make use of*) Ud. la computadora?
   - ❑ buscar información
   - ❑ componer música
   - ❑ diseñar gráficos
   - ❑ mandar y recibir el correo electrónico
   - ❑ escribir trabajos para sus clases
   - ❑ hacer compras
   - ❑ jugar a los videojuegos
   - ❑ navegar la red
   - ❑ organizar sus finanzas
   - ❑ publicar una página web
   - ❑ usar productos interactivos en CD-ROM
   - ❑ otro uso: ________________
3. ¿Qué le gusta más de las computadoras? ________________________________
4. ¿Qué le gusta menos? ________________________________

Después de ver

A. José Miguel tiene muchas ganas de comprar una computadora. ¿Cuánto recuerda Ud. de su visita a la tienda de equipo electrónico? Complete el siguiente párrafo con la forma correcta de las siguientes palabras y expresiones en los espacios en blanco.

comprar	estereofónico	planta baja
dejar	ir	vecindad
equipo	navegar	

Una tarde, Gustavo le muestra a José Miguel un anuncio de una tienda de ________________[1] electrónico que tiene una oferta especial. Como la tienda está en la ________________[2] de un edificio de su ________________,[3] deciden ir allá para mirar las computadoras. Pero, Gustavo le recomienda a José Miguel que todavía no ________________[4] una, sino que antes ________________[5] a varias tiendas para comparar los precios. Los jóvenes invitan a Paloma a acompañarlos. Pero primero, Gustavo le pide a ella que ________________[6] en casa su *walkman*. Dice que siempre que lo usa, él tiene que repetir lo que le dice varias veces. Gustavo cree que ella está loca para los aparatos ________________.[7]

En la tienda, una dependienta le muestra a José Miguel una computadora con monitor, ratón ergonómico y un módem interno. Luego, le muestra otra con CD-ROM interno y suficiente memoria para poder ________________[8] la red y utilizar programas de multimedia. Es la computadora que quiere José Miguel, pero no la compra hoy porque no tiene suficiente dinero.

B. En su opinión, ¿cuáles son las cuestiones (*issues*) más importantes con respecto a la calidad de la vida? Si indica que una cuestión le es importante, dé detalles para explicar por qué.

- ❑ cuestiones ecológicas

  ____

- ❑ cuestiones económicas

  ____

- ❑ cuestiones personales

  ____

- ❑ cuestiones morales

  ____

- ❑ cuestiones políticas

  ____

Capítulo 13

A SEGUNDA VISTA

Antes de ver

Contesta las siguientes preguntas sobre Ud. y la «cultura».

1. ¿Tiene Ud. interés en las actividades culturales? ¿Son una parte importante de su vida? ❑ sí ❑ no
2. ¿Qué actividad cultural le interesa más? ____________________
3. ¿Participa en esa actividad de alguna forma o sólo tiene afición por ella? ❑ Participo. ❑ Soy aficionado/a.
4. ¿Por qué le interesa tanto? ____________________
5. ¿Cuál es su artista favorito/a? ¿Por qué? ____________________

____

Después de ver

A. Parece que las relaciones entre Diego y Lupe se vuelven cada vez más estrechas (*close*), ¿no? ¿Cuánto recuerda Ud. de la conversación entre ellos? Todas las afirmaciones a continuación son falsas. Corríjalas, escribiendo oraciones completas.

1. Lupe duda que Diego esté tan cansado como dice porque no cree que haya estudiado mucho recientemente. ____________________

   ____
2. Lupe va a escribir su trabajo sobre los murales de José Clemente Orozco porque es su muralista preferido. ____________________

   ____
3. Diego cree que el arte moderno, por lo general, es muy feo, aunque es posible que existan algunos cuadros interesantes. ____________________

   ____
4. Lupe no cree que haya muchas cosas que le interesarían (*would interest*) a Diego en el Museo de Arte Moderno. ____________________

   ____

B. Piense en las respuestas que Ud. dio en **Antes de ver**. Imagínese que quiere introducir a alguien a la actividad cultural preferida por Ud. Ud. quiere que él/ella se lleve una buena impresión de esa actividad. Explique brevemente lo bueno de esa actividad y cuál es la mejor manera de apreciarla.

____

____

____

____

Capítulo 14

A SEGUNDA VISTA

Antes de ver

Conteste las siguientes preguntas sobre Ud. y el medio ambiente.

1. En su región, ¿hay un lugar al que se puede ir para dejar atrás por un rato el estrés de la vida diaria y sumergirse en un ambiente natural? ❑ sí ❑ no

   ¿Cuál es? ________________________________

2. ¿Va Ud. allí con frecuencia? ❑ sí ❑ no

3. ¿Qué hace Ud. personalmente para proteger o mejorar el medio ambiente?

   ____

   ____

Después de ver

A. Elisa Velasco no escribe solamente sobre los viajes, como se ve en este episodio. ¿Cuánto recuerda Ud. de su excursión al cráter del Pululahua? Llene cada espacio en blanco con la forma correcta de las siguientes palabras. Es necesario usar el participio pasado de los verbos.

acelerar	cubrir	gasolinera	recurso
aislamiento	denso	mecánico	
bello	finca	proteger	

Una tarde Elisa Velasco y José Miguel visitan el cráter del Pululahua, un volcán extinto que está al norte de Quito. Es un lugar muy ______________[1] dentro de una reserva geobotánica ______________[2] por el gobierno[a] del Ecuador. Un bosque ______________[3] cubre las laderas[b] del cráter y el fondo[c] fértil está ______________[4] por muchas pequeñas ______________[5] donde trabajan muchos agricultores.

Elisa busca en este ambiente natural la inspiración para su artículo sobre la protección de los ______________[6] naturales en el Ecuador. Mientras escribe en su computadora portátil, José Miguel explora un rato. Allí, en el ______________[7] y la tranquilidad del cráter, uno puede imaginar que se ha escapado por un rato del ritmo ______________[8] de la vida moderna.

Luego llega una señora cuyo[d] carro ha empezado a hacer ruidos extraños. La Sra. Velasco la invita a acompañarla a ella y a José Miguel a la población más cercana donde ellos van a buscar una ______________[9] porque necesitan llenar el tanque. Y allí la señora puede pedirle al ______________[10] que revise su carro.

[a]*government* [b]*slopes* [c]*bottom* [d]*whose*

B. En su opinión, ¿cuáles son los dos problemas de la vida moderna que tienen el mayor impacto en la vida de Ud. y sus amigos? ¿Por qué tienen tanto impacto en Uds.? ¿Cree que hay alguna manera de resolverlos? ¿Cuál es esa manera? Escriba sus respuestas a continuación.

Problema número 1: ______________________________

____

Razón de su impacto: ______________________________

____

Resolución: ______________________________

____

Problema número 2: ______________________________

____

Razón de su impacto: ______________________________

____

Resolución: ______________________________

____

Capítulo 15

A SEGUNDA VISTA

Antes de ver

Conteste las siguientes preguntas sobre los valores (*values*).

1. ¿Hay algunos valores compartidos (*shared*) por casi todos en nuestra sociedad? ❑ sí ❑ no
2. Si Ud. contestó que sí, ¿cuáles son? ______________________________

   ____
3. Si contestó que no, ¿por qué es así, en su opinión? ______________________________

   ____
4. En su opinión, cuáles son los lazos (*ties*) más fuertes entre la mayoría de los miembros de una sociedad? Ponga en orden de importancia los siguientes lazos, según lo que Ud. cree que es, en la realidad, no según lo que cree que debe ser.

   ____ de familia
   ____ de identidad sexual
   ____ económicos
   ____ étnicos/raciales
   ____ personales
   ____ políticos
   ____ regionales
   ____ religiosos

Después de ver

A. En este episodio, Lola le revela a su amiga Eva que está embarazada (*pregnant*). ¿Cuánto recuerda Ud. de su conversación? Todas las siguientes afirmaciones son falsas. Corríjalas, escribiendo oraciones completas.

1. Es viernes, y Lola va a un cumpleaños en Cádiz mientras Eva va a una boda en Sevilla.

   ____
2. Lola cree que Antonio, el nuevo novio de Susana, es el hombre más cariñoso y dulce del mundo.

   ____
3. Respecto al novio de Susana, Lola cree que, con tal de que tenga dinero y un coche rápido, lo demás no importa.

   ____
4. A Lola no le importa que Eva le cuente a su madre (de Lola) que está embarazada.

   ____
5. Lola le pide a Eva su opinión sobre quiénes deben ser los padrinos (*godparents*) del bebé.

   ____

B. Repase las respuestas que dio en **Antes de ver**. ¿Cuáles de esos valores cree Ud. que deberían (*should*) ser los más importantes en una sociedad ideal? ¿Y los menos importantes? ¿Por qué?

Capítulo 16

A SEGUNDA VISTA

Antes de ver

Conteste las siguientes preguntas sobre los puestos que ha tenido Ud.

1. ¿Cuál es el puesto más reciente que ha tenido Ud.? ______
2. ¿Todavía lo tiene? ❑ sí ❑ no ¿Renunció a él? ❑ sí ❑ no ¿Le gusta/gustaba? ❑ sí ❑ no
3. ¿Cuáles son/eran las responsabilidades que Ud. tiene/tenía? ______
4. ¿Qué cualidades tiene Ud. que le hacen/hacían apto/a para ese puesto? ______
5. ¿Se preparó mucho para la entrevista? ______
6. ¿Cómo se sentía antes de la entrevista para el puesto? ______
7. ¿Le presentó su currículum al entrevistador / a la entrevistadora? ❑ sí ❑ no

Después de ver

A. En este episodio, se ve que Lupe está en busca de (*in search of*) un puesto. ¿Cuánto recuerda Ud. del episodio? Conteste las siguientes preguntas, escribiendo oraciones completas.

1. ¿Qué requiere Lupe del puesto que busca? ______
2. ¿Cuáles son tres de los servicios que ofrece el banco? ______
3. ¿Por qué renunció Lupe a su puesto como recepcionista en la oficina de un abogado? ______
4. ¿Cuáles eran algunas de las responsibilidades de Lupe en la oficina del abogado? ______
5. ¿Cuáles son algunas de las cualidades que busca el banco en un/una aspirante para el puesto? ______

B. En su opinión, ¿cuáles son los puntos más fuertes que tiene Ud. como empleado/a potencial? Piense en el empleo que Ud. desea conseguir al graduarse. Escriba un párrafo corto persuasivo en que le presenta a un empleador / una empleadora posible algunas de sus cualidades positivas.

______

Capítulo 17

A SEGUNDA VISTA

Antes de ver

Conteste las siguientes preguntas sobre los acontecimientos actuales.

1. ¿Cuál es la noticia trascendental (*very important*) del momento? ______________________________
____
2. ¿Qué opina Ud. al respecto? ______________________________
____
3. ¿Cómo ha sido la cobertura (*coverage*)? ______________________________
____
4. En su opinión, ¿cómo se va a acabar? ______________________________
____

Después de ver

A. En este episodio, Manolo se reúne con sus amigos en un bar. ¿Cuánto recuerda Ud. de la discusión que tuvo lugar allí? Llene cada espacio en blanco con una palabra o frase de la lista a continuación.

acontecimiento	desempleo	política
apoyar	huelga	prensa
desastre	ley	protestar

Esta tarde, Lola no puede asistir a la tertulia, pero Manolo va sin ella. Maricarmen y Paco ya están discutiendo la ______________[1] cuando llega Manolo. Maricarmen cree que los ______________[2] recientes demuestran que el partido en poder —el que ______________[3] Paco— ha sido un ______________[4] y que sus líderes quieren dictar cómo deben vivir los demás. Manolo dice que el nuevo gobierno quiere votar una nueva ______________[5] antes de que nadie pueda ______________[6] en contra de ella. Según Paco, el problema es que, cuando el último gobierno dejó el poder, había varias ______________,[7] un desastre económico y mucho ______________.[8] De todos modos, los tres están de acuerdo en que no se puede creer todo lo que leen en la ______________.[9]

B. Haga el papel de reportero/a. Escriba una breve nota informativa sobre un acontecimiento reciente que, en su opinión, es muy importante. Incluya detalles que contesten las preguntas ¿qué?, ¿quién?, ¿dónde?, ¿cuándo? y ¿por qué?

____
____
____
____
____

Capítulo 18

A SEGUNDA VISTA

Antes de ver

Conteste las siguientes preguntas sobre Ud. y los viajes.

1. ¿Ha hecho Ud. un viaje... ? ❑ en autobús ❑ en tren ❑ en avión ❑ en crucero (*cruise ship*) ❑ de aventón (*hitchhiking*) ❑ en otro medio de transporte:
2. ¿Qué medio prefiere? ______________________________
3. ¿Qué es lo bueno de utilizar este medio? ______________________________
____
4. ¿Qué es lo malo? ______________________________
____

Después de ver

A. Bueno, casi ya ha terminado la estancia de Diego en México. Y parece que él y Lupe ahora tienen relaciones un poco más allá de la amistad, ¿verdad? ¿Cuánto recuerda Ud. del episodio? Llene los espacios en blanco con la forma correcta de las siguientes palabras.

alojamiento	desocupado	individual
avión	habitación	pasaje
baño	hotel	

DIEGO: Queremos hacerle varias preguntas sobre unos viajes que nos gustaría hacer. Primero, ¿cuánto cuesta un ______________[1] en autobús a Yucatán, digo, a Mérida?

AGENTE: ¿En autobús? ¿No quieren ir en ______________?[2]

DIEGO: Pues, el autobús sale más barato, y así podríamos ver un poco más del paisaje mexicano. (...)

AGENTE: Un pasaje en autobús, ida y vuelta, sale 600 pesos. ¿Ya tienen ______________[3] en Mérida?

LUPE: No, todavía no. Buscamos un ______________[4] que sea decente, pero que tampoco sea muy caro. (...)

AGENTE: Bueno, les puedo ofrecer ______________[5] en varios hoteles a precios muy razonables. A ver... ¿Cuándo piensan hacer el viaje?

DIEGO: La última semana de mayo.

AGENTE: Ajá... Eso va a estar un poco difícil. Casi todos los hoteles estarán completamente ocupados durante esa semana. Si viajaran una semana más tarde, encontrarían más habitaciones ______________.[6]

LUPE: Bueno, está bien. Entonces, la primera semana de junio.

AGENTE: Excelente. Les puedo ofrecer dos habitaciones ______________[7] con ______________[8] privado en el hotel Estrella del Mar.

B. Siempre se espera que un viaje sea fantástico, pero, es probable que todo el mundo haya hecho un viaje que resultó muy lejos de ser «ideal». Describa brevemente el peor viaje que Ud. haya hecho. ¿Por qué le resultó tan horrible? ¿Le habría salido mejor si Ud. hubiera hecho algo de manera diferente? Ahora que ha pasado el tiempo, ¿le parece más bien cómico que trágico el viaje?

____

____

____

____

____

C. Answers to Video Activities

A PRIMERA VISTA

PRIMEROS PASOS **Antes de ver A.** 1. S 2. D 3. S 4. D 5. S 6. D **B.** 1. c 2. e 3. d 4. a 5. f 6. b **Después de ver A.** 1. b 2. a 3. c 4. c 5. a 6. c

CAPÍTULO 1 **Después de ver A.** 1. b 2. literatura, inglés, antropología (sicología, arte moderno) 3. c 4. b 5., 6., 7. *Answers may vary.*

CAPÍTULO 2 **Antes de ver** *Horizontales:* 2. hermanos 6. madre 7. nietas 9. abuelo 10. esposo *Verticales:* 1. sobrino 3. esposa 4. mamá 5. primo 8. tío **Después de ver A.** 1. b 2. c 3. c 4. a 5. b

CAPÍTULO 3 **Después de ver A.** 1. b. JM d. P e. JM g. P 2. a, b, c, f 3. 40 4. 38 5. *bluejeans* 6. camiseta de rayas 7. Paloma

CAPÍTULO 4 **Después de ver A.** 1. d 2. e 3. f 4. b 5. c 6. a

CAPÍTULO 5 **Después de ver A.** 1. F 2. F 3. C 4. C 5. C 6. F 7. F

CAPÍTULO 6 **Después de ver A.** 1. a, c, e, f, g, i 2. b 3. a, c, e 4. a. M b. N c. L d. N e. A f. N g. A h. A

CAPÍTULO 7 **Antes de ver** *Horizontales:* 3. facturo 5. vacaciones 6. llegada 7. fotos 9. vuelta 10. maletero *Verticales:* 1. pasajero 2. atrasado 4. aeropuerto 8. sala **Después de ver A.** 1. b 2. b 3. b 4. a 5. a

CAPÍTULO 8 **Después de ver A.** 1. b 2. d 3. e 4. a 5. f 6. g 7. c

CAPÍTULO 9 **Después de ver A.** 1. b 2. a 3. c 4. c, d, f, g, i 5. a

CAPÍTULO 10 **Después de ver A.** 1. a 2. f 3. c 4. b 5. e 6. d

CAPÍTULO 11 **Después de ver A.** *Order of events:* 2, 1, 4, 3

CAPÍTULO 12 **Después de ver A.** 1. a 2. c 3. b 4. a 5. c

CAPÍTULO 13 **Después de ver A.** 1. b 2. f 3. a 4. d 5. c 6. e 7. g

CAPÍTULO 14 **Después de ver A.** 1. a 2. b 3. a 4. c 5. b

CAPÍTULO 15 **Antes de ver A.** a. 4 b. 2 c. 5 d. 6 e. 8 f. 1 g. 3 h. 7 **B.** *Answers may vary.* a. 2 b. 5 c. 3 d. 4 e. 1 f. 7 g. 6 h. 8 i. 9 **Después de ver A.** 1. e 2. f 3. c 4. d 5. b 6. a

CAPÍTULO 16 **Después de ver A.** 1. c 2. a 3. b 4. c

CAPÍTULO 17 **Después de ver A.** 1. c 2. a 3. c 4. a 5. a

CAPÍTULO 18 **Antes de ver** *Horizontales:* 1. champú 2. completo 6. alojamiento 8. huéspeda 9. pasaporte 10. botones *Verticales:* 1. copa 3. propina 4. formulario 5. viajeros 7. estanco **Después de ver A.** 1. c 2. a 3. b 4. f 5. e 6. g 7. d

A SEGUNDA VISTA

PRIMEROS PASOS **Después de ver A.** 1. soy 2. llamo 3. Mucho gusto 4. Qué tal 5. gracias 6. tres menos cuarto 7. gusta 8. soy 9. está 10. llama

CAPÍTULO 1 **Después de ver A.** 1. librería 2. buscan 3. es 4. antropología 5. favoritas 6. sicología 7. cantar 8. tomar 9. estudiamos

CAPÍTULO 2 **Después de ver A.** 1. hijo 2. prima 3. novio 4. viejas 5. parientes 6. tío 7. hermano 8. tiene 9. tía 10. jóvenes

CAPÍTULO 3 **Después de ver A.** 1. va 2. prefiere 3. tiene 4. tiene 5. Tengo 6. quiere 7. tiene 8. viene 9. vengo 10. quiere

CAPÍTULO 4 **Después de ver A. Paso 1.** *Possible answers:* 1. Lo que lleva Diego a la reunión con su profesor le importa mucho a la tía Matilde. 2. A Diego no le gusta vivir con su tía Matilde. 3. Hay una cama y un armario en la alcoba de Diego. 4. En esa casa, nadie se despierta a las cinco de la mañana. **Paso 2.** *agradables:* 1. Es amable. 2. Es cariñosa. *desagradables:* 1. Se baña a las cinco de la mañana y canta ópera en el baño. 2. Se acuesta a las nueve.

CAPÍTULO 5 **Después de ver A. Paso 1.** *Possible answers:* 1. Lola quiere ir al parque mañana porque hace muy buen tiempo. 2. Carolina Díaz quiere jugar con Marta esta tarde. 3. Está lloviendo en La Coruña mientras en Sevilla hace buen tiempo. 4. Este año Lola tiene unos estudiantes magníficos. 5. Manolo les invita a Carlos Suárez y su familia a visitarlo en Sevilla el próximo día. **Paso 2.** 1. contentos y cariñosos 2. desorganizado 3. juguetona

CAPÍTULO 6 **Después de ver A.** 1. recomienda 2. plato 3. rico 4. bistec 5. asado 6. ensalada 7. sopa 8. dice 9. atún **B.** 1. la mesa 2. los huevos 3. la sal 4. los vasos 5. la pera ("espera" → "es pera")

CAPÍTULO 7 **Después de ver A.** *Possible answers:* 1. El Sr. Gómez viajó a las Galápagos el año pasado; Elisa fue a Riobamba el mes pasado. 2. Elisa quiere ir en avión desde Quito y quedarse una semana en las Galápagos. 3. Elisa prefiere pagar con la tarjeta de crédito del periódico. 4. El Sr. Gómez y su esposa caminaron por la isla, observaron los animales, sacaron muchas fotos y descansaron.

CAPÍTULO 8 **Después de ver A.** *Answers may vary.*

CAPÍTULO 9 **Después de ver A.** 1. vino 2. era 3. aceptaron 4. tenía 5. iba 6. prometieron 7. salieron 8. quería 9. preguntó 10. entró 11. estaba 12. invitó

CAPÍTULO 10 **Después de ver A.** *Correction of false statements will vary.* 1. C 2. F: Marta tiene que guardar cama y quedarse en casa algunos días. 3. F: Esta mañana Lola se sintió muy mareada y no pudo comer. 4. F: Manolo se acuerda que él y Lola tenían que levantarse dos o tres veces cada noche. 5. F: Manolo se llevó una gran sorpresa cuando Lola entró en la tienda.

CAPÍTULO 11 **Después de ver A.** 1. me di con 2. se me rompió 3. se me perdieron 4. Se te cayó 5. me levanté

CAPÍTULO 12 **Después de ver A.** 1. equipo 2. planta baja 3. vecindad 4. compre 5. vaya 6. deje 7. estereofónicos 8. navegar

CAPÍTULO 13 **Después de ver A.** *Possible answers:* 1. Lupe no duda que Diego está cansado porque estudió mucho para su examen. 2. Lupe va a escribir su trabajo sobre Frida Kahlo porque es su pintora favorita. 3. A Diego le interesa el arte moderno y quiere ir al Museo de Arte Moderno con Lupe el próximo sábado. 4. Lupe cree que hay muchas cosas que le interesaría a Diego, como los cuadros de Kahlo y Rivera.

CAPÍTULO 14 **Después de ver A.** 1. bello 2. protegida 3. denso 4. cubierto 5. fincas 6. recursos 7. aislamiento 8. acelerado 9. gasolinera 10. mecánico

CAPÍTULO 15 **Después de ver A.** *Possible answers:* 1. Lola y Eva no tienen planes para la noche, a menos que sus maridos hayan hecho planes. 2. Susana cree que Antonio es el hombre más cariñoso y dulce del mundo; Lola cree que nadie es tan perfecto. 3. Lola cree que, si él trata a Susana con cariño y respeto, lo demás no importa. 4. Lola no quiere que su madre lo sepa antes de que ella se lo diga personalmente. 5. Lola y Manolo quieren que Eva y Jesús sean los padrinos del bebé.

CAPÍTULO 16 **Después de ver A.** *Possible answers:* 1. Lupe requiere que las horas sean flexibles. 2. El banco ofrece cuentas corrientes, cuentas de ahorros, cajeros automáticos (tarjetas de crédito y préstamos). 3. Lupe renunció el puesto porque ellos querían que ella trabajara la jornada completa. 4. Lupe contestaba el teléfono, hacía las citas para los clientes, organizaba el archivo, llevaba las cuentas y pagaba los gastos básicos de la oficina. 5. El banco busca una persona que sea amable, que aprenda rápidamente, que sepa escribir a máquina y utilizar una computadora y que tenga paciencia con los clientes.

CAPÍTULO 17 **Después de ver A.** 1. política 2. acontecimientos 3. apoya 4. desastre 5. ley 6. protestar 7. huelgas 8. desempleo 9. prensa

CAPÍTULO 18 **Después de ver A.** 1. pasaje 2. avión 3. alojamiento 4. hotel 5. habitaciones 6. desocupadas 7. individuales 8. baño

D. Videoscripts

MINIDRAMAS

Primeros pasos

Primera parte

MANOLO: ¡Hola, Maricarmen!
MARICARMEN: ¿Qué tal, Manolo? ¿Cómo estás?
MANOLO: Muy bien. ¿Y tú?
MARICARMEN: Regular. Nos vemos, ¿eh?
MANOLO: Hasta mañana.

ELISA VELASCO: Buenas tardes, señor Gómez.
MARTÍN GÓMEZ: Muy buenas, señora Velasco. ¿Cómo está?
ELISA VELASCO: Bien, gracias. ¿Y usted?
MARTÍN GÓMEZ: Muy bien, gracias. Hasta luego.
ELISA VELASCO: Adiós.

LUPE: Buenos días, profesor.
PROFESOR: Buenos días. ¿Cómo te llamas?
LUPE: Me llamo Lupe Carrasco.
PROFESOR: Mucho gusto, Lupe.
LUPE: Igualmente.

Tercera parte

PROFESOR: Me gusta mucho tu idea, Antonio. Es muy interesante.
ANTONIO: Gracias, profesor.
DIEGO: Perdón. ¿Es usted el profesor Salazar?
PROFESOR: Sí, yo soy.
DIEGO: Buenas tardes. Me llamo Diego González. Soy el estudiante de la Universidad de California.
PROFESOR: Ah, sí. El estudiante de Los Ángeles. Mucho gusto.
DIEGO: Igualmente.
PROFESOR: ¡Bienvenido a México! Él es Antonio Sifuentes. Es estudiante posgraduado en la facultad.
ANTONIO: ¿Qué tal, Diego?
DIEGO: Muy bien, gracias. ¿Y tú?
ANTONIO: Muy bien. Mucho gusto.
DIEGO: Igualmente, Antonio.
PROFESOR: ¡Ay! ¡Es tarde! Son las tres menos cuarto, y tengo una reunión con el director del Museo de Antropología a las tres. Con permiso.
ANTONIO: Cómo no, profesor.
PROFESOR: Diego, mañana voy a estar en mi oficina de las once a las doce. Mi oficina está en ese edificio.
DIEGO: Muy bien, profesor Salazar. Nos vemos mañana a las once.
PROFESOR: Claro que sí. ¡Hasta luego!
DIEGO/ANTONIO: Hasta mañana. Hasta luego.

ANTONIO: Es un profesor excelente. Es muy paciente y muy generoso con su tiempo. Bueno, Diego, ¿te gusta México?
DIEGO: Sí, me gusta mucho. ¿Tú eres de la Ciudad de México?
ANTONIO: Sí, soy de aquí. Pero, aquí se dice «D.F.», no «la Ciudad de México».
DIEGO: ¿Qué significa «D.F.»?
ANTONIO: Significa «Distrito Federal», como en tu país: Washington, D.C. Mira. Allí está una amiga mía. Se llama Lupe Carrasco. Vamos, te presento.
DIEGO: ¡Vamos!

Capítulo 1 En la universidad

DIEGO: ¡Lupe! ¿Cómo estás?
LUPE: Hola, Diego. Bien, gracias. ¿Y tú?
DIEGO: Excelente. ¿Compras libros para tus clases?
LUPE: Sí. Necesito comprar libros para la clase de literatura, la clase de inglés... y otras clases también.
DIEGO: Yo también necesito comprar libros.
LUPE: Pues, hasta luego.
DIEGO: Bueno, sí. Adiós.

DIEGO: ¡Ay, perdón!
LUPE: No hay por qué. ¡Ay, Diego!
DIEGO: ¡Lupe! ¿Qué haces?
LUPE: Busco un libro para la clase de antropología.
DIEGO: ¿Te gusta la antropología?
LUPE: Sí, me gusta mucho. Sobre todo, me gusta la antropología precolombina.
DIEGO: ¿En serio? Es mi materia favorita. ¿Qué clase tomas?
LUPE: Tomo la clase del profesor Salazar. Es una clase fascinante.
DIEGO: Yo también tomo esa clase. Así que somos compañeros... Bueno, Lupe, nos vemos en clase.
LUPE: Sí, nos vemos.

DIEGO: Y ahora, ¿qué libro buscas?
LUPE: Busco un libro para la clase de sicología y uno para el curso de arte moderno.
DIEGO: A mí no me gusta mucho la sicología. Pero sí me gusta el arte.
LUPE: Vamos... Pues, ¿qué más te gusta? ¿Qué te gusta hacer en tu tiempo libre?
DIEGO: ¿En mi tiempo libre? Pues... Me gusta mucho la música. También me gusta cantar, ¡pero necesito practicar más! ¿Qué te gusta a ti?
LUPE: Me gusta bailar. Bailo con frecuencia los fines de semana. ¿Bailas tú?
DIEGO: Sí, me gusta bailar también.
LUPE: También me gustan las fiestas donde hay mucha gente... Diego, debo comprar unas cosas más: cuadernos, lápices, plumas y un diccionario inglés-español. Y también necesito pagarlos. ¿Me acompañas?
DIEGO: Sí, con mucho gusto. Y ¿por qué no tomamos un café después?
LUPE: Está bien. Acepto. ¿Sabes? Como tenemos el mismo curso de antropología, ¿por qué no estudiamos juntos?
DIEGO: Creo que es una idea excelente. ¿Vamos?

Capítulo 2 La familia

ELISA: ¡Ay! Esto es imposible. Hay por lo menos cien fotos aquí.
JOSÉ MIGUEL: ¿Aló? Hola, Paloma. ¿Cómo estás? Bien, gracias. ¿A qué hora llegas? Ajá. Muy bien. Adiós. Mamá, Paloma y su novio llegan a las cuatro. Vamos a ir al cine.

ELISA: Muy bien... Espera... ¿Qué novio? ¿Alejandro?
JOSÉ MIGUEL: No, es su nuevo novio, Gustavo.
ELISA: Ay, ¡¿otro novio!?
JOSÉ MIGUEL: Sí. Oye, ¿qué haces?
ELISA: Tengo un álbum nuevo y quiero ordenar estas fotos. Pero son muchas y están tan desorganizadas.
JOSÉ MIGUEL: ¿Son todas fotos de la familia?
ELISA: Sí, de la familia.
JOSÉ MIGUEL: Pues, ¿te puedo ayudar?
ELISA: ¡Sí, gracias! ¿Por qué no tomas estas fotos? Sepáralas en dos grupos: un grupo de fotos antiguas y otro de fotos recientes.
JOSÉ MIGUEL: ¿Quién es este hombre?
ELISA: ¿Quién?
JOSÉ MIGUEL: El hombre alto. La niña morena eres tú, ¿no?
ELISA: Sí, la niña soy yo. El hombre es mi tío Ernesto. La señora es su esposa Amalia.
JOSÉ MIGUEL: ¿Es el tío Ernesto? ¡Qué cambio! En la foto se ve tan joven, pero ahora es viejo y tiene el pelo blanco.
ELISA: Sí, en la foto está más joven y tiene el pelo oscuro. Mira esta foto... Mira esta foto... Este muchacho es mi primo Marcelo. En la foto tiene seis años y está delgado. Ahora tiene treinta y tres años. Está muy gordo. ¡Todos cambiamos!
JOSÉ MIGUEL: ¿Quiénes son estas personas?
ELISA: Esta señora es mi abuela. Bonita, ¿no? El hombre a su lado es mi padre, tu abuelo. Se lo ve alto y fuerte. Y este... y este niño es mi hermano Miguel.
JOSÉ MIGUEL: ¿El papá de Paloma? Era muy pequeño, ¿no?
ELISA: Sí, debe tener dos o tres años en esta foto...

ELISA: Por fin terminamos.
PALOMA: ¡Buenas tardes, tía Elisa!
ELISA: ¡Hola! ¡Adelante!
PALOMA: Tía, quiero presentarte a mi novio, Gustavo. Gustavo, ésta es mi tía, Elisa Velasco.
GUSTAVO: Mucho gusto en conocerla, señora.
ELISA: El gusto es mío, Gustavo.
PALOMA: Y ya conoces a mi primo José Miguel.
JOSÉ MIGUEL: ¿Qué tal?
GUSTAVO: ¡Hola!
ELISA: Bueno, ya es hora de irse, ¿no? La película debe comenzar pronto. Gracias por ayudarme, hijo.
JOSÉ MIGUEL: De nada, mamá.
PALOMA: ¡Adiós!
GUSTAVO: ¡Hasta luego!
ELISA: No regreses muy tarde, ¿eh?
JOSÉ MIGUEL: ¡Chau!

Capítulo 3 De compras

JOSÉ MIGUEL: Oye, Paloma, ¿vas a la fiesta en casa de Eduardo este fin de semana?
PALOMA: No, no tengo ganas de ir a la fiesta. Creo que Gustavo y yo vamos al cine.
JOSÉ MIGUEL: Qué pena. Las fiestas de Eduardo siempre son muy buenas.
PALOMA: Sí, ya lo sé, pero prefiero ir al cine. ¡Mira! Hay rebajas en esta tienda. ¿Entramos un rato? Tengo que comprar unos *bluejeans,* y si hay rebajas, mejor.
JOSÉ MIGUEL: Bueno, pero sólo un rato. No tengo ganas de ir de compras hoy.
PALOMA: Vamos... Voy a buscar un par de *bluejeans.*

JOSÉ MIGUEL: Está bien.
EMPLEADA: Buenos días. ¿En qué puedo servirle?
JOSÉ MIGUEL: ¿Qué precio tienen estas camisas?
EMPLEADA: Están en rebaja. Cuestan 40.000 sucres cada una.
JOSÉ MIGUEL: Es un precio excelente.
EMPLEADA: Sí. Las camisas son de puro algodón, y las tenemos de muchos colores. Aquí tiene una verde, otra roja, otra amarilla y otra azul. ¿Qué talla usa?
JOSÉ MIGUEL: La 38, por lo general.
EMPLEADA: Mire. Estos pantalones son perfectos para esta camisa. Con este pantalón negro y esta camisa azul, Ud. está a la última moda.
JOSÉ MIGUEL: Me gustan mucho los pantalones. Y la camisa también. ¿Me los puedo probar?
EMPLEADA: Sí, cómo no. Por allí están los probadores.
PALOMA: ¿Vamos? Ya compré los *bluejeans*.
JOSÉ MIGUEL: Un momento. ¿Sabes? Esta tienda tiene ropa muy buena. Y los precios son razonables. Mira este pantalón... y esta camisa... ¿Y qué te parece esta camiseta?
PALOMA: Pues, a mí no me gustan las camisetas de rayas.
JOSÉ MIGUEL: Sí, tienes razón. Gracias. No quiero la camiseta.
PALOMA: ¿Estás listo ya? No tengo todo el día. Tengo que ir a mis clases.
JOSÉ MIGUEL: Bueno, primero voy a probarme los pantalones y la camisa. Luego nos vamos.
EMPLEADA: Por aquí, por favor.
PALOMA: «No tengo ganas de ir de compras hoy... » ¡Já!

Capítulo 4 En casa

MATILDE: ¡Diego! ¡Dieeeegoo! ¡Es hora de levantarte! ¡No quieres llegar tarde, ¿verdad?!
DIEGO: Sí, gracias, tía Matilde.
MATILDE: Diego, debes afeitarte hoy. Vas a hablar con tu profesor, ¿no?
DIEGO: Sí, tía...
MATILDE: Y creo que debes ponerte camisa y corbata también.
DIEGO: No te preocupes, tía. Hoy me visto bien. Tía Matilde tiene buenas intenciones, ¡pero ya no puedo más! Bueno, por lo menos mañana me despierto en mi nuevo apartamento...
MATILDE: Creo que debes ponerte esta camisa... y esta corbata... y estos pantalones.
DIEGO: Gracias, tía.

ANTONIO: Y esta es tu recámara. Una mesita de noche, un estante y una cama cómoda.
DIEGO: ¿Y eso?
ANTONIO: Eso es el clóset. Muy amplio, ¿no?
DIEGO: Sí. Hay mucho espacio. ¿Y la cocina?
ANTONIO: ¿Ves aquella puerta? Esa es la cocina. Todos comemos allí. Normalmente comemos juntos, cuando es posible.
DIEGO: ¿Y el baño?
ANTONIO: ¿Ves aquella puerta a la derecha? Bueno. Pues, ese es el baño.
DIEGO: ¡Ayy... !
ANTONIO: ¿Qué? ¿No te gusta la recámara?
DIEGO: No, Antonio, no es eso. Me gusta mucho mi recámara. Y también creo que voy a estar muy contento aquí. Es que... bueno, tía Matilde es muy amable, muy cariñosa, pero vivir con ella... ¡uf! Todos los días me despierta a las cinco porque canta mientras se baña... ¡Ópera! Además, se acuesta a las nueve de la noche y no puedo hacer nada después porque no quiero hacer mucho ruido.
ANTONIO: Pues, aquí no te levantamos a las cinco de la mañana. ¡Ni me gusta la ópera! ¡Te lo prometo!
DIEGO: Gracias, amigo. Dime, Antonio, ¿cómo es el horario de Uds.?

ANTONIO: Normalmente, yo me levanto a las siete y Juan se levanta a las seis y media. ¿A qué horas te levantas tú?
DIEGO: Si tengo clases, me levanto a las siete y media.
ANTONIO: ¡Perfecto! Primero Juan se baña y se afeita, después yo y por último tú.
DIEGO: ¿Y vuelven Uds. a casa para almorzar?
ANTONIO: Bueno, los lunes, miércoles y viernes sí vuelvo a casa para almorzar, porque no tengo clases por la tarde. Pero los martes y jueves almuerzo en la cafetería de la universidad. Juan no vuelve a casa para almorzar. Come en casa de su novia.
DIEGO: Muy bien. Entonces, los lunes, miércoles y viernes podemos almorzar aquí tú y yo. Antonio, creo que sí me va a gustar mucho vivir aquí.
ANTONIO: ¿Bueno? ¿Sí? ...Sí, cómo no... ¿De parte de quién?... Ah... sí... sí... Permítame tantito... Uh-huh... Sí. Diego, es tu tía Matilde. Va de compras y quiere preguntarte si necesitas vitaminas...
DIEGO: Hola, tía Matilde. ¿Cómo estás? Muy bien, ¿y tú? Sí, sí...

Capítulo 5 Las estaciones, el tiempo y un poco de geografía

MANOLO: Lola, no encuentro el cuaderno con los exámenes. ¿Sabes dónde está?
LOLA: Lo siento, querido. No sé. ¿Cómo es el cuaderno?
MANOLO: Es grande y amarillo. No sé dónde puede estar.
LOLA: Tal vez está dentro de la mesita de la entrada o en la cocina. ¿Hmm?
MANOLO: Es posible.
LOLA: Oye, Manolo. Dicen que mañana va a hacer buen tiempo. ¿Quieres ir al parque?
MANOLO: ¿Eh? No te oigo.
LOLA: ¡Dicen que mañana va a hacer soool! ¡Que si quieres ir al paarqueee!
MANOLO: ¿Por qué estás gritando?
LOLA: Perdona, cariño. ¿Quieres ir al parque mañana? Dicen que va a hacer sol y que la temperatura va a ser muy agradable, para el mes de abril. Podemos hacer un *picnic.*
MANOLO: Es una buena idea. Lo siento. Estoy un poco preocupado. Todavía no encuentro el cuaderno.
LOLA: Bueno, yo te ayudo. Voy a la habitación a buscarlos allí.
MANOLO: Ya lo cojo yo. ¿Diga?
CAROLINA: Buenos días. Habla Carolina Díaz. ¿Está Marta?
MANOLO: No, Carolina. Marta no está en este momento. Está en el parque con su tío abuelo. ¿Quieres dejarle un recado?
CAROLINA: Sí, muchas gracias. Me gustaría decirle que si quiere venir esta tarde a jugar conmigo. Hace buen tiempo y podríamos ir a jugar afuera.
MANOLO: Muy bien, Carolina. Yo le doy el recado. Saluda a tus padres de mi parte, por favor.
CAROLINA: Sí. Adiós.
MANOLO: Adiós. ... ¿Diga?
CARLOS: ¿Manolo? Soy Carlos Suárez.
MANOLO: ¡Ah, hombre! ¿Qué pasa? ¿Cómo estás? ¿Cómo te va por La Coruña?
CARLOS: Pues, mejor que el año pasado. Estoy muy contento con mi nuevo trabajo.
MANOLO: Me alegro. ¿Y qué tal están Begoña y los niños?
CARLOS: Bien, gracias. ¡Imagínate! ¡Ahora Raulito está más alto que Begoña! Todos estamos muy bien. ¿Y cómo están Lola y Marta?
MANOLO: Bien. Lola está muy ocupada con sus clases en la universidad, pero tiene unos estudiantes magníficos. Y Marta es tan buena como un ángel. Bueno, ¡no siempre! ¿Quieres hablar con Lola?
CARLOS: No puedo, Manolo. Sólo tengo un momentito. Begoña y los hijos me están esperando en el taxi. Sólo quiero decirte que mañana vamos a estar en Sevilla y queremos veros. ¿Qué te parece?

MANOLO: ¡Perfecto! Podemos ir al parque. Hace un tiempo maravilloso.

CARLOS: ¡Estupendo! Pues, aquí hace frío y está lloviendo a cántaros. Entonces, te llamo mañana. ¡Adiós y saludos a Lola!

MANOLO: Adiós, Carlos. Y saludos también a Begoña. Hasta mañana. Ah, Lola. Carlos te manda saludos. Él y su familia van a estar aquí en Sevilla mañana.

LOLA: ¡Qué bien!

MANOLO: ¿Y los exámenes?

LOLA: Bueno, no están encima de la estantería, y no están debajo de la cama. Y tampoco están detrás de la cómoda. Pero, Manolito...

MANOLO: ¿Sí?

LOLA: ¡Tus exámenes sí estaban dentro de tu portafolios!

Capítulo 6 *¿Qué le gusta comer?*

LOLA: A ver... No hay suficiente leche... Tampoco hay queso. ¿Cómo puede ser? ¡Acabo de hacer las compras el otro día! Comemos mucho en esta familia, me parece. ¿Hmm?

MANOLO: ¿Qué pasa, Lola?

LOLA: Mira... ¡Nunca hay comida en esta casa! Hay que comprar carne, patatas, agua mineral, de todo...

MANOLO: Bueno, no creo que sea necesario hoy.

LOLA: Pero, ¿cómo? ¿No ves? ¡No hay nada!

MANOLO: No importa. Hoy no vas a comprar nada.

LOLA: ¿Pero no me oyes, Manolo? No hay ni huevos, ni verduras, ni fruta...

MANOLO: Ya lo sé. Pero hoy no vas de compras. ¿Sabes? Es nuestro aniversario de bodas. Marta está con tus padres y tú y yo vamos a cenar fuera.

LOLA: Ay, Manolo. ¡Qué sorpresa! ¿Adónde vamos?

MANOLO: ¿Conoces el nuevo restaurante en el Hotel Castellano? Dicen que es excelente... ¡y muy romántico!

LOLA: No, no lo conozco. ¡Pero me parece estupendo!

MANOLO: Tengo unas reservaciones para las diez.

LOLA: Bueno, voy a cambiarme de ropa. Gracias, Manolo.

CAMARERO: Buenas noches, señores. ¿Qué les traigo de beber?

MANOLO: Una botella de vino tinto, creo. Rioja, ¿no?

LOLA: Sí, perfecto. ¿Y nos trae agua mineral, por favor? Con gas.

CAMARERO: Cómo no. Momento...

CAMARERO: ¿Ya saben lo que desean de comer los señores?

MANOLO: Creo que sí, pero, ¿qué recomienda Ud.?

CAMARERO: Hoy tenemos un plato especial: gambas al limón con arroz, un plato ligero y delicioso. Y también tenemos un salmón buenísimo que acaba de llegar esta tarde.

LOLA: ¡Qué rico! Yo quiero las gambas, por favor.

MANOLO: Eh, para mí, el bistec estilo argentino, poco asado. Y una ensalada mixta para dos.

CAMARERO: ¿Y para empezar? Tenemos una sopa de ajo muy rica.

LOLA: Para mí, una sopa, por favor.

MANOLO: Y para mí también. Ah, y le dice al chef que por favor le ponga un poco de atún a la ensalada.

CAMARERO: Muy bien, señor.

CAMARERO: Aquí tienen la cuenta los señores. Y como es su aniversario, permítanos invitarles a una copa.

LOLA: Ah, muy amable. Muchas gracias.

MANOLO: Sí, muchas gracias. Y, por favor, dígale al dueño que la comida aquí es deliciosa. Tiene un restaurante excelente.
CAMARERO: Muchas gracias, señor.

Capítulo 7 De vacaciones

SR. GÓMEZ: ¿Cómo está, Sra. Velasco?
ELISA: Muy bien, gracias, Sr. Gómez.
SR. GÓMEZ: ¿Cómo le fue en su viaje a Riobamba el mes pasado?
ELISA: Todo salió bien, gracias. Ud. me ayudó mucho.
SR. GÓMEZ: No hay de qué. Pase, por favor.
ELISA: Gracias.
SR. GÓMEZ: ¿Y sobre qué lugar va a escribir esta vez?
ELISA: Esta vez voy a escribir sobre las islas Galápagos.
SR. GÓMEZ: ¡Las Galápagos! ¡Qué bien!
ELISA: Ud. viajó a las islas Galápagos el año pasado, ¿verdad?
SR. GÓMEZ: Sí, fui con mi esposa en el mes de mayo. Fue una experiencia inolvidable. Y Ud., ¿cuándo piensa viajar?
ELISA: En unas tres semanas, como el doce o trece del próximo mes. Pero debo arreglar el viaje hoy.
SR. GÓMEZ: ¿Y cuánto tiempo piensa quedarse en las islas?
ELISA: Me gustaría pasar una semana allí. Quiero viajar en avión desde Quito. ¿Cuánto cuesta un boleto de ida y vuelta?
SR. GÓMEZ: Cuesta 615.000 sucres si Ud. viaja el sábado en la mañana.
ELISA: Está bien.
SR. GÓMEZ: ¿Desea que le haga una reservación de hotel también?
ELISA: Sí, por favor.
SR. GÓMEZ: Entonces, le hago las siguientes reservaciones: el avión sale de Quito a las islas el sábado 13 y seis noches de reservación en el hotel de la isla Santa Cruz.
ELISA: Perfecto. Muchas gracias.
SR. GÓMEZ: No hay por qué. ¿Cómo le gustaría pagar? ¿Lo de siempre?
ELISA: Sí, con tarjeta de crédito... ¡la del periódico, por supuesto!
SR. GÓMEZ: Está bien.
ELISA: ¿Qué hicieron Ud. y su esposa durante sus vacaciones en las Galápagos?
SR. GÓMEZ: Hicimos de todo. Caminamos por las islas, observamos los animales, saqué muchas fotos. Mi esposa nadó, tomó el sol, pero sobre todo, descansamos muchísimo. Las islas Galápagos son maravillosas. Y Ud., ¿va a tener tiempo para divertirse?
ELISA: Sí, espero que sí. Bueno, si tengo algunas preguntas más, ¿lo puedo llamar más tarde?
SR. GÓMEZ: Por supuesto, Sra. Velasco. Siempre es un placer verla. Que le vaya bien.
ELISA: Muchas gracias. Hasta la próxima.
SR. GÓMEZ: Adiós.

Capítulo 8 Los días festivos

JOSÉ JAIME: Tía Lola, vamos a darles de comer a las palomas.
LOLA: Sí, pero dile a Marta que tenga cuidado con el vestido. Aquí tienes un poco de pan para darles.
JOSÉ JAIME: Gracias.
ELENA: Lola, están allí las aceitunas? ¿Me las pasas, por favor?
LOLA: Sí, cómo no.
ELENA: Gracias. ¿Sabes? La ceremonia fue muy bonita. Y Marta estaba tan preciosa.
LOLA: Sí. Y se portó muy bien. Casi no me lo creo: su primera comunión. ¡Qué rápido pasan los años! Me di cuenta esta mañana, cuando Marta se vistió para la ceremonia...

JAIME: Lola, no te pongas triste. ¡Esta es una celebración feliz!
LOLA: Sí, ya lo sé...
ANA: Pues, Lola, yo me acuerdo de tu primera comunión. También fue una ceremonia bonita. ¡Ay, pero tú —te portaste bastante mal!
MANOLO: ¿Ah, sí? Cuéntanoslo, por favor. Lola nunca me lo mencionó antes.
ANA: Bueno, la ceremonia fue en la iglesia cerca de nuestra casa. ¿Te acuerdas, Lola?
LOLA: ¡Ay, mamá, por favor!
ANA: No te enfades, hija. Ay, bueno, durante la ceremonia, Lola y ese muchacho a su lado... ¿Cómo se llamaba ese chico?
LOLA: Ay, mamá... Ya no recuerdo.
ANA: Yo tampoco. Bueno, pues, durante la ceremonia los dos comenzaron a reírse mucho. Yo estaba muy avergonzada... Reírse así, ¡durante una ceremonia religiosa!
LOLA: Pero, mamá, no les contaste por qué nos reímos así. Es que había una señora cerca de nosotros que se durmió. ¡Hacía tanto ruido! De repente, el cabello de la señora se le movió así. Entonces nos dimos cuenta de que llevaba una peluca. ¡Qué gracioso! Ay... Yo me reí tanto que comencé a llorar. Fue algo inolvidable.
ANA: De todos modos, fue un acto de mala educación, reírse así de una señora, especialmente en la iglesia. ¡Pero *sí* fue muy divertido cuando se le cayó la peluca al suelo!
ELENA: ¿Sabéis? Deberíamos reunirnos con más frecuencia. ¿Os acordáis de la última Noche Vieja? ¡Nos divertimos tanto!
JAIME: Sí, lo pasamos muy bien. Fuimos a ese restaurante que está cerca de vuestra casa, y nos sirvieron aquellas tapas riquísimas, ¿eh?
LOLA: Sí. ¿Y os acordáis de la fiesta que hicimos durante las Navidades hace dos años? Fue en vuestra casa, mamá, y papá quiso sorprenderte con el árbol navideño...
PEDRO: Sí, pero tu madre ya había comprado un árbol. ¡Ese año tuvimos dos!

JAIME: Bueno, hasta otro, hermano.
MANOLO: ¡Y que sea pronto!
ELENA: Hasta luego. Nos divertimos mucho, ¿eh?
ANA: Que tengáis buen viaje.
PEDRO: Nos vais a mandar copias de las fotos, ¿no?
JAIME: Por supuesto que sí. Ha sido maravilloso veros. ¡Que haya suerte!
MANOLO: Cuídate.

Capítulo 9 El tiempo libre

LUPE: ¡Hola! ¡Soy Lupe! ¿Puedo pasar?
JUAN: ¡Sí, pásale, adelante!
ROCÍO: Mira, Juan. ¿Quieres ver esta película? Comienza en media hora.
JUAN: Perfecto. ¿Nos vamos?
LUPE: Hola, Juan, Rocío. ¿Cómo están?
JUAN: Hola, Lupe. Bien, gracias.
ROCÍO: ¿Qué onda, Lupe?
LUPE: Muy bien.
ANTONIO: ¡Hola, Lupe!
LUPE: Hola, Antonio. Oye, ¿está aquí Diego?
ANTONIO: No, no está. ¿Por qué?
LUPE: Ah, muy bien. Pues, el próximo fin de semana le quiero dar una fiesta sorpresa a Diego. Es su cumpleaños. Quiero invitar a todos Uds. a la fiesta.
ANTONIO: ¡Qué padre! ¿Y cuándo es la fiesta? ¿El viernes? ¿El sábado?
LUPE: El sábado. Rocío, ¿te gustaría venir?
ROCÍO: Ay, Lupe, me gustaría mucho, pero no puedo. Ya tengo planes para el sábado. Mis padres vienen al D.F. a visitarme, y vamos a ir al Ballet Folklórico esa noche.

JUAN: ¡Qué pena! Pero yo sí voy.

ANTONIO: Y yo también. Gracias por la invitación. ¿Puedo invitar a Mónica y a José Luis también?

LUPE: ¡Claro que sí! ¡Muy bien! Entonces, ¿por qué no vienen a mi casa a las siete? Y por favor, no le vayan a decir nada a Diego.

JUAN: No te preocupes. Él va a estar muy sorprendido. Pues, Rocío y yo salimos ahora mismo. Queremos ver la nueva película de Arau.

LUPE: Ah... Dicen que es la mejor del año.

ROCÍO: Ay, sí, tengo muchas ganas de verla. Bueno, ¡adiós!

ANTONIO: A ver, Lupe, siéntate. Pasas mucho tiempo con Diego. ¿Hay algo entre Uds.?

LUPE: No, no. Todavía no. Pero Diego es una buena persona. Tenemos mucho en común.

ANTONIO: ¿Sí? ¿Como qué?

LUPE: Pues, a los dos nos gusta hacer las mismas cosas: bailar, escuchar música, estudiar... Además, a los dos nos gustan mucho los animales. De niño, Diego tenía un perro negro y yo también tenía un perro negro. Qué casualidad, ¿no?

ANTONIO: Ah, sí, entiendo. Como los dos tenían perros negros cuando eran niños, eso quiere decir que son iguales.

LUPE: No, Antonio. Hay más. Diego vivía en el campo cuando era muy joven, igual que yo. Y los dos venimos de una familia muy grande. No sé. Es que... Diego es una de las personas más amables que conozco. ¡Y también es tan guapo!

ANTONIO: Bueno. No le vayas a decir a Diego, pero él me dijo que tú le interesas.

LUPE: ¿Sí? ¿Qué te dijo?

ANTONIO: Fue hace unos días. Diego me preguntó si tenías novio. Le dije que no. Yo le pregunté para qué quería saberlo. ¿Sabes? Me dijo que te iba a invitarte a un concierto.

LUPE: ¿Me va a invitar a un concierto? ¿Y qué tipo de concierto es?

ANTONIO: Un concierto de guitarra clásica.

LUPE: Y ¿cuándo es el concierto?

ANTONIO: Pues, creo que es el viernes. ¿Te gustaría ir?

LUPE: ¡Claro que sí! ¡Me gustaría mucho!

DIEGO: Hola. ¿Qué pasa? ¿Van Uds. al concierto?

ANTONIO: ¡Ah, no! Yo no la estaba invitando, Diego.

LUPE: Diego, Antonio me decía que tú querías invitarme a un concierto. Y, bueno, le decía que me gustaría mucho ir contigo. Ay, bueno, pues... ¿Me vas a invitar o no?

ANTONIO: Con permisito...

DIEGO: Pues, sí... sí. Bueno. Lupe, ¿quieres ir conmigo al concierto este viernes?

LUPE: Claro que sí. Me gustaría mucho ir contigo. Gracias. Oye, Diego, y ya que estamos haciendo planes para el fin de semana, ¿por qué no estudiamos juntos el sábado por la noche? ¿Como a las siete y media? ¿En mi casa?

DIEGO: De acuerdo.

LUPE: ¿Te espero?

DIEGO: Sí.

Capítulo 10 La salud

DRA. MÉNDEZ: ¿Así que no te sientes bien, Marta? Dime lo que te pasa.

MARTA: Anoche me dolió mucho el estómago. Y también la garganta.

LOLA: Sí, y ayer por la tarde estaba muy congestionada.

DRA. MÉNDEZ: ¿Sí? ¿Y cuándo comenzó a sentir estos síntomas?

LOLA: Fue unos días después de que se reunió con su amiga Carolina, quien ya estaba enferma.

DRA. MÉNDEZ: Ajá. Marta, saca la lengua, por favor. Di «ahhh».

MARTA: Ahhh...

DRA. MÉNDEZ: A ver... Respira. Más fuerte. Otra vez.
LOLA: ¿Qué pasa, doctora? ¿Es grave?
DRA. MÉNDEZ: No, no se preocupe. No es nada grave. Lo que tiene es un resfriado. Marta, debes guardar cama durante unos días y tomar muchos líquidos. Sra. Durán, voy a darle dos recetas. Las pastillas son para quitarle la congestión. Y el jarabe se lo puede dar cuando ella tosa.
LOLA: Muy bien, doctora.
DRA. MÉNDEZ: Y debes quedarte en casa algunos días.
MARTA: ¡Estupendo!
LOLA: Marta, por favor...
DRA. MÉNDEZ: Vamos.
LOLA: ¿Dra. Méndez? Esta mañana me sentí muy mareada, y no pude comer. Eh... Sospecho que estoy embarazada.
DRA. MÉNDEZ: Ah, ¿sí? Muy bien, pues, hagamos el análisis. Marta, ¿por qué no vas a la sala de espera? Hay allí varios libros que te van a interesar.
MARTA: Vale.

MANOLO: Bueno, ¿qué te dijo la doctora?
LOLA: Me dijo que Marta no tiene nada grave, lo cual es un alivio. Yo estaba algo preocupada. Y, claro, Marta se puso muy contenta cuando la doctora le dijo que no podía asistir a la escuela por varios días.
MANOLO: Pues, es natural... Recuerdo que cuando yo era niño, eso era lo mejor de estar enfermo.
LOLA: Manolo, ¿te acuerdas de nuestra Marta cuando era pequeña? ¡Qué preciosa era!
MANOLO: Sí... Todas las noches nos levantábamos dos o tres veces a cambiarle los pañales y a darle de comer... ¡uf!
LOLA: Manolo... ¿Te acuerdas del día en que nació Marta? Estaba tan pequeña y roja... ¿Y cuando regresamos del hospital?
MANOLO: Me acuerdo que te dabas miedo de cada estornudo, te preocupabas cada vez que tosía...
LOLA: Bueno, sí me preocupaba un poco... Pero eso es natural, ¿no?
MANOLO: Bueno, claro.
LOLA: Ah... Perfecto.
MANOLO: ¿Qué es lo «perfecto»?
LOLA: ¿Entramos un ratito, Manolo?
MANOLO: ¿Aquí? ¿Pero por qué? Esta es una tienda para señoras embarazadas.
LOLA: Sí, ya lo sé. Por eso...
MANOLO: Pero... pero... ¿¡Vamos a tener otro hijo?! ¡Lola, espera! ¡Lola!

Capítulo 11 *Presiones de la vida moderna*

MARÍA: ¡Elisa!
ELISA: Hola, mamá.
MARÍA: Hola, hija. ¿Cómo estás?
ELISA: Pues, estoy cansadísima y siento mucho estrés por el trabajo. Y... acabo de oír unas noticias no muy buenas.
MARÍA: ¿Qué noticias? ¿Qué pasó?
ELISA: Acabo de hablar con nuestra vecina, la Sra. Márquez. La pobre está sufriendo muchas presiones en estos días.
MARÍA: ¿Qué le pasa? Hace una semana que no hablo con ella.
ELISA: Pues, desafortunadamente, su hijo está muy enfermo. Entró en el hospital ayer, y los médicos creen que va a necesitar cirugía.

MARÍA: Ay, ¡qué lástima! Me acuerdo que, de joven, su hijo tenía que ir al hospital con frecuencia.

ELISA: La Sra. Márquez me dijo también que su esposo perdió el trabajo hace tres días. La pobre mujer está totalmente deprimida.

MARÍA: Ay, ¡qué mala suerte! ¿Por qué no vamos mañana en la tarde a visitarla? Tal vez la podemos ayudar de alguna manera.

ELISA: Muy buena idea, mamá. ¿Qué te pasa, hijo?

JOSÉ MIGUEL: ¡Qué horrible día! Tuve muy mala suerte hoy.

MARÍA: ¿Cómo? Cuéntanos cómo fue.

JOSÉ MIGUEL: No sé... Es que todo me salió mal. Fui al mercado esta mañana. Como iba muy distraído, me di con una señora en el camino. ¡Qué vergüenza! Estaba a punto de regresar a casa cuando se me rompió la bolsa. ¡Qué lío! Gracias a Dios, una señora me dio otra bolsa. También se me perdieron las llaves. No las pude encontrar. Por eso toqué a la puerta. ¿Ven? No sé qué me pasó hoy, pero tuve un día horrible. Bueno, mamá, aquí están las compras del mercado.

ELISA: ¡Ay! ¡José Miguel! ¡Se te cayó todo!

JOSÉ MIGUEL: ¡Lo siento, mamá! ¡Fue sin querer!

ELISA: Debes tener más cuidado, hijo.

JOSÉ MIGUEL: Perdóname. Parece que me levanté con el pie izquierdo hoy. ¡Qué lata!

ELISA: Ay, no vale la pena molestarte.

MARÍA: Bueno, pero hay algo bueno en todo esto.

ELISA: ¿Qué es?

MARÍA: ¡Que no llevamos una vida aburrida!

Capítulo 12 La calidad de la vida

GUSTAVO: Oye, José Miguel. ¿Todavía quieres comprar una computadora?

JOSÉ MIGUEL: Sí.

GUSTAVO: Mira. Esta tienda tiene una oferta especial.

JOSÉ MIGUEL: Déjame ver... No está mal. ¿Dónde queda la tienda?

GUSTAVO: Creo que está en esta vecindad... Sí, está en la planta baja de un edificio cerca de aquí. Aquí está la dirección. ¡Y está abierta hoy día!

JOSÉ MIGUEL: Ay, ¡cuánto me gustaría comprar una computadora!

GUSTAVO: Si quieres, yo te acompaño a la tienda. Pero te recomiendo que vayas a más tiendas para comparar los precios de cada una.

JOSÉ MIGUEL: Sí, claro. Además, me falta un poco del dinero. Así que no pienso comprar nada hoy. ¡Pero podemos mirar! Oye, Paloma... ¡Paloma! Paloma, quítate el *walkman*.

PALOMA: ¿Sí? ¿Qué pasa?

JOSÉ MIGUEL: Gustavo y yo vamos a una tienda de equipo electrónico para mirar las computadoras. ¿Quieres venir con nosotros?

PALOMA: ¡Sí, vamos!

GUSTAVO: Oye, Paloma. Quisiera que dejes este aparato aquí. El *walkman* me vuelve loco. Nunca oyes nada de lo que te digo cuando lo escuchas.

PALOMA: ¡Que sí!

GUSTAVO: ¡Que no! Tengo que repetirte lo que te digo varias veces hasta que me oigas.

PALOMA: Está bien, ¡pero no te enojes!

PALOMA: Voy a mirar el equipo de discos compactos. Ahora vuelvo. ¡Chau!

GUSTAVO: Esta mujer está loca por los aparatos estereofónicos.

JOSÉ MIGUEL: ¡Mira!

VENDEDORA: Buenas tardes. ¿En qué les puedo atender?

JOSÉ MIGUEL: Buenas tardes. Leímos su anuncio en el periódico. Quisiéramos ver las computadoras.

VENDEDORA: ¿Qué modelo buscan? Tenemos varios aquí. Este es nuevo. Viene con monitor, ratón ergonómico y un módem interno.
JOSÉ MIGUEL: Pero, no tiene lector de CD-ROM interno, ¿verdad? Prefiero uno que lo tenga.
VENDEDORA: Este modelo allí tiene lector de CD-ROM interno. Venga. Esta es la mejor de las que tienen CD-ROM.
JOSÉ MIGUEL: ¿Qué te parece, Gustavo?
GUSTAVO: No está mal... ¿Tiene suficiente memoria para navegar por el Internet?
VENDEDORA: Sí.
GUSTAVO: ¿Y se puede utilizar también un *browser* de páginas o programas de multimedia?
VENDEDORA: Este modelo es ideal para multimedia. Y lleva incluidos los programas necesarios para navegar la red.
JOSÉ MIGUEL: Ah, muy bien, porque pienso utilizar el Internet para ayudarme con mis trabajos en la universidad...

VENDEDORA: Así es cómo funciona...
PALOMA: ¿Encontraste la computadora que querías?
JOSÉ MIGUEL: Sí, pero no la voy a comprar hoy. No tengo suficiente dinero. Pero el precio de esta es excelente y tiene todo lo que quiero.
VENDEDORA: Si Ud. quiere, puede pagarla a plazos o con tarjeta de crédito.
JOSÉ MIGUEL: Muchas gracias, pero voy a esperar un poco más. Gracias por su atención.
VENDEDORA: De nada. Como ya tiene la información, puede volver cuando quiera.
JOSÉ MIGUEL: Gracias. ¿Vamos?
PALOMA: Vamos.
VENDEDORA: Hasta luego.

Capítulo 13 El arte y la cultura

DIEGO: Ya no puedo estudiar más. Estoy cansadísimo. Es la cuarta vez que leo el mismo párrafo y no me acuerdo de nada.
LUPE: No dudo que estás cansado. Estudiaste todo el día para tu examen.
DIEGO: Sí, pero todavía tengo que estudiar más. Es posible que este examen sea muy difícil; todo el mundo dice que los exámenes del profesor Ramírez son difíciles.
LUPE: Yo te conozco, Diego. Estoy segura que vas a salir bien en el examen.
DIEGO: Sí. Ojalá que tengas razón. ¿Ya sabes sobre qué vas a escribir tu trabajo para la clase de arte?
LUPE: Creo que sí. Me interesan mucho el arte y la vida de Frida Kahlo, así que voy a escribir algo sobre ella.
DIEGO: Kahlo pintó muchos autorretratos, ¿no?
LUPE: Sí, y sus autorretratos siempre tienen elementos simbólicos que representan sus emociones y su estado de ánimo. Sus cuadros me gustan muchísimo. Su esposo fue Diego Rivera, uno de los muralistas más famosos de México. Mira. Aquí ves uno de sus cuadros.
DIEGO: Conozco varios murales de Rivera. Los vi en el Palacio Nacional. Pero a mí me impresionan más los murales de José Clemente Orozco.
LUPE: Sí, Orozco fue un muralista excelente. Mira. Aquí ves uno de sus cuadros.
DIEGO: Así que vas a escribir sobre Frida Kahlo. ¿Qué más te interesa sobre ella?
LUPE: Bueno, me interesa mucho su arte, claro. Pero también me interesa porque llevó una vida muy difícil. Sufrió mucho, pero nunca dejó de apreciar la belleza de vivir... Oye, Diego. ¿Por qué no vamos al Museo de Arte Moderno este sábado? Allí podemos ver cuadros de Kahlo, de Rivera y de otros artistas importantes.
DIEGO: Me gustaría mucho ir, pero no creo que pueda. El examen es el lunes, y no estoy listo para él todavía. Saqué una buena calificación en el primer examen, pero el segundo fue más difícil. Temo que el tercero sea difícil también.
LUPE: Bueno, espero que salgas bien. Te ayudo a estudiar, si quieres.

DIEGO: Gracias. Pero, ¿por qué no vamos al Museo de Arte Moderno el próximo sábado? Todavía no lo conozco. ¿Dónde está?

LUPE: Está en el Bosque de Chapultepec. Es un museo excelente. Hay muchos cuadros famosos de artistas mexicanos del siglo XX. Muchos de esos cuadros son obras maestras.

DIEGO: A mí me gusta mucho el arte del siglo XX. ¿Qué más hay en el museo?

LUPE: Hay una colección de esculturas en el jardín. Se puede caminar por el jardín y ver todas las esculturas. Es muy agradable. Y es posible que haya una exposición en el edificio de al lado. Y también podemos ir al Castillo de Chapultepec, donde hay un mural de Orozco.

DIEGO: Creo que vas a ser una guía magnífica. ¿Crees que va a haber mucha gente?

LUPE: Sí. Estoy segura que va a haber mucha gente. Aquí en el D.F., las familias van los sábados al Bosque de Chapultepec. Pero no importa. Es parte de la gracia de Chapultepec. ¡Ojalá que no llueva ese día!

DIEGO: Bueno, te invito a tomar un cafecito. Temo que vaya a dormirme si no tomo un poco de café.

LUPE: Pues, acepto, ¡y con mucho gusto!

Capítulo 14 El medio ambiente

ELISA: Qué vista más bella, ¿no?

JOSÉ MIGUEL: Sí, es increíble. Me gusta mucho venir al cráter del Pululahua.

ELISA: A mí también. ¿Cuántas veces has estado aquí?

JOSÉ MIGUEL: No sé. Muchísimas. Varias veces contigo y unas cuantas más con amigos. Voy a explorar un rato.

ELISA: Muy bien. Pero ten cuidado, ¿eh? Yo voy a escribir un poco de mi artículo.

JOSÉ MIGUEL: Hasta pronto.

ELISA: Chau.

ELISA: (VO) Hoy día en el Ecuador, como en el resto del mundo, mucha gente está preocupada por las cuestiones del medio ambiente. La contaminación de las ciudades y sus afueras ha llegado a ser un problema muy grave. El desperdicio y la falta de los recursos naturales, tales como el petróleo, son algunas de las enormes desventajas de nuestro estilo de vida. La población mundial ha crecido enormemente en las últimas décadas, y el ritmo de la vida se ha vuelto muy acelerado. ¿Es posible que haya una manera de proteger el medio ambiente y a la vez desarrollar la economía del país? Un grupo estudiantil de Quito dice que sí y ha lanzado una campaña educativa para informar a la gente sobre este tema.

ELISA: Ay, tanta belleza. Y la gente la destruye con tanta facilidad... Ojalá que no sea demasiado tarde...

CONDUCTORA: ¡Eh, señora!

ELISA: ¿Sí, diga?

CONDUCTORA: Mire, tengo un problema. ¿Podría bajar a hablar con Ud.?

ELISA: ¡Claro! ¡Venga!

CONDUCTORA: Buenos días. Disculpe, señora. ¿Podría decirme a cuánto queda el pueblo más cercano?

ELISA: Bueno, hay un pueblo no muy lejos de aquí, como a unos diez minutos. Pero es muy pequeño. ¿Qué busca?

CONDUCTORA: Es el carro. Temo que tenga algo serio. Ha comenzado a hacer un ruido muy extraño, y quiero que lo revise un mecánico. ¿Sabe Ud. si hay un taller en el pueblo?

ELISA: Ay, lo dudo mucho. Pero hay otro pueblo más grande no muy lejos, y es muy posible que haya un taller allí. Siga todo derecho unos cinco kilómetros, y luego doble a la izquierda en la carretera para Quito. ¿Sabe? Se me ocurre algo. Nosotros vamos en esa dirección. La podemos acompañar. No me gusta que se quede sola en este camino con un carro que no arranca.

CONDUCTORA: Eso es muy amable de su parte, pero no se molesten.
JOSÉ MIGUEL: De veras, no es ninguna molestia. Necesitamos encontrar una gasolinera. Tenemos que llenar el tanque.
CONDUCTORA: Muchas gracias. Uds. me han ayudado muchísimo.
ELISA: No hay de qué. ¿Vamos?
CONDUCTORA: ¡Vamos!

Capítulo 15 La vida social

EVA: ¡Hola!
LOLA: ¿Qué tal, Eva?
EVA: ¿Cómo estás?
LOLA: ¡Por fin es viernes! Qué semana más larga, ¿eh?
EVA: ¿Qué vais a hacer este fin de semana?
LOLA: Pues, nos vamos a pasar el día con mi hermano en Cádiz. Es el cumpleaños de mi sobrino. Y el domingo no tenemos planes. ¿Y vosotros, qué hacéis?
EVA: El domingo vamos a una boda aquí en Sevilla. Se casa una prima mía. ¿Tenéis planes para esta noche?
LOLA: Creo que no, a menos que Manolo haya hecho planes.
EVA: ¿Y por qué no salimos todos juntos? ¡Hace tanto tiempo que no lo hacemos!
LOLA: Por mí, encantada. Vamos. Podemos ir a cenar o al cine. Hay dos o tres películas interesantes que a Manolo y a mí nos gustaría ver. También podemos llevar a las niñas. ¡Carolina y Marta ya son como hermanas! Se lo voy a preguntar a Manolo y te llamo después.
EVA: Muy bien. Yo también hablo con Jesús. Hablamos luego y entonces decidimos qué hacer, ¿vale?
LOLA: Estupendo.
EVA: Ah, ¡se me olvidó! ¿Has hablado con Susana?
LOLA: No. ¿Por qué?
EVA: Tiene un nuevo novio. Dice que está totalmente enamorada de él.
LOLA: ¡Qué bien! Por fin... Quedó tan deprimida después del divorcio. Bueno, cuéntame... ¿Lo conoces? ¿Cómo es?
EVA: Pues, se llama Antonio y es alto y moreno. Susana dice que fue amor a primera vista. Cree que no hay nadie ni más cariñoso, ni más dulce que él en todo el mundo.
LOLA: ¡Já! La pobre está completamente perdida. No hay nadie que sea tan perfecto.
EVA: Pasan mucho tiempo juntos. Según ella, se llevan muy bien y tienen mucho en común. Y dice que él tiene buen sentido de humor.
LOLA: Bueno, con tal de que la trate con cariño y respeto, lo demás no importa.
EVA: Susana quiere que nos reunamos todos para que lo conozcamos.
LOLA: Pues, dime cuándo. ¡Me gustaría mucho conocer a ese Príncipe Azul! Oye, Eva... ¿Me guardas un secreto?
EVA: Sí, ¡pero sólo si tu secreto no me meta en líos con Jesús!
LOLA: No, no... Nada de eso. Es que no quiero que lo sepa mi madre antes de que yo se lo diga personalmente.
EVA: Bueno, cuéntame, entonces.
LOLA: ¡Manolo y yo estamos esperando otro hijo!
EVA: ¡Lola! ¡Vaya sorpresa! ¡Cuánto me alegro!
LOLA: Y también Manolo y yo queremos pediros a ti y a Jesús que seáis los padrinos. Tenemos una amistad de muchos años, y os tenemos mucho cariño y confianza.
EVA: Ay, Lola, no hay nada que nos pudiera dar más alegría que ser vuestros compadres. Es un gran honor. ¡Enhorabuena, comadre! Oye, ¿y sabéis si es niño o niña?
LOLA: No, y no quiero saberlo. Prefiero que sea una sorpresa. Pero Manolo sí quiere saberlo.
EVA: Ya sabes cómo son los hombres...

Capítulo 16 *¿Trabajar para vivir o vivir para trabajar?*

DIEGO: Aquí buscan bibliotecaria... y aquí hay un anuncio para peluquera. O mejor, ¿por qué no solicitas este trabajo de mecánica? Ya te veo: ¡con toda la cara cubierta de aceite!

LUPE: Diego, no seas malo. Ya sabes que busco un trabajo o de vendedora o de recepcionista. O tal vez de cajera. Tiene que ser un puesto que tenga horas flexibles.

DIEGO: ¡Fíjate! En este anuncio buscan una recepcionista para un banco.

LUPE: ¿De veras? Puede ser el trabajo ideal. Déjame ver...

DIEGO: ¡Qué guapa!

LUPE: Gracias. Creo que estoy preparada para la entrevista. Pero, estoy un poco nerviosa. Quiero caerle bien a la directora de personal.

DIEGO: Lupe, cálmate. Dentro de unas pocas horas, tendrás un nuevo trabajo. Pero, ¿estás segura de que quieres trabajar en un banco?

LUPE: Sí. Será el trabajo ideal para mí. Las horas son convenientes y podré seguir tomando mis clases. Y también será muy buena experiencia.

DIEGO: Seguramente. Además, te ves maravillosa y muy profesional. Buena suerte. ¿Regresarás después de la entrevista?

LUPE: Sí, por supuesto. ¡Adiós!

SRA. IBÁÑEZ: Nuestro banco es un banco de servicio completo, Srta. Carrasco. Aquí les ofrecemos a nuestros clientes todos los servicios posibles: cuentas corrientes, cuentas de ahorros, cajeros automáticos, tarjetas de crédito, préstamos y otros servicios más. Como recepcionista, Ud. tendrá que contestar preguntas sobre todos estos servicios.

LUPE: Sí, entiendo, Sra. Ibáñez.

SRA. IBÁÑEZ: He hablado con varios aspirantes para el puesto de recepcionista, pero Ud. tiene el currículum más interesante. Veo que ha trabajado como recepcionista en la oficina de un abogado. ¿Por qué renunció a ese trabajo?

LUPE: Bueno, soy estudiante en la universidad. Me gustaba mucho el trabajo en la oficina del abogado, pero querían que trabajara la jornada completa. Desafortunadamente, no me era posible.

SRA. IBÁÑEZ: Y cuando trabajaba para el abogado, ¿cuáles eran sus responsabilidades?

LUPE: Contestaba el teléfono, hacía las citas con los clientes, organizaba el archivo... también le llevaba sus cuentas y pagaba los gastos básicos de la oficina. Eran las típicas responsabilidades de una recepcionista.

SRA. IBÁÑEZ: Ajá, entiendo. Srta. Carrasco, buscamos una persona que sea amable, que aprenda rápidamente, que sepa escribir a máquina y utilizar una computadora y que tenga paciencia con los clientes. Parece que Ud. cumple con estos requisitos. ¿Podrá asistir a un entrenamiento de seis horas la semana que viene?

LUPE: Sí, Sra. Ibáñez.

SRA. IBÁÑEZ: ¿Y podrá trabajar de vez en cuando en las otras sucursales del banco?

LUPE: ¡Claro que sí! No hay problema.

SRA. IBÁÑEZ: Muy bien. ¿Tiene alguna pregunta?

LUPE: Sí. Quisiera preguntarle cuál es el sueldo y cuáles son los días de trabajo. ¿Tendré que trabajar los sábados?

SRA. IBÁÑEZ: Aquí tiene. Este es el sueldo. Y normalmente, tendrá que trabajar los lunes, miércoles y viernes por la tarde. Es posible que, de vez en cuando, tenga que trabajar un sábado.

LUPE: El horario es perfecto para mis clases en la universidad. Y el sueldo también me parece justo.

SRA. IBÁÑEZ: Me alegro. Bueno, pues, ¡felicitaciones! El trabajo es suyo.

LUPE: ¡Muchas gracias, Sra. Ibáñez! Acepto su oferta con mucho gusto.

Capítulo 17 En la actualidad

MANOLO: Lola, ¿has visto las llaves?
LOLA: Están en la mesa, al lado del teléfono.
MANOLO: No, esas son tus llaves. Busco las mías.
LOLA: Ay, Manolo. No sé.
MANOLO: Ah. Aquí están. Lola, es una lástima que no puedas venir a la tertulia esta tarde. Te vamos a echar de menos.
LOLA: Ojalá que pudiera ir, pero Javier me pidió que escribiera una crítica de este artículo para el lunes. No me queda más tiempo. Y, además, tengo que cuidar al hermanito de Marta.
MARTA: ¡Yo quiero que sea hermanita!
MANOLO: Bueno, Marta. Ya veremos... Adiós, Lola.
LOLA: Hasta luego. Saludos a Paco y a Maricarmen.
MANOLO: Vale. Hasta luego.
MARTA: Adiós, papi.
MANOLO: Y, yo también quiero que sea hermanita.

MARICARMEN: No sé, Paco. Antes, esperaba que se mejorara la situación, pero ahora con los acontecimientos recientes...
PACO: Pero hay que darles un poco de tiempo. Acaban de ganar las elecciones.
MARICARMEN: ¿Cuánto tiempo necesitan? ¿Años? ¿Décadas? ¡¿Siglos?!
MANOLO: Ajá. Veo que habláis de política. Hola, Maricarmen. ¿Qué hay?
MARICARMEN: Hola, Manolo.
PACO: Sí, y como siempre, no estamos de acuerdo. Hola, Manolo. ¿Y Lola?
MANOLO: Tiene que trabajar esta tarde. Pero os manda saludos a los dos. Muy bien, ¿de qué hablamos hoy?
MARICARMEN: Hablamos del partido político de Paco. Y este, como siempre, cree que los líderes políticos de su partido tienen el derecho de dictar cómo viven los demás. Y yo, claro, no estoy de acuerdo.
PACO: Maricarmen, te equivocas. Es todo lo contrario. Mira. Mi partido ofrece soluciones razonables a los problemas más graves de hoy.
MANOLO: Hasta cierto punto, estoy de acuerdo con Maricarmen. ¿Viste las noticias del Canal 2 anoche? Paco, tu querido partido quería votar cuanto antes la nueva legislación, para que nadie más pudiera protestar.
PACO: ¡No, señor! No es así. ¿Siempre crees todo lo que dicen la prensa y la televisión? ¡Ojalá que el asunto fuera tan sencillo!
MARICARMEN: Pero Paco, no me parecen razonables las soluciones propuestas por tu partido. Es verdad que necesitamos nuevas leyes laborales, pero estas no resuelven nada.
PACO: ¡Al contrario! Maricarmen, el anterior presidente no había hecho nada en los últimos años. Mira las noticias. Hay huelgas, desempleo, desastres económicos...
MANOLO: ¡Paco! ¿Tú siempre crees todo lo que dicen la prensa y la televisión?
PACO: Pues, ¡parece que lo único en que estamos de acuerdo es en que *no* estamos de acuerdo!
MARICARMEN: Como siempre. Paco, Manolo, ¿queréis otra copa de vino? Yo voy a pedirme una más.
PACO: Sí, muchísimas gracias, Maricarmen.
MANOLO: Bueno.
MARICARMEN: Bueno, ¡parece que el camarero está de huelga también!
PACO: Ah, ¿y por qué no pides también más gambas? Están deliciosas.
MARICARMEN: Vale.
MANOLO: Oye, Paco. ¿Viste el periódico esta mañana?
PACO: Sí. ¿Por qué?
MANOLO: ¿Leíste el artículo de Fernando Villalba?
PACO: Ay, no comiences con él. ¡Parece imposible que alguien escribiera algo tan ridículo!

Capítulo 18 En el extranjero

DIEGO: ¡Qué rápido ha pasado el año! Ya casi terminan las clases.
LUPE: Sí, ¿verdad... ?
DIEGO: Lupe, pronto tendré que regresar a California. Pero antes, me gustaría mucho conocer un poco más de México. Si hiciera un pequeño viaje, ¿me acompañarías?
LUPE: ¡Por supuesto que sí! Sólo que me permitan dejar el trabajo un rato... Bueno, ¿adónde quieres ir? México es un país precioso. ¿Te gustaría ir a la playa? ¿a las montañas? ¿al desierto?
DIEGO: Me gustaría ir a Yucatán, para ver las ruinas de Chichen Itzá.
LUPE: Ajá, claro... ¡Así habla el futuro antropólogo! Bueno. Pues, entonces, tenemos que ir a la agencia para informarnos del viaje.
DIEGO: Eh, Lupe, eh... hay algo más. También me gustaría mucho que me acompañaras a California. Así podrías conocer a mis padres.
LUPE: ¡Me gustaría mucho!

DIEGO: ¡Señorita!
AGENTE: Buenos días. ¿En qué les puedo servir?
DIEGO: Queremos hacerle varias preguntas sobre unos viajes que nos gustaría hacer. Primero, ¿cuánto cuesta un pasaje en autobús a Yucatán, digo, a Mérida?
AGENTE: ¿En autobús? ¿No quieren ir en avión?
DIEGO: Pues, el autobús sale más barato, y así podríamos ver un poco más del paisaje mexicano. ¿Está bien, Lupe?
LUPE: Bueno, si quieres...
AGENTE: Un pasaje en autobús, ida y vuelta, sale 600 pesos. ¿Ya tienen alojamiento en Mérida?
LUPE: No, todavía no. Buscamos un hotel que sea decente, pero que tampoco sea muy caro. No tenemos el dinero para pagar un hotel de lujo.
AGENTE: Entiendo. Muy pocos estudiantes tienen mucho dinero. Bueno, les puedo ofrecer habitaciones en varios hoteles a precios muy razonables. A ver... ¿Cuándo piensan hacer el viaje?
DIEGO: La última semana de mayo.
AGENTE: Ajá... Eso va a estar un poco difícil. Casi todos los hoteles estarán completamente ocupados durante esa semana. Si viajaran una semana más tarde, encontrarían más habitaciones desocupadas.
LUPE: Bueno, está bien. Entonces, la primera semana de junio.
AGENTE: Excelente. Les puedo ofrecer dos habitaciones individuales con baño privado en el hotel Estrella del Mar. No es un hotel de lujo, pero es bueno y muy lindo. El precio de cada habitación es de 150 pesos por noche.
LUPE: Perfecto.
AGENTE: Y, ¿cuántos días piensan quedarse?
DIEGO: Unos cuatro o cinco días, nada más. Yo soy de California, y debo regresar pronto.
AGENTE: Muy bien... Tienen habitaciones reservadas para la primera semana de junio. ¿Sus nombres, por favor?
DIEGO: Sí, cómo no. Yo me llamo Diego González y la señorita es Guadalupe Carrasco.
AGENTE: Muy bien.
DIEGO: Gracias. Y ahora, quisiéramos preguntarle sobre otro viaje. Este es a los Estados Unidos. Lupe va a acompañarme a California por dos semanas.
AGENTE: Muy bien. ¿Y cuándo piensan viajar?
DIEGO: Bueno, creo que para la segunda o tercera semana de junio, yo debo estar...

LUPE: ¡Qué padre que tengan un precio especial para estudiantes! No lo puedo creer... ¡Me voy a California! ¡Dos semanas en Los Ángeles!

AGENTE: Ah, hay algo más. No se olvide de su pasaporte, Srta. Carrasco. Y como el Sr. González es ciudadano de los Estados Unidos, es muy posible que él pase por la aduana más rápidamente.

LUPE: ¿Y yo tengo que pasar por inmigración?

AGENTE: Claro, pero no hay problema. Ud. va a entrar como turista, y sólo se queda dos semanas. Sería un poco diferente si se quedara más tiempo. Bueno, ¡que disfruten de sus viajes!

DIEGO: Muchas gracias.

LUPE: Sí, gracias por todo.

EN CONTEXTO

Primeros pasos

MARIELA: ¡Muchas gracias!
RICARDO: De nada...
MARIELA: ¿Cómo te llamas?
RICARDO: Me llamo Ricardo. ¿Cómo se llama Ud.?
MARIELA: Yo me llamo Mariela Castillo. Mucho gusto, Ricardo.
RICARDO: Igualmente, Sra. Castillo.
MARIELA: No soy señora, soy señorita. Por el momento.
MADRE: Buenos días. Me llamo Margarita Salazar.
RICARDO: ¡Ella es mi mamá! Mamá, ella se llama Mariela. No es señora. ¡Es señorita! ¡Es la señorita Mariela!
MARIELA: Me llamo Mariela Castillo. Encantada, Sra. Salazar.
MADRE: Igualmente, Srta. Castillo. ¡Y bienvenida!
MARIELA: Muchas gracias
MADRE: Vamos, Ricardo.
MARIELA: ¡Adiós, Ricardo!
RICARDO: ¡Hasta luego, Srta. Mariela!

Capítulo 1 En la universidad

JUAN CARLOS: Buenos días... ¿Es la clase de economía?
EDUARDO: Sí, es la clase de economía.
JUAN CARLOS: ¿Qué tal? Soy Juan Carlos Alarcón.
EDUARDO: Buenos días. Me llamo Eduardo Robledo. Mucho gusto.
JUAN CARLOS: Igualmente. ¿Qué hora es?
EDUARDO: Son las once. Oye, ¿tomas también la clase de sociología con el profesor Ramón?
JUAN CARLOS: Sí, también tomo esa clase.
EDUARDO: ¿A qué hora es la clase de sociología? ¿Es a la una o a la una y media?
JUAN CARLOS: Es a la una y media, creo... Sí, a la una y media.
EDUARDO: Este grupo es excelente.
JUAN CARLOS: Sí, escucho su música con frecuencia. Me gusta mucho el jazz.
EDUARDO: Ah, ¿sí? Yo trabajo en el Café Azul. Allí tocan música jazz todos los fines de semana por la noche.
JUAN CARLOS: ¡Qué bacán! ¿A qué hora?
EDUARDO: A las diez.
JUAN CARLOS: ¡Perfecto! Entonces este fin de semana escucho jazz en tu café. Oye, ¿qué hora es?
EDUARDO: Son las once y cinco. ¿Dónde está la profesora? La clase es a las once.

Capítulo 2 La familia

ROBERTO: No entiendo. Ya son las tres. Mi prima Sabina debe estar aquí.
MARTÍN: No, todavía no son las tres. Es temprano. Yo tengo las tres menos cinco.
ROBERTO: Ah, bueno.
MARTÍN: ¿Cómo es tu prima?
ROBERTO: Es una chica joven. Tiene 16 años.
MARTÍN: Mmm... Mira... la chica allí es joven. ¿Es Sabina?
ROBERTO: No es ella. Esa chica es rubia. Sabina es morena.
MARTÍN: Ajá... Mira la chica allí. Es joven y morena. ¿Es tu prima?
ROBERTO: Eh... no. No es ella. Sabina es delgada. Esa chica que está allí es un poco gorda.

SABINA: ¡Hola!
ROBERTO: ¡Sabina! ¡Aquí estás! ¿Qué onda chiquita?
SABINA: ¿Cómo estás?
MARTÍN: Hola, yo soy Martín.
SABINA: Hola...

Capítulo 3 De compras

MARIELA: No. Gracias... Buenos días, señora.
VENDEDORA: Buenos días.
MARIELA: ¿De qué son las chaquetas?
VENDEDORA: Las chaquetas son de pura lana. Son muy bonitas, ¿verdad?
MARIELA: Sí, son bonitas. ¿Cuánto cuestan?
VENDEDORA: Cuestan 5.000 colones. Son, eh... muy buenas chaquetas.
MARIELA: No estoy segura. Es mucho.
VENDEDORA: ¡Pero el precio es una ganga! Son realmente buenas.
MARIELA: Sí, Ud. tiene razón, son chaquetas muy bonitas, pero de todos modos son un poco caras.
VENDEDORA: Vamos, señorita...
MARIELA: Bueno, voy a ver las chaquetas que tienen en el otro mercado. Muchas gracias. Adiós.
VENDEDORA: ¡Señorita! Puedo vender la chaqueta en 4.500 colones. ¿Está bien?
MARIELA: Sí, está bien. Muchas gracias, muy amable. Busco un regalo para mi hermana.
VENDEDORA: ¿Qué medidas usa? ¿Qué colores prefiere?
MARIELA: Mediano. Prefiere amarillo... o blanco. Ud. es de Argentina, ¿verdad?
VENDEDORA: Sí, soy argentina.
MARIELA: Buenos Aires es una ciudad tan linda.
VENDEDORA: Ah, sí, es lindísima. ¿Ud. estuvo alguna vez allá?

Capítulo 4 En casa

AGENTE: ¿Juan Carlos Alarcón?
JUAN CARLOS: ¿Sí?
AGENTE: Mucho gusto. Yo soy Amanda Villanueva, la agente.
JUAN CARLOS: Es un placer, señora.
AGENTE: Igualmente. Así que, ¿Ud. busca apartamento?
JUAN CARLOS: Sí. Prefiero vivir en un apartamento cerca del centro.
AGENTE: ¿Y qué tipo de apartamento prefiere? Tenemos muchísimos.
JUAN CARLOS: No quiero nada grande. Prefiero un apartamento con un solo dormitorio.
AGENTE: Muy bien. ¿Y qué más quiere?
JUAN CARLOS: Bueno... no necesito mucho. Prefiero un apartamento con sala, una ducha en el baño, una cocina con lavaplatos.
AGENTE: No hay problema. Tenemos muchísimos apartamentos así. ¿Y cuánto quiere pagar de alquiler?
JUAN CARLOS: Quiero pagar entre 600 y 700 soles. ¿Le parece posible?
AGENTE: Sí, es razonable. Mire... este apartamento tiene todo lo que quiere. Sala, un dormitorio, baño con ducha y lavaplatos en la cocina. ¿Quiere verlo? Está muy cerca de aquí, podemos caminar.
JUAN CARLOS: Sí, me gustaría verlo. Gracias.
AGENTE: Bueno, ¿vamos?
JUAN CARLOS: Vamos.

Capítulo 5 Las estaciones, el tiempo y un poco de geografía

AGENTE: ¿Ya tiene planes este año?
ROBERTO: Quiero hacer un viaje, pero no sé dónde ni cuándo todavía. Quiero bucear.
AGENTE: Bueno, tiene muchas opciones diferentes. ¿Adónde prefiere viajar?
ROBERTO: Prefiero viajar a una isla.
AGENTE: Bien... dicen que bucear en las islas del Caribe es maravilloso.
ROBERTO: ¿Es caro el Caribe?
AGENTE: Depende de la estación. En el invierno, cuesta más. En el verano, cuesta menos.
ROBERTO: Claro. ¿Y qué tiempo hace en el Caribe durante el verano?
AGENTE: Bueno, julio y agosto, por ejemplo, hace calor. Y llueve mucho también. Llueve casi todos los días.
ROBERTO: ¿Y qué tiempo hace durante el invierno?
AGENTE: Hace más fresco, y no llueve tanto.
ROBERTO: ¿Tiene alguna otra recomendación?
AGENTE: Hmm.... El país de Belice... tiene lugares maravillosos para bucear. Pero no es una isla.
ROBERTO: ¡Belice! ¡Qué buena idea!
AGENTE: Desde aquí no es muy caro el viaje.
ROBERTO: ¿Y qué tiempo hace en Belice?
AGENTE: Es muy húmedo, hace calor, hace mucho sol. Mire, aquí tiene unos folletos. Si quiere viajar a Belice, es más barato en verano, como siempre.
ROBERTO: Muchas gracias. Ud. puede hacer todas las reservaciones, ¿verdad? ¿como el avión y el hotel?
AGENTE: Sí, claro.
ROBERTO: ¿Cuándo necesito llamarla para arreglar el viaje?
AGENTE: Cuando quiera. Ya sabe...

Capítulo 6 ¿Qué le gusta comer?

MARIELA: ¡Hola, Sr. Valderrama!
VENDEDOR: Hola, Srta. Castillo. ¿Qué le doy hoy?
MARIELA: Voy a preparar una cena deliciosa. Es la primera vez que los padres de mi novio vienen a cenar. ¡Pienso causar una gran impresión!
VENDEDOR: ¿Qué va a preparar? Tal vez un buen pescado frito con arroz.
MARIELA: No, a mi novio no le gusta el pescado frito.
VENDEDOR: ¿Le gustan los camarones a su novio?
MARIELA: Sí, le gustan muchísimo.
VENDEDOR: Entonces, de primer plato, prepare un ceviche de camarones.
MARIELA: Muy bien consejo. De segundo plato voy a preparar unas chuletas de cerdo. A mí me gustan mucho las chuletas de cerdo.
VENDEDOR: Mire, Srta. Castillo, las zanahorias están buenísimas hoy. Van muy bien con las chuletas de cerdo.
MARIELA: Tiene toda la razón. Quisiera un cuarto de kilo. Y para el ceviche, necesito tomates y cebollas. ¿Me da medio kilo de cebollas y medio kilo de tomates, por favor?
VENDEDOR: Muy bien. ¿Y qué más?
MARIELA: ¿A cuánto está el kilo de espárragos?
VENDEDOR: El kilo de espárragos está a 500 colones.
MARIELA: Muy bien. Un cuarto de kilo de espárragos, entonces. Y me da también cuatro limones. ¡Qué buen tiempo hace hoy! ¿Verdad, Sr. Valderrama?
VENDEDOR: Ah, Srta. Castillo, donde Ud. está, siempre hace sol.
MARIELA: ¡Qué flores me echa, Sr. Valderrama!

Capítulo 7 De vacaciones

JUAN CARLOS: Buenas tardes. Un billete de ida y vuelta para Tarma, por favor. Sale a las dos y media, ¿verdad?
VENDEDORA DE BILLETES: Lo siento, pero ese tren está atrasado hoy. No sale hasta las seis y cuarto.
JUAN CARLOS: ¿Por qué? ¿Qué pasa?
VENDEDORA DE BILLETES: No estoy segura, pero parece que hay un problema mecánico.
JUAN CARLOS: ¡Pero sólo son las dos y cuarto! ¡Faltan todavía cuatro horas!
VENDEDORA DE BILLETES: De veras, lo siento. Pero no hay remedio.
JUAN CARLOS: Pero, los trenes en las otras líneas no están atrasados, ¿verdad?
VENDEDORA DE BILLETES: No, los otros trenes deben salir a la hora en punto.
JUAN CARLOS: ¿A qué hora sale el próximo tren para Chincheros?
VENDEDORA DE BILLETES: Sale cinco para las tres.
JUAN CARLOS: Bien. Un billete de ida y vuelta para Chincheros, por favor. Es que quiero escribir una guía turística sobre los pequeños pueblos peruanos, y no importa qué pueblo visito hoy.
VENDEDORA DE BILLETES: Ya veo. ¡Qué buena idea! Una guía sobre los pequeños pueblos. Muy interesante. ¿Prefiere Ud. un asiento de ventanilla o de pasillo?
JUAN CARLOS: Prefiero un asiento de ventanilla, por favor.
VENDEDORA DE BILLETES: ¿Y tiene equipaje para facturar?
JUAN CARLOS: No, sólo tengo esta mochila.
VENDEDORA DE BILLETES: Muy bien. El tren sale del andén número cinco.
JUAN CARLOS: Muchas gracias.
VENDEDORA DE BILLETES: De nada.

Capítulo 8 Los días festivos

EMPLEADO: Estos son los dos éxitos de este disco. Si quieres, puedes oírlos allá.
MUCHACHA: Gracias.
EMPLEADO: De nada.
ROBERTO: Buenos días.
EMPLEADO: Buenos días. ¿En que te puedo servir?
ROBERTO: Quisiera devolver este disco compacto.
EMPLEADO: Muy bien. Un momento... ¿Por qué quieres devolverlo?
ROBERTO: Ya lo tengo.
EMPLEADO: ¿Tienes el recibo?
ROBERTO: No, no tengo recibo. Me regalaron el disco para mi cumpleaños.
EMPLEADO: Lo siento, pero en ese caso no te puedo reembolsar el dinero. Necesitas un recibo para el reembolso.
ROBERTO: Qué pena. ¿Puedo cambiar el disco por otro?
EMPLEADO: Sí, eso está bien.
ROBERTO: Gracias. Oye, ¿no sabes si ya salió el nuevo disco de Ragazzi?
EMPLEADO: No, fíjate que no sale hasta el viernes. Todos lo estamos esperando. ¿Te gusta Ragazzi?
ROBERTO: Me encanta. Es mi grupo favorito.
EMPLEADO: A mí me encanta también. El guitarrista es increíble, ¿verdad?
ROBERTO: Es buenísimo. ¿Fuiste a su concierto el año pasado?
EMPLEADO: Sí, ¡qué padre! Fue el mejor concierto del año.
ROBERTO: Sabes, creo que me voy a esperar hasta el viernes para cambiar este disco.
EMPLEADO: Está bien.
ROBERTO: Nos vemos...
EMPLEADO: ¡Hasta luego! ¡Buen día!

Capítulo 9 *El tiempo libre*

AMALIA: ¡Hola, Mariela!
MARIELA: Hola, Amalia.
AMALIA: ¿Cómo estás?
MARIELA: Pura vida, ¿y vos?
AMALIA: Gracias, igual. ¿Qué hacés?
MARIELA: Quiero hacer algo interesante este fin de semana. ¿Vos tenés planes para mañana?
AMALIA: No, no tengo planes. Soy muy aburrida, nunca salgo de mi casa. ¿Por qué? ¿Querés hacer algo juntas?
MARIELA: Me encantaría. ¿Qué querés hacer?
AMALIA: Mmm... ¿Ir al cine? ¿Hay alguna película interesante?
MARIELA: A ver... la verdad es que no. No me interesan para nada estas películas. Pero podemos ir al teatro.
AMALIA: ¡Ay no! Fui al teatro el fin de semana pasado. No tengo ganas de ir otra vez.
MARIELA: ¡Me acabás de decir que sos muy aburrida y que nunca salís de casa!
AMALIA: Una pequeña exageración. Oíme, ¿por qué no vamos al museo? Hace mucho tiempo que no voy al museo.
MARIELA: ¡Pura vida! ¡Vamos al museo! Y después podemos ir a cenar. ¿Qué te parece?
AMALIA: Perfecto. ¿Por qué no cenamos en este restaurante nuevo? Dicen que es buenísimo.
MARIELA: Muy bien... voy a llamar para hacer una reservación. Buenas tardes. Quisiera reservar una mesa, por favor... para mañana... dos personas. A nombre de Mariela Castillo. ... Un momento, por favor... ¿A las ocho? A las ocho. Muchas gracias. Bueno, ya, ¿a cuál vamos? ¿Al de... ?

Capítulo 10 *La salud*

FARMACÉUTICO: Buenas tardes, Juan Carlos. ¿Cómo estás hoy? ¿Mejor?
JUAN CARLOS: Pues, me duele mucho la garganta y estoy bien resfriado.
FARMACÉUTICO: ¿Fuiste a ver al médico?
JUAN CARLOS: Tuve una consulta esta mañana.
FARMACÉUTICO: ¿Y qué te dijo?
JUAN CARLOS: Tengo una infección respiratoria. Me dio una receta para un antibiótico.
FARMACÉUTICO: Ah, sí, este antibiótico es muy bueno. Pero es importante que tomes todas las pastillas, ¿sabes? No dejes de tomarlas en cuanto te sientas mejor.
JUAN CARLOS: Sí, lo sé. Las voy a tomar todas. ¿Me puede recomendar un jarabe para la tos?
FARMACÉUTICO: Claro... personalmente, prefiero este. Pero te recomiendo que no lo tomes si vas a manejar. Puede darte sueño.
FARMACÉUTICO: ¿Y adónde vas ahora?
JUAN CARLOS: Voy a regresar a mi casa, a acostarme y dormir.
FARMACÉUTICO: Muy bien, Juan Carlos. Dormir es una de las mejores medicinas, ¿verdad?
JUAN CARLOS: Sí, lo sé.
FARMACÉUTICO: Hasta luego. ¡Que te sientas mejor!
JUAN CARLOS: Muy bien. Adiós. Y, ¡gracias!

Capítulo 11 *Presiones de la vida moderna*

ROBERTO: Esto es imposible... estoy totalmente perdido. Esta es la calle Milagros. Acabo de venir de la calle Ibáñez. ¡El bar debe estar cerca! No lo entiendo. Eh... Disculpe, señor...
SEÑOR: ¿Sí?
ROBERTO: Perdone la molestia... pero estoy perdido. Busco el bar «La copa alegre». ¿Lo conoce Ud.?
SEÑOR: No estoy seguro. ¿Me puede decir en qué calle queda?

ROBERTO: Queda en la calle Santiago de Chile.
SEÑOR: Ah, sí. Conozco el bar. Mire, es muy fácil llegar. No queda lejos. ¿Ve Ud. el teléfono?
ROBERTO: Sí.
SEÑOR: Esa es la calle Martín Gómez. Doble a la derecha en esa calle. Luego camine dos cuadras y doble a la izquierda en la avenida Flores. ¿Me entiende?
ROBERTO: Sí... doblo a la derecha en la calle Martín Gómez. Luego a la izquierda en la avenida Flores.
SEÑOR: Así es. Luego camine una cuadra y doble a la derecha en la calle Santiago de Chile. Siga derecho y a unos cien metros va a ver el bar a la izquierda.
ROBERTO: Bien... a ver si entiendo bien. A la derecha en Martín Gómez, a la izquierda en Flore, a la derecha en la calle Santiago de Chile; y el bar está a la izquierda.
SEÑOR: Exactamente.
ROBERTO: Muchísimas gracias, señor.
SEÑOR: No hay de qué, joven.
ROBERTO: Es Ud. muy amable.
SEÑOR: Qué la vaya bien.
ROBERTO: Igualmente, señor.

Capítulo 12 La calidad de la vida

ESTUDIANTE: Disculpe, Srta. Castillo. ¿Me puede ayudar?
MARIELA: Claro que sí.
ESTUDIANTE: Gracias, muy amable. Es que no sé manejar bien este programa.
MARIELA: A ver... ¿qué es lo que intenta hacer?
ESTUDIANTE: Quiero mandar este documento por correo electrónico a mi profesor, pero no funciona.
MARIELA: Vamos a ver. Con permiso...
ESTUDIANTE: ¿Quiere Ud. hacerlo?
MARIELA: No. Prefiero que Ud. lo haga. Así aprende mejor. Bien. Primero, abra su cuenta de correo electrónico. No, es mejor que no abra el documento. Bien, ahora le sugiero que ponga primero la dirección electrónica del profesor en ese espacio. Cuidado, un error tipográfico y no funciona.
ESTUDIANTE: Ya está.
MARIELA: Ahora, con el ratón, escoja «adjuntar documento» del menú. Y es necesario que elija el documento que quiere mandar.
ESTUDIANTE: Es éste.
MARIELA: Hmmm...
ESTUDIANTE: Ya. Listo, ¿no?
MARIELA: Sí. Haga «click » para mandarlo, y...
ESTUDIANTE: ¿Qué es eso?
MARIELA: ¡Es mi teléfono celular! ¿Aló? Un momentito...

Capítulo 13 El arte y la cultura

VENDEDORA: Estos tejidos vienen de Chincheros, en el Cuzco.
JUAN CARLOS: Sí. Chincheros es muy conocido por sus tejidos.
VENDEDORA: Son de primera calidad. Conozco a una familia allá que me los teje.
JUAN CARLOS: ¿Y la cerámica?
VENDEDORA: Las piezas de cerámica son reproducciones de cerámica antigua.
JUAN CARLOS: El original de esta pieza está en el museo de Lima, ¿verdad? Es una buena reproducción.
VENDEDORA: Sí, lo es. Todas mis artesanías son muy buenas. ¿Quiere llevarse esa pieza? Le rebajo un poco el precio, por ser mi primera venta.
JUAN CARLOS: ¿En cuánto me la deja? Soy un estudiante pobre.

VENDEDORA: Ay, otro estudiante pobre. Todos los estudiantes que vienen a mi puesto son pobres, ¿sabe? A ver... se la dejo en sesenta soles.
JUAN CARLOS: Ajá. ¿Y las máscaras? Son de Huancayo, ¿verdad?
VENDEDORA: Sí, muy bien, joven. Son de Huancayo. Ud. sabe mucho de artesanías.
JUAN CARLOS: Es un pasatiempo mío. Viajo mucho por el Perú. Quiero publicar algún día una guía turística sobre los pequeños pueblos peruanos.
VENDEDORA: Me alegra mucho que haya jóvenes con interés en los pequeños pueblos. La mayoría se pasa la vida en las grandes ciudades.
JUAN CARLOS: ¿Qué precio tiene esta máscara?
VENDEDORA: Bueno, a Ud., nuestro joven viajero, se la dejo en un precio especial. Si me compra la cerámica y la máscara, sólo le pido cien soles en total. Fíjese, ¡qué ganga!
JUAN CARLOS: Muy amable. ¿Cien soles me dijo? Qué pena, no tengo tanto dinero. ¿Por qué no quedamos en ochenta soles?
VENDEDORA: ¡Ay joven! Déjeme un margen de ganancia. ¡Ni para Ud., ni para mí!

Capítulo 14 El medio ambiente

ROBERTO: ¡Este carro me tiene como loco, Miguel! ¡Es la tercera vez que lo arreglas este año!
MIGUEL: Sí, ya lo sé, Roberto. Primero le arreglé los frenos... luego fue la transmisión. ¿Y cómo están los frenos y la transmisión?
ROBERTO: ¡Los frenos y la transmisión están bien! ¡No sé qué pasa, pero este carro tonto simplemente no quiere arrancar!
MIGUEL: Cálmate, Roberto. Vamos a ver... Dime, viejo, ¿qué te pasa esta vez? ¿Por qué no arrancas, eh? ¿Qué tienes? ¿Qué necesitas?
ROBERTO: Lo que necesita este carro es ser reciclado para convertirlo en lata de aluminio.
MIGUEL: Bueno. No hace falta que lo insultes, Roberto. ¿Por qué no me explicas qué pasó?
ROBERTO: Muy bien. Ayer tuve un día horrible. Primero me desperté tarde y por eso llegué tarde al trabajo. Después del trabajo, se me perdieron las llaves.
MIGUEL: El carro, Roberto. El carro.
ROBERTO: Ah, sí. Bueno, salí del trabajo. Metí la llave e intenté arrancar el motor y nada. Absolutamente nada.
MIGUEL: ¿Se prendieron las luces dentro del carro?
ROBERTO: Sí, las luces se prendieron. Y no es la batería, Miguel. La batería es nueva.
MIGUEL: Ajá... ajá... ajá...
ROBERTO: ¿Qué es? ¿Algo muy caro? ¿O muy difícil de arreglar?
MIGUEL: Roberto, estás nervioso. Cálmate. Lo que pasa es muy sencillo. Mira. ¿Qué pasa con este Roberto, eh? Tiene que tomar la vida con más calma, ¿no?

Capítulo 15 La vida social

RECEPCIONISTA: Buenos días, oficina de la consejera Valenzuela. ¿En qué le puedo servir?
MARIELA: Muy buenos días. ¿Me comunica con la consejera Valenzuela, por favor?
RECEPCIONISTA: Disculpe, ¿de parte de quién?
MARIELA: Soy Mariela Castillo.
RECEPCIONISTA: Un momento, por favor. Lo siento, pero la consejera está con un cliente en este momento. ¿Quiere dejar un recado?
MARIELA: Bueno, lo que quiero es hacer una cita.
RECEPCIONISTA: No hay problema. Yo le puedo ayudar con una cita. ¿Qué día de la semana prefiere Ud.?
MARIELA: Prefiero el viernes, si es posible.
RECEPCIONISTA: Tenemos una cita el viernes a las nueve de la mañana. ¿Está bien?
MARIELA: Sí, está bien. Una pregunta...

RECEPCIONISTA: ¿Sí?
MARIELA: Quiero hablar con la consejera Valenzuela sobre la posibilidad de empleo para una persona con mi educación y experiencia. ¿Debo traer una copia de mi currículum?
RECEPCIONISTA: Sí, siempre es recomendable tener una copia de su currículo.
MARIELA: Muy bien. Muchas gracias.
RECEPCIONISTA: De nada, Srta. Castillo. La vemos el viernes a las nueve de la mañana. ¡Adiós!
MARIELA: Gracias a Ud. ¡Adiós!

Capítulo 16 *¿Trabajar para vivir o vivir para trabajar?*

JUAN CARLOS: Buenas tardes.
EMPLEADO: Buenas tardes.
JUAN CARLOS: Gracias.
EMPLEADO ¿En qué lo puedo atender?
JUAN CARLOS: Quisiera abrir unas cuentas.
EMPLEADO: ¿Y qué tipo de cuentas quiere Ud. abrir?
JUAN CARLOS: Necesito una cuenta corriente y una cuenta de ahorros. ¿Ganan intereses sus cuentas corrientes?
EMPLEADO: Depende del tipo de cuenta corriente. Si Ud. elige esta cuenta, gana intereses mensualmente, con tal de que mantenga un mínimo de cien soles en la cuenta.
JUAN CARLOS: ¿Qué pasa si el balance de la cuenta baja de los cien soles?
EMPLEADO: En ese caso le cargamos una multa a su cuenta.
JUAN CARLOS: ¿Y el otro tipo de cuenta corriente? ¿Cómo es?
EMPLEADO: Es más sencillo. No requiere un balance mínimo, pero tampoco gana intereses.
JUAN CARLOS: Prefiero esta cuenta. No quiero pagar multas. Y la cuenta de ahorros, ¿gana intereses?
EMPLEADO: Sí, y tampoco requiere un balance mínimo.
JUAN CARLOS: Dígame. ¿Tiene este banco cajeros automáticos?
EMPLEADO: Sí, claro. Tenemos un cajero automático afuera, y también puede utilizar, sin pagar, los cajeros automáticos de las otras sucursales del banco.
JUAN CARLOS: ¿Y funciona la tarjeta del cajero automático en otros bancos y otras ciudades?
EMPLEADO: Sí, funciona, pero si no es una sucursal de nuestro banco hay que pagar cinco soles por el servicio.
JUAN CARLOS: Muy bien.
EMPLEADO: ¿Tiene toda la información que necesita?
JUAN CARLOS: Sí, gracias. Estoy listo. Quiero abrir mis cuentas con este cheque, por favor.
EMPLEADO: Muy bien. ¿Cuántos soles quiere depositar en la cuenta corriente y cuántos en la cuenta de ahorros?
JUAN CARLOS: En la cuenta corriente, quiero depositar 600 soles. Y en la cuenta de ahorros, 700 soles.
EMPLEADO: ¿Apellido paterno?

Capítulo 17 *En la actualidad*

DUEÑA: ¡Roberto, hijo! ¿Cómo estás? ¡Estaba muy preocupada! ¿Por qué no viniste ayer?
ROBERTO: Doña Beatriz, no debe preocuparse. Me levanté tarde ayer y tuve que apurarme para llegar al trabajo.
DUEÑA: Tuve mucho miedo ayer. ¡No sabes cuántos crímenes hay hoy en día!
ROBERTO: Lo siento, doña Beatriz. Fue sin querer. A ver. ¿Qué necesito hoy? un periódico liberal, un periódico conservador, una revista internacional, dos revistas políticas...
DUEÑA: ¡Cuántas revistas y periódicos! ¿Qué pasa, Roberto? ¿Vendes en la otra esquina? ¿Tienes tu propio puesto?
ROBERTO: Es importante informarse, doña Beatriz.
DUEÑA: Sí, tienes toda la razón. Debes ser la persona más informada de México.

ROBERTO: ¿Cuánto le debo, doña Beatriz?
DUEÑA: Eh son... Son sesenta y ocho.
ROBERTO: ¿Me puede cambiar un billete de 200 pesos?
DUEÑA: No, Roberto. Es muy temprano. ¿No tienes uno más pequeño?
ROBERTO: Sí, un billete de cien pesos. ¿Está bien?
DUEÑA: Muy bien. Bueno... A ver... Treinta y dos, es tu cambio.
ROBERTO: Gracias, doña Beatriz. Nos vemos mañana, ¿no?
DUEÑA: Claro, hijo. ¡Y no me vuelvas a dar otro susto! ¡Ay! Si yo fuera tu madre...
ROBERTO: ¡Hasta mañana, doña Beatriz!
DUEÑA: ¡Adiós!... Ay, muchacho...

Capítulo 18 En el extranjero

SENORA: Gracias.
EMPLEADO: Con mucho gusto, señora. ¡La próxima persona, por favor! Buenos días, señorita.
MARIELA: Buenos días, señor. Necesito estampillas para tarjetas postales.
EMPLEADO: ¿Son postales para correo doméstico, o correo internacional?
MARIELA: Esta tarjeta es para correo doméstico. Esta tarjeta va al Uruguay, y a los Estados Unidos.
EMPLEADO: Estampillas para correo doméstico cuestan cincuenta colones. Para correo internacional, setenta y cinco colones. Muy bien. ¿Hay algo más?
MARIELA: Sí. Quisiera mandar este paquete a Francia. ¿Cuánto cuesta?
EMPLEADO: Eso depende de cómo quiera mandarlo, señorita. Por correo aéreo le cuesta 1.230 colones, pero llega en dos semanas. Si desea mandarlo por barco, le cuesta solamente 780 colones.
MARIELA: ¿Y cuánto tarda en llegar si lo mando por barco?
EMPLEADO: Debe llegar en unos dos meses.
MARIELA: Es un regalo navideño y como todavía nos faltan tres meses para Navidad, por barco está bien.
EMPLEADO: Cómo no, señorita. Por favor, escriba aquí el contenido del paquete y el valor. Es para la aduana. ¿Necesita algo más?
MARIELA: No, gracias. Es todo.
EMPLEADO: Muy bien, son 980 colones en total.
MARIELA: Gracias.

ENFOQUE CULTURAL SEGMENTS

Capítulo 1 Los Estados Unidos

Los Estados Unidos es un país de gran diversidad.

Casi la totalidad de su población está compuesta de inmigrantes de distintas partes del mundo.

La población hispanoamericana es una de las de mayor crecimiento en los últimos años en los Estados Unidos.

Su influencia es cada vez más fuerte. Esto se evidencia en la comida, el arte y las costumbres.

Los Estados Unidos es un auténtico mosaico de razas.

Capítulo 2 México

México. Su capital es México, Distrito Federal. El D.F., como se conoce, es la ciudad más grande y poblada de México.

Los mexicanos aman sus raíces. Ellos conservan hermosas tradiciones que muestran al mundo el orgullo que sienten por su pasado.

El arte en México es muy variado: va desde las antiguas edificaciones y arte pre-hispánico hasta el colorido muralismo mexicano.

Ciudades prehispánicas como Teotihuacán... coloniales como Oaxaca... como Guadalajara con todo el sabor de las costumbres mexicanas... las playas soleadas como Acapulco y Cancún... son sólo una muestra de la diversidad y la belleza de México.

Capítulo 3 Nicaragua

Nicaragua es el país más grande de América Central.

Su capital es Managua. En Managua está la antigua Catedral, que resistió el terremoto de 1972.

Los mercados son muy populares. En Masaya está el mercado artesanal más grande de Nicaragua.

Granada es un pueblo de arquitectura colonial. Caminar por sus calles es como estar en el siglo XVIII.

Nicaragua tiene más de 40 volcanes. Son muy conocidos el Masaya y el Momotombo.

En el lago de Nicaragua, hay muchas islas habitadas por personas... y animales.

Dentro de la literatura nicaragüense, sobresale la poesía de Rubén Darío, y en el arte, la pintura primitivista.

Nicaragua es un pueblo sencillo y valiente. La hermosa Nicaragua nos recuerda siempre las raíces y la historia de América Central.

Capítulo 4 Costa Rica

Costa Rica es conocida por ser una tierra de paz. Su capital es San José.

Los «ticos», como se conoce a los costarricenses, son personas amables y alegres.

La biodiversidad en los bosques de Costa Rica es una de las mayores del mundo.

Su sistema de parques nacionales, refugios y reservas biológicas protege la vida silvestre de Costa Rica.

Las playas de Costa Rica son famosas. Algunas de ellas son el lugar de desove de la tortuga Baula.

El cráter del volcán Poás es uno de los más grandes del mundo.

El verdor de sus bosques y montañas durante la estación lluviosa, el atractivo de sus playas doradas en la estación seca y la calidez de un pueblo hospitalario son los tesoros que tiene Costa Rica.

Capítulo 5 Guatemala

Guatemala está hacia el norte, en América Central. Su capital actual es Ciudad de Guatemala.

Antigua Guatemala fue la capital hasta 1773. Es una de las ciudades más viejas y hermosas de América.

Tikal fue el mayor centro ceremonial de la cultura maya durante la época clásica.

Estas ruinas incluyen plazas, una acrópolis, pirámides y templos.

Las ruinas de Tikal están en medio de la selva tropical. Son un sitio único, bello.

Los indios mayas-quichés se visten con trajes coloridos que ellos fabrican. Esta cultura tiene una visión hermosa sobre la creación del hombre y del mundo.

Capítulo 6 Panamá

Panamá es el istmo que une a América Central con América del Sur.

Este país tiene fama internacional por su canal.

El canal de Panamá es un canal interoceánico que comunica el mar Caribe con el océano Pacífico.

Es una de las vías fluviales más importantes del mundo.

El canal de Panamá está rodeado de selvas vírgenes.

La ciudad de Panamá es la capital del país. Es una ciudad moderna que está en la costa del Pacífico.

En el Casco Viejo, hay edificaciones muy viejas.

Pero la atracción principal de Panamá es su gente simpática.

Capítulo 7 Honduras

Honduras. La capital de este país de América Central es Tegucigalpa. Esta ciudad tiene algunos edificios de gran interés cultural.

Al oeste de la capital están las ruinas mayas de Copán. Entre sus atracciones están la Plaza Grande y la Acrópolis.

Honduras tiene varios parques nacionales. Su fauna incluye, entre otros, jaguares, monos, lagartos y aves.

Las islas y playas caribeñas de Honduras son famosas y bellas.

El arte, la comida y los bailes son muestras de la cultura popular de los hondureños.

Esta gente alegre refleja el carácter amable de los pueblos centroamericanos.

El Salvador

El Salvador es un país muy pequeño. San Salvador es su capital y es la ciudad más grande del país.

En San Salvador, hay varios mercados populares. Ahí se encuentran mercancías de todo género: comestibles, hierbas medicinales, artesanía.

Las pupusas son la comida más popular de El Salvador. Son como tortillas de masa de maíz, rellenas de queso, frijoles fritos o de chicharrón.

Las ruinas mayas de Tazumal son las ruinas más importantes y mejor preservadas del país.

En El Salvador hay más de 25 volcanes inactivos. Esto permite hacer caminatas hasta el cráter de algunos de estos volcanes.

Como en otros países de Centroamérica, la belleza de El Salvador está lejos de la ciudad en sus verdes bosques y montañas.

Capítulo 8 Cuba

Cuba es la isla mayor de Las Antillas. Su capital es La Habana y fue fundada en 1519 con el nombre de San Cristóbal de la Habana.

La Habana Vieja es una joya colonial. Su centro histórico está colmado de construcciones de este estilo.

El paseo de Malecón es uno de los sitios más concurridos de la ciudad. Las noches habaneras se llenan de música al caer el sol.

Cuba es testigo de gran riqueza cultural. En Santiago de Cuba nacieron el son cubano y el bolero. La alegría del pueblo cubano contagia a quienes recorren sus calles.

Cuba, su historia y el sabor de su gente, resultan un paseo inolvidable.

Capítulo 9 Colombia

Colombia está en el extremo norte de América del Sur. Su capital es Bogotá.

Colombia tiene ciudades muy importantes, como Medellín, Barranquilla y Cartagena. Algunas de estas ciudades son muy desarrolladas.

La economía colombiana es bastante estable. La industria textil es una de las más importantes de Colombia.

Colombia tiene bellas playas, valles y montañas.

Los colombianos son personas muy alegres. Cada año celebran varios carnavales, desfiles y festivales. La música y los bailes son un elemento muy importante en la cultura de este país.

Colombia, un país de grandes atracciones.

Capítulo 10 Venezuela

Venezuela está hacia el noreste de América del Sur.

Su gente es cálida, al igual que su clima.

La capital de Venezuela es Caracas. Es una de las ciudades más grandes y modernas de Sudamérica.

Simón Bolívar, «el Libertador» de América del Sur, era nativo de Caracas.

El principal recurso económico de Venezuela es el petróleo. Venezuela es uno de los mayores productores de petróleo del mundo.

La naturaleza de Venezuela es muy variada: costas, playas, ríos y los enormes tepuyes.

Los tepuyes son unas montañas únicas, que tienen la cima plana.

Ciudades hermosas y naturaleza dramática son dos de los grandes atractivos turísticos que tiene Venezuela.

Capítulo 11 Puerto Rico

Esta hermosa isla fue descubierta por Cristóbal Colón en 1493. Su capital es San Juan.

Puerto Rico se conoce también como Borinquen; a los puertorriqueños se les llama boricuas.

Algunas edificaciones, como los fuertes San Felipe del Morro, el castillo de San Cristóbal y el palacio de la Fortaleza, son un legado de la arquitectura militar española.

Puerto Rico es uno de los lugares más bellos de América. Con toda razón, en su canto a Puerto Rico, el gran poeta Gautier la llamó la Perla de los Mares.

Sus playas, bosques y montañas son algunas de las maravillas que encantan a todo el que visita esta joya del Caribe.

Capítulo 12 *Perú*

Perú limita con el océano Pacífico, en América del Sur. Lima es la capital de Perú.

La cuenca del Amazonas ocupa gran parte de Perú. La vida silvestre de esta zona es espectacular.

Los Andes peruanos son uno de los lugares más bellos del continente. Ahí viven muchos indígenas. Ellos hablan quechua.

En los Andes se encuentra el cóndor y también la llama.

Cusco fue la capital de imperio incaico. Es un pueblo colonial hermoso.

Al oeste de Cusco están las ruinas de Machu Picchu, la ciudad perdida de los Incas.

Perú: su gente y cultura están llenas de magia.

Capítulo 13 *Bolivia*

Hacia el centro de América del Sur está Bolivia.

Este país del altiplano tiene una cultura muy rica.

Esta cultura mantiene las mismas tradiciones, valores y creencias de las antiguas civilizaciones.

En Bolivia, muchas personas son de ascendencia amerindia.

La lengua oficial es el español. También se hablan el quechua y el aymará, dos lenguas indígenas.

La Paz es la capital de Bolivia y la ciudad más alta del mundo.

El lago Titicaca es un lugar sagrado para los incas.

Su belleza geográfica, desde los Andes hasta los bosques amazónicos, y el misterio de su pasado hacen de Bolivia un enigmático y llamativo país.

Ecuador

En Ecuador está una de las ciudades más hermosas de América del Sur: Quito, su capital. El centro de Quito es famoso por su valor histórico.

La arquitectura es colonial. Esto se nota en sus calles, casas, iglesias y palacios.

La iglesia de San Francisco es la iglesia más vieja de Ecuador. Fue construida por los españoles en el siglo XVI.

Ecuador tiene también lugares de gran belleza natural.

Hacia el oeste de Ecuador, en el océano Pacífico, está el archipiélago de Galápagos. En esas islas habitan muchas especies marinas y aves. Las islas Galápagos son un paraíso para los amantes de la naturaleza.

Capítulo 14 Argentina

Por la extensión de su territorio, Argentina ocupa el segundo lugar en América del Sur.

Buenos Aires, su capital, está junto al río de la Plata. Este río es considerado el «mar» de los argentinos.

Los «porteños», como se les conoce a los bonaerenses, son en su mayoría descendientes de inmigrantes europeos.

La influencia europea se nota en el arte y la arquitectura de la capital argentina.

La Avenida 9 de Julio es una de las avenidas más anchas del mundo.

El tango es el baile típico de Argentina. Lugares como el barrio «La Boca» de Buenos Aires inspiraron tangos muy famosos.

Este hermoso ritmo que vibra al son del bandoneón nos hace sentir la pasión de una ciudad que no descansa nunca: Buenos Aires.

Capítulo 15 Chile

Chile es un país famoso por su geografía única. Tiene al oeste la costa del océano Pacífico; al este, la Cordillera de los Andes. Hacia el sur tiene tierras heladas. Al norte de Chile está el desierto Atacama, el lugar más seco del planeta Tierra.

Santiago, la capital de Chile, es una ciudad inmensa de amplias calles y plazas, iglesias, parques y edificios modernos.

La cultura chilena es una mezcla de las influencias europea e indígena. Esto se ve en su música, arquitectura, arte y literatura.

Chile, un hermoso país, de contrastes culturales y naturales.

Capítulo 16 Paraguay

Muy al sur del continente está Paraguay.

Su capital es Asunción. Es la ciudad más grande de Paraguay. Presencia una mezcla de arquitectura antigua y edificios modernos.

El río Paraguay separa la región este del país de la región del Chaco.

Otro río importante es el Paraná. Es la única salida que tiene Paraguay al mar.

En el río Paraná se construyó la represa de Itaipú. Esta es la represa hidroeléctrica más grande del mundo.

Hacia el sur de Paraguay están las ruinas de las antiguas misiones jesuitas.

Las cataratas del Iguazú están entre Paraguay, Brasil y Argentina... La belleza de Paraguay llega hasta ese majestuoso lugar.

Uruguay

Uruguay es uno de los países más pequeños de Hispanoamérica.

La capital es Montevideo. Esta ciudad está junto al estuario del río de la Plata.

Es una ciudad muy pintoresca. Su arquitectura es un mosaico de estilos colonial español, italiano y Art-Deco.

En la Ciudad Vieja hay varios edificios y monumentos de interés histórico.

Montevideo tiene también edificios modernos. Los centros comerciales son muy grandes y muy visitados por los jóvenes uruguayos.

Lejos de la ciudad, en las pampas uruguayas, viven los gauchos. Los gauchos viven de la ganadería y la agricultura.

Pequeño en tamaño pero grande en colorido y sorpresas... así es Uruguay.

Capítulo 17 La República Dominicana

La República Dominicana está en el corazón del Caribe. Santo Domingo, su capital, fue la primera ciudad que se fundó en el Nuevo Mundo.

Esta ciudad tiene una historia muy rica. En ella se fundaron la primera catedral, el primer monasterio y la primera universidad del Nuevo Mundo. Por todo esto, es considerada patrimonio cultural de la humanidad.

La mayoría de su gente lleva sangre taína en sus venas. Los dominicanos son personas hospitalarias.

La riqueza natural de la República Dominicana hace de esta isla un lugar único y privilegiado.

La República Dominicana es, sin duda, un auténtico paraíso tropical.

Capítulo 18 España

España está en la Península Ibérica, en Europa meridional. Su capital es Madrid.

España cuenta con verdaderas joyas arquitectónicas.

En el Escorial, municipio Madrid, está el monasterio famoso de San Lorenzo. Este fue construido por Felipe II para conmemorar el triunfo de los españoles en la batalla de San Quintín. La Giralda en Sevilla, construida en la época almohade en el siglo XII. La Alhambra de Granada, una exquisita muestra de arte islámico, la bella Toledo con su arquitectura medieval.

Todos estos lugares hermosos son los que hablan de la historia de España.

XI. Answers to *¡Repasemos!* Exercises (Workbook/Laboratory Manual)

PRIMEROS PASOS

Repasemos

A. Listening Passage.

Después de escuchar
Paso 1. (Corrections of false statements will vary.)
1. F Julia es de Tegucigalpa.
2. C
3. F Julia no habla guaraní.
4. F Se habla portugués en Brasil.
5. C
6. F El español no es la única lengua que se habla en Latinoamérica.

Paso 2
1. La palabra idioma es sinónimo de <u>lengua</u>.
2. Julia es de Honduras: es hondureña. Susana es de Paraguay: es <u>paraguaya</u>.
3. Susana habla guaraní y <u>español</u> (o <u>castellano</u>).
4. En Belice se habla <u>inglés</u>.

B. Entrevista (Answers will vary.)
1. ¿Cómo te llamas? Me llamo <u>Horacio Quintana</u>.
2. ¿Cómo estás hoy? Estoy <u>bien</u>.
3. ¿Eres paciente y flexible? Sí, soy paciente y flexible. (No, no soy paciente y flexible.)
4. ¿Te gusta jugar al tenis? Sí, me gusta jugar al tenis. (No, no me gusta jugar al tenis.)
5. ¿A qué hora es la clase de español? La clase de español es a la <u>una de la tarde</u> (<u>a las diez de la mañana</u>).
6. ¿Cuántos estudiantes hay en la clase de español? Hay <u>veinticinco</u> estudiantes (en la clase de español).

CAPÍTULO 1

A.
1. Deseo trabajar.
2. Necesitamos trabajar.
3. Necesitamos comprar un diccionario.
4. Necesitamos pagar el diccionario.
5. Necesita buscar unos libros.

B. ANA: ¡Hola, Daniel! ¿Qué tal? (¿Cómo estás?)
DANIEL: Bien, gracias. ¿A qué hora regresas a casa hoy?
ANA: A las dos. Trabajo a las cuatro.
DANIEL: ¿Cuántas horas trabajas hoy?
ANA: Seis. Y esta noche necesito estudiar. Mañana hay un examen de historia.
DANIEL: ¡Pobre! Trabajas mucho.
ANA: Pues, necesito pagar mis libros y la matrícula. Hasta mañana.
DANIEL: Adiós. Hasta luego.

C. Listening Passage.

Después de escuchar
1. Para expresar el concepto de «major», se usa la palabra especialización (o carrera) en español.
2. Por lo general, no hay semestres en el año académico hispánico.
3. Julia toma cursos en relación con las ciencias políticas.
4. También toma una lengua extranjera: el inglés.
5. En Salamanca, hay muchos estudiantes extranjeros.

D. Entrevista (Answers will vary.)
1. ¿Qué clases tomas este semestre? Tomo español, matemáticas y ciencias políticas.
2. ¿Quién enseña tu clase de español? La profesora (El profesor) Jiménez enseña la clase.
3. ¿A qué hora es tu clase de español? (Mi clase de español) Es a las diez de la mañana.
4. ¿Qué hay en tu cuarto? (En mi cuarto) Hay un estante, un escritorio, una cama y dos lámparas.
5. ¿Tocas un instrumento musical? Sí, toco un instrumento musical. (No, no toco un instrumento musical.)
6. ¿Qué compras en la librería? Compro libros, bolígrafos y papel en la librería.

CAPÍTULO 2

A. Possible answers:

1. Hay siete (seis) personas en la familia Rivera.
2. (Los padres) Son de México.
3. El padre trabaja en IBM. La madre es ama de casa (trabaja en una oficina).
4. Estudia música en UCLA. Tiene veinte años. Es moreno, delgado y romántico. No es trabajador; es perezoso.
5. (La otra señora) Es la abuela. Tiene sesenta años. Es muy amable y simpática.
6. El coche es pequeño y nuevo y la casa es grande y vieja, y son de la abuela (de los padres).

B. Listening Passage.

Después de escuchar
Paso 1. (Corrections of false statements will vary.)
1. C
2. F Los abuelos participan activamente en el cuidado de los nietos.
3. F Por lo general, las personas viejas no viven en asilos.
4. C
5. C

Paso 2
1. La madre de mi madre es mi abuela materna.
2. Mis suegros son los padres de mi esposo/a.
3. Los bisnietos son los hijos de los nietos.
4. Por lo general, las familias hispanas son más grandes que las familias estadounidenses.

C. Entrevista (Answers will vary.)
1. ¿Vives con tus padres? Sí, vivo con mis padres. (No, no vivo con mis padres.)
2. ¿Escribes cartas a tus parientes? Sí, escribo cartas a mis parientes. (No, no escribo cartas a mis parientes.)
3. ¿Cuántas personas hay en tu familia? Hay cinco personas en mi familia.
4. ¿Cómo es tu familia? Mi familia es grande, simpática y amable.
5. ¿De dónde son tus abuelos? Mis abuelos son de los Estados Unidos.
6. ¿Debes comprar regalos para tus parientes? Sí, debo comprar regalos para mis parientes.

CAPÍTULO 3

A.
1. (El Sr. Rivera) Quiere comprar un par de sandalias y una camisa. Busca una camisa de rayas.
2. (Llega a la tienda) A las once y media.
3. Todas (las camisas) son caras.
4. No, por fin compra una camisa de quince dólares.
5. Todas (las sandalias) son caras también.
6. (Tiene que ir) A una zapatería (A la Zapatería Galán).
7. Regresa (a casa) contento con sus compras.

B. Listening Passage.

Después de escuchar
1. c 2. b 3. c 4. a

C. Entrevista (Answers will vary.)
1. ¿Cuál es tu color favorito? Mi color favorito es el azul.
2. ¿Qué ropa llevas hoy? (Hoy) Llevo una camiseta y *bluejeans*.
3. ¿Adónde te gusta ir de compras? Me gusta ir de compras al centro comercial.
4. ¿Tienes ganas de ir al centro este fin de semana? Sí, tengo ganas de ir al centro este fin de semana. (No, no tengo ganas de ir al centro este fin de semana.)
5. ¿Qué prefieres, la ropa cara o la ropa barata? Prefiero la ropa barata.
6. Por lo general, ¿cuánto pagas por un par de zapatos de tenis? Pago cien dólares (por un par de zapatos de tenis).
7. Y ¿cuánto pagas por un par de *bluejeans*? Pago cincuenta dólares (por un par de *bluejeans*).

CAPÍTULO 4

A.
1. nuestros
2. los
3. después de
4. vuelvo
5. voy
6. biblioteca
7. la
8. al
9. mis
10. vamos
11. a
12. de
13. cansada
14. mis
15. mi
16. vamos
17. leemos
18. miramos
19. Por
20. mis
21. ves
22. los
23. nos divertimos

B. Listening Passage.

Después de escuchar. (Corrections of false statements will vary.)
1. ND
2. F Alma no vive en el centro de la ciudad de Panamá. (Alma vive en las afueras de la ciudad.)
3. F Su casa es (bastante) grande.
4. C
5. F La casa de Alma (sí) tiene patio.

C. Entrevista (Answers will vary.)
1. ¿Te levantas tarde o temprano los domingos? Me levanto tarde/temprano (los domingos).
2. ¿A qué hora almuerzas, normalmente? (Normalmente,) Almuerzo a la una (al mediodía).
3. ¿Qué días de la semana tienes clases? Tengo clases los lunes, miércoles y viernes.
4. ¿Dónde te diviertes más, en la universidad o en una fiesta? Me divierto más en una fiesta.
5. ¿Qué traes todas las días a la clase de español? Traigo el libro de español a clase (todos los días).
6. ¿Adónde vas después de la clase de español? (Después de la clase de español) Voy a la biblioteca (a otra clase).
7. ¿Qué muebles tienes en tu alcoba? (En mi alcoba,) Tengo una cama, una mesita y una lámpara.
8. ¿En qué cuarto de tu casa o apartamento te gusta estudiar? Me gusta estudiar en la cocina.

CAPÍTULO 5

B. Listening Passage.

Después de escuchar. (Corrections of false statements will vary.)
1. F Nicanor no es de Vermont. (Es de Santo Domingo.)
2. C
3. C
4. F En Sudamérica hace frío en algunas regiones.
5. F A Nicanor no le gustaría vivir en Los Andes.
6. F Cuando es verano en el Hemisferio Norte, es invierno en el Hemisferio Sur.

C. Entrevista (Answers will vary.)
1. ¿Cuál es la fecha de hoy? Hoy es el 21 de marzo.
2. ¿Cuándo es tu cumpleaños? (Mi cumpleaños) Es el 14 de julio.
3. ¿Qué tiempo hace en el invierno en la ciudad donde tú vives? Hace frío (en la ciudad donde vivo).
4. ¿Qué ropa te pones cuando hace calor? (Cuando hace calor,) Me pongo pantalones cortos y una camiseta.
5. ¿Qué te gusta hacer cuando estás en casa? (Cuando estoy en casa,) Me gusta leer y cocinar.
6. ¿Qué estás haciendo en este momento? (En este momento) Estoy escribiendo y practicando el español.

CAPÍTULO 6

A. Possible answers:

(A.)
1. (José y Miguel) Llaman a Tomás para invitarlo a cenar en el restaurante El Toledano.
2. Deciden llevarlo allí porque es el cumpleaños de Tomás y quieren celebrarlo con él.
3. Tomás no conoce este lugar, pero le gusta mucho la idea de salir con sus amigos.
4. Pasan por él a las nueve y cuarto.

(B.) 1. Después de llegar al restaurante, encuentran una mesa desocupada lejos del escenario porque hay mucha gente.
2. (Hay tanta gente) Porque la comida es buena y la música también.
3. Tomás pide ______, y José y Miguel piden ______.
4. Durante la cena escuchan música.
5. Después de comer, José y Miguel pagan la comida.
6. Salen muy contentos y satisfechos con la comida en El Toledano.

B. Listening Passage.

Después de escuchar

1. En España, los españoles van con frecuencia a un café o a un bar para pasar el tiempo con los amigos y los compañeros.
2. En los bares, sirven tapas que son pequeños platos de comidas diversas.
3. Julia dice que prefiere la ciudad de Sevilla para divertirse. Allí no hace frío en el invierno y la gente puede salir muy tarde todo el año.

C. Entrevista (Answers will vary.)

1. ¿Conoces un buen restaurante? ¿Cómo se llama? Sí, conozco un buen restaurante. Se llama El Fondo San Miguel. (No, no conozco un buen restaurante.)
2. ¿Conoces al dueño de ese restaurante? Sí, conozco al dueño. (No, no conozco al dueño.)
3. ¿Dónde comes cuando tienes mucha prisa? (Cuando tengo mucha prisa,) Como en McDonald's.
4. ¿Qué pides en un restaurante cuando tienes mucho dinero? (Cuando tengo mucho dinero,) Pido un bistec.
5. ¿Qué te gusta beber cuando tienes sed? (Cuando tengo sed,) Me gusta beber agua.
6. ¿Qué plato especial sabes preparar? Sé preparar la paella. (No sé preparar ningún plato.)
7. ¿Dónde vas a cenar esta noche, en un restaurante o en casa? Voy a cenar en casa esta noche.

CAPÍTULO 7

B. Listening Passage.

Antes de escuchar
Paso 2. 1. e 2. c 3. d 4. b 5. a

Después de escuchar. 1, 2, 4, 5, 7

C. Entrevista (Answers will vary.)

1. ¿Adónde fuiste para tus últimas vacaciones? Fui a México (para mis últimas vacaciones).
2. ¿Cómo viajaste? ¿En avión? ¿En tren? Viajé en avión (tren, autobús).
3. ¿Le mandaste tarjetas postales a alguien? Sí, le mandé tarjetas postales a alguien (a mis amigos). (No, no le mandé tarjetas postales a nadie.)
4. ¿Adónde te gustaría viajar para tus próximas vacaciones? Me gustaría viajar a España.
5. ¿Con quién te gustaría viajar? Me gustaría viajar con mi mejor amigo/a.
6. ¿Qué te gusta muchísimo y qué odias? Me gusta muchísimo ir al cine. Odio tomar los exámenes.

CAPÍTULO 8

B. Listening Passage.

Después de escuchar. 1, 3, 4, 5, 6

C. Entrevista (Answers will vary.)
1. ¿Qué te regalaron tus amigos para tu último cumpleaños? (Mis amigos) Me regalaron unos discos compactos.
2. ¿Dónde fue tu última fiesta de cumpleaños? (Mi última fiesta de cumpleaños) Fue en casa de unos amigos.
3. ¿Cuál es tu fiesta o día festivo favorito? Mi día festivo favorito es la Navidad.
4. ¿En qué días festivos se reúnen tú y tu familia? Mi familia y yo nos reunimos para (durante) la Navidad.
5. ¿Cómo te sientes durante una típica fiesta familiar? (Durante una típica fiesta familiar) Me siento muy feliz.
6. ¿Qué haces en las fiestas estudiantiles? (En las fiestas estudiantiles,) (Yo) Bailo y hablo con mis amigos.
7. ¿Cómo te vestiste para ir a la última fiesta estudiantil? (Para ir a la última fiesta estudiantil) Me puse (Llevé/Me vestí con) ropa muy elegante.

CAPÍTULO 9

A. Verb forms for answers:

1. me despertaba
2. me bañaba/duchaba
3. me cepillaba los dientes
4. me vestía
5. desayunaba
6. me despedía
7. iba a la escuela
8. asistía a clases
9. almorzaba
10. conversaba y me reía con los amigos
11. volvía a casa
12. estudiaba
13. me sentaba a cenar a las seis
14. si no tenía que estudiar
15. miraba la televisión
16. leía
17. le decía «buenas noches»
18. me quitaba la ropa
19. me acostaba

B. Listening Passage.

Después de escuchar. (Corrections of false statements will vary.)
1. F Los más adinerados a veces tienen otra casa fuera de la ciudad.
2. F Normalmente los abuelos (sí) pasan tiempo con sus hijos y nietos.
3. F Los domingos se almuerza por dos o tres horas.
4. F Por lo general, los padres (sí) pasan tiempo con sus hijos durante el fin de semana.

C. Entrevista (Answers will vary.)
1. ¿Qué haces en tus ratos libres? (En mis ratos libres,) (Yo) Voy al cine y leo novelas.
2. ¿Qué hacías en tus ratos libres cuando eras más joven? (Cuando era más joven,) (Yo) Paseaba en bicicleta y nadaba (en mis ratos libres).
3. En tu opinión, ¿cuál fue la mejor película del año? (En mi opinión,) La mejor película del año fue *You Can Count On Me*.
4. ¿Cuál es el quehacer doméstico que menos te gusta? ¿Por qué? El quehacer doméstico que menos me gusta es pasar la aspiradora porque es muy aburrido.
5. ¿Qué aparatos domésticos tienes en tu cocina? En mi cocina tengo un lavaplatos, un refrigerador y una tostadora.
6. ¿Dónde vivías cuando tenías cinco años? Vivía en Texas (cuando tenía cinco años).

CAPÍTULO 10

A. 1. Descubrieron que la mitad de los estudiantes no tenían muy buena salud física.
2. Corren el riesgo de un ataque cardíaco.
3. Sufre de sobrepeso.
4. Los padres les ofrecen camaradería y también queman calorías.
5. Empiezan a desaparecer las barreras tradicionales que complican los logros atléticos.
6. Hay que ser serios y no consumir drogas.
7. Lo más importante es que aprendan a soñar (a creer en sí mismos).

B. Listening Passage.

Después de escuchar. (Corrections of false statements will vary.)
1. F El sistema médico más común en los países hispanos es el de medicina socializada.
2. F El gobierno no controla el sistema médico en los Estados Unidos.
3. C
4. C
5. C

C. Entrevista (Answers will vary.)
Hablando de la última vez que estuviste enfermo/a.
1. ¿Cuántos días guardaste cama la última vez que estuviste enfermo/a? La última vez que estuve enfermo/a, guardé cama por cuatro días.
2. ¿Qué síntomas tenías? Tenía fiebre y un resfriado.
3. ¿Fuiste al médico? Sí, fui al médico. (No, no fui al médico.)

Hablando de la salud en general.
4. ¿Qué haces para mantener la buena salud? Hago ejercicio, como bien y no fumo.
5. ¿A quién llamas cuando no te sientes bien? (Cuando no me siento bien,) Llamo al médico.
6. ¿Qué le aconsejas a una persona que fuma? Le aconsejo que deje de fumar.

CAPÍTULO 11

A. 1. hicimos 2. tenía 3. alemana 4. estudiaba 5. Nos quedamos 6. Llegamos 7. por 8. al 9. fuimos 10. a 11. nos sirvió 12. nos llevó 13. varios 14. tocaba 15. bebía 16. bailaba 17. nos invitó 18. conocimos 19. quienes 20. viajamos 21. antigua 22. Nuestra 23. magnífica 24. tuvimos 25. despedirnos 26. rápidos 27. modernos

B. Listening Passage.

Después de escuchar. (Some answers will vary.)
1. ¿Por qué perdió el conocimiento el hombre? Perdió el conocimiento porque saltó del autobús.
2. ¿Qué le dolía después del accidente? Le dolían la cabeza y la pierna.
3. El accidentado parece muy deprimido. ¿Por qué? Porque es muy torpe y tiene mala suerte.
4. ¿Qué crees que va a decir o hacer el médico? Creo que el médico le va a decir que debe tener más cuidado.
5. ¿Dónde crees que trabaja el accidentado? Creo que trabaja en una oficina.

C. Entrevista (Answers will vary.)

1. ¿Cuánto tiempo hace que estudias en esta universidad? Hace dos años que estudio en esta universidad.
2. ¿Cuánto tiempo hace que conociste a tu mejor amigo/a? Hace quince años que conocí a mi mejor amigo/a.
3. ¿Se te olvidó apagar las luces del coche alguna vez? Sí, se me olvidó apagar las luces del coche una vez. (No, no se me olvidó apagar las luces del coche ninguna vez.)
4. ¿Se te perdieron las llaves del coche alguna vez? Sí, se me perdieron las llaves del coche una vez. (No, no se me perdieron las llaves del coche ninguna vez.)
5. ¿Eras muy torpe cuando tenías doce años? Sí, era muy torpe (cuando tenía doce años). (No, no era muy torpe...)
6. ¿Sufrías muchas presiones cuando estabas en la escuela secundaria? Sí, sufría muchas presiones (cuando estaba en la escuela secundaria). (No, no sufría muchas presiones [cuando estaba en la escuela secundaria]).

CAPÍTULO 12

A. Paso 1. 1. conocieron 2. visitaba 3. dijeron 4. iban 5. se puso 6. invitó 7. aceptaron 8. quedaron 9. prometió 10. iba 11. volvieron 12. llevaron 13. Se despidieron 14. prometieron

Paso 2. 1. Fueron a las sierras centrales de California. 2. Era un turista del sur de Francia que visitaba los Estados Unidos. 3. Le dijeron que iban a hacer un viaje a Francia en mayo. 4. Se puso muy contento y los invitó a visitarlo en su casa. 5. Pasaron una semana juntos. 6. Lo llevaron al aeropuerto en Los Ángeles. 7. Se prometieron verse pronto en Europa.

B. Listening Passage.

Después de escuchar. 2, 4, 6, 7

C. Entrevista (Answers will vary.)

1. ¿Tienes que pagar alquiler donde vives? ¿Cuánto pagas al mes? Sí, tengo que pagar alquiler donde vivo. Pago trescientos dólares al mes. (No, no tengo que pagar alquiler donde vivo.)
2. ¿Cómo es tu vecindad? (Mi vecindad) Es muy bonita y está cerca de la universidad.
3. ¿Qué le dices a un niño que se está portando mal? Le digo que se porte bien.
4. ¿Qué quieres que haga tu mejor amigo/a? Quiero que mi mejor amigo/a me llame todos los días.
5. ¿Qué aparatos electrónicos tienes? Tengo un disco compacto y un radio portátil.
6. ¿Qué aparatos electrónicos te gustaría tener? Me gustaría tener una grabadora.

CAPÍTULO 13

A. 1. Si quieres aprender a hablar francés, debes practicar más. 2. El profesor duda que podamos hablar bien antes de terminar el tercer año. 3. Acabamos de tomar nuestro segundo examen. Ahora vamos a celebrar. 4. ¿Te acuerdas de lo fácil que fue el primer examen? ¡Este fue dificilísimo! 5. El profesor Larousse insiste (en) que empecemos a estudiar más. Tengo que ir al laboratorio todos los días. 6. ¿Por qué no le pides a Marcel Dupont que te ayude? 7. ¿Es cierto que pienses tomar el quinto semestre de francés? 8. ¡Ahora quiero olvidarme de los estudios y de la universidad!

B. Paso 1. 1. antropología física, lingüística, arqueología y etnología 2. interpreta 3. la misma capacidad 4. iguales 5. respetables 6. vivir en paz

Paso 2. 1. Es cierto que todas las culturas son respetables. 2. Espero que todos los pueblos puedan vivir en paz. 3. Es posible que todas las razas sean iguales.

C. Listening Passage.

Después de escuchar
1. a, c 2. c 3. b 4. a, d 5. c 6. d

D. Entrevista (Answers will vary.)
1. ¿Fuiste a un concierto el año pasado? Sí, fui a un concierto la semana pasada. (No, no fui a ningún concierto el año pasado.)
2. ¿Cuál es tu actor favorito o tu actriz favorita? Mi actor favorito (Mi actriz favorita) es Benicio del Toro.
3. ¿Visitaste algún museo el año pasado? ¿Cuál? Sí, visité dos museos el año pasado. (No, no visité ningún museo el año pasado.)
4. ¿Qué tipo de arte te gusta? Me gusta el arte moderno.
5. ¿Qué es lo primero que haces cuando llegas a casa después de tu última clase? Lo primero que hago es comer algo.
6. ¿Qué temes con respecto a tus clases? Temo que mis profesores me den muchas tareas.

CAPÍTULO 14

A.
2. se anunció
3. habían cruzado
4. se escaparon
5. Viajaron
6. llegaron
7. tuvo
8. tomó
9. había venido
10. pasó
11. pudo
12. empezó
13. estaban
14. habían desaparecido
15. murió
16. tuvo
17. pensaban
18. había desaparecido

B. Listening Passage.

Después de escuchar. (Corrections of false statements will vary.)
1. F Las personas que viven en los países hispanos (sí) están acostumbrados a conducir.
2. F No hay muchos autos japoneses en España, y aunque hay muchos Ford, hay más marcas europeas.
3. F Sí, se venden marcas europeas en Latinoamérica.
4. F El precio de la gasolina es más alto en España.
5. C

C. Entrevista (Answers will vary.)
1. ¿Dónde prefieres vivir, en la ciudad o en el campo? Prefiero vivir en la ciudad / el campo.
2. ¿Hay mucha contaminación en el lugar donde vives? Sí, hay mucha contaminación en el lugar donde vivo. (No, no hay mucha contaminación en el lugar donde vivo.)
3. ¿Qué has hecho este año para proteger el medio ambiente? (Este año,) He reciclado las latas y las botellas.
4. ¿Qué arreglos le puedes hacer tú al coche? Puedo revisar el aceite. (No puedo hacer ningún arreglo a mi coche.)
5. ¿Has chocado con alguien alguna vez? Sí, he chocado con alguien una vez. (No, no he chocado con nadie.) (Nunca he chocado.)
6. ¿Obedeces el límite de velocidad cuando conduces? Sí, lo obedezco. (No, no lo obedezco.)
7. ¿Cuánto tiempo hace que recibiste la licencia de manejar? Recibí mi licencia de manejar hace cinco años.

CAPÍTULO 15

A. 1. Espera que lo pueda ayudar.
2. Tiene una novia que vive lejos de él, pero otra chica quiere que salga con ella y le gusta la otra chica también.
3. Le parece que no pueden ser novios de verdad.
4. No desea traicionar a su novia.
5. analice / traicione / la quiere / salga

B. Listening Passage.

Después de escuchar
1. España 2. los Estados Unidos 3. España 4. los Estados Unidos 5. España 6. España, los Estados Unidos

C. Entrevista (Answers will vary.)
1. ¿En qué año naciste? Nací en 1982.
2. ¿En qué ciudad has vivido la mayor parte de tu vida? He vivido la mayor parte de mi vida en Chicago.
3. ¿Has conocido a una persona que te guste mucho este año? Sí, he conocido a alguien que me gusta mucho. (No, no he conocido a nadie que me guste mucho.)
4. ¿Conoces a alguien que se haya casado recientemente? Sí, conozco a alguien que se ha casado recientemente. (No, no conozco a nadie que se haya casado recientemente.)
5. ¿Trabajan tus padres para que tú puedas asistir a la universidad? Sí, mis padres trabajan para que yo pueda asistir a la universidad. (No, mis padres no trabajan para que yo pueda asistir a la universidad.)
6. ¿Con quién te llevas mejor, con tus amigos o con tu familia? Me llevo mejor con mis amigos / mi familia.

CAPÍTULO 16

B. Listening Passage.

Después de escuchar
1. los Estados Unidos 2. el mundo hispánico 3. el mundo hispánico 4. los Estados Unidos 5. el mundo hispánico 6. el mundo hispánico 7. los Estados Unidos

C. En el periódico. First ad:
1. Necesito un año de experiencia para este puesto.
2. Es para ambos sexos.
3. Debe tener la edad de 25 a 45 años.
4. La empresa ofrece un sueldo y prestaciones muy atractivas.
5. No lo dice.

Second ad:
1. Necesito de uno a tres años de experiencia para el puesto de secretaria. Para el puesto de auxiliar de contabilidad, no lo dice.
2. No lo dice.
3. No lo dice.
4. La empresa ofrece sueldo según aptitudes, prestaciones superiores a las de la ley y buen ambiente de trabajo.
5. Según la empresa, el ambiente es magnífico.

D. Entrevista (Answers will vary.)

1. ¿Qué harás este año para ahorrar dinero? Comeré más en casa y saldré menos.
2. ¿Hasta cuando piensas vivir en tu casa o apartamento actual? Pienso vivir allí hasta el próximo año.
3. ¿Dónde vivirás algún día? Algún día viviré en otro país.
4. ¿Qué profesión tendrás algún día? Algún día seré arquitecto.
5. Cuando vayas a una entrevista, ¿qué harás para caerle bien al entrevistador? Me vestiré muy bien y sonreiré mucho.
6. ¿Cómo será el mundo del futuro? Habrá una computadora en cada casa y todo el mundo trabajará en casa.

CAPÍTULO 17

A.
1. La reunificación de las dos Alemanias. (La desintegración de la Unión Soviética.)
2. (Ha habido intervenciones militares.) En África, en el sur de Asia y en algunas regiones de Hispanoamérica.
3. El conflicto en el Oriente Medio pone en peligro a la paz del mundo.
4. Dos problemas son la contaminación del aire y de los océanos y ríos y la destrucción de la capa de ozono.
5. Sugiere que todavía existe el temor a las intervenciones militares.

B. Listening Passage.

Después de escuchar

Noticia 1: Fuerte maremoto en Nicaragua, de más de siete (7) puntos en la escala Richter.
Noticia 2: Tema: el desempleo Mes: agosto
Noticia 3: Visita de Juan Carlos I, rey de España. Duración de la visita: tres (3) días
Noticia 4: Propuesta del partido de oposición para subir el precio de la gasolina, el tabaco y el alcohol, el primero en un cinco (5) por ciento y los dos últimos en un diez (10) por ciento. El próximo noticiero de amplio reportaje será a las dos (2) de la tarde.

C. Descripción. (Answers will vary.)

1. ¿Cree Ud. que a este matrimonio le gusten las campañas políticas? Sí, creo que le gustan. No, no creo que le gusten.
2. ¿Le gustan a Ud. las campañas políticas? Sí, me gustan. (No, no me gustan.)
3. ¿Cómo se informan las personas del dibujo acerca de las elecciones? Se informan por la televisión.
4. ¿Sigue Ud. las campañas políticas en la televisión, en la radio o en el periódico? Las sigo en la televisión y el periódico.

D. Entrevista (Answers will vary.)

1. ¿Quién querías que ganara las últimas elecciones presidenciales? Quería que Nader ganara las últimas elecciones.
2. ¿Qué esperabas que hiciera el nuevo gobierno? Esperaba que el nuevo gobierno creara más puestos de trabajo.
3. ¿A qué partido vas a apoyar en las próximas elecciones? Voy a apoyar al partido Verde. (No voy a apoyar a ningún partido.)
4. ¿Con quién discutes de política? Discuto de política con mis amigos.
5. ¿Cómo te enteras de los acontecimientos mundiales? Me entero de los acontecimientos mundiales por la televisión y el periódico.
6. ¿Crees que los reporteros son imparciales? Sí, creo que son imparciales. (No, no creo que sean imparciales.)

CAPÍTULO 18

A. 1. tenía (tendría) 2. haría 3. fuera 4. pasaran 5. acabara 6. tocaron 7. iría 8. encontraría 9. terminé 10. era 11. decidí 12. Llamé 13. podía (podría) 14. saliera 15. tuviera 16. encantaría

B. Listening Passage.

Antes de escuchar. (Answers will vary depending on students' knowledge.)

1. ¿Dónde viven los cubanoamericanos principalmente? Viven principalmente en Miami.
2. Muchos cubanos llegaron a los Estados Unidos dentro de un corto período de tiempo. ¿Por qué emigraron? Emigraron porque no les gustaba el gobierno de Cuba.
3. ¿Qué tipo de gobierno existe en Cuba hoy día? ¿Cómo se llama la persona que gobierna Cuba actualmente? El tipo de gobierno en Cuba es el comunismo. Fidel Castro gobierna Cuba.
4. ¿Pueden los ciudadanos norteamericanos viajar libremente a Cuba? No, los ciudadanos norteamericanos no pueden viajar libremente a Cuba.

Después de escuchar

1. c 2. a 3. c 4. a

C. En el periódico. 1. F 2. F 3. F 4. C

D. Entrevista (Answers will vary.)

1. ¿Qué tiene que hacer un viajero antes de entrar en su país de origen? Tiene que pasar por la aduana.
2. ¿Has viajado al extranjero? ¿Adónde? Sí, he viajado a México. (No, no he viajado al extranjero.)
3. ¿Adónde viajarías si pudieras? Viajaría a España.
4. ¿En qué tipo de hotel te quedarías en el extranjero? Me quedaría en un hotel de lujo.
5. Si estuvieras en Madrid, ¿qué harías? Iría a muchos bares para comer tapas.
6. ¿Has visto muchos turistas extranjeros en la ciudad donde vives? Sí, he visto muchos. (No, no he visto muchos/ninguno.)